Estimating Software Costs

ABOUT THE AUTHOR

CAPERS JONES is a leading authority in the world of software estimating, measurement, metrics, productivity, and quality. He designed IBM's first automated software estimating tool in 1973. He also designed both the SPQR20® and Checkpoint® commercial software cost-estimating tools. He was the founder and chairman of Software Productivity Research (SPR), where he retains the title of Chief Scientist Emeritus. While he was chairman of SPR, the company brought out the leading KnowledgePlan® estimating tool under his direction. Jones frequently speaks at conferences such as IEEE Software, International Function Point Users Group (IFPUG), the Project Management Institute (PMI), the Software Process Improvement Network (SPIN), the Computer Aid (CAI) conference series, and at scores of in-house corporate and government events. Capers Jones has been named to the Computer Aid advisory board in 2007. *Estimating Software Costs* is his 14th book.

Estimating Software Costs: Bringing Realism to Estimating, Second Edition

Capers Jones

New York   Chicago   San Francisco   Lisbon   London   Madrid
Mexico City   Milan   New Delhi   San Juan   Seoul
Singapore   Sydney   Toronto

The **McGraw·Hill** Companies

Cataloging-in-Publication Data is on file with the Library of Congress

McGraw-Hill books are available at special quantity discounts to use as premiums and sales promotions, or for use in corporate training programs. For more information, please write to the Director of Special Sales, Professional Publishing, McGraw-Hill, Two Penn Plaza, New York, NY 10121-2298. Or contact your local bookstore.

Estimating Software Costs: Bringing Realism to Estimating, Second Edition

Copyright © 2007 by The McGraw-Hill Companies. All rights reserved. Printed in the United States of America. Except as permitted under the Copyright Act of 1976, no part of this publication may be reproduced or distributed in any form or by any means, or stored in a database or retrieval system, without the prior written permission of publisher.

1 2 3 4 5 6 7 8 9 0   DOC DOC   0 1 9 8 7

ISBN-13: 978-0-07-148300-1
ISBN-10:   0-07-148300-4

Sponsoring Editor
Wendy Rinaldi

Editorial Supervisor
Janet Walden

Project Manager
Madhu Bhardwaj,
International Typesetting
and Composition

**Acquisitions
Coordinator**
Mandy Canales

Copy Editor
Claire Splan

Proofreader
Raina Trivedi

Indexer
Claire Splan

Production Supervisor
Jean Bodeaux

Composition
International Typesetting
and Composition

Illustration
International Typesetting
and Composition

Art Director, Cover
Jeff Weeks

Cover Designer
Pattie Lee

*This book is dedicated to colleagues
who were among the pioneers of software
measurement and software cost estimating:
Al Albrecht, Dr. Barry Boehm, Tom DeMarco,
Steve Kan, Larry Putnam, Howard Rubin,
and Tony Salvaggio*

Contents

Foreword

Once when discussing a project then already months behind schedule, a puzzled executive observed that "every project we do comes in late." Turning to his cowering CIO, he further fumed, "We give you reasonable deadlines *up front*! Why can't you manage to them?" A knowing look passed between the CIO and a certain consultant who shall remain nameless. Setting the date before the requirements are set is the oldest problem in the software book, but the CIO had no credibility when he argued for different dates, since he lacked the one thing he needed to command the respect of his bosses: a well-defined, consistently applied, and rigorously executed software estimation process.

In its first fifty years, the business of software development acquired a notorious reputation for out-of-control schedules, massive cost overruns, and imperceptible quality control. Project estimation, planning, and quality management were frequently so primitive and haphazard that most large software development projects ran late and exceeded their original budgets. Indeed, many such projects were canceled before they ever reached completion, typically after wasting vast quantities of human and financial resources.

Of course, the worst cases of project failure—the really big fiascos—were often covered up by organizations, since public knowledge of the worst failures would severely impact the market value and public perception of otherwise successful companies.

Naturally, each project had its own story, but a common thread seemed to run through the worst cases. Most overruns and failures to deliver were based on careless, arbitrary, and/or grossly optimistic cost, effort and duration estimates that were typically created with manual, "seat of the pants" estimation techniques. From the beginning of software cost estimation, the "seat of the pants" approach was immensely popular, and as the comic in an old burlesque routine used to say, "It's been following us around ever since."

Early on, it was fairly easy to estimate the anticipated size of software applications, since the few programming languages were very similar and closely resembled actual machine instructions. In this sense, form and function were, if only for a brief time, very nearly equal. Similarly, individual programmer productivity was reasonably easy to predict, expressed usually as "lines of code per month." Thus, a project manager could build a "back-of-the-envelope" estimate by dividing total estimated size by the average productivity, yielding an estimate of the number of months needed to write the code.

Today, when coding can consume as little as 5 percent of a software project's lifecycle, such primitive estimation techniques seem almost comical. Nevertheless, in many organizations the process works about the same way it did 50 years ago. In reality, "back of the envelope" is just a nicer way of saying "seat of the pants," and from an even casual survey of cost and schedule overruns, one might say that the "seat of the pants" is wearing a little thin.

It would be a great relief to say that all that is changing in these latter days of enlightenment, marked by whiz-bang development tools, off-the-shelf enterprise applications that do it all right out of the box (well, almost), black-belted six-sigma samurais, and process improvement gurus with their amply documented how-to's and must-do's. It ought to be getting so much better now. However, if one were to guess, it's likely that 50 years from *now* it will still be said that in its infancy—and now in its presumed adolescence—the software industry was most notable for its stubborn and almost entirely successful resistance to anything like standard engineering disciplines, including in particular rigorous, repeatable calibration, measurement, and estimation.

Thankfully, there have been brave voices in the software wilderness over the years, who studied and sought to remedy the basic problem of poor software project estimation. Capers Jones, Founder and Chief Scientist of Software Productivity Research, LLC (SPR), is perhaps the most widely published and read of this small group of passionate pioneers. From his early work in linguistics and programming language dynamics to his development of a highly successful line of commercial parametric estimating models, including today's SPR KnowledgePlan®, Jones has been a consistent advocate for a more formalized software cost-estimation process.

In 1998, Jones published the first edition of *Estimating Software Costs*, which comprehensively surveyed the history of software estimation, as well as the full range of estimation tools and techniques available to project managers at the time. With this current revised second edition, he expands the scope of his study to include observations and commentary on the current state of estimation in numerous new outposts on the software development landscape, including extreme programming, Agile methods, and ever more extensive ERP and COTS solutions.

In addition, Jones provides the latest data from SPR's research on the myriad of factors affecting project estimation.

Jones continues to argue that organizations must abandon the concept of software estimation as a linear application of industrial principles. His central thesis is that successful software development is not a simple matter of matching a number of people to a number of work units in order to achieve arbitrary budgets and deadlines—an approach that continues to lead to the "endless project" phenomenon, otherwise known as the "death march," the "train wreck," or the "black hole." (Frequently, this approach also leads to a new CIO.) He reminds us that the software process itself remains exceptionally people-oriented and so is somewhat resistant to the influence of newer and better technologies. He points out that ever-advancing tools and methodologies have indeed tended to improve productivity over time, but costs have not always declined proportionately, and the people on a project—their skills, their perceptions, even their feelings—can still matter the most. Somehow, estimates must take these into account.

The overarching problem with poor estimation continues to be excessive optimism, brought on largely by poor methods and arbitrary expectations. However, most software cost estimation is still done by individual project managers working with primitive, homegrown methods. Some are successful, but the ubiquity of cost overruns, schedule slippages, and canceled projects across every industry suggests that most are not. Something needs to change, and Capers Jones effectively argues that formal, rigorous estimation methods—and institutional commitment to use them—are the necessary agents of this change.

–Doug Brindley
President, Software Productivity Research LLC

Preface

In the ten years between the first and the second editions of this book, many changes have taken place in the computer industry and also in the technology of software cost estimating.

More than 20 new development methodologies have appeared, including about a dozen kinds of "Agile" development. Object-oriented (OO) methods are expanding in popularity. Use cases and the unified modeling language (UML) have joined the mainstream of software design methods. The Software Engineering Institute has issued the new capability maturity model integration (CMMI). All of these new approaches are being used on software projects where accurate cost and schedule estimates are important.

Some of these new methods have created new metrics for estimation and measurement. Thus in 2007 software project managers may have to understand not only lines of code and function point metrics, but also Cosmic function points, engineering function points, object points, story points, web object points, use case points, and perhaps 30 others. However, these new metrics are still experimental and lack large volumes of historical data. Standard function point metrics have been used to measure more than 25,000 software projects. So far as can be determined, all of the other metrics put together have been used to measure less than 300 projects, or perhaps 10 projects per metric.

There has also been significant research into estimating methods, and also research into the reasons for inaccurate estimation. While estimating errors are still common, we now know the primary causes of such errors. There are four of them:

- Software projects grow at a rate of about 2 percent per month during development.
- Excessive numbers of bugs or defects throw off testing schedules.
- Producing paper documents often costs more than source code.
- Accurate estimates may be arbitrarily replaced by optimistic estimates.

Now that we know the major sources of software cost-estimating errors, we can begin to control them. The three main technical sources of software cost-estimating errors are actually capable of being eliminated from software cost estimates. But the fourth source of error, the arbitrary replacement of accurate estimates with optimistic ones, remains troublesome.

Once created, software cost estimates must be approved by the clients for whom the software project is being created and sometimes by higher management as well. When clients or higher management face urgent business needs, there is a strong tendency for them to reject accurate cost estimates. This is because building large or complex software applications remains time consuming and expensive.

Thus, instead of starting a software project with a true cost estimate based on team and technical capabilities, many software projects are forced to use external business dates as deadlines. They are also forced to use budgets that are lower than necessary to include all needed functions. These are sociological issues and they are difficult to solve.

The best solution to avoid replacement of accurate estimates is to support the estimate with historical data from similar projects. If history proves that a specific kind of project has never been built any faster or cheaper than the formal cost estimate, then the estimate might survive. Without solid historical data, the estimate will probably be rejected and replaced. This means that benchmarking, or the collection of accurate historical data, is an important precursor to accurate estimation.

Collecting historical data and designing and building software cost-estimating tools have been my main occupations since 1971. My estimation work started at IBM when a colleague and I were asked to collect data about the factors that affected software costs.

After spending a year on collecting cost data within IBM and reviewing the external literature on software costs, it seemed possible to construct a rule-based automated estimating tool that could predict software effort, schedules, and costs for the main activities of IBM's systems software development projects; that is, requirements, design, design reviews, coding, code inspections, testing, user documentation, and project management.

A proposal was given to IBM senior management to fund the development of a software cost-estimating tool. The proposal was accepted, and work commenced in 1972. From that point on, I've designed and built a dozen software cost-estimating tools for individual companies or for the commercial estimating market. The purpose of this book is to show some of the kinds of information needed to build software cost models, and to present an insider's view of the cost-estimating business.

The book tries to cover the fundamental issues involved with software cost estimating. A number of other estimating and metrics specialists have contributed ideas and information and are cited many times.

The work of such other estimating specialists as Allan Albrecht, Dr. Barry Boehm, Frank Freiman, Don Galorath, Dr. Randall Jensen, Steve McConnell, Larry Putnam, Dr. Howard Rubin, and Charles Symons are discussed, although as competitors we do not often share proprietary information with each other.

In my view and also in the view of my competitors, accurate software cost estimating is important to the global economy. Every software project manager, every software quality assurance specialist, and many software engineers, systems analysts, and programmers should understand the basic concepts of software cost estimation. This is a view shared by all of the commercial software cost-estimating vendors.

All of us in the commercial software cost-estimating business know dozens of manual estimating algorithms. All of us in the cost-estimating business use manual estimating methods from time to time on small projects, but not one of us regards manual estimation methods as being sufficient for handling the full life-cycle estimates of major software projects. If manual methods sufficed, there would be no commercial software estimating tools.

It is an interesting phenomenon that most of the major overruns and software disasters are built upon careless and grossly optimistic cost estimates, usually done manually. Projects that use formal estimating tools, such as the competitive tools COCOMO II, GECOMO, SLIM, PRICE-S, ProQMS, SEER, SoftCost, or my company's tools (SPQR/20, CHECKPOINT, or KnowledgePlan), usually have much better track records of staying within their budgets and actually finishing the project without serious mishap.

The reason that manual estimating methods fail for large systems can be expressed in a single word: *complexity*. There are hundreds of factors that determine the outcome of a software project, and it is not possible to deal with the combinations of these factors using simple algorithms and manual methods.

This book illustrates the kinds of complex estimating problems that triggered the creation of the cost-estimating and software project management tool industries. The problems of large-system estimation are the main topic of concern, although estimating methods for small projects are discussed, too.

Estimation is not the only project management function that now has automated support. The book also attempts to place the subject of estimation tools in context with other kinds of project management tools, and to point out gaps where additional kinds of tools are needed.

Software cost-estimating tools are now part of a suite of software project management tools that includes cost estimating, quality estimating, schedule planning (often termed *project management*), methodology or process management, risk analysis, departmental budgeting, milestone tracking, cost reporting, and variance analysis.

These disparate tools have not yet reached the level of sophisticated and seamless integration that has been achieved in the domain of word processing coupled with spreadsheets, databases, and graphical tools, but that level of integration is on the horizon.

Because software cost estimating is a very complex activity involving scores of factors and hundreds of adjustments, this book has a fairly complex structure. It is divided into six main sections and 24 individual chapters.

Section 1 includes an introduction to the topic of software cost estimation, and a survey of the features of software cost-estimating tools. Section 1 also covers the business aspects of software project management, such as how much tools are likely to cost and what kind of value they create. Section 1 assumes no prior knowledge on the part of the reader.

Section 2 deals with several methods for creating early estimates, long before a project's requirements are completely understood. Early estimation from partial knowledge is one of the most difficult forms of estimation, and yet one of the most important. Far too often, early estimates end up being "engraved in stone" or becoming the official estimate for a software project.

This section discusses both manual estimating methods using rules of thumb and the somewhat more sophisticated preliminary estimating methods offered by commercial software estimating tools.

Section 3 deals with the methods of sizing various software artifacts. All commercial software estimating tools need some form of size information in order to operate, and there are a surprisingly large number of ways for dealing with size.

As this book is being written, sizing based on function point metrics is dominant in the software estimating world, but sizing based on lines of code, and on less tangible materials, also occurs. There are also some new experimental metrics such as "use case points" and "object points." However, these are primarily experimental and lack significant amounts of historical data. There are also a number of specialized metrics in the object-oriented domain. While interesting and useful for OO projects, the specialized OO metrics cannot be used for side-by-side comparisons between OO projects and conventional projects.

Section 4 deals with how software cost-estimating tools handle adjustment factors. There are more than 100 known factors that can influence the outcomes of software projects, including the capabilities of the team, the presence or absence of overtime, the methodologies and tools used, and even office space and ergonomics.

Although commercial software cost-estimating tools offer default values for many important topics, the ranges of uncertainty are so great that users are well advised to replace generic "industry averages" with specific values from their own enterprises for key parameters, such as average salary levels, burden rates, staff experience levels, and other factors that can exert a major impact on final results.

Section 5 deals with the principles of activity-based cost estimation for ten activities that occur with high frequency on many software projects:

- Requirements gathering and analysis
- Prototyping
- Specifications and design
- Formal design inspections
- Coding
- Formal code inspections
- Change management, or configuration control
- User documentation
- Testing
- Project management

There are, of course many more than ten activities, but these ten were selected because they occur with high frequency on a great many software projects. Unless the estimates for these ten activities are accurate, there is little hope for accuracy at the gross project level.

Section 6 deals with the principles of activity-based cost estimating for 21 kinds of maintenance and enhancement activities. Maintenance estimating is far more complex than development estimating, since the age and structure of the base application has a severe impact.

There are also a number of very specialized kinds of maintenance estimating that can be quite expensive when they occur, but do not occur with high frequency—error-prone module removal, field service, and dealing with *abeyant* defects, which occur when a user runs an application but cannot be replicated at the maintenance repair facility. Section 6 also deals with several new forms of maintenance that are extremely costly— special dates, expansion of the number of digits in phone numbers, changing daylight savings time, and similar problems that affect hundreds of applications.

– Capers Jones

Acknowledgments

As always, thanks to my wife, Eileen Jones, for making this book possible in many ways. She handles all of our publishing contracts, and by now knows the details of these contracts as well as some attorneys. Thanks also for her patience when I get involved in writing and disappear into our computer room. Also thanks for her patience on holidays and vacations when I take my portable computer.

Appreciation is due to Michael Bragen, Doug Brindley, and Peter Katsoulas of Software Productivity Research LLC. Doug, Michael, and Peter are continuing to develop and refine tools based on some of my estimating algorithms. Thanks to Chas Douglis for his help over many years.

Appreciation is also due to Charles Douglis and Mark Pinis for their design of SPR's KnowledgePlan estimating tool.

Thanks to Tony Salvaggio and Michael Milutis of ComputerAid for providing many opportunities to discuss estimation and benchmarking with their clients and their colleagues. Thanks also for their interest in publishing my reports on their web site.

Appreciation is due to hundreds of colleagues who are members of the International Function Point Users Group (IFPUG). Without IFPUG and the ever-expanding set of projects measured using function points, estimating technology would not have reached the current level of performance.

Thanks are due to Dave Shough, a colleague at IBM who helped me collect data for my first estimating tool. Thanks, too, to Dr. Charles Turk, another IBM colleague and a world-class APL expert, who built the first estimating tool that I designed. Appreciation is due to the late Ted Climis of IBM, who sponsored much of my research on software costs.

Special appreciation is due to Jim Frame, who passed away in October 1997 just as the first edition of this manuscript was being finished. Jim was the Director of IBM's Languages and Data Facilities laboratories, and the immediate sponsor of my first studies on software cost estimation. Jim was later ITT's vice president of programming, where he also supported software cost-estimation research. The software industry lost a leading figure with his passing. Jim's vision of the important role software plays in modern business inspired all who knew him.

Great appreciation is due to all of my former colleagues at Software Productivity Research for their aid in gathering the data, assisting our clients, building the tools that we use, and for making SPR an enjoyable environment. Special thanks to the families and friends of the SPR staff, who had to put up with lots of travel and far too much overtime. Thanks to my former colleagues Mark Beckley, Ed Begley, Chuck Berlin, Barbara Bloom, Julie Bonaiuto, William Bowen, Michael Bragen, Doug Brindley, Kristin Brooks, Tom Cagley, Lynne Caramanica, Debbie Chapman, Sudip Charkraboty, Craig Chamberlin, Carol Chiungos, Michael Cunnane, Chas Douglis, Charlie Duczakowski, Gail Flaherty, Dave Garmus, Richard Gazoorian, James Glorie, Scott Goldfarb, Jane Green, David Gustafson, Wayne Hadlock, Bill Harmon, Shane Hartman, Bob Haven, David Herron, Steve Hone, Jan Huffman, Peter Katsoulas, Richard Kauffold, Heather McPhee, Scott Moody, John Mulcahy, Phyllis Nissen, Jacob Okyne, Donna O'Donnel, Mark Pinis, Tom Riesmeyer, Janet Russac, Cres Smith, John Smith, Judy Sommers, Bill Walsh, Richard Ward, and John Zimmerman. Thanks also to Ajit Maira and Dick Spann for their service on SPR's board of directors.

Many other colleagues work with us at SPR on special projects or as consultants. Special thanks to Allan Albrecht, the inventor of function points, for his invaluable contribution to the industry and for his outstanding work with SPR. Without Allan's pioneering work in function points, the ability to create accurate baselines and benchmarks would probably not exist.

Many thanks to Hisashi Tomino and his colleagues at Kozo Keikaku Engineering in Japan. Kozo has translated several of my prior books into Japanese. In addition, Kozo has been instrumental in the introduction of function point metrics into Japan by translating some of the relevant function point documents.

Much appreciation is due to the client organizations whose interest in software assessments, benchmarks and baselines, measurement, and process improvements have let us work together. These are the organizations whose data make estimation tools possible.

There are too many groups to name them all, but many thanks to our colleagues and clients at Andersen Consulting, AT&T, Bachman, Bellcore, Bell Northern Research, Bell Sygma, Bendix, British Air, CBIS, Charles Schwab, Church of the Latter Day Saints, Cincinnati Bell, CODEX, Computer Aid, Credit Suisse, DEC, Dunn & Bradstreet, Du Pont, EDS, Finsiel, Ford Motors, Fortis Group, General Electric, General Motors, GTE, Hartford Insurance, Hewlett-Packard, IBM, Informix, Inland Steel, Internal Revenue Service, ISSC, JC Penney,

JP Morgan, Kozo Keikaku, Language Technology, Litton, Lotus, Mead Data Central, McKinsey Consulting, Microsoft, Motorola, Nippon Telegraph, NCR, Northern Telecom, Nynex, Pacific Bell, Ralston Purina, Sapiens, Sears Roebuck, Siemens-Nixdorf, Software Publishing Corporation, SOGEI, Sun Life, Tandem, TRW, UNISYS, U.S. Air Force, U.S. Navy Surface Weapons groups, US West, Wang, Westinghouse, and many others.

Thanks also to my colleagues in software estimation: Allan Albrecht, Barry Boehm, Carol Brennan, Tom DeMarco, Don Galorath, Linda Laird, Steve McConnell, Larry Putnam, Don Reifer, Howard Rubin, Frank Freiman, Charles Symons, and Randall Jensen. While these researchers into software cost estimating may be competitors, they are also software cost-estimating pioneers and leading experts. Without their research, there would be no software cost-estimation industry. The software industry is fortunate to have researchers and authors such as these.

Appreciation is also due to those who teach software cost estimating and introduce this important topic to their students. Dr. Victor Basili and Professor Daniel Ferens have both done a great deal to bridge the gap between academia and the business world by introducing real-world estimation tools into the academic domain.

– Capers Jones

Introduction to Software Cost Estimation

Software cost estimation is a complex activity that requires knowledge of a number of key attributes about the project for which the estimate is being constructed. Cost estimating is sometimes termed "parametric estimating" because accuracy demands understanding the relationships among scores of discrete parameters that can affect the outcomes of software projects, both individually and in concert. Creating accurate software cost estimates requires knowledge of the following parameters:

- *The sizes of major deliverables, such as specifications, source code, and manuals*
- *The rate at which requirements are likely to change during development*
- *The probable number of bugs or defects that are likely to be encountered*
- *The capabilities of the development team*
- *The salaries and overhead costs associated with the development team*
- *The formal methodologies that are going to be utilized (such as the Agile methods)*
- *The tools that are going to be utilized on the project*

- *The set of development activities that are going to be carried out*
- *The cost and schedule constraints set by clients of the project being estimated*

Although the factors that influence the outcomes of software projects are numerous and some are complex, modern commercial software cost-estimation tools can ease the burden of project managers by providing default values for all of the key parameters, using industry values derived from the integral knowledge base supplied with the estimation tools.

In addition, software cost-estimation tools allow the construction of customized estimating templates that are derived from actual projects and that can be utilized for estimating projects of similar sizes and kinds.

This section discusses the origins and evolution of software cost-estimation tools and how software cost estimation fits within the broader category of software project management. In addition, this section discusses the impact of software cost-estimation tools on the success rates of software projects and uses this data to illustrate the approximate return on investment (ROI) from software cost-estimating and project management tools.

1

Introduction

Software cost estimating has been an important but difficult task since the beginning of the computer era in the 1940s. As software applications have grown in size and importance, the need for accuracy in software cost estimating has grown, too.

In the early days of software, computer programs were typically less than 1000 machine instructions in size (or less than 30 function points), required only one programmer to write, and seldom took more than a month to complete. The entire development costs were often less than $5000. Although cost estimating was difficult, the economic consequences of cost-estimating errors were not very serious.

Today some large software systems exceed 25 million source code statements (or more than 300,000 function points), may require technical staffs of 1000 personnel or more, and may take more than five calendar years to complete. The development costs for such large software systems can exceed $500 million; therefore, errors in cost estimation can be very serious indeed.

Even more serious, a significant percentage of large software systems run late, exceed their budgets, or are canceled outright due to severe underestimating during the requirements phase. In fact, excessive optimism in software cost estimation is a major source of overruns, failures, and litigation.

Software is now the driving force of modern business, government, and military operations. This means that a typical Fortune 500 corporation or a state government may produce hundreds of new applications and modify hundreds of existing applications every year. As a result of the host of software projects in the modern world, software cost estimating is now a mainstream activity for every company that builds software.

In addition to the need for accurate software cost estimates for day-to-day business operations, software cost estimates are becoming a significant aspect in litigation. Over the past fifteen years, the author and his colleagues have observed dozens of lawsuits where software cost estimates were produced by the plaintiffs, the defendants, or both. For example, software cost estimation now plays a key part in lawsuits involving the following disputes:

- Breach of contract suits between clients and contractors
- Suits involving the taxable value of software assets
- Suits involving recovering excess costs for defense software due to scope expansion
- Suits involving favoritism in issuance of software contracts
- Suits involving wrongful termination of software personnel

From many viewpoints, software cost estimating has become a critical technology of the 21st century because software is now so pervasive.

How Software Cost-Estimating Tools Work

There are many kinds of automated tools that experienced project managers can use to create cost, schedule, and resource estimates for software projects. For example, an experienced software project manager can create a cost-estimate and schedule plan using any of the following:

- Spreadsheets
- Project management tools
- Software cost-estimating tools

A frequently asked question for software cost-estimating tool vendors is "Why do we need your tool when we already have spreadsheets and project management tools?"

The commercial software-estimating tools are differentiated from all other kinds of software project management tools and general-purpose tools, such as spreadsheets, in these key attributes:

- They contain knowledge bases of hundreds or thousands of software projects.
- They can perform size predictions, which general-purpose tools cannot.
- They can automatically adjust estimates based on tools, languages, and processes.
- They can predict quality and reliability, which general-purpose tools cannot.

- They can predict maintenance and support costs after deployment.
- They can predict (and prevent) problems long before the problems actually occur.

Unlike other kinds of project management tools, the commercial software cost-estimating tools do not depend upon the expertise of the user or project manager, although experienced managers can refine the estimates produced. The commercial cost-estimating tools contain the accumulated experience of many hundreds or thousands of software projects.

Because of the attached knowledge bases associated with commercial cost-estimating tools, novice managers or managers faced with unfamiliar kinds of projects can describe the kind of project being dealt with, and the estimating tool will construct an estimate based on similar projects derived from information contained in its associated knowledge base.

Figure 1.1 illustrates the basic principles of modern commercial software cost-estimating tools.

The starting point of software estimation is the size of the project in terms of either logical source code statements, physical lines of code, function points, or, sometimes, all three metrics. The project's size can be derived from the estimating tool's own sizing logic, supplied by users as an explicit input, or derived from analogy with similar projects stored in the estimating tool's knowledge base. Even for Agile projects and those using iterative development, at least approximate size information can be created.

Once the basic size of the project has been determined, the estimate can be produced based on the specific attributes of the project in question. Examples of the attributes that can affect the outcome of the estimate include the following:

- The rate at which project requirements may change
- The experience of the development team with this kind of project
- The process or methods used to develop the project ranging from Agile to Waterfall

Figure 1.1 Software-estimating principles.

- The specific activities that will be performed during development
- The number of increments, iterations, or "sprints" that will be used
- The programming language or languages utilized
- The presence or absence of reusable artifacts
- The development tool suites used to develop the project
- The environment or ergonomics of the office work space
- The geographic separation of the team across multiple locations
- The schedule pressure put on the team by clients or executives
- Contractual obligations in terms of costs, dates, defects, or features

Using commercial estimating tools, these project attributes can either be supplied by the user or inherited from similar projects already stored in the estimating tool's knowledge base. In a sense estimating tools share some of the characteristics of the object-oriented paradigm in that they allow inheritance of shared attributes from project to project.

In software-estimating terminology, these shared attributes are termed *templates*, and they can be built in a number of ways. For example, estimating-tool users can point to an existing completed project and select any or all of the features of that project as the basis of the template. Thus, if the project selected as the basis of a template were a systems software project, used the C programming language, and utilized formal design and code inspections, these attributes could be inherited as part of the development cycle and could become part of an estimating template for other projects.

Many other attributes from historical projects can also be inherited and can become aspects of software-estimating templates. For example, a full estimating template can contain inherited attribute data on such topics as the following:

- The experience of the development team in similar applications
- The process or methodology used to develop the application
- The SEI capability maturity level of the organization
- The standards that will be adhered to, such as ISO, DoD, IEEE, and so forth
- The tools used during design, coding, testing, and so forth
- The programming language or languages utilized
- The volumes of reusable artifacts available
- The ergonomics of the programming office environment

Since software projects are not identical, any of these inherited attributes can be modified as the need arises. However, the availability of templates makes the estimation process quicker, more convenient, and more reliable because templates substitute specific knowledge from local projects for generic industry default values.

Templates can also be derived from sets of projects rather than from one specific project, or can even be custom-built by the users, using artificial factors. However, the most common method of template development is to use the automatic template construction ability of the estimating tool, and simply select relevant historical projects to be used as the basis for the template.

As a general rule, software-estimating templates are concerned with four key kinds of inherited attributes: (1) *personnel*, (2) *technologies*, (3) *tools*, and (4) the *programming environment*, as illustrated by Figure 1.2.

Three of these four factors—the experience of the personnel, the development process, and the technology (programming languages and support tools)—are fairly obvious in their impact. What is not obvious, but is equally important, is the impact of the fourth factor—*environment*.

The environment factor covers individual office space and the communication channels among geographically dispersed development teams. Surprisingly, access to a quiet, noise-free office environment is one of the major factors that influences programming productivity.

The ability to include ergonomic factors in an estimate is an excellent example of the value of commercial software cost-estimating tools. Not only do they contain the results of hundreds or thousands of completed projects, but the tools contain data about influential factors that many human project managers may not fully understand.

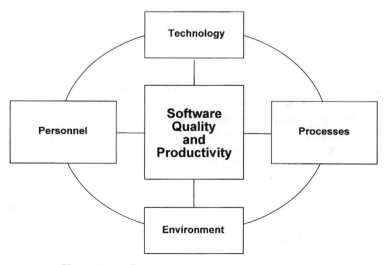

Figure 1.2 Key estimate factors.

The four key sets of attributes must be considered whether estimating manually or using an automated estimating tool. However, one of the key features of commercial software-estimating tools is the fact that they are repositories containing the results of hundreds or thousands of software projects, and so the effect of these four attribute areas can be examined, and their impacts can be analyzed.

There is a standard sequence for software cost estimation, which the author has used for more than 35 years. This sequence can be used with manual software cost estimates, and also mirrors the estimation stages in the software-estimation tools that the author has designed. There are ten steps in this sequence, although the sequence starts with 0 because the first stage is a pre-estimate analysis of the requirements of the application.

Step 0: Analyze the Requirements

Software cost estimation at the project level cannot be performed unless the requirements of the project are well understood. Therefore, before estimating itself can begin, it is necessary to explore and understand the user requirements. At some point in the future it should be possible to create estimates automatically from the requirements specifications, but the current level of estimating technology demands human intervention.

A common estimating activity today is to analyze the software requirements and create function point totals based on those requirements. This provides the basic size data used for formal cost estimation. Function point analysis is usually performed manually by certified function point counting personnel. A time is rapidly approaching when function point totals can be derived automatically from software requirements, and this method may appear in commercial software cost-estimation tools within a few years.

It is a known fact that requirements for large systems cannot be fully defined at the start of the project. This fact is the basis for the Agile methods, extreme programming, Scrum, and a number of others. This fact is also embedded in the algorithms for several commercial software estimating tools. Once the initial requirements are understood, the average rate of growth of new requirements is about 2 percent per calendar month. This growth can be planned for and included in the estimate.

Step 1: Start with Sizing

Every form of estimation and every commercial software cost-estimating tool needs the sizes of key deliverables in order to complete an estimate. Size data can be derived in several fashions, including the following:

- Size prediction using an estimating tool's built-in sizing algorithms
- Sizing by extrapolation from function point totals
- Sizing by analogy with similar projects of known size
- Guessing at the size using "project manager's intuition"
- Guessing at the size using "programmer's intuition"
- Sizing using statistical methods or Monte Carlo simulation

For Agile methods and those projects using iterative development, sizing of the entire application may be deferred until the early increments are complete. However, even for Agile and iterative projects it is possible to make an approximate prediction of final size just by comparing the nature of the project to similar projects or using size approximations based on the class, type, and nature of the software. Later in this book examples are given of such sizing methods.

The basic size of the application being estimated is usually expressed in terms of function points, source code statements, or both. However, it is very important to size all deliverables and not deal only with code. For example, more than 50 kinds of paper documents are associated with large software projects, and they need to be sized also. Of course, when using one of the commercial software estimating tools that support documents sizing, these sizes will automatically be predicted.

Source code sizing must be tailored to specific programming languages, and more than 600 languages are now in use. About one-third of software projects utilize more than a single programming language. More than a dozen kinds of testing occur, and each will require different volumes of test cases.

Sizing is a key estimating activity. If the sizes of major deliverables can be predicted within 5 to 10 percent, then the accuracy of the overall estimate can be quite good. If size predictions are wildly inaccurate, then the rest of the estimate will be inaccurate, too. As mentioned earlier, empirical evidence from large software projects indicates that requirements grow at an average rate of about 2 percent per calendar month from the end of the requirements phase until the start of the testing phase. The total growth of requirements can exceed 50 percent of the volume of the initial requirements when measured with function points. A major problem with estimating accuracy has been ignoring or leaving out requirements creep. Modern cost-estimating tools can predict requirements growth and can include their costs and schedules in the estimate.

The technologies available for sizing have been improving rapidly. In the early days of software cost estimation, size data had to be supplied by users, using very primitive methods. Now modern software cost-estimating tools have a number of sizing capabilities available, including support for very early size estimates even before the requirements are firm.

Step 2: Identify the Activities to Be Included

Once the sizes of key deliverables are known, the next step is to select the set of activities that are going to be performed. In this context the term *activities* refers to the work that will be performed for the project being estimated, such as requirements, internal design, external design, design inspections, coding, code inspections, user document creation, meetings or Scrum sessions, change control, integration, quality assurance, unit testing, new function testing, regression testing, system testing, and project management. Accurate estimation is impossible without knowledge of the activities that are going to be utilized.

Activity patterns vary widely from project to project. Large systems utilize many more activities than do small projects. Waterfall projects utilize more activities than Agile projects. For projects of the same size, military and systems software utilize more activities than do information systems. Local patterns of activities are the ones to utilize, because they reflect your own enterprise's software development methodologies.

Modern software cost-estimating tools have built-in logic for selecting the activity patterns associated with many kinds of software development projects. Users can also adjust the activity patterns to match local variations.

Step 3: Estimate Software Defect Potentials
and Removal Methods

The most expensive and time-consuming work of software development is the work of finding bugs and fixing them. In the United States the number of bugs or defects in requirements, design, code, documents, and bad-fixes averages five per function point. Average defect removal efficiency before delivery is 85 percent. The cost of finding and repairing these defects averages about 35 percent of the total development cost of building the application. The schedule time required is about 30 percent of project development schedules. Defect repair costs and schedules are often larger than coding costs and schedules. Accuracy in software cost estimates is not possible if defects and defect removal are not included in the estimates. The author's software cost-estimating tools include full defect-estimation capabilities, and support all known kinds of defect-removal activity. This is necessary because the total effort, time, and cost devoted to a full series of reviews, inspections, and multistage tests will cost far more than source code itself.

Defect estimation includes predictive abilities for requirements defects, design defects, coding defects, user documentation defects, and a very troubling category called *bad fix defects*. The phrase *bad fix* refers to new defects accidentally injected as a by-product of repairing previous defects. Bad fix defects average about 7 percent of all defect repairs. Some estimating tools can predict bad fixes.

Estimating tools that support commercial software can also predict duplicate defect reports, or bugs found by more than one customer. It is also possible to estimate *invalid defect reports*, or bug reports that turn out not to be the fault of the software, such as user errors or hardware problems.

The ability to predict software defects would not be very useful without another kind of estimation, which is predicting the *defect-removal efficiency* of various kinds of reviews, inspections, and test stages. Modern software cost-estimating tools can predict how many bugs will be found by every form of defect removal, from desk checking through external beta testing.

Step 4: Estimate Staffing Requirements

Every software deliverable has a characteristic *assignment scope*, or amount of work that can be done by a single employee. For example, an average assignment for an individual programmer will range from 5000 to 15,000 source code statements (from about 50 up to 2000 function points).

However, large systems also utilize many specialists, such as system architects, database administrators, quality assurance specialists, software engineers, technical writers, testers, and the like. Identifying each category of worker and the numbers of workers for the overall project is the next step in software cost estimation.

Staffing requirements depend upon the activities that will be performed and the deliverables that will be created, so staffing predictions are derived from knowledge of the overall size of the application and the activity sets that will be included. Staffing predictions also need to be aware of "pair programming" or two-person teams, which are part of some of the new Agile methods.

For large systems, programmers themselves may comprise less than half of the workforce. Various kinds of specialists and project managers comprise the other half. Some of these specialists include quality assurance personnel, testing personnel, technical writers, systems analysts, database administrators, and configuration control specialists. If the project is big enough to need specialists, accurate estimation requires that their efforts be included. Both programming and other kinds of noncoding activities, such as production of manuals and quality assurance, must be included to complete the estimate successfully.

Step 5: Adjust Assumptions Based on Capabilities and Experience

Software personnel can range from top experts with years of experience to rank novices on their first assignment. Once the categories of technical workers have been identified, the next step is to make adjustments based on typical experience levels and skill factors.

Experts can take on more work, and perform it faster, than can novices. This means that experts will have larger assignment scopes and higher production rates than average or inexperienced personnel.

Other adjustments include work hours per day, vacations and holidays, unpaid and paid overtime, and assumptions about the geographic dispersal of the software team. Adjusting the estimate to match the capabilities of the team is one of the more critical estimating activities.

While estimating tools can make adjustments to match varying degrees of expertise, these tools have no way of knowing the specific capabilities of any given team. Many commercial estimating tools default to "average" capabilities, and allow users to adjust this assumption upward or downward to match specific team characteristics.

Step 6: Estimate Effort and Schedules

Effort and schedule estimates are closely coupled, and often are performed in an iterative manner.

Accurate effort estimation requires knowledge of the basic size of the application plus the numbers and experience levels of the software team members and the sizes of various deliverables they are expected to produce, such as specifications and user manuals.

Accurate schedule estimation requires knowledge of the activities that will be performed, the number of increments or "sprints" that will be carried out, the sizes of various deliverables, the overlap between activities with mutual dependencies, and the numbers and experience levels of the software team members.

Schedule and effort estimates are closely coupled, but the interaction between these two dimensions is complicated and sometimes is counterintuitive. For example, if a software project will take six months if it is developed by one programmer, adding a second programmer will not cut the schedule to three months. Indeed, a point can be reached where putting on additional personnel may slow down the project's schedule rather than accelerating it.

The complex sets of rules that link effort and schedules for software projects are the heart of the algorithms for software cost-estimating tools.

As an example of one of the more subtle rules that estimating tools contain, adding personnel to a software project within one department will usually shorten development schedules. But if enough personnel are added so that a second department is involved, schedules will stretch out. The reason for this is that software schedules, and also productivity rates, are inversely related to the number of project managers engaged. There are scores of rules associated with the interaction of schedules and effort, and some of these are both subtle and counterintuitive.

In fact, for very large software projects with multiple teams, the rate at which development productivity declines tends to correlate more closely to the number of managers that are engaged than to the actual number of programmers involved. This phenomenon leads to some subtle findings, such as the fact that projects with a small span of control (less than six developers per manager) may have lower productivity than similar projects with a large span of control (12 developers per manager).

Step 7: Estimate Development Costs

Development costs are the next-to-last stage of estimation and are very complex. Development costs are obviously dependent upon the effort and schedule for software projects, so these factors are predicted first, and then costs are applied afterwards.

Costs for software projects that take exactly the same amount of effort in terms of hours or months can vary widely due to the following causes:

- Average salaries of workers and managers on the project
- The corporate burden rate or overhead rate applied to the project
- Inflation rates, if the project will run for several years
- Currency exchange rates, if the project is developed internationally

There may also be special cost topics that will have to be dealt with separately, outside of the basic estimate:

- License fees for any acquired software needed
- Capital costs for any new equipment
- Moving and living costs for new staff members
- Travel costs for international projects or projects developed in different locations
- Contractor and subcontractor costs
- Legal fees for copyrights, patents, or other matters
- Marketing and advertising costs

- Costs for developing videos or CD-ROM tutorial materials and training
- Content acquisition costs if the application is a web-based product

On the whole, developing a full and complete cost estimate for a software project is much more complex than simply developing a resource estimate of the number of work hours that are likely to be needed. Many cost elements, such as burden rates or travel, are only indirectly related to effort and can impact the final cost of the project significantly.

The normal pattern of software estimation is to use hours, days, weeks, or months of effort as the primary estimating unit, and then apply costs at the end of the estimating cycle once the effort patterns have been determined.

Step 8: Estimate Maintenance and Enhancement Costs

Software projects often continue to be used and modified for many years. Maintenance and enhancement cost estimation are special topics, and are more complex than new project cost estimation.

Estimating maintenance costs requires knowledge of the probable number of users of the application, combined with knowledge of the probable number of bugs or defects in the product at the time of release.

Estimating enhancement costs requires good historical data on the rate of change of similar projects once they enter production and start being used. For example, new software projects can add 10 percent or more in total volume of new features with each release for several releases in a row, but then slow down for a period of two to three years before another major release occurs.

Many commercial estimating tools can estimate both the initial construction costs of a project and the maintenance and enhancement cost patterns for more than five years of usage by customers.

There is no actual limit on the number of years that can be estimated, but because long-range projections of user numbers and possible new features are highly questionable, the useful life of maintenance and enhancement estimates runs from three to five years. Estimating maintenance costs ten years into the future can be done, but no estimate of that range can be regarded as reliable because far too many uncontrollable business variables can occur.

Step 9: Present Your Estimate to the Client and Defend It Against Rejection

Once a cost estimate is prepared, the next step is to present the estimate to the client who is going to fund the project. For large systems and applications of 5000 function points or larger (equivalent to roughly 500,000 source code statements) about 60 percent of the initial estimates will be rejected by the client. Either the estimated schedule will be too long, the costs will be too high, or both. Often the client will decree a specific delivery date much shorter than the estimated date. Often the client will decree that costs must be held within limits much lower than the estimated costs. Projects where formal estimates are rejected and replaced by arbitrary schedules and costs derived from external business needs rather than team capabilities have the highest failure rates in the industry. About 60 percent of such projects will be cancelled and never completed at all. (At the point of cancellation, both costs and schedules will already have exceeded their targets.) Of the 40 percent of projects that finally do get completed, the average schedule will be about one year late, and the average cost will be about 50 percent higher than targets.

The best defense against having a cost estimate rejected is to have solid historical data from at least a dozen similar projects. The second-best defense against have a cost estimate rejected is to prepare a full activity-based estimate that includes quality, paperwork, requirements creep, all development activities, and all maintenance tasks, You will need to prove that your estimate has been carefully prepared and has left nothing to chance. High-level or phase-level estimates that lack detail are not convincing and are easy to reject.

Cautions About Accidental Omissions from Estimates

Because software-estimating tools have such an extensive knowledge base, they are not likely to make the kinds of mistakes that inexperienced human managers make when they create estimates by hand or with general-purpose tools and accidentally omit activities from the estimate.

For example, when estimating large systems, coding may be only the fourth most expensive activity. Human managers often tend to leave out or underestimate the non-code work, but estimating tools can include these other activities.

- Historically, the effort devoted to finding and fixing bugs by means of reviews, walkthroughs, inspections, and testing takes more time and costs more than any other software activities. Therefore, accurate cost estimates need to start with quality predictions, because defect-removal costs are often more expensive than anything else.

- In second place as major cost elements are the expenses and effort devoted to the production of paper documents, such as plans, specifications, user manuals, and the like. For military software projects, paperwork will cost twice as much as the code itself. For large civilian projects greater than 1000 function points or 100,000 source code statements, paper documents will be a major cost element and will approach or exceed the cost of the code.

- In third place for many large projects are the costs and schedules of dealing with "creeping requirements" or new features added to the project after the requirements phase. All software projects will grow due to creeping requirements and therefore this factor should be an integral part of the estimates for all major software projects.

- For some large distributed applications that involve multiple development locations or subcontractors, the costs of meetings and travel among the locations can cost more than the source code and may be in fourth place in the sequence of all software costs. A frequent omission from software cost estimates is the accidental exclusion of travel costs (airlines, hotels, etc.) for meetings among the development teams that are located in different cities or different countries. For very large kinds of systems, such as operating systems, telecommunication systems, or defense systems, which may involve distributed development in half a dozen countries and a dozen cities, the costs of travel can exceed the cost of coding significantly, and this topic should not be left out by accident.

- Many software cost estimates—and many measurement systems, too—cover only the core activities of software development and ignore such topics as project management and support (i.e., program librarians, secretaries, administration, etc.). These ancillary activities are part of the project and can, in some cases, top 20 percent of total costs. This is far too much to leave out by accident.

- The software domain has fragmented into a number of specialized skills and occupations. It is very common to accidentally leave out the contributions of specialists if their skills are needed only during portions of a software development cycle. Some of the specialist groups that tend to be accidentally omitted from software cost estimates include quality assurance specialists, technical writing specialists, function point specialists, database administration specialists, performance tuning specialists, network specialists, and system administration specialists. The combined contributions of these and other specialists may total more than 20 percent of all software development costs and should not be omitted by accident.

- The most common omission from internal software cost estimates for information systems are the costs expended by users during requirements definition, prototyping, status reviews, phase reviews, documentation, inspections, acceptance testing, and other activities where the developers have a key role. Since user representatives are not usually considered to be part of the project team, their contributions to the project are seldom included in software cost estimates, and are seldom included in measurement studies, either. The actual amount of effort contributed by users to major software development projects can approach 20 percent of the total work in some cases, which is not a trivial amount and is far too significant to leave out by accident. Some commercial software cost-estimating tools keep a separate chart of accounts for user activities and allow user efforts to be added to total project costs, if desired.

- For many projects, maintenance after delivery quickly costs more than the development of the application itself. It is unwise to stop the estimate at the point of delivery of the software without including at least five years of maintenance and enhancement estimates. Since maintenance (defect repairs) and enhancements (adding new features) have different funding sources, many estimating tools separate these two activities. Other forms of maintenance work, such as customer support or field service, may also be included in post-release estimates.

A key factor that differentiates modern commercial software cost-estimating tools from general-purpose tools, such as spreadsheets and project management tools, is the presence of full life-cycle historical data. This gives them the ability to estimate quality and to estimate the sizes and costs of producing paper deliverables, the probable volumes of creeping requirements, and the costs of coding and testing.

When considering acquisition of a software cost-estimating tool, be sure that the knowledge base includes the kind of software you are interested in. The real-life cost and schedule results of information systems, systems software, commercial software, military software, and embedded software are not identical, and you need to be sure the estimating tool contains data on the kinds of software you are concerned with. Some tools support all classes of software, but others are more narrow in focus.

Software Cost Estimating and Other Development Activities

Software cost estimating is not a "standalone" activity. The estimates are derived in large part from the requirements of the project, and will be strongly affected by the tools, process, and other attributes associated with the project. A cost estimate is a precursor for departmental budgets, and also serves as a baseline document for comparing accumulated costs against projected costs.

For any project larger than trivial, multiple cost estimates will be prepared during the course of development, including but not limited to the following:

- A rough pre-requirements guesstimate
- An initial formal estimate derived from the project requirements
- One or more midlife estimates, which reflect requirements changes
- A final cost accumulation using project historical data

In addition, since the software industry is somewhat litigious, cost estimates may also be prepared as a by-product of several kinds of litigation, including the following:

- Litigation for breach of contract between software clients and outsource companies
- Litigation involving the taxable value of software in tax disputes

In the course of developing a software project, historical data will steadily be accumulated. This means that after the first rough guesstimate and the initial requirements estimate, future estimates will need to interleave historical data with predicted data. Therefore, software-estimating tools need the ability to capture historical data and to selectively display both historical data and predicted values.

Figure 1.3 illustrates how software cost estimation fits into the context of other key software development activities.

As can be seen from Figure 1.3, estimating is closely aligned with other key development phases. When done well, software cost estimates are among the most valuable documents in the entire software world, because they make a software project real and tangible in terms of the resources, schedules, and costs that will be required.

However, cost estimates that are poorly constructed and grossly inaccurate are key factors in almost every major software disaster. The best advice for those charged with constructing software cost estimates is the following:

- Be accurate.
- Be conservative.
- Base the estimate on solid historical data.
- Include quality, since software quality affects schedules and costs.
- Include paper documents, since they can cost more than source code.
- Include project management.

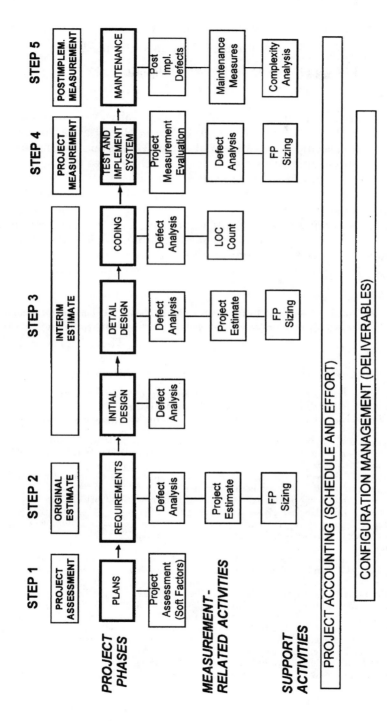

Figure 1.3 Software cost estimation and other activities.

- Include the effects of creeping requirements.
- Do not exaggerate the effect of tools, languages, or methods.
- Get below phases to activity-level cost estimates.
- Be prepared to defend the assumptions of your estimate.

Even with the best estimating tools, accurate software cost estimating is complicated and can be difficult. But without access to good historical data, accurate software cost estimating is almost impossible. Measurement and estimation are twin technologies and both are urgently needed by software project managers.

Measurement and estimation are also linked in the commercial software cost-estimation marketplace, since many of the commercial estimating companies are also benchmark and measurement companies. As better historical data becomes available, the features of the commercial software cost-estimating tools are growing stronger.

References

Barrow, Dean, Susan Nilson, and Dawn Timberlake: *Software Estimation Technology Report*, Air Force Software Technology Support Center, Hill Air Force Base, Utah, 1993.

Boehm, Barry: *Software Engineering Economics*, Prentice-Hall, Englewood Cliffs, N.J., 1981.

———: *Software Cost Estimation with COCOMO II*, Prentice-Hall, Englewood Cliffs, NJ;

Brown, Norm (ed.): *The Program Manager's Guide to Software Acquisition Best Practices*, Version 1.0, U.S. Department of Defense, Washington, D.C., July 1995.

Charette, Robert N.: *Software Engineering Risk Analysis and Management*, McGraw-Hill, New York, 1989.

———: *Application Strategies for Risk Analysis*, McGraw-Hill, New York, 1990.

Cohn, Mike: *Agile Estimating and Planning* (Robert C. Martin Series), Prentice-Hall PTR, Englewood Cliffs, NJ, 2005.

Coombs, Paul: *IT Project Estimation: A Practical Guide to the Costing of Software*, Cambridge University Press, Melbourne, Australia.

DeMarco, Tom: *Controlling Software Projects*, Yourdon Press, New York.

———: *Deadline*, Dorset House Press, New York, 1997.

Department of the Air Force: *Guidelines for Successful Acquisition and Management of Software Intensive Systems*; vols. 1 and 2, Software Technology Support Center, Hill Air Force Base, Utah, 1994.

Dreger, Brian: *Function Point Analysis*, Prentice-Hall, Englewood Cliffs, N.J., 1989.

Galorath, Daniel D. and Michael W. Evans: *Software Sizing, Estimation, and Risk Management*, Auerbach, Philadelphia, PA, 2006.

Garmus, David, and David Herron: *Measuring the Software Process: A Practical Guide to Functional Measurement*, Prentice-Hall, Englewood Cliffs, N.J., 1995.

Garmus, David and David Herron: *Function Point Analysis: Measurement Practices for Successful Software Projects*, Addison-Wesley, Boston, Mass., 2001.

Grady, Robert B.: *Practical Software Metrics for Project Management and Process Improvement*, Prentice-Hall, Englewood Cliffs, N.J., 1992.

——— and Deborah L. Caswell: *Software Metrics: Establishing a Company-Wide Program*, Prentice-Hall, Englewood Cliffs, N.J., 1987.

Gulledge, Thomas R., William P. Hutzler, and Joan S. Lovelace (eds.): *Cost Estimating and Analysis—Balancing Technology with Declining Budgets*, Springer-Verlag, New York, 1992.

Howard, Alan (ed.): *Software Metrics and Project Management Tools*, Applied Computer Research (ACR), Phoenix, Ariz., 1997.

IFPUG Counting Practices Manual, Release 4, International Function Point Users Group, Westerville, Ohio, April 1995.

Jones, Capers: *Critical Problems in Software Measurement*, Information Systems Management Group, 1993a.

———: *Software Productivity and Quality Today—The Worldwide Perspective*, Information Systems Management Group, 1993b.

———: *Assessment and Control of Software Risks*, Prentice-Hall, Englewood Cliffs, N.J., 1994.

———: *New Directions in Software Management*, Information Systems Management Group.

———: *Patterns of Software System Failure and Success*, International Thomson Computer Press, Boston, 1995.

———: *Applied Software Measurement*, 2nd ed., McGraw-Hill, New York, 1996.

———: *The Economics of Object-Oriented Software*, Software Productivity Research, Burlington, Mass., April 1997a.

———: *Software Quality—Analysis and Guidelines for Success*, International Thomson Computer Press, Boston, 1997b.

———: *The Year 2000 Software Problem—Quantifying the Costs and Assessing the Consequences*, Addison-Wesley, Reading, Mass., 1998.

———: *Software Assessments, Benchmarks, and Best Practices*, Addison-Wesley, Boston, Mass, 2000.

Kan, Stephen H.: *Metrics and Models in Software Quality Engineering*, 2nd edition, Addison-Wesley, Boston, Mass., 2003.

Kemerer, C. F.: "Reliability of Function Point Measurement—A Field Experiment," *Communications of the ACM*, **36:** 85–97 (1993).

Keys, Jessica: *Software Engineering Productivity Handbook*, McGraw-Hill, New York, 1993.

Laird, Linda M. and Carol M. Brennan: *Software Measurement and Estimation: A practical Approach*; John Wiley & Sons, New York, 2006.

Lewis, James P.: *Project Planning, Scheduling & Control*, McGraw-Hill, New York, New York, 2005.

Marciniak, John J. (ed.): *Encyclopedia of Software Engineering*, vols. 1 and 2, John Wiley & Sons, New York, 1994.

McConnell, Steve: *Software Estimation: Demystifying the Black Art*, Microsoft Press, Redmond, WA, 2006.

Mertes, Karen R.: *Calibration of the CHECKPOINT Model to the Space and Missile Systems Center (SMC) Software Database (SWDB)*, Thesis AFIT/GCA/LAS/96S-11, Air Force Institute of Technology (AFIT), Wright-Patterson AFB, Ohio, September 1996.

Ourada, Gerald, and Daniel V. Ferens: "Software Cost Estimating Models: A Calibration, Validation, and Comparison," in *Cost Estimating and Analysis: Balancing Technology and Declining Budgets*, Springer-Verlag, New York, 1992, pp. 83–101.

Perry, William E.: *Handbook of Diagnosing and Solving Computer Problems*, TAB Books, Blue Ridge Summit, Pa., 1989.

Pressman, Roger: *Software Engineering: A Practitioner's Approach with Bonus Chapter on Agile Development*, McGraw-Hill, New York, 2003.

Putnam, Lawrence H.: *Measures for Excellence—Reliable Software on Time, Within Budget:* Yourdon Press/Prentice-Hall, Englewood Cliffs, N.J., 1992.

———, and Ware Myers: *Industrial Strength Software—Effective Management Using Measurement*, IEEE Press, Los Alamitos, Calif., 1997.

Reifer, Donald (ed.): *Software Management*, 4th ed., IEEE Press, Los Alamitos, Calif., 1993.

Rethinking the Software Process, CD-ROM, Miller Freeman, Lawrence, Kans., 1996. (This CD-ROM is a book collection jointly produced by the book publisher, Prentice-Hall, and the journal publisher, Miller Freeman. It contains the full text and illustrations of five Prentice-Hall books: *Assessment and Control of Software Risks* by Capers Jones; *Controlling Software Projects* by Tom DeMarco; *Function Point Analysis* by Brian Dreger; *Measures for Excellence* by Larry Putnam and Ware Myers; and *Object-Oriented Software Metrics* by Mark Lorenz and Jeff Kidd.)

Rubin, Howard: *Software Benchmark Studies for 1997*, Howard Rubin Associates, Pound Ridge, N.Y., 1997.

Roetzheim, William H., and Reyna A. Beasley: *Best Practices in Software Cost and Schedule Estimation*, Prentice-Hall PTR, Upper Saddle River, N.J., 1998.

Stukes, Sherry, Jason Deshoretz, Henry Apgar, and Ilona Macias: *Air Force Cost Analysis Agency Software Estimating Model Analysis—Final Report*, TR-9545/008-2, Contract F04701-95-D-0003, Task 008, Management Consulting & Research, Inc., Thousand Oaks, Calif., September 1996.

Stutzke, Richard D.: *Estimating Software-Intensive Systems: Projects, Products, and Processes*, Addison-Wesley, Boston, Mass, 2005.

Symons, Charles R.: *Software Sizing and Estimating—Mk II FPA (Function Point Analysis)*, John Wiley & Sons, Chichester, U.K., 1991.

Wellman, Frank: *Software Costing: An Objective Approach to Estimating and Controlling the Cost of Computer Software*, Prentice-Hall, Englewood Cliffs, N.J., 1992,

Yourdon, Ed: *Death March—The Complete Software Developer's Guide to Surviving "Mission Impossible" Projects*, Prentice-Hall PTR, Upper Saddle River, N.J., 1997.

Zells, Lois: *Managing Software Projects—Selecting and Using PC-Based Project Management Systems*, QED Information Sciences, Wellesley, Mass., 1990.

Zvegintzov, Nicholas: *Software Management Technology Reference Guide*, Dorset House Press, New York, 1994.

2

The Origins of Software Cost Estimation

The software industry began in the 1950s. Almost immediately software estimation started to cause problems. In the 1960s when computers began to be used for business purposes by corporations, software-estimation problems started to attract top-management attention. Software projects soon gained a reputation for having more cost and schedule overruns than any other aspect of business operations. Consequently, a number of large corporations began to assign specialists to look for improved methods of software-cost estimation.

Software development and maintenance are both difficult domains for cost-estimation purposes. Software is highly labor-intensive, so individual human variances exert a major impact. Also, unlike with many physical constructs, such as buildings or automobiles, the requirements and design for software projects tend to change significantly during the development cycle. Indeed, the average rate for new requirements after the requirements phase averages 2 percent per calendar month. A few projects have noted requirements growth of more than 5 percent per month during the subsequent design and coding phases. There are also many different kinds of software, many different processes or methods for building software, and many hundreds of programming languages in which the code itself might be written. For example, the schedule and cost results of projects that are exactly the same size can vary widely for various kinds of software, such as the following:

- Web-based development projects
- Internal information systems projects
- External outsourced projects
- Systems software projects

- Embedded software projects
- Commercial software projects
- Military software projects

Within these seven discrete forms of software, schedules for exactly the same size of application can vary by more than three to one, and costs can vary by more than six to one.

Further, software projects do not scale up very well. The tools and methods needed to successfully build a large system of, say, 10,000 function points or 1 million source code statements are quite different from those needed for small applications of 10 function points or 1000 source code statements. For example some of the new Agile methods and extreme programming (XP) have been very successful for projects below 1000 function points or 50,000 Java statements in size. But they have not yet been successful for applications of 10,000 function points or 50,000 Java statements in size. They have not even been attempted for applications of 100,000 function points or 5 million Java statements in size.

The overall result of the combination of these factors is that software cost estimating is a complicated activity that requires the ability to deal with a host of overlapping variables, including but not limited to the following:

- Requirements volatility
- Class and type of software being estimated
- Size of the final application
- Team capabilities
- Multiple occupation groups employed
- Standard and overtime pay required
- Processes and methods used
- Tools and equipment available
- Programming languages used
- Reusable artifacts available

The Early History of Software Cost Estimation

From the start of the software era in the 1950s until roughly 1970, software cost estimating was performed manually, using simple rules of thumb or local estimating algorithms developed through trial and error methods. (Indeed, even today simple rules of thumb and manual methods are numerically the most frequently used methods of developing software cost estimates, in spite of the many problems of these crude approaches.)

By the late 1960s, computer usage had become widespread and therefore software applications were growing in both size and numbers. Software cost estimating first began to be discussed as an important technology in the late 1960s. Joel Aron of IBM gave a presentation on software cost estimating at a NATO conference in 1969 (Aron 1970). Both of the estimating pioneers, Dr. Barry Boehm and Larry Putnam, first began to explore software cost estimation in the late 1960s.

By the late 1960s and early 1970s, a number of researchers independently began to explore the possibilities of building automated software cost-estimating tools. It is no coincidence that the software cost estimating pioneers all worked for large corporations that were experiencing difficulties in building large software systems. Such large companies and organizations as the Army, the Air Force, IBM, RCA, TRW, and Hughes Aircraft were among the first to fund formal research studies for improved methods of software cost estimating.

Some of these pioneering researchers succeeded well enough to bring out internal estimating tools that later evolved into commercial software cost-estimating tools, and thus created the modern software cost-estimating industry. As this edition is being written there are at least 50 commercial software cost-estimating tools sold in the United States, and perhaps 25 sold elsewhere. However, the cost-estimating industry is young enough so that many of the software cost-estimating pioneers are still active in the commercial estimating business although some are approaching retirement.

Some of the pioneering estimating researchers included Allan Albrecht at IBM on the East Coast, Dr. Barry Boehm at TRW, Frank Freiman at RCA, Dr. Randall Jensen at Hughes, Colonel Larry Putnam in the U.S. Army, and the author at IBM on the West Coast. All of these estimating pioneers began their research into software cost estimation at roughly the same time. All of these estimation researchers were facing the same problem in their respective organizations: Software applications were growing in size and importance, and no one knew how to predict the costs of these troublesome projects with high accuracy.

In 1973, the author and his colleague Dr. Charles Turk at IBM San Jose built IBM's first automated estimation tool for systems software. This early software cost-estimation tool was called *IPQ*, short for *Interactive Productivity and Quality* estimator. Since that name proved awkward, an expanded version of the tool created in 1974 was renamed *DPS*, for *Development Planning System*.

A number of papers and reports on software cost estimation based on DPS were presented at external conferences and in a 1977 IBM Technical Report (Jones 1977).

Although he did not develop a software-estimating tool himself, Dr. Fred Brooks of IBM captured the need for better software-estimating methods in his classic book *The Mythical Man-Month* (Brooks 1974). This book described the development problems of IBM's OS/360 operating system, which was the first software application built by IBM that topped 1 million source code statements in its first release, and was also the first IBM software product that missed its delivery date by a long enough period for the delay to be published in the major software journals and newspapers, to the considerable embarrassment of IBM executives.

Also around 1974, Dr. Randall Jensen and his colleagues at Hughes Aircraft were at work on the software cost-estimating methodology that later grew into the commercial SEER software cost-estimating tool (Jensen and Tonies 1979).

Around 1975, Allan Albrecht and his colleagues at IBM White Plains were developing the original version of the function point metric, which has become a major feature of modern software estimation.

The function point metric is a synthetic metric based on five external attributes of software applications: (1) inputs, (2) outputs, (3) inquires, (4) logical files, and (5) interfaces.

The function point metric stays constant regardless of the programming language used to implement the software. This property of invariance across multiple programming languages greatly eased sizing and estimating the non-coding portions of software projects, such as requirements, design, specifications, creation of user manuals, and the like. As a result, most of the modern software cost-estimating tools now support function point metrics as well as lines-of-code-metrics.

In tracing the origins of software cost estimating, the commercial software-estimation business dates back only to the early 1970s. In 1977, the PRICE-S software-estimation model designed by Frank Freiman was marketed as the first commercial software-estimation tool in the United States. (The PRICE-H hardware-estimation tool had come out earlier in 1973.)

The PRICE-S tool was originally developed and marketed by RCA. However, the tool has changed hands many times and is now marketed by Lockheed-Martin. It is a sign that cost estimating is important when a tool survives far longer than the company that first created it. In this case, RCA was acquired by General Electric, followed by Martin-Marietta, which became Lockheed-Martin after a merger.

In October 1979, Allan Albrecht, then at IBM, gave a paper on function point metrics at a joint IBM/SHARE/GUIDE conference in Monterey,

California (Albrecht 1979). At the same time, IBM put the structure of the function point metric into the public domain. Since function point metrics are now supported by more than 30 software-estimation tools in the United States and by 15 tools overseas, the publication of function point metrics was a very significant step in software cost estimating.

In 1979, the second commercial estimation tool reached the U.S. market. This was the software life-cycle management (SLIM) tool developed by Larry Putnam of Quantitative Software Management (QSM). Putnam developed his original concepts for the SLIM model while serving in the U.S. Army, where he was often engaged in the estimation of military software projects. In 1978, Putnam published a report on a generalized macroestimating method in *IEEE Transactions on Software Engineering* (Putnam 1978).

In 1981, Dr. Barry Boehm, who worked at TRW at the time, published his monumental book on *Software Engineering Economics* (Boehm 1981), which contained the essential algorithms of the *constructive cost model* (COCOMO). Since the COCOMO algorithms were first described in print, at least a dozen commercial software-estimating tools have been derived from the COCOMO estimation method. Today, COCOMO remains the only software-estimating model whose algorithms are not treated as trade secrets. Dr. Boehm and his colleagues have developed a new COCOMO II software cost-estimating model, which supports function point metrics and adds additional features, such as sizing logic, that were not part of the original COCOMO model.

Also in 1981, the first worldwide publication of Allan Albrecht's paper on function points occurred when the paper was included in the present author's book *Programming Productivity—Issues for the Eighties* (Jones 1981).

In 1982, Tom DeMarco, a well-known software management consultant, published his classic book *Controlling Software Projects* (DeMarco 1982), which contained an independent form of functional metric that, by coincidence, duplicated some of the features of Albrecht's function point. (This situation brings to mind the publication of two independent theories of evolution by Darwin and Wallace, with Darwin getting the most recognition because he published first.)

The DeMarco function point, sometimes called the *bang* metric, is supported by several software cost-estimating tools. Several features of the original DeMarco function point have resurfaced in a recent metric termed *Boeing 3D function points* and in several other function point variants, as well.

In 1983, Charles Symons, a British software-estimating researcher working at the management consulting group of Nolan, Norton & Company (later acquired by KPMG Peat Marwick), published a description of an alternative function point metric that he termed *Mark II function points*, which became widely used in the United Kingdom (Symons 1991). (More recently Charles Symons has been a lead developer on another new form of function point metric termed "cosmic function points.")

The Mark II method differed from the Albrecht function point in a number of respects, and it has become a popular metric for estimation and measurement in the United Kingdom, Canada, and Hong Kong. Further, the Mark II variant was the first of at least 36 other function point variations.

The Mark II function point metric includes entities and relationships as parameters, and also has an expanded set of adjustment factors for dealing with complexity, with the result that Mark II function point counts tend to be larger than Albrecht function point counts for many applications with complex data structures.

In 1983, Dr. Howard Rubin's ESTIMACS model reached the commercial market. Dr. Rubin is a professor at Hunter College, and is also a well-known software management consultant.

Dr. Rubin's original work on the ESTIMACS cost-estimating model was derivative of some of IBM's internal estimating methodology for information systems projects. ESTIMACS supported an early form of function point metric prior to IBM's major revision of function points in 1984, which is the basis of today's standard function point.

(The *MACS* portion of the name *ESTIMACS* refers to the MACS corporation, which was the original vendor of the ESTIMACS tool. This corporation was acquired by Computer Associates, but the name of the estimating tool was not changed.)

The Expansion and Use of Functional Metrics for Software Cost Estimating

Starting in the 1970s, Albrecht and his colleagues at IBM measured the sizes of many projects using both LOC-metrics and function point metrics. The results showed useful but not perfect correlations between the two metrics.

The dual measurement of both lines of code and function points led to *backfiring*, or direct conversion from LOC-metrics to function point metrics and vice versa. The term "backfiring" denotes the direct mathematical conversion of logical source code statements into an equivalent volume of function points.

Backfiring is used primarily for estimating maintenance and enhancement projects for aging legacy applications, where the specifications may be missing and the original development personnel have changed jobs.

By 1984 enough data had been collected that it was possible to start publishing conversion ratios between logical source code statements and function point metrics. The early reports covered only 20 of the more common programming languages. However, the use of backfiring became so common that the table of conversion rates between source code statements and function points now includes almost 500 programming languages (Jones 1996).

In 1985 the author's SPQR/20™ (short for *software productivity, quality, and reliability*) estimation tool reached the commercial market. The SPQR/20 estimation tool was the first commercial software estimator built explicitly to support function point metrics and to include bidirectional backfiring support. That is, logical statements could be converted into equivalent function point totals, or vice versa. SPQR/20 was also the first software-estimation tool to use function points for the sizing logic for specifications, user documents, and source code.

The SPQR/20 tool also integrated quality, risk, and reliability estimating with effort, cost, and schedule estimating, and it produced maintenance and enhancement estimates for five years after the initial deployment of a software project. This was a pioneering attempt to integrate all of the following key predictable factors into a single tool:

- Sizing of all deliverables
- Staffing by activity
- Schedules by activity
- Effort by activity
- Costs by activity
- Quality and defect severity levels
- Defect removal efficiency
- Reliability
- Risks
- Maintenance
- Enhancements

By 1986, usage of function point metrics had grown so rapidly that the nonprofit International Function Point Users Group (IFPUG) was founded by a number of users of this metric. The IFPUG organization was started in Toronto, Canada, a city that has pioneered a number of interesting software technologies. (IFPUG moved its headquarters to Westerville, Ohio, in 1988 and became a nonprofit corporation in the United States.)

As function point usage grew, the IFPUG organization recognized that counting was complex enough that standards would be required.

Also, it was desirable to develop a certification examination to ensure that counting would be consistent from project to project. In 1986 Allan Albrecht, the inventor of function point metrics, developed the first IFPUG-certified course for function point counting.

Although Allan Albrecht, who is an electrical engineer, envisioned function points as a metric for all kinds of software, the historical fact that function points were first used for information systems slowed down the acceptance of functional metrics within the real-time and embedded-software domains.

Between the early 1970s and 1987, the nucleus of the current software cost-estimating industry was created. Most of the original estimating pioneers all developed their own estimating methods, which have become the basis of the current software-estimating business, as shown in Table 2.1.

These pioneering commercial software-estimating tools, plus the invention and publication of function point metrics, mark the emergence of the modern software cost-estimation industry.

Many of the more recent estimating tools are derived at least in part from the work of the software-estimating pioneers. For example, at least 20 commercial estimating tools (12 in the United States and 8 overseas) use portions of the COCOMO algorithms published by Dr. Barry Boehm.

About the same number of commercial estimating tools use the backfiring method published by Allan Albrecht and Capers Jones for converting lines-of-code data based on logical statement counts into equivalent function point data.

Because accurate software cost estimation depends upon data derived from accurate measurement of software projects, it is no coincidence that some of the software cost-estimating pioneers are also well known

TABLE 2.1   Commercial Software Estimation from 1974 Through 1986

Estimation pioneer	Methods or tools	Year of availability
Dr. Randall Jensen	SEER	1974
Frank Freiman	PRICE-S	1977
Allan Albrecht	IBM function points	1978
Larry Putnam	SLIM	1979
Dr. Barry Boehm	COCOMO	1981
Tom DeMarco	DeMarco function points	1982
Charles Symons	Mark II function points	1983
Dr. Howard Rubin	ESTIMACS	1983
Allan Albrecht and Capers Jones	Backfiring (LOC to function points)	1984
Capers Jones	SPQR/20	1985
Allan Albrecht and Capers Jones	SPR feature points	1986

as measurement experts. Indeed, a majority of the published books that contain quantitative measurement data for software projects have been written by the software cost-estimating pioneers.

The linkage between software measurement and software estimation is so strong that outside of the data collected and published by software cost-estimating specialists, there are very few other industry collections of quantitative data on software productivity, costs, and quality.

Some of the function point groups, such as the IFPUG benchmark committee and the Australian function point users group, have published limited volumes of benchmark data.

There are some interesting military software data collections and also some government software data collected by the National Aeronautics and Space Administration (NASA). However, military software developers and, to an extent, governmental software developers use standards and approaches that are not totally commensurate with civilian methods or results. Also, comparatively little of the governmental software data has found its way into commercial books dealing with software productivity or quality.

Several Air Force databases contain significant quantities of project-level data and are sometimes used for calibrating software cost-estimating tools: The Electronic Systems Center (ESC) and Space and Missile Systems Center (SMC) databases are good examples, as is the data collected by the Rome Air Development Center (RADC).

In recent years the nonprofit function point organizations in various countries have begun to publish collections of benchmark data, with the function groups in Australia (Australian Software Metrics Association [ASMA]), the Netherlands Function Point Users Group (NEFPUG), and the International Function Point Users Group (IFPUG) in the United States having the largest numbers of projects to date. In 2006 a new consortium of organizations began to make plans for gathering benchmark information that includes assessment data as well as quantitative data. Some of the participants in this new consortium include the Software Engineering Institute, the David's Consulting Group, and Software Productivity Research LLC.

Function points have become so common that even the consulting groups that do not market estimating tools use function point metrics as the basis for their comparative benchmark studies, and they often compare their results against some of the published studies produced by the software-estimating companies.

The bulk of the published data on software productivity, costs, schedules, and quality still derives from the books and articles published by software-estimating tool developers, who continue to measure and collect data at a combined rate of several hundred software projects every month.

References

Albrecht, A. J.: "Measuring Application Development Productivity," *Proceedings of the Joint IBM/SHARE/GUIDE Application Development Symposium*, October 1979, reprinted in Capers Jones, *Programming Productivity—Issues for the Eighties*, IEEE Computer Society Press, New York, 1981, pp. 34–43.

Aron, J. D.: "Estimating Resources for Large Programming Systems," *Software Engineering Techniques*, NATO Conference Report, Rome, October 1969, April 1970, pp. 68–84.

Boehm, Barry: *Software Engineering Economics*, Prentice-Hall, Englewood Cliffs, N.J., 1981.

Brooks, Fred: *The Mythical Man-Month*, Addison-Wesley, Reading, Mass., 1974, rev. 1995.

DeMarco, Tom: *Controlling Software Projects*, Yourdon Press, New York, 1982.

Jensen, R. W., and C. C. Tonies: *Software Engineering*, Prentice-Hall, Englewood Cliffs, N.J., 1979.

Jones, Capers: *Program Quality and Programmer Productivity*, IBM Technical Report TR 02.764, IBM, San Jose, Calif., January 1977.

————: "Measuring Programming Quality and Productivity," *IBM Systems Journal*, **17**(1): 39–63 (1978).

————: *Programming Productivity—Issues for the Eighties*, IEEE Press, rev. 1986.

————: *Programming Productivity*, 2d ed., McGraw-Hill, 1986.

————: *Critical Problems in Software Measurement*, Information Systems Management Group, 1993a.

————: *Software Productivity and Quality Today—The Worldwide Perspective*, Information Systems Management Group, 1993b.

————: *Assessment and Control of Software Risks*, Prentice-Hall, 1994.

————: *New Directions in Software Management*, Information Systems Management Group.

————: *Patterns of Software System Failure and Success*, International Thomson Computer Press, Boston, 1995.

————: *Applied Software Measurement*, 2d ed., McGraw-Hill, 1996.

Putnam, Lawrence H.: "A General Empirical Solution to the Macro Software Sizing and Estimation Problem," *IEEE Transactions on Software Engineering*, **SE-4**(4): 345–361 (1978).

————: *Measures for Excellence—Reliable Software On Time, Within Budget*, Yourdon Press/Prentice-Hall, Englewood Cliffs, N.J., 1992.

Rubin, Howard: *Software Benchmark Studies For 1997*, Howard Rubin Associates, Pound Ridge, N.Y., 1997.

Symons, Charles R.: *Software Sizing and Estimating—Mk II FPA (Function Point Analysis)*, John Wiley & Sons, Chichester, U.K, 1991.

Six Forms of Software Cost Estimation

Among our clients about 80 percent of large corporations utilize automated software-estimation tools. About 30 percent utilize two or more automated estimation tools, sometimes for the same project. About 15 percent employ cost-estimating specialists. In large companies, manual estimates are used primarily for small projects below 500 function points in size or for "quick and dirty" estimates where high precision is not required.

However, for small companies with less than 100 software personnel, only about 25 percent utilize automated software-estimation tools. The primary reason for this is that small companies only build small software projects, where high-precision estimates are not as important as for large systems.

Software cost estimates can be created in a number of different fashions. In order of increasing rigor and sophistication, the following six methods of estimating software costs are used by corporations and government groups that produce software.

- Manual software-estimating methods

    1. Manual project-level estimates using rules of thumb

    2. Manual phase-level estimates using ratios and percentages

    3. Manual activity-level estimates using work-breakdown structures

- Automated software-estimating methods

    1. Automated project-level estimates (macro-estimation)

    2. Automated phase-level estimates (macro-estimation)

    3. Automated activity-level or task-level estimates (micro-estimation)

The most accurate forms of software cost estimation are the last ones in each set: cost estimating at either the activity or the task level. Only the very granular forms of software cost estimation are usually rigorous enough to support contracts and serious business activities. Let us consider the pros and cons of each of these six estimating methods.

Overview of Manual Software-Estimating Methods

Manual estimates for software projects using simple rules of thumb constitute the oldest form of software cost estimation, and this method is still the most widely used, even though it is far from the most accurate.

An example of an estimating rule of thumb would be "Raising the function point total of an application to the 0.4 power will predict the schedule of the project in calendar months from requirements until delivery." Another and more recent example would be "for a story that contains five story points, it can be coded in 30 hours of ideal time."

Examples of rules of thumb using the lines-of-code-metrics might be "JAVA applications average 500 non-commentary code statements per staff month" or "JAVA applications cost an average of $10 per line of code to develop."

About the only virtue of this simplistic kind of estimation is that it is easy to do. However, simplistic estimates using rules of thumb should not serve as the basis of contracts or formal budgets for software projects.

Manual phase-level estimates using ratios and percentages are another common and long-lived form of software estimation. Usually, the number of phases will run from five to eight, and will include such general kinds of software work as: (1) requirements gathering, (2) analysis and design, (3) coding, (4) testing, and (5) installation and training.

Manual phase-level estimates usually start with an overall project-level estimate and then assign ratios and percentages to the various phases. For example, suppose you were building an application of 100 function points, or roughly 10,000 COBOL source code statements in size. Using the rules of thumb from the previous example, you might assume that if this project will average 500 source code statements per month, then the total effort will take 20 months.

Applying typical percentages for the five phases previously shown, you might next assume that requirements would comprise 10 percent of the effort, analysis and design 20 percent, coding 30 percent, testing 35 percent, and installation and training 5 percent.

Converting these percentages into actual effort, you would arrive at an estimate for the project that showed the following:

Requirements	2 staff months
Analysis and design	4 staff months
Coding	6 staff months
Testing	7 staff months
Installation	1 staff month
TOTAL	20 staff months

The problems with simple phase-level estimates using ratios and percentages are threefold:

- The real-life percentages vary widely for every activity.

- Many kinds of software work span multiple phases or run the entire length of the project.

- Activities that are not phases may accidentally be omitted from the estimate.

As an example of the first problem, for small projects of less than 1000 lines of code or 10 function points, coding can total about 60 percent of the total effort. However, for large systems in excess of 1 million lines of code or 10,000 function points, coding is often less than 15 percent of the total effort. You cannot use a fixed percentage across all sizes of software projects.

As an example of the second problem, the phase-level estimating methodology is also weak for activities that span multiple phases or run continuously. For example, preparation of user manuals often starts during the coding phase and is completed during the testing phase. Project management starts early, at the beginning of the requirements phase, and runs throughout the entire development cycle.

As an example of the third problem, neither *quality assurance* nor *technical writing* nor *integration* are usually identified as phases. But the total amount of effort devoted to these three kinds of work can sometimes top 25 percent of the total effort for software projects. There is a common tendency to ignore or to underestimate activities that are not phases, and this explains why most manual estimates tend toward excessive optimism for both costs and schedules.

The most that can be said about manual phase-level estimates is that they are slightly more useful than overall project estimates and are just about as easy to prepare. However, they are far from sufficient for contracts, budgets, or serious business purposes.

The third form of manual estimation, which is to estimate each activity or task using a formal work-breakdown structure, is far and away the most accurate of the manual methods.

This rigorous estimating approach originated in the 1960s for large military software projects and has proven to be a powerful and effective method that supports other forms of project management, such as critical path analysis. (Indeed, the best commercial estimating tools operate by automating software estimates to the level of activities and tasks derived from a work-breakdown structure.)

The downside of manual estimating via a detailed work-breakdown structure of perhaps 50 activities, or 250 or so tasks, is that it is very time consuming to create the estimate initially, and it is even more difficult to make modifications when the requirements change or the scope of the project needs to be adjusted.

Overview of Automated Software-Estimating Methods

The first two forms of automated estimating methods are very similar to the equivalent manual forms of estimation, only faster and easier to use. The forms of automated estimation that start with general equations for the staffing, effort, and schedule requirements of a complete software project are termed *macro-estimation*.

These macro-estimation tools usually support two levels of granularity: (1) estimates to the level of complete projects, and (2) estimates to the level of phases, using built-in assumptions for the ratios and percentages assigned to each phase.

Although these macro-estimation tools replicate the features of manual estimates, many of them provide some valuable extra features that go beyond the capabilities of manual methods.

Recall that automated software-estimation tools are built on a knowledge base of hundreds, or even thousands, of software projects. This knowledge base allows the automated estimation tools to make adjustments to the basic estimating equations in response to the major factors that affect software project outcomes, such as the following:

- Adjustments for levels of staff experience
- Adjustments for software development processes
- Adjustments for specific programming languages used
- Adjustments for the size of the software application
- Adjustments for work habits and overtime

The downside of macro-estimation tools is that they do not usually produce estimates that are granular enough to support all of the important software-development activities. For example, many specialized activities tend to be omitted from macro-estimation tools, such as the production of user manuals, the effort by quality-assurance personnel, the effort by database administrators, and sometimes even the effort of project managers.

The automated estimating tools that are built upon a detailed work-breakdown structure are termed *micro-estimating* tools. The method of operation of micro-estimation is the reverse of that of macro-estimation.

The macro-estimation tools begin with general equations for complete projects, and then use ratios and percentages to assign resources and time to specific phases.

The micro-estimation tools work in the opposite direction. They first create a detailed work-breakdown structure for the project being estimated, and then estimate each activity separately. When all of the activity-level or task-level estimates are complete, the estimating tool then sums the partial results to reach an overall estimate for staffing, effort, schedule, and cost requirements. The advantages of activity-based micro-estimation are the following:

- The granularity of the data makes the estimates suitable for contracts and budgets.

- Errors, if any, tend to be local within an activity, rather than global.

- New or unusual activities can be added as the need arises.

- Activities not performed for specific projects can be backed out.

- The impact of specialists, such as technical writers, can be seen.

- Validation of the estimate is straightforward, because nothing is hidden.

- Micro-estimation is best suited for Agile projects.

A critical aspect of software estimation is the chart of accounts used, or the set of activities for which resource and cost data are estimated. The topic of selecting the activities to be included in software project estimates is a difficult issue and cannot be taken lightly. There are four main contenders:

- Project-level measurements
- Phase-level measurements
- Activity-level measurements
- Task-level measurements

Before illustrating these four concepts, it is well to begin by defining what each one means in a software context, with some common examples.

A *project* is defined as the implementation of software that satisfies a cohesive set of business and technical requirements. Under this definition, a project can be either a standalone program, such as an accounting application or a compiler, or a component of a large software system, such as the supervisor component of an operating system. The manager responsible for developing the application, or one of the components of larger applications, is termed the *project manager.*

Software projects can be of any size, but those where software cost-estimating and project management tools are utilized are most commonly those of perhaps 1000 function points, or 100,000 source code statements, and larger. Looking at the project situation from another view, in a cost-estimating and project management context, formal project estimates and formal project plans are usually required for projects that will require more than five staff members and will run for more than about six calendar months.

A *phase* is a chronological time period during which much of the effort of the project team is devoted to completing a major milestone or constructing a key deliverable item. There is no exact number of phases, and their time intervals vary. However, the phase concept for software projects implies a chronological sequence starting with requirements and ending with installation or deployment.

An example of a typical phase structure for a software project might include the following:

1. The requirements phase

2. The risk analysis phase

3. The design and specification phase

4. The coding phase

5. The integration and testing phase

6. The installation phase

7. The maintenance phase

Of course, some kinds of work, such as project management, quality assurance, and the production of user documents, span multiple phases. Within a phase, multiple kinds of activities might be performed. For example, the testing phase might have as few as one kind of testing or as many as a dozen discrete forms of testing.

The phase structure is only a rough approximation that shows general information. Phases are not sufficient or precise enough for cost estimates that will be used in contracts or will have serious business implications.

An *activity* is defined as the sum of the effort needed to complete a key milestone or a key deliverable item. For example, one key activity is gathering user requirements. Other activities for software projects would be completion of external design, completion of design reviews on the external design, completion of internal or logical design, completion of design reviews on the logical design, completion of database design, completion of a test plan, completion of a user's guide, and almost any number of others.

There are no limits on the activities utilized for software projects, but from about 15 to 50 key deliverables constitute a normal range for software cost-estimating purposes. Activities differ from phases in that they do not assume a chronological sequence; also, multiple activities are found within any given phase. For example, during a typical software project's testing phase it would be common to find the following six discrete testing activities:

1. New function testing

2. Regression testing

3. Component testing

4. Integration testing

5. Stress testing

6. System testing

A *task* is defined as the set of steps or the kinds of work necessary to complete a given activity. Using the activity of unit testing as an example, four tasks normally included in that activity might comprise the following:

1. Test case construction

2. Test case running or execution

3. Defect repairs for any problems found

4. Repair validation and retesting

There is no fixed ratio of the number of tasks that constitute activities, but from 4 to perhaps 12 tasks for each activity are very common patterns.

Of these four levels of granularity, only activity and task estimates will allow estimates with a precision of better than 10 percent in repeated trials. Further, neither project-level nor phase-level estimates will be useful in modeling process improvement strategies, or in carrying out "what if" alternative analysis to discover the impact of various tools, methods, and approaches. This kind of modeling of alternative scenarios is a key feature of automated software-estimating approaches, and a very valuable tool for software project managers.

Estimating only at the level of full projects or at phase levels correlates strongly with cost and schedule overruns, and even with litigation for breach of contract.

This is not to say that phase-level or even project-level estimates have no value. These concise estimating modes are very often used for early sizing and estimating long before enough solid information is available to tune or adjust a full activity-level estimate.

However, for projects that may involve large teams of people, have expenses of more than $1 million, or have any kind of legal liabilities associated with missed schedules, cost overruns, or poor quality, then a much more rigorous kind of estimating and planning will be necessary.

A fundamental problem with the coarse estimating approaches at the project and phase levels is that there is no way of being sure what activities are present and what activities (such as user manual preparation) might have been accidentally left out.

Also, data estimated to the levels of activities and tasks can easily be rolled up to provide phase-level and project-level views. The reverse is not true: You cannot explode project-level data or phase-level data down to the lower levels with acceptable accuracy and precision. If you start an estimate with data that is too coarse, you will not be able to do very much with it.

Table 3.1 gives an illustration that can clarify the differences. Assume you are thinking of estimating a project such as the construction of a small switching system. Shown are the activities that might be included at the levels of the project, phases, and activities for the chart of accounts used to build the final cost estimate.

Even more granular than activity-based cost estimates would be the next level, or task-based cost estimates. Each activity in Table 3.1 can be expanded down a level (or even more). For example, activity 16 in Table 3.1 is identified as unit testing. Expanding the activity of *unit testing* down to the task level might show six major tasks:

Activity	Tasks
Unit testing	1. Test case creation
	2. Test case validation
	3. Test case execution
	4. Defect analysis
	5. Defect repairs
	6. Repair validation

Assuming that each of the 25 activities in Table 3.1 could be expanded to a similar degree, then the total number of tasks would be 150. This level

TABLE 3.1   Project-, Phase-, and Activity-Level Estimating Charts of Accounts

Project level	Phase level	Activity level
Project	1. Requirements	1. Requirements
	2. Analysis	2. Prototyping
	3. Design	3. Architecture
	4. Coding	4. Planning
	5. Testing	5. Initial design
	6. Installation	6. Detail design
		7. Design review
		8. Coding
		9. Reused code acquisition
		10. Package acquisition
		11. Code inspection
		12. Independent verification and validation
		13. Configuration control
		14. Integration
		15. User documentation
		16. Unit testing
		17. Function testing
		18. Integration testing
		19. System testing
		20. Field testing
		21. Acceptance testing
		22. Independent testing
		23. Quality assurance
		24. Installation
		25. Management

of granularity would lead to maximum precision for a software project estimate, but it is far too complex for manual estimating approaches, at least for ease and convenience of use.

Although some large software systems consisting of multiple components may actually reach the level of more than 3000 tasks, this is a misleading situation. In reality, most large software systems are really comprised of somewhere between half a dozen and 50 discrete components that are built more or less in parallel and are constructed using very similar sets of activities. The absolute number of tasks, once duplications are removed, seldom exceeds 100, even for enormous systems that may top 10 million source code statements or 100,000 function points.

Only in situations where hybrid projects are being constructed so that hardware, software, microcode, and purchased parts are being simultaneously planned and estimated will the number of activities and tasks top 1000, and these hybrid projects are outside the scope of software cost-estimating tools. Indeed, really massive and complex hybrid projects will stress any kind of management tool.

For day-to-day software estimation, somewhere between 10 and 30 activities and perhaps 30 to 150 tasks will accommodate almost any software application in the modern world and will allow estimates with sufficient precision for use in contracts and business documents.

Estimating to the activity level is the first level suitable for contracts, budgets, outsourcing agreements, and other serious business purposes. Indeed, the use of simplistic project or phase-level estimates for software contracts is very hazardous and may well lead to some kind of litigation for breach of contract.

Estimating at the activity level does not imply that every project performs every activity. For example, small MIS projects and client/ server applications normally perform only 10 or so of the 25 activities that are shown previously. Systems software such as operating systems and large switching systems will typically perform about 20 of the 25 activities. Only large military and defense systems will routinely perform all 25.

However, it is better to start with a full chart of accounts and eliminate activities that will not be used. That way you will be sure that significant cost drivers, such as user documentation, are not left out accidentally because they are not part of just one phase.

Table 3.2 illustrates some of the activity patterns associated with six general kinds of software projects:

- Web-based applications
- Management information systems (MIS)
- Contract or outsourced projects
- Systems software projects
- Commercial software projects
- Military software projects

As can be seen from Table 3.2, activity-based costing makes visible some important differences in software-development practices. This level of granularity is highly advantageous in software contracts and is also very useful for preparing detailed schedules that are not likely to be exceeded for such trivial reasons as accidentally omitting an activity.

Now that the topic of activity-based estimating has been discussed, it is of interest to illustrate some of the typical outputs that are available from commercial software-estimating tools. Table 3.3 illustrates a hypothetical 1000–function point systems software project written in the C programming language.

The granularity of the estimate is set at the activity level, and the project is assumed to have started on January 6, 1997. In this example,

TABLE 3.2   Typical Activity Patterns for Six Software Domains

Activities performed	Web-based	MIS	Outsource	Commercial	Systems	Military
01 Requirements		X	X	X	X	X
02 Prototyping	X	X	X	X	X	X
03 Architecture		X	X	X	X	X
04 Project plans		X	X	X	X	X
05 Initial design		X	X	X	X	X
06 Detail design		X	X	X	X	X
07 Design reviews		X	X	X	X	X
08 Coding	X	X	X	X	X	X
09 Reuse acquisition	X		X	X	X	X
10 Package purchase		X	X		X	X
11 Code inspections				X	X	X
12 Independent verification and validation				X		
13 Configuration management		X	X	X	X	X
14 Formal integration		X	X	X	X	X
15 Documentation	X	X	X	X	X	X
16 Unit testing	X	X	X	X	X	X
17 Function testing		X	X	X	X	X
18 Integration testing		X	X	X	X	X
19 System testing		X	X	X	X	X
20 Field testing				X	X	X
21 Acceptability testing		X	X		X	X
22 Independent testing						X
23 Quality assurance			X	X	X	X
24 Installation and training		X	X		X	X
25 Project management		X	X	X	X	X
Activities	5	16	20	21	22	25

the average burdened salary level for all project personnel is set at $5000 per month.

Although most of the outputs from this illustrative example are straightforward, several aspects might benefit from a discussion. First, note that 20 out of the 25 activities are shown, which is not uncommon for systems software in this size range.

Second, note that the overlapped schedule and the waterfall schedule are quite different. The waterfall schedule of roughly 120 calendar months is simply the arithmetic sum of the schedules of the various activities used. This schedule would probably never occur in real life, because software projects always start activities before the previous activities are completed. As a simple example, design usually starts when the requirements are only about 75 percent complete. Coding usually starts when the design is less than 50 percent complete, and so on.

The overlapped schedule of just over 18 months reflects a much more common scenario, and assumes that nothing is really finished when the next activity begins.

The third aspect of this example that merits discussion is the fact that unpaid overtime amounts to almost 42 staff months, which is about 14 percent of the total effort devoted to the project. This much unpaid overtime is a sign of three important factors:

- The software personnel are exempt, and don't receive overtime payments.

- Schedule pressure is probably intense for so much unpaid overtime to accrue.

- There are major differences between *real* and *apparent* productivity rates.

If the unpaid overtime is left out (which is a common practice), then the apparent productivity rate for this project is 3.78 function points per staff month, or 473 source code statements per staff month.

If the unpaid overtime is included, then the real productivity rate for this project is 3.27 function points per staff month, or 409 source code statements per staff month. It can easily be seen that the omission or inclusion of unpaid overtime can exert a major influence on overall productivity rates.

Although coding is the most expensive single activity for this project, and costs almost $322,200 out of the total cost of just over $1,320,000, that is still only a little over 24 percent of the total cost for the project.

By contrast, the nine activities associated with defect removal (quality assurance, reviews, inspections, and testing) total to about $383,000 or roughly 29 percent of the overall development cost.

The activities associated with producing paper documents (plans, requirements, design, and user manuals) total to more than $394,000 or about 30 percent of the development cost.

Without the granularity of going down at least to the level of activity-based costs, the heavy proportion of non-coding costs might very well be underestimated, and it would be difficult to ascertain if these costs were even present in the estimate. With activity-based costs, at least errors tend to be visible and, hence, can be corrected.

The overlap in project schedules is difficult to see from just a list of start and stop dates. This is why calendar intervals are usually shown visually in the form of Gantt charts, critical path networks, or PERT charts.

Figure 3.1 illustrates a Gantt chart that would accompany an activity-based cost estimate such as the one shown in Table 3.3. The provision of graphs and charts is a standard feature of a number of software cost-estimating tools, because graphical outputs make the visualization of key information easier to comprehend.

Many estimating tools allow users to switch back and forth between numerical and graphical output, to print out either or both kinds, and in some cases, to actually make adjustments to the estimate by manipulating the graphs themselves.

Analyzing the Gantt chart, it is easy to see why the waterfall schedule and the overlapped schedule differ by a ratio of almost 8 to 1. The sum of the schedules for the individual software activities is never equal to the elapsed time, because most activities are performed in parallel and overlap both their predecessor and their successor activities.

Incidentally, the kinds of Gantt chart information shown in both Table 3.3 and Fig. 3.1 are standard output from such software-estimating tools as CHECKPOINT, KnowledgePlan, SLIM, and a number of others.

However, if schedule information were needed down to the level of tasks, or even below that to the level of individual employees, then the data would usually be exported from a cost-estimating tool and imported into a project-planning tool, such as Microsoft Project.

The kinds of information shown in Table 3.3 and Figure 3.1 are only a few of the kinds of data that modern software cost-estimating tools can provide. Many of the other capabilities will be illustrated later in this book, as will some of the many other kinds of reports and analyses.

For example, software cost-estimating output reports also include quality and reliability estimates, maintenance and enhancement estimates, analyses of risks, and sometimes even evaluations of the strengths and weaknesses of the methods and tools being applied to the software project being estimated.

Strength and weakness analysis is also a useful capability for other purposes, such as moving up the Software Engineering Institute (SEI) capability maturity model. Since modern software cost-estimation tools, many of which include measurement capabilities, can include as many as a hundred or more influential factors, their ability to focus on topics

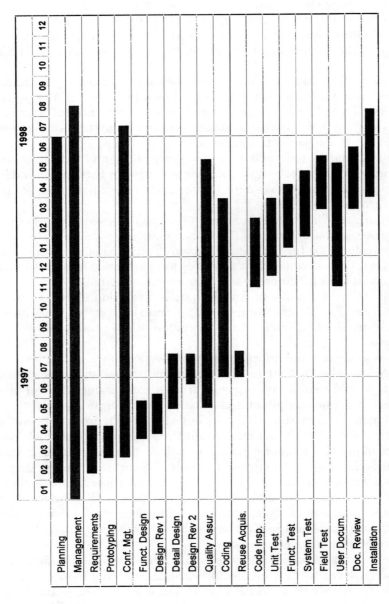

Figure 3.1 Sample Gantt chart output from a software cost-estimating tool.

TABLE 3.3 Example of Activity-Based Software Cost Estimating
Project type: Systems software of 1000 function points (125,000 C statements)
Project start: January 6, 1997
First delivery: July 15, 1998

Activity	Start date	End date	Schedule, months	Effort, months	Staffing	Cost, $
Planning	1/6/97	6/29/98	17.71	13.54	0.76	67,700
Management	1/6/97	8/15/98	17.40	19.45	1.12	97,250
Requirements	2/14/97	4/4/97	1.61	6.86	4.26	34,300
Prototyping	2/27/97	3/30/97	1.02	2.39	2.34	11,950
Configuration management	3/15/97	7/20/98	16.50	8.50	0.52	42,500
Functional design	3/6/97	5/12/97	2.20	15.72	7.15	78,600
Design reviews 1	3/24/97	5/12/97	1.61	3.92	2.43	19,600
Detail design	4/29/97	8/7/97	2.27	16.07	7.08	80,350
Design reviews 2	6/9/97	7/7/97	0.92	4.20	4.57	21,000
Quality assurance	4/3/97	7/28/98	15.80	5.50	0.35	27,500
Coding	5/15/97	4/15/98	9.01	64.44	7.15	322,200
Reuse acquisition	7/1/97	7/13/97	0.39	0.29	0.74	1,450
Code inspections	11/1/97	3/25/98	3.37	11.60	3.44	58,000
Unit test	11/13/97	4/8/98	4.89	5.19	1.06	25,950
Function test	1/30/98	5/5/98	5.01	16.08	3.21	80,400
System test	2/13/98	4/25/98	4.07	20.57	5.05	102,850
Field test	4/20/98	6/1/98	1.45	4.28	2.95	21,400
User documents	11/15/97	5/25/97	6.20	26.70	4.31	133,500
Document reviews	2/1/98	5/5/98	5.65	5.27	0.93	26,350
Installation	4/15/98	7/20/98	3.10	13.43	4.33	67,150
Average staff level					14.47	
Overlapped schedule			18.24			
Waterfall schedule			120.18			
Paid effort and costs				264.00		1,320,000
Unpaid overtime				41.64		
Total effort				305.64		
Cost per function point						1,320.00
Cost per SLOC					10.56	

where the project is either better or worse than industry norms is a great asset for process-improvement work.

In spite of the advantages derived from using software cost-estimation tools, surveys by the author at software project management and metrics conferences indicate that the most accurate forms of software cost estimation are not the most widely used.

The frequency of use among a sample of approximately 500 project managers interviewed during 2004 and 2005 is as shown in Table 3.4.

TABLE 3.4   Frequency of Usage of Software Cost-Estimating Methods

Estimating methodology	Project management usage
Manual software estimating	42%
Automated software estimating	58%
Total	100%

The fact that manual estimating methods, which are known to be inaccurate, are still rather widely utilized is one of the more troubling problems of the software project management domain.

Comparison of Manual and Automated Estimates for Large Software Projects

A comparison by the author of 50 manual estimates with 50 automated estimates for projects in the 5000–function point range showed interesting results. The manual estimates were created by project managers who used calculators and spreadsheets. The automated estimates were also created by project managers or their staff estimating assistants using several different commercial estimating tools. The comparisons were made between the original estimates submitted to clients and corporate executives, and the final accrued results when the applications were deployed.

Only four of the manual estimates were within 10 percent of actual results. Some 17 estimates were optimistic by between 10 percent and 30 percent. A dismaying 29 projects were optimistic by more than 30 percent. That is to say, manual estimates yielded lower costs and shorter schedules than actually occurred, sometimes by significant amounts. (Of course several revised estimates were created along the way. But the comparison was between the initial estimate and the final results.)

By contrast 22 of the estimates generated by commercial software-estimating tools were within 10 percent of actual results. Some 24 were conservative by between 10 percent and 25 percent. Three were conservative by more than 25 percent. Only one automated estimate was optimistic, by about 15 percent.

(One of the problems with performing studies such as this is the fact that many large projects with inaccurate estimates are cancelled without completion. Thus for projects to be included at all, they had to be finished. This criterion eliminated many projects that used both manual and automated estimation.)

Interestingly, the manual estimates and the automated estimates were fairly close in terms of predicting coding or programming effort.

But the manual estimates were very optimistic when predicting requirements growth, design effort, documentation effort, management effort, testing effort, and repair and rework effort. The conclusion of the comparison was that both manual and automated estimates were equivalent for actual programming, but the automated estimates were better for predicting noncoding activities.

This is an important issue for estimating large software applications. For software projects below about 1000 function points in size (equivalent to 125,000 C statements), programming is the major cost driver, so estimating accuracy for coding is a key element. But for projects above 10,000 function points in size (equivalent to 1,250,000 C statements), both defect removal and production of paper documents are more expensive than the code itself. Thus accuracy in estimating these topics is a key factor.

Software cost and schedule estimates should be accurate, of course. But if they do differ from actual results, it is safer to be slightly conservative than it is to be optimistic. One of the major complaints about software projects is their distressing tendency to overrun costs and planned schedules. Unfortunately, both clients and top executives tend to exert considerable pressures on managers and estimating personnel in the direction of optimistic estimates. Therefore a hidden corollary of successful estimation is that the estimates must be defensible. The best defense is a good collection of historical data from similar projects.

References

Barrow, Dean, Susan Nilson, and Dawn Timberlake: *Software Estimation Technology Report*, Air Force Software Technology Support Center, Hill Air Force Base, Utah, 1993.

Boehm, Barry: *Software Engineering Economics*, Prentice-Hall, Englewood Cliffs, N.J., 1981.

———: *Software Cost Estimation with COCOMO II*, Prentice-Hall, Englewood Cliffs, N.J.; 2000.

Brown, Norm (ed.): *The Program Manager's Guide to Software Acquisition Best Practices*, Version 1.0, U.S. Department of Defense, Washington, D.C., July 1995.

Charette, Robert N. *Software Engineering Risk Analysis and Management*, McGraw-Hill, New York, 1989.

———: *Application Strategies for Risk Analysis*, McGraw-Hill, New York, 1990.

Cohn, Mike: *Agile Estimating and Planning* (Robert C. Martin Series), Prentice-Hall PTR, Englewood Cliffs, N.J., 2005.

Coombs, Paul: *IT Project Estimation: A Practical Guide to the Costing of Software*, Cambridge University Press, Melbourne, Australia, 2003.

DeMarco, Tom: *Controlling Software Projects*, Yourdon Press, New York, 1982.

———: *Deadline*, Dorset House Press, New York, 1997.

Department of the Air Force: *Guidelines for Successful Acquisition and Management of Software Intensive Systems*; vols. 1 and 2, Software Technology Support Center, Hill Air Force Base, Utah, 1994.

Dreger, Brian: *Function Point Analysis*, Prentice-Hall, Englewood Cliffs, N.J., 1989.

Galorath, Daniel D. and Michael W. Evans: *Software Sizing, Estimation, and Risk Management*, Auerbach, Philadelphia PA, 2006.

Garmus, David, and David Herron: *Measuring the Software Process: A Practical Guide to Functional Measurement*, Prentice-Hall, Englewood Cliffs, N.J., 1995.
———: *Function Point Analysis: Measurement Practices for Successful Software Projects*, Addison-Wesely, Boston, Mass., 2001.
Grady, Robert B.: *Practical Software Metrics for Project Management and Process Improvement*, Prentice-Hall, Englewood Cliffs, N.J., 1992.
——— and Deborah L. Caswell: *Software Metrics: Establishing a Company-Wide Program*, Prentice-Hall, Englewood Cliffs, N.J., 1987.
Gulledge, Thomas R., William P. Hutzler, and Joan S. Lovelace (eds.): *Cost Estimating and Analysis—Balancing Technology with Declining Budgets*, Springer-Verlag, New York, 1992.
Howard, Alan (ed.): *Software Metrics and Project Management Tools*, Applied Computer Research (ACR), Phoenix, Ariz., 1997.
IFPUG Counting Practices Manual, Release 4, International Function Point Users Group, Westerville, Ohio, April 1995.
Jones, Capers: *Critical Problems in Software Measurement*, Information Systems Management Group, 1993a.
———: *Software Productivity and Quality Today—The Worldwide Perspective*, Information Systems Management Group, 1993b.
———: *Assessment and Control of Software Risks*, Prentice-Hall, Englewood Cliffs, N.J., 1994.
———: *New Directions in Software Management*, Information Systems Management Group, ISBN 1-56909-009-2, 1994.
———: *Patterns of Software System Failure and Success*, International Thomson Computer Press, Boston, 1995.
———: *Applied Software Measurement*, 2d ed., McGraw-Hill, New York, 1996.
———: *The Economics of Object-Oriented Software*, Software Productivity Research, Burlington, Mass., April 1997a.
———: *Software Quality—Analysis and Guidelines for Success*, International Thomson Computer Press, Boston, 1997b.
———: *The Year 2000 Software Problem—Quantifying the Costs and Assessing the Consequences*, Addison-Wesley, Reading, Mass., 1998.
———: *Software Assessments, Benchmarks, and Best Practices*, Addison-Wesley, Boston, Mass, 2000.
Kan, Stephen H.: *Metrics and Models in Software Quality Engineering, 2nd edition*, Addison-Wesley, Boston, Mass., 2003.
Kemerer, C. F.: "Reliability of Function Point Measurement—A Field Experiment," *Communications of the ACM*, **36:** 85–97 (1993).
Keys, Jessica: *Software Engineering Productivity Handbook*, McGraw-Hill, New York, 1993.
Laird, Linda M. and Carol M. Brennan: *Software Measurement and Estimation: A practical Approach*; John Wiley & Sons, New York, 2006.
Lewis, James P.: *Project Planning, Scheduling & Control*, McGraw-Hill, New York, 2005.
Marciniak, John J. (ed.): *Encyclopedia of Software Engineering*, vols. 1 and 2, John Wiley & Sons, New York, 1994.
McConnell, Steve: *Software Estimation: Demystifying the Black Art*, Microsoft Press, Redmond, WA, 2006.
Mertes, Karen R.: *Calibration of the CHECKPOINT Model to the Space and Missile Systems Center (SMC) Software Database (SWDB)*, Thesis AFIT/GCA/LAS/96S-11, Air Force Institute of Technology (AFIT), Wright-Patterson AFB, Ohio, September 1996.
Ourada, Gerald, and Daniel V. Ferens: "Software Cost Estimating Models: A Calibration, Validation, and Comparison," in *Cost Estimating and Analysis: Balancing Technology and Declining Budgets*, Springer-Verlag, New York, 1992, pp. 83–101.
Perry, William E.: *Handbook of Diagnosing and Solving Computer Problems*, TAB Books, Blue Ridge Summit, Pa., 1989.
Pressman, Roger: *Software Engineering: A Practitioner's Approach with Bonus Chapter on Agile Development*, McGraw-Hill, New York, 2003.

Putnam, Lawrence H.: *Measures for Excellence—Reliable Software on Time, Within Budget:* Yourdon Press/Prentice-Hall, Englewood Cliffs, N.J., 1992.

———, and Ware Myers: *Industrial Strength Software—Effective Management Using Measurement*, IEEE Press, Los Alamitos, Calif., 1997.

Reifer, Donald (ed.): *Software Management*, 4th ed., IEEE Press, Los Alamitos, Calif., 1993.

Rethinking the Software Process, CD-ROM, Miller Freeman, Lawrence, Kans., 1996. (This CD-ROM is a book collection jointly produced by the book publisher, Prentice-Hall, and the journal publisher, Miller Freeman. It contains the full text and illustrations of five Prentice-Hall books: *Assessment and Control of Software Risks* by Capers Jones; *Controlling Software Projects* by Tom DeMarco; *Function Point Analysis* by Brian Dreger; *Measures for Excellence* by Larry Putnam and Ware Myers; and *Object-Oriented Software Metrics* by Mark Lorenz and Jeff Kidd.)

Rubin, Howard: *Software Benchmark Studies for 1997*, Howard Rubin Associates, Pound Ridge, N.Y., 1997.

Roetzheim, William H., and Reyna A. Beasley: *Best Practices in Software Cost and Schedule Estimation*, Prentice-Hall PTR, Upper Saddle River, N.J., 1998.

Stukes, Sherry, Jason Deshoretz, Henry Apgar, and Ilona Macias: *Air Force Cost Analysis Agency Software Estimating Model Analysis—Final Report*, TR-9545/008-2, Contract F04701-95-D-0003, Task 008, Management Consulting & Research, Inc., Thousand Oaks, Calif., September 1996.

Stutzke, Richard D.: *Estimating Software-Intensive Systems: Projects, Products, and Processes*; Addison-Wesley, Boston, Mass, 2005.

Symons, Charles R.: *Software Sizing and Estimating—Mk II FPA (Function Point Analysis)*, John Wiley & Sons, Chichester, U.K., 1991.

Wellman, Frank: *Software Costing: An Objective Approach to Estimating and Controlling the Cost of Computer Software*, Prentice-Hall, Englewood Cliffs, N.J., 1992.

Yourdon, Ed: *Death March—The Complete Software Developer's Guide to Surviving "Mission Impossible" Projects*, Prentice-Hall PTR, Upper Saddle River, N.J., 1997.

Zells, Lois: *Managing Software Projects—Selecting and Using PC-Based Project Management Systems*, QED Information Sciences, Wellesley, Mass., 1990.

Zvegintzov, Nicholas: *Software Management Technology Reference Guide*, Dorset House Press, New York, 1994.

Software Cost-Estimating Tools and Project Success and Failure Rates

The author and his colleagues at Software Productivity Research (SPR) were commissioned to do several studies of the patterns of failure and success associated with software projects. The first full results were published in *Patterns of Software System Failure and Success* (Jones 1995). More recent results were published in 2003, 2004, and 2006.

The attributes of *success* included delivering the system on time or early, staying within budgets, providing high quality levels, and providing high levels of user satisfaction.

The attributes of *failure* included cancellation of the project in mid-development, or severe schedule or cost overruns, or both. Poor quality and low user satisfaction were also aspects of failure.

The studies explored six kinds of large software projects: (1) systems software, (2) military software, (3) information systems software, (4) outsourced software, (5) commercial software, and (6) end-user software.

The studies also explored six size ranges an order of magnitude apart, starting with very small projects of 1 function point in size and culminating with massive systems of 100,000 function points in size.

Using six size ranges from 1 to 100,000 function points (FP), Table 4.1 shows the approximate frequency of various kinds of outcomes, ranging from finishing early to total cancellation. This table is taken from *Patterns of Software Systems Failure and Success* (Jones 1995).

The study concentrated on the failures and successes of large systems in the 10,000–function point (500,000–source code statement) and higher range, since failures are more common than successes for large systems, and large-system failures can be enormously expensive.

TABLE 4.1   Software Project Outcomes by Size of Project

	Probability of selected outcomes, %				
	Early	On Time	Delayed	Canceled	Total
1 FP	14.68	83.16	1.92	0.25	100
10 FP	11.08	81.25	5.67	2.00	100
100 FP	6.06	74.77	11.83	7.33	100
1,000 FP	1.24	60.76	17.67	20.33	100
10,000 FP	0.14	28.03	23.83	48.00	100
100,000 FP	0.00	13.67	21.33	65.00	100
Average	5.53	56.94	13.71	23.82	100

The root causes of software success and failure include technical factors, social and cultural factors, and management factors. The study found that there is an almost infinite number of ways to fail in building software applications, and only a few ways to succeed.

As can easily be seen from Table 4.1, small software projects are successful in the majority of instances, but the risks and hazards of cancellation or major delays rise quite rapidly as the overall application size goes up. Indeed, the development of large applications in excess of 10,000 function points is one of the most hazardous and risky business undertakings of the modern world.

Of the ways to succeed, the capabilities of the project management team had a very strong impact. Conversely, on the failures or projects that were canceled or ran very late, poor project management practices were universally noted.

The attributes most strongly associated with successful software projects include the use of automated software cost-estimating tools and automated software project management tools, effective quality control, and effective tracking of software-development milestones.

For larger software projects in excess of 1000 function points, or roughly 100,000 source code statements, success rates correlate strongly with four kinds of estimation or prediction rigor:

- Formal sizing of major deliverables (specifications, source code, test cases, and user manuals)
- Formal cost estimating down to the level of activities and tasks
- Formal quality estimating for all defect categories (requirements, design, code, documentation, and bad-fix defects)
- Formal schedule planning down to the level of individual workers

and three kinds of measurement rigor:

- Accurate resource and cost tracking during development
- Accurate milestone tracking during development
- Accurate defect tracking during development

The major difference between successful and unsuccessful software projects can be encapsulated by two key words: *no surprises*. With successful projects, development evolves painlessly from careful estimating, planning, and quality control. There are no unexpected delays due to sloppy planning, and no protracted nightmarish testing delays when the software is discovered not to work.

To summarize the kinds of tools most often associated with successful software projects, they include the following capabilities:

- Automated sizing of major deliverables
- Automated cost estimating
- Automated defect estimating
- Automated project planning
- Automated defect tracking
- Automated project resource tracking
- Automated project milestone tracking

Tools alone don't make a successful project, of course. In addition to sophisticated project management tools and development tools, successful software projects also make use of other rigorous approaches, including but not limited to the following:

- Careful requirements analysis
- Formal design and code inspections
- Testing by trained specialists
- Effective quality-assurance groups

As we have observed on hundreds of projects, effective estimating and planning methods, coupled with careful measurements and quality control, are high on the list of methods that can optimize software projects.

Probabilities of Software Project Success or Failure

The author and his colleagues at Software Productivity Research often deal with topics where multiple factors simultaneously impact the outcome of a project. A useful way of showing the range of possible outcomes is to illustrate what happens when every factor is either the best that it can be or the worst, and to ignore intermediate situations.

The author has found that the upper limit of convenience and effectiveness for this approach is to deal with four factors. The various combinations of four factors result in 16 possible outcomes, and it is usually possible to assign failure or success probabilities to each of the 16 combinations.

It is even possible to assign specific quality and productivity levels to the combinations, although that is not done in this book.

The reason that four factors is the convenient upper limit is that each additional factor would double the number of possible combinations, so that five factors would generate 32 possibilities, six factors would generate 64 combinations, and so on.

Table 4.2 illustrates the probability results of 16 combinations of four major management factors that affect software cancellations and schedules:

- Use of automated versus manual estimating tools
- Use of automated versus manual planning methods
- Use of automated versus manual progress-tracking methods
- Use of optimal versus minimal quality-control approaches

The phrase *automated estimating* implies usage of one or more of the commercial software-estimating tools, such as ABT Bridge Modeler, BYL, CHECKPOINT, COCOMO II, GECOMO, KnowledgePlan, PRICE-S, ProQMS, SEER, SLIM, SOFTCOST, SPQR/20, or others within this class.

The phrase *automated planning* implies usage of one or more of the commercial software planning or project management tools, such as ABT Project Manager's Workbench (PMW), CA SUPERPROJECT, Microsoft Project, PINNACLE, Primavera, TIMELINE, or one of many others within this class.

The phrase *formal tracking* implies a monthly summation of accomplishments, milestones, and potential problems encountered by every manager on a project. The lower-level progress reports are summarized upward to provide an overall status report of the health of the project. Formal tracking also implies usage of automated tools that can produce variance reports showing the difference between budgeted and actual expenditures, as well as variances in schedule and milestone achievement.

The phrase *optimal quality control* is defined to mean utilizing formal design and code inspections, formal and automated defect tracking, and formal testing by trained specialists as well as unit testing by the developers themselves.

The phrase *minimal quality control* is defined to mean a failure to utilize pretest inspections, a lack of effective defect tracking, and testing by ordinary generalists.

Although quality control is technical in nature, it is primarily driven by management decisions. In several significant disasters the technical staff recommended using such approaches as formal inspections and testing, but were overruled by management for the stated reason that "there is no time in the schedule."

TABLE 4.2   **Probability of Canceled, Delayed, On-Time, or Early Software Project
Completion Associated with Estimation and Project Management Factors**
(Best-practice project management factors appear in boldface type)

	Probability of selected outcomes, %			
	Canceled	Delayed	On time	Early
Manual estimates Manual plans Informal tracking Minimal quality control	40	45	15	0
Manual estimates **Automated plans** Informal tracking Minimal quality control	37	42	20	1
Manual estimates Manual plans **Formal tracking** Minimal quality control	35	39	24	2
Automated estimates Manual plans Informal tracking Minimal quality control	33	36	28	3
Manual estimates Manual plans Informal tracking **Optimal quality control**	30	32	34	4
Manual estimates **Automated plans** **Formal tracking** Minimal quality control	27	28	40	5
Automated estimates **Automated plans** Informal tracking Minimal quality control	23	26	45	6
Automated estimates Manual plans **Formal tracking** Minimal quality control	20	23	50	7
Manual estimates **Automated plans** Informal tracking **Optimal quality control**	18	20	54	8
Manual estimates Manual plans **Formal tracking** **Optimal quality control**	16	17	58	9
Automated estimates Manual plans Informal tracking **Optimal quality control**	13	15	62	10

TABLE 4.2   Probability of Canceled, Delayed, On-Time, or Early Software Project Completion Associated with Estimation and Project Management Factors *(Continued)*
(Best-practice project management factors appear in boldface type)

	Probability of selected outcomes, %			
	Canceled	Delayed	On time	Early
Automated estimates	10	12	67	11
Automated plans				
Formal tracking				
Minimal quality control				
Manual estimates	8	10	69	13
Automated plans				
Formal tracking				
Optimal quality control				
Automated estimates	5	8	72	15
Manual plans				
Formal tracking				
Optimal quality control				
Automated estimates	3	6	74	17
Automated plans				
Manual tracking				
Optimal quality control				
Automated estimates	1	2	78	19
Automated plans				
Formal tracking				
Optimal quality control				

Since the probability of a successful or unsuccessful outcome varies with the size range of the project being developed, the probabilities shown here are assumed to be for a system of nominally 5000 function points in size. This is roughly equivalent to about 525,000 source code statements in a procedural language such as COBOL or FORTRAN.

For smaller projects, successful outcomes would be more prevalent. For larger projects, unsuccessful outcomes would be more prevalent. There are commercial software estimating tools, such as CHECKPOINT, KnowledgePlan, SLIM, and SPQR/20, that can predict the specific failure probabilities of software projects of any arbitrary size and combination of technologies. It is recommended that tools such as these be utilized for dealing with the actual risk probabilities. The information in Table 4.2 simply indicates approximate outcomes and should not be used for serious planning purposes.

The margin of error in the information in Table 4.2 is high, but the overall combinations of factors are derived from empirical observations, and they illustrate that too much carelessness can lead to disaster.

Obviously, this picture is incomplete and omits all midrange situations between the best and the worst. There are also many other factors that can affect software projects besides the four shown here.

However, the overall situation is quite clear and is supported by many empirical observations. Carelessness, poor estimating, poor planning, poor tracking, and minimal quality control are strongly associated with canceled projects, overruns, and various disasters.

Conversely, usage of automated estimating and planning tools, careful monthly tracking, and excellence in terms of software quality are strongly associated with software projects that are successful in terms of schedule adherence, cost control, customer satisfaction, and other beneficial attributes.

The seeds of major software disasters are usually sown in the first three months of commencing the software project. Hasty scheduling, irrational commitments, unprofessional estimating techniques, and carelessness of the project management function are the factors that tend to introduce terminal problems. Once a project blindly lurches forward toward an impossible delivery date, the rest of the disaster will occur almost inevitably.

The literature on software successes and failures is out of balance, in that books on failures outnumber books on successes by a huge margin. This is not necessarily bad, but it does imply that software is a very troublesome discipline.

References

Brooks, Fred: *The Mythical Man-Month*, Addison-Wesley, Reading, Mass., 1974, rev. 1995.

Charette, Robert N.: *Software Engineering Risk Analysis and Management*, McGraw-Hill, New York, 1989.

———: *Application Strategies for Risk Analysis*, McGraw-Hill, New York, 1990.

DeMarco, Tom: *Deadline*, Dorset House Press, New York, 1997.

Jones, Capers: *Assessment and Control of Software Risks*, Prentice-Hall, ISBN 0-13-741406-4, 1994.

Ewusi-Mensah, Kweku: *Patterns of Software Systems Failure and Success*, International Thomson Computer Press, Boston, 1995.

———: *Software Development Failures*, MIT Press, Cambridge, MA, 2003.

———: *Why Flawed Software Projects Are Not Cancelled in Time*, Cutter IT Journal, vol. 10., no 12, December 2003, pp. 12–17.

———:*Software Project Management Practices / Failure Versus Success*, Projects & Profits, Vol. 6, no 4, April 2006, pp 17–26.

_____*Social and Technical Reasons for Software Project Failures*, Crosstalk, Vol. 19, No. 6, June 2006, pp 4–8.

Perry, William E.: *Handbook of Diagnosing and Solving Computer Problems*, TAB Books, Blue Ridge Summit, Pa., 1989.

Yourdon, Ed: *Death March—The Complete Software Developer's Guide to Surviving "Mission Impossible" Projects*, Prentice-Hall PTR, Upper Saddle River, N.J., 1997.

Sources of Error in Software Cost Estimation

One of the first questions software project managers ask is how accurate the software cost-estimating tools are. That question is surprisingly difficult to answer, since accuracy can be judged only in the context of precisely measured software projects. Most companies, universities, and government agencies do not have historical data that is precise enough to be used to judge the relative accuracy of software cost-estimation tools. Surprisingly, the accuracy of some software cost-estimating tools is much higher than the accuracy of historical data!

Indeed, as determined by performing assessment and benchmark studies, the historical cost data for an average software project is only about 50 percent complete. Most cost-tracking systems omit early requirements, unpaid overtime, the work of specialists, the technical work performed by users, project management, travel costs, and many other factors that will be discussed later in this chapter.

A very common phenomenon occurs when companies or researchers first evaluate a software cost-estimating tool. Comparisons are made between the estimating tool and locally available historical data. These estimates almost always show large discrepancies of 50 to 100 percent or more between what the estimating tool predicts and the historical results.

The variances are always in the same direction: The estimating tool predicts higher costs and longer schedules than what the local historical data indicates. The natural tendency is to assume that the estimating tool is inaccurate. However, it often happens that the error resides in the historical data itself. Most of what passes for historical data in the software industry is incomplete and omits perhaps 50 percent of the real work performed on software projects.

Before the topic of software-estimation accuracy can be properly discussed, it is necessary to understand the gaps and errors that are endemic in software measurement data. Only when the errors of historical data have been corrected is it possible to judge the relative accuracy of estimation methods.

Following are the three major sources of error observed in software historical data. These three problems are almost universal, and unless they are corrected it is very difficult to utilize historical data for calibrating estimation tools. Observations on these problems have been made as a result of software process assessments, and are derived from studies within about 600 companies and government organizations. The three major problems are:

- Failure to include all activities that were performed
- Failure to include all classes of workers who participate
- Failure to include unpaid overtime

Normally, software project historical data is accumulated in some kind of a general project cost-tracking system. These cost-tracking systems are seldom designed for, or optimized for, collecting data on software projects. Their most common problem is that they lack an effective chart of accounts that matches a full software life cycle.

The most common omissions from cost-tracking systems include the following:

- Work performed before the cost-tracking system was initialized, such as requirements determination
- Work performed by nonprogramming personnel, such as technical writers, database administrators, or quality-assurance staffers
- Work performed by project management, especially second-level or higher managers
- Technical work performed by users when they participate in testing or create their own user documentation

Note that it is intrinsically difficult to quantify activities that are omitted from formal cost-tracking systems. However, from interviewing several hundred project personnel and asking them to reconstruct how they spent their time, the following tentative values can be assigned to these missing elements:

- From 5 to 10 percent of a software project's effort will be expended before the cost-tracking system is turned on.
- From 15 to 30 percent of the work on a project will be performed by workers who are not included in typical cost-tracking systems.

- Management effort will amount to between 10 and 20 percent of the overall project and may not be tracked in some companies.

- User participation in the technical work of software projects amounts to between 5 and 20 percent of the total effort and is almost never tracked.

- Unpaid overtime by exempt professional staff and management amounts to between 5 and 15 percent of software project effort, with the largest amount of overtime being utilized on the most important and largest projects.

Other problems with historical data collection also occur. Here are a few observations that have been noted during software process assessments:

- When a project begins to run low on funding, there is a tendency to charge time to other projects.

- Some personnel refuse to use the cost-tracking system at all.

- Some complex systems projects utilize other kinds of personnel besides software engineers, such as electrical engineers or mechanical engineers. These engineers may be engaged in software design work and sometimes even in coding, but they do not regard themselves as software personnel and don't record their time when doing software work.

- Some enterprises have no cost-tracking systems at all and, hence, have no historical data of any kind.

Since problems with historical data are so endemic, it is a fair question to ask how software-estimating tool vendors accumulated enough information to build the tools in the first place. (Note that the author is also a developer of commercial software cost-estimating tools.)

From informal conversations with competitive estimating-tool vendors (such as Dr. Barry Boehm of COCOMO, Larry Putnam of SLIM, and Dr. Howard Rubin of ESTIMACS), it appears that all have encountered problems of inaccurate historical data and have compensated for this problem in one or more of three ways:

- By excluding projects where the data is incomplete

- By correcting the missing data based on interviews with project team members

- By building activity-based cost-estimating tools

As a general rule, historical data that is not granular should be avoided. Data collected only to the level of complete projects, for example, without any breakdown by activities or tasks, is seldom accurate enough to be useful for estimating purposes.

TABLE 5.1   Patterns of Missing Software Cost Data by Industry

Software subindustry	Percentage of missing data	Most common omissions
Military software	10	Unpaid overtime
Contracted or outsourced software	10	Unpaid overtime
Systems software	12	Unpaid overtime and documentation
Commercial software	15	Unpaid overtime, non-code tasks, and requirements
Information systems	35	Unpaid overtime, user activities, non-code tasks, specialists, and project managers
End-user software	75	Everything but coding

Also, data that is granular only to the level of phases (such as require-ments, design, coding, testing, and installation) is also of questionable value. Many activities span multiple phases. To name but a few, con-figuration control, integration, and the preparation of user manuals normally span at least two phases. Therefore, phase-level data cannot be safely used for estimating multiphase work.

Some industries are better than others in recording software effort, schedule, cost, and quality information. Among the clients served by Software Productivity Research, the patterns of errors typically noted are presented in Table 5.1.

The problem of incomplete historical data is common enough that the patterns of gaps can be illustrated. Table 5.2 is derived from the compan-ion volume to this book, *Applied Software Measurement* (Jones 1996a).

Only about 5 activities out of a possible 25 are routinely accurate enough that the data is usable for cost-estimation purposes. The effect of the missing or incomplete data is to drive up apparent productivity rates and make projects seem cheaper than they really are.

The chart of accounts shown in Table 5.2 illustrates the approximate level of granularity that is needed to accumulate historical data with enough precision to judge the accuracy of software-estimation tools.

Historical data that is only aggregated to the level of complete proj-ects is not useful for serious study, since there is no way of knowing what activities were or were not performed and did or did not affect the total costs and resources.

There are at least two levels below the activity level that are necessary for really fine-tuning estimating tools: tasks and subtasks. For example, if *unit testing* is considered to be a standard activity, then the following three tasks are the key subcomponents of normal unit testing:

1. Preparing test cases

2. Running test cases

3. Repairing bugs or defects

TABLE 5.2   Common Gaps in Historical Software Cost and Resource Data

Activities performed	Completeness of historical data
01 Requirements	Missing or incomplete
02 Prototyping	Missing or incomplete
03 Architecture	Incomplete
04 Project planning	Incomplete
05 Initial analysis and design	Incomplete
06 Detail design	Incomplete
07 Design reviews	Missing or incomplete
08 Coding	Complete
09 Reusable code acquisition	Missing or incomplete
10 Purchased package acquisition	Missing or incomplete
11 Code inspections	Missing or incomplete
12 Independent verification and validation	Complete
13 Configuration management	Missing or incomplete
14 Integration	Missing or incomplete
15 User documentation	Missing or incomplete
16 Unit testing	Incomplete
17 Function testing	Incomplete
18 Integration testing	Incomplete
19 System testing	Incomplete
20 Field testing	Incomplete
21 Acceptance testing	Missing or incomplete
22 Independent testing	Complete
23 Quality assurance	Missing or incomplete
24 Installation and training	Missing or incomplete
25 Project management	Missing or incomplete
26 Total project resources, costs	Incomplete

Because every activity will have from three to five tasks connected with it, and some tasks can have from three to five subtasks, the most granular level of precision can exceed 1000 data elements.

Judging the Accuracy of Software Cost Estimates

Because the author's company designs and builds software cost-estimating tools, he is frequently asked three general questions about the accuracy of estimates:

- How accurate are our company's tools in terms of how their results compare to historical data?

- How accurate are our company's tools in terms of how their estimates compare to estimates from competitive estimating tools?

- How accurate are our company's tools in terms of how their estimates compare to manual cost estimates?

The first question has already been discussed, with the surprising result that cost estimates both from our tools and from competitive estimating tools are often more accurate than historical data, due to "leakage" from cost-tracking systems.

A significant study was performed by Air Force Captain Karen R. Mertes as a master's thesis at the Air Force Institute of Technology, using validated Air Force data (Mertes 1996). This study showed that when the historical data is accurate, estimates usually come within 10 percent, and sometimes come closer than 5 percent.

The second question about competitive tools is difficult for the author to answer, since it involves comparing our products against our competitors'. That question obviously involves a conflict of interest, and it is better addressed by university studies or independent research. Because the United States military services produce so much software and use so many estimating tools, much of the comparative research about software cost estimation is performed in a military context. The Air Force Software Technology Support Center (STSC) at Hill Air Force Base in Utah produced an interesting comparison of no less than 31 software cost estimation tools that contrasts features and discusses partial accuracy from limited trials (Barrow et al. 1993). The estimating tools included were ASSET-R, CA-ESTIMACS, CA-FPXpert, CB COCOMO, CEIS, CHECKPOINT, COCOMO1, COCOMOID, CoCoPro, COSTAR, COSTEXPERT, COSTMODL, GECOMO Plus, GHL COCOMO, ESTIMATE, PRICE-S, PROJECT BRIDGE, REVIC, SASET, SECOMO, SEER-SEM, SEER-SSM, SIZE PLANNER, SIZE Plus, SIZEEXPERT, SLIM, SOFTCOSST-R, SPQR/20, SWAN, and SYSTEM-4. Another Air Force comparison using a smaller number of tools but a greater amount of validated data was performed jointly between Maxwell Air Force Base and the Air Force Institute of Technology (Ourada and Ferens 1995). This study included eight estimating tools (REVIC, COCOMO, PRICE-S, SEER, SASET, SYSTEM-4, CHECKPOINT, and COSTMODL). Another interesting military estimating comparison, by the well-known software cost-estimating expert, Professor Daniel Ferens of the Air Force Institute of Technology (AFIT), was published in one of the special cost-estimating issues of *American Programmer* magazine (Ferens 1996). An older and fairly rare study of civilian software cost-estimating models was performed by MIT and included six software cost models from the 1985 era (Kemerer 1987).

The third question has been answered independently by a number of software-estimating tool vendors, and the results are identical:

- Manual estimates are usually highly optimistic for costs and schedules.

- Automated estimates are usually accurate or conservative for costs and schedules.

The author collected a sample of 50 manual software cost estimates from our company's clients for projects where both the initial formal cost estimate and the final accumulated costs were known. Figure 5.1 shows that only 4 of these 50 manual estimates came within plus or minus 5 percent of the historical costs, and the majority of manual estimates were optimistic to a significant degree.

Because the manual estimates were produced by colleagues and clients, interviews and discussions were able to pinpoint the reasons for the optimism. Here are some examples cited by project managers whose estimates proved to be optimistic:

"I could not get approval for an accurate estimate, so I had to change it."

"The project doubled in size after the requirements."

"Debugging and testing took longer than we thought."

"The new CASE tools we were using didn't work right and slowed us down."

"We didn't have any estimating tools available at the time the estimate was needed."

"I lost some of my developers and had to find replacements."

By contrast, Figure 5.2 illustrates the accuracy ranges of 50 automated software cost estimates.

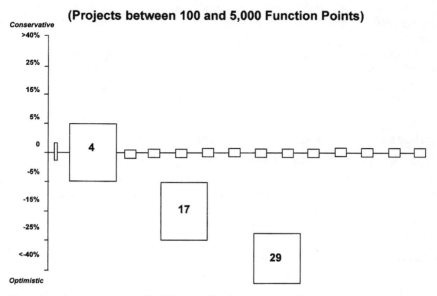

Figure 5.1   Accuracy ranges for 50 manual software cost estimates.

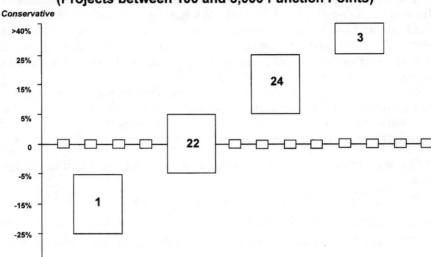

Figure 5.2 Accuracy ranges for 50 automated software cost estimates.

It is interesting that a much higher percentage of automated methods came within plus or minus 5 percent than with manual methods. Even more interesting is the fact that the direction of error is reversed.

Automated estimating tools are usually conservative when they are not accurate, while manual methods are usually optimistic. Indeed, only 1 of the 50 automated estimates was on the optimistic side.

Accuracy within plus or minus 5 percent is the desired goal of estimating, but if errors do occur the fail-safe mode is to be conservative rather than optimistic. For bidding purposes, deliberate optimism is sometimes used, but in the long run accuracy and conservatism are the best choices.

Classes of Software Estimation Errors

Once the problem of incomplete or missing historical data has been overcome, it is possible to evaluate the accuracy of estimation tools and methods themselves. There are 12 common problems that tend to occur with software estimates:

- Metrics errors
- Scaling errors
- Executive and client errors

- Sizing errors
- Activity-selection errors
- Assignment-scope errors
- Production-rate errors
- Creeping user requirements
- Critical path errors
- Staffing build-up errors
- Technology adjustment errors
- Special or unique situations

Let us consider the implications of these sources of error individually.

Metrics Errors

The most common error in software estimating is derived from the very common usage of *lines-of-code* (LOC) metrics. Although LOC-metrics were proven to be unreliable for software estimation as long ago as 1978, the technique is still among the most widely utilized.

There are problems with LOC-metrics associated with variations in the way code is counted, but these are not the source of the main problem. The main problem with LOC-metrics is the fact that more than half of all software effort is not directly related to source code. This means that LOC-metrics tend to paradoxically move in the wrong direction when used with high-level languages.

To illustrate the problem with LOC-metrics as an estimation method, Table 5.3 shows three examples of the same program. The first example is written in macro assembly language, the second is written in Ada 83,

TABLE 5.3   Implementation of the Same Program in Three Languages

	Macro assembly	Ada 83	C++
Source code required, LOC	10,000	3,500	2,500
Effort per activity, staff months			
Requirements	1.0	1.0	1.0
Design	3.0	2.0	0.5
Coding	5.0	1.5	1.0
Testing	4.0	1.5	1.0
Documentation	2.0	2.0	2.0
Management	2.0	1.0	0.5
Total project, months	18.0	10.0	7.5
Total project, LOC/staff month	555	350	333
Coding and testing, % total project	28%	15%	13%

and the third example is written in C++. However, all three examples perform exactly the same functions.

As may be seen from the examples, apparent productivity expressed in LOC-metrics declines as the power of the language increases. This phenomenon causes problems for estimation when LOC-metrics are used by the unwary.

For example, suppose a manager has some historical data based on assembly language, with a rate of 600 LOC per month. It is natural to assume that more powerful languages such as Ada or C++ will improve productivity, as indeed they often do. (Note that pure coding for the prior examples had rates of 2000 LOC per month for assembly, 2300 for Ada, and 2500 for C++.)

It often happens that unwary or inexperienced software managers get trapped into making false estimating assumptions along these lines: "We've been getting 600 LOC per month for our assembly-language projects, and Ada is a much more powerful language. I'll use 700 LOC per month as the rate for estimating our new Ada project."

This common estimating problem is comprised of two separate components:

- Historical data that is not granular enough to show activities is dangerous for estimating work.

- The LOC-metrics itself is flawed and dangerous for cross-language measurement or estimation purposes.

This problem is very common when estimates are performed manually. But it can also occur with some of the older LOC-based estimation tools that do not vary their assumptions from language to language. Most modern software-estimating tools allow the specific language or sets of languages used to be identified, and then adjust the estimation algorithms to match the specifics of the language set.

There are alternate metrics that do not exhibit the paradoxical rate reversal associated with lines of code. The function point metric, for example, is free from the distortions and errors that occur with LOC-metrics.

As an example, since all three versions of the program in Table 5.3 are identical in functionality, their function point total would stay constant regardless of language. Assume that the program illustrated contains 50 function points. When productivity is expressed in terms of function points per staff month, the results correlate exactly with the increased power of the higher level languages:

Assembly-language version	=	2.80 function points per staff month
Ada version	=	5.00 function points per staff month
C++ version	=	6.60 function points per staff month

The ability of function points to measure and estimate economic productivity across multiple languages is one of the reasons why the usage of this metric has been expanding at more than 50 percent per year. By about 1992, the nonprofit International Function Point Users Group (IFPUG) had become the largest software measurement association in the United States. When the membership of the 21 current international affiliates is considered, the function point metric is now the most widely used software metric in the world.

Scaling Errors

Another common source of estimating error is the naive assumption that data collected from small programs can safely be used to estimate large systems. Large systems (more than 1 million source code statements or 10,000 function points) differ from small programs (less than 10,000 source code statements or 100 function points) in two major ways:

- Large systems require more activities than small programs.
- The costs of large systems do not follow the same profile as small programs.

Using the chart of accounts from Table 5.1 as a reference point, small programs seldom perform more than about 10 of the 25 activities that are listed. Large civilian systems, on the other hand, routinely perform at least 20 of the 25 activities, and large military projects perform all 25.

Not only do large systems perform more activities, but the effort required for various kinds of work changes notably as software projects grow in size. Table 5.4, derived from *Applied Software Measurement* (Jones 1996), highlights the distribution of effort for programs and systems of various sizes.

As may be seen from Table 5.4, it is not at all safe to use data taken from applications of one size range as the basis for estimating applications of a significantly different size.

TABLE 5.4   Variations in Software Effort Associated with Application Size

Size, function points	Size, KLOC	Coding, %	Paperwork, %	Defect removal, %	Management and support, %
1	0.1	70	5	15	10
10	1	65	7	17	11
100	10	54	15	20	11
1,000	100	30	26	30	14
10,000	1,000	18	31	35	16

The most common form of scaling error is the assumption that data from small projects of 100 function points or less (roughly 10,000 source code statements) can be used for large systems of 1000 function points or more (roughly 100,000 source code statements). The reason is that project managers see many more small projects than large systems. A project manager may be responsible for several small projects in the course of a typical business year, but be responsible for the estimation of a large system only a few times in an entire career. Therefore, project managers know quite a bit about small-project estimating, but very little about large-system estimating.

Executive and Client Errors

One of the most severe sources of software-estimation error centers around corporate politics, or the fact that senior executives and client executives have the authority to arbitrarily reject valid estimates. Most software cost estimates must go through several layers of management approval and client approval before being finalized.

What often happens is that the original estimate created by a software project manager is either accurate or conservative. However, this initial estimate is outside the envelope of an acceptable schedule or acceptable costs in the minds of the executives who must approve the estimate. Therefore, the project manager is directed to recast the estimate in order to lower costs or shorten schedules or both.

What has happened is that the real estimate is no longer the creation of the software project manager responsible for the project. The real estimate has become the subjective opinion of a client or senior executive. Usually, such mandated estimates are made in the total absence of any kind of serious, professional estimating methodology, and without any estimating tools at all.

When performing autopsies on canceled software projects or on projects that exceeded their schedules and budgets by more than 50 percent, more than half of these disasters are seen to have had initial conservative estimates that were arbitrarily rejected by senior executives or by client executives. Unfortunately, the project managers were still assigned the blame for the disaster or overrun even though they had tried to estimate accurately.

Sizing Errors

Yet another common software-estimating error is that of mistakes in predicting the sizes of various deliverables. Sizing errors are very common for all external deliverables, including the quantity of source code, the number of screens, and the number of pages in both course materials and user documentation.

Sizing errors are also endemic when dealing with internal deliverables, such as pages of specifications, pages of planning documents, test cases, and the like.

Predicting source code size, documentation quantities and sizes, and test-cases are standard functions of modern software-estimating tools, although they are missing from those developed prior to about 1985. (Historical note: SPQR/20, which was released in 1985, appears to be the first commercial software-estimating tool that included sizing logic for source code, documentation volumes, and test cases. This tool pioneered the usage of function points as the uniform basis for sizing all software deliverables.)

More recent software-estimating tools can predict the size of more than 50 paper documents, the number of test cases for 18 kinds of testing, and source code size for almost 600 programming languages.

Activity-Selection Errors

Activity-selection errors are those of omitting necessary work from an estimate, such as accidentally omitting the costs of user documentation. Activity selection from a repertoire of more than 20 activities (or even several hundred tasks), with the estimating tool automatically adjusting its selection to match military, civilian, and project class or type characteristics, is now a standard function of modern software-estimating tools.

Users can override activity-selection logic or produce custom activity lists. Several modern software cost-estimating tools support the creation of *templates* that utilize historical projects or custom templates created by the user as the basis for activity and task selection.

Activity-selection errors are very common when performing manual estimates. For example, a project manager within a major computer company once received funding for a project with an approved estimate that accidentally omitted the costs of producing the user manuals.

Activity-selection errors also have another unfortunate manifestation: Software tool vendors and programming language vendors tend to make advertising claims based on comparisons of unlike activities. For example, an ad for a fourth-generation language cited productivity results of more than 100 function points per staff month, and the ad claimed that these results were "10 times greater than COBOL." However, when the vendor was queried about the activities that went into the claim, it was discovered that requirements, design, user documentation, and project management were not included. In fact, the only activities that were included for the language being advertised were coding and unit testing. However, the COBOL projects used for the comparison did include requirements, design, documentation, and other normal project activities.

Failure to define the tasks and activities when either measuring or estimating software is an embarrassingly common problem within the software industry. Table 5.5 shows the patterns of tasks that are typical for several kinds of software projects. Table 5.5 is also derived from the author's companion book, *Applied Software Measurement* (Jones 1996).

TABLE 5.5   Software Development Activities Associated with Six Subindustries (Percentage of Staff Months by Activity)

Activities performed	Web-based	MIS	Outsource	Commercial	System	Military
01 Requirements		7.50	9.00	4.00	4.00	7.00
02 Prototyping	10.00	2.00	2.50	1.00	2.00	2.00
03 Architecture		0.50	1.00	2.00	1.50	1.00
04 Project plans		1.00	1.50	1.00	2.00	1.00
05 Initial design		8.00	7.00	6.00	7.00	6.00
06 Detail design		7.00	8.00	5.00	6.00	7.00
07 Design reviews			0.50	1.50	2.50	1.00
08 Coding	35.00	20.00	16.00	23.00	20.00	16.00
09 Reuse acquisition	5.00		2.00	2.00	2.00	2.00
10 Package purchase		1.00	1.00		1.00	1.00
11 Code inspections				1.50	1.50	1.00
12 Independent verification and validation						1.00
13 Configuration management		3.00	3.00	1.00	1.00	1.50
14 Formal integration		2.00	2.00	1.50	2.00	1.50
15 User documentation	10.00	7.00	9.00	12.00	10.00	10.00
16 Unit testing	40.00	4.00	3.50	2.50	5.00	3.00
17 Function testing		6.00	5.00	6.00	5.00	5.00
18 Integration testing		5.00	5.00	4.00	5.00	5.00
19 System testing		7.00	5.00	7.00	5.00	6.00
20 Field testing				6.00	1.50	3.00
21 Acceptance testing		5.00	3.00		1.00	3.00
22 Independent testing						1.00
23 Quality assurance			1.00	2.00	2.00	1.00
24 Installation and training		2.00	3.00		1.00	1.00
25 Project management		12.00	12.00	11.00	12.00	13.00
Total	100.0	100.0	100.0	100.0	100.0	100.0
Activities	5	16	20	21	22	25

As can easily be seen, it would be dangerous to construct a formal software cost estimate without full and complete knowledge of the activities that are going to be part of the development cycle for the project in question.

The large variations in activity sets from class to class illustrate why gross estimates at the project or phase level are seldom as accurate as those at the activity level. It is too hard to validate gross estimates because the inner structure of the work to be performed is invisible.

Although project-level and phase-level estimates were the norm from the 1960s through the early 1990s, activity-level cost estimates are rapidly becoming the norm.

Assignment-Scope Errors

Assignment-scope errors are those of miscalculating the quantity of work that can be handled by the staff, so that they become overloaded. The phrase *assignment scope* denotes the amount of work assigned to one staff member.

Assignment-scope prediction in terms of both natural metrics (pages of specifications, source code, and number of test cases) and synthetic metrics (function points and feature points) is now a standard function of modern software cost-estimating tools. Templates defined by users or created from historical project data can also be used.

Assignment scopes have now been worked out from empirical observations for the following occupation groups:

- Software development engineers and/or programmers
- Software maintenance engineers and/or programmers
- Systems analysts
- Technical writers
- Quality-assurance specialists
- Configuration control specialists
- Integration specialists
- Testing specialists
- Customer-support specialists
- Project managers

However, there are almost 100 software occupations that can be found in large software-producing companies, such as IBM, AT&T, Microsoft, and the like. There are quite a few specialized occupation groups where the quantity of work that can be assigned to one person is still uncertain. Examples of occupations where assignment scopes fluctuate from project to project and company to company include the following:

- Administrative specialists
- Database administration specialists
- Network specialists
- Multimedia specialists
- Human factors specialists
- System performance specialists
- Process specialists

As of 2007, there are some unresolved problems surrounding specialists and assignment scopes. For example, how many different kinds of specialists are needed to support a general software population of 1000?

Research in this topic is made difficult by the fact that many companies do not even have records or job titles for some of the specialist occupations. For example, companies that use "member of the technical staff" as a blanket job title covering a host of occupations are essentially unable to do research into an important topic.

The topic of specialization and assignment scope is becoming more and more important in the context of four recent trends:

- Downsizing, or major layoffs of personnel in large companies
- Business process reengineering
- The increasing frequency of outsourcing arrangements, which transfer employees to the outsource company

In all four situations, knowledge of the kinds and quantities of specialists employed by an enterprise is a significant factor.

Production-Rate Errors

The phrase *production rate* denotes the amount of work that one person can complete in a standard time period, such as an hour, a work day, a work week, or a work month.

Production-rate errors are those of excessive optimism, such as assuming coding rates in excess of 3000 statements per month. Production-rate estimation using both natural metrics, such as source code, and synthetic metrics, such as function points, is now a standard function of modern software cost-estimating tools. Templates defined by users or created from historical data can also be used.

Production rates expressed in terms of natural metrics have long been a part of the software-estimation process. For example, estimating programming effort by lines of code per month, estimating technical writing time by pages written per month, and estimating testing by test runs per hour all date back to the 1950s. The problem with natural metrics is that they do not allow aggregation or summarization of unlike tasks.

More recently, the synthetic function point metric has been used to provide a uniform base for exploring the comparative performance of all activities and tasks. Table 5.6 shows current average production rates in function points for the 25-activity chart of accounts already discussed in Table 5.5.

TABLE 5.6   Productivity Ranges for Software Development Activities

Activities performed	Function points per month			Work hours per function point		
	Minimum	Mode	Maximum	Maximum	Mode	Minimum
01 Requirements	50.00	175.00	350.00	2.64	0.75	0.38
02 Prototyping	25.00	150.00	250.00	5.28	0.88	0.53
03 Architecture	100.00	300.00	500.00	1.32	0.44	0.26
04 Project plans	200.00	500.00	1500.00	0.66	0.26	0.09
05 Initial design	50.00	175.00	400.00	2.64	0.75	0.33
06 Detail design	25.00	150.00	300.00	5.28	0.88	0.44
07 Design reviews	75.00	225.00	400.00	1.76	0.59	0.33
08 Coding	15.00	50.00	200.00	8.80	2.64	0.66
09 Reuse acquisition	400.00	600.00	2000.00	0.33	0.22	0.07
10 Package purchase	350.00	400.00	1500.00	0.38	0.33	0.09
11 Code inspections	75.00	150.00	300.00	1.76	0.88	0.44
12 Independent verification and validation	75.00	125.00	200.00	1.76	1.06	0.66
13 Configuration management	1000.00	1750.00	3000.00	0.13	0.08	0.04
14 Formal integration	150.00	250.00	500.00	0.88	0.53	0.26
15 User documentation	20.00	70.00	100.00	6.60	1.89	1.32
16 Unit testing	70.00	150.00	400.00	1.89	0.88	0.33
17 Function testing	25.00	150.00	300.00	5.28	0.88	0.44
18 Integration testing	75.00	175.00	400.00	1.76	0.75	0.33
19 System testing	100.00	200.00	500.00	1.32	0.66	0.26
20 Field testing	75.00	225.00	500.00	1.76	0.59	0.26
21 Acceptance testing	75.00	350.00	600.00	1.76	0.38	0.22
22 Independent testing	100.00	200.00	300.00	1.32	0.66	0.44
23 Quality assurance	30.00	150.00	300.00	4.40	0.88	0.44
24 Installation and training	150.00	350.00	600.00	0.88	0.38	0.22
25 Project management	15.00	100.00	200.00	8.80	1.32	0.66
Cumulative results	1.90	6.75	13.88	69.38	19.55	9.51
Arithmetic mean	133	284.8	624	2.78	0.78	0.38

As can be seen, there are wide variances for every activity. However, it is very useful to be able to explore the relative productivity of every activity and task using a common metric. This kind of research is opening up many new avenues for improved estimation accuracy.

Another aspect of necessary production-rate adjustments are those required to deal with variances in the number of work hours per day and the probable amount of unpaid overtime applied.

Both work hours and unpaid overtime vary extremely from project to project, company to company, industry to industry, and country to country. Table 5.7 shows the approximate values for the United States for six subindustries.

As can be seen, the typical work-hour pattern for commercial software houses, such as Microsoft or Oracle, is quite a bit longer than for internal software producers. Variances such as this are even more extreme internationally, when it is necessary to include the very significant differences in vacation periods and holidays for projects that span the Atlantic or Pacific and involve European or Asian development teams as well as American development teams.

This kind of data on work patterns is so highly variable from company to company and country to country that it is unsafe to use "industry norms" for estimating actual projects. Instead, each estimate should use local values for work hours and effective work hours.

Creeping User Requirements

Omission of creeping requirements refers to the very common phenomenon of failing to adjust an estimate for the growth rate in unplanned requirements after the conclusion of the formal requirements phase.

The phenomenon of creeping requirements is so common that predicting the amount of requirements creep and adjusting the estimate accordingly have become standard functions of modern cost-estimating tools.

TABLE 5.7   Representative Software Work Hours per Day in Six Subindustries

Software class	Work hours per 8-h day	Unpaid overtime per day	Total work hours per day
End user	3.5	0.0	3.5
MIS	5.5	1.0	6.5
Outsource	7.0	1.5	8.5
Commercial	7.0	2.0	9.0
System	6.0	1.0	7.0
Military	6.5	1.0	7.5
Average	5.9	1.1	7.0

One of the useful by-products of function points is their ability to perform direct measurement of creeping user requirements. Every change that a user might need after the initial requirements are agreed to will almost certainly affect one or more of the five basic function point parameters:

- Inputs
- Outputs
- Inquiries
- Logical files
- Interfaces

From long-range observations of several hundred projects, it can be stated that creeping requirements average about 2 percent per month from the day of the initial agreement on requirements until the commencement of testing. Thus, for a project that has a schedule of 2 years or 24 months from requirements until testing, it can be expected that the functional content will grow by roughly 50 percent.

The utility of function points for monitoring and measuring project growth explains why so many consulting and outsourcing companies are adopting function points as the basis of their contracts. For example, the current average cost of building one function point in the United States is just over $1000.

Suppose a contract is agreed to for producing an application of 1000 function points in size for a cost of $1000 per function point, or $1 million in all. Now suppose that six months into the contract, the client identifies a need for an additional 100 function points. Under the basic terms of the contract, the new functionality might be added to the contract for a price of $100,000.

Some vendors are even adopting a sliding scale, with the cost per function point going up for changes added later in the development cycle. The methodology of using function points as the basis for software contracts is clarifying a number of important issues and making the contracts easier to administer.

However, vendors should be alerted to a new problem that is showing up in breach of contract lawsuits by unhappy clients. Usually the first year of an outsourcing arrangement is complex, with many personnel changing positions and needing time to adjust to the new arrangement. The outsource company's managers and technical staff also need time to understand the applications in depth. As a result, the first year of an outsource contract usually has a temporary reduction in productivity of perhaps 5 percent compared to the year preceding the outsourcing agreement.

However, it is not uncommon for outsource contracts to commit the vendor to annual improvements in development or maintenance productivity, or both. If the client has performed a function point baseline analysis prior to starting the outsource contract, then it will be easy to measure the performance of the outsourcer during the first year. If the outsource vendor promised to achieve, for example, a 5 percent increase in productivity in the first year but the actual results were a 5 percent reduction, then litigation for breach of contract is a common response by the client.

Outsource vendors should be aware that while using function points as the basis of contracts makes the contracts easy to administer and has many advantages, the function point metric is accurate enough that empty promises and false claims will quickly become visible.

Critical Path Errors

Software development is a complex net of hundreds of interlinked activities. A very common estimating problem is failure to identify the critical path though this network of activities, so that delays in some key component or deliverable ripples downstream and lengthens the final delivery schedule.

The most common variety of critical path error is associated with debugging and testing. It is obvious that final integration and delivery of a software project cannot occur if the software is not working. From a sample of 64 IBM software projects and 20 ITT software projects that ran late by at least six months, insufficient time was allowed in the schedule for debugging and testing on every project. The root cause of the problem was an unwise attempt by senior executives to compress schedules by skimping on quality control and testing. This approach usually backfires, and stretches out the schedule rather than shortening it.

These same projects exhibited an interesting pathology. Until testing began, there was no overt sign or evidence that the projects were in trouble; indeed, they seemed to be ahead of schedule. However, when the cost and time profiles of the late projects were examined and compared to similar projects that were delivered close to their nominal schedules, the true situation emerged.

The late projects had skimped on front-end reviews, inspections, and quality control. This gave a false appearance of speeding through the development cycle. When the problems were finally encountered as testing began, there were so many of them and they were so severe that schedule recovery was impossible. Figure 5.3 illustrates the very different curves that differentiate pathological projects from healthy projects.

Note how deceptive the early phases are for projects on the pathological curve. All of the short-cuts during requirements and design and the failure to utilize inspections come back to haunt testing and maintenance.

How Quality Affects Software Estimation

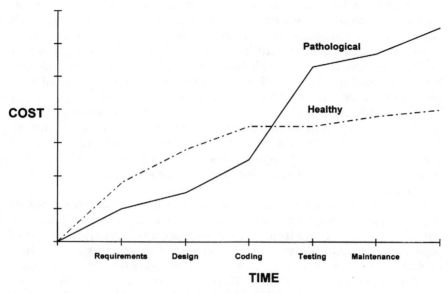

Figure 5.3 Cost comparison of pathological and healthy projects.

Staffing Build-Up Errors

This problem is only intermittent, but can be severe when it occurs. For many military and defense contractors, and some civilian contractors, the total complement of personnel needed to complete a contract is not actually employed or available. When a contract is won, there is an immediate need to start a hiring campaign or find subcontractors to do the work.

The problem of staffing build-up errors can occur when there is a shortage of available personnel or the subcontracting process takes longer than anticipated. If a contract assumes, for example, that 100 software engineers will be available on a certain date, and only 20 are present on that date, all of the subsequent activities and schedules are likely to be thrown out of kilter.

Technology Adjustment Errors

The most subtle and complex of the sources of estimating errors are those dealing with adjusting the estimate to match the effects of various tools, languages, and methodologies.

As of 2007 there are more than 600 programming languages in use, and more than 5000 tools aimed at aspects of software development. There are also more than 150 specification and design methods, and more than 50 varieties of software methodology, such as information engineering, the object-oriented paradigm, various structured approaches, and the like.

To add to the difficulty of this topic, many of the tools and approaches are being marketed with productivity or quality claims that lack any kind of empirical evidence. There is also a continuous influx of new topics, which have little or no supporting data of any kind.

For example, Agile methods and Quality Function Deployment (QFD) are now starting to be used for software, but most such usages are so new that the results are not yet known. Multimedia applications, virtual reality applications, and applications intended for massively parallel computing platforms are also too new to have accumulated much historical data.

There are also some important topics that have a very steep learning curve. For example, the object-oriented paradigm has such a steep learning curve that the first projects developed using various kinds of object-oriented analysis usually take longer and are more expensive than projects of the same size and nature developed using the older structured methods, such as the Yourdon or Warnier-Orr design approaches.

This means that both estimating-tool vendors and their clients can encounter situations that are outside the boundary of current versions of estimating tools. Although this is a regrettable situation, software is not unique in having to deal with new phenomena. Not many years ago, most patients with Lyme disease were misdiagnosed because that illness had not yet been identified or typed.

The best of the estimating tools and methods attempt to stay current with advances in technologies by implementing annual upgrades to the factors that are included. For example, ten years ago, or even five years ago, there were no estimating tools that allowed client/server applications to be identified as a discrete type of project for estimating purposes. However, now that client/server applications are exploding in popularity, most estimating-tool vendors are preparing updates that support this technology.

As this book is being written, JAVA applications are just starting to be measured with enough precision to develop useful software cost-estimating algorithms. There will always be an *event horizon* for software-estimating tools, or a gap between the newest software technologies and the algorithms used by the estimating tools.

Special or Unique Situations

The phrase *special or unique situations* refers to uncommon factors that can affect a specific project, but which do not occur with enough regularity to fit into standard estimating algorithms or common templates. A few examples of special situations that can affect project costs will clarify the point:

- Closure of an office or evacuation of staff due to weather conditions
- Closure of an office or evacuation of staff due to fire or natural disaster
- Voluntary termination of more than 50 percent of project team members
- Major layoffs or downsizing of project personnel
- Illness or incapacity of key team members
- Physical relocation of a project team from one city to another
- Injunctions or legal actions that freeze project specifications or source code
- Sale or merger of companies that affects specific projects
- Travel costs for trips among geographically dispersed projects
- Moving, living, and real-estate costs for hiring new employees

These are only examples of special situations that, when they do occur, must be factored in to a final software cost estimate.

Range of Impact of Estimating Errors

Estimating-tool vendors are often asked questions about how accurate their tools are. It is even more significant to note how far out of balance an estimate can be if one or more of the 12 error conditions are present when the estimate is prepared. Following are the ranges of impact associated with each of the 12 problems.

When an estimate includes *metrics errors*, such as using LOC rates from one language for estimating productivity on a project using another language, the observed range of deviation can exceed 100 percent. That is, an error can be off by more than 100 percent if the languages vary widely, such as using data from assembly language to estimate projects written in an object-oriented language such as C++.

When an estimate includes *scaling errors*, such as using data from a small project to estimate a large system, the observed range of deviation can approach an order of magnitude, or 1000 percent. It might be thought that such errors would never occur in real life, but unfortunately they do. A major government software project in excess of 15,000 function points, or 15 million lines of code, was estimated using data drawn from projects of less than 500 function points, or 50,000 lines of code. This is one of the reasons why the project is running more than four years behind schedule: The schedule was absurd in the way it was developed.

When an estimate includes *executive errors*, where schedules or costs are constrained by executive or client decree, the results are always in the same direction: The projects take longer and cost more. The typical range of political errors is about 50 percent for schedules and 100 percent for costs. That is, the real project takes almost twice as long and costs almost as much as the forced estimate. This phenomenon is associated with another troublesome situation: canceled projects. It often happens that the initial estimates of projects that are canceled without being completed had been subjected to political manipulation.

When an estimate includes *sizing errors*, the range of deviation is more or less proportional to the difference between the true size and the anticipated size. Experienced project managers have been observed to average about plus or minus 15 percent in estimating the size of deliverables, if the requirements are stable. Inexperienced managers can fluctuate widely, and have errors that approach 100 percent or more. Sizing errors are more common for manual estimates than for automated ones, but some of the older estimating tools, such as COCOMO clones, still require that users input size themselves. Modern estimating tools with full sizing logic derived from function points can usually (but not always) come within 15 percent of estimating key deliverables, such as the volume of source code and the size of user documentation.

When an estimate includes *task-selection errors*, the range of uncertainty can exceed an order of magnitude, or 1000 percent. The worst case would be to estimate only coding, and exclude all other activities. Task-selection errors are much more common for manual estimates than for automated ones. Most modern estimating tools have a full repertoire of activities and tasks available and will suggest the appropriate set for any given project. The more sophisticated estimating tools will vary their task lists to match civilian or military norms and large systems or small projects.

When an estimate includes *assignment-scope errors*, the range of uncertainty can approach 100 percent. Normally, assignment-scope errors result in too few people for the work at hand. Here, too, the problem is more common for manual estimates than for automated ones. This problem is particularly severe for maintenance estimates and for estimates of customer support. In real life, some people are able to handle much larger assignment scopes than others. Experienced personnel, for example, can often handle tasks that are two or three times larger than those that novices can deal with.

When an estimate includes *production-rate errors*, the range of uncertainty usually matches the difference between the true rate and the anticipated rate. Suppose a technical writer is estimated to be able to write 75 pages per month, and can only average 50 pages per month.

It is difficult to generalize the impact of production-rate errors, since production rates are highly specific to the activities being performed and to the skill and experience of the personnel doing the work.

When an estimate includes *creeping user requirements errors*, the range of uncertainty more or less matches the volume of unplanned functionality. As stated previously, function points are now being used to make direct measurements of unplanned functions, and the average is about 1 percent per month from the end of requirements to the commencement of testing. Thus, for a two-year project, perhaps 25 percent requirements creep might occur. Some modern estimating tools can predict probable volume of creeping requirements.

When an estimate includes *critical path errors*, both the schedules and the costs will appear to be running better than planned until testing begins, whereupon the entire project comes to a shuddering halt for an indefinite period. This problem normally results in schedule slippages of about 25 percent and cost overruns in excess of 35 percent, although unpaid overtime is so enormous during the testing of projects with critical path errors that the cost overruns might be hidden.

When an estimate includes *staffing build-up errors*, the range of uncertainty matches the difference between the planned and available personnel. If you expect to have ten people start a project and you only have five available, then the error is obviously 100 percent. This error condition does not lend itself to generalization and must be dealt with in the context of specific projects.

When an estimate includes *technology adjustment errors*, the observed range of uncertainty appears to be as much as 150 percent. This problem is particularly severe when technologies are initially deployed. There is always a short-term reduction in productivity as personnel climb the learning curve. Unfortunately, there is a tendency by tool vendors and by project managers to assume that there will be immediate productivity gains. On the whole, estimating tools do a better job of dealing with this factor than do manual estimates, but this problem requires very thoughtful consideration.

When an estimate includes *special or unique situation errors*, there is usually no way of dealing with the problem ahead of time. Here is an example of a special and unique situation that could not be anticipated: The cooling pipe for an air conditioning system of an office building in Cambridge, Massachusetts burst and dropped over 500 gallons of cooling fluid onto the main development computer owned by a software company, shutting down development on a critical project for almost a week.

Another example of a special and unique situation occurred during one of the California earthquakes, when the roof of a programming laboratory in Palo Alto collapsed, causing software development to be temporarily suspended until the staff could be relocated to other quarters.

As another example of a special case, in litigation involving a payment dispute between a contract programmer and a small software company, the judge ordered the source code of the product to be frozen until the issue was decided. The case ran on for more than a year, and the company was unable to even fix bugs in the product, eventually resulting in bankruptcy.

Another special case involved a midwestern manufacturing company where a popular CIO was fired after a merger with another company, whose CIO took over the position. More than 50 percent of the software personnel in the original company resigned in protest, shutting down at least a dozen major software projects.

Software estimation is still a young technology, with only about 35 years of history as of 2007. Although the technology of software estimation is imperfect, it is rapidly improving. Of particular value in improving the ability to estimate projects has been the advent of better measurement, and also of functional metrics.

Better measurement is starting to provide a nucleus of firm schedule, resource, cost, and quality data that can be used as a jumping-off place for estimation. Functional metrics are free of the paradoxical quirks of the older LOC-metrics, which produced erroneous results for high-level languages. Further, functional metrics are allowing research to occur on topics that were previously obscure, such as the impact of specialization. The overall prognosis for improved estimation is very favorable.

References

Barrow, Dean, Susan Nilson, and Dawn Timberlake: *Software Estimation Technology Report*, Software Technology Support Center, OO-ALC/TISE, Hill Air Force Base, Utah, March 1993.

Ferens, Daniel V.: "Software Cost Estimating in the DoD Environment," *American Programmer*, **9**(7):28–34 (1996).

Jones, Capers: *Patterns of Software System Failure and Success*, International Thomson Computer Press, Boston, 1995.

————: *Applied Software Measurement*, 2d ed., McGraw-Hill, New York, 1996a.

————: *Table of Programming Languages and Levels* (8 Versions from 1985 through July 1996), Software Productivity Research, Burlington, Mass., 1996b.

————: *Software Quality—Analysis and Guidelines for Success*, International Thomson Computer Press, Boston, 1997.

————: *Software Assessments, Benchmarks, and Best Practices*, Addison-Wesley Longman, Boston, MA, 2000.

————: *Why Flawed Software Projects Are Not Cancelled in Time;* Cutter IT Journal, vol. 10., no 12, December 2003, pp. 12–17.

————: *Software Project Management Practices / Failure Versus Success*, Projects & Profits, Vol. 6, no 4; April 2006, pp 17–26.

————: *Social and Technical Reasons for Software Project Failures*, Crosstalk, Vol. 19, No. 6, June 2006; pp 4–8.

Kan, Stephen H.: *Metrics and Models in Software Quality Engineering*, Addison-Wesley, Reading, Mass., 1995.

Kemerer, Chris F.: "An Empirical Validation of Software Cost Estimation Models," *Communications of the ACM*, **30:**416–429 (1987).

Mertes, Karen R.: *Calibration of the CHECKPOINT Model to the Space and Missile Systems Center (SMC) Software Database (SWDB)*, Thesis AFIT/GCA/LAS/96S-11, Air Force Institute of Technology (AFIT), Wright-Patterson AFB, Ohio, September 1996.

Ourada, Gerald L., and Daniel V. Ferens: "Software Cost Estimating Models: A Calibration, Validation, and Comparison," in *Cost Estimating and Analysis: Balancing Technology and Declining Budgets*, Springer-Verlag, New York, 1992, pp. 83–101.

2

Preliminary Estimation Methods

Software cost estimates must be produced long before there is sufficient knowledge about a software project to be truly accurate. Two forms of preliminary estimation are discussed in this section:

- *Manual estimates using rules of thumb*

- *Preliminary estimates using the approximation modes of commercial estimating tools*

Accurate software estimating is too difficult for simple rules of thumb. Yet in spite of the availability of more than 50 commercial software-estimating tools, simple rules of thumb remain a common approach. The "lines-of-code" or LOC-metrics is known to be troublesome for modern high-level programming languages. Yet rules of thumb based on LOC continue to be used for projects where the results are likely to be incorrect.

The function point metric has now been used on many thousands of software projects. A family of simple rules of thumb based on function points can now be applied to estimating software sizes, schedules, effort, costs, and quality.

For newer projects using newer methodologies such as the Agile approach, Scrum, and the like, many new rules of thumb are evolving using new metrics such as object points, story points, use case points, web object points, and more.

Simple rules of thumb are not a substitute for formal cost estimates produced using such tools as COCOMO II, the CAI estimation tool, SEER, KnowledgePlan, Price S, True S, or SLIM, but they are capable of providing rough early estimates or "sanity checks" for estimates produced using more formal methods. The more accurate forms of manual software cost estimating involve activity-based costing. These methods are more complex than simple rules of thumb, but are also more powerful.

Many commercial software-estimating tools recognize the fact that estimates must be created before there is adequate information about a project and the factors that will affect its outcome. Therefore, commercial estimating tools offer a variety of approximation modes for creating early estimates from partial knowledge. These early estimates are not particularly accurate, but they are usually better than wild guesses.

The most powerful of the preliminary estimating methods use templates derived from similar projects. With template estimation, at least the same kinds of projects are used as the starting point.

Manual Software-Estimating Methods

This chapter includes a variety of rules of thumb that have been derived primarily from several thousand projects that utilized the traditional "waterfall" model of software development. The next chapter includes some rules of thumb derived from projects that use the Agile approaches, object-oriented methods, and some special situations such as deploying enterprise resource planning (ERP) applications.

The phrase *manual software cost estimation* refers to estimating methods that are simple enough that they can be performed mentally or, at least, using nothing more sophisticated than a pocket calculator.

Manual estimating methods remain widely used approaches to software cost estimating as the second edition of this book is being written. Manual estimating methods are useful for the following purposes:

- Early estimates before requirements are known
- Small projects needing only one or two programmers
- Low-value projects with no critical business impacts

However, there are a number of situations where manual estimates are not very useful and indeed may be hazardous:

- Contract purposes for software development or maintenance
- Projects larger than 100 function points or 10,000 source code statements
- Projects with significant business impact

Manual methods are quick and easy, but not very accurate. Accurate estimating methods are complex and require integration of many kinds of information. When accuracy is needed, avoid manual estimating methods.

As pointed out in Chapter 4, a comparative study of 50 estimates produced manually and 50 estimates produced by commercial estimating tools noted two significant results:

- Manual estimates were wrong by more than 35 percent more than 75 percent of the time. The maximum errors exceeded 50 percent for both costs and schedules. The errors with manual estimates were always on the side of excessive optimism, or underestimating true costs and actual schedules.

- Automated estimates came within 5 percent of actual costs about 45 percent of the time. The maximum errors were about 30 percent. When errors occurred, they were usually on the side of conservatism, or estimating higher costs and longer schedules than actually occurred.

Of course, automated estimating tools can achieve optimistic results, too, if users do things such as exaggerate staff experience, understate application size or complexity, minimize paperwork and quality control, and ignore learning curves. These are common failures with manual estimates, and they can be carried over into the automated estimation domain, too.

In spite of the plentiful availability of commercial software-estimating tools, the author receives dozens of e-mail and phone messages containing requests for simple rules of thumb that can be used manually or with pocket calculators.

This chapter provides a number of rules of thumb that are interesting and sometimes useful. Readers are cautioned that rules of thumb are not suitable for formal estimates, major projects, or software with important schedule, cost, or business implications.

Rules of Thumb Based on Lines-of-Code-Metrics

For many years manual estimating methods were based on the lines-of-code (LOC) metrics, and a number of workable rules of thumb were developed for common procedural programming languages, such as Assembly, COBOL, FORTRAN, PASCAL, PL/I, and the like.

These LOC rules of thumb usually start with basic assumptions about coding productivity rates for various sizes of software projects, and then use ratios or percentages for other kinds of work, such as testing, design, quality assurance, project management, and the like.

Tables 6.1 and 6.2 illustrate samples of the LOC-based rules of thumb for procedural languages in two forms: Table 6.1 uses *months* as the unit

TABLE 6.1   Rules of Thumb Based on LOC-Metrics for Procedural Languages
(Assumes 1 work month = 132 work hours)

Size of program, LOC	Coding, LOC per month	Coding effort, months	Testing effort, %	Non-code effort, %	Total effort, months	Net LOC per months
1	2500	0.0004	10.00	10.00	0.0005	2083
10	2250	0.0044	20.00	20.00	0.0062	1607
100	2000	0.0500	40.00	40.00	0.0900	1111
1,000	1750	0.5714	50.00	60.00	1.2000	833
10,000	1500	6.6667	75.00	80.00	17.0000	588
100,000	1200	83.3333	100.00	100.00	250.0000	400
1,000,000	1000	1000.0000	125.00	150.00	3750.0000	267

for work, while Table 6.2 uses *hours* as the unit for work. Both hourly and monthly work metrics are common in the software literature, with the hourly form being common for small programs and the monthly form being common for large systems.

Both tables show seven size ranges for software, with each one being an order of magnitude larger than its predecessor.

The column labeled "Testing Effort, %" denotes the relative amounts of time for testing versus coding. As can be seen, the larger the project, the greater the amount of testing required.

The column labeled "Non-code Effort, %" denotes the host of activities other than pure programming that are associated with software projects and need to be included in the estimate:

- Requirements definition
- External design
- Internal design
- Change management

TABLE 6.2   Rules of Thumb Based on LOC-Metrics for Procedural Languages
(Assumes 1 work month = 132 work hours)

Size of program, LOC	Coding, LOC per hour	Coding effort, hours	Testing effort, %	Non-code effort, %	Total effort, hours	Net LOC per hour
1	18.94	0.05	10.00	10.00	0.06	15.78
10	17.05	0.59	20.00	20.00	0.82	12.18
100	15.15	6.60	40.00	40.00	11.88	8.42
1,000	13.26	75.43	50.00	80.00	173.49	5.76
10,000	11.36	880.00	75.00	100.00	2,420.00	4.13
100,000	9.09	11,000.00	100.00	150.00	38,500.00	2.60
1,000,000	7.58	132,000.00	125.00	150.00	495,000.00	2.02

- User documentation
- Project management

As software applications grow in size, a larger and larger proportion of total effort must be devoted to paperwork and other non-coding activities.

As can be seen, the *monthly* form of normalizing effort is fine for large systems but is not very convenient for the smaller end of the spectrum. Conversely, the *hourly* form is inconvenient at the large end.

Also, the assumption that a work month comprises 132 hours is a tricky one, since the observed number of hours actually worked in a month can run from less than 120 to more than 170. Because the actual number of hours varies from project to project, company to company, and country to country, it is best to replace the generic rate of 132 with an actual or specific rate derived from local conditions and work patterns.

While LOC-based estimating rules of thumb served for many years, they are rapidly dropping from use because software technologies have changed so much that it is difficult, and even dangerous, to apply them under some conditions.

Usage of the LOC-metrics obviously assumes the existence of some kind of procedural programming language where programmers develop code using some combination of alphanumeric information, which is the way such languages as COBOL, C, FORTRAN, and hundreds of others operate.

However, the development of Visual Basic and its many competitors, such as Realizer, has changed the way many modern programs are developed. Although these visual languages do have a procedural source code portion, quite a bit of the more complex kinds of "programming" are done using button controls, pull-down menus, visual worksheets, and reusable components. In other words, programming is being done without anything that can be identified as a *line of code* for measurement or estimation purposes.

Also, the object-oriented programming languages and methods, such as Objective C, Smalltalk, Eiffel, and the like, with their class libraries, inheritance, and polymorphism, have also entered a domain where attempting to do estimates using conventional lines of code is not a very effective approach.

As the 21st century unfolds, the volume of programming done using languages where the LOC-metrics no longer works well for estimating purposes is rising rapidly. By perhaps 2025 more than 70 percent of the new software applications will be developed using either object-oriented languages or visual languages, or both.

Over and above the fact that the LOC-metrics is difficult to apply for many modern programming languages, there are deep and serious

TABLE 6.3   Rank Order of Large System Software Cost Elements

1. Defect removal (inspections, testing, and finding and fixing bugs)
2. Producing paper documents (plans, specifications, and user manuals)
3. Meetings and communication (clients, team members, and managers)
4. Programming or coding
5. Project management
6. Change management

economic problems with attempting to use LOC-metrics for measurement and estimation purposes.

Most of the important kinds of software, such as operating systems, billing systems, aircraft navigation systems, word processors, spreadsheets, and the like, are quite large compared to the sizes of applications built 20 years ago.

Twenty years ago, a programming application of 100,000 LOC was viewed as rather large. Even IBM's main operating system, OS/360, was only about 1 million LOC in size during its first year of release, although the modern incarnation, MVS, now tops 10 million LOC.

Today, a size of 100,000 LOC is more or less an entry-level size for a modern Windows XP application. Many software packages can top 1,000,000 LOC, while things like major operating systems are in the 20-million-LOC domain and up.

For large systems in the 1 million–source code statement size range, programming itself is only the fourth most expensive activity. The three higher-cost activities cannot really be measured or estimated effectively using the LOC-metrics. Also, the fifth and sixth major cost elements, project management and change management, cannot easily be estimated or measured using the LOC-metrics either. (See Table 6.3.)

If these non-coding activities are not measured separately, the overall project can be measured using LOC, but such measures have a disturbing property: They will penalize high-level languages and make low-level languages seem to have higher productivity rates than high-level languages.

As can easily be seen, the usefulness of a metric such as lines of code, which can only measure and estimate one out of the six major software cost elements, is a significant barrier to economic understanding.

Rules of Thumb Based on Ratios and Percentages

Software projects obviously include a lot more kinds of work than just coding. A fairly large family of manual estimating methods has developed based on the use of ratios and percentages.

These rules assume a *cascade* form of estimation. First, the overall project is estimated in its entirety. Second, ratios and percentages are applied to apportion the overall effort into the desired sets of phases or activities.

The basic problem with ratio-based estimation is the false assumption that there are constant ratios between coding and other key activities, such as testing, project management, integration, and the like. In fact, the ratios vary significantly, based on five sets of independent variables:

- The class of the application (systems software, information systems, web-based, etc.)
- The size of the application
- The programming language or languages utilized
- The presence or absence of reusable materials
- The methodology used such as Agile methods, waterfall methods, spiral methods etc.

The complexity of the interactions of these five sets of variables is why commercial software cost-estimating tools contain hundreds of rules and adjustment factors.

There are too many combinations of factors to illustrate all of them, but it is instructive to view how the percentages applied to key software activities vary in response to the class and size of the application.

Table 6.4 uses only seven major activities in order to highlight the percentage of coding effort against the background of non-coding activities.

Table 6.4 shows some of the changes in ratios among five different classes of applications. Note that for end-user applications there is very little work except coding and testing, because when users are building their own software they obviously know what their own requirements are, and they don't need personal user's guides.

TABLE 6.4   Percentages of Development Effort by Software Class
(Assumes application of 1000 function points or 100,000 source code statements)

Activity	End-user projects	MIS projects	Systems projects	Commercial projects	Military projects
Requirements definition	0	7	8	4	10
Design	10	12	15	10	15
Coding	60	25	18	25	18
Testing	30	30	30	36	22
Change management	0	6	10	5	12
Documentation	0	8	7	10	10
Project management	0	12	12	10	13
Total	100	100	100	100	100

By contrast, for military software projects, the activities associated with requirements, design, and documentation total roughly twice the effort devoted to coding itself: 35 percent versus 18 percent.

When we consider ratios based on various size ranges of applications, we also see huge differences that prevent any single ratio or percentage from being a safe general estimating method.

Table 6.5 shows five size plateaus an order of magnitude apart, starting with small applications of 10 function points (roughly 1000 source code statements) and running up to enormous systems of 100,000 function points (roughly 10 million source code statements).

At the small end of the spectrum, coding is the dominant activity in terms of effort, but at the large end of the spectrum, coding itself is only 15 percent of the total effort. The main cost drivers at the large end of the spectrum are the activities associated with finding and fixing bugs and the activities associated with producing various kinds of paper documents, such as requirements, plans, specifications, and user manuals.

At the intersection between rules of thumb based on ratios and those based on lines of code is an important topic that is not well covered in the software literature: the amount of reusable source code taken from similar applications or from other sources.

Table 6.6 gives reuse percentages noted among SPR's clients for a variety of programming languages. It is interesting that in spite of the emphasis that the object-oriented community places on software reuse, the language that typically has the largest volume of reusable code for common applications is Visual Basic.

When reusable material is present in substantial volumes during a software development project, it will obviously affect the schedule, effort, and cost results from an estimating standpoint.

Software reusability is an important topic with many poorly understood aspects. For example, software reuse is only valuable if the reused material approaches zero-defect quality levels. Reusing poor-quality source code is dangerous and expensive.

TABLE 6.5   Percentages of Development Effort by Software Size
(Assumes procedural languages, such as COBOL or C)

Activity	10-FP projects	100-FP projects	1000-FP projects	10,000-FP projects	100,000 FP projects
Requirements definition	5	5	7	8	9
Design	5	6	10	12	13
Coding	50	40	30	20	15
Testing	27	29	30	33	34
Change management	1	4	6	7	8
Documentation	4	6	7	8	9
Project management	8	10	10	12	12
Total	100	100	100	100	100

TABLE 6.6   Approximate Amount of Reusable Code by Language

Language	Average reuse, %
Visual Basic	60.00
Eiffel	55.00
Smalltalk	50.00
JAVA	50.00
Objective C	45.00
Ada 95	35.00
C++	27.50
SQL	25.00
Ada	25.00
COBOL	17.50
FORTRAN	15.00
Macro assembly	15.00
C	12.50
Pascal	12.50
Jovial	10.00
CMS2	10.00
PL/I	7.50
Basic assembly	5.00
Average	26.15

The ratios for software reuse shown in Table 6.6 are only approximate and can vary widely. For example, there can be Visual Basic applications with less than 10 percent reused code, while some basic assembly applications can top 40 percent in terms of code reuse.

In general, the languages that endorse and facilitate reuse, such as the object-oriented family of languages and the Visual Basic family, have far more sources of reusable code than do such languages as COBOL, where reuse is merely accidental.

The overall conclusion is that the use of simplistic ratios and percentages for software cost estimating is a very hazardous practice unless the estimator has experience-based ratios derived from projects of the same size, same class, same programming language, and that utilize the same volume of reusable materials.

There is no single set of ratios or percentages that can be universally applied to software projects. This lack of universal constants is true in every other human activity. Knowing the average cost of buying an automobile in the United States is obviously irrelevant to buying your own personal automobile. You start with the kind of automobile and set of features that you want, check the averages for that combination, and then try to negotiate with dealers for a better cost.

It is astonishing that project managers would use simple ratios and percentages for software projects that cost millions of dollars, and yet use much more sophisticated costing techniques for buying automobiles, home appliances, houses, clothes, food, or any other personal purchases.

Rules of Thumb Based on Function Point Metrics

Since function point metrics were first published in the late 1970s, their use has swept through the software world, and function points are now among the most widely used of any metric in all countries that develop significant volumes of software, such as the United States, Japan, South Korea, China, Germany, Australia, and Canada.

Function point metrics solve some of the more difficult problems for software cost estimation and cost measurement, and it is interesting to explore the origin and evolution of functional metrics.

In the middle 1970s, the IBM corporation was the world's largest and most successful producer of mainframe software. However, IBM's success and innovation led to some new and unexpected problems.

By the middle 1970s, IBM's software community was topping 25,000 members, and the costs of building and maintaining software were becoming a significant portion of the costs and budgets for new products.

Programming languages were exploding in number, and within IBM applications were being developed in assembly language, APL, COBOL, FORTRAN, RPG, PL/I, PL/S (a derivative of PL/I), and perhaps a dozen others. Indeed, many software projects at IBM and elsewhere used several languages concurrently, such as COBOL, RPG, and SQL, as part of the same system.

Also, the sizes of IBM's average software applications were growing from the 10,000 lines of code typical for the old IBM 1401 computers to well over 100,000 lines of code for the IBM 360 and IBM 370 computers.

The combination of larger applications and dozens of programming languages meant that manual estimates based on the lines-of-code-metrics were causing cost and schedule overruns of notable proportions. The problems of IBM in this era are captured very well in Dr. Fred Brooks's classic book *The Mythical Man-Month* (Brooks 1974), which was revised and reissued to commemorate the 20th anniversary of its first publication.

Allan J. Albrecht and his colleagues at IBM White Plains were tasked with attempting to develop an improved methodology for sizing, estimating, and measuring software projects. The method they developed is now known as *function point analysis*, and the basic metric they developed is termed a *function point*.

Although the actual rules for counting function points are rather complex, the essential concepts behind the function point metric are simple: Base the size of applications on external characteristics that do not change because of the programming language or languages used.

In essence, a *function point* consists of the weighted totals of five external aspects of software applications:

- The types of *inputs* to the application
- The types of *outputs* that leave the application
- The types of *inquiries* that users can make
- The types of *logical files* that the application maintains
- The types of *interfaces* to other applications

In October 1979, Allan Albrecht presented the function point metric at a conference in Monterey, California, sponsored jointly by IBM and two IBM user groups, SHARE and GUIDE. Concurrently, IBM placed the basic function point metric into the public domain.

What Albrecht and his colleagues at IBM were attempting to do was to create a software metric that had the following ten important design goals:

- The metric can be used to measure software productivity.
- The metric can be used to measure software quality.
- The metric can be used to measure software in any known programming language.
- The metric can be used to measure software in any combination of languages.
- The metric can be used to measure all classes of software (real-time, MIS, systems, etc.)
- The metric can be used to measure any software task or activity and not just coding.
- The metric can be used in discussions with clients.
- The metric can be used for software contracts.
- The metric can be used for large-scale statistical analysis.
- The metric can be used for value analysis.

On the whole, the function point metric meets all ten goals fairly well. This is not to say that function points have no problems of their own, but they meet the ten criteria far better than the older lines-of-code-metrics. Indeed, given the advent of visual languages and object-oriented software, the lines-of-code-metrics does not currently meet any of the ten criteria at all.

As the usage of function points expanded, a nonprofit organization, the International Function Point Users Group (IFPUG), was formed. IFPUG has now become one of the largest measurement associations in the world, and there are affiliated organizations in at least 20 other countries. (For additional information on this group, readers can visit their web site, www.IFPUG.org.)

IFPUG took over responsibility from IBM for modernizing and updating the basic counting rules for function points, which have gone through a number of major and minor sets of revisions. On average, IFPUG issues a major revision about every three years, and minor revisions once or twice a year. The most common reason for a revision is to include new kinds of software or new environments, such as web-based applications or embedded applications.

This chapter contains a number of simple rules of thumb that cover various aspects of software development and maintenance. The rules assume the Version 4.5 function point counting rules published by IFPUG. Adjustments would be needed for the British Mark II function point rules, for COSMIC function point rules, or the older IFPUG rules. Also, these rules would need adjustments for some of the many function point variations, such as the Boeing 3D function point, object points, use-case points, feature points, or the DeMarco *bang* function point.

However, rules of thumb are far too limited to cover every aspect of software development. So this section also discusses the usage of simple table-driven *templates* that allow somewhat finer levels of estimation. Here, too, the table-driven method is not as accurate as a commercial estimating tool, but can be performed quickly and can provide a rough check on more formal and rigorous estimating approaches.

Strong cautions must be given yet again:

- Simple rules of thumb are *not* accurate.

- Simple rules of thumb should *not* be used for contracts, bids, or serious business purposes.

- No manual software-estimating methodology can give rapid response when assumptions change and requirements creep.

The following rules of thumb are known to have a high margin of error. They are being published in response to many requests to the author for simple methods that can be used manually or with pocket calculators. Also, an understanding of the limitations of manual estimating methods can give a greater appreciation for the need for more formal automated methods.

The best that can be said is that the rules of thumb are easy to use, and can provide a "sanity check" for estimates produced by other and hopefully more rigorous methods.

Function Point Sizing Rules of Thumb

Predicting the sizes of various deliverables is the usual starting point for software cost estimating. The function point metric has transformed sizing from a very difficult task into one that is now both easy to perform and comparatively accurate, although the accuracy of early sizing methods applied prior to the availability of information that can lead to function point analysis is not great.

Sizing Function Point Totals Prior to Completion of Requirements

It often happens that software cost estimates are required long before there is enough solid information to actually create an accurate estimate. Since the function point metric is the basis for so many subsequent estimating stages, it is very difficult to produce a reasonable software cost estimate prior to the completion of the requirements, which comprise the first software document with enough information to derive function point totals.

However, there are function point sizing methods that can be used to create a rough approximation of function point totals long before requirements are complete, although this method has a high margin of error.

Software Productivity Research (SPR) uses a multipart taxonomy for defining software projects in terms of scope, class, and type, in order to identify a project when entering information into the software cost-estimating tools.

These project-identification checklists are organized using more or less the same principle as the Richter scale for earthquakes; that is, the larger numbers have more significance than the smaller numbers.

This property can be utilized to produce very early size approximations of function points before almost any other facts are known about the software projects in question. Admittedly, this crude form of sizing is far too inaccurate for serious cost-estimating purposes, but it has the virtue of being usable before any other known form of sizing is possible.

To use the scope, class, and type of taxonomy for guessing at the approximate size of the software, it is only necessary to sum the list values for the scope, class, and type and raise the total to the 2.35 power. This calculation sequence will yield a rough approximation of function points, assuming IFPUG Version 4 is the counting method. Table 6.7 summarizes the scope, class, and type lists in numeric order.

The kind of information needed to use this sizing approximation method is usually known on the very first day that requirements begin, so very early sizing is possible even if the size approximation

TABLE 6.7   Examples of Scope, Class, and Type Values

Scope	Class	Type
1 Subroutine	1 Individual software	1 Nonprocedural
2 Module	2 Shareware	2 Web applet
3 Reusable module	3 Academic software	3 Batch
4 Disposable prototype	4 Single location—internal	4 Interactive
5 Evolutionary prototype	5 Multilocation—internal	5 Interactive GUI or web-based
6 Standalone program	6 Contract project—civilian	6 Batch database
7 Component of system	7 Time sharing	7 Interactive database
8 Release of system	8 Military services	8 Client/server
9 New system	9 Internet	9 Mathematical
10 Compound system	10 Leased software	10 Systems
	11 Bundled software	11 Communications
	12 Marketed commercially	12 Process control
	13 Outsource contract	13 Trusted system
	14 Government contract	14 Embedded
	15 Military contract	15 Image processing
		16 Multimedia
		17 Robotics
		18 Artificial intelligence
		19 Neural net
		20 Hybrid: mixed

is rather imprecise. To utilize this rough sizing method, it is only necessary to do three things:

- Apply the numeric list values to the project to be sized in terms of the scope, class, and type factors.
- Sum the numeric values from the three lists.
- Raise the total to the 2.35 power.

For example, assume you are building an application with the following three attributes:

Scope = 6 (standalone program)
Class = 4 (internal—single site)
Type = 8 (client/server)
Sum   = 18

Raising 18 to the 2.35 power yields a value of 891, which can be utilized as a very rough approximation of function points, assuming the IFPUG Version 4.1 rules. Incidentally, client/server applications are often in the 1000–function point range, so this is not a bad starting point.

Let us try this method again on a different form of application. Suppose you were building a small personal application with the following properties:

Scope = 4 (disposable prototype)
Class = 1 (individual program)
Type   = 1 (nonprocedural)
Sum   = 6

Raising 6 to the 2.35 power gives a value of 67, which can serve as a rough approximation of the application's function point total. Here, too, since most personal applications are less than 100 function points in size, this is not a bad way of beginning even if the true size will vary.

Applying this same method to a more significant military software project, the results might be the following:

Scope =   9 (new system)
Class = 15 (military contract)
Type   = 13 (trusted system)
Sum   = 37

Raising 37 to the 2.35 power gives a value of 4844 function points, which again can serve as a rough approximation of the application's function point total until enough information is available to perform a proper function point analysis. Here, too, military software projects at the system level are often in the 5000–function point range in size (or larger), so this approximation method is enough to see that the application will not be a trivial one.

This very crude function point size approximation method is not recommended for any purpose other than estimating size prior to full requirements definition, when almost nothing is known about a software project and some form of sizing is needed to complete an early estimate.

Incidentally, it would be possible to use this taxonomy with other metrics such as object points, Cosmic function points, or engineering function points. The only change would be that the combination would have to use different powers to match the other metrics. However, those powers are not known by the author, so the groups that control these other metrics would have to provide such information.

It should be noted that the SPR scope, class, and type lists are changed from time to time to add new kinds of software or to adjust the rank placements as empirical evidence suggests that changes are needed. These changes mean that users of the methods should feel free to experiment with other power settings besides 2.35, or even to develop their own list sequences. This kind of early sizing is essentially a form of pattern matching. Now that thousands of software projects exist, this method uses only a basic taxonomy to attempt to find applications with similar patterns. It is theoretically possible that this pattern matching approach could be extended to bring in historical data from such projects, and even to provide links to reusable components from similar projects.

The fundamental operating principle of this early sizing method is that useful information about software projects can be derived from a taxonomy that can rank a software application in a fashion that allows rough size information to be derived merely from the ranking itself.

Even the first column, or scope portion, of this taxonomy can be used for rough sizing purposes. Table 6.8 shows the "average" sizes of various kinds of projects, assuming a rough expansion factor of 100 logical source code statements for every function point.

In Table 6.8 most of the terms are self-explanatory. However, item 10, *compound system*, is a large system that is actually comprised of several systems linked together. An example of a compound system would be the SAP R3 integrated business suite, although that is much larger than 15,000 function points (closer to 250,000 function points). It is comprised of a number of linked *systems*, which taken together constitute the entire SAP product.

A modern example of a compound system would be Microsoft Office, which comprises the separate applications of word processing, spreadsheet, database, graphics, and personal scheduler, all integrated and working together. In fact, Microsoft Office is in the 25,000–function point size range, with each of the individual applications running about 3000 to 5000 function points, plus the OLE capabilities to share information making up the total.

Because triangulating a software project in terms of its scope, class, and type is possible as early as the first day that requirements definition begins, this method can be utilized very early in a development cycle, long before any other kind of information is available.

Users are urged to experiment with their own ranking systems and taxonomies, and also with varying the power used to achieve the function point approximations.

TABLE 6.8   Size Approximations Using Only the Scope Factor

Application scope	Size, function points	Size, source lines of code
1 Subroutine	1	100
2 Module	3	300
3 Reusable module	5	500
4 Disposable prototype	7	700
5 Evolutionary prototype	10	1,000
6 Standalone program	25	2,500
7 Component of system	100	10,000
8 Release of system	5,000	500,000
9 New system	10,000	1,000,000
10 Compound system	25,000	2,500,000

Sizing by Analogy

Another form of rapid sizing is simply browsing a list of the sizes of applications that have been measured and selecting one or more similar projects to serve as an approximate size basis for the new project that is about to be estimated, as shown by Table 6.9.

TABLE 6.9   Approximate Sizes of Selected Software Applications
(Sizes based on IFPUG Version 4 and SPR logical statement rules)

Application	Type	Purpose	Primary language	Size, KLOC	Size, FP	LOC per FP
Graphics Design	Commercial	CAD	Objective C	54	2,700	20.00
IEF	Commercial	CASE	C	2,500	20,000	125.00
Visual Basic	Commercial	Compiler	C	375	3,000	125.00
IMS	Commercial	Database	Assembly	750	3,500	214.29
CICS	Commercial	Database	Assembly	420	2,000	210.00
Lotus Notes	Commercial	Groupware	Mixed	350	3,500	100.00
MS Office Proj.	Commercial	Office tools	C	2,000	16,000	125.00
SmartSuite	Commercial	Office tools	Mixed	2,000	16,000	125.00
MS Office SB	Commercial	Office tools	C	1,250	10,000	125.00
Word 7.0	Commercial	Office tools	C	315	2,500	126.00
Excel 6.0	Commercial	Office tools	C	375	2,500	150.00
MS Project	Commercial	Project management	C	375	3,000	125.00
KnowledgePlan	Commercial	Project management	C++	134	2,500	56.67
CHECKPOINT	Commercial	Project management	Mixed	225	2,100	107.14
Function Point Control	Commercial	Project management	C	56	450	125.00
SPQR/20	Commercial	Project management	Quick Basic	25	350	71.43
WMCCS	Military	Defense	Jovial	18,000	175,000	102.86
Aircraft Radar	Military	Defense	Ada 83	213	3,000	71.00
Gun Control	Military	Defense	CMS2	250	2,336	107.00
Airline Reservation	MIS	Business	Mixed	2,750	25,000	110.00
Insurance Claims	MIS	Business	COBOL	1,605	15,000	107.00
Telephone billing	MIS	Business	C	1,375	11,000	125.00
Tax Preparation (Personal)	MIS	Business	Mixed	180	2,000	90.00
General Ledger	MIS	Business	COBOL	161	1,500	107.00
Order Entry	MIS	Business	COBOL/SQL	106	1,250	85.00
Human Resource	MIS	Business	COBOL	128	1,200	107.00
Sales Support	MIS	Business	COBOL/SQL	83	975	85.00
Budget Preparation	MIS	Business	COBOL/SQL	64	750	85.00

TABLE 6.9 Approximate Sizes of Selected Software Applications *(Continued)*
(Sizes based on IFPUG Version 4 and SPR logical statement rules)

Application	Type	Purpose	Primary language	Size, KLOC	Size, FP	LOC per FP
Windows XP	Systems	Operating system	C	25,000	85,000	129.41
MVS	Systems	Operating system	Assembly	12,000	55,000	218.18
UNIX V5	Systems	Operating system	C	6,250	50,000	125.00
DOS 5	Systems	Operating system	C	1,000	4,000	250.00
5ESS	Systems	Telecommunication	C	1,500	12,000	125.00
System/12	Systems	Telecommunication	CHILL	800	7,700	103.90
Total				68,669	542,811	126.51
Average				2,020	15,965	126.51

Sizing by analogy is a feature of automated cost-estimating models, but as more and more projects are measured, it will be increasingly common to see published tables of applications sizes using both function points and source code statements. Table 6.9 gives an example of such a table.

Sizing Source Code Volumes

Now that thousands of software projects have been measured using both function points and lines of code (LOC), empirical ratios have been developed for converting LOC data into function points, and vice versa. The following rules of thumb are based on *logical statements* rather than *physical lines*.

(The physical LOC-metrics has such wide and random variations from language to language and programmer to programmer that it is not suited for sizing, for estimating, or for any other serious purpose.)

Rule 1: Sizing Source Code Volumes

One function point = 320 statements for basic assembly language
One function point = 213 statements for macro assembly language
One function point = 128 statements for the C programming language
One function point = 107 statements for the COBOL language
One function point = 107 statements for the FORTRAN language
One function point = 80 statements for the PL/I language
One function point = 71 statements for the ADA 83 language
One function point = 53 statements for the C++ language
One function point = 50 statements for the JAVA language
One function point = 15 statements for the Smalltalk language

---

The overall range of noncommentary logical source code statements to function points ranges from more than 300 statements per function point for basic assembly language to less than 15 statements per function point for object-oriented languages and many program generators.

However, since many procedural languages, such as C, Cobol, Fortran, and Pascal, are close to the 100-to-1 mark, that value can serve as a rough conversion factor for the general family of procedural source code languages.

For object-oriented programming languages with full class libraries, such as Actor, Eiffel, Objective-C, C++, JAVA, and Smalltalk, the range is from perhaps 14 to about 50 statements per function point, and a value such as 20 statements per function point can serve as a rough approximation.

These code-sizing rules of thumb have a high margin of error, and need specific adjustments based on individual *dialects* of programming languages. Also, individual programming styles can vary significantly. Indeed, in a controlled study within IBM where eight programmers implemented the same specification using the same language, a 5-to-1 variation in the number of source code statements was noted, based on individual interpretations of the specification.

Note that these rules for sizing source code can also be reversed. It often happens when dealing with aging legacy applications, and sometimes for small enhancement and maintenance projects, that source code volumes are known earlier in the development cycle than is possible to calculate function points.

Direct conversion from source code volumes to an equivalent count of function points is termed *backfiring*. Although the accuracy of backfiring is not great, because individual programming styles can cause wide variations in source code counts, it is easy and popular.

Indeed, for some aging legacy applications where the specifications are missing and the source code is the only remaining artifact, backfiring provides the only effective method for arriving at function point values.

There is another situation where backfiring is very popular, too: small enhancements and maintenance projects. The normal method of calculating function points has trouble with small projects below about 15 function points in size because the weighting factors have lower limits; this creates a floor at about 15 function points, below which the normal method ceases to work effectively.

However, the backfiring method of conversion between logical statements has no lower limit and can even be used for sizes as small as a fraction of a function point. For example, making a 1–source code statement change to a COBOL application has a size of about 0.001 function points. There is no way to calculate such a tiny fraction of a function point using normal methods.

Because maintenance and enhancement projects are very common, and because aging legacy applications are also common, the backfiring method for approximating function points is actually the most widely used method in the world for deriving function point totals.

Backfiring is a common feature of software cost-estimating tools, and is found in at least 30 commercial software cost-estimating tools in the United States, as well as in those developed in Europe and elsewhere.

Note that for backfiring to work well, the starting point should be *logical statements* rather than physical lines of source code. However, it is possible to cascade from physical lines to logical statements, although the accuracy is reduced somewhat.

Sizing Paper Deliverables

Software is a very paper-intensive industry. More than 50 kinds of planning, requirements, specification, and user-related document types can be created for large software projects. For many large systems, and especially for large military projects, producing paper documents costs far more than producing the source code.

The more common kinds of paper documents associated with software applications include:

- Requirements
- Cost estimates
- Development plans
- Functional specifications
- Change requests
- Logic or internal specifications
- Project status reports
- User manuals
- Test plans
- Bug or defect reports

Document types that occur from time to time, but not for every application, include:

- Contracts between clients and outsource vendors
- Use cases
- Design inspection reports
- Code inspection reports

- Quality assurance reports
- Translations of documents into other languages
- Training and tutorial materials
- Sales and marketing plans for commercial software

Paperwork volumes correlate fairly closely to the size of the application, using either function points or source code metrics. Small projects create comparatively few paper documents, and they themselves are not very large.

Also, some development methods tend to create more or less documentation than other methods. For example, the Agile development methods typically produce a very sparse or lean document set. At the other end of the spectrum, projects that are created using military standards or that require ISO certification tend to produce much larger document sets than average.

Overall, large systems in the 10,000–function point or 1 million–source code statement range often produce large numbers of documents, and some of these are very large indeed. For example, some sets of specifications have topped 60,000 pages.

For a few really large systems in the 100,000–function point range, the specifications can actually exceed the lifetime reading speed of a single person, and could not be finished even by reading eight hours a day for an entire career!

The following rule of thumb encompasses the sum of the pages that will be created in requirements, internal and external specifications, development and quality plans, test plans, user manuals, and other business-related software documents.

However, if you are following ISO 9000–9004 standards, you should use 1.17 as the power rather than 1.15. If you are following older military standards, such as DoD 2167, you should use 1.18 as the power rather than 1.15, because military projects produce more paperwork than any other kind of software application.

Rule 2: Sizing Software Plans, Specifications, and Manuals

Function points raised to the 1.15 power predict approximate page counts for paper documents associated with software projects.

A simple corollary rule can be used to predict the approximate volume of text that the pages will contain: Pages multiplied by 400 words per page predict the approximate number of English words created for the normal page size used in the United States (i.e., 8.5- by 11-in paper stock) with single-spaced type, using a 12-point type such as Times Roman. The actual capacity is greater than 400 words, but the inclusion of graphics and tables must be factored in.

Obviously, adjustments must be made for European A4 paper, where the capacity is closer to 500 words, once again assuming that graphic elements and tables will also be present, and that a 12-point type is selected.

Paperwork is such a major element of software costs and schedules that it cannot safely be ignored. Indeed, one of the major problems with the LOC-metrics is that it tends to conceal both the volumes of paper deliverables and the high costs of software paperwork.

Sizing Creeping User Requirements

One of the most severe problems of the software world is that of dealing with the emergence of new and changing requirements after the completion of the initial requirements phase.

The function point metric is extremely useful in measuring the rate at which requirements creep. In fact, the usage of *cost per function point* is now starting to occur in software contracts and outsourcing agreements. For contract purposes, cost per function point is used with a sliding scale that becomes more expensive for features added later in the development cycle.

Rule 3: Sizing Creeping User Requirements

Creeping user requirements will grow at an average rate of 2 percent per month from the design through coding phases. On an average, software applications will grow by at least 15 percent during development.

Assume that you and your clients agree during the requirements definition to develop an application of exactly 1000 function points. This rule of thumb implies that every month thereafter during the subsequent design and coding phases the original requirements will grow by a rate of 20 function points.

Since the overall schedule for a generic 1000–function point project would be about 16 calendar months, and the design and coding phases would be about half that, or 8 calendar months, this rule implies that about 16 percent new features would be added due to creeping requirements. The final total for the application would be 1160 function points rather than the initial value of 1000 function points.

In real life, the observed range of creeping requirements ranges from close to 0 to more than 5 percent per month. The better requirements methods, such as joint application design (JAD), prototypes, and requirements inspections, can reduce the rate of creep to well below 1 percent per month.

However, quick requirements methods, such as those often found with rapid application development (RAD), the Agile approach, or client/server projects, can cause the rate of creep to top 5 percent per month and throw the project into turmoil.

Because internal information systems have no visible penalties associated with creeping requirements, they tend to grow almost uncontrollably. For contract software and outsourcing arrangements, there may be financial penalties for adding requirements late in the development cycle.

For software development contracts, perhaps the most effective way of dealing with changing user requirements is to include a sliding scale of costs in the contract itself. For example, suppose a hypothetical contract is based on an initial agreement of $500 per function point to develop an application of 1000 function points in size, so that the total value of the agreement is $500,000.

The contract might contain the following kind of escalating cost scale for new requirements added downstream:

Initial 1000 function points	$500 per function point
Features added more than 3 months after contract signing	$600 per function point
Features added more than 6 months after contract signing	$700 per function point
Features added more than 9 months after contract signing	$900 per function point
Features added more than 12 months after contract signing	$1200 per function point
Features deleted or delayed at user request	$150 per function point

Similar clauses can be utilized with maintenance and enhancement outsource agreements, on an annual or specific basis such as the following:

Normal maintenance and defect repairs	$125 per function point per year
Mainframe to client/server conversion	$200 per function point per system

The advantage of the use of function point metrics for development and maintenance contracts is that they are determined from the user requirements and cannot be unilaterally added or deleted by the contractor.

One of the many problems with the older LOC-metrics is that there is no objective way of determining the minimum volume of code needed to implement any given feature. This means that contracts based on cost per LOC could expand without any effective way for the client to determine whether the expansions were technically necessary.

Function points, on the other hand, cannot be unilaterally determined by the vendor and must be derived from explicit user requirements. Also, function points can easily be understood by clients, while the LOC-metrics is difficult to understand in terms of why so much code is needed for any given contract.

Sizing Test-Case Volumes

The function point metric is extremely useful for test-case sizing, since the structure of function point analysis closely parallels the items that need to be validated by testing.

Rule 4: Sizing Test-Case Volumes

Function points raised to the 1.2 power predict the approximate number of test cases created.

Commercial software-estimating tools can predict the number of test cases for more than 15 discrete forms of testing, and can deal with the specifics of unit testing, new function testing, system testing, and all of the other varieties. This simple rule of thumb encompasses the sum of all test cases in all forms of testing, which is why rules of thumb should be used with caution.

A simple corollary rule can predict the number of times each test case will be run or executed during development: Assume that each test case would be executed approximately four times during software development.

Of course, there are at least 18 separate forms of testing used for software projects. In addition, companies are split between those where developers perform testing, where professional test personnel perform testing, and even where independent test organizations perform testing. The true complexity of testing requires much more work than a simple rule of thumb for acceptable precision in estimating results.

Sizing Software Defect Potentials

The *defect potential* of an application is the sum of bugs or errors that will occur in five major deliverables:

- Requirements errors
- Design errors
- Coding errors
- User documentation errors
- Bad fixes, or secondary errors introduced in the act of fixing a prior error

One of the many problems with LOC-metrics is the fact that more than half of all software defects are found in requirements and design, and hence the LOC-metrics is not capable of either predicting or measuring their volume with acceptable accuracy.

Because the cost and effort for finding and fixing bugs is usually the largest identifiable software cost element, ignoring defects can throw off estimates, schedules, and costs by massive amounts.

Rule 5: Sizing Software Defect Potentials

Function points raised to the 1.25 power predict the approximate defect potential for new software projects.

A similar corollary rule can predict the defect potentials for enhancements. In this case, the rule applies to the size of the enhancement rather than to the base that is being updated: Function points raised to the 1.27 power predict the approximate defect potential for enhancement software projects, using the enhancement (and not the base system) as the basis for applying the rule. The higher power used in the enhancement rule is because of the latent defects lurking in the base product that will be encountered during the enhancement process. The same rule can be used for maintenance projects such as defect repairs, although these may be so small (less than one function point) that the rule becomes ineffective.

The function point metric has been very useful in clarifying the overall distribution of software defects. Indeed, almost the only literature on the volume of non-code defects uses function point metrics for expressing the results. The approximate U.S. average for software defects during development for new projects is shown in Table 6.10.

As can easily be seen from Table 6.10, there are more software defects found outside the code than within it. Data expressed using the older

TABLE 6.10   U.S. Averages for Software Defect Levels During Development

Defect origin	Defects per function point
Requirements	1.00
Design	1.25
Code	1.75
User documents	0.60
Bad fixes	0.40
Total	5.00

LOC-metrics almost never deals with non-coding defects, such as those in requirements, specifications, and user manuals.

There are two other important categories of defects where empirical evidence has not yet accumulated enough data to derive useful rules of thumb: (1) errors in databases, and (2) errors in test cases themselves.

Research on database errors is handicapped by the fact that there is no *data point* metric for normalizing database sizes or defect rates.

This same problem is true for test cases. However, assessments and interviews with commercial software companies indicate that errors in test cases are sometimes more plentiful than errors or bugs in the software itself!

A very preliminary rule of thumb for test-case errors would be about 1.8 defects per function point. This rule is derived by simply dividing the function point total of the application by the number of errors fixed in test cases.

Hopefully, more reliable data will become available for test-case errors in the future, and data quality will be able to be measured if a data point size metric can be created.

Sizing Software Defect-Removal Efficiency

The defect potential is the life-cycle total of errors that must be eliminated. The defect potential will be reduced by somewhere between 85 percent (approximate industry norms) and 99 percent (best-in-class results) prior to actual delivery of the software to clients. Thus, the number of delivered defects is only a small fraction of the overall defect potential.

Rule 6: Sizing Defect-Removal Efficiency for Test Steps

Each software test step will find and remove 30 percent of the bugs that are present.

An interesting set of rules of thumb can size the number of defects that might be found and can approximate the defect-removal efficiency of various reviews, inspections, and tests.

Testing has a surprisingly low efficiency in actually finding bugs. Most forms of testing will find less than one bug or defect out of every three that are present. The implication of this fact means that a series of between 6 and 12 consecutive defect-removal operations must be utilized to achieve very high-quality levels.

A typical set of test steps for medium-sized software projects in the 5,000–function point size range would include

1. Unit testing by developers
2. New function testing
3. Regression testing
4. Performance testing
5. System testing
6. Acceptance testing

If each of these six test stages removed 30 percent of the latent defects, the cumulative efficiency of the whole series would be about 88 percent. Assume you start with 1000 defects and remove 30 percent with each test step. The results would be 1000, 700, 490, 343, 240, 168, and 117 defects still latent at the end.

This is why major software producers normally use a multistage series of design reviews, code inspections, and various levels of testing from unit test through system test.

The rather low defect-removal efficiency level of most common forms of testing explains why the U.S. average for defect-removal efficiency is only about 85 percent unless formal design and code inspections are utilized.

Rule 7: Sizing Formal Inspection Defect-Removal Efficiency

Each formal design inspection will find and remove 65 percent of the bugs present.
Each formal code inspection will find and remove 60 percent of the bugs present.

In fact, the defect-removal efficiency of formal design and code inspections is so much higher than testing that it is useful to show a separate rule for these activities.

It is easy to see from Rule 7 why most of the software organizations that produce really high quality software with more than 95 percent cumulative defect-removal efficiency utilize formal pretest inspections at the design and code levels.

Incidentally, although formal inspections are not inexpensive, they have such a strong effect on defect removal that the increase in testing speed and reduction in testing and maintenance costs that they trigger give them one of the best returns on investment of any known software technology.

As an added benefit, if you do use formal design and code inspections before testing begins, you will find that the overall cumulative efficiency of the inspections and test steps together may well top 95 percent on average, and achieve 99 percent defect removal efficiency levels from time to time.

Rule 8: Post-Release Defect-Repair Rates

Maintenance programmers can repair 10 bugs per staff month.

To complete the set of quality-related rules of thumb, Rule 8 deals with the rate at which bugs can be repaired after software applications are released.

Rule 8, or maintenance repair rates, has been around the software industry for more than 30 years and still seems to work. However, some of the state-of-the-art maintenance organizations that utilize complexity analyzers and code-restructuring tools and have sophisticated maintenance work benches available can double the rate and may even top 20 bugs per month.

Rules of Thumb for Schedules, Resources, and Costs

After the sizes of various deliverable items and potential defects have been quantified, the next stage in an estimate is to predict schedules, resources, costs, and other useful results.

Some of the rules of thumb for dealing with schedules, resources, and costs are compound, and require joining several individual rules together. However, these combinations are simple enough to be done with a pocket calculator, spreadsheet, or even in your head if you are good with mental calculations.

Assignment Scope and Production-Rate Logic

Software rules of thumb and both manual and automated estimating methods utilize algorithms and relationships based on two key concepts:

- The *assignment scope* (A scope) is the amount of work for which one person will be responsible on a software project.

- The *production rate* (P rate) is the amount of work that one person can perform in a standard time period, such as a work hour, work week, work month, or work year.

Both assignment scopes and production rates can be expressed using any convenient metric, such as function points, source code statements, or "natural" deliverables, such as words or pages.

For example, assume that you are responsible for estimating an application of 50,000 source code statements in size using the C programming language. If an average assignment for programmers in your organization is 10,000 source code statements, then this project will require five programmers.

If an average programmer in your organization can code at a rate of 2000 C statements each month, then the project will require 25 months of effort.

By combining the results of the assignment-scope and production-rate rules, you can derive useful estimates with a pocket calculator.

Let us look at the kinds of information that can be derived using A-scope and P-rate logic. We will also include an average monthly salary rate in order to derive a complete cost estimate.

Monthly pay	$6,000
Project size	50,000 C statements
A scope	10,000 C statements
P rate	2,000 C statements per month
Staff	5 programmers (50,000 divided by the A scope of 10,000)
Effort	25 months (50,000 divided by the P rate of 2,000)
Schedule	5 months (25 months of effort divided by 5 programmers)
Cost	$150,000 (25 months of effort at $6000 per month)

This logic is not foolproof, but is often useful for creating quick and rough estimates. However, to use assignment scopes and production rates well, you need to know the averages and ranges of these factors within your own organization. This is one of the reasons why software measurements and software cost estimating are so closely aligned. Measurements supply the raw materials needed to construct accurate cost estimates.

Indeed, companies that measure software projects well can create local rules of thumb based on their own data that will be much more useful than generic rules of thumb based on overall industry experience.

Estimating Software Schedules

Schedule estimation is usually the highest priority topic for clients, project managers, and software executives. Rule 9 calculates the approximate interval from the start of requirements until the first delivery to a client.

Rule 9: Estimating Software Schedules

Function points raised to the 0.4 power predict the approximate development schedule in calendar months.

**TABLE 6.11   Software Schedules in Calendar Months
from Start of Requirements to Delivery**
(Assumes 1000 function points from requirements to delivery)

Power	Schedule in calendar months	Projects within range
0.32	9.12	Agile projects
0.33	9.77	Scrum, Crystal, etc.
0.34	10.47	
0.35	11.22	
0.36	12.02	O-O software
0.37	12.88	Client/server software
0.38	13.80	Outsourced software
0.39	14.79	MIS software
0.40	15.85	Commercial software
0.41	16.98	Systems and embedded software
0.42	18.20	Civilian government software
0.43	19.50	Military software
0.44	20.89	
0.45	22.39	

Note that Rule 9 is a generic rule that would need adjustment between civilian and military projects. Because military software usually takes more time, raising function point totals to about the 0.45 power gives a better result.

Among our clients, the range of observed schedules in calendar months varies from a low of about 0.32 to a high of more than 0.45. In general, smaller, simpler projects would match the lower power levels, while larger, more complex projects would match the higher power levels. Also, standards that add complexity and extra paperwork to software development, such DoD 2167 or ISO 9001, tend to push the schedule power level above the 0.4 average value.

Table 6.11 illustrates the kinds of projects whose schedules are typically found at various power levels, assuming a project of 1000 function points in size.

The use of function points for schedule estimation is one of the more useful by-products of function points developed in recent years. As with all rules of thumb, the results are only approximate and should not be used for serious business purposes such as contracts. However, as a sanity check these rules of thumb are fairly useful. Readers are urged to explore historical data within their own organizations and to develop schedule power tables based on their own local results, rather than on industry averages.

Estimating Software Staffing Levels

The next rule of thumb is concerned with how many personnel will be needed to build the application. Rule 10 is based on the concept of *assignment scope* or the amount of work for which one person will normally be responsible.

Rule 10: Estimating Software Development Staffing Levels

Function points divided by 150 predict the approximate number of personnel required for the application.

Rule 10 includes software developers, quality assurance, testers, technical writers, database administrators, and project managers.

The rule of one technical staff member per 150 function points obviously varies widely based on the skill and experience of the team and the size and complexity of the application. This rule simply provides an approximate starting point for more detailed staffing analysis. If you are only interested in programming and not in analysis, design, technical writing, etc. then use a value of 500 function points. Thus if you are concerned with building a 10,000–function point application (1,000,000 LOC), then some 20 programmers will be needed. However, if you use pair programming, the assignment scope will be cut in half.

Rule 11: Estimating Software Maintenance Staffing Levels

Function points divided by 750 predict the approximate number of maintenance personnel required to keep the application updated.

A corollary rule can estimate the number of personnel required to maintain the project during the maintenance period.

The implication of Rule 11 is that one person can perform minor updates and keep about 750 function points of software operational. (Another interesting maintenance rule of thumb is: Raising the function point total to the 0.25 power will yield the approximate number of years that the application will stay in use.)

Among our clients, the best-in-class organizations are achieving ratios of up to 3500 function points per staff member during maintenance. These larger values usually indicate a well-formed geriatric program, including the use of complexity analysis tools, code-restructuring tools, reengineering and reverse-engineering tools, and full configuration control and defect tracking of aging legacy applications.

Rule 11 will vary with programming languages. For low-level languages such as Assembler, an assignment scope of about 250 function points would be used. For higher-level languages such as JAVA, 750 would be used. For really experienced maintenance personnel, the assignment scope will be about 1500 function points.

Rule 12: Estimating Software Development Effort

Multiply software development schedules by the number of personnel to predict the approximate number of staff months of effort.

Estimating Software Development Effort

The last development rule of thumb in this chapter is a hybrid rule that is based on the combination of Rules 9 and 10.

Since this is a hybrid rule, an example can clarify how it operates. Assume you are concerned with a project of 1000 function points in size.

- Using Rule 9, or raising 1000 function points to the 0.4 power, indicates a schedule of about 16 calendar months.

- Using Rule 10, or dividing 1000 function points by 150, indicates a staff of about 6.6 full-time personnel.

- Multiplying 16 calendar months by 6.6 personnel indicates a total of about 106 staff months to build this particular project.

(Incidentally, another common but rough rule of thumb defines a *staff month* as consisting of 22 working days with 6 productive hours each day, or 132 work hours per month.)

Hybrid rules are more complex than single rules, but at least this hybrid rule includes the two critical factors of staffing and schedules.

Rules of Thumb Using Activity-Based Cost Analysis

There are manual software cost-estimating methodologies that are more accurate than simple rules of thumb, but they require work sheets and more extensive calculations in order to be used. Of these more complex manual methods, the approaches that lead to activity-based cost estimates are often the most useful and also the most accurate in the hands of experienced project managers.

It has been known for many years that military software projects have much lower productivity rates than civilian software projects. It has also been known for many years that large systems usually have much lower productivity rates than small projects. A basic question that our measurement methods should be able to answer is, "Why do these productivity differences occur?"

It is the ability to explore some of the fundamental reasons why productivity rates vary that gives activity-based measurements a strong advantage that can lead to significant process improvements.

Data measured only to the project level is inadequate for any kind of in-depth economic analysis or process comparison. This is also true for data based on rudimentary phase structures, such as "requirements, design, coding, integration, and testing."

However, when activity-based cost analysis is used, it becomes fairly easy to answer questions such as the one posed at the beginning of this section. For example, military software projects have lower productivity rates than civilian software projects because military software projects perform many more activities than do civilian projects of the same size.

SPR has analyzed many software development methodologies from around the world, and has constructed a generic checklist of 25 activities that occur with high frequency. This list of activities is used for baseline cost collection, for schedule measurement, and as the basis for exploring the effectiveness of various kinds of tools and practices.

One of the interesting by-products of exploring software projects down to the activity level is the set of *patterns* that are often associated with various sizes and kinds of software projects.

To illustrate some of the variations at the activity level, Table 6.12 gives examples of activity pattern differences noted during SPR assessment and baseline studies for various classes of software based on the checklist of 25 activities that SPR utilizes for data collection.

Table 6.12 illustrates the patterns noted for six general kinds of software: (1) end-user software, (2) management information systems (MIS), (3) outsource projects, (4) commercial software vendors, (5) systems software, and (6) military software.

It is very interesting to realize that much of the observed difference in productivity rates among various industries and kinds of software is due to the fact that they do not all build software using the same sets or patterns of activities. It takes much more work to build U.S. military software than any other kind of software in the world. This is because Department of Defense standards mandate activities such as *independent verification and validation* and *independent testing* that civilian software projects almost never use.

Over and above the average values shown, there can be other significant variations. For example, small client/server projects may only perform 8 of the 16 activities listed under the MIS domain, which simultaneously explains why client/server productivity can be high and client/server quality low, since many of the quality-related activities are conspicuously absent in the client/server domain.

From activity-based analysis such as this, it becomes easy to understand a number of otherwise ambiguous topics. For example, it can

TABLE 6.12 Typical Activity Patterns for Six Software Domains

Activities performed	End user	MIS	Outsource	Commercial	Systems	Military
01 Requirements		X	X	X	X	X
02 Prototyping	X	X	X	X	X	X
03 Architecture		X	X	X	X	X
04 Project plans		X	X	X	X	X
05 Initial design		X	X	X	X	X
06 Detail design		X	X	X	X	X
07 Design reviews		X	X	X	X	X
08 Coding	X	X	X	X	X	X
09 Reuse acquisition	X		X	X	X	X
10 Package purchase		X	X		X	X
11 Code inspections				X	X	X
12 Independent verification and validation						X
13 Configuration management		X	X	X	X	X
14 Formal integration		X	X	X	X	X
15 Documentation	X	X	X	X	X	X
16 Unit testing	X	X	X	X	X	X
17 Function testing		X	X	X	X	X
18 Integration testing		X	X	X	X	X
19 System testing		X	X	X	X	X
20 Field testing				X	X	X
21 Acceptance testing		X	X		X	X
22 Independent testing						X
23 Quality assurance			X	X	X	X
24 Installation and training		X	X		X	X
25 Project management		X	X	X	X	X
Activities	5	18	21	20	23	25

easily be seen why U.S. military software projects are more expensive than any other kind of software, since they perform more activities.

Variation in activity patterns is not the only factor that causes productivity differences, of course. The experience and skill of the team, the available tools, programming languages, methods, processes, and a host of other factors are also important. However, the impact of these other factors cannot be properly understood unless the cost and effort data for the project is accurate and is also granular down to the level of the activities performed.

If your software cost-tracking system "leaks" large but unknown amounts of effort, and if you collect data only to the level of complete projects, you will not have enough information to perform the kind of multiple regression analysis necessary to evaluate the impact of the other factors that influence software productivity and cost results.

To illustrate the approximate amount of effort and costs required for specific activities, Table 6.13 shows the average amount of work hours per function point for each of the 25 activities in the standard SPR chart of accounts for software projects, although there are, of course, large variations for each activity.

The information shown in Table 6.13 illustrates the basic concept of activity-based costing. It is not a substitute for one of the commercial software cost-estimating tools that support activity-based costs in a much more sophisticated way, such as allowing each activity to have its own unique cost structure and varying the nominal hours expended based on experience, methods, tools, and so forth.

In this table, the "Staff FP Assignment" column represents the average number of function points assigned to one staff member.

The "Monthly FP Production" column represents the typical amount of a particular activity that one person can accomplish in one month.

The "Work Hours per FP" column represents the number of hours for each function point, assuming in this case that 132 hours are worked each month. Obviously, this column will change if the number of available monthly hours changes.

To use the data in Table 6.13, you need to know at least the approximate function point size of the application in question. Then, select the set of activities that you believe will be performed for the application. After that, you can add up the work hours per function point for each activity.

You can do the same kind of selection and aggregation with costs, of course, but you should replace the default compensation level of $5000 per staff month and the default burden or overhead rate of 100 percent with the appropriate values from your own company or organization.

Note that Table 6.13 uses a generic chart of accounts that includes both civilian and military activities. For example, activity 12 is *independent verification and validation*, which is required by many military contracts but is seldom or never used for civilian projects.

Once activity-based costing is started, it can be extended to include many other activities in a similar fashion. For example, the set of activities shown here is common for development projects. If you are concerned with the maintenance of aging legacy applications, with porting software

TABLE 6.13   Example of Activity-Based Chart of Accounts
(Assumes new development projects)

Assumptions	
Work hours per month	132
Unpaid overtime per month	0
Average monthly salary	$5,000
Burden rate	100%
Burdened monthly rate	$10,000
Burdened hourly rate	$76

Activities	Staff FP assignment	Monthly FP production	Work hours per FP	Burdened cost per FP	Staffing per 1000 FP
01 Requirements	250.00	175.00	0.75	$57.14	4.00
02 Prototyping	350.00	150.00	0.88	66.67	2.86
03 Architecture	2000.00	300.00	0.44	33.33	0.50
04 Project plans	1000.00	500.00	0.26	20.00	1.00
05 Initial design	250.00	175.00	0.75	57.14	4.00
06 Detail design	250.00	150.00	0.88	66.67	4.00
07 Design reviews	200.00	225.00	0.59	44.44	5.00
08 Coding	150.00	50.00	2.64	200.00	6.67
09 Reuse acquisition	250.00	600.00	0.22	16.67	4.00
10 Package purchase	5000.00	400.00	0.33	25.00	0.20
11 Code inspections	150.00	150.00	0.88	66.67	6.67
12 Independent verification and validation	2000.00	125.00	1.06	80.00	0.50
13 Configuration management	1000.00	1750.00	0.08	5.71	1.00
14 Integration	2000.00	250.00	0.53	40.00	0.50
15 User documentation	750.00	70.00	1.89	142.86	1.33
16 Unit testing	150.00	150.00	0.88	66.67	6.67
17 Function testing	350.00	150.00	0.88	66.67	2.86
18 Integration testing	700.00	175.00	0.75	57.14	1.43
19 System testing	2500.00	200.00	0.66	50.00	0.40
20 Field (beta) testing	1500.00	225.00	0.59	44.44	0.67
21 Acceptance testing	750.00	350.00	0.38	28.57	1.33
22 Independent testing	2500.00	200.00	0.66	50.00	0.40
23 Quality assurance	2000.00	150.00	0.88	66.67	0.50
24 Installation and training	5000.00	350.00	0.38	28.57	0.20
25 Project management	750.00	100.00	1.32	100.00	1.33
Cumulative results	203.39	6.75	19.55	1481.03	4.92

from one platform to another, or with bringing out a new release of a commercial software package, then you will need to deal with other activities outside of those shown in the table.

Table 6.14 illustrates a similar chart of accounts as might be used for an enhancement project in the civilian software domain. While some of the activities are identical between new projects and enhancements, enhancements often have some unique activities, such as analyzing the base system, restructuring the base system (if necessary), regression testing, and several others. These *enhancement-only* activities are shown in boldface type in the table to set them off from common activities.

Neither table should be regarded as anything more than an example to illustrate the concept of activity-based cost estimating. What are actually

TABLE 6.14   Example of Activity-Based Chart of Accounts
(Assumes enhancement projects)

Assumptions	
Work hours per month	132
Unpaid overtime per month	0
Average monthly salary	$5,000
Burden rate	100%
Burdened monthly rate	$10,000
Burdened hourly rate	$76

Activities	Staff FP assignment	Monthly FP production	Work hours per FP	Burdened cost per FP	Staffing per 1000 FP
01 Requirements	250.00	175.00	0.75	$57.14	4.00
02 **Base analysis**	1000.00	300.00	0.44	33.33	1.00
03 **Restructuring base**	3000.00	1000.00	0.13	10.00	0.33
04 Project plans	1000.00	500.00	0.26	20.00	1.00
05 Initial design	300.00	200.00	0.66	50.00	3.33
06 Detail design	300.00	175.00	0.75	57.14	3.33
07 Design reviews	200.00	225.00	0.59	44.44	5.00
08 Coding	150.00	50.00	2.64	200.00	6.67
09 Reuse acquisition	250.00	600.00	0.22	16.67	4.00
10 New inspections	150.00	150.00	0.88	66.67	6.67
11 **Base inspections**	500.00	150.00	0.88	66.67	2.00
12 Configuration management	1000.00	1750.00	0.08	5.71	1.00
13 Integration	2000.00	250.00	0.53	40.00	0.50
14 User documentation	750.00	70.00	1.89	142.86	1.33
15 Unit testing	150.00	150.00	0.88	66.67	6.67
16 New function testing	350.00	150.00	0.88	66.67	2.86
17 **Regression testing**	1000.00	150.00	0.88	66.67	1.00
18 Integration testing	700.00	175.00	0.75	57.14	1.43
19 System testing	2500.00	200.00	0.66	50.00	0.40
20 **Repackaging**	2500.00	300.00	0.44	33.33	0.40
21 Field (beta) testing	3000.00	225.00	0.59	44.44	0.33
22 Acceptance testing	2500.00	200.00	0.66	50.00	0.40
23 Quality assurance	2000.00	150.00	0.88	66.67	0.50
24 Installation and training	5000.00	350.00	0.38	28.57	0.20
25 Project management	750.00	100.00	1.32	100.00	1.33
Cumulative results	218.18	6.94	19.02	1496.48	4.58

needed are similar tables that match your organization's charts of accounts and substitute your organization's data for generic industry data.

However, both tables do illustrate the levels of granularity that are needed to really come to grips with the economic picture of software development. Data collected only to the level of projects or a few phases is too coarse to really understand software economics with enough precision to plan significant process improvements.

Tables 6.13 and 6.14 are generic in nature and do not assume any particular methodology or formal process.

However, there are also specific activity patterns associated with object-oriented (OO) development, information engineering (IE), rapid application development (RAD), and a host of methodologies and software processes. The fundamental concept of activity-based costing can still be used, even though the activities and their patterns will vary, as will the specific values for the activities in question.

Summary and Conclusions

Simple rules of thumb are never very accurate, but continue to be very popular. The main sizing and estimating rules of thumb and the corollary rules presented here are all derived from the use of the function point metric. Although function point metrics are more versatile than the older lines-of-code-metrics, the fact remains that simple rules of thumb are not a substitute for formal estimating methods.

These rules of thumb and their corollaries have a high margin of error and are presented primarily to show examples of the kinds of new project management information that function point metrics have been able to create. At least another dozen or so rules of thumb also exist for other predicting phenomena, such as annual software enhancements, optimal enhancement sizes, software growth rates during maintenance, and many other interesting topics.

Software estimating using rules of thumb is not accurate enough for serious business purposes. Even so, rules of thumb continue to be the most widely used estimating mode for software projects. Hopefully, the limits and errors of these simplistic rules will provide a motive for readers to explore more accurate and powerful estimation methods, such as commercial estimating tools.

Manual estimating methods using work sheets that drop down to the level of activities, or even tasks, are more accurate than simple rules of thumb, but they require a lot more work to use. They also require a lot more work when assumptions change.

Replacing work sheets with automated spreadsheets eliminates some of the drudgery, but neither worksheets nor spreadsheets can deal with some of the dynamic estimating situations, such as creeping user requirements or improvements in tools and processes during project development. This is why automated estimating tools usually outperform manual estimating methods.

Software measurement and estimation are becoming mainstream issues as software becomes a major cost element in corporations and government organizations. In order to use collected data for process improvements or industry benchmark comparisons, it is important to address and solve three problems:

- Leakage from cost-tracking systems must be minimized or eliminated.

- Accurate normalization metrics, such as function points, are needed for benchmarks to be economically valid.

- Cost and effort data needs to be collected down to the level of specific activities to understand the reasons for software cost and productivity-rate variances.

Activity-based software costing is not yet a common phenomenon in the software industry, but the need for this kind of precision is already becoming critical.

The literature on manual estimating methods is the largest of almost any project management topic, with a number of books offering algorithms, rules of thumb, or empirical results taken from historical data.

References

Albrecht, A. J.: "Measuring Application Development Productivity," *Proceedings of the Joint IBM/SHARE/GUIDE Application Development Symposium*, October 1979, reprinted in Capers Jones, *Programming Productivity—Issues for the Eighties*, IEEE Computer Society Press, New York, 1981, pp. 34–43.

Barrow, Dean, Susan Nilson, and Dawn Timberlake: *Software Estimation Technology Report*, Air Force Software Technology Support Center, Hill Air Force Base, Utah, 1993.

Boehm, Barry: *Software Engineering Economics*, Prentice-Hall, Englewood Cliffs, N.J., 1981.

———: *Software Cost Estimation with COCOMO II*, Prentice-Hall, Englewood Cliffs, N.J, 2000

Brooks, Fred: *The Mythical Man-Month*, Addison-Wesley, Reading, Mass., 1974, rev. 1995.

Brown, Norm (ed.): *The Program Manager's Guide to Software Acquisition Best Practices*, Version 1.0, U.S. Department of Defense, Washington, D.C., July 1995.

Charette, Robert N.: *Software Engineering Risk Analysis and Management*, McGraw-Hill, New York, 1989.

———: *Application Strategies for Risk Analysis*, McGraw-Hill, New York, 1990.

Cohn, Mike: *Agile Estimating and Planning* (Robert C. Martin Series), Prentice-Hall PTR, Englewood Cliffs, N.J., 2005.

Coombs, Paul, *IT Project Estimation: A Practical Guide to the Costing of Software*, Cambridge University Press, Melbourne, Australia, 2003.

DeMarco, Tom: *Controlling Software Projects*, Yourdon Press, New York, 1982.

———: *Deadline*, Dorset House Press, New York, 1997.

Department of the Air Force: *Guidelines for Successful Acquisition and Management of Software Intensive Systems*; vols. 1 and 2, Software Technology Support Center, Hill Air Force Base, Utah, 1994.

Dreger, Brian: *Function Point Analysis*, Prentice-Hall, Englewood Cliffs, N.J., 1989.

Galorath, Daniel D. and Michael W. Evans: *Software Sizing, Estimation, and Risk Management*, Auerbach, Philadelphia PA, 2006.

Garmus, David, and David Herron: *Measuring the Software Process: A Practical Guide to Functional Measurement*, Prentice-Hall, Englewood Cliffs, N.J., 1995.

———: *Function Point Analysis: Measurement Practices for Successful Software Projects*, Addison-Wesley, Boston, Mass., 2001.

Grady, Robert B.: *Practical Software Metrics for Project Management and Process Improvement*, Prentice-Hall, Englewood Cliffs, N.J., 1992.

——— and Deborah L. Caswell: *Software Metrics: Establishing a Company-Wide Program*, Prentice-Hall, Englewood Cliffs, N.J., 1987.

Gulledge, Thomas R., William P. Hutzler, and Joan S. Lovelace (eds.): *Cost Estimating and Analysis—Balancing Technology with Declining Budgets*, Springer-Verlag, New York, 1992.

Howard, Alan (ed.): *Software Metrics and Project Management Tools*, Applied Computer Research (ACR), Phoenix, Ariz., 1997.

IFPUG Counting Practices Manual, Release 4, International Function Point Users Group, Westerville, Ohio, April 1995.

Jones, Capers: *Critical Problems in Software Measurement*, Information Systems Management Group, 1993a.

———: *Software Productivity and Quality Today—The Worldwide Perspective*, Information Systems Management Group, 1993b.

———: *Assessment and Control of Software Risks*, Prentice-Hall, Englewood Cliffs, N.J., 1994.

———: *New Directions in Software Management*, Information Systems Management Group; 1994.

———: *Patterns of Software System Failure and Success*, International Thomson Computer Press, Boston, 1995.

———: *Applied Software Measurement*, 2d ed., McGraw-Hill, New York, 1996.

———: *The Economics of Object-Oriented Software*, Software Productivity Research, Burlington, Mass., April 1997a.

———: *Software Quality—Analysis and Guidelines for Success*, International Thomson Computer Press, Boston, 1997b.

———: *The Year 2000 Software Problem—Quantifying the Costs and Assessing the Consequences*, Addison-Wesley, Reading, Mass., 1998.

———: *Software Assessments, Benchmarks, and Best Practices*, Addison-Wesley, Boston, Mass, 2000.

Kan, Stephen H.: *Metrics and Models in Software Quality Engineering, 2nd edition*, Addison-Wesley, Boston, Mass., 2003.

Kemerer, C. F.: "Reliability of Function Point Measurement—A Field Experiment," *Communications of the ACM*, **36:** 85–97 (1993).

Keys, Jessica: *Software Engineering Productivity Handbook*, McGraw-Hill, New York, 1993.

Laird, Linda M. and Carol M. Brennan: *Software Measurement and Estimation: A Practical Approach*, John Wiley & Sons, New York, 2006.

Lewis, James P.: *Project Planning, Scheduling & Control*, McGraw-Hill, New York, 2005.

Marciniak, John J. (ed.): *Encyclopedia of Software Engineering*, vols. 1 and 2, John Wiley & Sons, New York, 1994.

McConnell, Steve: *Software Estimation: Demystifying the Black Art*, Microsoft Press, Redmond, WA, 2006.

Mertes, Karen R.: *Calibration of the CHECKPOINT Model to the Space and Missile Systems Center (SMC) Software Database (SWDB)*, Thesis AFIT/GCA/LAS/96S-11, Air Force Institute of Technology (AFIT), Wright-Patterson AFB, Ohio, September 1996.

Ourada, Gerald, and Daniel V. Ferens: "Software Cost Estimating Models: A Calibration, Validation, and Comparison," in *Cost Estimating and Analysis: Balancing Technology and Declining Budgets*, Springer-Verlag, New York, 1992, pp. 83–101.

Perry, William E.: *Handbook of Diagnosing and Solving Computer Problems*, TAB Books, Blue Ridge Summit, Pa., 1989.

Pressman, Roger: *Software Engineering: A Practitioner's Approach with Bonus Chapter on Agile Development*, McGraw-Hill, New York, 2003.

Putnam, Lawrence H.: *Measures for Excellence—Reliable Software on Time, Within Budget:* Yourdon Press/Prentice-Hall, Englewood Cliffs, N.J., 1992.

———, and Ware Myers: *Industrial Strength Software—Effective Management Using Measurement*, IEEE Press, Los Alamitos, Calif., 1997.

Reifer, Donald (ed.): *Software Management*, 4th ed., IEEE Press, Los Alamitos, Calif., 1993.

Rethinking the Software Process, CD-ROM, Miller Freeman, Lawrence, Kans., 1996. (This CD-ROM is a book collection jointly produced by the book publisher, Prentice-Hall, and the journal publisher, Miller Freeman. It contains the full text and illustrations of five Prentice-Hall books: *Assessment and Control of Software Risks* by Capers Jones; *Controlling Software Projects* by Tom DeMarco; *Function Point Analysis* by Brian Dreger; *Measures for Excellence* by Larry Putnam and Ware Myers; and *Object-Oriented Software Metrics* by Mark Lorenz and Jeff Kidd.)

Roetzheim, William H., and Reyna A. Beasley: *Best Practices in Software Cost and Schedule Estimation*, Prentice-Hall PTR, Upper Saddle River, N.J., 1998.

Rubin, Howard: *Software Benchmark Studies for 1997*, Howard Rubin Associates, Pound Ridge, N.Y., 1997.

Stukes, Sherry, Jason Deshoretz, Henry Apgar, and Ilona Macias: *Air Force Cost Analysis Agency Software Estimating Model Analysis—Final Report*, TR-9545/008-2, Contract F04701-95-D-0003, Task 008, Management Consulting & Research, Inc., Thousand Oaks, Calif., September 1996.

Stutzke, Richard D.: *Estimating Software-Intensive Systems: Projects, Products, and Processes*; Addison-Wesley, Boston, Mass., 2005.

Symons, Charles R.: *Software Sizing and Estimating—Mk II FPA (Function Point Analysis)*, John Wiley & Sons, Chichester, U.K., 1991.

Wellman, Frank: *Software Costing: An Objective Approach to Estimating and Controlling the Cost of Computer Software*, Prentice-Hall, Englewood Cliffs, N.J., 1992,

Yourdon, Ed: *Death March—The Complete Software Developer's Guide to Surviving "Mission Impossible" Projects*, Prentice-Hall PTR, Upper Saddle River, N.J., 1997.

Zells, Lois: *Managing Software Projects—Selecting and Using PC-Based Project Management Systems*, QED Information Sciences, Wellesley, Mass., 1990.

Zvegintzov, Nicholas: *Software Management Technology Reference Guide*, Dorset House Press, New York, 1994.

Manual Estimating Methods Derived from Agile Projects and New Environments

In the ten years between the writing of the first and second editions of this book, a number of interesting new ideas and methods for software development have arisen or increased in usage. All of these have created new challenges for estimating team sizes, schedules, effort, costs, and quality. The most widely known of these new concepts include:

- Agile software development methods
- Clean room development
- Component-based development (CBD)
- Crystal development approach
- Dynamic system development method (DSDM)
- Enterprise resource planning (ERP)
- Extreme programming (XP)
- Feature-driven development (FDD)
- International outsourcing
- ISO 9000-9004 quality standards
- Iterative development
- Object-oriented development (OO)
- Quality function deployment (QFD)
- Pattern-based development
- Rapid Application Development (RAD)

- Scrum
- Software Engineering Institute (SEI) CMM and CMMI levels
- Six-sigma for Software
- Spiral software development
- Unified modeling language (UML)
- Use cases for software requirements
- Web-based applications

Some of these methods do not encompass a complete development cycle from requirements to deployment. For others, there is still insufficient data to have developed useful rules of thumb or effective estimating algorithms. For the second edition of this book, usage has been sufficient in recent years to provide at least preliminary estimating rules of thumb for eight of these new approaches:

- Agile software development methods
- Component-based development (CBD)
- Dynamic system development method (DSDM)
- Enterprise resource planning (ERP)
- Extreme programming (XP)
- International outsourcing
- Object-oriented development (OO)
- SEI CMM and CMMI levels

Some partial rules of thumb and preliminary algorithms are provided for the methods that lack insufficient data for complete sets of rules of thumb.

Within the next few years information will no doubt become sufficient to provide estimating algorithms for the other methods. However, since new development approaches are being developed at a rate of one or two per calendar year, it is actually impossible to stay current with the very latest software technologies.

Other recent authors also provide rules of thumb for some of the newer software development methods. For example, Steve McConnell's book *Software Estimation: Demystifying the Black Art* (Microsoft Press, 2006) touches upon the Agile methods, object-oriented development, Scrum, and several other new approaches. The sixth edition of Roger Pressman's monumental book *Software Engineering—A Practitioner's Approach* (McGraw-Hill, 2005) discusses many new methods such as the Agile approach, the object-oriented approach, Scrum, the CMM, etc.

After a new method is developed, it has to be used on a reasonable number of projects. This usually takes at least two years. Then a statistically significant sample of these projects needs to collect sufficient data for analysis and derivation of estimating algorithms. The whole process from creation of a new method until estimating algorithms can be developed is normally about a five–calendar year cycle. To gather information on maintenance and to calculate defect-removal efficiency levels, another year is needed.

One issue with some of the new methods discussed in this chapter is the fact that only a few practitioners are interested in measurement, metrics, and collection of historical data. This issue can delay the discovery of useful information for several years. New development methods might be effective, but until historical data is collected, there is no way to validate their effectiveness.

Although there is some overlap among these approaches, each has a number of enthusiasts and each has developed its own literature. Therefore it seems best to provide rules of thumb and estimating algorithms in the context of each of these new disciplines.

However, as general background information for readers, all of these various software development methods need to address 30 historical problems that have affected software projects for more than 50 years. In fact, very little progress in solving most of these problems has been noted for at least the last 30 years:

1. Initial requirements are seldom more than 50 percent complete.

2. Requirements grow at about 2 percent per calendar month during development.

3. About 20 percent of initial requirements are delayed until a second release.

4. Finding and fixing bugs is the most expensive software activity.

5. Creating paper documents is the second most expensive software activity.

6. Coding is the third most expensive software activity.

7. Meetings and discussions are the fourth most expensive activity.

8. Most forms of testing are less than 30 percent efficient in finding bugs.

9. Most forms of testing touch less than 50 percent of the code being tested.

10. There are more defects in requirements and design than in source code.

11. There are more defects in test cases than in the software itself.

12. Defects in requirements, design, and code average 5.0 per function point.

13. Total defect-removal efficiency before release averages only about 85 percent.

14. About 15 percent of software defects are delivered to customers.

15. Delivered defects are expensive and cause customer dissatisfaction.

16. About 5 percent of modules in applications will contain 50 percent of all defects.

17. About 7 percent of all defect repairs will accidentally inject new defects.

18. Software reuse is only effective for materials that approach zero defects.

19. About 5 percent of software outsource contracts end up in litigation.

20. About 35 percent of projects > 10,000 function points will be cancelled.

21. About 50 percent of projects > 10,000 function points will be one year late.

22. The failure mode for most cost estimates is to be excessively optimistic.

23. Productivity rates in the U.S. are about 10 function points per staff month.

24. Assignment scopes for development are about 150 function points.

25. Assignment scopes for maintenance are about 750 function points.

26. Development costs about $1200 per function point in the U.S.

27. Maintenance costs about $150 per function point per calendar year.

28. After delivery applications grow at about 7 percent per calendar year during use.

29. Average defect repair rates are about ten bugs or defects per month.

30. Programmers need about ten days of annual training to stay current.

So far as can be determined neither conventional software development nor any of the new approaches are totally successful in addressing all 30 of these problems. The Agile methods, for example, address problems 1, 2, 3, 4, 5, and 6 quite well but are silent on many of the other problems, except for problem 26 where Agile methods are somewhat better than average.

The Agile methods have concentrated to a significant degree on problem 5, paperwork costs. In fact, for a majority of Agile projects problems 5 and 7 have changed places. Meetings and discussions have been elevated to the number two spot in the expense hierarchy, and paperwork has dropped down significantly. Sometimes paper costs have come close to vanishing. Of course, for projects using the unified modeling language (UML) and use cases, paperwork costs continue as the number two cost driver.

The large number of alternative development approaches in the software engineering literature is a good indication that none of these approaches has solved all 30 of the problems cited above. If all or even a majority of the problems had been solved, then the method that solved them would probably become the standard approach. Since there are many competing software engineering approaches, it is apparent that none have yet succeeded in solving all 30 problems, or at least none have yet published convincing results supported by reliable data.

Metrics Used for Rules of Thumb

This book uses function point metrics as the basic unit of measure for some of the rules of thumb. The specific form of function point metric is that defined by the International Function Point Users Group (IFPUG), using counting rules version 4.1.

Many users of the new generation of software development methods are not familiar with function point metrics. It is not necessary to know how function points are counted in order to understand data based on function points. But for those who would like a deeper understanding of the origins and counting rules, *Function Point Analysis* by David Garmus and David Herron (Addison-Wesley, 2001) is a good primer. This book includes information on counting function points for object-oriented (OO) projects and for some of the other newer development methods.

Function point metrics are calculated from the requirements of a software application, using weighted combinations of five parameters: inputs, outputs, inquiries, interfaces, and logical files. The rules are rather complex, and accurate counting of function points usually requires several days training plus working through a number of examples. A certification exam is administered by the IFPUG organization, and there are more than 1000 certified function point counters in the U.S. at the time of this writing.

From the point of view of new and emerging software engineering methods, it is significant that function point totals can be derived from many different representation methods, including but not limited to Agile stories; various forms of diagramming that are part of the unified modeling language (UML); use cases; and older methods such as text-based specifications, flowcharts, HIPO diagrams, and many other forms of representation.

Function point metrics are independent of the kind of software being developed. Function point metrics have been used for information systems, enterprise resource planning packages, operating systems, embedded software, process control applications, weapons systems software, and even microcode.

Function point metrics can be used to measure every activity that is part of a software life cycle: requirements, analysis, design, inspections, coding, testing, documentation, integration, configuration control, management, maintenance, and even more. In a more recent context function points can be used to measure Scrum sessions, sizes and effort of creating Agile stories, and the effort to create use cases. The size of both use cases and stories can be measured with function points too.

Function points can be used to measure productivity using "function points produced per staff month" or some variant such as "work hours per function point." Function points can be used to measure quality using "defects per function point." In fact, function points can be used to measure the quality of specific items such as requirements, specifications, source code, and user documents.

Function point metrics are also independent of the programming language or languages used to implement a software application. The fact that function point metrics are language-independent has led to a useful (but not extremely accurate) approach for approximating function point totals called "backfiring." Because the function point total for a specific application is independent of the volume of source code, it is interesting to measure both the function point totals of applications and the source code volumes.

For every known programming language and dialect, and there are more than 600 of these, there are rules of thumb that show the approximate number of logical source code statements that are equivalent to one function point. For example in this book, Java examples are assumed to average about 50 statements per function point. The C programming language examples are assumed to average about 125 statements per function point.

A few examples of typical values for the number of source code statements per function point are shown in Table 7.1.

For backfiring purposes, the column labeled "Mean" is the approximate value that represents the number of source code statements per function point. Of course, due to the fact that thousands of programmers may use the same language and all may have slightly different programming styles, there is a broad range of source code statements per function point.

The column labeled "Language Level" predates the development of function point metrics. In the early 1970s within IBM, the relative power of a programming language was approximated by calculating

TABLE 7.1   Ratios of Logical Source Code Statements to Function Points for Selected Programming Languages Using Version 4.1 of the IFPUG Rules

Language	Nominal level	Source statements per function point		
		Low	Mean	High
Basic assembly	1.00	200	320	450
Macro assembly	1.50	130	213	300
C	2.50	60	128	170
FORTRAN	3.00	75	107	160
COBOL	3.00	65	107	150
PASCAL	3.50	50	91	125
PL/I	4.00	65	80	95
Ada 83	4.50	60	71	80
C++	6.00	30	53	125
Java	6.40	29	50	78
Ada 95	6.50	28	49	110
Visual Basic	10.00	20	32	37
Smalltalk	15.00	15	21	40
SQL	27.00	7	12	15

the number of statements in basic assembly language that would be required to equal one statement in the language of interest. For example, it took about three assembly statements to create the functionality of one COBOL statement. Therefore COBOL was deemed to be a "level 3 language." Although this method is no longer widely used, it does provide a useful shorthand way of discussing languages of various degrees of power.

Historically, backfiring was developed during the early days of function point usage when both lines of code and function point totals were counted for hundreds of software applications.

The backfiring approach is most widely used for legacy applications where the specifications may no longer be current, but the source code exists and can be counted. This property is also useful for deriving function points for some of the new Agile methods where prototypes supplant written specifications.

The overall advantage of function point metrics is that they are so widely used that most benchmark studies are now based on function points. In the United States, more than 25,000 software projects have been measured using function point metrics, and with this large sample it is possible to establish fairly good benchmark information for almost any kind of software project using any kind of software development methodology.

In fact the kinds of benchmark data included in this book would not be possible with the older "lines-of-code" metrics or with some of the very specialized object-oriented (OO) metrics. Similar data might eventually be possible with story points, use-case points, object points, or some of the other function point derivatives but none is available in 2007. This is because there is no large collection of historical data that used these metrics. Also, there are no standard conversion rules between various OO metrics and standard IFPUG function points. Two possible exceptions involve "story points" and use cases. Although the results vary, it appears that one story point is approximately equal to two IFPUG function points. It appears that one use case is approximately equal to 35 function points.

Some of the specific metrics used in this book for rules of thumb include

- **Development Productivity**   The U.S. average is about ten function points per staff month. This is equivalent to about 500 Java statements per staff month. This value includes all activities from requirements through delivery, and it includes analysts, programmers, managers, and specialists such as software quality assurance.

- **Development Assignment Scope**   This is the average amount of work assigned to one person. The U.S. average for assignment scope is about 150 function points. This is equivalent to about 7500 Java statements. The metric includes analysts, programmers, managers, and specialists such as technical writers or software quality assurance staff.

- **Development Schedule**   Software development schedules grow longer as applications get larger. One interesting property of function point metrics is that schedule rules of thumb in calendar months can be approximated by raising the size of the application in function points to a specific power. The U.S. average is about the 0.4 power. Thus if you are building an application of 1000 function points in size, raising 1000 to the 0.4 power yields a result of 15.8, which approximates the number of calendar months from the start of a project until it is delivered.

- **Defect Potential**   This metric represents the sum of defects or bugs found in requirements, design, code, documentation, and "bad fixes." The latter category represents new bugs accidentally injected when repairing older bugs. The current U.S. average for defect potential is about 5.0 per function point. The values for each source of defect are

Defect source	Defects per function point
Requirements	1.00
Design	1.25
Code	1.75
Documents	0.60
Bad Fixes	0.40
TOTAL	5.00

The value of 5.00 defects per function point is a static value that does not change for either small or large software applications. A useful rule of thumb that does change is to raise the size of the application in function points to the 1.25 power. This will give a reasonable approximation of a software project's defect potential. For example, if you are building an application of 1000 function points, raising 1000 to the 1.25 power yields 5623 bugs or defects in all sources.

- **Defect-Removal Efficiency** This metric is easy to understand and easy to use on projects. It does not require a knowledge of function points. The development team records all bugs or errors found during development. Users report all bugs for a predetermined period such as 90 days after delivery. Then the two values are summed, and the percentage found before release is calculated. This value is known as defect removal efficiency. If the developers find 90 bugs during development, and the users find ten bugs in the first three months of usage, the total number of bugs is 100. The defect removal efficiency is 90 percent in this example. The current U.S. average is only about 85 percent. The best in class projects in the best companies approaches 99 percent. From the author's observations as an expert witness in lawsuits involving cancelled software projects, it appears that failing software projects are often less than 80 percent efficient in finding defects.

- **Bad Fix Injection** It has been known for many years that not all bug fixes are correct. Some of them accidentally introduce new bugs. The U.S. average for bad fix injection is about 7 percent. That is, for every 100 bugs you fix, seven of your fixes will introduce a new bug. However, for large applications with error-prone modules, the bad fix injection rates can top 50 percent. Bad fix injection rates are also elevated for some (but not all) modules that are high in essential and cyclomatic complexity.

- **Maintenance Assignment Scope** This is the average amount of a legacy application that one person can maintain in the course of a year. The tasks included in the maintenance assignment scope are assumed to be fixing latent bugs are performing minor updates. The U.S. average is about 750 function points, which is equivalent to about 37,500 Java statements.

- **Cost per Function Point** Cost information is extremely variable due to large differences in team composition and use of specialists, large differences in average salary, large differences in overhead rates, and large differences in unpaid overtime. That being said, average cost for development in the United States is about $1200 per function point. The average cost for maintenance of legacy applications is about $150 per function point per calendar year. However, the range for development runs from less than $250 per function point for some small Agile projects up to more than $5000 per function point for some large defense systems. The range for maintenance runs from less than $50 per function point per year to more than $600 per function point per year for "error-prone modules" in large systems.

The following sets of rules of thumb for new technologies have a high margin of error. However, by publishing rules of thumb that might need revision or be incorrect, it is hoped that future studies will refine the rules and correct any current errors.

Rules of Thumb for Manual Software Cost Estimates

Following are rules of thumb for eight kinds of software project that have emerged or become popular in the ten years between the first edition of this book and the second edition.

Agile Software Development

Because of the well-known failures of software projects, many researchers have been seeking alternative approaches. The genesis of the set of "Agile" methods can be traced to the publication of the "Agile manifesto" in 2001. This manifesto recommended collaborative development, meeting evolving requirements with working versions, and growing the final application organically from a number of iterations.

The essence of Agile development is that requirements for software projects will always be fluid and changing. Rather than attempting to document every known requirement prior to starting development, under the Agile methods small teams of developers build working versions of key features in very short intervals called "time boxes" or "increments." In order to do this, there must be daily contact with the application's customer and with each other.

Since the Agile development has increased to the point where perhaps 15 percent of software projects below 1000 function points in size now use some of the Agile concepts. In the United States probably 5000 or more software projects have used the Agile concepts, primarily for projects at the smaller end of the size spectrum.

The Agile methods include requirements in the form of *stories* and have enough interesting characteristics to begin to develop some specialized estimating and planning approaches. Mike Cohn's book *Agile Estimating and Planning* (Prentice-Hall PTR, 2005) is among the first to tackle some of the project management issues of the Agile approach.

Some of the Agile methods develop requirements via user stories, each of which describes a typical usage pattern for a software application. A metric called *story points* has been devised for assigning a relative size to each story. Thus stories can range from one to about five story points in size.

Once enumerated, story points can be used to estimate velocity, in terms of the number of story points that can be developed in one iteration or sprint. If the project uses time boxes, then that is equivalent to the number of stories that can be developed in a typical time box, such as two weeks or a month. As this book is written, stories can vary in size from team to team and project to project. A rough value of about eight hours to develop the code for one story is not an uncommon starting point.

Some Agile projects use a concept called "ideal time." *Ideal time* is time that is fully devoted to a task, without interruptions such as phone calls or conversations. Ideal time is sometimes used for predicting the velocities of building the next iteration. A ratio of about 2 to 1 between ideal time and clock time would not be uncommon, i.e., 40 minutes of concentrated work and 20 minutes of something else in one hour. A metric termed *e factor*, or environmental factor can be derived by dividing ideal time by clock time. Thus 40 minutes of concentrated work in an hour yields an e factor of 0.66.

Although there are no formal conversion rules between story points and standard IFPUG function points, some preliminary observations indicate that a typical story point is more or less equivalent to two IFPUG function points in size. If so, then one story point would also be roughly equivalent to 100 Java statements. Recall, however, that function points are standardized while story points are flexible and can vary in size.

A similar conversion factor can be applied to use cases. One use case is approximately equal to 35 function points. If so, then one use case would be roughly equivalent to 1750 Java statements. Here, too, function points are standardized while use cases are flexible and can vary in size.

Above 10,000 function points the use of Agile drops down and more conventional methods remain the norm. This is due in part to the fact that really large applications where development teams can top 50 people may have trouble applying some of the Agile concepts.

However, the Agile method has been proposed for large reengineering projects of legacy applications. When reengineering legacy software, the main set of features to be developed is already known and understood. This means that cost and schedule estimates can be made earlier than with applications where fluid requirements are likely to expand the time and cost envelopes.

Although the average size of Agile projects is small, the method has been used on a number of projects in the size range of about 2000 function points or 100,000 Java statements. These have been done in about 100 business days using time boxes.

The Agile approach is popular with its practitioners and has generally been successful when deployed for suitable projects. However, because the Agile method embraces rapidly changing requirements, it is not easy to predict either the final size of an Agile application or its ultimate delivery date. That implies that the Agile approach may not be a good choice for fixed-price development contracts on large projects.

Following are some rules of thumb for Agile software projects using function point metrics:

- The average size of an Agile application is about 500 function points or roughly 25,000 Java statements.

- A typical Agile project will start with a two-week planning and organization period during which the team will come together and scope out the nature of the overall project. Then on average, an Agile project will have five increments or releases at two-week intervals. Each increment will average about 100 function points or 5000 Java statements in size.

- Historical data indicates fairly short schedules under Agile methods. Raising the size of the application in function points to about the 0.33 power will yield an approximate schedule in calendar months from inception to delivery. Thus raising a typical 500–function point Agile project to the 0.33 power indicates an approximate schedule of about 7.7 months from inception to delivery.

- A typical Agile team will consist of five full-time personnel: two sets of programmers who work cooperatively, and a client representative. A technical writer might also be involved if needed.

- A typical Agile assignment scope is about 100 function points or 5000 Java statements. This is the amount of work that is typically assigned to one person.

- An average Agile production rate is about 36 function points or 1800 Java statements per staff month.

- Because of the comparatively small sizes of Agile applications, their defect potentials would probably be only about 3.5 per function point. The defect potential for an average Agile project of 500 function points in size will be about 1750 defects from all sources: requirements, design, code, documents, and bad fixes.

- Because of the small sizes of the increments, the daily contact with the client, and the pair-programming concept, the defect-removal efficiency levels of Agile projects is about 92 percent. About 1610 out of 1750 defects will be found before deployment.

- The bad-fix injection rate for Agile projects is about 2 percent. An average Agile project of 500 function points in size will have about 32 defects accidentally injected while fixing prior defects.

- A typical number of delivered defects for an Agile project of 500 function points in size will be about 170, or 0.34 per function point. Of these less than five will be high-severity defects. About 50 will be medium-severity defects. About 115 will be low-severity defects.

- Once deployed, an average Agile project can be maintained by a single maintenance programmer. In fact one maintenance programmer can probably handle two or three typical Agile projects for defect repairs and minor enhancements. A typical maintenance assignment scope for Agile projects will be about 1500 function points.

At the low end of the size spectrum (below 1000 function points), the Agile methods are rapidly becoming the norm. Both Agile productivity rates and quality levels compare favorably to more traditional levels.

Although Agile methods started with small projects, attempts are being made to scale up the approach to larger applications. These attempts have been boosted by Microsoft's recent experiments with Agile methods for some of their commercial products. All of Microsoft's commercial products are larger than 10,000 function points in size. Windows XP is larger than 100,000 function points in size, which would be equivalent to more than 5,000,000 Java statements.

Although not many Agile projects to date have actually utilized function point metrics, that metric is in fact the most reliable for studying economic productivity, quality, and other quantitative projects. Lines-of-code-metrics are seriously deficient. Some of the specialized object-oriented metrics can be used within the OO domain, but have no ability to compare OO projects with standard projects. Neither story points nor use case points nor object points can be used for side-by-side comparisons of projects using different methodologies. However, function point metrics are very useful for comparisons between different methods, different programming languages, different sized applications, and different sets of technologies.

Component-Based Development

The idea of building software applications from libraries of reusable components has been circulating through the software world since the late 1960s. In a sense, operating systems such as IBM's MVS and Microsoft Windows are a form of reusable components, since these systems provide basic control features that no longer have to be written from scratch. Database applications are another example of successful components that have become widespread.

The basic concept of component-based development is to construct software applications from libraries of reusable components and thereby minimize the amount of custom code that must be created to meet all user requirements. Ideally the components will be certified to perform as advertised, approach zero-defect levels, and use standard interface techniques.

Reusable components can either be acquired from commercial vendors or developed and stored for use within an enterprise, or both.

In recent years approaches such as JavaBeans, object request broker architecture, CORBA, and others have attempted to facilitate component development and deployment, with reasonable but mixed results. Several thousand projects have utilized component-based development, but only a handful have provided solid data on their results.

Following are some rules of thumb for component-based software projects:

- The average size of a component-based application is about 5000 function points or roughly 250,000 Java statements.

- An average reusable component will be about 200 function points in size, or 10,000 Java statements.

- Reusable components will provide about 60 percent of the functionality in the application. Custom code will provide about 40 percent of the functionality.

- For the overall schedule of a component-based project, raise the application size in function points to about the 0.36 power. The result will yield the approximate schedule from inception to delivery. Raising a typical component-based application to the 0.36 power indicates a schedule of just over 21 calendar months from inception to delivery.

- Selecting, qualifying, and adapting the reusable components will require about 30 percent as much effort as developing equivalent custom code. Typical production rates for acquiring reusable components and adapting them averages about 30 function points per staff month, which is equivalent to about 1500 Java statements per staff month.

- Building a successful component for later reuse will require about 30 percent more effort than simply building the component for one-time custom use. This is because of the need for greater care in defect removal and for documenting features and interfaces. Reusable components are themselves developed at a rate of about six function points per staff month or 300 Java statements per staff month.

- Developing the custom code that links to and uses the reusable components proceeds at a rate of about ten function points per staff month or 500 Java statements per staff month on average.

- Unfortunately, many reusable components are not at zero-defect levels. A typical reusable component of 200 function points or 10,000 Java statements will contain about 50 latent defects or 0.25 per function point.

- The bad-fix injection rate against reusable components is about 5 percent. Therefore, for a typical reusable component where 50 defects are found, about three bad fixes will accidentally inject fresh defects while repairing prior defects.

There are some fairly serious barriers that must be overcome before software reuse can even approach its economic potential. Here is a short summary of the major obstacles:

- You cannot safely reuse garbage. Successful reuse demands that the reusable materials be certified to levels of quality that approach or achieve zero defects. The primary barrier to successful reuse is poor quality control and careless practices that are common today.

- When you set out to reuse something you have to construct that artifact with reuse in mind. It is usually not possible to casually extract reusable artifacts from ordinary software projects for high-volume corporate reuse. The second barrier is finding the time and funds to construct reusable materials initially, given the intense schedule and cost pressure most software projects are under. Software life cycles, estimating tools, planning tools, company standards, and design methods need to include specific capabilities for dealing with reusable materials. As the situation now stands, most software management tools and practices have no provision for reuse.

- Once you accumulate a useful library of reusable artifacts you need to offer some incentives to project managers and technical personnel to make use of the materials. This is not as easy as it sounds, and requires both cultural and financial changes to current practices. For example, your current measurement system may not give credit for reuse. There may also be a staff resistance to making use of someone else's work. In general, a successful reuse program must deal with social issues as well as technical issues.

There are many other important factors associated with reuse besides the ones discussed here, but the basic points are clear enough. Reuse has the best potential for improving financial software costs and schedules of any known technology, but there are serious barriers that must be eliminated before reuse can take its place as a major software technology.

Dynamic System Development
Method (DSDM)

The concepts of the Dynamic System Development Method originated in the United Kingdom as an extension to the older Rapid Application Development (RAD) protocols. DSDM is aimed primarily at information technology projects, and is supported by a non-profit consortium of companies and organizations that use and modify the DSDM approach.

DSDM shares some aspects of other Agile methods such as time-boxed increments and integral support for flexible fast-changing requirements. DSDM also overlaps other methods such as Scrum and the unified modeling language (UML).

Since DSDM originated in the United Kingdom, that remains the area with the greatest usage. Several hundred applications have been built using DSDM principles in the United Kingdom. Some key features of DSDM include continuous involvement by users, extensive use of time-boxed prototypes for all features as they are defined, and iterative development. Testing occurs for all of the prototypes and of course for the final consolidated application with all features present.

A typical DSDM project life cycle includes

- Feasibility study
- Business study
- Functional model iteration
- Prototype of initial functional model
- Design of additional features and increments
- Iterative development and testing of features and increments
- Deployment of all features and training of users

The DSDM approach has attempted to select useful features from a number of the Agile methods, and appears to have made their selections judiciously. Following are some approximate rules of thumb for DSDM projects with an unfortunately high margin of error. This is due in part to the fact that the United Kingdom uses several variants of function point metrics such as Mark II and COSMIC function points, as well as standard IFPUG function points. Since the function point variants lack accurate conversion factors to the IFPUG method, there is some ambiguity in all results. (This book uses IFPUG function points for all data.)

- The average size of a DSDM application is about 1,500 function points or roughly 75,000 Java statements.
- A typical DSDM project will start with four weeks of feasibility and business study. After that a typical DSDM project will have ten

increments or releases at two-week intervals. Each increment will average about 150 function points or 7500 Java statements in size. At the end, final integration, system testing, acceptance testing, and deployment will take about a month.

- Raising the application size in function points to the 0.33 power will generate an approximate schedule in calendar months from inception to deployment. Raising a typical project of 1500 function points to the 0.33 power indicates a schedule of just over 11 calendar months from inception to delivery.

- A typical DSDM team for a 1500–function point project will consist of about ten software engineering personnel and at least one user representative. A technical writer might also be involved if needed.

- A typical DSDM assignment scope is about 125 function points or 6250 Java statements. This is the amount of work that is typically assigned to one person.

- A typical DSDM production rate is about 12 function points or 600 Java statements per staff month.

- Because of the comparatively small sizes of DSDM applications, their defect potentials average only about 4.0 per function point. The defect potential for an average Agile project of 1500 function points in size will be about 6000 defects from all sources: requirements, design, code, documents, and bad fixes.

- Because of frequent reviews and testing of DSDM materials, the defect-removal efficiency level of DSDM projects is about 90 percent. About 5400 out of 6000 defects will be found before deployment.

- The bad-fix injection rate for DSDM projects is about 3 percent. A typical DSDM project of 1500 function points in size will have about 160 defects accidentally injected while fixing prior defects.

- A typical number of delivered defects for a DSDM project of 1500 function points in size will be about 700, or 0.46 per function point. Of these about 15 will be high-severity defects. About 150 will be medium-severity defects. About 535 will be low-severity defects.

- Once deployed, an average DSDM project can be maintained by a single maintenance programmer. A typical DSDM maintenance assignment scope project will be about 1500 function points so one maintenance staff member will probably be sufficient for defect repairs and minor code updates.

DSDM is an interesting hybrid of Agile, RAD, and other approaches. To date DSDM is used primarily in the United Kingdom, but seems to be working well.

Enterprise Resource
Planning (ERP) Deployment

The most important point to understand about ERP deployment is that modern ERP tools are enormous. Because they attempt to support almost every aspect of a modern business, they average around 250,000 function points in size. This is equivalent to about 12,500,000 Java statements. (Note that ERP tools are not written in Java, but that language is so widespread that it is convenient for expressing size information.)

As background for understanding the economics of ERP packages, recall that software development in corporate environments has traditionally been funded and driven by the specific needs of operating units: sales, marketing, purchasing, manufacturing, finance, human resources, taxation, quality assurance, and so forth.

Although these disparate operating units are part of the same companies, they have historically operated as semi-independent groups under their own executives and with their own budgets. In many large corporations, each of the main operating units had their own dedicated software development and maintenance groups.

It often happens that the software created to support a particular business operation is so unique that it is difficult to interface with the software created in support of other business operations. The result has been a patchwork collection of independent applications that do not communicate with others easily (or at all), built on top of databases with unique structures and data elements. Therefore, while local unit-level information and data processing needs are usually met, many companies have had trouble gaining a clear perspective or useful data at the corporate level.

The fundamental ERP vision is that to be successful, enterprises need to integrate all of their business applications so that they communicate, and to pool all of their disparate data into an enterprise-wide data warehouse.

Since the aging legacy applications built by the companies themselves cannot easily be blended or integrated, the ERP concept has been to provide a cohesive set of applications that are already integrated. Further, most ERP architectures are built on the concept of sharing information in the presence of continuous growth and changing business needs. Therefore, the installation of ERP packages provide much better cross-unit integration of data and information than companies have had in the past.

As ERP packages expand their markets, there is an increasing need to estimate the schedules and costs of deploying and customizing the ERP packages. There is also a need to estimate the downstream schedules and costs of building custom applications in an ERP environment or customizing some of the ERP components.

Examples of the major business components of ERP applications and their approximate sizes include

Manufacturing	50,000 function points
Bill of materials	
Capacity planning	
Workflow management	
Quality control	
Cost management	
Supply Chains	25,000 function points
Inventory	
Order entry	
Purchasing	
Supply chain planning	
Finance	50,000 function points
General ledger	
Cash flow	
Accounts payable	
Accounts receivable	
Projects	20,000 function points
Cost accounting	
Billing	
Time and expense management	
Human Resources	30,000 function points
Payroll	
Benefits	
Time and attendance	
Health care plans	
Customer Relationships	25,000 function points
Marketing	
Sales	
Call centers	
Warranties	
Data Warehouses	50,000 function points
All relevant corporate data	
Full ERP Package	250,000 function points

Of course, not every company uses every ERP feature. A more typical ERP deployment in a large manufacturing company would probably utilize about 150,000 function points out of the total feature set of 250,000 function points.

Considering the historical results of ERP deployment, raising the function point total of the ERP features to be deployed to the 0.23 power will generate an approximate schedule in calendar months for installation, customization, and training. Applying this rule of thumb to a feature set of 150,000 function points yields 15.5 calendar months.

What is somewhat surprising is that as large as they are, ERP applications do not really supply 100 percent of necessary business functions to run a large enterprise. The total quantity of function points found in large corporations' portfolios often exceeds 1,000,000. Thus it can be seen that as big as they are, ERP features comprise only about 25 percent of the capabilities needed to run a modern enterprise.

The main advantage of ERP applications is consistency in interfaces, and easy sharing of important data across many departments and organizations of large enterprises. Also, ERP packages are fairly cost-effective compared to attempting to build similar feature sets.

Typical ERP clients would have to spend perhaps $1000 per function point if they set out to build the most widely used ERP features for themselves. Assume a typical ERP installation that uses 150,000 function points. At a development cost of $1000 per function point, it would cost about $150,000,000 to replicate the ERP features. By contrast, the ERP package can be leased for less than $5 per function point.

Although ERP deployment can sometimes be lengthy and difficult, the schedules for building custom software are far longer. An approximate development schedule in calendar months can be calculated by taking the size of the desired application in function points and raising it to the 0.4 power. Thus, to build the features of a 150,000–function point ERP installation would take about 117 months or almost ten years. By contrast, most ERP packages can be fully deployed and operational in 16 months or less.

The generalized capabilities of ERP application suites often require significant tailoring for specific clients. The adjustments consist of modifications to ERP tables, and perhaps some custom code development.

As a provisional rule of thumb, assume that about 5 percent of the ERP features require tailoring for a specific client. Thus, for the 150,000–function point ERP installation discussed above, roughly 7500 function points would require modification or adjustment. Since ERP vendors provide tools and trained consultants, a rate of about 75 function points per staff month might be anticipated for the modifications and customization. That would imply about 100 staff months or 2,200 staff days of effort to tailor a 150,000 function point ERP installation and customize 7,500 function points. At a nominal cost of $2500 per day, customization of the ERP package would cost about $5,500,000. This may sound like quite a bit, but compared to the average development effort of ten function points per staff month for ordinary COBOL applications, it is rather efficient.

Most complex tools such as ERP applications require substantial training and sometimes consulting assistance to be used effectively.

A provisional rule of thumb is that every ERP user will need about five days of training to get up to speed on the new ERP way of doing business. Since a typical ERP deployment will have about 1000 users, the overall need for training adds up to about 5000 class days. At a nominal cost of $250 per student day, ERP training might cost $1,250,000. Training is usually spread over about a three-month calendar period.

Another way of understanding training is to interview some of the consulting companies that provide it. At a conference for the German ERP tool, SAP, about 25 training consultants were interviewed. The average response by the training partners was that SAP clients should expect to spend about $2 in training for every $1 of the first year lease. The range of responses ran from a low of $1.25 to a high of $5 although the high response also included some consulting.

A general rule of thumb for software training is that users of application packages need about one day of instruction for every 5000 function points in the package. Since users of ERP packages will typically use between 10,000 and 25,000 function points of ERP features in their normal jobs, somewhere between two days and five days of training per user should be anticipated.

One important topic that is not discussed as widely as it should be is the fact that ERP packages, like all other large software applications, contain defects or bugs. Typically, ERP packages start with defect potentials of about 6.0 per function point due to their large sizes. Defect-removal efficiency before their initial release is about 90 percent. Thus, for an ERP package of 250,000 function points the total defect volume would be 1,500,000 defects. At first deployment, as many as 150,000 defects would still be present. About 1000 would be high-severity defects, 20,000 would be medium-severity defects, and 129,000 would be low-severity defects.

Unfortunately, the bad-fix injection rate on such large and complex applications is about 7 percent, so secondary defects with ERP packages are an issue for several years.

However, after deployment latent defects will be found, reported by customers, and fixed at a rate of perhaps 40 percent per calendar year overall. The more critical high-severity defects will be found at a rate of about 70 percent during the initial year of deployment, and then about 60 percent per year after that. Thus, after several years of deployment and usage, the ERP packages achieve reasonable levels of stability.

Another fairly serious issue with ERP packages is that of "error-prone modules." It was discovered in the 1970s that large software applications have an unequal distribution of defects. About 5 percent of their modules typically contain about 50 percent of all reported defects. ERP applications are very large, and from customer reports, some of these may have error-prone modules.

Error-prone modules are the most expensive and troublesome entities in software. The bad-fix rate against error-prone modules can top
50 percent. In fact, they are often so complex that they become even worse
as a direct result of trying to fix defects. Usually, isolation and redevelopment is the only effective solution for curing error-prone modules.

Once deployed, ERP packages need continuous maintenance and
updates. As a result, users should expect to have about one full-time
person for about every 50,000 function points of the ERP features that
they use. This person will report bugs or defects to the vendor, and also
install updates and defect repairs from the vendor.

Although this volume of defects may seem high, it is roughly in the
same range as all other large software systems such as the operating systems that control our computers, the office suites that we use
for word processing and spreadsheets, and many others. Overall, the
volume of defects in ERP packages is somewhat lower than the numbers
of defects in custom-built applications that provide the same features.

The overall impact that ERP packages are having on the business
world is significant. What ERP has done is to create an integrated suite
of powerful business applications that support all of the major operating
units of typical companies—finance, sales, marketing, manufacturing,
human resources, and so forth.

In a sense, the ERP vendors are doing for business operations what
packages such as Windows XP and Microsoft Office have done for end-
user applications: integrating all necessary features into a single cohesive whole that can share information among all components.

As ERP usage expands internationally, many questions have arisen
as to how function point metrics can be used in ERP environments.
Fortunately, exploring the economic advantages of packages such as
ERP is one of the main reasons why function point metrics were originally developed.

In addition, questions have arisen as to whether software cost-
estimating tools can handle the costs and schedules of building applications in ERP environments. Here, too, a number of commercial estimating tools can deal with building and maintaining applications in an
ERP environment, and even with some of the expenses of acquiring and
tailoring ERP applications themselves.

Extreme Programming (XP)

Extreme programming is another variant on the Agile methods. It also
includes aspects of object-oriented (OO) development. Extreme programming originated in the Chrysler Corporation in the early 1990s.
It became popular after the 1999 publication of Kent Beck's book
Extreme Programming Explained (Addison-Wesley, 2000). In 2003 Matt

Stephens and Douglas Rosenberg published *Extreme Programming Refactored* (Apress L.P.), which opposed some of the extreme programming concepts.

Extreme programming has some interesting characteristics that set it off from some of the other Agile approaches. Among these characteristics are

- Simplicity of design is a major objective.
- Plans are based on individual features rather than the full system.
- Test cases are written before the code.
- Unit tests are designed first and intended to be automated.
- Test cases are the primary method for defining requirements.
- Requirements are defined and implemented serially with direct user involvement.
- Programmers work in pairs and review each other's materials.
- Features are built individually in two-week time boxes.
- Integration is continuous and daily builds and releases can occur.
- Changes to previous releases are called "refactoring."

Following are some rules of thumb for XP:

- The average size of an XP application is about 300 function points or roughly 15,000 Java statements.
- A typical XP project will start with a one-week planning and organization period during which the team will come together and scope out the nature of the overall project. Then on average an XP project will have four iterations or releases at two-week intervals. Each increment will average about 75 function points or 3750 Java statements in size. There may be an additional week at the end for final testing, deployment, and user training.
- Historical data indicates fairly short schedules under XP methods. Raising the size of the application in function points to about the 0.25 power will yield an approximate schedule in calendar months from inception to delivery for projects smaller than 500 function points. (There is little data available for XP projects larger than 500 function points.) Raising 500 function points to the 0.25 power indicates a schedule of just over four calendar months from inception to delivery.
- A typical XP team will consist of three full-time personnel: a pair of programmers who work cooperatively, and a client representative. A technical writer might also be involved if needed.

- A typical XP assignment scope is about 100 function points or 5000 Java statements. This is the amount of work that is typically assigned to one person.

- An average Agile production rate is about 40 function points or 2000 Java statements per staff month.

- Because of the comparatively small sizes of XP applications, their defect potentials would probably be only about 3.0 per function point. The defect potential for an average XP project of 300 function points in size will be about 900 defects from all sources: requirements, design, code, documents, and bad fixes.

- Because of the small sizes of the releases, careful testing of every release, daily contact with the client, and the pair-programming concept, the defect-removal efficiency level of XP projects is about 95 percent. About 855 out of 900 defects will be found before deployment.

- The bad-fix injection rate for XP projects is about 2 percent. An average Agile project of 300 function points in size will have about 17 defects accidentally injected while fixing prior defects.

- A typical number of delivered defects for an Agile project of 300 function points in size will be about 55, or 0.18 per function point. Of these about three will be high-severity defects. About 12 will be medium-severity defects. About 40 will be low-severity defects.

- Once deployed, a typical XP project can be maintained by a part-time maintenance programmer. In fact, one maintenance programmer can probably handle five or more XP projects for defect repairs and minor enhancements. A typical maintenance assignment scope for Agile projects will be about 1500 function points or 75,000 Java statements.

Although the XP approach has both enthusiasts and detractors, it seems to work well enough for applications at the low end of the size spectrum (below 500 function points).

The ability of the XP approach to scaling up to the larger sizes is not known, because such work has not yet been reported. But when used for small applications, XP productivity rates and quality levels compare favorably to more traditional levels and even to some of the other Agile alternatives.

The XP method has proven to be somewhat eclectic. In fact, XP is probably used in conjunction with other approaches more often than it is used in a pure form. There are reports of the successful merger of the XP approach with the capability maturity model (CMM) and with six-sigma quality control approach. The fluidity of the XP method and the rigor of the CMM and six-sigma methods sound like odd combinations, but seemingly they can be blended together.

Microsoft has been exploring the XP approach internally. Since Microsoft's applications are quite large (about 100,000 function points for Windows and Microsoft Office) it will be interesting to see how well XP scales up into the Microsoft internal environment.

International Outsourcing

Perhaps the most important long-range rule of thumb for international outsourcing is the fact that inflation is a global issue. Salaries and benefits in countries that are sophisticated enough to be major outsourcers can be expected to rise in the future. There may be cost savings from international outsourcing in the near future, but for the long run overseas costs are going to go up fairly rapidly. Expect off-shore costs to rise at rates equal to or greater than U.S. inflation rates.

A second important rule of thumb is that not all outsource agreements are beneficial to both parties. Some agreements will be terminated, and some will end up in court. Following are very significant rules of thumb about outsource litigation odds:

Outsource results after 24 months	
Generally satisfactory to both parties	70 percent
Some dissatisfaction by client or vendor	15 percent
Dissolution of agreement planned	10 percent
Litigation between client and vendor probable	4 percent
Litigation between client and vendor in progress	1 percent

When litigation does occur between outsource clients and vendors, several chronic problems have been observed:

- The client charges that the vendor failed to perform the terms of the contract such as costs, quality, or completion of milestones.

- The vendor charges that the client unilaterally expanded the scope of the contract by adding requirements or activities to those agreed upon.

Once the problems begin to occur, the human relations between the clients and vendors usually spiral downhill until a dissolution of the agreement occurs, or even litigation.

If you have determined that international outsourcing is at least a potential option for your company, then you will need to evaluate possible outsourcing partners. You may choose to evaluate the potential outsource partners with your own staff, or you can choose one or more of the external management consultants who specialize in this area.

A fundamental decision in outsourcing is to decide whether a domestic or an international outsource partner is preferred. The international

outsource companies from countries such as China, India, Ireland, or
Russia can usually offer attractive short-term cost reductions.

Do not enter into an outsource agreement solely on the basis of current cost reductions. Be sure to include quality levels and defect-removal
efficiency levels in the contract. Paying low costs for buggy software is
a bad investment.

If you are considering an international outsource partner, some of the
factors to include in your evaluation are

- The expertise of the candidate partners for the kinds of software your
  company utilizes

- The availability of satellite or reliable broad-band communication
  between your sites and the outsource location

- The local copyright, patent, and intellectual property protection within
  the country where the outsource vendor is located

- The probability of political upheavals or factors that might interfere
  with transnational information flow

- The basic stability and economic soundness of the outsource vendor,
  and what might occur should the vendor encounter a severe financial
  downturn

- The technical sophistication of the vendor in terms of their use of
  six-sigma methods, or their current level on the capability maturity
  model (CMM).

Some of the general topics to consider when evaluating potential outsource partners that are either domestic or international include the
following:

- The expertise of the outsource vendor within your industry, and for
  the kinds of software your company utilizes. (If the outsource vendor
  serves your direct competitors, be sure that adequate confidentiality
  can be assured.)

- The satisfaction levels of current clients who use the outsource vendor's services. You may wish to contact several clients and find out
  their first-hand experiences. It is particularly useful to speak with
  clients who have had outsource contracts in place for more than two
  or three years, and hence can talk about long-term satisfaction.

- Whether or not any active or recent litigation exists between the outsource company and either current or past clients. Although active
  litigation may not be a "show-stopper" in dealing with an outsource
  vendor, it is certainly a factor you will want to find out more about if
  the situation exists.

- How the vendor's own software performance compares against industry norms in terms of productivity, quality, reuse, and other quantitative factors. For this kind of analysis, the usage of the function point metric is now the most widely used in the world, and far superior to any alternative metrics. If the outsource vendor has no data on their own quality or productivity, be cautious. They may not be very sophisticated themselves.

- The kinds of project management tools that the vendor utilizes. Project management is a weak link of the software industry and the leaders tend to utilize a suite of software project management tools including cost-estimation tools, quality-estimation tools, software-planning tools, software-tracking tools, and several others. If your candidate outsource vendor has no quantitative estimating or measurement capabilities, it is unlikely that their performance will be much better than your own.

Some of the software your company owns may have such a significant competitive value that you do not want to outsource it, or even to let any other company know of its existence. One of the basic preparatory steps before initiating an international outsource arrangement is to survey your major current systems and arrange security or protection for valuable software assets with high competitive value.

- Identification of systems and programs that have high competitive value or that utilize proprietary or trade-secret algorithms. These systems may well be excluded from more general outsource arrangements. If they are to be included in an outsource contract, then special safeguards for confidential factors should be negotiated. Note also that preservation of proprietary or competitive software and data is very delicate when international outsource contracts are utilized. Be sure that local patent, copyright, and intellectual property laws are sufficient to safeguard your sensitive materials. You may need attorneys in several countries.

- Analysis of the databases and files utilized by your software applications, and the development of a strategy for preservation of confidential data under the outsource arrangement. If your databases contain valuable and proprietary information on topics such as trade secrets, competitors, specific customers, employee appraisals, pending or active litigation, or the like, you need to ensure that this data is carefully protected under any outsource arrangement.

On the whole, outsource agreements work best if the client has a realistic expectation of what is likely to occur. Outsource agreements are likely to fail if the client expects miraculous improvements in productivity, major reductions in schedules, or some other tremendous improvement. Of course, the vendors should not promise miraculous agreements in order to get the business.

Some other rules of thumb in the area of international outsourcing are

- Expect to spend about six calendar months in finding a suitable outsource partner.

- Expect that the one-time costs of moving software to the outsource vendor and getting their staff up to speed will cost about 20 percent of your current average annual budget for software development.

- Do not expect annual cost savings of more than 10 percent per year compared to your current levels for new development. You may occasionally get savings of more than 10 percent, but that is comparatively rare.

- Do not expect annual maintenance cost savings of more than about 20 percent per year compared to your current levels for defect repairs, routine maintenance, and small enhancements.

- Do not expect annual cost savings of more than about 25 percent for activities that need a lot of human interactions, such as call-center support or responding to user requests for dealing with problems.

- Insist on high quality levels, proof of satisfactory defect-removal efficiency, and speed of defect repairs. It would be prudent to ask for 95 percent defect-removal efficiency levels, with the calculations being based on bugs reported within 90 days of deployment. Ask that defect repair intervals not exceed five calendar days for high-severity defects or ten calendar days for defects of medium-severity levels.

As a final note of caution, the author has worked as an expert witness in 15 breach of contract lawsuits between outsource vendors and their clients. On average outsource vendors have better development methods than their clients, but not every outsourced project will be done using state of the art methods. Clients do need to exercise care in developing the contract and they need to maintain a vigilant oversight over important projects.

Successful outsource development projects usually have defect potentials of less than 5.0 per function point coupled with defect-removal efficiency levels of about 94 percent. However, outsource projects that end up in court for breach of contract have averaged more than 6.0 defects per function point coupled with defect-removal efficiency levels that are about 80 percent, for the projects that were actually deployed. The outsource projects that were cancelled before completion did not have sufficient data to determine final defect-removal efficiency levels, although they did run around 6.0 defects per function point.

For major projects of 10,000 function points the differences between successful projects and those in litigation are both interesting and alarming. The successful projects remove about 47,000 out of a potential defect total of 50,000. The projects heading to court only remove about 48,000 out of 60,000 potential defects. The successful projects are deployed with about 3,000 latent defects, while the disasters are deployed with about 12,000 latent defects. Error-prone modules were also very troublesome with the disasters.

High-severity defects in the successful projects total about 250, while high-severity defects in the litigation projects often top 2000. From these kinds of results, it is obvious why quality and defect-removal efficiency should be part of outsource contracts.

For some reason, litigation involving outsourced development work is more likely to end up in litigation than outsourced maintenance work. Of the cases where the author has worked, only one lawsuit has involved maintenance problems, while 14 involved development problems.

Object-Oriented (OO) Development

Object-oriented programming languages such as Smalltalk, C++, Objective-C, and Java have been in use for more than 30 years with good success. Object-oriented design methods originated in the early 1990s, but finally reached common ground in 1996 with the publication of the unified modeling language (UML) in 1996 by Grady Booch, Ivar Jacobsen, and James Rumbaugh. (They are known collectively as "the three amigos" after a film comedy of the same name.) The UML and object-oriented design approaches are powerful but baroque. Empirical data supporting their effectiveness remains somewhat sparse.

The object-oriented domain has created a sort of parallel universe to conventional software development. This universe tends to have its own nomenclature, conferences, programming languages, design approaches, development methods, and even its own special kinds of metrics and measurements.

The last point, object-oriented metrics, has been unfortunate for economic analysis. Some of the topics in experimental OO metrics include methods per class, coupling between objects, degree of cohesion of objects, and a number of others that are relevant to the OO domain.

Most of the OO metrics only work in an OO context and cannot be used for side-by-side economic comparisons of OO projects and conventional projects. However, the OO metrics have led to some experimental cost and schedule estimating methods for OO projects. For side-by-side comparisons between OO projects and conventional projects, the OO metrics are not effective. Fortunately, function point metrics can be used for side-by-side analysis.

Several researchers have developed experimental "object point" metrics for OO projects. These experimental object points attempt to apply the principles of function point metrics to OO applications. However, as the second edition of this book is being written, there is not enough experience with the object point metrics to judge their accuracy or impact on either sizing or cost estimating. As a general rule, variations to standard function point metrics have not been successful in attracting widespread usage or in developing useful benchmarks and estimating algorithms.

Object-oriented software applications have ranged in size from small projects of less than 100 function points up to really large systems in excess of 25,000 function points in size. Unlike some of the Agile approaches that tend to specialize at the small end of the size spectrum, the OO methods do seem to scale up to the large end.

A major claim by the OO approach is that reusability is both possible and indeed featured at both the design and code levels. At the code level, this claim of reuse has been verified, but at the design level the results are not yet definitive. When all of the dozen key artifacts are examined that might be reused, the OO approach has concentrated on the technical artifacts of code and design. The artifacts associated with quality control and project management are more or less outside the current range of the OO methods:

Reusable artifact	Support by OO methodology
Reusable source code	Supported and common
Reusable architecture	Supported and common
Reusable screens	Supported and common
Reusable human interfaces	Supported and common
Reusable requirements	Supported partially
Reusable designs	Supported partially
Reusable test cases	Supported partially
Reusable data	Supported partially
Reusable cost estimates	Support lacking
Reusable project plans	Support lacking
Reusable test plans	Support lacking
Reusable user documents	Support lacking

Because OO projects vary widely in size, and also encompass information systems, embedded applications, military projects and many other types, the rules of thumb shown here will need to be adjusted to match the specific kind of project being considered.

- The average size of an OO application is about 2500 function points or roughly 125,000 Java statements.

- If the UML is used for design of an average OO application of 2500 function points, expect about 0.5 pages per function point or 1250 pages in all.

- Design errors using UML will typically run to about 0.25 per function point, or about 625 errors in an average project of 2500 function points. Design inspections are a useful adjunct to the UML approach.

- Each use case will represent an average of about 35 function points. The overall range seems to be from a low of 15 to a high of 75 function points per use case.

- Historical data indicates somewhat shorter than average schedules under OO methods. Raising the size of the application in function points to about the 0.35 power will yield an approximate schedule in calendar months from inception to delivery. Thus raising a typical OO project of 2500 function points in size to the 0.35 power yields a result of about 15.5 calendar months from inception to deployment.

- A typical OO assignment scope is about 200 function points or 10,000 Java statements. This is the amount of work that is typically assigned to one person.

- An average OO production rate is about 18 function points or 900 Java statements per staff month.

- The overall defect potentials of OO projects would probably be about 4.5 per function point. The defect potential for an average OO project of 2500 function points in size will be about 11,250 defects from all sources: requirements, design, code, documents, and bad fixes.

- Typical defect removal efficiency levels for OO projects are about 92 percent. About 10,350 out of 11,250 defects will be found before deployment.

- The bad-fix injection rate for OO projects is about 4 percent. An average OO project of 2500 function points in size will have about 400 defects accidentally injected while fixing prior defects.

- A typical number of delivered defects for an OO project of 2500 function points in size will be about 1200, or 0.4 per function point. Of these less than 25 will be high-severity defects. About 150 will be medium-severity defects. About 1025 will be low-severity defects.

- Once deployed, an average OO project can be maintained by a single maintenance programmer. A typical maintenance assignment scope for OO projects will be about 2500 function points.

The object-oriented methods are firmly established and continue to grow in terms of numbers of projects and practitioners. OO productivity rates and quality levels compare favorably to more traditional levels. However, there remains a shortage of fully measured OO projects where effort, costs, schedules, and quality levels have been measured accurately. For some additional insights into OO project management, see *Object Lessons* by Dr. Tom Love (SIGS Books Inc, 1993) and

Object Solutions: Managing the Object-Oriented Project by Grady Booth (Pearson Education, 1995). *Software Engineering – A Practitioner's Approach* by Roger Pressman (McGraw-Hill, 2005) discusses both OO management and management of some of the Agile methods as well.

The margin of error for the OO rules of thumb reported here is high, but without publication of preliminary results there would be no incentive to develop more accurate results.

Capability Maturity Model (CMM)

The history of the capability maturity model (CMM) can be traced to the year 1984, when the famous Software Engineering Institute (SEI) was first incorporated. The primary originator of the CMM approach is Watts Humphrey, and several extensions were later added by Dr. Bill Curtis during his tenure at the SEI. The early versions of the CMM began to achieve popularity by about 1993.

Due to the success of the original CMM the SEI began to broaden its horizon to include entire systems and not just software. To that end, the expanded Capability Maturity Model Integration (CMMI) was published in 1996. Utilization of the CMMI has been slower than the CMM due in part to the increased complexity of the CMMI concepts.

Other topics that have been melded with the CMM and CMMI include Watts Humphrey's personal software process (PMP) and team software process (TMP).

Because the original CMM is almost 20 years old and has been utilized by hundreds of companies and thousands of software projects, there is fairly good empirical data available. Indeed, there have been several studies commissioned by the Air Force and other groups that have explored the value of the CMM.

The newer CMMI has less than ten years of practical usage, and hence somewhat less available data.

One of the early, major, and continuing activities of the SEI was the development of a formal evaluation or assessment schema for evaluating the capabilities of defense contractors. Indeed, Watts Humphrey's book on this topic, *Managing the Software Process* (Addison-Wesley, 1989) became a best-seller.

The SEI assessment data is collected by means of on-site interviews using both a standard questionnaire and also observations and informal data. Once collected, the assessment data is analyzed, and used to place a software organization on one of the five plateaus of the well-known SEI capability maturity model, or CMM as it is now widely called. Although the assessment and maturity level concepts can be considered separately, most people regard the two as being a linked set.

Formal SEI software assessments are performed by the SEI and by a dozen or so licensed consulting organizations. There are also less formal "SEI-style" assessments that companies can perform on their own, or that are done by consultants that are not licensed by the SEI but who use assessment approaches derived from the published SEI materials.

Because of the importance of very large systems to the Department of Defense, the SEI assessment approach originally dealt primarily with the software processes and methodologies used by very large companies that produced very large systems. The original SEI assessment approach was derived from the best practices used by leading corporations such as IBM and ITT, which employ from 5000 to more than 25,000 software professionals, and which could safely build systems in excess of 1,000,000 lines of code or 10,000 function points.

The SEI assessment data is collected in part using a questionnaire that contains about 150 binary questions, such as:

"Does the software quality assurance function have a management reporting channel separate from the software development project management (Yes or No)?"

Based on the patterns of answers to the SEI assessment questions, the final result of the SEI assessment process is to place the software organization on one of the levels of a five-point maturity scale. The five plateaus on the SEI maturity level are

SEI maturity level	Meaning	Frequency of occurrence
1 = Initial	Chaotic	75.0 percent
2 = Repeatable	Marginal	15.0 percent
3 = Defined	Adequate	8.0 percent
4 = Managed	Good to excellent	1.5 percent
5 = Optimizing	State of the art	0.5 percent

It is immediately obvious that the distribution of software organizations is severely skewed toward the low end of the scale. A similar kind of skew would occur if you were to look at the distribution of candidates selected to enter the Olympics for events such as down-hill skiing. Most ordinary citizens could not qualify at all. Very few athletes could make it to the Olympic tryouts, even fewer would represent their countries, and only three athletes from around the world would win medals in each event.

The SEI assertions about quality and productivity were initially made without any kind of study or empirical evidence being collected. In fact, the SEI assessment approach itself still does not include the collection of quantitative benchmark information on either productivity rates or quality levels. This was a serious flaw in the SEI assessment procedure. However, after more than 20 years of SEI assessments, enough quantitative data has been collected to show the average results or performance ranges of the five SEI maturity levels.

Eventually, the Air Force commissioned several studies to explore this fundamental question. As data began to be collected, it became evident that there was quite a bit of overlap among the various SEI maturity levels. For example, in terms of both quality and productivity, the best software projects from level 1 organizations were occasionally superior to the worst developed by level 3 organizations.

The reason was that some smaller companies cannot afford some of the infrastructure and special departments assumed by the SEI CMM concept. Some small companies with capable personnel could achieve rather good results even at level 1. Conversely, achieving levels 3, 4, and 5 on the SEI CMM scale do not guarantee that all software projects will be successful, although it does raise the statistical probabilities for success.

There is now evidence from studies such as the ones carried out by Quantitative Software Methods (QSM) in 1993 and Software Productivity Research (SPR) in 1994 that indicates that when organizations do move from CMM level 1 up to level 3, their productivity and quality levels tend to improve. Although this is encouraging for the SEI CMM concept, these studies have been rather small with only a few companies and projects examined.

More recently, the SEI has been attempting to broaden the set of factors included under the assessment and CMM umbrella. Indeed, SEI factors dealing with personnel skills and human relations has been published. It is a positive sign that the SEI now recognizes the gaps and missing components of the original CMM approach, and is attempting to eliminate them.

Because the original CMM has been in use twice as long as the newer CMMI, more information is available for the CMM than for the CMMI. The following rules of thumb are derived from the CMM, but similar results can be expected from the CMMI.

Although the average size of projects that are developed by organizations that use the CMM approach is only about 2000 function points, the major benefits from using the CMM and CMMI occur on really large applications in the 10,000–function point range. Therefore, the rules of thumb shown here are all based on applications of 10,000 function points in size.

There is another difference in these rules of thumb also. The prior rules showed some data in terms of Java, which has an approximate value of 50 source code statements per function point. Because Java is not yet common in the defense and large-system world where the CMM approach is used, these rules of thumb are based on the C programming language. The C language has an approximate value of 125 source code statements per function point.

Because the results vary widely among the five levels of the CMM, all of the following rules of thumb show the variations among all five levels.

The first set of rules of thumb show the per capita expenses and the time in calendar months to move from CMM level 1 to CMM level 5:

Cost per capita and schedule to reach CMM 5		
CMM level	Cost per capita	Calendar months
CMM 1	$0	0
CMM 2	$3,500	18
CMM 3	$3,000	18
CMM 4	$3,500	12
CMM 5	$2,000	12
TOTAL	$12,000	60

The second set of rules of thumb illustrates the odds that a software project of 10,000 function points in size (roughly 1,250,000 C statements) will be delayed by at least one year compared to its original plan, or terminated without ever being completed.

Schedule delays and project cancellation by CMM level		
CMM level	12-Month delays	Termination
CMM 1	35%	40%
CMM 2	30%	30%
CMM 3	20%	12%
CMM 4	10%	4%
CMM 5	5%	2%

The major reason for canceling a large software project is because it has exceeded its planned schedule and budget by so many months that the return on investment has switched from positive to negative.

The next set of rules of thumb shows the approximate schedules in calendar months from the start of the project to delivery. The column labeled "Exponent" is the power that might be used to derive a schedule. Raising the project size of 10,000 function points to each power will yield the approximate monthly schedule.

Schedule months from start to delivery by CMM level		
CMM level	Exponent	Calendar months
CMM 1	0.45	63
CMM 2	0.44	58
CMM 3	0.43	52
CMM 4	0.42	48
CMM 5	0.41	44

The main reason that schedules slip is because of poor quality. Large software applications are notoriously error-prone. The next set of rules of thumb show defect potentials and removal efficiency levels. The defect potential is the sum of possible defects in requirements, design, code, documents, and "bad fixes." The removal efficiency is the percent of defects eliminated before delivery of the application after all formal inspections and test stages have been completed.

Defect potentials and removal efficiency by CMM level			
CMM level	Defect potential per function point	Removal efficiency	Delivered defects per function point
CMM 1	6.00	85.00%	0.90
CMM 2	4.50	89.00%	0.50
CMM 3	4.00	93.00%	0.28
CMM 4	3.00	95.00%	0.15
CMM 5	2.50	97.00%	0.08

The final set of rules of thumb shows approximate monthly productivity rates by CMM levels. The results are expressed in terms of both "function points per staff month" and also "lines of code per staff month." The LOC data assumes the C programming language in these rules of thumb.

Monthly productivity rates by CMM level		
CMM level	Function points per staff month	Lines of code per staff month
CMM 1	3.00	375
CMM 2	3.50	438
CMM 3	5.00	625
CMM 4	7.50	938
CMM 5	9.00	1125

Once software applications are deployed, they need to be maintained because latent defects will be reported and minor changes will occur. Major updates are called *enhancements* and are dealt with as new development projects. A key metric for routine maintenance tasks is that of the *assignment scope,* or the quantity of code or function points that one maintenance programmer can support in the course of a typical calendar year.

Because of the high volume of latent defects in applications developed at levels 1 and 2 of the CMM, the maintenance assignment scopes are rather small. Ease of maintenance demands excellence in pre-deployment quality control, such as is found with levels 3, 4, and 5 of the CMM.

	Maintenance assignment scopes after deployment	
CMM level	Assignment scope function points	Assignment scope lines of code
CMM 1	500	62,500
CMM 2	750	93,750
CMM 3	1500	187,500
CMM 4	2000	250,000
CMM 5	2500	312,500

Because the CMM results seem to be so good, it might be asked why they have not been universally adapted. The CMM results are beneficial primarily for really large systems in the 10,000–function point range or systems larger than 1,000,000 source code statements in size. For smaller projects below 1000 function points in size, the costs and overhead of the CMM methodology are so expensive that the benefits are very low and may even turn negative.

Software Methods with Only Partial Rules of Thumb

A number of interesting methods lack sufficient data to derive useful rules of thumb. That doesn't mean that the methods are bad; it only means that more research is needed. Following are some software development approaches that need additional research and more empirical data.

Cleanroom Development

The word *cleanroom* was derived from the facilities used to manufacture computer chips, where the air is filtered to prevent contamination. In a software context, the cleanroom approach refers to some unique development practices created by the late Dr. Harlan Mills of IBM's Research Division.

Under the cleanroom method, mathematical proofs of correctness are used as defect prevention and removal methods. The proofs must be complete before the code is tested.

Unfortunately, in spite of the emphasis on quality that is part of the cleanroom method, there is insufficient data to know either the defect potentials or defect-removal efficiency of cleanroom projects.

It is obvious from cleanroom characteristics that the method would only work on small programs with finite and unchanging requirements. Adding new features in mid-development would obviously require new correctness proofs as well. To date the cleanroom approach has been used experimentally, but has not yet found its way into the mainstream of software development. Also, how maintenance and enhancements would be performed using the cleanroom approach is not fully defined.

Crystal Development Approach

The term *crystal* is taken from a monograph entitled "Crystal Clear" by Alastair Cockburn, which was later expanded and published as a book (Addison-Wesley, 1994). The term was also adopted by Jim Highsmith in his books and articles.

The crystal methodology is an amalgamation of some of the principles of Agile development. Crystal has been characterized as being more flexible than extreme programming, but lighter and more agile than conventional methods. The stated targets of the crystal approach are small teams who are building small to medium applications. Thus, crystal should apply to software applications between about 100 and 1500 function points in size.

Although Crystal is beginning to grow in popularity, there is insufficient data to provide useful rules of thumb for schedules, costs, defect potentials, or defect-removal efficiency. It can be stated that crystal team sizes are typically five or less, and that crystal schedules are usually less than six months duration.

Feature-Driven Development (FDD)

Feature-driven development is another of the emerging set of Agile development methods. It attempts to meld together a number of best practices from both the Agile and conventional development methods.

This approach originated for a fairly large software project in Singapore. It is an amalgamation of both object-oriented (OO) principles and the Agile concepts. Its salient feature is that the entire set of functions for large systems are defined as sets of specific features, which will then be implemented using iterative approaches.

The FDD method does utilize design and code inspections, so quality control is a priority of the approach. The utilization of formal inspections indicates that defect-removal efficiency levels should be at or above 95 percent. The use of decomposition into specific small features indicates that defect potentials should be at or below about 4.5 per function point. However, these are theoretical statements, and not actual rules of thumb. FDD seems promising and hopefully additional data will soon be available.

ISO 9000-9004 Quality Standards

The International Organization for Standardization (ISO) has, over the years, published a wide variety of standards, and a substantial set of standards dealing with quality issues. The most relevant standard for software projects is ISO 9000-3. However, all of the ISO standards ranging from 9000 through 9004 have aspects that may apply to software projects. Some of these standards concern creating quality plans, some with performing quality audits, and in the case of ISO 9000-3 actually measuring software quality.

Because ISO certification may be necessary in order to sell products to certain European governmental clients and to some corporations, quite a few companies have adopted the ISO standards and gone through the certification process.

Unfortunately, in a software context, there is insufficient data available to judge either the defect potentials or the defect-removal efficiency levels of companies and projects that are certified under any of the ISO 9000-9004 standards. To date there is insufficient data to determine whether software projects in companies using ISO 9000-9004 standards have defect potentials lower than U.S. norms (about 5.0 per function point), or defect-removal efficiency levels higher than U.S. norms (about 85 percent).

The one ISO topic where data is available is in the peripheral area of the volume of documentation required. The set of measurements and reports associated with ISO 9000-9004 standards total to about 0.6 pages per function point. This may not sound like much, but for a 1500–function point project, that approximates 900 pages of plans and reports.

It is obvious that the various ISO standards are not part of the set of Agile approaches, because the paperwork volumes are so extensive.

Iterative or Incremental Development

The basic concepts of iterative development are actually older than the computer era—they originated in the 1930s for manufacturing of complex hardware devices such as aircraft and weapons systems. In fact, a case can be made that iterative development may be one of the oldest concepts in the history of human construction. There is evidence that the construction of Stonehenge used a form of iterative development more than 3000 years ago.

The basic concepts of iterative development seem to be fundamentally valid. When you are building a really large and complex structure, it is almost impossible to design every feature that will eventually be needed. It is better to start by building a smaller working version and begin to use it. Then the experiences of users can guide the designers in the planning and construction of additional features.

Applied to software, if the overall size of a hypothetical application ends up at 10,000 function points, the first working version might be only 2500 function points in size. Then additional features will be added in the form of three additional increments, each of which is 2500 function points in size.

The advantages of the iterative method are twofold. First, the time and costs of building the initial increment will be only a small fraction of those required to build the entire application. Second, the day-to-day experiences of the users with each increment will provide valuable ideas to the designers, so that succeeding increments are more user friendly and have a better fit to the true requirements of the application than trying to guess them before construction starts.

From an estimating standpoint iterative development is an interesting problem. Many standard software-estimating methods can be used to predict the schedules and costs of each individual increment. That is not a problem. But how long will each increment be used in order to gain enough solid information to build the next increment in the series?

Also, if the software application is to be developed under a fixed-price contract or there is a maximum budget for the entire system, how can these costs be determined before even the first increment has been designed and developed?

One way of dealing with these issues is to adopt a hybrid approach. At the start of the project there will be a serious attempt to predict the size and features of the overall application. Then, the full set of features will be subdivided into a series of useful increments that can be built individually. The goal is to start construction with a nucleus of really key features in the first increment, and then add the less obvious features further along.

The fundamental concepts of iterative development were part of the evolutionary chain that led to the Agile methods. The ambiguity of building software that might contain a random number of iterations built to random schedules also led to the concept of time boxes or attempting to define features that could be constructed in specific intervals, which range from a low of two weeks to a maximum of six months. Once a specific time box has been selected, then estimating its completion is straightforward. But predicting the total number of time boxes and selecting their optimum duration needs some knowledge of the overall scope and size of the entire application. For example two-week time boxes are too small for applications in the 10,000–function point size range, but a six-month time box is too big for an application in the 1000–function point size range.

Because of the high variability of the iterative method, no single set of algorithms or rules of thumb will apply universally. However, a few provisional rules of thumb can be stated:

- For applications larger than 10,000 function points in size, each increment should contain about 25 percent of the total functionality. Plan for four iterations, with about one calendar month of usage between the first five iterations over about a 40-month period.

- For applications smaller than 2500 function points in size, each increment should contain about 20 percent of the total functionality. Plan for five iterations with about two weeks of usage between the first three iterations over about a 22-month period.

- Because of the gaps between iterations, schedules for iterative projects can be approximately derived by raising the overall size in function points to the 0.40 power.

- Due to the nature of iterative design, defect potentials are somewhat lower than average and run about 4.5 defects per function point.

- Defect-removal efficiency levels for iterative projects hover at about an average level of 85 percent cumulatively.

- The failure rate or cancellation of projects due to excessive schedule delays, cost overruns, or defect levels seems to be lower for iterative projects than for waterfall projects. This seems to be due to the fact that users become dependent upon the early increments, rather than to the intrinsic merits of the iterative approach itself.

Iterative development is a useful method for building software applications in a real-world environment of ambiguous and rapidly changing requirements. But iterative development is far from being a panacea. Estimating iterative projects has aspects that are both easy and hard. It is easy to estimate any specific increment, but predicting the overall results for the full set of increments is challenging.

Pattern-Based Software Development

The concepts of pattern-based development originated in the 1980s by practitioners of the Smalltalk object-oriented language. *Design Patterns: Elements of Reusable Object Oriented Software* by Erich Gamma (Addison-Wesley, 1995) identified 23 common patterns that occurred in many software applications. By encapsulating these patterns in standard design representations, they could be reused in many software applications. For that matter, some of the code that embodies the patterns could be reused as well.

Since the idea surfaced that many software applications shared common functions that could be defined as patterns and then made reusable, the concept of pattern-based development has been expanding from design and code to include some additional deliverables. In fact, as of 2006 pattern-based development is probably achieving the widest range of reusability of any current methodology.

Reusable artifact	Support by pattern methodology
Reusable source code	Supported and common
Reusable designs	Supported and common
Reusable screens	Supported and common
Reusable human interfaces	Supported and common
Reusable requirements	Supported and increasing
Reusable architecture	Supported and increasing
Reusable project plans	Supported and increasing
Reusable test plans	Supported and increasing
Reusable user documents	Supported and increasing
Reusable test cases	Supported partially
Reusable data	Supported partially
Reusable cost estimates	Support lacking

A quick review of the history of software reuse indicates that programmers spontaneously reused about 15 percent of code from application to application. Later when the object-oriented methods appeared, the volume of reusable code jumped up to perhaps 50 percent, and about 35 percent of design documents were added to the set of reusable materials.

With pattern-based development, we are approaching the range of more than 60 percent reusable design materials and more than 60 percent reusable code as well. There is an unanswered question as to whether or not reuse of design and code can eventually top 90 percent.

The pattern-based methodology is beginning to bring reusable requirements into the equation, and with reusable requirements and designs available, then reusable test libraries are possible too. Reusable sections from user manuals are also possible.

Unfortunately, pattern-based development is still in rapid evolution. Also, very few projects that have utilized design and code patterns have been measured in order to collect data on quality, costs, schedules, or other quantifiable aspects of development. Thus, only a very few and very preliminary rules of thumb can be discussed for pattern-based development:

- The average size of a pattern-based OO application is about 2000 function points or roughly 100,000 Java statements.

- About 75 percent of the design features used in pattern-based applications will be derived from standard patterns. About 15 different patterns will show up in a pattern-based application. Reuse in the pattern-based applications is higher than average.

- About 60 percent of the code used in pattern-based applications will be reused from class libraries or from available sources.

- Preliminary data indicates very short average schedules for pattern-based applications, due in part to reuse and borrowing. Raising the size of the application in function points to about the 0.3 power will yield an approximate schedule in calendar months from inception to delivery. Thus, raising the size of a typical pattern-based project of 2000 function points to the 0.3 power yields a result of about ten calendar months from inception to deployment.

- A typical pattern-based assignment scope is about 300 function points or 30,000 Java statements due to extensive reuse. This is the amount of work that is typically assigned to one person.

- On average pattern-based production rates are about 34 function points or 1700 Java statements per staff month (assuming that reusable code exists).

- The overall defect potentials of pattern-based projects are typically about 3.0 per function point. The defect potential for a typical pattern-based project of 2000 function points in size will be about 6000 defects from all sources: requirements, design, code, documents, and bad fixes. This is much lower than average, due to the fact that defects in most of the patterns themselves have previously been eliminated.

- Pre-delivery defect removal for pattern-based applications would be about 90 percent. Thus, about 5400 out of 6000 defects would be found for a 2000–function point pattern-based application. (Unfortunately, there is not enough data to know the bad-fix injection rate.)

- The number of defects at delivery of a 2000–function point pattern-based application would be about 0.3 per function point, or 600 in all. Of these about six would be high-severity defects, 40 would be medium-severity defects, and 554 would be low-severity defects.

- Once deployed, a typical pattern-based project can be maintained by one maintenance programmer for defect repairs and minor updates. A typical maintenance assignment scope for pattern-based projects will be about 2000 function points.

The pattern-based approach is technically interesting and is likely to expand in usage. This statement assumes that the pattern concept is extended to all major deliverables, and that the patterns are widely understood.

The total quantity of patterns required to build any arbitrary software project is currently unknown. However, it can be hypothesized that about 50 design patterns and perhaps 60 requirements patterns could probably replicate the features of any existing software application.

Quality Function Deployment (QFD)

Quality Function Deployment (QFD) originated in Japan in a manufacturing environment. Its salient features are attempting to capture customer quality needs in an explicit fashion, and then responding to each of those needs also in an explicit fashion. Other data, such as competitive responses, may also be included.

QFD is not a full life cycle approach, but rather is a particularly comprehensive approach to identifying customer requirements as they pertain to quality. Thus QFD is often an adjunct to the six-sigma approach.

One of the interesting artifacts of the QFD approach is a matrix that shows customer needs on one axis and development solutions to those needs on the other. Because the top of this matrix has a peak that connects the two views, the QFD method is sometimes nicknamed "the house of quality." At a distance, a QFD diagram does somewhat resemble the front view of a normal small house with a peaked roof.

The usage of QFD for software projects in the United States is not yet sufficient to create useful rules of thumb. Some very preliminary observations derived from discussions with clients who did utilize QFD for software are the following:

- The QFD diagrams themselves average about 0.1 pages of diagrams per function points.

- Efforts to collect the quality data from customers and construct QFD diagrams proceed at an approximate rate of 500 function points per staff month.

- Applications that use the QFD diagrams typically have defect potentials below 4.0 per function point. Apparently the QFD diagrams do eliminate many requirement issues and a few design issues as well. Coding defect levels are not visibly affected.

- Defect-removal efficiency levels for the projects that utilize QFD diagrams seems to be about 90 percent, or perhaps 5 percent better than U.S. averages. The reason for this is not that QFD actually raises testing and inspection efficiency levels, but rather that QFD eliminates a significant volume of requirement and design defects where efficiency levels are usually lower than for coding defects.

The primary users of the QFD approach in the United States have been a few large and quite sophisticated manufacturing organizations. These used QFD for their manufactured products, and the approach migrated to their software community.

Rapid Application Development (RAD)

The set of methods entitled Rapid Application Development, or RAD, emerged in the 1970s and 1980s as one of the first alternatives to the traditional waterfall software development approach.

Because the traditional waterfall method started with a lengthy requirements gathering and analysis process followed by an even more lengthy design and specification process, the RAD approach tried to cut down these time intervals by substituting prototypes and working code for written requirements and specifications. Thus RAD was a member of the iterative development set of methodologies, and one of the precursors to the newer Agile development methodologies.

While the concepts of prototypes work rather well for some kinds of software, they are not a perfect fit for others. For fairly small projects below 1000 function points in size, where the users or clients are available every day for discussions and experimenting with the prototype, RAD tended to be successful. But for large and complex applications above 10,000 function points in size, or for those that had many different kinds of users and offered many different kinds of functionality, RAD was not successful.

There is not enough available data on RAD for a full set of rules of thumb or for predictive algorithms, but the following provisional information may be useful.

- For applications below 1000 function points in size, RAD schedules can be approximated by raising the size of the application in function points to the 0.38 power. Thus, for an application of 1000 function points, the schedule would be about 13 calendar months from inception to delivery.

- For applications above 5000 function points in size, RAD schedules can be approximated by raising the size of the application in function points to the 0.4 power. Thus, for an application of 5000 function points, the schedule would be about 30 calendar months.

- Defect potentials with RAD approximate U.S norms of about 5.0 per function point from all sources of defects.

- Defect-removal efficiency levels with RAD approximate U.S. norms of about 85 percent. Thus, delivered defects with RAD also approximate U.S. norms of about 0.75 per function point.

The RAD approach was applied to several hundred projects in the 1980s and early 1990s, but in recent years RAD has been supplanted by some of the newer Agile methods.

Scrum

The word "scrum" requires an explanation. It is not an acronym or an abbreviation. It is taken from soccer, and refers to a kind of mass collision of players that sometimes takes place in the middle of the field.

When the Scum concept is applied to software, it defines one of the Agile methods. Some of the salient features of Scrum lie in its terminology. For example, the Scrum method utilizes one-month time boxes that are called "sprints." Features awaiting development are in a backlog queue. Each backlogged item should have a cost and schedule estimate for production.

The Scrum approach also features daily team meetings that are somewhat like abbreviated inspections in that problems and issues are surfaced and examined.

Another interesting approach is the role of the "scrummaster." Ordinarily, Scrum teams are fairly democratic and self-organizing. The role of the scrummaster is to serve more or less as an interface between the team and the outside world and to deal with any problems or issues that might affect the project.

Scrum is somewhat eclectic and has welcomed some of the concepts of extreme programming and object-oriented programming.

While the majority of Scrum projects have been less than 2000 function points in size and developed by teams that total less than ten people, it has been asserted that the Scrum approach could be scaled up to any arbitrary size.

However, since customer requirements are gathered by having one or more customers as part of the Scrum team, it is obvious that applications that might be used by thousands of people in hundreds of ways might not be amenable to the Scrum approach. For example, it would not be the preferred method for a new release of Microsoft Windows, for the next SAP release, or a missile defense system.

Because measurement and collection of historical data is not a special focus of the Scrum approach, there is not enough current information to create a complete set of rules of thumb. From partial information, some preliminary rules of thumb are

- Scrum schedules can be approximated by raising the size of the application in function points to the 0.36 power. Thus, for an application of 2000 function points the approximate schedule from inception to deployment would be about 15 calendar months.

- The volume of paperwork in the form of pages of requirements and specifications are greatly reduced. Paperwork volumes are only about 50 percent of normal waterfall projects. A typical information technology project creates about 0.55 pages per function point for requirements, and another 0.55 pages per function point for design. Scrum projects are down to or below 0.25 pages per function point for each.

- Defect potentials with Scrum seem to be better than average and run to about 4.0 per function point. Requirements and design errors are reduced by larger volumes than coding errors. Thus the defect potential for a Scrum application of 2000 function points in size would be about 8000 defects.

- Defect-removal efficiency levels with Scrum seem to be better than average, and may top 92 percent due to the daily meetings and frequent informal inspections that are integral parts of the Scrum approach. Finding and fixing 92 percent of 8000 defects would indicate that 7360 defects would be found, leaving 640 defects still present at delivery. Of these about ten would be high-severity defects, 60 would be medium-severity defects, and 570 would be low-severity defects.

- There is insufficient data to judge the bad-fix injection rate of Scrum projects. However, other Agile methods seem to range from 2 percent to about 5 percent bad-fix injections.

- There is not a lot of history about maintenance of Scrum projects after deployment, but from the few examples that do exist it appears that maintenance assignment scopes are in the range of 1000 function points or 50,000 Java statements.

The Scrum approach seems to be expanding in terms of usage as this second edition is being written. In part this is due to the merits of the approach itself, and in part it is due to the increasing numbers of books and training materials.

In 2005 Microsoft announced that it was starting to use Agile methods, extreme programming, and the Scrum approach on various projects. Microsoft has not always been at the forefront of adopting innovative approaches internally, so their endorsement of Scrum, XP, and the Agile approach is interesting.

Six-sigma for Software

The term "six-sigma" is a statistical phrase that refers to the number of defects per million chances of making a defect. A six-sigma defect rate would be no more than 3.4 defects per million opportunities. The concept originated in Motorola in the mid 1980s and was originally applied to manufacturing operations.

For a 10,000–function point project in the C programming language, the total quantity of code would be about 1,250,000 source code statements. The average defect potential for such a system would be about 6.0 defects per function point or 60,000 defects in all. (The number of pure coding defects would be about 1.75 per function point or 17,500 in all.) Average defect-removal efficiency for such a system would be about 83 percent, so the number of latent defects at delivery would be about 10,200. By contrast, achieving a six-sigma quality level for such a large application would mean no more than about four defects in total. In fact, no software project to date has ever actually achieved a six-sigma quality level.

Another way of looking at six-sigma in a software context would be to achieve a defect-removal efficiency level of about 99.9999 percent. Since the average defect-removal efficiency level in the United States is only about 85 percent, and less than one project in 1000 has even topped 98 percent, it can be seen that actual six-sigma results are beyond the current state of the art.

Although achieving actual six-sigma quality levels is beyond the current state of the art for software, the kinds of defect measurements and statistical analysis of software projects that is part of the six-sigma methodology is actually quite useful and has been successful. The six-sigma approach has also been melded with the Software Engineering Institute's capability maturity model, with fairly good success.

When software projects are measured in companies that utilize the six-sigma approach for their software projects, such as Lockheed Martin and Motorola, the actual results are better than U.S. averages. In general the defect potentials of companies using the six-sigma approach are below the 5.0 defects per function point U.S. average, while defect-removal efficiency levels are at or above 95 percent.

Achieving a 95 percent average on defect-removal efficiency is about 10 percent higher than U.S. norms. These results are even better considering that they are derived from large and complex systems in the 5000–function point size range. Typically such systems would top 6.0 defects per function point and achieve only about an 83 percent defect-removal efficiency level.

It happens that the projects measured in six-sigma organizations also utilized other methods such as formal design and code inspections and formal testing. While the available data on six-sigma for software shows results that are better than average, it is not yet sufficient to demonstrate that it was the six-sigma method itself that was responsible for the good results.

The general principles of the six-sigma approach elevate statistical quality control and quality measurements to high levels of importance. These topics are valuable for the construction of large software projects in the 10,000–function point size range. In fact, the value of the six-sigma concepts appears to be proportional to the size of the applications that organizations build.

That being said, the six-sigma methods would seem to be highly suitable for companies that build really large systems such as operating systems and ERP applications that top 100,000 function points or 10,000,000 source code statements in size. Thus, organizations such as IBM, Microsoft, Oracle, SAP, and government groups such as the Department of Defense, National Security Agency, or the Veterans Administration are likely candidates for six-sigma methods.

Spiral Software Development

The "spiral" form of software development was created by the famous software engineering researcher Dr. Barry Boehm. Dr. Boehm is also a pioneer in software cost estimating, and the creator of the well-known COCOMO and COCOMO II cost-estimating tools. The spiral method was first discussed in the 1980s and began to attract users, primarily in the large-systems domain.

In 2006 the Department of Defense formally endorsed the spiral method, and in fact has specified that the spiral approach be utilized on some new and large software projects that are out to bid. This endorsement by the Department of Defense is going to have a major influence on the defense contracting community.

Spiral development is a form of iterative development, but it includes some noteworthy special features. As with the other forms of iterative development, the overall set of features for a large application are divided into subsets, each of which will be developed separately. For a 10,000–function point application, there would probably be four subsets, each of 2500 function points in size. For each subset or iteration, a spiral software project includes four large phases:

- Planning
- Risk analysis
- Engineering
- Customer evaluation

The most significant difference between the spiral approach and other forms of iterative development is the "risk analysis" phase. This activity is intended to consider every known technical risk that can affect the outcome of the project, and find solutions for as many as possible.

Risk analysis was not usually a formal part of the older waterfall approach, and is missing from some of the Agile and object-oriented methods too. However, it is a valuable adjunct to the development process for large systems in the 10,000–function point size range. These large applications have traditionally had the highest failure rates and the longest schedule delays of almost any kind of engineered product. Therefore, the inclusion of a risk-analysis phase is a step in the right direction. The only caveat about the risk analysis phase is that the skill set needed to perform an effective risk analysis is not very common.

There is not a great deal of available data on the results of using the spiral model, but the few projects that we have data for, seem to have achieved good results. Defect potentials were apparently below U.S. averages of about 5.0 defects per function point, while defect-removal efficiency levels were higher than 90 percent, which is also better than average.

Since the projects that utilized the spiral method were in the large system category in the defense sector, development schedules are not particularly rapid. This is due to the huge volume of paperwork and the extensive oversight requirements that the government burdens the defense community with. Actual design and coding are about as fast as anywhere else, but the overhead of the defense sector is enormous. Therefore, schedules can be approximated by raising the size of the application in function points to about the 0.45 power.

Unified Modeling Language (UML)

Object-oriented programming was developed before object-oriented design. The need for a solid method of representing OO designs was recognized by a number of researchers, including James Rumbaugh, Grady Booch, and Ivar Jacobsen. Each of these did some pioneering work in the area of OO design, and in fact created some interesting design approaches. When they became aware of one another's work, they decided that it would be more effective to consolidate their efforts. Thus, the unified modeling language, or UML, was created.

The UML was first published in 1996, and has been gathering users and experience over more than a ten-year period. The UML is somewhat eclectic and attempted to utilize valuable approaches such as use cases and class-responsibility-collaboration (CRC) cards.

It should be noted that the UML is not static, but in fact is designed to be an extensible language and is evolving. Version 2.0 is the current form and was adopted by the Object Management Group in 2004.

The UML is not a single representation, but uses a variety of visual diagrams and text-based methods in order to show several aspects of software applications. In fact, a total of about 13 different kinds of diagrams are present in the UML. These can be subdivided into three main groups:

- The functional model reflects an application from the point of view of the user, and typically is based on use cases.

- The object model shows the OO aspects of the application and is based on class diagrams.

- The dynamic model shows internal operations of the application, and uses techniques such as action diagrams and state-change descriptions.

Although the UML has many adherents and has probably been used on more than 1000 software projects, not very many of these have been measured well enough to derive rules of thumb or algorithms concerning the UML. Some preliminary observations about the UML include

- The volume of UML documents for an average OO application is between about 0.4 and 0.7 pages per function point. A typical volume would be about 0.5 pages per function point.

- Design errors using UML will typically run to about 0.25 per function point. Expect one error for about every two pages of UML design. Formal design inspections would be a useful adjunct to the UML approach.

- Bad fixes, or new defects accidentally introduced when fixing prior defects, seems to approximate about 5 percent for UML design documents.

- For use cases alone, each use case will represent an average of about 35 function points. The overall range seems to be from a low of 15 to a high of 75 function points per use case.

The International Function Point Users Group (IFPUG) has been developing material on the rules for counting function points from UML specifications. Although function point metrics are not yet common for OO projects, they can be useful for estimating the effort and costs for producing designs and specifications, and also for measuring defect rates in design documents.

It is technically possible to develop an automated tool that would provide counts of function point totals from UML specifications without the cost of manual counts. However, as this book is being written such tools are not commercially available.

A great many people are using the UML, and a great many people are working on refining and extending its capabilities. There is a need for more reliable data on UML volumes, on defects found within UML designs, and on the costs, schedules, and work required to produce designs when using the UML.

Use Cases for Software Requirements

Use cases are a fairly new way of capturing the requirements and user specifications for software applications. Use cases were originally developed in the mid-1980s by Ivar Jacobsen, who later contributed his ideas to the UML. As a result, uses cases are one of the standard diagramming techniques that have become part of the UML. However, use cases are also deployed outside of the UML and have become a fairly popular approach in their own right.

Use cases are intended to describe how various kinds of users (termed "actors") interact with a software application. The actors can be live people, or they can be other software packages.

As with many specification approaches, use cases can have varying levels of detail, ranging from bare sketches to quite detailed descriptions.

Because of the popularity of use cases and their fairly wide deployment, it should be possible to provide solid algorithms and estimating approaches. However, only a few of the projects that have utilized use cases have also captured information on the costs, quality, and results of their usage.

It is interesting that there is a special metric called *use case points* that is somewhat similar in concept to function point metrics. Use case points accumulate the total numbers of actors, relationships, and other aspects of the use case methodology to develop a total value for the project being estimated. Once the size in use case points is determined, then effort and schedule algorithms can be applied.

Because function point counters frequently have to deal with specifications containing use cases, some preliminary data is also available from them. Because the literature on function point metrics is so widespread, most data is expressed using function point metrics rather than use case metrics.

- Each use case will represent an average of about 35 function points. The overall range seems to be from a low of 15 to a high of 75 function points per use case. Thus for a typical application of 1500 function points in size (roughly 75,000 Java statements), expect about 42 use case diagrams. In other words, a single use case defines the usage pattern of about 1785 Java statements.

- The effort required to create use cases proceeds at a rate of about 250 function points per staff month. Thus for a typical application of 1500 function points, expect to spend about six staff months creating use cases. This is equivalent to creating seven use cases per staff month.

- It will probably take about four test cases to handle the testing of a single use case. The range of test cases is from about two to eight test cases per use case. Thus for a typical application of 1500 function points in size with 42 use case diagrams, expect to create about 170 test cases.

- Design errors in use cases typically run to about 0.15 per function point. Expect one error for about every three use case diagrams. Formal design inspections would be a useful adjunct to the use case approach. For a typical application of 1500 function points in size, expect about 225 use case errors.

- Bad fixes, or new defects accidentally introduced when fixing prior defects, seems to approximate about 5 percent for use case design documents. If you make 225 initial use case errors, expect about 11 new errors as accidental byproducts of fixing the initial errors.

There is very little empirical data on the defect-removal efficiency levels associated with either testing use cases or from formal inspections of use cases. However, formal inspections of other kinds of design documents are typically about 65 to 80 percent efficient in finding defects. An initial value of about 75 percent design inspection removal efficiency can be used as a preliminary value until better data is available.

Web-Based Applications

Over the past ten years, web-based applications have exploded in numbers. There are now more than 1,000,000 web-based applications in the United States alone. The annual creation of new web-based applications is in excess of 100,000 per year and rising.

Not only are the numbers of web-based applications rising exponentially, but there is also a rapid evolution in the methods of designing and building web applications. Scores of new web-design and web-construction tools are showing up in the commercial marketplace each year.

Web-based design and construction methodologies run the gamut from formal waterfall-based approaches through the leanest of Agile approaches. Some of the web applications built by major organizations such as the Internal Revenue Service or state governments typically use traditional development methods. But the web applications of small companies often use Agile methods or commercial web tools. There are also hundreds of web outsource companies. In fact almost every town in America has several web service companies that can design and build web sites and web applications for small local companies.

Web-based applications resemble older styles of software applications in many respects, but a number of unique features must be considered in web-based software applications:

- High performance and sub-second response times are mandatory for web applications.

- High security and resistance to hackers are necessary for many web applications.

- Unusual attributes such as sound and video are part of many web applications.

- Users of web applications may number in the millions, each with different needs.

- Web application development schedules are usually less than 12 calendar months.

- Web content (data, graphics) can change in real-time.

- Customer responses can be captured at once.

- Failures and downtime are very serious issues for web applications.
- Errors in web content are troublesome and difficult to solve.

Because of the variability of web-based applications and their development approaches, it is hard to derive rules of thumb that can be applied universally. Also, the great majority of web applications have not devoted much effort or time to gathering historical data or performing process assessments. Thus there is a shortage of historical data, in spite of the large number of web applications built over the past few years. A few preliminary rules of thumb for web applications follow:

- The average size of a web application is about 2000 function points or roughly 100,000 Java statements.
- About 70 percent of the features used in web applications will be borrowed from existing web applications or taken from web construction tools. Reuse in the web domain is higher than almost any other.
- Historical data indicates very short average schedules for web applications, due in part to reuse and borrowing. Raising the size of the application in function points to about the 0.3 power will yield an approximate schedule in calendar months from inception to delivery. Thus raising a typical web project of 2000 function points in size to the 0.3 power yields a result of about ten calendar months from inception to deployment.
- A typical web assignment scope is about 250 function points or 15,000 Java statements due to extensive reuse. This is the amount of work that is typically assigned to one person.
- An average web production rate is about 40 function points or 2000 Java statements per staff month.
- The overall defect potentials of web projects are probably about 3.5 per function point. The defect potential for an average web project of 2000 function points in size will be about 7000 defects from all sources: requirements, design, code, documents, and bad fixes.
- Pre-delivery defect removal for web applications is about 88 percent. Thus about 6160 out of 7000 defects would be found for a 2000–function point web application.
- About 840 defects would be present at deployment. Of these about ten would be high-severity defects, 50 would be medium-severity defects, and 780 would be low-severity defects.
- Because of typical patterns of web usage, about 95 percent of high- and medium-severity latent defects will be discovered in web applications within the first 90 days of usage.

■ Once deployed, an average web project can be maintained by two maintenance programmers. A typical maintenance assignment scope for OO projects will be about 1000 function points. However, for web applications there may be a need for around-the-clock maintenance. There may also be a need for backup maintenance personnel in case the primary maintainers are sick or incapacitated. In addition, the content of the web site is not the responsibility of the software maintenance group. If there are changes, errors, or updates to the data files, images, sounds, or other content features, they are outside the scope of ordinary software maintenance.

Web-based applications are perhaps the most interesting and rapidly changing field of the computer era. Both the technology of constructing web applications and the sophistication of web applications are changing on a daily basis.

Summary and Conclusions

Software engineering and software project management are dynamic and rapidly changing occupations. New methodologies have been evolving at the rate of about two per year for the past ten years. There is no sign that these inventive new methods will slow down, and some signs that they will increase in number.

Software estimating is also dynamic. Estimating tool vendors and all who are concerned with accuracy of estimation must devote time and energy to stay current with evolving technologies.

However, to repeat a caution from earlier in this chapter, it takes about five years from when a new technology is introduced to be able to analyze its results statistically and derive estimating algorithms that can be used to predict future results. It takes at least another year to be able to estimate a new method's impact on maintenance costs. There is an unavoidable lag between the first deployment of a new method, and the ability to estimate that method's impact on productivity, schedules, costs, quality, and maintenance.

References

The Agile Alliance web site (http://www.Agilealliance.org/home).
Ambler, S.: *Process Patterns—Building Large-Scale Systems Using Object Technology*, Cambridge University Press, SIGS Books, 1998.
Artow, J. and I. Neustadt: *UML and the Unified Process*, Addison-Wesley, Boston, Mass., 2000.
Beck, K: *Extreme Programming Explained: Embrace Change*, Addison-Wesley, Boston, Mass., 1999.
Booch, Grady: *Object Solutions: Managing the Object-Oriented Project*, Addison-Wesley, Reading, Mass., 1995.

————, Ivar Jacobsen, and James Rumbaugh: *The Unified Modeling Language User Guide, Second Edition*, Addison-Wesley, Boston, Mass., 2005.

Boehm, Barry: "A Spiral Model of Software Development and Enhancement: Proceedings of the Int. Workshop on Software Process and Software Environments," ACM Software Engineering Notes, Aug. 1986, pp. 22–42.

"Capability Maturity Model Integration, Version 1.1," Software Engineering Institute, Carnegie-Mellon Univ., Pittsburgh, PA, March 2003 (http://www.sei.cmu.edu/cmmi/)

Chidamber, S.R. and C.F. Kemerer: "A Metrics Suite for Object-Oriented Design," *IEEE Trans. on Software Engineering*, Vol. SE20, No. 6, June 1994, pp. 476–493.

Cockburn, Alistair: *Agile Software Development*, Addison-Wesley, Boston, Mass., 2001.

Cohen, D., M. Lindvall and P. Costa: "An Introduction to Agile Methods," *Advances in Computers*,Elsevier Science, New York, 2004, pp. 1–66

Cohen, Lou: *Quality Function Deployment: How to Make QFD Work for You*, Prentice-Hall PTR, Englewood Cliffs, NJ- Mass., 1995

Cohn, Mike: *Agile Estimating and Planning*, Prentice-Hall PTR, Englewood Cliffs, N.J., 2005.

————: *User Stories Applied: For Agile Software Development*, Addison-Wesley, Boston, Mass., 2004.

Enterprise Resource Planning (http://en.wikipedia.org/wiki/Enterprise_resource_ planning).

Feature Driven Development (http://en.wikipedia.org/wiki/Feature_Driven_ Development).

Fernandini, Patricia: *A Requirements Pattern—Succeeding in the Internet Economy*, Addison-Wesley, Boston, Mass., 2002.

Fuqua, Andrew M.: *Using Function Points in XP—Considerations*, Springer Berlin/ Heidelberg, 2003.

Gack, Gary: "Applying Six-Sigma to Software Implementation Projects" (http://software. isixsigma.com/library/content/c040915b.asp).

Gamma, Erich, Richard Helm, Ralph Johnson, and John Vlissides: *Design Patterns: Elements of Reusable Object Oriented Design*, Addison-Wesley, Boston Mass., 1995.

Garmus, David and David Herron: *Function Point Analysis*, Addison-Wesley Longman, Boston, Mass., 2001.

————: *Measuring the Software Process: A Practical Guide to Functional Measurement*, Prentice-Hall, Englewood Cliffs, N.J., 1995.

Hallowell, David L.: "Six Sigma Software Metrics, Part 1" (http://software.isixsigma.com/ library/content/03910a.asp).

Highsmith, Jim: *Agile Software Development Ecosystems*, Addison-Wesley, Boston, Mass., 2002.

Humphrey, Watts: *TSP—Leading a Development Team*, Addison-Wesley, Boston, Mass., 2006.

————: *Managing the Software Process*, Addison-Wesley, Reading, Mass., 1989.

International Function Point Users Group (IFPUG) (http://www.IFPUG.org).

International Organization for Standards, ISO 9000 / ISO 14000 (http://www.iso.org/iso/ en/iso9000-14000/index.html).

Jeffries, R. et al: *Extreme Programming Installed*, Addison-Wesley, Boston, Mass., 2001.

Jones, Capers: *Applied Software Measurement*, McGraw-Hill, New York, 1996.

————: "Sizing Up Software," *Scientific American*, New York, December 1998; Vol. 279, No. 6; pp 104–109.

————: *Software Assessments, Benchmarks, and Best Practices*, Addison-Wesley Longman, Boston, Mass., 2000.

————: *Conflict and Litigation Between Software Clients and Developers*, Software Productivity Research, Burlington, Mass., 2003.

Kan, Stephen H.: *Metrics and Models in Software Quality Engineering, Second Edition*, Addison-Wesley Longman, Boston, Mass., 2003.

Koirala, Shavisprasad: "How to Prepare Quotations Using Use Case Points" (http://www .codeproject.com/gen/design/usecasepoints.asp).

Larman, Craig and Victor Basili: "Iterative and Incremental Development—A Brief History," *IEEE Computer Society*, June 2003, pp 47–55.

Love, Tom: *Object Lessons*, SIGS Books, New York, 1993.

McConnell, Steve: *Software Estimating: Demystifying the Black Art*, Microsoft Press, Redmond, WA 2006.

Mills, H., M. Dyer, and R. Linger: "Cleanroom Software Engineering," *IEEE Software*, 4, 5 (Sept. 1987), pp. 19–25.

Pressman, Roger: *Software Engineering—A Practitioner's Approach, Sixth Edition*, McGraw-Hill, New York, 2005.

Quality Function Deployment (http://en.wikipedia.org/wiki/Quality_function_ deployment).

Rapid Application Development (http://en.wikipedia.org/wiki/Rapid_application_ development).

Stapleton, J.: *DSDM—Dynamic System Development in Practice*, Addison-Wesley, Boston, Mass., 1997.

Stephens M. and D. Rosenberg: *Extreme Programming Refactored: The Case Against XP*, APress L.P., Berkeley, Calif., 2003.

Chapter

8

Automated Estimates from Minimal Data

Among software project managers, having full information about a software project to create an initial cost is a rarity. Estimates are demanded by both clients and senior management before the requirements are known, before the team is assembled, and before the tools and methods are selected. The majority of early cost estimates have to be produced in a hurry with less than complete information about the factors that will influence the outcome of the project.

This chapter discusses some of the estimating features that commercial estimating-tool vendors and researchers have developed to allow useful estimates from imperfect and partial information. These early estimates have the advantage of being easy and very quick to create. Often, from the time an estimating tool is turned on until the estimate is finished is a matter of less than five minutes. Of course, no one can expect high precision from estimates that are based only on a few known factors.

The commercial software-estimating tools are usually calibrated so that *average* performance is the assumed value for all settings and adjustments. This means that when you are creating an initial cost estimate and don't yet know all of the information needed for high precision, you can simply accept the average settings for such topics as assignment scopes, available work hours, or team experience levels and create preliminary estimates using these default settings until more accurate information is known later.

To give a framework for discussing the sequence of activities that must be completed when constructing an initial software cost estimate for a project, three stages can highlight the basic sequence of software-estimating activities:

1. Recording administrative and project information
2. Preliminary sizing of key deliverables
3. Producing a preliminary cost estimate

As a general sequence describing the way early software estimation works, these three stages apply both to software cost-estimation tools and to manual software cost-estimation methods.

As we move through the stages of preparing software cost estimates, note that the same factors that influence the outcome of the estimate are also key factors for software measurement purposes. This explains why so many of the software cost-estimating vendors are also measurement experts and have benchmarking services: You cannot build an effective software cost-estimating tool without substantial historical data from which to derive the algorithms.

For any kind of software cost estimate, some kind of input information has to be provided by the users, sizing of various deliverables must occur, adjustments to basic estimates for experience and complexity and other factors must be made, and all of the pieces of the estimate must be totaled at the end to produce the final estimate.

We'll begin our tour of automated estimating by examining the minimum kinds of information needed to do preliminary, early estimates. Then we will move to the more extensive kinds of information needed to calibrate and adjust the estimate for optimal precision.

Let us now consider the three software cost-estimating stages in sequence, starting with the minimum amount of information that has to be provided in order to allow at least a rough estimate using commercial software-estimating tools.

Stage 1: Recording Administrative and Project Information

Since software cost estimates will have a life expectancy that can run from weeks up to several years, the first kind of information that needs to be recorded is administrative information, such as the name of the project for which the estimate is being prepared, and some information about the participants in the estimating process so that they can be contacted if needed.

Most items of administrative information are straightforward and readily available and are known even before the requirements begin. A few optional topics are exceptions, however, such as recording a *standard industry classification* or identifying the starting date of the project in question.

Following are samples of some of the questions used by the author and other vendors of commercial software cost-estimating tools to collect basic administrative information when performing software cost estimates.

This administrative information is optional in terms of getting some kind of estimate out of a commercial software-estimating tool. However, to keep one project's estimate from being confused with another, at least the names of the project, the project manager, and the person preparing the estimate should be recorded. Also, this kind of administrative information will allow an estimate to be picked up after a period of weeks or months without confusion as to which project it deals with.

Software Estimating Administrative Information

Security level	_____
Project name	_____
Estimate number	_____
Estimating tool	_____
Project description	_____
Industry classification (NAIC)	_____
Organization	_____
Location	_____
Project manager	_____
Estimate completed by	_____
Current date (mm/dd/yyyy)	_____
Project start (mm/dd/yyyy)	_____
Desired delivery (mm/dd/yyyy)	_____

The *security level* is optional for many estimates, but is an important item for military and classified software projects. Security may also have relevance for software estimates in competitive situations, such as bids, or for software estimates being prepared in the course of litigation, such as tax cases or breach of contract cases.

The *project name* is included for convenience in telling one estimate from another, since any large company may have dozens of ongoing software projects in any given month.

The *estimate number* is useful in distinguishing early estimates from later estimates. For example, an estimate numbered 1 for a particular project is not likely to be as firm as an estimate numbered 6 for the same project.

For estimates that are being prepared for litigation, it is important to record the name of the *estimating tool*. Also, some large enterprises have as many as half a dozen different software cost-estimating tools available, so it is useful to record which tool is used for which estimate. Of course, most of the commercial software cost-estimating tools identify themselves on their printed outputs and also on screen, but some in-house estimation tools may not do this.

The *project description* is optional and, of course, does not affect the outcome of a project at all. Its purpose is to facilitate separating one project from another if a company does a lot of similar kinds of work. For example, as the Eurocurrency conversion work expands throughout the world, project descriptions might be used for such purposes as "Euro conversion for project A," "Euro conversion for project B," and so on.

The *Industry classification (NAIC) code* is optional, but can be very useful. The North American Industry Classification (NAIC) codes replaced the older Standard Industry Classification codes (SIC) in 2002. Both coding methods were developed by the U.S. Department of Commerce to assist in performing statistical studies of trends within industries. Many large-scale economic studies utilize NAIC or SIC codes, including software benchmarking studies.

The full set of NAIC codes and their definitions are available from the Government Printing Office in Washington, D.C., or even as advertisements from such companies as Dun and Bradstreet.

The purpose of recording the optional NAIC codes is to allow benchmark comparisons of your projects with similar projects within the same industry. Although use of the NAIC code is purely optional, if you want to compare your projects against a knowledge base of projects from within your own industry, then use of the NAIC code is recommended.

The *current date* in most commercial software cost-estimating tools is automatically taken from the internal date field of the computer itself, although users can, of course, change this if they wish. Sometimes 15 or 20 "what if" estimates may be run for the same project on the same day, so it can even be useful to record the time of day for a specific estimate. Some commercial software cost-estimating tools will utilize the current date for the start date of the project unless the user inputs a specific start date.

A very important piece of information for software cost estimating is the *project start date* of the project being estimated. However, the start date of a project is also one of the most tricky and elusive pieces of information in the entire domain of software cost estimating.

The reason that determining the start date of a project is ambiguous is because quite a lot of informal exploratory work can take place before it is decided that a software application should be built or is required.

Ideally, the start date reflects the date on which effort on the formal requirements gathering commenced. However, in real-life estimating, the best that can usually be achieved is a more or less arbitrary start-ing point selected by the project manager, a client, or technical staff members who pick a date that approximates the kickoff point for the project being estimated.

If the start date is omitted as a specific input, the usual default by commercial software cost-estimating tools is to use the current day's date as the starting date.

The *desired delivery date* for the software project is optional but can also be very useful. If the delivery date predicted by the estimating tool is much longer than the desired delivery date, then obviously the project has to be speeded up, cut down in size, or both.

Some commercial software cost-estimating tools include an *advice* mode. If the predicted date for the completion of the project is signifi-cantly later than the desired delivery date, the estimating tool will offer suggestions about approaches that might bring the two closer together or make them identical.

A Software Taxonomy: Defining the Nature, Scope, Class, and Type of Project

After recording basic (and largely optional) administrative information about the project being estimated, the next kind of input information to consider is the fundamental issue of taxonomy, that is, "What kind of software project is this one?"

Software projects come in a wide variety of classes and types—systems software, embedded software, civilian projects, military projects, and a host of other designations.

Each of these variations in terms of the class and type of the applica-tion can affect the outcome of the project in real life, and hence must be considered when performing a software cost estimate.

At least some kind of information about the nature of a software project must be supplied, in order to achieve estimates of even marginal precision. It is also important to record this information for measurement purposes.

In the domain of defining a taxonomy for pinning down the exact form of a software project, there are many variations from estimating tool to estimating tool. In the estimating tools that the author has designed and built, four terms are used to differentiate software projects into families or categories with enough precision to use the results for soft-ware-estimation purposes:

- Project nature
- Project scope
- Project class
- Project type

The term *project nature* refers to whether the application being estimated is a new project, an enhancement to existing software, a maintenance project, or a conversion project.

This question is important when using automated estimating tools, because different factors will affect each choice. For example, estimating an enhancement project requires dealing with the size and complexity of an existing software application.

The term *project scope* refers to whether the estimate is to be performed for something small, such as a module, or something large, such as a system. This question is also important when using automated estimating tools, because here, too, different factors will be evaluated for large systems that may not be present when estimating small projects.

The term *project class* refers to the business arrangement under which the project is to be built; that is, whether it will be built for internal purposes or for delivery to clients, or whether it will be built to civilian or military norms.

The term *project type* refers to the nature of the software itself; that is, whether the software will be an information system, systems software, embedded software that might reside onboard an airplane, or something else.

Although in real life there may be unlimited possibilities for these four terms, when using an automated estimating tool it is necessary to limit the choices to those that the rules of the estimating tool are capable of evaluating.

PROJECT NATURE: _____

1. New program development
2. Enhancement (new functions added to existing software)
3. Maintenance (defect repair to existing software)
4. Conversion or adaptation (migration to new platform)
5. Reengineering (reimplementing a legacy application)
6. Package modification (revising purchased software)

The *nature* question occurs early in the sequence of gathering information, because it is used to guide the choice of further questions later on. For example, if the project being estimated is identified as an *enhancement*, then obviously information will be needed about the existing software that is being updated.

The second topic of importance is the *scope* of the project, or whether the estimate is being prepared for something small, like a module, or something large, like a major software system.

The *scope* topic is not a substitute for detailed size information, but serves to narrow the set of downstream factors that need to be evaluated. For example, if a project is identified as a *system*, then activities such as architecture, user documentation, and system testing are likely to be performed.

PROJECT SCOPE: _____

1. Subroutine
2. Module
3. Reusable module
4. Disposable prototype
5. Evolutionary prototype
6. Standalone program
7. Component of a system
8. Release of a system
9. New system (initial release)
10. Compound system (linked integrated systems)

On the other hand, if the project is identified as a *module*, then many system-level activities, such as architecture, system testing, and creation of a user's guide, are not likely to occur.

The next topic of concern is a very important one for software cost-estimating purposes: the *class*, or business rationale, for the project being estimated. The software class is one of the factors that has real-life implications as well as implications in software cost estimating.

As a general rule, the further down the class list a project is placed, the larger it is, the more expensive it becomes, and the greater the proportion of costs associated with the production of paper documents becomes.

When considering the class of a project, note that projects identified as *external* differ in many important ways from projects identified as *internal*. The external projects are designed to be delivered to customers or clients, and, hence, often have more extensive testing and more complete sets of user documentation.

Also, the set of external projects are much more likely to end up in some kind of litigation or arbitration should major quality flaws or other deficiencies slip out into production. The class of an application is very important for both measurement and estimation purposes.

Consider the implications of the class parameter on real-life software cost elements. For the first class on the list, *personal programs*, there may be no written requirements, no specifications, no user documentation, and no project paperwork of any kind, and the entire costs of the project may be devoted to coding and debugging.

PROJECT CLASS: _____

1. Personal program, for private use
2. Personal program, to be used by others
3. Academic program, developed in an academic environment
4. Internal program, for use at a single location
5. Internal program, for use at multiple locations
6. Internal program, developed by external contractor
7. Internal program, with functions used via time sharing
8. Internal program, using military specifications
9. External program, to be put in public domain or on the Internet
10. External program, leased to users
11. External program, bundled with hardware
12. External program, unbundled and marketed commercially
13. External program, developed under commercial contract
14. External program, developed under government contract
15. External program, developed under military contract

For the last class on the list, *military contract software*, the production of paper documents will absorb more than 50 percent of the total cost of building the application, while coding costs will usually be less than 20 percent.

There are other important assumptions that can be derived from the class parameter. For example, the class of *internal software projects* usually has smaller and less sophisticated user manuals than the class of *external software projects.*

Another significant piece of information that needs to be recorded is the *type* of software, or whether the software is real-time, embedded, or perhaps even a hybrid project consisting of multiple categories of software under the same system umbrella.

The *type* parameter is a very troubling one and also is quite volatile. Many new kinds or types of software projects tend to appear, and it is tough work for estimating vendors to stay current with all possible types. For example, for the second edition of this book the type labeled Web applications, has exploded in numbers. When the first edition of this book was published in 1996, web applications were less than 1 percent of all projects. Now web applications have topped 10 percent of all projects, and continue to increase in numbers.

The *type* parameter is significant in evaluating the kind of quality-control approaches that are likely to be associated with the software projects. Before a new type parameter can be added to a software cost-estimating tool, enough projects of that type must be measured so that estimating algorithms can be developed and refined.

As can be seen, the general rankings of the nature, scope, class, and type parameters more or less follow the pattern of the Richter scale for evaluating earthquake power. In other words, the larger numbers have more serious consequences than the smaller numbers.

Also, the combination of nature, scope, class, and type parameters provides a useful *pattern* for browsing a cost-estimation knowledge base and selecting similar projects that can be used as a starting point for sizing by analogy or even as a jumping-off place for performing a rough early version of the current estimate. One of the main purposes of recording nature, scope, class, and type is to facilitate pattern matches when seeking historical projects whose data may be relevant.

To leave software for a moment and consider other human activities where approximation and preliminary estimates occur, think of the stages of purchasing an automobile or building a home. For example, consider the differences in Case X and Case Y for purchasing an automobile.

	Case X	Case Y
Nature	Used automobile	New automobile
Class	U.S. manufacture	German manufacture
Type	4 cylinders; economy	8 cylinders; luxury
Scope	2-door coupe	4-door station wagon

If your criteria for purchasing an automobile approximates Case X, then you can probably acquire one for less than $15,000. However, if your criteria are similar to Case Y, you will no doubt have to spend more than $50,000 and possibly more than $90,000.

Simply placing your choices into a taxonomy of possibilities is enough to understand the probable cost ranges for the kinds of automobiles you are interested in. There is a great deal of useful information contained in a well-formed taxonomy, and for software cost estimating the ability to slot a proposed project into the right combination of nature, class, type, and scope is sufficient to estimate the probable costs and schedules within tolerable boundaries.

From a real-life standpoint, consider the huge differences in costs and schedules that are likely to be found between the following two combinations of software estimating input parameters, even if nothing else is known about the projects except these four topics:

	Case A	Case B
Project name	Travel expenses	Gun Control System
Project nature	1 (new program)	1 (new program)
Project scope	4 (disposable prototype)	9 (new system)
Project class	1 (personal program)	15 (military contract)
Project type	1 (nonprocedural)	14 (embedded software)

PROJECT TYPE: _____

1. Nonprocedural (generated, query, spreadsheet)
2. World Wide Web application
3. Batch applications program
4. Interactive applications program
5. Interactive GUI applications program
6. Batch database applications program
7. Interactive database applications program
8. Client/server applications program
9. Scientific or mathematical program
10. Systems or support program
11. Communications or telecommunications program
12. Process-control program
13. Trusted system
14. Embedded or real-time program
15. Graphics, animation, or image-processing program
16. Multimedia program
17. Robotics, or mechanical automation program
18. Artificial intelligence program
19. Neural net program
20. Hybrid project (multiple types)

For hybrid projects:

Primary type : _____   Secondary type : _____

Although there is not yet enough information to produce a formal cost estimate, it is obvious that Case B is going to cost a lot more than Case A. Without even knowing any more details than the combinations of nature, scope, class, and type, we can already draw some useful inferences.

For example, it is probable that Case A will be less than 50 function points or 2500 Java source code statements in size, since more than 95 percent of programs identified as *personal* and *prototypes* are below this size.

Case B, on the other hand, will probably be larger than 5000 function points or 250,000 Java source code statements in size, since more than 50 percent of military applications identified as *systems* are above this size range.

In fact before any actual requirements are gathered, it is possible to use pattern matching from project nature, scope, class, and type to predict a probable application size in terms of function points, use case points, story points, and even lines of code. Summing the nature, scope, class, and type numbers and raising that total to the 2.35 power will give a useful approximation of size in terms of function points. For example, Case A totals to 7, and raising that to the 2.35 power yields about 97 function points or roughly 4800 Java statements. Case B totals to 39, and raising that to the 2.35 power yields about 5500 function points or 275,000 Java statements.

Since each use case is equivalent to about 35 function points, it can be predicted that Case A will need perhaps three use cases, while Case B might need 157 use cases. Thus, knowing nothing about a project but its taxonomy can yield useful early size information.

Further, it is also obvious that Case A is going to be developed in a way that will differ in many important ways from that of Case B. For example, Case B will no doubt follow various military development standards, such as DoD 2167A or DoD 498, while Case A may follow no standards of any kind.

Not only that, but we can begin to extract similar projects from our cost-estimation database in order to evaluate them as potential templates for use in estimating the current project.

We can also begin to see why manual software cost-estimating is a complex activity that is easy to get wrong, and rather difficult to get right. The permutations of the 6 nature questions, 8 scope questions, 15 class questions, and 20 type questions lead to 14,400 possible combinations. Each of these 14,400 possibilities will have a characteristic set of activities, methods, languages, and tools that can further impact the results of a cost estimate.

And we have not yet even started to consider other important topics, such as the size of the application, its complexity, the rate at which requirements are likely to change, and the experience levels of the development team!

There is now another important piece of information to consider: the *project goals* of the project as given to the project manager by the clients or by higher management.

This factor is very important in real life, and hence is important to know when performing software cost estimates, also. Six varieties of goals are found for software projects, but unfortunately Goal 2, or *shortest schedule*, is perhaps the most common even though it is one of the most dangerous of all.

When using automated software estimating these six goals exert a considerable impact on estimating assumptions, as follows:

- For Goal 1, or *standard estimate*, normal staffing complements and no excessive schedule pressures are assumed.

- For Goal 2, or *shortest schedule with extra staff*, there is an implied assumption that staffing complements will be expanded by perhaps a ratio of 2 to 1. More subtle, there is also an assumption that management does not know or understand much about software quality, so such activities as formal inspections will probably be absent or truncated. This goal would often be found on "good enough"—style projects, and sometimes on Rapid Application Development projects.

PROJECT GOALS:

1. Find the standard estimate of schedule, staff, and quality.
2. Find the shortest development schedule with extra staff.
3. Find the lowest effort with reduced staff.
4. Find the highest quality with normal staff.
5. Find the highest quality with shortest schedule.
6. Find the highest quality with least effort.

- For Goal 3, or *lowest effort*, there is an assumption that this is a background project with no great rush to have it completed. Therefore, the smallest staffing complement noted on similar projects will be assumed.

- Goal 4, or *highest quality*, combines the assumption of normal staffing complements with the assumption that quality is significant, and hence assumes that such approaches as specifications and inspections will be followed more or less rigorously.

- Goal 5, or *highest quality with shortest schedule*, is not a bad choice, and is often used for outsource projects, systems software, and commercial software. This goal assumes additional staffing, but does not assume that quality-control approaches will be bypassed or abbreviated.

- Goal 6, or *highest quality and least effort*, seldom occurs because schedule pressure is so endemic in the software industry. When it does occur, the assumptions are for a reduced staffing complement coupled with significant attention to quality control. This goal is sometimes used after a major round of downsizing, when many personnel have been laid off more or less concurrently.

Work Patterns, Staff Salaries, and Overhead Rates

Most commercial software cost-estimating tools provide default values for such topics as compensation, burden rates, and work patterns. However, the range of possible values for each of these factors is very broad, so it is normal to make adjustments for local conditions.

This kind of information is very important for software cost-estimating purposes. In real life as well as in setting up an estimating tool, it is important to know if the personnel will be available full time or will have other commitments.

It is also important to know typical work patterns, in terms of the length of the normal working week, normal working day, and vacations; number of holidays; and so forth.

Most software cost-estimating tools provide some kind of default values for these assumptions, but defaults and average values should really be replaced by actual local information if it is available.

In companies that use commercial software-estimating tools, basic information about work patterns and compensation rates can be inherited from project to project or can be set up as corporate default values for use by all estimates within a given company, or at least within a given location, where such attributes are likely to be more or less constant from project to project.

Staff availability: _____
(Default = 100%)

Exempt technical staff: _____
(Default = 100%)

Average work week: _____
(Default = 5 days)

Work hours per day: _____
(Default = 8.0)

Effective work hours per day: _____
(Default = 6.0)

Overtime hours per week: _____
(Default = 0 hours)

Work days per year: _____
(Default = 220)

Overtime premium pay: _____
(Default = 50%)

Average salary (monthly):   _____
(Default = $5,000)

There is a need for accurate data on these topics. The need is vital for estimates of critical projects where unpaid or paid overtime is likely to be needed. There can be a tremendous difference in both schedules and costs between a project that is averaging ten hours of unpaid technical staff overtime every week and a project of the same size and kind with no overtime, or even with part-time personnel who divide the work day with other projects.

This kind of information is also very important for estimates that are international, since work patterns vary widely between North America, Europe, the Pacific Rim, and South America.

For example, overtime is very common in the United States and Japan, but is much less common in Germany and Canada. Indeed, in Germany some computer facilities close down on weekends and even shut down the power to their computer systems, so that weekend work is almost impossible.

Examples of typical software cost-estimating information dealing with personnel costs, work patterns, and overtime follow.

The *availability* factor deals with whether project personnel will be fully assigned to the current project or will be splitting their time among multiple projects.

Exempt is the term used by the U.S. Bureau of Labor Statistics for salaried personnel who do not receive overtime payments. Most U.S. software technical personnel fall into this category, and also tend to work rather long weeks. Personnel who are paid on an hourly basis and do receive overtime pay are termed *nonexempt*.

The *work week* parameter is very significant for international cost estimates. For example, the normal U.S. work week consists of 5 days of 8 hours duration, or 40 hours in all. The normal Japanese work week, on the other hand, consists of 5.5 days of 8 hours duration, or 44 hours in all. The normal Canadian work week consists of 5 days but only 7 hours duration, or 35 hours in all, although the Canadian work week can vary between summer and winter.

The *work hours per day* parameter deals with the nominal amount of time during which employees are expected to be present and available for work assignments. However, in real life most of us don't actually work that amount of time on a daily basis.

The *effective work hours per day* parameter deals with the amount of effective time available, once lunch periods, coffee breaks, and other nonwork activities are backed out. This is an equivalent definition to the "ideal time" ratio used by some of the Agile methods for estimating sprints or development intervals.

The *overtime hours* parameter is a key factor for dealing with project schedules and also project costs. In spite of the importance of this parameter, it is often ignored or set to zero value, when in fact extensive overtime occurs on many software projects.

The *work days per year* parameter is very significant for international estimates, since the number of public holidays and vacation days varies widely from country to country. Although the nominal work year in the United States is about 220 days, the nominal work year in much of Western Europe is only about 200 days due to much longer vacation periods.

The *overtime premium pay* parameter is the adjustment to base pay rates for normal, scheduled overtime by nonexempt employees. Overtime can become very complicated, and sometimes will have different rates on holidays from normal weekday rates, and Sundays may also have different rates from Saturdays.

The *average salary* parameter is really an oversimplification used primarily for early software cost estimates before the staff complement is fully known. This parameter is simply the average monthly compensation rate for all project personnel, including both managers and technical staff members.

The phrase *burden rate* refers to the costs for taxes, medical benefits, building rents, utilities, and a host of other indirect items that are needed to keep a company running. These costs are usually applied on top of staff compensation, and the total is then used for contracts and cost-estimating purposes. The range of burden rates is very wide, and can run from less than 15 percent for companies operating out of small home offices to more than 300 percent for large defense contractors.

The *burdened compensation* parameter refers to the sum of salary expenses plus administrative expenses that must be factored into the cost estimate.

The *currency* parameter is important for international cost estimates, because, for example, the values of Australian, Canadian, and American dollars are not the same. The currency parameter was updated in many commercial software cost-estimating tools in order to support the new unified European currency, which was phased in over several years, beginning on January 1, 1999.

The work pattern and compensation information is an example of the kind of data that is often inherited from other projects, using the ability to construct templates offered by many software estimating tools.

Stage 2: Preliminary Sizing of Key Deliverables

We're now almost at the point where we can provide a rough or preliminary estimate for the project, but before we can do this we need to determine at least the approximate size of the project.

Size determination has long been one of the most difficult and troublesome aspects of software cost estimating, although technical advances over the last 20 years have made sizing easier and more accurate than in the early days of the industry.

Modern software cost-estimating tools support a variety of sizing methods, including but not limited to the following:

- Size supplied by users as explicit inputs
- Size approximations based on scope, class, and type
- Size approximations based on function points

- Size approximations based on statistical reconstruction
- Sizing by analogy with previously measured projects
- Size approximations based on business situations
- Size approximations based on Monte Carlo simulations
- Size approximations based on physical lines of source code
- Size approximations based on logical source code statements
- Size based on use case points, object points, story points, or other new metrics

Software Project Sizing Provided by Users

The oldest method for dealing with size used by software cost-estimating tools was to ask that size information be provided by the users as an explicit input, in the form of the estimated volume of source code. This method was common in the software-estimating tools that came out in the 1970s, such as PRICE-S, SLIM, and COCOMO, and it is still supported in more recent software cost-estimating tools, such as CHECKPOINT, COCOMO II, and KnowledgePlan, although advanced sizing logic is now available, too.

Although many modern estimating tools now include sizing logic and can help the user to determine project sizes, all of them still allow users to input an explicit size value if they wish to do so. Most commercial estimating tools permit the size to be expressed in terms of function points, source code volumes, or both. Indeed, many modern software cost-estimating tools can convert size between function points and source code statements in either direction. A few also accept size inputs using object points, use case points, and other new metrics.

Of course, for size information using source code for estimating purposes, it is also necessary to know the programming languages involved. Therefore, a corollary piece of information would be to identify the languages for the project, usually by means of some kind of checklist of the languages supported by the estimating tool.

Today these checklists run up to more than 600 languages, but the earlier software cost-estimating tools usually supported between 10 and 30 programming languages.

By about 1985, software estimating tools began to appear that could accept size information entered using either lines of code or function points, and the tool itself would convert data in both directions. This was made possible by a technique called *backfiring*, which was developed via empirical observations of the number of source code statements required to encode one function point in various languages.

The development of the backfiring methodology meant that size information could initially be stated either in terms of source code counts or function point counts, based on the preference of the estimating-tool users. Typical generic size questions might resemble the following:

Software Application Size Assumptions

Programming language(s):   _____

Application size in noncommentary source code statements: _____

Application size in physical lines of code: _____

Source code statements per function point: _____

Source code counting method: _____

Application size in function points: _____

Function point counting method: _____

With question sets such as the preceding, the user could supply partial information and the estimating tool would complete the missing elements. For example, a user who supplied only source code statement counts would also be able to see size expressed in terms of function points, and vice versa. However, a user would have to supply either source code size or function point size, because the backfire size conversion equations needed a starting point of one form or the other.

If the application being estimated uses only a single programming language, then entering explicit size data is straightforward, if not always easy. However, about one-third of the applications in the United States and elsewhere use multiple programming languages. Indeed, sometimes as many as a dozen discrete languages can be found within the same application, although two-language pairs are far more common.

Mixed language applications are very common among all classes of software—systems, military, information systems, and commercial. Some of the more common programming language combinations include the following:

- Ada and CMS2
- Ada and Jovial
- Ada and Assembly
- Basic and Assembly
- Basic and C
- C and Assembly
- C and C++
- C++ and Assembly
- COBOL and database languages
- COBOL and PL/I

- COBOL and Query languages
- COBOL and RPG
- COBOL and SQL
- COBOL, SQL, and database languages
- Generators mixed with procedural languages
- Java and HTML

The presence of combinations of programming languages makes sizing using the LOC-metrics more complicated, but software estimating tools now support mixed language sizing and also size conversions between source code volumes and equivalent function point totals in situations where as many as a dozen languages might be in use within the same application.

Although the methods for dealing with multiple programming languages vary from tool to tool, the following example of a mixed-language worksheet would not be uncommon. This sample worksheet shows an application of 500 function points that uses four different languages: COBOL, SQL, RPG II, and FOCUS.

Users of estimating tools cannot be expected to know the levels of programming languages nor the number of statements required to encode one function point. Therefore, the software cost-estimating tools usually provide some kind of pull-down menu with this kind of information.

The information on the ratios of source code statements to function points are sometimes expressed in terms of maximum, average, and minimum values, or sometimes in terms of only a single default value. In either case, users can adjust the ratio in response to local conditions or in situations where they feel the default value may be incorrect.

Users can input any of the factors that they know, and the estimating tool will solve for the unknown factors. For example, users could supply size in KLOC, and the estimating tool would produce function points, or vice versa.

The four languages shown here are merely an example of how mixed-language applications are dealt with in terms of sizing. Essentially, any combination involving any number of programming languages can be dealt with by modern software cost-estimating tools. Note that both source code and function point metrics are now supported by the great majority of software estimating tools, so sizing can be based on either metric or on both concurrently.

It is possible to do the same kind of conversion between source code and function points for mixed languages using a pocket calculator if the language levels are known, but one of the advantages of automated software cost-estimating tools is that they can do this set of calculations

Multiple Language Size Aggregation

Number of languages: 4

Function point method: IFPUG Version 3.4

Language	KLOC	Language levels	Source statements per function point	Function points
COBOL	15.00	3.00	106.67	141
SQL	1.00	25.00	12.80	78
RPG II	10.00	5.00	64.00	156
FOCUS	5.00	8.00	40.00	125
Total	31.00	5.16	62.00	500

in a fraction of a second, while it takes human beings a great deal longer even if they know all of the language levels.

With automated software estimating tools, factors such as the ratio of source code statements to function points are normally provided by the tools themselves, using pull-down lists or tables similar to Tables 8.1 and 8.2.

Table 8.1 illustrates a small sample of 16 programming languages listed in alphabetical order, with both the level and the approximate number of source code statements per function point illustrated.

Tables 8.1 and 8.2 use IFPUG Version 3.4 as the basis of the expansion factors. Adjustments to such a table for IFPUG Version 4.0 or for other variants, such as the British Mark II function point method, are also possible, but they require somewhat different ratios of source code to function points. This rather complex issue will be dealt with further on in the book.

The information in Tables 8.1 and 8.2 merely represents typical languages and values that can be found in dozens of commercial software estimating tools. Many other kinds of information may also be shown, such as the range of possible values for each language, the number of projects in the sample for each language, complexity assumptions, and so forth.

The same set of 16 languages is shown in another format, listed in descending order by language level, in Table 8.2.

In addition, users of software cost-estimating tools also have the ability to modify the language tables by adding languages of their choice, or by changing the default values for the levels of programming languages that are contained in the table.

TABLE 8.1   Software Language Levels in Ascending Order of Alphabetic Sequence

Language	Level	Source code statements per function point
Ada 83	4.50	71.12
Ada 95	6.00	53.33
Algol	3.00	106.67
Assembly (basic)	1.00	320.00
Assembly (macro)	1.50	213.33
C	2.50	128.00
C++	5.00	64.00
COBOL	3.00	106.67
FORTRAN	3.00	106.67
Jovial	3.00	106.67
Java	6.00	50.00
Objective-C	12.00	26.67
PowerBuilder	20.00	16.00
Smalltalk	15.00	21.33
SQL	25.00	12.80
Visual Basic	10.00	32.00
Average	7.63	92.35

A surprisingly large number of companies have developed unique, proprietary languages that only they use. For example, the ITT corporation developed a variant of PL/I for electronic switching systems, called ESPL/I, which was only used within ITT. Many other companies have also created unique languages that they alone utilize.

TABLE 8.2   Software Language Levels in Ascending Order of Level or Statements per Function Point

Language	Level	Source code statements per function point
Assembly (basic)	1.00	320.00
Assembly (macro)	1.50	213.33
C	2.50	128.00
Algol	3.00	106.67
COBOL	3.00	106.67
FORTRAN	3.00	106.67
Jovial	3.00	106.67
Ada 83	4.50	71.12
C++	5.00	64.00
Ada 95	6.00	53.33
Java	6.00	50.00
Visual Basic	10.00	32.00
Objective-C	12.00	26.67
Smalltalk	15.00	21.33
PowerBuilder	20.00	16.00
SQL	25.00	12.80
Average	7.63	92.35

Over and above the 600 or so programming languages that are available in commercial form, such as C, COBOL, and Smalltalk, the author and his colleagues have encountered at least another 200 proprietary languages in the course of their assessment and benchmarking studies.

Proprietary languages are hard to deal with in the context of software cost estimation, because their levels or the numbers of source code statements per function point are seldom known, and the proprietary languages are not included as standard choices in the estimating tools. However, about 99 percent of these proprietary languages are actually minor variants to *public* languages, such as PL/I, so it is practical to assume that the levels of the public and private languages are in the same general range.

A quick analysis of the most common programming languages at ten-year intervals between 1967 and 2007 illustrates the rapid evolution of programming languages, as shown in Table 8.3.

New programming languages continue to be created at the rate of perhaps six per year. It is an unanswered question why the software industry needs more than 600 programming languages.

Automated Sizing Approximation Methods

While size data supplied by users is fairly common, it often happens that project managers, who are the most common users of estimating tools, don't have enough information to determine the size of the application.

In this situation, the user could guess at the size, but guesses are seldom satisfactory. Modern commercial software cost-estimating tools provide a wide variety of sizing approximation methods that can be used for early estimates before requirements are firm. Not every software estimating tool supports every method, but some form of size approximation is a common feature.

The sizing problem is usually dealt with in a series of sequential operations. The first step in the sequence is to determine the size of the overall application in terms of a major metric, such as function points, source code statements, use case points, object points, story points, or another metric of choice.

TABLE 8.3   Most Common Programming Languages from 1967 to 2007

Year	Languages
1967	Assembly
1977	COBOL and FORTRAN
1987	COBOL, C, and Ada
1997	Visual Basic and Java
2007	Java, C, and HTML

Once this overall size is determined, the sizes of a variety of other artifacts and deliverables can be projected, including but not limited to the following:

- The sizes of specifications
- The sizes of user manuals
- The number of test cases to be created
- The probable numbers of defects or bugs
- The number of screens that need to be developed

The sizing of these secondary items will be discussed later in the book. However, before the secondary topics can be considered it is necessary to deal with the primary size topics of function point totals and source code volumes.

Sizing Based on Function Point Ranges   There are several forms of size approximation based on the usage of function point metrics in a more subjective way than a formal function point analysis.

These approximation methods do not require that users have enough information at hand to actually perform accurate counts of the real function point totals of the applications in question.

An early form of function point sizing that utilized approximate ranges instead of exact counts was developed in 1985. This approximation methodology only asked that the user select an approximate range for each of the function point methods, and then the tool itself would narrow down the choices based on nature, class, and type logic, as follows.

Probable Values for Function Point Input Parameters

	None	<10	11–25	26–50	>50
Inputs	1	2	3	4	5
Outputs	1	2	3	4	5
Logical Files	1	2	3	4	5
Inquiries	1	2	3	4	5
Interfaces	1	2	3	4	5

To use this form of approximation, the user would simply select one of the five integer values from 1 through 5, and the estimating tool would examine the choices and select a value for the factors in question.

Since this method has been in use for more than 20 years, it has been utilized hundreds or even thousands of times. When comparing the early approximation results against final sizes, after function points have actually been counted, the approximated values tend to be on the low side.

Analysis reveals that the difference between the initial approximation and the final size often vary because of creeping requirements, or features added later in the development cycle after the first or early estimate is performed. Interestingly, the approximate size estimate and the first actual count of function points tend to be rather close, but after that point creeping requirements need to be dealt with.

The realization that creeping user requirements need to be included in software size-estimating methodology is an important topic, and has led to some useful methods for approximating the rate at which requirements creep is likely to occur, which will be discussed later.

Sizing Based on Function Point Reconstruction A second form of early approximation based on function point logic was developed in 1989, although it can also be performed manually if historical data is readily available.

This form of approximate sizing from function point metrics is based on the existence of a knowledge base of projects within the estimating tool itself. This second form of approximation assumes that users might know some of the function point information, but not all of it. By examining similar projects within the knowledge base, it becomes possible to reconstruct the missing function point elements using the statistics of similar projects.

This second approximation method is based on pattern-matching concepts. For software applications of significant size ranges, such as those larger than 1000 function points, there is a natural sequence during the requirements phase in which the elements of function point counting are uncovered.

The output types are usually the first item known or defined during the requirements phase, while the inquiry types are often the last. Table 8.4 shows the usual sequence.

Suppose you were concerned with creating a preliminary estimate for a software project that has the set of known attributes shown for

TABLE 8.4 Normal Sequence of Function Point Discovery

Function point element	Normal sequence of enumeration	Normal chronology from start of project
Outputs	Usually known first	Within the first month
Inputs	Usually known second	Within two months
Interfaces	Usually known third	Within three months
Logical files	Usually known fourth	Within four months
Inquiries	Usually known last	Within five months

Case A, but not yet enough information to attempt a formal function point analysis.

Case A

Project name	New Account Entry
NAIC code	60 (depository Institutions)
Start date	January 6, 2007
Burdened cost	$7500
Project goals	1 (normal effort)
Project nature	1 (new program)
Project scope	5 (standalone program)
Project class	5 (internal, multiple locations)
Project type	8 (client/server)
Language	PowerBuilder
FP method	IFPUG Version 4
Project size	?
External inputs	?
External outputs	30
External inquiries	?
Internal logical files	?
External interface files	?

However, at this point in the requirements cycle a need for 30 kinds of outputs has been identified.

Surprisingly, although only the number of outputs has been enumerated, this partial information is enough to produce a preliminary size estimate by analysis of projects that share the same kinds of overall

---

Statistical Reconstruction of Missing Function Point Elements

Function Types	Number	Weight		Raw total
External inputs	35	×	4 =	140*
External outputs	30	×	5 =	150
External inquiries	45	×	4 =	180*
Internal logical files	10	×	10 =	100*
External interfaces	5	×	7 =	35*
Raw total				605*
Complexity adjustment				105%
Adjusted function points				636*

*Omitted values synthesized from similar projects.

attributes, such as nature, scope, class, and type, and that also have about 30 external outputs.

In fact, so long as any one of the attributes is known, then the missing attributes can be created by statistical analysis of similar applications. Should the user know two or more of the missing attributes, the accuracy of the preliminary size estimate can improve to acceptable levels.

By aggregating other projects in the knowledge base that have the same signatures in terms of nature, scope, class, and type and averaging their function point elements, it is possible to create a *synthetic* size estimate that might resemble the above, although this particular example is hypothetical and merely represents what might occur.

This method of approximation works reasonably well for projects that plan to use function point metrics but are simply too early in defining requirements to be able to derive accurate counts.

But there are many projects where neither the project managers nor the technical staff are familiar with function points, and they may not have a clue as to any of the function point parameters at all. Obviously, this form of approximation is not effective for such projects.

However, the next form of approximation, *sizing by analogy*, can be utilized regardless of whether function points or source code metrics (or neither) constitute the starting point.

This method can also be performed manually, but it requires access to a significant amount of historical data for similar projects that can be scanned.

Sizing by Analogy   One of the conveniences of automated estimating tools is that their built-in knowledge bases can ease some of the more difficult aspects of software cost estimation.

Size approximation by analogy is based on browsing a catalog of similar projects and seeking examples similar to the one being estimated as the starting point for size analysis. Sizing by analogy is an excellent example of how estimation tools can ease a tricky problem. If a project starts with a good taxonomy showing its nature, scope, class, and type, then selecting similar projects is quite straightforward.

Sizing by analogy is the last of the approximation methods that will be discussed, and it is the most useful and potentially the most accurate of any of the approximate sizing methods.

Any software cost estimation and/or measurement tool that keeps a directory of projects already estimated or measured can assist in performing at least a rudimentary form of sizing by analogy.

However, in order to make the sizing task easy, the tool should also offer a summary list of projects with helpful identifying information, such as the type of project and the business purpose. The list in Table 8.5 is derived from the SPR historical data files and illustrates the kind of information needed to make sizing by analogy convenient.

TABLE 8.5   Approximate Sizes of Selected Software Applications
(Sizes based on IFPUG 4 and SPR logical statement rules)

Application	Type	Purpose	Primary language	Size, KLOC	Size, FP	LOC per FP
Airline Reservations	MIS	Business	Mixed	2,750	25,000	110.00
Insurance Claims	MIS	Business	COBOL	1,605	15,000	107.00
Telephone Billing	MIS	Business	C	1,375	11,000	125.00
Tax Preparation (Personal)	MIS	Business	Mixed	180	2,000	90.00
General Ledger	MIS	Business	COBOL	161	1,500	107.00
Order Entry	MIS	Business	COBOL/ SQL	106	1,250	85.00
Human Resource	MIS	Business	COBOL	128	1,200	107.00
Sales Support	MIS	Business	COBOL/ SQL	83	975	85.00
Budget Preparation	MIS	Business	COBOL/ SQL	64	750	85.00
Graphics Design	Commercial	CAD	Objective C	54	2,700	20.00
IEF	Commercial	CASE	C	2,500	20,000	125.00
Visual Basic	Commercial	Compiler	C	375	3,000	125.00
IMS	Commercial	Database	Assembly	750	3,500	214.29
CICS	Commercial	Database	Assembly	420	2,000	210.00
WMCCS	Military	Defense	Jovial	18,000	175,000	102.86
Aircraft Radar	Military	Defense	Ada 83	213	3,000	71.00
Gun Control	Military	Defense	CMS2	225	2,336	107.00
Lotus Notes	Commercial	Groupware	Mixed	350	3,500	100.00
MS Office Professional	Commercial	Office tools	C	2,000	16,000	125.00
SmartSuite	Commercial	Office tools	Mixed	2,000	16,000	125.00
MS Office Standard	Commercial	Office tools	C	1,250	10,000	125.00
Word 7.0	Commercial	Office tools	C	315	2,500	126.00
Excel 6.0	Commercial	Office tools	C	375	2,500	150.00
Windows XP5	Systems	Operating system	C	11,000	85,000	129.41
MVS	Systems	Operating system	Assembly	12,000	55,000	218.18
UNIX V5	Systems	Operating system	C	6,250	50,000	125.00
ERP	Commercial	ERP	C	315	250,000	125.00
MS Project	Commercial	Project management	C	375	3,000	125.00
Knowledge Plan	Commercial	Project management	C++	134	2,500	56.67
CHECKPOINT	Commercial	Project management	Mixed	225	2,100	107.14

TABLE 8.5   Approximate Sizes of Selected Software Applications *(Continued)*
(Sizes based on IFPUG 4 and SPR logical statement rules)

Application	Type	Purpose	Primary language	Size, KLOC	Size, FP	LOC per FP
Function Point Control	Commercial	Project management	C	56	450	125.00
SPQR/20	Commercial	Project management	Quick Basic	25	350	71.43
5ESS	Systems	Telecommunication	C	1,500	12,000	125.00
System/12	Systems	Telecommunication	CHILL	800	7,700	103.90
Total				68,669	542,811	126.51
Average				2,020	15,965	126.51

This list covers only a small set of sample projects, simply to illustrate some of the kinds of information that are useful when browsing through sets of software projects. Of course, software estimating tools can also provide subsets of projects to cut down on the amount of work needed to find useful analogies. Pattern-matching will eventually become a major feature of software estimating tools.

It would obviously be tedious to browse through huge lists of 1000 or more projects, so using search logic to subset the overall listing into more manageable segments is a more convenient approach.

For example, a user might restrict the search logic to include only those projects with selected characteristics, such as the following set:

- Web project types
- Online business purposes
- Java programming language

On the other hand, another user might wish to restrict the search logic to a totally different set of criteria, such as the following:

- Military project types
- Weapons systems
- Ada 95 programming language

Although the current discussion deals only with using similar projects as the basis for sizing new projects, the same fundamental concept of starting with projects stored in an estimating tool's knowledge base can also be used to construct estimation templates that include not only size data but also attribute and adjustment factors. Building templates from historical project data will be discussed more fully in the next section, which discusses detailed estimating methods. The concept of inheriting attributes from historical projects is essentially the same concept as inheritance in the object-oriented world. Selecting appropriate projects via pattern matching is also logically similar to OO patterns.

Sizing by analogy need not be limited to a single project. It might be of interest to evaluate half a dozen or more similar projects and use the average size of this sample as the starting point for estimating a new project.

Several commercial software estimation tools have built-in statistical features that can easily handle aggregation and averaging of sizes and other quantifiable data, and that can also produce standard deviations and other statistical information of possible value.

Sizing the Impact of Creeping Requirements   One of the classic problems of software size estimation is that of *creeping requirements,* or new features added in mid-development after the first software cost estimate has been created.

The software requirements gathering process can affect the rate at which requirements creep if methods of proven effectiveness are known. The most effective techniques for minimizing the disruptive effect of uncontrolled creeping requirements include the following:

- Joint application design (JAD)
- Prototyping of key features and outputs
- Quality Function Deployment (QFD)
- Developing requirements via user stories
- Formal requirements inspections
- Using iterative development with precise sizing only for the current sprint or increment
- Contractual penalties for late requirements
- Automated configuration control tools
- Software estimating tools with creep-prediction features
- Use of function point metrics during development

Fortunately, the advent of function point metrics allows the rate of creeping requirements to be measured directly. Recall that the function point sizes of software projects are normally enumerated four times during software development:

- A rough function point approximation before requirements are complete
- A formal function point sizing at the end of the requirements phase

- A midcourse function point sizing at the end of the design phase
- A final function point sizing at the end when the software is delivered

These four points of reference, coupled with other kinds of information, such as project schedules, allow the rate of requirements creep to be anticipated with reasonable, but not perfect, precision.

Table 8.6 shows the approximate rate at which software requirements creep for six size ranges an order of magnitude apart, from 1 function point through 1000 function points. It illustrates typical scenarios where no concentrated effort has been applied to reducing the impact of creeping user requirements. In situations where effective requirements approaches are used, such as JAD sessions and requirements inspections, the rate of creeping requirements can be much lower than the data shown.

Of course, the opposite case may be true as well: The rate of creeping requirements growth may sometimes be *worse* than Table 8.6 indicates. This situation can be devastating for fixed-price contracts, and greatly troubling for any kind of schedule and cost-containment method. Of course, Agile methods, Scrum, and iterative development were designed specifically to deal with large volumes of changing requirements.

In the absence of any other information, it can be assumed that software requirements will creep or grow at an average monthly rate of about 2 percent from the end of the requirements phase through the design and coding phases. This situation may be tolerable for applications with development schedules of less than 12 months, but for major systems with three- to five-year development cycles, the steady accumulation of unplanned requirements can be a major contributing factor to cost and schedule overruns.

Incidentally, changes in software project requirements can be negative as well as positive. It often happens that towards the end of the design or coding phases, when it becomes apparent that planned schedules will be missed, it may be necessary to defer some features to a follow-on release.

TABLE 8.6   Approximate Rate of Creeping Software Requirements

Delivered size, FP	Schedule, months	Planned size, FP	Creep size, FP	Percentage of requirements creep
1	1.00	1.00	0.00	0.00
10	2.51	9.50	0.50	5.00
100	6.31	92.00	8.00	8.00
1000	15.85	850.00	150.00	15.00
10000	39.81	6500.00	3500.00	35.00
100000	100.00	55000.00	45000.00	45.00

TABLE 8.7 Growth and Deferral Pattern of Function Point Volumes for an Application of 1000 Function Points

Month	Phase	FP per month	Cumulative FP	Percent per month
January	Requirements	250	250	25.0
February		350	600	35.0
March		350	950	35.0
April	Design	75	1025	7.50
May		38	1063	3.80
June		24	1087	2.40
July		45	1132	4.50
August	Coding	25	1157	2.50
September		18	1175	1.80
October		10	1185	1.0
November		10	1195	1.0
December	Testing	5	1200	0.50
January		1200	1000	220.0
February		0	1000	0.0
March		0	1000	0.0
April		0	1000	0.0
May		0	1000	0.0
June	Deployment	0	1000	0.0
Total		1000	1000	100

Table 8.7 illustrates a typical pattern of both growth and deferral in function point totals for an application of a nominal 1000 function points at delivery with an 18-month development cycle.

Note that the growth pattern for function points illustrated by Table 8.7 represents the function point total as defined in the application's requirements and specifications. The function point metric is not an appropriate tool for monitoring the rate at which software applications are constructed, because software is not built one function point at a time.

An examination of Table 8.7 reveals some common but interesting trends. Note that at its peak in the month of December, the project is actually up to 1200 function points in total size.

At that point, it is suddenly realized that the project will miss its schedule severely, so it is decided to defer features that total 200 function points to a later release.

This combination of functional expansion and contraction is very common for applications in the 1000–function point size range and larger. In fact, our assessment and benchmarking studies indicate that less than 25 percent of projects larger than 1000 function points actually contain all of the intended features in the initial release.

Since creeping software requirements are an endemic problem for the software industry, modern software cost-estimating tools can offer at least some assistance by predicting the probable volume of unplanned requirements and their consequences on schedules and costs. Predicting the rate at which unplanned requirements will grow is also useful in an Agile context for planning future increments or sprints.

During early estimating sessions, these creeping requirements predictions can either be ignored or can be added to the final estimate, based on the preference of the user of the estimating tool.

Once the programming languages and size of the application have been entered into a cost-estimating tool, there is enough information to produce a rough but useful software cost estimate.

At this point, the estimating tool has knowledge of only ten kinds of information: nature, scope, class, type, goals, programming language, burdened salary rate, size of the application in terms of either function points or source code (or both), and the start date of the project.

Therefore, early cost estimates will not include adjustments based on team experience, complexity, tools, methods, or any of several hundred factors that are known to influence the outcomes of software projects.

In spite of the need to further refine the estimate with adjustment factors, the fact that it is now possible to create a rough estimate using only ten parameters is a useful feature of modern software cost-estimating tools.

It should be noted as an important fact that the same parameters that are useful for early software cost estimating should also be recorded when projects are measured and historical data is collected.

In the context of using the estimate for comparison purposes, it is also useful to record the NAIC industry code. This will facilitate comparing the estimate against similar projects from the same industry. The NAIC code does not affect the outcome of an estimate, but does make it easier to do comparisons with like projects.

Stage 3: Producing a Preliminary Cost Estimate

Once the administrative data for a software project, the cost and burden-rate data, work-habit data, and user-supplied size data have been provided, there is enough information available to create a rough preliminary cost estimate.

This preliminary estimate based on minimal information cannot be very accurate, because none of the major adjustment factors have been dealt with. However, the fact that preliminary estimates at this point can be done at all is encouraging.

The early estimating situation brings to mind Samuel Johnson's observation made while looking at a dog that had been trained to walk on its hind legs: "It isn't done well, but it is surprising that it can be done at all."

Once the ten basic inputs have been entered into a software cost-estimating tool, it is very easy to create a preliminary estimate.

Usually, it is only necessary to switch the tool from *input* mode to *estimate* mode. Some software cost-estimating tools even support concurrent inputs and estimates, so that the effect of each new or changed input shows up at once in an immediate, real-time revision of the estimated results.

Consider the same two Cases A and B that were discussed earlier. The following example illustrates the minimum amount of ten kinds of information needed to produce early software cost estimates for these two projects.

	Case A	Case B
Project Name	Travel Expenses	Gun Control System
NAIC code	73 (Services)	97 (national security)
Start date	January 6, 1997	January 6, 1997
Burdened cost	$6000	$12,000
Project goals	1 (normal effort)	4 (highest quality)
Project nature	1 (new program)	1 (new program)
Project scope	1 (disposable prototype)	7 (major system)

	Case A	Case B
Project class	1 (personal program)	15 (military contract)
Project type	1 (nonprocedural)	14 (embedded software)
Language	Visual Basic	Ada 95
FP method	IFPUG Version 4	IFPUG Version 4
Project size	15 FP 480 LOC	250 KLOC (4688 FP)
Count method	SPR logical statements	SEI physical lines

Five of the ten factors are always known even very early in the requirements phase, and only the start date, burdened salary rate, choice of programming languages, and the size of the application are problematic. The SIC code is not always readily known, but some software estimating tools provide a pull-down list of these codes.

While all of the factors are of use, the factors that actually affect the numeric results of an estimate are the following:

- Project goals
- Project nature
- Project scope
- Project class
- Project type
- Project size

At this point, the user can actually create a rough preliminary estimate for both Case A and Case B. There is not much point in dropping down to a task-level estimate at this point, because none of the adjustment factors that can influence project outcomes, such as complexity, experience, tools, methods, processes, and the like, have yet been dealt with.

The usual mode of cost-estimating tools when presented with incomplete adjustment information is to assume that the project will be *average* in terms of the missing elements. That is, there will be no adjustments of any kind based on complexity, experience, or the other key adjustment parameters.

At this point, if the estimating tool is switched from *input* to *estimate* mode, a preliminary software cost estimate can be created from the minimum information that has been provided.

Table 8.8 illustrates Case A, which is a simple travel expense application produced as a prototype.

Although this project is a comparatively small one, the cost estimate still provides some useful information. For example, the estimated cost of the project is $1363.64. This is not terribly expensive for custom software, but since it is possible to buy travel accounting software packages for less than $100, it may be that building a custom one might be construed as a waste of time. This simple example illustrates one of

TABLE 8.8 Preliminary Estimate for Case A (Personal Software)

Project information			
Category	Input	Category	Input
Project name	Travel Expenses	Start date	January 6, 2007
Project class	Personal	Project scope	Disposable prototype
Project type	Nonprocedural	Project goals	Normal
Language	Visual Basic	SIC code	73 (services)
Monthly rate	$6,000		
Source code size	480 (SPR logical statements)		
Function point size	15 (IFPUG 4)		

Activity	Start date	Completion date	Schedule, days	Staff	Effort, days	Cost
Coding	1/6/07	1/8/07	3	1	3	$818.18
Testing	1/7/07	1/9/07	2	1	2	545.45
Total/average	1/6/07	1/9/07	5	1	5	1363.64

Rate summary	
FP per month	66.00
LOC per month	2114.00
Cost per FP	$90.91
Cost per LOC	$2.84

the useful properties of software cost-estimating tools: They facilitate business decisions, such as make-or-buy analyses.

In fairness, it is highly unlikely that anyone would bother to run a small personal application through a commercial software cost-estimating tool. However, commercial software cost-estimating tools can handle projects as small as a one-line maintenance change (equivalent to perhaps one-hundredth of a function point) to as large as a 30 million–source code statement defense system (equivalent to perhaps 300,000 function points). They can easily deal with small sprints or the development of iterations as part of Agile projects.

Now let us examine the estimate for Case B, which is a much larger and more serious undertaking. Recall that Case B is a military software project produced under military specifications and standards.

For larger projects such as this, the normal work metric would be *months* rather than *days*, although users can select whatever work metric they wish to see (i.e., hours, days, months, or years), and the estimating tool will handle the conversion automatically.

As can be seen when examining Table 8.9, this project will not be a trivial one in terms of effort, schedules, and costs, even though all of the information is not yet at hand to refine the estimate.

The *latent* information derived merely from knowing the scope, nature, class, and type plus preliminary size data is quite enough to draw useful conclusions and generate a rough estimate.

Although only a few basic facts about both applications have been provided, the knowledge base and rules within the cost-estimating tool know that military projects utilize several activities that are rare or nonexistent in the civilian world, as follows:

- Critical design reviews
- Independent verification and validation
- Independent testing

These three activities are applied to the estimate simply because the project is identified as a military project. If the estimate was to be produced for the same kind of application, but it was identified as a civilian project, then these three activities would not be automatically included.

Note that in Case A, size was originally provided by the user in the form of function points and was then converted into the equivalent size in terms of logical source statements, using a backfiring utility function found within most commercial software estimating tools.

In Case B, size was originally provided in the form of SEI-style physical lines of code, or KLOC (units of 1000 LOC), and was then converted

TABLE 8.9   **Preliminary Estimate for Case B (Military Software)**

Project information			
Category	Input	Category	Input
Project name	Gun Control System	Start date	January 6, 2007
Project class	Military	Project scope	System
Project type	Embedded	Project goals	Highest quality
Language	Ada 95	SIC code	97 (national security)
Monthly rate	$12,000		
Source code size	250,000 (SEI physical lines)		
Function point size	4,688 (IFPUG 4)		

Activity	Start date	Completion date	Schedule, months	Staff	Effort, months	Cost
Requirements	1/6/07	6/20/07	6.13	19.00	116.50	$1,398,000
Prototype	2/6/07	7/27/07	6.35	10.00	63.50	762,000
Design	5/15/07	12/20/07	9.43	20.00	188.50	2,262,000
Critical design review	12/10/07	1/20/08	1.20	26.00	31.25	375,000
Coding	9/15/07	7/15/07	10.02	23.50	235.40	2,824,800
Code inspections	5/3/08	7/20/08	2.70	26.00	70.25	843,000
Testing	6/10/08	1/20/09	8.67	31.00	268.75	3,225,000
Independent verification and validation	10/2/08	2/12/09	4.71	7.00	33.00	396,000
Independent testing	11/1/08	1/27/09	2.96	8.00	23.70	284,400
Quality assurance	3/15/08	4/20/09	13.05	4.00	52.20	626,400
User documents	3/1/08	4/10/09	13.45	7.75	104.25	1,251,000
Management	/6/08	4/26/09	28.00	5.00	140.00	1,680,000
Total/average	1/6/08	4/26/09	28.00	15.60	1327.30	15,927,600

Rate summary	
FP per month	3.53
LOC per month	188.35
Cost per FP	$3397.53
Cost per LOC	$63.71

into the equivalent size in terms of function points, also using the back-firing size-conversion feature.

However, backfiring from physical lines is very problematic because individual programming styles vary so widely. For accuracy when back-firing, logical statement counts rather than physical line counts should be used whenever possible.

This form of bidirectional backfiring conversion between function point metrics and logical statement counts of software is a standard feature of perhaps 30 commercial software cost-estimating tools and is rapidly becoming a universal project management approach.

Neither the estimate for Case A nor for Case B is very accurate at this point, but both are probably useful for considering the general effort, cost, and schedule situations for the projects in question.

Note also that both estimates were produced using minimal information and, hence, minimal time on the part of the project manager or person producing the estimate. Preliminary estimates of this kind can be created in less than a minute if the ten basic facts for the projects being estimated are known and automated estimating tools are available.

Summary and Conclusions

Sizing approximations and preliminary cost estimates are not particularly accurate, but they are accurate enough for gross business decisions, such as whether to proceed with a project into the requirements phase, where more details will become available.

If preliminary estimates are used only as gates to determine whether projects should proceed or be terminated, they serve a useful purpose.

However, preliminary estimates using minimal information should definitely *not* serve as the basis for contracts, outsourcing agreements, or budgets for major projects.

In order to achieve a level of estimating accuracy suitable for important business decisions, many more factors need to be considered and included in the estimate. Actual software projects are built by real people, using tools and development processes that can affect the outcome of the project in significant ways. Here, too, general information can get the estimate started, but in order to achieve a satisfactory precision, a number of adjustments and refinements need to be made.

None of the approximation methods discussed thus far in this book are perfect or can offer great precision. But all are useful and have a place in software cost estimation. However, early estimates using approximate information are only the beginning stage of software cost estimation. Let us now explore how to refine the estimate by dealing with some of the more detailed sizing and adjustment factors.

The literature on early estimation and approximation is sparse, but is growing fairly rapidly under the influence of the usage of function point metrics. The authors who provide useful rules of thumb for early estimation can be divided into such sets as: (1) those who use lines-of-code-metrics; (2) those who use function point metrics; (3) those who use both lines-of-code and function point metrics; and (4) those who use object points, use case points, story points, or something else, which is a very mixed category including object-oriented metrics, Halstead software-science metrics, and a variety of other metrics, such as simply using number of personnel or number of work hours.

References

The Agile Alliance home page (http://www.agilealliance.org/home).

Ambler, S.: *Process Patterns—Building Large-Scale Systems Using Object Technology*, Cambridge University Press, New York, NY, SIGS Books, 1998.

Artow, J. and I. Neustadt: *UML and the Unified Process*, Addison-Wesley, Boston, Mass., 2000.

Beck, K.: *Extreme Programming Explained: Embrace Change*, Addison-Wesley, Boston, Mass., 1999.

Booch Grady, Object Solutions: Managing the Object-Oriented Project; Addison-Wesley, Reading, MA; 1995.

Booch, Grady, Ivar Jacobsen, and James Rumbaugh: *The Unified Modeling Language User Guide, Second Edition*, Addison-Wesley, Boston, Mass., 2005.

Boehm, Barry: *Software Engineering Economics*, Prentice-Hall, Englewood Cliffs, N.J., 1981.

Chidamber, S.R. and C.F. Kemerer: "A Metrics Suite for Object-Oriented Design," *IEEE Trans. on Software Engineering*, Vol. SE20, No. 6, June 1994, pp. 476–493.

Cockburn, Alistair: *Agile Software Development*, Addison-Wesley, Boston, Mass., 2001.

Cohn, Mike: *Agile Estimating and Planning*, Prentice-Hall PTR, Englewood Cliffs, N.J., 2005.

———: *User Stories Applied: For Agile Software Development*, Addison-Wesley, Boston, Mass., 2004.

DeMarco, Tom: *Controlling Software Projects*, Yourdon Press, New York, 1982.

———: *Why Does Software Cost So Much?*, Dorset House, New York, 1995.

Department of the Air Force: *Guidelines for Successful Acquisition and Management of Software Intensive Systems*, vols. 1 and 2, Software Technology Support Center, Hill Air Force Base, Utah, 1994.

Dreger, Brian: *Function Point Analysis*, Prentice-Hall, Englewood Cliffs, N.J., 1989.

Fuqua, Andrew M.: *Using Function Points in XP—Considerations*, Springer Berlin/ Heidelberg, 2003.

Galea, R. B.: *The Boeing Company: 3D Function Point Extensions, V2.0, Release 1.0*, Boeing Information Support Services, Seattle, Wash., June 1995.

Garmus, David, and David Herron: *Measuring the Software Process: A Practical Guide to Functional Measurement*, Prentice-Hall, Englewood Cliffs, N.J., 1995.

Grady, Robert B.: *Practical Software Metrics for Project Management and Process Improvement*, Prentice-Hall, Englewood Cliffs, N.J., 1992.

———, and Deborah L. Caswell: *Software Metrics: Establishing a Company-Wide Program*, Prentice-Hall, Englewood Cliffs, N.J., 1987.

Humphrey, Watts S.: *Managing the Software Process*, Addison-Wesley/Longman, Reading, Mass., 1989.

———: *A Discipline of Software Engineering*, Addison-Wesley, Reading, Mass., 1995.

IFPUG Counting Practices Manual, Release 4.1, International Function Point Users Group, Westerville, Ohio, 2000.

———: Release 4, International Function Point Users Group, Westerville, Ohio, April 1995.

International Function Point Users Group (IFPUG) (http://www.IFPUG.org).

Jones, Capers: *SPQR/20 Users Guide*, Software Productivity Research, Cambridge, Mass., 1986.

———: *Critical Problems in Software Measurement*, Information Systems Management Group, Carlsbad, CA 1993.

———: *Assessment and Control of Software Risks*, Prentice-Hall, Englewood Cliffs, NJ 1994.

———: *New Directions in Software Management*, Information Systems Management Group, Carlsbad, CA, 1994.

———: *Patterns of Software System Failure and Success*, International Thomson Computer Press, Boston, Mass., 1995.

———: *Applied Software Measurement, Second Edition*, McGraw-Hill, New York, 1996a.

————: *Table of Programming Languages and Levels* (8 Versions from 1985 through July 1996), Software Productivity Research, Burlington, Mass., 1996b.

————: *The Economics of Object-Oriented Software*, Software Productivity Research, Burlington, Mass., April 1997a.

————: *Software Quality—Analysis and Guidelines for Success*, International Thomson Computer Press, Boston, Mass., 1997b.

————: "Sizing Up Software," *Scientific American*, New York, December 1998, Vol. 279, No. 6, pp 104–109.

————: *Software Assessments, Benchmarks, and Best Practices*; Addison-Wesley Longman, Boston, Mass., 2000.

Kan, Stephen H.: *Metrics and Models in Software Quality Engineering, Second Edition;*, Addison-Wesley, Boston, Mass., 2003.

Kemerer, C. F.: "Reliability of Function Point Measurement—A Field Experiment," *Communications of the ACM*, **36:**85–97 (1993).

McConnell, Steve: *Software Estimating: Demystifying the Black Art*, Microsoft Press, Redmond, Wa, 2006.

Pressman, Roger: *Software Engineering—A Practitioner's Approach, Sixth Edition*, McGraw-Hill, New York, 2005.

Putnam, Lawrence H.: *Measures for Excellence—Reliable Software on Time, Within Budget*, Yourdon Press/Prentice-Hall, Englewood Cliffs, N.J., 1992.

————, and Ware Myers: *Industrial Strength Software—Effective Management Using Measurement*, IEEE Press, Los Alamitos, Calif., 1997.

Rethinking the Software Process, CD-ROM, Miller Freeman, Lawrence, Kans., 1996. (This CD-ROM is a book collection jointly produced by the book publisher, Prentice-Hall, and the journal publisher, Miller Freeman. It contains the full text and illustrations of five Prentice-Hall books: *Assessment and Control of Software Risks* by Capers Jones; *Controlling Software Projects* by Tom DeMarco; *Function Point Analysis* by Brian Dreger; *Measures for Excellence* by Larry Putnam and Ware Myers; and *Object-Oriented Software Metrics* by Mark Lorenz and Jeff Kidd.)

Roetzheim, William H., and Reyna A. Beasley: *Best Practices in Software Cost and Schedule Estimation*, Prentice-Hall PTR, Upper Saddle River, N.J., 1998.

Rubin, Howard: *Software Benchmark Studies for 1997*, Howard Rubin Associates, Pound Ridge, N.Y., 1997.

Symons, Charles R.: *Software Sizing and Estimating—Mk II FPA (Function Point Analysis)*, John Wiley & Sons, Chichester, U.K., 1991.

————: "ISMI—International Software Metrics Initiative—Project Proposal" (private communication), June 15, 1997.

————: "Software Sizing and Estimating: Can Function Point Methods Meet Industry Needs?" (unpublished draft submitted to the IEEE for possible publication), Guild of Independent Function Point Analysts, London, U.K., August 1997.

Whitmire, S. A.: "3-D Function Points: Scientific and Real-Time Extensions to Function Points," *Proceedings of the 1992 Pacific Northwest Software Quality Conference*, June 1, 1992.

3

Sizing Software Deliverables

Software projects consist of far more than just source code. A modern software project is surrounded by a host of artifacts and deliverable items that need to be both sized and estimated. Software projects can include text-based documents, graphical and multimedia materials, source code, and test cases and test scripts. In addition, although these are not planned artifacts, software projects are also accompanied by large numbers of bugs or defects. Here, too, both sizing and estimating technologies are needed.

This section discusses the kinds of sizing methods that are found in software cost-estimating tools for dealing with all classes of deliverable items and all major kinds of software artifacts.

Sizing Software Deliverables

Up until this point our discussion of software cost estimating has dealt primarily with surface issues that are not highly complex. We are now beginning to deal with some of the software cost-estimating issues that are very complex indeed.

It will soon be evident why software cost-estimating tools either must be limited to a small range of software projects or else must utilize hundreds of rules and a knowledge base of thousands of projects in order to work well.

It is easier to build software estimating tools that aim at specific domains, such as those aimed only at military projects or at management information systems projects, than to build estimating tools that can work equally well with information systems, military software, systems and embedded software, commercial software, web applets, object-oriented applications, and the myriad of classes and types that comprise the overall software universe.

In this section we will begin to delve into some of the harder problems of software cost estimating that the vendors in the software cost-estimating business attempt to solve, and then we will place the solutions into our commercial software cost-estimating tools.

General Sizing Logic for Key Deliverables

One of the first and most important aspects of software cost estimating is that of *sizing*, or predicting the volumes of various kinds of software deliverable items. Sizing is a very complex problem for software cost estimating, but advances in sizing technology over the past 30 years have been impressive.

Software cost-estimating tools usually approach sizing in a sequential or *cascade* fashion. First, the overall size of the application is determined,

TABLE 9.1   Software Artifacts for Which Size Information Is Useful

1.	Use cases for software requirements
2.	User stories for software requirements
3.	Classes and methods for object-oriented projects
4.	Function point sizes for new development
5.	Function point sizes for reused material and packages
6.	Function point sizes for changes and deletions
7.	Function point sizes for creeping requirements
8.	Function point sizes for reusable components
9.	Function point sizes for object-oriented class libraries
10.	Source code to be developed for applications
11.	Source code to be developed for prototypes
12.	Source code to be extracted from a library of reusable components
13.	Source code to be updated for enhancement projects
14.	Source code to be changed or removed during maintenance
15.	Source code to be updated from software packages
16.	Screens to be created for users
17.	Screens to be reused from other applications
18.	Text-based paper documents, such as requirements and specifications
19.	Text-based paper documents, such as test plans and status reports
20.	Percentages of text-based paper documents that are reused
21.	Graphics-based paper documents, such as data flow diagrams or control flows
22.	Percentages of graphics elements that are reused
23.	Online HELP text
24.	Graphics and illustrations
25.	Multimedia materials (music and animation)
26.	Defects or bugs in all deliverables
27.	New test cases
28.	Existing test cases from regression test libraries
29.	Database contents
30.	Percentage of database contents that are reused

using source code volumes, function point totals, use cases, stories, object points, screens, or some other metric of choice. Then the sizes for other kinds of artifacts and deliverable items are predicted based on the primary size in terms of LOC, function points, or whatever metric was selected.

Before discussing how sizing is performed, it is useful to consider some 30 examples of the kinds of software artifacts for which sizing may be required. The main software artifacts are shown in Table 9.1.

Although this list is fairly extensive, it covers only the more obvious software artifacts that need to be dealt with. Let us now consider the sizing implications of these various software artifacts at a somewhat more detailed level.

Sizing Methods Circa 2007

One of the major historical problems of the software engineering world has been the need to attempt to produce accurate cost estimates for software projects before the requirements are fully known.

The first step in software cost estimating requires a knowledge of the size of the application in some tangible measurement such as lines of code, function points, object points, use cases, story points, or some other alternative.

The eventual size of the application is, of course, derived from user requirements of the application. Thus sizing and understanding user requirements are essentially the same problem.

Empirical data from hundreds of measured software projects reveals that a full and perfect understanding of user requirements is not usually possible to achieve at one time. User requirements tend to unfold and grow over time. In fact, the measured rate of this growth of user requirements averages 2 percent per calendar month, from the end of the nominal "requirements phase" through the subsequent design and coding phases.

The total accumulated growth in requirements averages about 25 percent more than initially envisioned, but the maximum growth in requirements has exceeded 100 percent. That is, the final application ends up being about twice as large as initially envisioned.

Historically, the growth in requirements after the formal requirements phase has led to several different approaches for dealing with this phenomenon, such as the following:

- Improved methods of requirements gathering such as joint application design (JAD), where clients work side by side with designers using formal methods that are intended to gather requirements with few omissions.

- Freezing requirements for the initial release at some arbitrary point. Additional requirements are moved into subsequent releases.

- Including anticipated growth in the initial cost estimates. Often the first estimate will include an arbitrary "contingency factor" such as an additional 35 percent for handling unknown future requirements that occur after the estimate is produced.

- Various forms of iterative development, where pieces of the final application are developed and used before starting to build the next set of features.

- Various forms of Agile development, where development commences when only the most important and obvious features are understood. As experiences with using the first features accumulate, additional features are planned and constructed. The features for the final application may not be understood until a number of versions have been developed and used. For some of the Agile approaches, clients are part of the team and so the requirements evolve in real time.

Software applications are a different kind of engineering problem from designing a house or a tangible object such as an automobile.

Before construction starts on a house, a full set of design blueprints are developed by the architect, using inputs from the owners. It does happen that the owners may make changes afterwards, but usually the initial blueprint is more than 95 percent complete.

Unfortunately for the software world, clients usually demand cost estimates for 100 percent of the final application at a point in time where less than 50 percent of the final features are understood. A key challenge to software estimating specialists and software project managers is to find effective methods for sizing applications in the absence of full knowledge of their final requirements.

Some of the methods that have developed for producing software application size and cost estimates in the absence of full requirements include the following:

- Pattern matching, or using historical data from similar projects as the basis for both predicting the final size and costs of a new project.

- Using historical data on the average rate of requirements growth to predict the probable amount of growth from the time of the first estimate to the end of the project.

- Using various mathematical or statistical methods to attempt a final size prediction from partial requirements.

- Using arbitrary rules of thumb to add "contingency" amounts to initial estimates to fund future requirements.

- Attempting to limit requirements growth by freezing requirements at a specific point, and deferring all additions to future versions that will have their own separate cost estimates.

- Producing formal cost estimates only for the features and requirements that are fully understood, and delaying the production of a full cost estimate until later when the requirements are finally defined.

Let us consider the pros and cons of these six methods for dealing with sizing software applications in the absence of full requirements.

Pattern Matching from Historical Data

In 2007, about 70 percent of all software applications are repeats of legacy applications that have lived past their prime and need to be retired. However, only about 15 percent of these legacy applications have reasonably complete historical data available in terms of schedules, costs, and quality. What the legacy applications do have available is a known size. However this size data may only be available in terms of source code. Also, the programming language for the legacy software is probably not going to be the same as that of the new replacement application.

For example, if you are replacing a legacy order entry system circa 1990 with a new application, the size of the legacy application might be 5000 function points and 135,000 COBOL source statements in size.

The new version will probably include all of the existing legacy features, and some new features as well. You might also be planning to use an object-oriented method of developing the new version and the Smalltalk programming language.

You can assume that the set of features for the new application will be larger than the old but the source code volume might not be. Using the legacy application as the starting point, and some suitable conversion rules, you might predict that the new version will be about 6000 object points in size. The volume of code in the Smalltalk programming language might be about 36,000 Smalltalk statements since Smalltalk is a much more powerful language than COBOL.

As an additional assumption since you are using OO methods and code, you probably will have about 50 percent reusable code so you will only be developing about 3000 object points and 18,000 new Smalltalk statements.

Of course, this is not a perfect approach to sizing, but if you do happen to have historical size information available from one or more similar legacy applications, you can be reasonably sure that you will not understate the size of the new application. The new application will almost certainly be somewhat larger than the old in terms of features.

If you have access to a large volume of historical data from a consulting company or benchmark group you might be able to evaluate a number of similar legacy applications. Doing this requires a benchmark database and a good taxonomy of application nature, class, scope, and type in order to ensure appropriate matches.

Pattern matching from legacy applications is the only method that can be used before requirements gathering is started. Thus, pattern matching provides the earliest chronology for creating a cost estimate that does not depend almost exclusively on guesswork.

Using Historical Data to Predict Growth in Requirements

It is a proven fact that for large software applications, the requirements are *never* fully defined at the end of the nominal requirements phase. It is also a proven fact that requirements typically grow at a rate of about 2 percent per calendar month assuming a standard waterfall development model and a normal requirements gathering and analysis process.

This growth continues during the subsequent design and coding phases, but stops at the testing phase. For an application with a six-month design phase and a nine-month coding phase, the cumulative growth will be about 30 percent in new features.

(However, if you are using one of the Agile methods that concentrates exclusively on the most obvious and important initial requirements, the monthly rate of growth in new requirements will be about 15 percent per calendar month. For an Agile application with a one-month design phase and four months of sprints or iterations, the cumulative growth in requirements will be about 75 percent in new features.)

Thus, historical data from past projects that show the rate at which requirements evolve and grow during the development cycle can be used to estimate the probable size of the entire application. Incidentally, predicting the growth of requirements over time is a useful adjunct to the method of "earned value" costing.

Several commercial software cost-estimating tools include features that attempt to predict the volume of growth of requirements after the requirements phase. The actual calculations, of course, are somewhat more complex than the simple examples discussed here.

Mathematical or Statistical Attempts to Extrapolate Size from Partial Requirements

Recall from Chapters 6, 7, and 8 that the taxonomy of nature, class, type, and scope places a software application squarely among similar applications. In fact, once an application has been placed in this taxonomy, simply raising the sum to the 2.35 power will yield a rough approximation of the function point total for the application as illustrated in Chapter 8. Similar rules can be applied to predict the number of object points, use case points, or other metrics.

One of the characteristics of applications that occupy the same place in a taxonomy is that such applications often have very similar distributions of function point values for the five elements: inputs, outputs, inquiries, logical files, and interfaces.

Assume that the taxonomy of your new application matches a legacy application that had 50 inputs, 75 outputs, 50 inquiries, 15 logical files, and 10 interfaces. When analyzing early requirements for the new application, you will probably start with "outputs" since that is the most common starting place for understanding user needs.

If you ascertain that your new application will have 80 outputs, then you have enough information to make a mathematical prediction of likely values for the missing data on inputs, inquiries, logical files, and interfaces. Thus, you can predict about 53 inputs, 80 outputs, 53 inquiries, 17 logical files, and 11 interfaces.

We started with knowledge only of the outputs, and used mathematical extrapolation to predict the missing values.

Similar kinds of predictions could also be made with object points or use case points. However, there is comparatively little historical data available that is expressed in terms of either object points or use case points.

Some commercial software cost-estimating tools do include extrapolation features from partial knowledge. It should be noted that there are two drawbacks to sizing using this approach: (1) you need firm knowledge of the size of at least one factor, and (2) you need access to historical data from similar projects.

Also, from time to time new applications will not actually match the volumes of inputs, outputs, inquiries, etc., from legacy or historical projects. Thus, this method occasionally will lead to erroneous sizing.

Arbitrary Rules of Thumb for Adding Contingency Factors

The oldest and simplest method for dealing with incomplete requirements is to add a contingency factor to each cost estimate. These contingency factors are usually expressed as simple percentages of the total cost estimate. For example, back in the 1970s IBM used the following sliding scale of contingency factors for software cost estimates:

Phase 1 requirements cost estimate:	35 percent
Phase 2 design cost estimate:	20 percent
Phase 3 coding cost estimate:	15 percent
Phase 4 testing cost estimate:	5 percent

The rationale for these contingency factors is that the extra money would be used to fund requirements that had not been understood or present at the time of each cost estimate. In other words, although expressed in terms of dollars, contingency factors are inserted to deal with the growth of unknown requirements and to handle the increase in size that these requirements will cause.

While the contingency factors were moderately successful in the 1970s, they gradually ran into technical difficulties. As typical IBM applications grew in size from less than 1000 function points in the 1970s to more than 10,000 function points in the 1990s, the contingency factors needed to be increased. This is because for large systems, less is known early and more growth occurs later on.

To use simple percentage contingency factors on applications in the 10,000–function point range, the values would have to approximate the following:

Phase 1 requirements cost estimate:	50 percent
Phase 2 design cost estimate:	35 percent
Phase 3 coding cost estimate:	20 percent
Phase 4 testing cost estimate:	10 percent

However, such large contingency factors are psychologically unsettling to executives and clients. They feel uncomfortable with estimates that are based on such large adjustment factors.

Freezing Requirements
at Fixed Points in Time

Since the 1970s some large corporations such as AT&T, IBM, and Microsoft have had firm cut-off dates for all features that were intended to go out in a specific releases. After the initial release of a large system such as the AT&T ESS5 switching system, IBM's MVS operating system, and Microsoft's Windows XP operating system, future releases are planned at fixed intervals.

For example, IBM would plan a maintenance release for bug repairs six months after the initial release of an application, and then add new features 12 months after the initial release. Maintenance releases and new-feature releases would then continue to alternate on those schedules for about five calendar years. After about 36 months there would be a "mid-life kicker" or a release with quite a lot of interesting new features.

New features would be targeted for a specific release, but if there were problems that made a feature miss its planned release, it had to wait for another 12 months before going out. This sometimes led to rushing and poor quality in order to meet the deadline for an important new feature.

It also happens that for very large systems in the 10,000–function point range (equivalent to 500,000 Java statements or 1,250,000 C statements) the initial release usually contains only about 80 percent of the features that were originally intended. An analysis of large IBM applications by the author in the 1970s found that 20 percent of planned features missed the first release. However, about 30 percent of the features in the first release were not originally planned, but occurred later in the form of creeping requirements. This is a fairly typical pattern.

For large applications that are likely to last for five or ten years once deployed, having fixed release intervals is a fairly effective solution. Development teams soon become comfortable with fixed release intervals and can plan accordingly.

Also, customers or clients usually prefer a fixed release interval because it makes their maintenance and support planning easier and helps keep costs level over time. The one exception to the advantages of fixed release intervals is the case of high-severity defects, which need to be fixed and released as quickly as possible.

For example, users of Microsoft Windows receive very frequent updates from Microsoft when security breaches or other critical problems are found in Windows XP or Microsoft Office.

Producing Formal Cost Estimates
Only for Subsets of the Total Application

Some of the Agile approaches attempt to avoid the problems of complete sizing and cost estimating in the absence of full requirements by producing cost estimates only for the next iteration or sprint that will be produced. The overall or final cost for the application is not attempted, on the grounds that it is probably unknowable until customers have used the early releases and decided what they want next.

This method does avoid large errors in sizing and cost estimating. But that is because the predictions of the final size and final costs are not attempted initially. Currently in 2007, this approach is used mainly for internal projects where the costs and schedule are not subject to contractual requirements. It is not currently the method of choice for fixed-price contracts or for other software applications where the total cost must be known for legal or corporate reasons.

The approach of formal estimates only for the next sprint or iteration does fit in reasonably well with the "earned value" approach, although not very many Agile projects have reported using earned value measurements to date.

However, as more and more Agile projects are completed there will be a steady accumulation of historical data. Within a few years, there should be enough information to know the total numbers of stories, story points, use cases, sprints, and other data from hundreds of Agile projects.

Within perhaps five or ten years, pattern matching approaches will begin to be widely available in an Agile context. Once there is a critical mass of completed Agile projects with historical data available, then it will be possible to use this information to predict overall sizes and costs for new applications.

This means that the Agile development teams will have to record historical information, which will add slightly to the effort for developing the applications.

The same kinds of patterns are starting to be developed for object-oriented projects. At some point in the near future, pattern matching will begin to be effective not only for the technical features of OO applications, but also for predicting costs, schedules, staffing, quality, and other business features as well.

Function Point Variations Circa 2007

Over and above the function point metric defined by IFPUG, there are close to 40 other variants that do not give the same results as the IFPUG method. Further, many of the function point variants have no published conversion rules to standard IFPUG function points or much data of any kind in print.

This means that the same application can appear to have very different sizes, based on whether the function point totals follow the IFPUG counting rules, the British Mark II counting rules, COSMIC function point counting rules, object-point counting rules, the SPR feature point counting rules, the Boeing 3D counting rules, or any of the other function point variants. Thus, application sizing and cost estimating based on function point metrics must also identify the rules and definitions of the specific form of function point being utilized.

These variants have introduced serious technical challenges into software benchmarks and economic analysis. Suppose you were a metrics consultant with a client in the telecommunications industry who wanted to know what methods and programming languages gave the best productivity for PBX switching systems. This is a fairly common kind of request.

You search various benchmark data bases and find 21 PBX switching systems that appear to be relevant to the client's request. Now the problems start:

- Three of the PBXs were measured using "lines of code." One counted physical lines, one counted logical statements, and one did not define which method was used.

- Three of the PBXs were object-oriented. One was counted using object points and two were counted with use case points.

- Three of the PBXs were counted with IFPUG function points.

- Three of the PBXs were counted with COSMIC function points.

- Three of the PBXs were counted with NESMA function points.

- Three of the PBXs were counted with Feature points.

- Three of the PBXs were counted with Mark II function points

As of 2007, there is no easy technical way to provide the client with an accurate answer to what is really a basic economic question. You cannot average the results of these 21 similar projects nor do any kind of useful statistical analysis because of the use of so many different metrics.

Prior to this book there have been no published conversion rules from one metric variant to another. Although this book does have some tentative conversion rules, they are not viewed by the author as being accurate enough to use for serious business purposes such as providing clients with valid comparisons between projects counted via different approaches.

In the author's opinion, the developers of alternate function point metrics have a professional obligation to provide conversion rules from their new metrics to the older IFPUG function point metric. It is not the job of IFPUG to evaluation every new alternative.

Also, IFPUG itself introduced a major change in function point counting rules in 1994, when Version 4 of the rules was published. The Version 4 changes eliminated counts of some forms of error messages (over substantial protest, it should be noted) and, hence, reduced the counts from the prior Version 3.4 by perhaps 20 percent for projects with significant numbers of error messages.

The function point sizes in this book are based on IFPUG counts, with Version 4.1 being the most commonly used variant. However, from time to time points require that the older Version 3.4 form be used. The text will indicate which form is utilized for specific cases.

Over and above the need to be very clear as to which specific function point is being used, there are also some other issues associated with function point sizing that need to be considered.

The rules for counting function points using most of the common function point variants are rather complex. This means that attempts to count function points by untrained individuals generally lead to major errors. This is unfortunate, but is also true of almost any other significant metric.

Both the IFPUG and the equivalent organization in the United Kingdom, the United Kingdom Function Point (Mark II) Users Group, offer training and certification examinations. Other metrics organizations, such as the Australian Software Metrics Association (ASMA) and the Netherlands Software Metrics Association (NESMA) may also offer certification services. However, most of the minor function point variants have no certification examinations and have very little published data.

When reviewing data expressed in function points, it is important to know whether the published function point totals used for software cost estimates are derived from counts by certified function point counters, from attempts to create totals by untrained counters, or from four other common ways of deriving function point totals:

- Backfiring from source code counts, either manually or using tools such as those marketed by ViaSoft

- Automatic generation of function points from requirements and design, using tools

- Deriving function points by analogy, such as assuming that Project B will be the same size as Project A, a prior project that has a function point size of known value

- Counting function points using one of the many variations in functional counting methods (i.e., SPR feature points, Boeing 3D function points, COSMIC function points, Netherlands function points, etc.)

(Of course it is also important to know whether data expressed in lines of code is based on counts of physical lines or logical statements, just as it is important to know whether distance data expressed in *miles* refers to statute miles or nautical miles, or whether volumetric data expressed in terms of *gallons* refers to U.S. gallons or Imperial gallons.)

As a result of the lack of written information for legacy projects, the method called "backfiring," or direct conversion from source code statements to equivalent function point totals, has become one of the most widely used methods for determining the function point totals of legacy applications. Since legacy applications far outnumber new software projects, this means that backfiring is actually the most widely used method for deriving function point totals.

Backfiring is highly automated, and a number of vendors provide tools that can convert source code statements into equivalent function point values. Backfiring is very easy to perform, so that the function point totals for applications as large as 1 million source code statements can be derived in only a few minutes of computer time.

The downside of backfiring is that it is based on highly variable relationships between source code volumes and function point totals. Although backfiring may achieve statistically useful results when averaged over hundreds of projects, it may not be accurate by even plus or minus 50 percent for any specific project. This is due to the fact that individual programming styles can create very different volumes of source code for the same feature. Controlled experiments by IBM in which eight programmers coded the same specification found variations of about 5 to 1 in the volume of source code written by the participants.

Also, backfiring results will vary widely based upon whether the starting point is a count of physical lines, or a count of logical statements. In general, starting with logical statements will give more accurate results. However, counts of logical statements are harder to find than counts of physical lines.

In spite of the uncertainty of backfiring, it is supported by more tools and is a feature of more commercial software estimating tools than any other current sizing method. The need for speed and low sizing costs explains why many of the approximation methods, such as backfiring, sizing by analogy, and automated function point derivations, are so popular: They are fast and cheap, even if they are not as accurate. It also explains why so many software-tool vendors are actively exploring automated rule-based function point sizing engines that can derive function point totals from requirements and specifications, with little or no human involvement.

Since function point metrics have splintered in recent years, the family of possible function point variants used for estimation and measurement include at least 38 choices (see Table 9.2).

Note that this listing is not stated to be 100 percent complete. The 38 variants shown in Table 9.2 are merely the ones that have surfaced in the

TABLE 9.2   Function Point Counting Variations Circa 2007

1.	The 1975 internal IBM function point method
2.	The 1979 published Albrecht IBM function point method
3.	The 1982 DeMarco bang function point method
4.	The 1983 Rubin/ESTIMACS function point method
5.	The 1983 British Mark II function point method (Symons)
6.	The 1984 revised IBM function point method
7.	The 1985 SPR function point method using three adjustment factors
8.	The 1985 SPR backfire function point method
9.	The 1986 SPR feature point method for real-time software
10.	The 1994 SPR approximation function point method
11.	The 1997 SPR analogy-based function point method
12.	The 1997 SPR taxonomy-based function point method
13.	The 1986 IFPUG Version 1 method
14.	The 1988 IFPUG Version 2 method
15.	The 1990 IFPUG Version 3 method
16.	The 1995 IFPUG Version 4 method
17.	The 1989 Texas Instruments IEF function point method
18.	The 1992 Reifer coupling of function points and Halstead metrics
19.	The 1992 ViaSoft backfire function point method
20.	The 1993 Gartner Group backfire function point method
21.	The 1994 Boeing 3D function point method
22.	The 1994 object point method
23.	The 1994 Bachman Analyst function point method
24.	The 1995 Compass Group backfire function point method
25.	The 1995 Air Force engineering function point method
26.	The 1995 Oracle function point method
27.	The 1995 NESMA function point method
28.	The 1995 ASMA function point method
29.	The 1995 Finnish function point method
30.	The 1996 CRIM micro–function point method
31.	The 1996 object point method
32.	The 1997 data point method for database sizing
33.	The 1997 Nokia function point approach for telecommunications software
34.	The 1997 full function point approach for real-time software
35.	The 1997 ISO working group rules for functional sizing
36.	The 1998 COSMIC function point approach
37.	The 1999 story point method
38.	The 2003 use case point method

software measurement literature or been discussed at metrics conferences. No doubt, at least another 20 or so variants may exist that have not yet published any information or been presented at metrics conferences.

With some reluctance, the author is providing a table of conversion factors between some of the more common function point variants and standard IFPUG function points (see Table 9.3). The accuracy of the conversion ratios is questionable in 2007. Hopefully, even the publication of incorrect conversion rules will lead to refinements and more accurate rules in the future. This is an area that needs a great deal of research.

TABLE 9.3   Approximate Conversion Ratios to IFPUG Function Points
(Assumes Version 4.1 of the IFPUG Counting Rules)

Function point method	From IFPUG function points	To IFPUG function points	Java statements per function point
Story Points	50.00%	200.00%	100
Taxonomy-Based	85.00%	117.65%	59
IBM Original	90.00%	111.11%	56
IFPUG Version 4.1	100.00%	100.00%	50
Feature Points	100.00%	100.00%	50
NESMA	105.00%	95.24%	48
Full Function Points	110.00%	90.91%	45
Object Points	110.00%	90.91%	45
3D Function Points	110.00%	90.91%	45
Backfire: Logical LOC	112.00%	89.29%	45
COSMIC Function Points	115.00%	86.96%	43
Engineering Function Pts.	115.00%	86.96%	43
IFPUG Version 3.0	120.00%	83.33%	42
Mark II Function Points	120.00%	83.33%	42
Use Case Points	125.00%	80.00%	40
Backfire: Physical LOC	130.00%	76.92%	38

Table 9.3 uses IFPUG 4.1 as its base. If you want to convert 100 IFPUG function points to COSMIC function points, use the "From IFPUG…" column. The result would be about 115 COSMIC function points. Going the other way, if you start with 100 COSMIC function points and want to convert to IFPUG, use the "To IFPUG…" column. The result would be about 87 IFPUG function points.

If you want to perform conversions among the other metrics, you will need to do a double conversion. For example, if you want to convert use case points into COSMIC function points, you will have to convert both values into IFPUG first. If you start with 100 use case points, that is equal to about 80 IFPUG function points. Then you would use the "From IFPUG…" value of 115 percent for COSMIC, and the result would be about 92 COSMIC function points.

The software industry has long been criticized for lacking good historical data and for inaccurate sizing and estimating of many applications. Unfortunately, the existence of so many different metrics is exacerbating an already difficult challenge for software estimators.

Reasons Cited for Creating Function Point Variations

The reasons why there are at least 38 variations in counting function points deserve some research and discussion. First, it was proven long ago in the 1970s that the lines-of-code-metrics cannot measure software productivity in an economic sense and is harmful for activity-based cost analysis. Therefore, there is a strong incentive to adopt some form of functional metric because the older LOC method has been proven to be unreliable.

However, the mushrooming growth of function point variations can be traced to other causes. From meetings and discussions with the developers of many function point variants, the following reasons have been noted as to why variations have been created.

First, a significant number of variations were created due to a misinterpretation of the nature of function point metrics. Because the original IBM function points were first applied to information systems, a belief grew up that standard function points don't work for real-time and embedded software. This belief is caused by the fact that productivity rates for real-time and embedded software are usually well below the rates for information systems of the same size measured with function points.

Almost all of the function point variants yield larger counts for real-time and embedded software than do standard IFPUG function points.

The main factors identified as differentiating embedded and real-time software from information systems applications include the following:

- Embedded software is high in algorithmic complexity.
- Embedded software is often limited in logical files.
- Embedded software's inputs and outputs may be electronic signals.
- Embedded software's interfaces may be electronic signals.
- The user view for embedded software may not reflect human users.

These differences are great enough that the real-time and systems community has been motivated to create a number of function point variations that give more weight to algorithms, give less weight to logical files, and expand the concept of inputs and outputs to deal with electronic signals and sensor-based data rather than human-oriented inputs and outputs, such as forms and screens. Are these alternative function point methods really useful? There is no definitive answer, but from the point of view of benchmarking and international comparisons they have caused more harm than they have created value.

Another phenomenon noted when exploring function point variations is the fact that many function point variants are aligned to national borders. The IFPUG is headquartered in the United States, and most of the current officers and committee chairs are U.S. citizens.

There is a widespread feeling in Europe and elsewhere that in spite of the association having *international* in its name, IFPUG is dominated by the United States and may not properly reflect the interests of Europe, South America, the Pacific Rim, or Australia. Therefore, some of the function point variants are more or less bounded by national borders, such as the Netherlands function point method and the older British Mark II function point method.

If function points are to remain viable into the next century, it is urgent to focus energies on perfecting one primary form of functional metric rather than dissipating energies into the creation of scores of minor function point variants, many of which have no published data and have only a handful of users.

Even worse, while many months of effort have been spent developing 38 function point variants, some major measurement and metrics issues are almost totally unexamined. As will be pointed out later in this chapter, the software engineering community lags physics and engineering in understanding and measuring complexity. Also, there are no effective measurements for database volumes or database quality. There are no effective measurements or metrics that can deal with intangible value. There are no good measurements or metrics for customer service. It would be far more useful for software engineering if metrics research began to concentrate on important topics that are beyond the current measurement state of the art, rather than dissipating energies on scores of minor function point variants.

Regardless of the reasons, the existence of so many variations in counting function points is damaging to the overall software metrics community and is not really advancing the state of the art of software measurement.

As the situation currently stands, the overall range of apparent function point counts for the same application can vary by perhaps two to one, based on which specific varieties of function point metrics are utilized. This situation obviously requires that the specific form of function point be recorded in order for the size information to have any value.

Although the large range of metric choices all using the name "function points" is a troublesome situation, it is not unique to software. Other measurements outside the software arena also have multiple choices for metrics that use the same name. For example, it is necessary to know whether statute miles or nautical miles are being used; whether American dollars, Australian dollars, or Canadian dollars are being used; and whether American gallons or Imperial gallons are being used. It is also necessary to know whether temperatures are being measured in Celsius or Fahrenheit degrees. There are also three ways of calculating the octane rating of fuel, and several competing methods for calculating fuel efficiency or miles per gallon. There are even multiple ways of calculating birthdays.

However, the explosion of the function point metric into 38 or so competitive claimants must be viewed as an excessive number of choices. Hopefully, the situation will not reach the point seen among programming languages, where 600 or more languages are competing for market share.

Volume of Function Point Data Available

The next table is an attempt to quantify the approximate number of software projects that have been measured using various forms of metrics. IFPUG Version 4.1 is in the majority, but due to the global preponderance of aging legacy applications, various forms of backfiring appear to be the major sources of global function point data for maintenance projects.

The information in Table 9.4 is derived from discussions with various benchmarking companies, from the software metrics literature, and from informal discussions with function point users and developers during the course of software assessment and benchmarking studies. The table has a high margin of error and is simply a rough attempt to evaluate the size of the universe of function point data and lines of code data when all major variations are included.

TABLE 9.4: Approximate Numbers of Projects Measured

Metric used	New projects	Maintenance projects	Total projects	Percent
IFPUG Version 4.1	17,000	6,000	23,000	16.05%
Physical LOC	10,000	8,000	18,000	12.56%
IFPUG Version 3.0	15,000	2,500	17,500	12.21%
Gartner Backfire	10,000	6,000	16,000	11.17%
Backfire: Physical LOC	3,500	12,000	15,500	10.82%
Uncertified Counters	7,000	5,000	12,000	8.37%
Backfire: Logical LOC	2,000	7,500	9,500	6.63%
Mark II Function Points	5,000	1,000	6,000	4.19%
NESMA Function Points	4,000	1,500	5,500	3.84%
IBM Original	3,500	1,000	4,500	3.14%
Logical LOC	3,000	1,000	4,000	2.79%
Use Case Points	2,500	100	2,600	1.81%
Story Points	2,500	25	2,525	1.76%
COSMIC Function Points	1,100	300	1,400	0.98%
SPR Function Points	800	500	1,300	0.91%
DeMarco Bang Metric	800	350	1,150	0.80%
Feature Points	750	300	1,050	0.73%
Object Points	800	200	1,000	0.70%
Full Function Points	300	75	375	0.26%
Engineering Function Pts.	100	50	150	0.10%
3D Function Points	75	50	125	0.09%
Taxonomy-Based	100	10	110	0.08%
TOTALS	89,825	53,460	143,285	100.00%

Because aging legacy applications comprise the bulk of all software projects in the world, the various forms of backfiring, or direct conversion between source code statements and function points, is the most widely utilized method for enumerating function points, especially for legacy applications. All of the major software benchmarking companies (e.g., Davids, Gartner Group, SPR, etc.) utilize backfiring for their client studies and, hence, have substantial data derived from backfiring.

Curiously, none of the major function point groups, such as IFPUG, the United Kingdom Function Point Users Group, or the Netherlands Software Metrics Association, have attempted any formal studies of backfiring, or even made any visible contribution to this popular technology. The great majority of reports and data on backfiring come from the commercial benchmark consulting companies, such as the David's Consulting Company, Gartner Group, Rubin Systems, and Software Productivity Research.

As stated, the margin of error with Table 9.4 is very high, and the information is derived from informal surveys at various function point events in the United States, Europe, and the Pacific Rim. However, there seems to be no other source of this kind of information on the distribution of software projects among the various forms of function point analysis.

It is also curious that none of the function point user associations, such as IFPUG or the United Kingdom Function Point Users Group, have attempted to quantify the world number of projects measured using function points. IFPUG has attempted some benchmarking work, but only in the context of projects measured using the IFPUG Version 4 counting rules.

Unfortunately, the major function point associations, such as IFPUG in the United States, the British Mark II users group, NESMA, ASMA, and others, tend to view each other as political rivals and, hence, ignore one another's data or sometimes even actively disparage one another.

Consider yet another issue associated with function point metrics. The minimum weighting factors assigned to standard IFPUG function points have a lower limit or cut-off point. These limits mean that the smallest practical project where such common function point metrics as IFPUG and Mark II can be used is in the vicinity of 10 to 15 function points. Below that size, the weighting factors tend to negate the use of the function point metric.

Because of the large number of small maintenance and enhancement projects, there is a need for some kind of *micro–function point* that can be used in the zone that runs from a fraction of a single function point up to the current minimum level where normal function points apply.

Since it is the weighting factors that cause the problem with small projects, one obvious approach would be to use unadjusted function point counts for small projects without applying any weights at all. However, this experimental solution would necessitate changes in the logic of software estimating tools to accommodate this variation.

The huge numbers of possible methods for counting function points are very troublesome for software cost-estimating tool vendors and for all those who build metrics tools and software project management tools. None of us can support all 38 variations in function point counting, so most of us support only a subset of the major methods.

Software Complexity Analysis

The topic of complexity is very important for software cost estimation because it affects a number of independent and dependent variables, such as the following:

- High complexity levels can increase bug or defect rates.
- High complexity levels can lower defect-removal efficiency rates.
- High complexity levels can decrease development productivity rates.
- High complexity levels can raise maintenance staffing needs.
- High complexity levels can lengthen development schedules.
- High complexity levels increase the number of test cases needed.
- High complexity levels affect the size of the software application.
- High complexity levels change backfiring ratios.

Unfortunately, the concept of *complexity* is an ambiguous topic that has no exact definition agreed upon by all software researchers. When we speak of complexity in a software context, we can be discussing the difficulty of the problem that the software application will attempt to implement, the structure of the code, or the relationships among the data items that will be used by the application. In other words, the term *complexity* can be used in a general way to discuss problem complexity, code complexity, and data complexity.

The scientific and engineering literature encompasses no fewer than 30 different flavors of complexity, some or all of which may be found to be relevant for software applications. Unfortunately, most of the forms of scientific complexity are not even utilized in a software context. The software engineering community is far behind physics and other forms of engineering in measuring and understanding complexity.

In a very large book on software complexity, Dr. Horst Zuse (Software Complexity: Measures and Methods; Walter de Gruyter, Berlin 1990) discusses about 50 variants of structural complexity for programming alone.

It is perhaps because of the European origin—functional metrics are not as dominant there as in the United States—but in spite of the book's large size and fairly complete treatment, Zuse seems to omit all references to function point metrics and to the forms of complexity associated with functional metrics.

When software sizing and estimating tools utilize complexity as an adjustment factor, the methods tend to be highly subjective. Some of the varieties of complexity encountered in the scientific literature that show up in a software context include the following:

- *Algorithmic complexity* concerns the length and structure of the algorithms for computable problems. Software applications with long and convoluted algorithms are difficult to design, to inspect, to code, to prove, to debug, and to test. Although algorithmic complexity affects quality, development productivity, and maintenance productivity, it is utilized as an explicit factor by only a few software cost-estimating tools.

- *Code complexity* concerns the subjective views of development and maintenance personnel about whether the code they are responsible for is complex or not. Interviewing software personnel and collecting their subjective opinions is an important step in calibrating more formal complexity metrics, such as cyclomatic and essential complexity. A number of software estimating tools have methods for entering and adjusting code complexity based on ranking tables that run from *high* to *low* complexity in the subjective view of the developers.

- *Combinatorial complexity* concerns the numbers of subsets and sets that can be constructed out of N components. This concept sometimes shows up in the way that modules and components of software applications might be structured. From a psychological vantage point, combinatorial complexity is a key reason why some problems seem harder to solve than others. However, this form of complexity is not utilized as an explicit estimating parameter.

- *Computational complexity* concerns the amount of machine time and the number of iterations required to execute an algorithm. Some problems are so high in computational complexity that they are considered to be noncomputable. Other problems are solvable but require enormous quantities of machine time, such as cryptanalysis or meteorological analysis of weather patterns. Computational complexity is sometimes used for evaluating the performance implications of software applications, but not the difficulty of building or maintaining them.

- *Cyclomatic complexity* is derived from graph theory and was made popular for software by Dr. Tom McCabe (IEEE Transactions on Software Engineering, Vol SE2, No. 4 1976). Cyclomatic complexity is a measure of the control flow of a graph of the structure of a piece of software. The general formula for calculating cyclomatic complexity of a control flow graph is edges − nodes + unconnected parts × 2. Software with no branches has a cyclomatic complexity level of 1. As branches increase in number, cyclomatic complexity levels also rise. Above a cyclomatic complexity level of 20, path flow testing becomes difficult and, for higher levels, probably impossible.

Cyclomatic complexity is often used as a warning indicator for potential quality problems. Cyclomatic complexity is the most common form of complexity analysis for software projects and the only one with an extensive literature. At least 20 tools can measure cyclomatic complexity, and these tools range from freeware to commercial products. Such tools support many programming languages and operate on a variety of platforms.

- *Data complexity* deals with the number of attributes associated with entities. For example, some of the attributes that might be associated with a human being in a typical medical office database of patient records could include date of birth, sex, marital status, children, brothers and sisters, height, weight, missing limbs, and many others. Data complexity is a key factor in dealing with data quality. Unfortunately, there is no metric for evaluating data complexity, so only subjective ranges are used for estimating purposes.

- *Diagnostic complexity* is derived from medical practice, where it deals with the combinations of symptoms (temperature, blood pressure, lesions, etc.) needed to identify an illness unambiguously. For example, for many years it was not easy to tell whether a patient had tuberculosis or histoplasmosis because the superficial symptoms were essentially the same. For software, diagnostic complexity comes into play when customers report defects and the vendor tries to isolate the relevant symptoms and figure out what is really wrong. However, diagnostic complexity is not used as an estimating parameter for software projects.

- *Entropic complexity* is the state of disorder of the component parts of a system. Entropy is an important concept because all known systems have an increase in entropy over time. That is, disorder gradually increases. This phenomenon has been observed to occur with software projects because many small changes over time gradually erode the original structure. Long-range studies of software projects in maintenance mode attempt to measure the rate at which entropy increases and determine whether it can be reversed by such approaches as code restructuring. Surrogate metrics for evaluating entropic complexity are the rates at which cyclomatic and essential complexity change over time, such as on an annual basis. However, there are no direct measures for software entropy.

- *Essential complexity* is also derived from graph theory and was made popular by Dr. Tom McCabe (IEEE Transactions on Software Engineering, Vol SE2, No. 4 1976). The essential complexity of a piece of software is derived from cyclomatic complexity after the graph of the application has been simplified by removing redundant paths. Essential complexity is often used as a warning indicator for potential quality problems. As with cyclomatic complexity, a module with no branches at all has an essential complexity level of 1. As unique branching sequences increase in number, both cyclomatic and essential complexity levels will rise. Essential complexity and cyclomatic complexity are supported by a variety of software tools.

- *Fan complexity* refers to the number of times a software module is called (termed *fan in*) or the number of modules that it calls (termed *fan out*). Modules with a large fan-in number are obviously critical in terms of software quality, since they are called by many other modules. However, modules with a large fan-out number are also important, and they are hard to debug because they depend upon so many extraneous modules. Fan complexity is relevant to exploration of reuse potentials. Fan complexity is not used as an explicit estimating parameter, although in real life this form of complexity appears to exert a significant impact on software quality.

- *Flow complexity* is a major topic in the studies of fluid dynamics and meteorology. It deals with the turbulence of fluids moving through channels and across obstacles. A new subdomain of mathematical physics called *chaos theory* has elevated the importance of flow complexity for dealing with physical problems. Many of the concepts, including chaos theory itself, appear relevant to software and are starting to be explored. However, the application of flow complexity to software is still highly experimental.

- *Function point complexity* refers to the set of adjustment factors needed to calculate the final adjusted function point total of a software project. Standard U.S. function points as defined by the IFPUG have 14 complexity adjustment factors. The British Mark II function point uses 19 complexity adjustment factors. The SPR function point and feature point metrics use three complexity adjustment factors. Function point complexity is usually calculated by reference to tables of known values, many of which are automated and are present in software estimating tools or function point analysis tools.

- *Graph complexity* is derived from graph theory and deals with the numbers of edges and nodes on graphs created for various purposes. The concept is significant for software because it is part of the analysis of cyclomatic and essential complexity, and also is part of the operation of several source code restructuring tools. Although derivative metrics, such as cyclomatic and essential complexity, are used in software estimating, graph theory itself is not utilized.

- *Halstead complexity* is derived from the *software-science* research carried out by the late Dr. Maurice Halstead (Elements of Software Science, Elsevier North Holland, New York, 1977) and his colleagues and students at Purdue University. The Halstead software science treatment of complexity is based on four discrete units: (1) number of unique operators (i.e., verbs), (2) number of unique operands (i.e., nouns), (3) instances of operator occurrences, and (4) instances of operand occurrences.
The Halstead work overlaps linguistic research, in that it seeks to enumerate such concepts as the vocabulary of a software project. Although the Halstead software-science metrics are supported in some software cost-estimating tools, there is very little recent literature on this topic.

- *Information complexity* is concerned with the numbers of entities and the relationships between them that might be found in a database, data repository, or data warehouse. Informational complexity is also associated with research on data quality. Unfortunately, all forms of research into database sizes and database quality are handicapped by the lack of metrics for dealing with data size, or for quantifying the forms of complexity that are likely to be troublesome in a database context.

- *Logical complexity* is important for both software and circuit design. It is based upon the combinations of AND, OR, NOR, and NAND logic conditions that are concatenated together. This form of complexity is significant for expressing algorithms and for proofs of correctness. However, logical complexity is utilized as an explicit estimating parameter in only a few software cost-estimating tools.

- *Mnemonic complexity* is derived from cognitive psychology and deals with the ease or difficulty of memorization. It is well known that the human mind has both temporary and permanent memory. Some kinds of information (i.e., names and telephone numbers) are held in temporary memory and require conscious effort to be moved into permanent memory. Other kinds of information (i.e., smells and faces) go directly to permanent memory.
Mnemonic complexity is important for software debugging and during design and code inspections. Many procedural programming languages have symbolic conventions that are very difficult to either scan or debug because they oversaturate human temporary memory. Things such as nested loops that use multiple levels of parentheses—that is, (((…)))—tend to swamp human temporary memory capacity.

Mnemonic complexity appears to be a factor in learning and using programming languages, and is also associated with defect rates in various languages. However, little information is available on this potentially important topic in a software context, and it is not used as an explicit software estimating parameter.

- *Organizational complexity* deals with the way human beings in corporations arrange themselves into hierarchical groups or matrix organizations. This topic might be assumed to have only an indirect bearing on software, except for the fact that many large software projects are decomposed into components that fit the current organizational structure rather than the technical needs of the project. For example, many large software projects are decomposed into segments that can be handled by eight-person departments, whether or not that approach meets the needs of the system's architecture.

  Although organizational complexity is seldom utilized as an explicit estimating parameter, it is known that large software projects that are well organized will outperform similar projects with poor organizational structures.

- *Perceptional complexity* is derived from cognitive psychology and deals with the arrangements of edges and surfaces that appear to be simple or complex to human observers. For example, regular patterns appear to be simple while random arrangements appear to be complex. This topic is important for studies of visualization, software design methods, and evaluation of screen readability. Unfortunately, the important topic of the perceptional complexity of various software design graphics has only a few citations in the literature, and none in the cost-estimating literature.

- *Problem complexity* concerns the subjective views of people asked to solve various kinds of problems about their difficulty. Psychologists know that increasing the number of variables and the length of the chain of deductive reasoning usually brings about an increase in the subjective view that the problem is complex. Inductive reasoning also adds to the perception of complexity. In a software context, problem complexity is concerned with the algorithms that will become part of a program or system. Determining the subjective opinions of real people is a necessary step in calibrating more objective complexity measures.

- *Process complexity* is mathematically related to flow complexity, but in day-to-day software work it is concerned with the flow of materials through a software development cycle. This aspect of complexity is often dealt with in a practical way by project management tools that can calculate critical paths and program evaluation and review technique (PERT) diagrams of software development processes.

■ *Semantic complexity* is derived from the study of linguistics and is concerned with ambiguities in the definitions of terms. Already cited in this book are the very ambiguous terms *quality, data,* and *complexity.* The topic of semantic complexity is relevant to software for a surprising reason: Many lawsuits between software developers and their clients can be traced back to the semantic complexity of the contract when both sides claim different interpretations of the same clauses. Semantic complexity is not used as a formal estimating parameter.

■ *Syntactic complexity* is also derived from linguistics and deals with the grammatical structure and lengths of prose sections, such as sentences and paragraphs. A variety of commercial software tools are available for measuring syntactic complexity, using such metrics as the FOG index. (Unfortunately, these tools are seldom applied to software specifications, although they would appear to be valuable for that purpose.)

■ Topologic complexity deals with rotation and folding patterns. This topic is often explored by mathematicians, but it also has relevance for software. For example, topological complexity is a factor in some of the commercial source code restructuring tools.

As can be seen from the variety of subjects included under the blanket term *complexity*, this is not an easy topic to deal with. From the standpoint of sizing software projects, 6 of the 24 flavors of complexity stand out as being particularly significant:

■ Cyclomatic complexity

■ Code complexity

■ Data complexity

■ Essential complexity

■ Function point complexity

■ Problem complexity

Each of these six forms tends to have an effect on either the function point total for the application, the volume of source code required to implement a set of software requirements, or both. Although not every software estimating tool uses all six of these forms of complexity, the estimating tools that include sizing logic utilize these complexity methods more often than any of the others.

If these six aspects of complexity are rated as high, based on either the subjective opinions of the technical staff who are building the software or on objective metrics, then application sizes are likely to be larger than if these topics are evaluated as being of low complexity.

These same topics also affect software quality, schedules, and costs. However, many other aspects of complexity affect the effort to build software. For estimating the costs and schedules associated with software projects, all 24 of the forms of complexity can be important, and the following 12 of them are known to affect project outcomes in significant ways:

- Algorithmic complexity
- Cyclomatic complexity
- Code complexity
- Data complexity
- Entropic complexity
- Essential complexity
- Function point complexity
- Mnemonic complexity
- Organizational complexity
- Problem complexity
- Process complexity
- Semantic complexity

It has been known for many years that complexity of various forms tends to have a strong correlation with application size, elevated defect levels, reduced levels of defect-removal efficiency, elevated development and maintenance costs, lengthened schedules, and the probability of outright failure or cancellation of a software project.

The correlations between complexity and other factors are not perfect, but are strong enough so that best-in-class companies utilize automated tools for measuring the complexity of source code. As complexity rises, the probability of errors also tends to rise, although the data on the correlations between complexity and defect rates has some exceptions.

Complexity analysis is an intermediate stage of another software technology, too. Most of the commercial code restructuring tools begin with a complexity analysis using cyclomatic complexity or essential complexity, and then automatically simplify the graph of the application and rearrange the code so that cyclomatic and essential complexity are reduced.

Although complexity analysis itself works on a wide variety of programming languages, the code restructuring tools were originally limited to COBOL. In recent years, C and FORTRAN have been added, but there are many hundreds of languages for which automatic restructuring is not possible.

Complexity analysis plays a part in backfiring, or direct conversion from lines-of-code (LOC) metrics to function point metrics. Because the volume of source code needed to encode one function point is partly determined by complexity, it is useful to have cyclomatic and essential complexity data available when doing backfiring. In principle, the complexity-analysis tools could generate the equivalent function point totals automatically, and some vendors are starting to do this.

Much of the literature on software complexity concentrates only on code, and sometimes concentrates only on the control flow or branching sequences. While code complexity is an important subject and well worthy of research, it is far from the only topic that needs to be explored.

Software Productivity Research uses multiple-choice questions to elicit information from software development personnel about their subjective views of several kinds of complexity. SPR normally interviews half a dozen technical personnel for each project and questions their perceptions of the factors that influenced the project, using several hundred multiple-choice questions.

It is relevant to show how perceived complexity increases with some tangible examples. Five plateaus for problem complexity, code complexity, and data complexity are shown in Table 9.5, illustrating examples of the factors at play in the ranges between simple and highly complex in the three domains.

Over the years thousands of software development personnel have been interviewed using this form of complexity questionnaire, and data has also been collected on schedules, costs, defect levels, and defect-removal efficiency levels.

As might be suspected, software projects where the answers are on the high side of the scale (4s and 5s) for problem, code, and data complexity tend to have much larger defect rates and much lower defect-removal efficiency levels than projects on the lower end of the scale (1s and 2s).

However, some interesting exceptions to this rule have been observed. From time to time highly complex applications have achieved remarkably good quality results with few defects and high levels of defect-removal efficiency. Conversely, some simple projects have approached disastrous levels of defects and achieved only marginal levels of defect-removal efficiency.

The general reason for this anomaly is because software project managers tend to assign the toughest projects to the most experienced and capable technical staff, while simple projects are often assigned to novices or those with low levels of experience.

The SPR complexity factors also play a key role in the logic of backfiring or direct conversion from logical source code statements into

TABLE 9.5   Examples of Software Complexity Analysis Questions

Problem complexity

1. Simple algorithms and simple calculations
   All problem elements are well understood.
   Logic is primarily well understood.
   Mathematics are primarily addition and subtraction.

2. Majority of simple algorithms and simple calculations
   Most problem elements are well understood.
   Logic is primarily deductive from simple rules.
   Mathematics are primarily addition and subtraction, with few complex operations.

3. Algorithms and calculations of average complexity
   Some problem elements are "fuzzy" and uncertain.
   Logic is primarily deductive, but may use compound rules with IF, AND, OR, or CASE conditions.
   Mathematics may include statistical operations, calculus, or higher math.

4. Some difficult and complex calculations
   Many problem elements are "fuzzy" and uncertain.
   Logic is primarily deductive, but may use compound rules with IF, AND, OR, or CASE conditions; some inductive logic or dynamic rules may be included; some recursion may be included.
   Mathematics may include advanced statistical operations, calculus, simultaneous equations, and nonlinear equations.

5. Many difficult and complex calculations
   Most problem elements are "fuzzy" and uncertain.
   Logic may be inductive as well as deductive. Deductive logic may use compound, multilevel rules involving IF, AND, OR, or CASE conditions; recursion is significant.
   Mathematics includes significant amounts of advanced statistical operations, calculus, simultaneous equations, nonlinear equations, and noncommutative equations.

Code complexity

1. Nonprocedural (generated, database, spreadsheet)
   Simple spreadsheet formulas or elementary queries are used.
   Small modules with straight-through control flow are used.
   Branching logic use is close to zero.

2. Built with program skeletons and reusable modules
   Program or system is of a well-understood standard type.
   Reusable modules or object-oriented methods are used.
   Minimal branching logic is used.

3. Well structured (small modules and simple paths)
   Standard IF/THEN/ELSE/CASE structures are used consistently.
   Branching logic follows structured methods.

4. Fair structure, but some complex paths or modules
   IF/THEN/ELSE/CASE structures are partially used.
   Some complicated branching logic is used.
   Memory or timing constraints may degrade structure.

5. Poor structure, with many complex modules or paths
   IF/THEN/ELSE/CASE structures are used randomly or not at all.
   Branching logic is convoluted and confusing.
   Severe memory or timing constraints degrade structure.

TABLE 9.5   Examples of Software Complexity Analysis Questions *(Continued)*

Data complexity

1. Simple data, few variables, and little complexity
    Single file of basic alphanumeric information is used.
    Few calculated values are used.
    Minimal need for validation.

2. Several data elements, but simple data relationships
    Single file of primarily alphanumeric information is used.
    Some calculated values are used.
    Some interdependencies exist among records and data.
    Some need for validation exists.

3. Multiple files, switches, and data interactions
    Several files of primarily alphanumeric information are used.
    Some calculated or synthesized values are used.
    Substantial need exists for validation.
    Some data may be distributed among various hosts.

4. Complex data elements and complex data interactions
    Multiple file structures are used.
    Some data may be distributed among various hosts.
    Some data may not be alphanumeric (i.e., images or graphics).
    Many calculated or synthesized values are used.
    Substantial need exists for validation.
    Substantial interdependencies exist among data elements.

5. Very complex data elements and complex data interactions
    Multiple and sometimes incompatible file structures are used.
    Data is distributed among various and incompatible hosts.
    Data may not be alphanumeric (i.e., images or graphics).
    Many calculated or synthesized values are used.
    Substantial need exists for validation.
    Substantial interdependencies exist among data elements.

equivalent function points. For the purposes of backfiring, the sum of the problem, code, and data complexity scores are used to provide a complexity adjustment multiplier (see Table 9.6).

For example, a COBOL application of average complexity with a sum of 9 for the individual complexity scores will probably require approximately 107 source code statements in the procedure and data divisions to encode 1 function point.

A low-complexity application with a sum of 3 for the complexity factors might require only about 75 source code statements in the procedure and data divisions to encode 1 function point.

A high-complexity application with a sum of 15 for the factors might require as many as 140 source code statements in the procedure and data divisions to encode 1 function point.

Complexity is a very important topic for software. Indeed, the complexity of some software applications appears to be as great as that of almost any kind of product constructed by the human species.

TABLE 9.6   SPR Backfire Complexity Adjustments

Sum of problem, data, and code complexity scores	Code size adjustment multiplier
3	0.70
4	0.75
5	0.80
6	0.85
7	0.90
8	0.95
9	1.00
10	1.05
11	1.10
12	1.15
13	1.12
14	1.25
15	1.30

A great deal more research is needed on all forms of software complexity, and particularly on complexity associated with algorithms, visualization, software requirements, specifications, test cases, and data complexity.

Software Sizing with Reusable Components

As the second edition is being drafted, an increasingly large number of software projects are being constructed using reusable components of various kinds. The topic of reuse is very large and includes many more artifacts than source code alone. For example, it is possible to reuse any or all of the following software artifacts:

- Reusable architectures
- Reusable requirements
- Reusable use cases or stories
- Reusable designs
- Reusable class libraries
- Reusable source code modules
- Reusable source code components
- Reusable cost estimates
- Reusable project plans
- Reusable data
- Reusable user manuals
- Reusable graphics

- Reusable test plans
- Reusable test cases

To facilitate subsequent reuse, every reusable object should have its measured size included as part of the basic information that accompanies the reused artifact. However, as of 2007 the majority of reusable objects and artifacts lack accurate size information.

Sizing methods for dealing with reusable artifacts are not yet perfected as this book is being written, but they are starting to evolve. The eventual solution will probably be to enumerate function point totals, object point totals, or totals in some other metric for all major reusable artifacts, so that when software projects are constructed from reusable components their overall size can be summed from the function point sizes of the individual components.

Thus, it might be possible in the future to estimate a project that consists of 7 reusable components, each of 100 function points in size, plus a separate portion that must be developed uniquely that is 300 function points in size. Thus, the overall project as delivered will be 1000 function points, but it will be constructed from 700 function points of reusable components and one unique component of 300 function points.

A basic difficulty of this approach is the fact that generic reusable components may have features that are not needed or used by a specific application. For example, suppose that for a reusable component of 100 function points, only half of these, or 50 function points, are actually going to be utilized in the application being estimated.

The current solution to this problem is to assign a size label to the overall reusable component, and then use percentages to deal with the portions being used. For example, in the case just cited the gross size of the component is 100 function points, and if 50 percent of these features are to be utilized, then the net size in the current application would be 50 function points.

However, the introduction of percentages is intellectually unsatisfying and lacks precision. As this book is being written, there are no other available methods for dealing with partial utilization of reusable artifacts. Of course, improvements in the development of reusable objects might also minimize the quantities of included material that is not actually utilized.

Since functional metrics reflect the user's view of the features needed or desired, it is obvious that if 1000 users are going to utilize portions of the same artifact, their personal needs will vary widely.

Consider a basic application, such as a modern Windows-based word processor, whose total size in terms of all features is perhaps 5000 function points. Modern word processors are so feature-rich that it is doubtful if any single user utilizes more than a fraction of their available capacity.

For example, in writing this book using Microsoft Word it is unlikely that the author utilized more than about 10 percent of the total feature set of this product, or perhaps 500 function points out of a possible 5000 function points.

However, on any given business day millions of people are using Microsoft Word simultaneously, so all of us together probably exercise every known feature of this product on a daily basis, even though no single user needs more than a small fraction of the total capabilities.

This simple example illustrates a key point when dealing with software reusability. It is important to keep separate records for what is *delivered* to clients, what is *developed* by the project team, and what is *reused* from component or class libraries.

In the past, the size of what got delivered and the size of what was developed were close to being the same, and reuse usually amounted to less than 15 percent by volume. As component reuse, patterns, frameworks, object-oriented class libraries, and other forms of reuse become common there will be a marked transformation in the ratios of reused material to custom development. It is not impossible to envision future software projects where close to 100 percent of the major artifacts are reused and custom development hovers below 1 percent.

Incidentally, the use of ratios and percentages to distinguish the proportion of reused material for any given artifact is now a feature of the sizing logic of several commercial software cost-estimating tools. Users can now specify the percentage of reuse for such key artifacts as specifications, source code, user manuals, test cases, and so forth. The estimating tools will suggest default values based on empirical data, but users are free to modify the default assumptions for each artifact.

Overview of the Basic Forms of Software Sizing Metrics

The first edition of this book included a tutorial section on counting function points using the general rules from IFPUG. However, counting rules from IFPUG and other metrics groups tend to change annually. Also, many other function point variants exist and it is not possible to discuss the counting rules for all of these in less than about 500 pages.

For this second edition, a different approach is being used. Instead of a primer on IFPUG function point analysis, there are short discussions and pointers to sources of information about both IFPUG function points and other common sizing metrics. For those who actually wish to learn to count function points or the other metrics, taking a formal course followed by a certification examination is the best path. Tutorial books are also a good option. Because of rapid changes in counting rules and measurement technology, it is also useful to search the web for recent information.

It should be noted that actually counting functional metrics is not a trivial task. Usually, several days of training, numerous case studies, and guidance from a certified expert are needed to do this job well. Once a candidate has learned to count function points, passing a certification examination is the next step before actually attempting to count function points for clients or for situations where accuracy is needed. Counting function points is not a task for partly trained amateurs.

A controlled study found that certified function point counters who had passed the IFPUG exam had only about a 3 percent variation when counting the trial applications used for the study. Uncertified counters, on the other hand, can vary by more than 30 percent when counting the same application. Thus, certification is an important step in dealing with function point metrics with acceptable accuracy.

Following are short discussions of the more common metrics used for sizing circa 2007:

- **3D Function Points**   This variant was developed inside the Boeing corporation and published circa 1995. The 3D approach was intended for counting function points in a real-time environment. The 3D method produces larger counts for real-time software than standard IFPUG function points. Current usage circa 2007 is not known.

- **Backfiring from Physical LOC**   Backfiring is a method of converting the size of an application from source code volumes into an approximate number of function points. It is used primarily for legacy applications where code exists but no supporting specifications, so that conventional function point counting is impossible. Backfiring is as old as the function point metric itself. Allan Albrecht and his colleagues in IBM measured both source code volumes and function points while function point metrics were being developed and calibrated in the early 1970s. The starting point for backfiring can either be physical lines or logical statements. The Software Engineering Institute (SEI) has endorsed counts of physical lines of code as a metric for software projects. However, depending upon the programming language, there can be ranges of more than 3 to 1 between counts of physical lines of code and counts of logical statements. Backfiring from physical lines of code may sometimes come close actual counts of function points, but this form of backfiring can be off by more than 50 percent.

- **Backfiring from Logical Statements**   Mathematical conversion from source code volumes to function point metrics can start using counts of physical lines of code or counts of logical statements. Because some languages (such as Quick Basic) allow multiple statements to be placed on a single physical line, there are often major differences between counts of physical lines of code and counts of logical statements. In other languages (such as COBOL), a single logical statement can span several physical lines, such as might be found in case statements or "if...then" statements. Because of the random and uncertain nature of physical lines, backfiring from counts of logical statements is more consistent and often yields results that are closer to actual counts of function points. Unfortunately, it is harder to get accurate counts of logical statements. When used for backfiring purposes, conversion from logical statements often matches actual function point counts within about 20 percent. The main source of information on backfiring from logical statements is a large catalog of programming languages published by Software Productivity Research LLC (SPR). As of 2007, this catalog contains more than 600 languages and dialects. This catalog includes information on the number of logical source code statements for every known programming language. It also contains information on the ranges, since programmers tend to code in different styles. As might be expected, the observed range is directly proportional to the numbers of programmers who use a particular language. Common languages such as C and Java have very large ranges.

- **Complexity Metrics**   Complexity is an important topic that can affect the sizes of applications, their defect rates, their schedules, and their costs. Unfortunately, the software engineering community uses only fairly primitive methods for dealing with complexity. For sizing purposes, a subjective evaluation of complexity is part of the calculations for counting function point metrics. For evaluating software quality and defect levels, Tom McCabe's cyclomatic and essential complexity metrics have long been used. The actual impact of various kinds of complexity on software size, costs, and error rates remains ambiguous circa 2007.

- **COSMIC Function Points**   Cosmic function points are one of the newer and more important variants to IFPUG function points. The word "COSMIC" stands for "Common Software Measurement Consortium," which is an organization centered in Europe and the United Kingdom. The COSMIC function point method evolved from Dr. Alain Abran's older "full function point" method coupled with some aspect of Charles Symon's Mark II function point method. Members of the COSMIC group come mainly from Europe and the United Kingdom, although Canada, Japan, and Australia also have members. There are few if any members of the COSMIC organization from the United States. As with most function point variants, COSMIC function points produce larger totals for real-time software than do IFPUG function points. The COSMIC organization offers training and certification examinations. However, the COSMIC organization has not dealt with backfiring in a formal way, nor have they published conversion rules between IFPUG function points and COSMIC function points. The COSMIC approach is one of four methods certified by the International Standards Association.

- **Engineering Function Points**   This function point variant was published circa 1994 by Donald Ulmholtz and Arthur Leitgab. This metric starts with the usual IFPUG method but adds a new data element—algorithms. Therefore, engineering function points actually overlap the older feature point metric from 1986 that also added algorithms to the function point rules. There are few recent citations about engineering function points. Usage as of 2007 is unknown.

- **Feature Points**   The feature point metric was developed by the author circa 1986, in collaboration with Allan Albrecht, the inventor of function points. (Albrecht worked for Software Productivity Research for several years after retiring from IBM.) Feature points differed from IFPUG function points in several respects. A new parameter, "algorithms," was introduced. The weight assigned to the "logical file" parameter was reduced. The method was developed to solve a psychological problem rather than an actual measurement problem. There was a misapprehension that function point measurements only applied to information systems. By using the name "feature points" and by introducing the algorithm parameter, a metric was introduced that appealed to the telecommunications and real-time domain. For more than 90 percent of all applications function points and feature points generated the same totals. Only for a few applications with a great many algorithms would feature points yield higher totals. Feature points were one of the few function point variants to offer conversion rules to standard IFPUG counts. After standard IFPUG function points began to be used for real-time and telecommunications software, there was no need for feature points. The primary citation and examples of feature points were in the author's book *Applied Software Measurement* (McGraw-Hill publisher, 1996). Usage as of 2007 is unknown.

- **Full Function Points**   This metric was developed by Dr. Alain Abran of the University of Quebec. As with many function point variations, full function points yield higher counts for real-time software than standard IFPUG function points. Full function points had some usage in Canada, the United Kingdom, and Europe. The method had few if any users in the United States. The full function point metric was one of the precursors to the new COSMIC function point. The full function point method evolved over several years and had several different sets of counting rules. Conversion from full function points to IFPUG function points is not precise, but it has been observed that full function points create larger totals than IFPUG for real-time software by perhaps 15 percent. Full function points were publicized circa 1998.

Now that the COSMIC approach has been released, usage of full function points circa 2007 is unknown.

- **IFPUG Function Points**   IFPUG stands for "International Function Point Users Group." This is the oldest and largest software metrics association, with about 3000 members in perhaps 25 countries. IFPUG is a non-profit organization. Their web site is www.IFPUG .org. As background, function points were invented by Allan Albrecht and his IBM colleagues circa 1975. IBM was the keeper of function point counting rules from 1975 until 1986 when IFPUG was formed in Toronto, Canada. IFPUG moved to the United States in 1998. IFPUG publishes and updates the counting rules for function points (the current version is 4.1) and also runs training courses and certification exams. As of 2007, about 1500 people have passed the IFPUG certification exam. IFPUG function points consist of the totals of five external attributes of software: inputs, outputs, inquiries, logical files, and interfaces. Totals of these attributes are summed, and then adjusted for complexity. This sounds quite simple, but the actual counting rules are more than 100 pages long. It usually takes from two to three days of training before the certification exam can be successfully passed. As of 2007, IFPUG function points are in use for information systems, embedded software, real-time software, weapons systems, expert systems, and essentially all other forms of software. In side-by-side trials with some of the other function point variants, IFPUG tends to create somewhat lower totals than the other variants for real-time software. The IFPUG approach is one of four methods certified by the International Standards Organization.

- **ISO Standard 19761 for Functional Sizing**   The International Organization of Standards (ISO) has defined an overall standard for sizing software. This is ISO 19761, which was published in 2003. Currently, four function point methods have received ISO certification: COSMIC function points, IFPUG function points, Mark II function points, and NESMA function points. As this book is written, none of the object-oriented metrics such as object points, web object points, and use case points have been certified by ISO, nor have any of the lines-of-code-metrics. Backfiring has not been certified either. It should be noted that ISO certification does not guarantee accuracy of counts, nor consistency among unlike counting methods. However, ISO certification does indicate that a specific metric has followed a reasonable set of rules and is theoretically capable of being used to create fairly accurate size data.

- **Mark II Function Points**   The Mark II function point method is the oldest variant to standard IFPUG function points. The Mark II approach was first announced in London by Charles Symons in 1983.

The Mark II approach was also documented in Symon's book, *Software Sizing and Estimating Mk II FPA (function point analysis)* (John Wiley & Sons publisher, 1991). As with the other function point variants, the Mark II approach tends to produce higher totals than IFPUG function points for real-time and embedded software. Usage of the Mark II approach was most widespread in the United Kingdom, but there was also usage in other countries with historical ties to the U.K. such as Hong Kong, Ireland, and Australia. The Mark II method for evaluating complexity does contain some interesting extensions to the IFPUG approach. Some of these methods have migrated into the newer COSMIC function point approach. The Mark II approach is one of four methods certified by the International Standards Organization.

- **NESMA Function Points** The acronym "NESMA" stands for the Netherlands Software Metrics Association. NESMA originated under a different name: Netherlands Function Point Users Group, or NEFPUG, in 1989. They changed their name circa 1995. The NESMA organization has about 120 member companies, almost 1000 individual members, and is a major European source for metrics information and function point certification. NESMA produces a function point standards manual that is based on IFPUG 4.1, but has some extensions and differences. As a result, the NESMA method for counting function points and the IFPUG method come fairly close to producing the same totals, but NESMA typically generates large totals for real-time software. The NESMA method is one of four approaches certified by the International Standards Organization.

- **Object Points** There are several metrics that use the name "object points." One of these was defined by D.R. Banker in 1994; there are also object points supported by Dr. Barry Boehm's COCOMO II cost-estimating tool. Another method termed "web object points" was defined by the well-known software consultant, Donald Riefer, in 2002. Banker's version of object points uses screens and reports to generate a kind of function point. This method is not actually derived from the object-oriented programming method. The second method, by Reifer, includes parameters based on multimedia files, scripts, links, hypertext, and other attributes of modern web-based applications. The Reifer approach adds these new parameters to standard IFPUG function points. As might be expected from the new parameters, it will produce larger counts than IFPUG function points for web-based applications. The Reifer approach also includes and supports back-firing, which is a rare feature among the function point variants. In spite of using the term "object points," neither the Banker nor Reifer methods are actually derived from the canons of object-oriented programming. Usage of object points as of 2007 is unknown. However, the Reifer method was intended to operate in a COCOMO II environment, which is a widely used software cost-estimating tool. Therefore, the Reifer variant may have several hundred users.

- **SPR Function Points** Software Productivity Research developed a minor function point variation in 1986 to simplify and speed up calculations. The SPR function point metric was developed in conjunction with Allan Albrecht, the inventor of function points. The main difference between SPR function points and standard function points was in simplifying the complexity adjustments. The SPR approach used three factors for complexity, each of which could be evaluated via a five-point scale: problem complexity, data complexity, and code complexity. The last factor, "code complexity," was used to adjust the results when backfiring. It was not used for forward function point estimation. The SPR approach was designed to come as close as possible to the standard IFPUG method. However, the method in use at the time was IFPUG 3.0. The SPR approach was not updated to match IFPUG 4.0 or 4.1 because other methods supplanted it. The primary publication of the SPR approach was in the author's book *Applied Software Measurement, Second Edition* (McGraw-Hill publisher, 1996). There were several hundred users of SPR function points in the 1990s, and some still use the method in 2007.

- **Story Points** The term "story points" stems from a method used by the Agile development approach and by extreme programming (XP) in gathering requirements. User requirements are documented in the form of "user stories," which are roughly analogous to use cases but more informal. Because user stories can range from very small to rather large, there was a need to have some form of metric for judging the relative size of a user story. The purpose of story points was to facilitate estimating the schedules and resources needed to develop the code for the story. Currently, story points are a subjective metric without certification or formal counting rules. In fact, one way of ascertaining the number of story points in a user story is called the "poker game" because team members open with their estimate of the number of story points, and other team members can check or raise. Because of the popularity of Agile and XP, there are hundreds or even thousands of users of story points circa 2007. However, the literature on story point sizes is sparse. Needless to say, story points are not certified by the International Standards Organization (ISO). From examining some stories and looking at story points, it can be hypothesized that a story point is more or less equivalent to two function points. An entire story is more or less equivalent to about 20 function points.

- **Use Case Points**   Use cases are one of the methods incorporated into the unified modeling language (UML), although they can be used separately if desired. Because of the widespread deployment of UML for object-oriented (OO) software, use cases have become quite popular since about 2000. A use case describes what happens to a software system when an actor (typically a user) sends a message or causes a software system to take some action. Use case points start with some of the basic factors of IFPUG function points, but add new parameters such as "actor weights." Use case points also include some rather subjective topics such as "lead analyst capability" and "motivation." Since both use case points and IFPUG function points can be used for object-oriented software, some side-by-side results are available. As might be expected from the additional parameters added, use case points typically generate larger totals than IFPUG function points by about 25 percent. One critical problem limits the utility of use case points. Use case points have no relevance for software projects where use cases are not being utilized. Thus, for dealing with economic questions such as the comparative productivity of OO projects versus older procedural projects that don't capture requirements with use cases, the use case metric will not work at all. Because of the popularity of UML and use cases, the use case metric probably has several hundred users circa 2007. However, the use case metric is not one of those certified by the International Standards Organization. There are currently no certification exams for measuring the proficiency of metrics specialists who want to count with use cases. The approach is growing in numbers, but would benefit from more training courses, more text books, and either creating a user association or joining forces with an existing user group such as IFPUG, NESMA, or one of the others. Since use case metrics are irrelevant for older projects that don't deploy use cases, the lack of conversion rules from use case metrics to other metrics is a major deficiency.

There are many complicated metrics used in daily life that we have learned to utilize and often take for granted, although few of us actually know how these metrics are counted or derived. For example, in the course of a normal day we may use the metrics of horsepower, octane ratings, and perhaps British thermal units (BTUs). We might discuss caloric content or cholesterol levels in various kinds of food. We may also discuss wind-chill factors. For day-to-day purposes, it is only sufficient that we know how to use these metrics and understand their significance. Very few people actually need to know how to calculate octane ratings or horsepower, so long as we feel fairly confident that published data is calculated honestly.

In the same vein, very few people need to understand how to count function points, but every software project manager and technical staff member should understand how to use them and should know ranges of productivity and quality results.

For example, every project manager should understand the following generic ranges of software productivity levels:

- Projects of less than 5 function points per staff month (more than 26 work hours per function point) indicate performance that is below U.S. averages for all software projects.

- Projects between 5 and 10 function points per staff month (13 to 26 work hours per function point) approximate the normal range for U.S. software projects.

- Projects between 10 and 20 function points per staff month (7 to 13 work hours per function point) are higher than U.S. averages for software projects. Many object-oriented OO projects are in this range.

- Projects above 20 function points per staff month (7 work hours per function point) are significantly better than U.S. averages for software projects. Many Agile projects are in this range, in part because many Agile projects are quite small.

Of course, this kind of generic information needs to be calibrated for the specific class of software being considered, and also for the size of specific applications. Small projects of less than 100 function points in size often top 20 function points per staff month, but for larger projects above 1000 function points in size such results are extremely rare.

Function point metrics are difficult to calculate but easy to understand. The basic range of performance using function point metrics should be known by all software practitioners even if they only know such generalities as the following:

- A delivered defect rate of more than 1.50 bugs per function point is very bad.

- A delivered defect rate of less than 0.75 bugs per function point is normal.

- A delivered defect rate of less than 0.10 bugs per function point is very good.

Understanding productivity and quality data expressed in terms of function points should be part of the training of every software manager. Knowing how to count function points is a skill that is needed only by a comparatively few specialists.

In summary, the main strengths of function point metrics are the following:

- Function points stay constant regardless of the programming languages used.
- Function points are a good choice for full-life-cycle analysis.
- Function points are a good choice for software reuse analysis.
- Function points are a good choice for object-oriented economic studies.
- Function points are supported by many software cost-estimating tools.
- Function points can be mathematically converted into logical code statements for many languages.

The main weaknesses of function point metrics are the following:

- Accurate counting requires certified function point specialists.
- Function point counting can be time-consuming and expensive.
- Function point counting automation is of unknown accuracy.
- Function point counts are erratic for projects below 15 function points in size.
- Function point variations have no accurate conversion rules to IFPUG function points.
- Many function point variations have no backfiring conversion rules.

Although the technical strengths of function points are greater than their weaknesses, the politics and disputes among the function point splinter groups is distressing. The multiplicity of function point variants is confusing to non-specialists and somewhat embarrassing to the function point community itself.

On the other hand, the problems of using lines-of-code-metrics for sizing and estimating are even greater than those of functional metrics. The most effective strategy would probably be to concentrate on developing one or more *standard* functional metrics with rigorous conversion logic between the standard and older alternatives.

Source Code Sizing

Source code sizing is the oldest sizing method for software and has been part of the feature sets of software cost-estimating tools since the 1970s. In general, for such common programming languages as COBOL or C, automated software cost-estimating tools can now do a very capable job of source code size prediction as early as the requirements phase, and often even before that, by using some of the approximation methods discussed earlier.

However, sizing for modern *visual* programming languages has added some complexity and some ambiguity to the source code sizing domain. For such languages as Visual Basic, Realizer, Forte, PowerBuilder, and many others, some of the "programming" does not utilize source code statements at all.

Sizing source code when the language utilizes button controls, pull-down menus, or icons in order to create functionality is a difficult task that taxes software cost-estimating tools. But the usage of such controls for programming development is a fast-growing trend that will eventually dominate the software language world. It is also a trend that basically negates the use of source code metrics for some of the languages in question, although function points work perfectly well.

When the software industry began in the early 1950s, the first metric developed for quantifying the output of a software project was the metric termed *lines of code* (LOC). Almost at once some ambiguity occurred, because a line of code could be defined as either of the following:

- A physical line of code
- A logical statement

Physical lines of code are simply sets of coded instructions terminated by pressing the ENTER key of a computer keyboard. For some languages physical lines of code and logical statements are almost identical, but for other languages there can be major differences in apparent size based on whether physical lines or logical statements are used.

Table 9.7 illustrates some of the possible code counting ambiguity for a simple COBOL application, using both logical statements and physical lines.

TABLE 9.7   Sample COBOL Application Showing Sizes of Code Divisions Using Logical Statements and Physical Lines of Code

Division	Logical statements	Physical lines
Identification division	25	25
Environment division	75	75
Data division	300	350
Procedure division	700	950
Dead code	100	300
Comments	200	700
Blank lines	100	100
Total lines of code	1500	2500

As can be seen from this simple example, the concept of what actually comprises a line of code is surprisingly ambiguous. The size range can run from a low of 700 LOC if you select only logical statements in the procedure division to a high of 2500 LOC if you select a count of total physical lines. Almost any intervening size is possible, and most variations are in use for productivity studies, research papers, journal articles, books, and so forth.

Bear in mind that Table 9.7 is a simple example using only one programming language for a new application. The SPR catalog of programming languages contains more than 600 programming languages, and more are being added on a daily basis. Furthermore, a significant number of software applications utilize two or more programming languages at the same time. For example, such combinations as COBOL and SQL, Ada and Jovial, and Java and HTML are very common. SPR has observed one system that actually contains 12 different programming languages.

There are other complicating factors, too, such as the use of macro instructions and the inclusion of copybooks, inheritance, class libraries, and other forms of reusable code. There is also ambiguity when dealing with enhancements and maintenance, such as whether to count the base code when enhancing existing applications.

Obviously, with so many variations in how lines of code might be counted, it would be useful to have a standard for defining what should be included and excluded. Here we encounter another problem. There is no true international standard for defining code counting rules. Instead, there are a number of published local standards which, unfortunately, are in conflict with one another.

Citing just two of the more widely used local standards, the SPR code-counting rules published in 1991 are based on logical statements while the SEI code-counting standards are based on physical lines of code. Both of these conflicting standards are widely used and widely cited, but they differ in many key assumptions.

As an experiment, the author carried out an informal survey of code-counting practices in such software journals as *American Programmer, Byte, Application Development Trends, Communications of the ACM, IBM Systems Journal, IEEE Computer, IEEE Software, Software Development,* and *Software Magazine.*

About a third of the published articles using LOC data used physical lines, and another third used logical statements, while the remaining third did not define which method was used and, hence, were ambiguous in results by several hundred percent. While there may be justifications for selecting physical lines or logical statements for a particular research study, there is no justification at all for publishing data without stating which method was utilized!

To summarize, the main strengths of physical LOC are as follows:

- The physical LOC-metrics is easy to count.
- The physical LOC-metrics has been extensively automated for counting.
- The physical LOC-metrics is used in a number of software estimating tools.

The main weaknesses of physical LOC are as follows:

- The physical LOC-metrics may include substantial dead code.
- The physical LOC-metrics may include blanks and comments.
- The physical LOC-metrics is ambiguous for mixed-language projects.
- The physical LOC-metrics is ambiguous for software reuse.
- The physical LOC-metrics is a poor choice for full-life-cycle studies.
- The physical LOC-metrics does not work for some visual languages.
- The physical LOC-metrics is erratic for direct conversion to function points.
- The physical LOC-metrics is erratic for direct conversion to logical statements.

The main strengths of logical statements are as follows:

- Logical statements exclude dead code, blanks, and comments.
- Logical statements can be mathematically converted into function point metrics.
- Logical statements are used in a number of software estimating tools.

The main weaknesses of logical statements are as follows:

- Logical statements can be difficult to count.
- Logical statements are not extensively automated.
- Logical statements are a poor choice for full-life-cycle studies.
- Logical statements are ambiguous for some visual languages.
- Logical statements may be ambiguous for software reuse.
- Logical statements may be erratic for direct conversion to the physical LOC-metrics.

Although not as exotic as the modern visual programming languages, a number of important business applications have been built with spreadsheets such as Excel and Lotus. The mechanics of entering a spreadsheet formula are more or less equivalent to using a *statement* in a programming language. The spreadsheet macro languages actually are programming languages, if not very elegant ones. However, using the built-in spreadsheet facilities for creating graphs from numeric tables is not really *programming* as it is traditionally defined.

Even more troublesome in the context of sizing are some of the add-on features associated with spreadsheets, such as templates, backsolving features, functions for statistical operations, for "what you see is what you get" printing, and a host of others.

For example, Case Study A earlier in this book illustrated a cost estimate for a small personal travel expense program that was to be created in Visual Basic. Several commercial spreadsheets already have travel expense templates available, so that if the application were intended for a spreadsheet rather than for Visual Basic, little or no programming would even be needed.

Indeed, even in the context of Visual Basic, travel expense controls are available from commercial vendors, which would cut down on the amount of procedural code that might have to be created.

Of course, reused software code in any fashion adds complexity to the task of software sizing also. Spontaneous reuse by programmers from their own private libraries of algorithms and routines has been part of programming since the industry began.

More extensive, formal reuse of software artifacts from certified libraries or commercial sources is not as common as private reuse, but is rapidly becoming a trend of significant dimensions.

As mentioned previously, there are more than 500 variations and dialects of commercial programming languages in existence, and perhaps another 200 or so proprietary "private" languages have been developed by corporations for their own use.

Also, many software applications utilize multiple languages concurrently. About one-third of U.S. software projects contain at least two programming languages, such as COBOL and SQL. Perhaps 10 percent of U.S. software applications contain three or more languages, and a few may contain as many as a dozen languages simultaneously.

The technology of source code size prediction for traditional procedural programming languages has been eased substantially by the advent of function point metrics. Because function points are normally calculated or derived during requirements definition, and because source code volumes can be predicted once function point totals are known, it is now possible to create reasonably accurate source code size estimates much earlier in the development cycle than ever before.

However, even with the help of function points source code sizing has some problems remaining, as shown in Table 9.8.

TABLE 9.8   Software Sizing Problems Circa 2007

1. Sizing source code volumes for proprietary programming languages
2. Sizing source code volumes for visually oriented programming languages
3. Sizing source code volumes for spreadsheet applications
4. Sizing source code volumes for microcode programming languages
5. Sizing very small updates below the levels at which function points are accurate
6. Sizing the volume of reusable code from certified component libraries
7. Sizing the volume of borrowed code taken from other applications
8. Sizing the volume of base, existing code when updating legacy applications
9. Sizing the volume of commercial software packages when they are being modified
10. Sizing changes and deletions to legacy applications, rather than new code
11. Sizing temporary scaffold code that is discarded after use
12. Sizing code volumes in disposable prototypes
13. Standardizing the forms of complexity that affect sizing logic
14. Validating or challenging the rules for backfiring lines of code to function points
15. Measuring the rate of unplanned growth to software artifacts during development

The same application can vary by as much as 500 percent in apparent size depending upon which code counting method is utilized. Consider the following example in the BASIC programming language:

```
BASEPAY = 0: BASEPAY5HOURS*PAYRATE: PRINT BASEPAY
```

This example is obviously one physical line of code. However, this example contains three separate logical statements. The first statement sets a field called *BASEPAY* to zero value. The second statement performs a calculation and puts the result in the field called *BASE-PAY*. The third statement prints out the results of the calculation.

It is clearly important to know whether physical lines or logical statements are implied when using the phrases *lines of code* (LOC), *1000 lines of code* (KLOC), and *1000 source lines of code* (KSLOC). (There is no difference numerically between KLOC and KSLOC.)

As a general rule, sizing source code volumes lends itself to rule-based parsing engines that can examine large volumes of source code quickly. While such engines are commercially available for such common languages as COBOL and C, the organizations that utilize proprietary or obscure languages often build their own counting tools.

Unfortunately, there is little or no consistency in the rules themselves, and almost every conceivable variation can be and has been utilized. The wide variations in methods for enumerating source code volumes cast severe doubts on the validity of large-scale statistical studies based on LOC-metrics.

If one-third of the journal articles use physical lines of code, one-third use logical statements, and one-third don't state which method is used, then it is obvious that the overall data based on LOC-metrics needs some serious scrubbing before any valid conclusions might be derived from it.

Once the primary size of a software project is determined using function points, source code statements, or both, then a host of other software artifacts can be sized in turn. Let us now consider some of the sizing ranges for such derivative software artifacts as paper documents, test cases, and bugs or defects.

Sizing Object-Oriented Software Projects

The object-oriented (OO) paradigm has been expanding rapidly in terms of numbers of projects developed. The OO paradigm presents some interesting challenges to software cost-estimating and sizing tool vendors, since OO development methods are not perfectly congruent with the way software is developed outside of the OO paradigm.

The OO community has been attempting to quantify the productivity and quality levels of OO projects. To this end, several OO metrics have been developed including use case points and several flavors of object points. Because of the special needs of the OO paradigm the traditional LOC-metric was not a suitable choice.

Although function point metrics can actually demonstrate the productivity advantages of the OO paradigm and have been used for OO economic analysis knowledge of functional metrics remains comparatively sparse among the OO community even in 2007.

Curiously, the function point community is very knowledgeable about the OO paradigm, but the reverse is not true. For example, Software Engineering Management Research Lab at the University of Montreal has produced an interesting report that mapped the older Jacobsen OO design method into equivalent function point analysis and generated function point sizes from Jacobsen's design approach.

A fairly extensive form of software research has started among OO metrics practitioners to develop a new and unique kind of sizing and estimating for OO projects, based on a specialized suite of metrics that are derived from the OO paradigm itself. For example, research at the University of Pittsburgh has attempted to build a complete OO metrics suite.

Similar research is ongoing in Europe, and a suite of OO metrics termed MOOD has been developed in Portugal. There are also *object point* metrics, which attempt to build a special kind of function point keyed to the OO paradigm. Use case points and web object points are also used by OO practitioners.

In the United States the work of Chidamber and Kemerer is perhaps the best known. Some of the OO metrics suggested by Chidamber, Darcy, and Kemerer include the following:

- **Weighted Methods per Class (WMC)**   This metric is a count of the number of methods in a given class. The *weight* portion of this metric is still under examination and is being actively researched.

- **Depth of Inheritance Tree (DIT)**   This is the maximum depth of a given class in the class hierarchy.
- **Number of Children (NOC)**   This is the number of immediate subclasses of a given class.
- **Response for a Class (RFC)**   This is the number of methods that can execute in response to a message sent to an object within this class, using up to one level of nesting.
- **Lack of Cohesion of Methods (LCOM)**   This metric is a count of the number of disjoint method pairs minus the number of similar method pairs. The disjoint methods have no common instance variables, while the similar methods have at least one common instance variable.

As this edition is being written, the OO metrics are still somewhat experimental and unstandardized. None of the OO metrics, for example, have been certified by the International Standards Organization nor do they follow the guidelines of the ISO standard for functional sizing.

In the past, both LOC and function point metrics have splintered into a number of competing and semi-incompatible metric variants. There is some reason to believe that the OO metrics community will also splinter into competing variants, possibly following national boundaries. The main strengths of OO metrics are as follows:

- The OO metrics are psychologically attractive within the OO community.
- The OO metrics appear to be able to distinguish simple from complex OO projects.
- The OO metrics can measure productivity and cost within the OO paradigm.
- The OO metrics can measure quality within the OO paradigm.

The main weaknesses of OO metrics are as follows:

- The OO metrics do not support studies outside of the OO paradigm.
- The OO metrics do not deal with full-life-cycle issues.
- The OO metrics have not yet been applied to testing.
- The OO metrics have not yet been applied to maintenance.
- The OO metrics have no conversion rules to LOC-metrics.
- The OO metrics have no conversion rules to other function point metrics.
- The OO metrics lack automation.

- The OO metrics lack certification.

- The OO metrics do not adhere to the ISO standards for functional sizing.

- The OO metrics are not supported by software estimating tools.

Because of the rapid growth of the OO paradigm, the need for sizing and estimating metrics within the OO community is fairly urgent. Upon examination, use case points, web object points, object points, metrics for object-oriented software engineering (MOOSE) and metrics for object-oriented design (MOOD) metrics suites have some interesting technical features. Unfortunately, the OO metrics researchers have lagged in creating conversion rules between OO metrics and older metrics. This means that none of the OO metrics are able to deal with side-by-side comparisons between OO projects and procedural projects. This limits the usefulness of OO metrics to operating purely within an OO context, and bars them from dealing with larger economic and quality issues where statistical analysis of many kinds of projects are part of the analysis.

Sizing Text-Based Paper Documents

Software is a very paper-intensive occupation and tends to put out massive quantities of paper materials. In fact, for large military software projects the creation and production of paper documents is actually the major cost element; it is more expensive than the source code itself and is even more expensive than testing and defect removal.

For civilian projects, paperwork is not quite as massive as for military projects, but it can still run up to many thousands of pages for large systems above 5000 function points in size. Indeed, it is the high cost of software paperwork that was the impetus in creating some of the Agile development approaches. Extensive paperwork in the form of large and possibly ambiguous requirements documents and formal specifications are viewed by the Agile community as barriers to effective development rather than necessary precursors to coding.

Some of the major categories of paper documents produced for software projects include but are not limited to the following ten categories:

- Planning documents
- Requirements
- Specifications
- User manuals
- Training materials

- Marketing materials
- Defect reports
- Financial documents
- Memos and correspondence
- Contracts and legal documents

Sizing paper deliverables is a major feature of software cost-estimating tools and is a major topic for real-life software projects.

Sizing paper documents is especially important in a military software context, because military standards trigger the production of more paper than any other triggering factor in human history. The classic DoD 2167 standard has probably caused the creation of more pages of paper than any other technical standard in the world. Even the newer DoD 498 standard tends to generate significant volumes of paper materials.

Interestingly, the newer ISO 9000–9004 quality standards are giving DoD 2167 quite a good race for the record for most paperwork produced for a software project.

Curiously, many of these required military software documents were not really needed for technical reasons, but are there because the Department of Defense has a long-standing distrust of its many vendors. This distrust has manifested itself in the extensive oversight requirements and the massive planning, reporting, and specification sets mandated by such military standards as DoD 2167 or DoD 498.

The same sense of distrust is also found in the ISO 9000–9004 standard set and in ISO 9001 in particular. For an activity as common as performing software inspections and testing software applications, it should not be necessary to create huge custom test plans for every application. What the ISO standards and the DoD standards might have included, but did not, are the skeleton frameworks of review, inspection, and test plans with an assertion that special test-plan documentation would be needed only if the standard plans were *not* followed.

For commercial software projects, the internal specifications are not as bulky as for military or for systems software, but the external user manuals and the tutorial information are both large and sometimes even elegant, in terms of being produced by professional writers and professional graphics artists.

Among our civilian client organizations paperwork production ranks as the second most expensive kind of work on large systems, and is outranked only by the costs of defect removal, such as testing.

(Coding, by the way, is often as far down the list of software elements as fourth place. Coding expenses on large systems often lag behind paperwork costs, defect-removal costs, and meetings and communications costs.)

A minor but tricky issue for sizing software paperwork volumes is that of adjusting the size estimate to match the kind of paper stock being used.

For example, a normal page of U.S. office paper in the 8.5- by 11-inch format holds about 500 English words, although the inclusion of graphics and illustrations lowers the effective capacity to around 400 words. However, the common European A4 page size holds about 600 English words, while legal paper holds about 675 English words.

By contrast, the smaller page size used by the U.S. civilian government agencies only holds about 425 words. Thus, in order to predict the number of pages in specifications and user manuals, it is obvious that the form factor must be known.

Of course, the full capacity of a printed page for holding text is seldom utilized, because space is often devoted to the inclusion of graphical materials, which will also be discussed as an interesting sizing problem.

Table 9.9 illustrates how function point metrics are now utilized for producing size estimates of various kinds of paper documents. The table assumes normal 8.5- by 11-inch U.S. paper and IFPUG Version 4.1 function point rules.

Table 9.9 and the following illustrate a major benefit of function point metrics in the context of software sizing and cost estimating. Because the function point total for an application stays constant regardless of which programming language or languages are utilized, function points provide a very stable platform for sizing and estimating non-code artifacts, such as paper documents.

In fact, some of the LOC-based estimating tools don't deal with paper deliverables or non-coding work at all.

Table 9.9 shows selected size examples, drawn from systems, MIS, military, and commercial software domains. In this context, *systems software* is that which controls physical devices, such as computers or telecommunication systems.

TABLE 9.9   Number of Pages Created per Function Point for Software Projects

	Systems software	MIS software	Military software	Commercial software	Average
Project plans	0.30	0.20	0.45	0.25	0.30
Requirements	0.45	0.50	0.85	0.30	0.53
Functional specifications	0.80	0.55	1.75	0.60	0.93
Logic specifications	0.85	0.50	1.65	0.55	0.89
Test plans	0.25	0.10	0.55	0.25	0.29
User tutorials	0.30	0.15	0.50	0.85	0.45
User reference	0.45	0.20	0.85	0.90	0.60
Online HELP	0.15	0.30	0.25	0.65	0.34
Total	3.55	2.50	6.85	4.35	4.31

MIS stands for *management information systems software* and refers to the normal business software used by companies for internal operations.

Military software constitutes all projects that are constrained to follow various military standards.

Commercial software refers to ordinary packaged software, such as word processors, spreadsheets, and the like.

This kind of sizing for software documentation is now a standard feature of several commercial software cost-estimating tools. Indeed, as many as 50 discrete document types may be found on very large software projects. Table 9.10 is a summary list of the various kinds of paper documents associated with software projects.

TABLE 9.10   Examples of Paper Documents Associated with Software Projects

Requirements and specification documents
1. Normal requirements specifications
2. Joint application design (JAD) requirements specifications
3. Quality Function Deployment (QFD) requirements specifications
4. Rapid Application Development (RAD) requirements specifications
5. Initial functional specifications
6. Final functional specifications
7. Internal logic specifications
8. Software reuse specifications
9. State-change specifications
10. Interface and dependency specifications
11. Security and confidentiality specifications
12. Database design specifications

Planning and control documents
1. Software project development schedule plans
2. Software project development tracking reports
3. Software project development cost estimates
4. Software project development cost-tracking reports
5. Software project milestone reports
6. Software project value analysis
7. Software project marketing plans
8. Software project customer support plans
9. Software project documentation plans
10. Software ISO 9000–9004 supporting documents
11. Software project inspection plans
12. Software project inspection tracking reports
13. Software project internal test plans
14. Software project test result reports
15. Software project external test plans
16. Software project external test results
17. Software prerelease defect-tracking reports
18. Software postrelease defect-tracking reports
19. Software project development contracts
20. Software litigation documentation

TABLE 9.10   Examples of Paper Documents Associated with Software Projects *(Continued)*

User reference and training documents
1.   Installation guides
2.   User tutorial manuals
3.   User reference manuals
4.   Programmers guides
5.   System programmers guides
6.   Network administration guides
7.   System maintenance guides
8.   Console operators guides
9.   Messages and return codes manuals
10.   Quick reference cards
11.   Online tutorials
12.   Online HELP screens
13.   Error messages
14.   Icon and graphic screens
15.   READ-ME files
16.   Audio training tapes
17.   Video training tapes
18.   CD-ROM training materials

Although few projects will produce all of the kinds of information listed in Table 9.10, many software projects will create at least 20 discrete kinds of paper and online documentation. Given the fact that between 20 percent and more than 50 percent of software project budgets can go to the production of paper and online documents, it is obvious that paperwork sizing and cost estimating are important features of modern software cost-estimating tools.

Several commercial software estimating tools can even predict the number of English words in the document set, as well as the numbers of diagrams that are likely to be present, and can change the page-count estimates based on type size or paper size.

Since the actual sizing algorithms for many kinds of paper documents are proprietary, Table 9.11 is merely derived by assuming a ratio of 500 words per page, taken from Table 9.11.

As can easily be seen from Tables 9.10 and 9.11, software is a very paper-intensive occupation, and accurate software cost estimating cannot ignore the production of paper documents and achieve acceptable accuracy. Far too great a percentage of overall software costs are tied up in the creation, reviewing, and updating of paper documents for this cost factor to be ignored.

To illustrate the overall magnitude of software paperwork, the author has worked on several large systems in the 10,000–function point category where the total volume of pages in the full set of design and specification documents exceeded 60,000 pages.

TABLE 9.11   Number of English Words per Function Point for Software Projects

	Systems software	MIS software	Military software	Commercial software	Average
Project plans	120	80	180	100	120
Requirements	180	200	340	120	210
Functional specifications	320	220	700	240	370
Logic specifications	340	200	660	220	355
Test plans	100	40	220	100	115
User tutorials	120	60	200	340	180
User reference	180	80	340	360	240
Online HELP	60	120	100	260	135
Total	1420	1000	2740	1740	1725

As a more extreme case, the sum of the paper documents for a proposed new operating system that IBM was considering would have totaled more than 1 million pages. The specifications would have been so large that reading them would exceed the lifetime reading speed of normal adults if they read steadily for eight hours every day for an entire career!

Should it have gone to completion, the full set of paper documents for the "Star Wars" strategic defense initiative, following normal military standards, would have exceeded 1 billion pages, and the sum of the English words would have exceeded 500 billion.

Although the document size information in this book is based on U.S. paper sizes and English words, software is an international discipline. Some software cost-estimating tools can deal with the same problems as they might be encountered in France, Germany, Japan, or other countries that both use different languages and have different conventions for paper sizes.

In addition, some kinds of software, such as commercial packages, need to be *nationalized*, or translated into multiple languages. For example, the author's own KnowledgePlan cost-estimating tool is available in English, Japanese, and French versions. Large commercial software vendors, such as Computer Associates, IBM, and Microsoft, may have software materials translated into more than a dozen languages.

Another tricky but important aspect of dealing with software paperwork costs is producing estimates for multinational projects, where the primary specifications are in a single language, such as English, but the development team may comprise personnel from France, Japan, Russia, the Ukraine, and many other countries as well. Although the developers may be able to deal with English-language specifications, there may be a need for supplemental materials created in other languages.

Some cost-estimating tools can also estimate the added costs for translating tutorial materials, HELP screens, and even source code comments from one natural language to another.

Translation costs can be a rather complicated topic for languages that do not use the same kinds of symbols for representing information. For example, translating materials from English into Japanese or Chinese written forms is a great deal more costly than merely translating English into French or Spanish. Indeed, automated translation tools are available that can facilitate bidirectional translations between English and many European languages.

Another critical aspect of sizing software paperwork volumes is the fact that the volumes are not constant, but grow during the development cycle (and afterwards) in response to creeping user requirements.

Thus, software paperwork sizing algorithms and predictive methods must be closely linked to other estimating capabilities that can deal with creeping user requirements, deferrals of features, and other matters that cause changes in the overall size of the application.

It is obvious why visualization is such an important technology for software, and why software cost-estimating tools need to be very thorough in sizing and estimating paperwork for large software applications. Indeed, for almost all large systems in excess of 1000 function points in size, the total effort devoted to the construction of paper documents is actually greater than the effort devoted to coding. In the case of large military systems, the effort devoted to the creation of paper documents can be more than *twice* as costly as coding.

Sizing Graphics and Illustrations

Software specifications, software user manuals, software training materials, and sometimes online software tutorials often make extensive use of graphics and visual information. The kinds of graphical materials associated with software projects include but are not limited to the following categories:

- Application design graphics
- Planning and scheduling graphics
- Charts derived from spreadsheets
- Illustrations in user manuals
- Graphical user interfaces (GUIs)
- Photographs and clip art

Graphics sizing is a complicated undertaking because there are so many possibilities. In the modern world of web-based applications, graphics are the primary user interface. Indeed, some of the graphical elements are dynamic in the form of video or animation. For example, in just the software design category alone there are at least 50 major dialects of graphical software specification methods in existence, such as those listed in Table 9.12.

Not only are there many different dialects or flavors of graphics-based software specification methods, but many projects use combinations of these diverse approaches rather than a single pure approach. For example, it is very common to see a mixture of flowcharts, one or more of the object-oriented specification methods, and some kind of entity-relationship charts all in the specifications for a single project.

Even more difficult from the standpoint of software sizing and cost estimating, a significant number of companies have developed unique and proprietary variants of common design methods that only they utilize. For example, the ITT corporation used the structured analysis and design technique (SADT) in both its pure form, and also in the form of a customized ITT variation created for switching software projects.

TABLE 9.12   Forms of Graphical Software Design Representations

1.	Conventional flowcharts
2.	Control-flow diagrams
3.	Data-structure diagrams
4.	Gane & Sarson data-flow diagrams
5.	DeMarco bubble diagrams
6.	Entity-relationship diagrams
7.	Chen entity-relationship diagrams
8.	James Martin entity-relationship diagrams
9.	James Martin information engineering diagrams
10.	Texas Instruments information engineering diagrams
11.	Nassi-Shneiderman diagrams
12.	Chapin chart diagrams
13.	Decision tables
14.	Hierarchy plus input, output, process (HIPO) diagrams
15.	Yourdon structured design diagrams
16.	Yourdon object-oriented diagrams
17.	Shlaer-Mellor object-oriented analysis diagrams
18.	Unified modeling language (UML) object-oriented diagrams
19.	Use cases and various object-oriented diagrams
20.	Customized object-oriented diagrams
21.	Six-sigma graphical representations
22.	Petri nets
23.	State-transition diagrams
24.	Warnier-Orr diagrams
25.	Structured analysis and design technique (SADT) diagrams
26.	Merise diagrams
27.	Quality function deployment (QFD) house diagrams
28.	Root-cause analysis fishbone diagrams

Table 9.13 illustrates the approximate volumes of graphic items per function point in various document types. A *graphic item* can be any of the following:

- A flowchart page
- An entity-relationship chart
- A data-flow diagram
- A control-flow diagram
- A use case diagram
- A UML diagram (in about 13 flavors)
- A Gantt chart
- A PERT chart
- A Kiviat graph
- A graph from a spreadsheet, such as Excel or Lotus
- An illustration from a graphics package, such as PowerPoint
- A photograph

Needless to say, Table 9.13 has a significant margin of error and should be used only to gain an understanding of the significant volumes of graphical materials that are likely to be produced for software projects.

The ability of modern software cost-estimating tools to deal with the size ranges of both text and graphics is one of the features that makes such tools useful.

Too often, manual estimates by software project managers tend to ignore or understate the non-coding portions of software projects,

TABLE 9.13 Number of Graphics Items per Function Point for Software Projects

	Systems software	MIS software	Military software	Commercial software	Average
Plan graphics	0.30	0.20	0.45	0.25	0.30
Requirements graphics	0.15	0.20	0.35	0.15	0.21
Function graphics	0.30	0.25	0.60	0.25	0.35
Logic graphics	0.45	0.25	1.00	0.30	0.50
Test graphics	0.10	0.03	0.25	0.10	0.12
Tutorial graphics	0.25	0.10	0.30	0.60	0.31
Reference graphics	0.25	0.10	0.50	0.60	0.36
HELP graphics	0.10	0.20	0.20	0.40	0.23
Total	1.90	1.33	3.65	2.65	2.38
Graphics per page	0.54	0.53	0.53	0.61	0.55
Graphics per 1000 words	1.34	1.33	1.33	1.52	1.38

because the managers have comparatively little familiarity with the paper and graphics side of software.

Sizing Bugs or Defects

As software projects grow from less than 1000 function points to more than 10,000 function points in size, the costs, effort, and schedules associated with defect-removal operations tend to become the largest and costliest component of the entire project.

Also, when software projects miss their schedules (as in the case of the Denver airport) it is almost always due to a quality problem that keeps the software from running well enough to go into full production.

Of all of the factors that need to be estimated carefully, the number of bugs or errors is the most critical. Two major aspects of bug or defect prediction are now features of several software cost-estimating tools:

- Predicting the number of bugs by origin point and severity levels
- Predicting the efficiency of various inspections and tests in removing bugs

Software defect prediction is another area where commercial software cost-estimating tools can outperform even experienced human managers. The reason is that software cost-estimating tools are operating from the basis of several thousand projects, while human managers may see fewer than 50 projects in their entire careers.

The function point metric has expanded the ability to create accurate quality estimates and defect predictions. Prior to the advent of function point metrics, much of the software quality literature and most of the defect-prediction algorithms dealt only with coding defects. Now that function points are widely used, the ability to measure and predict software defects has expanded to include five significant categories:

- Requirements defects
- Design and specification defects
- Coding defects
- User documentation defects
- Bad fixes, or secondary defects

Three new kinds of software defect prediction capabilities are not yet found in commercial software cost-estimating tools, but research is nearing the stage where predictive algorithms can be developed:

- Test-case defects
- Data and database defects
- Web content defects

All three of these new categories of software defects have cost and schedule implications. Research performed at IBM indicates that software test cases sometimes contain more defects or errors than the software the test cases have been created to test!

The whole topic of *data quality* is becoming increasingly important. Research into data quality has suffered from the fact that there is no known metric for normalizing database volumes or data defects. In other words, there is no *data point* metric that is the logical equivalent to the *function point* metric.

Now that web projects are exploding in numbers and business importance, errors in web content are increasing in both number and economic consequences.

The well-known aphorism that "you can't manage what you can't measure" has long been true for software quality. For about 50 years, less than 5 percent of U.S. companies had measurement programs for software quality. Similar proportions have been noted in the United Kingdom and in Europe. Therefore, attempts to improve software quality tended to resemble the classic probability example called the *drunkard's walk*. Quality improvements would lurch erratically in different directions and not actually get very far from the origin point.

When exploring why software quality measurements have seldom been performed, a basic issue has always been that the results were not very useful. A deeper analysis of this problem shows that an important root cause of unsuccessful quality measurement can be traced to the use of the flawed LOC-metrics.

Quality measurements based on lines of code have tended to ignore quality problems that originate in requirements and design and are of no use at all in measuring defects in related documents, such as user manuals. LOC-metrics have no relevance for databases and web content either. When the problems and errors of non-code software deliverables were accumulated, it was discovered that more than half of all software errors or defects were essentially invisible using LOC-metrics.

Historically, software quality was measured in terms of defects per 1000 source code statements, or 1000 lines of code (KLOC).

Unfortunately, the KLOC metric contains a built-in paradox that causes it to give erroneous results when used with newer and more powerful programming languages, such as Ada, object-oriented languages, or program generators.

The main problem with the KLOC metric is that this metric conceals, rather than reveals, important quality data. For example, suppose a company has been measuring quality in terms of defects per KLOC. A project coded in FORTRAN might require 10,000 LOC, and might contain 200 bugs, for a total of 20 defects per KLOC.

Now, suppose the same project could be created using a more powerful language, such as C++, which would require only 2000 lines of code and contain only 40 bugs. Here, too, there are 20 defects per KLOC, but the total number of bugs is actually reduced by 80 percent.

In the preceding FORTRAN and C++ examples, both versions provide the same functions to end users, and so both contain the same number of function points. Assume both versions contain 100 function points.

When the newer defects per function point metric is used, the FORTRAN version contains 2.00 defects per function point, but the C++ version contains only 0.40 defects per function point. With the function point metric, the substantial quality gains associated with more powerful high-level languages can now be made clearly visible.

Another problem with LOC-metrics is the difficulty of measuring or exploring defects in non-code deliverables, such as requirements and specifications. Here, too, function point metrics have illuminated data that was previously invisible.

Based on a study published in the author's book *Applied Software Measurement* (McGraw-Hill, 1996, the average number of software errors in the United States is about five per function point. Note that software defects are not found only in code, but originate in all of the major software deliverables, in approximately the quantities shown in Table 9.14.

These numbers represent the total numbers of defects that are found and measured from early software requirements definitions throughout the remainder of the life cycle of the software. The defects are discovered via requirement reviews, design reviews, code inspections, all forms of testing, and user problem reports.

Unmeasured and practically unmeasurable in 2007 are defects found in test cases, in databases, and in web content. From the author's attempts to quantify these, some very preliminary numbers are now possible:

- Test case errors approximate 2.0 defects per function point.

- Database errors approximate 6.0 defects per function point.

- Web content errors approximate 4.0 defects per function point.

TABLE 9.14   U.S. Averages in Defects per Function Point Circa 2007

Defect origins	Defects per function point
Requirements	1.00
Design	1.25
Coding	1.75
Documentation	0.60
Bad fixes	0.40
Total	5.00

In other words, the volume of "invisible" defects that have not yet been measured because of a lack of suitable metrics is possibly more than twice as large as the volume of defects that are currently being measured.

U.S. averages using function points lend themselves to graphical representation. The graph in Figure 9.1 shows defect-potentials and defect-removal efficiency levels as the two axes. The graph also identifies three zones of some significance:

- The central zone of average performance, where most companies can be found.

- The zone of best-in-class performance, where top companies can be found.

- The zone of professional malpractice, where companies that seem to know nothing at all about quality can be found.

It is very revealing to overlay a sample of an enterprise's software projects on this graph. Note that the *defects per FP* axis refers to the total defect potential, which includes errors in the requirements, specifications, source code, user manuals, and bad fix categories.

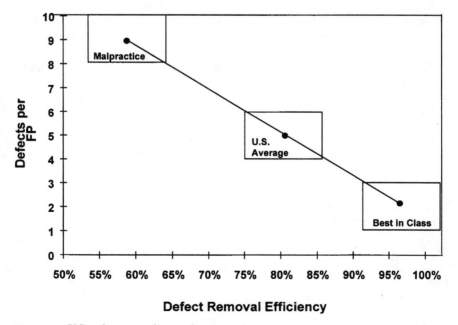

Figure 9.1   U.S. software quality performance ranges.

Complementing the function point metric are measurements of defect-removal efficiency, or the percentages of software defects removed prior to delivery of the software to clients.

The U.S. average for defect-removal efficiency, unfortunately, is currently only about 85 percent, although top-ranked projects in such leading companies as AT&T, IBM, Motorola, Raytheon, and Hewlett-Packard achieve defect-removal efficiency levels well in excess of 99 percent on their best projects and average close to 95 percent.

All software defects are not equally easy to remove. Requirements errors, design problems, and bad fixes tend to be the most difficult. Thus, on the day when software is actually put into production, the average quantity of latent errors or defects still present tends to be about 0.75 per function point, distributed as shown in Table 9.15, which also shows approximate ranges of defect-removal efficiency by origin point of software defects.

Note that at the time of delivery, defects originating in requirements and design tend to far outnumber coding defects. Data such as this can be used to improve the upstream defect-prevention and defect-removal processes of software development.

The best results in terms of defect removal are always achieved on projects that utilize formal pretest inspections of design, code, and other major deliverables, such as user manuals, and even test cases.

It is obvious that no single defect-removal operation is adequate by itself. This explains why best-in-class quality results can be achieved only from synergistic combinations of defect prevention, reviews or inspections, and various kinds of test activities.

The best software projects within the organizations that constitute roughly the upper 10 percent of the groups that SPR has assessed have achieved remarkably good quality levels. Following are software quality targets derived from best-in-class software projects and organizations:

- Defect potentials of less than 2.5 defects per function point. (Sum of defects found in requirements, design, code, user documents, and bad fixes.)

TABLE 9.15   Defect-Removal Efficiency by Origin of Defect
(Expressed in defects per function point)

Defect origins	Defect potentials	Removal efficiency	Delivered defects
Requirements	1.00	77%	0.23
Design	1.25	85%	0.19
Coding	1.75	95%	0.09
Documentation	0.60	80%	0.12
Bad fixes	0.40	70%	0.12
Total	5.00	85%	0.75

- Cumulative defect-removal efficiency averages higher than 95 percent. (All defects found during development, compared to first year's customer-reported defects.)

- Average less than 0.025 user-reported defects per function point per year. (Measured against valid, unique defects.)

- Achieve 90 percent *excellent* ratings from user-satisfaction surveys. (Measured on topics of product quality and service.)

- Allow zero error-prone modules in released software. (Modules receiving more than 0.8 defects per function point per year.)

- Improve software quality via defect prevention and defect removal at more than 40 percent per year. (Baseline is the current year's volume of customer-reported defects.)

If your organization is approaching or achieving these results, then you are part of a *world-class* software production organization.

There are thousands of ways to fail when building software applications, and only a very few ways to succeed. It is an interesting phenomenon that the best-in-class companies in terms of quality all use essentially similar approaches in achieving their excellent results. The 12 attributes of the best-in-class quality organizations are listed in Table 9.16.

The similarity of approaches among such companies as AT&T, Bellcore, Hewlett-Packard, IBM, Microsoft, Motorola, Raytheon, and so forth is quite striking when side-by-side benchmark comparisons are performed.

The SEI maturity level concept is one of the most widely discussed topics in the software literature. SPR was commissioned by the U.S. Air Force to perform a study on the economic impact of various SEI capability maturity levels (CMM). Raw data was provided to SPR on levels 1, 2, and 3 by an Air Force software location.

TABLE 9.16   Common Attributes Noted in Best-in-Class Software Organizations

1. Effective quality and removal efficiency measurements
2. Effective defect prevention (i.e., JAD, QFD, etc.)
3. Automated defect and quality estimation
4. Automated defect tracking
5. Complexity analysis tools
6. Test coverage analysis tools
7. Test automation tools
8. Test library control tools
9. Usage of formal design and code inspections
10. Formal testing by test specialists
11. Formal quality-assurance group
12. Executive and managerial understanding of quality

In terms of quality, the data available indicated that for maturity levels 1, 2, and 3 average quality tends to rise with CMM maturity level scores. However, this study had a limited number of samples. By contrast, the U.S. Navy has reported a counterexample, and has stated that at least some software produced by a level 3 organization was observed to be deficient.

There is clearly some overlap among the various SEI levels. Some of the software projects created by organizations at SEI level 2 are just as good in terms of quality as those created by SEI level 3. Indeed, there are even good- to excellent-quality projects created by some SEI level 1 organizations. Table 9.17 shows some suggested quality targets for the five plateaus of the SEI capability maturity model.

Above level 3 these targets are somewhat hypothetical, but from observations of organizations at various CMM levels the results would seem to be within the range of current technologies through level 4.

For level 5, the hardest part of the target would be dropping the potential defect level down to 1 per function point. Achieving a 99 percent cumulative defect-removal efficiency level is actually possible with current technologies for projects using formal inspections, testing specialists, and state-of-the-art testing tools.

As can be seen, the combination of function point metrics and defect-removal efficiency metrics are beginning to clarify quality topics that have long been ambiguous and intangible. Some of the examples shown here are now standard features of software cost-estimating tools.

It cannot be overemphasized that quality estimates and cost estimates are closely coupled, because the costs and schedule time required for defect-removal operations make up the largest component of software expense elements.

Software quality measurement and estimation should not be limited only to source code. Every major software deliverable should be subject to careful quality analysis, including but not limited to software requirements, specifications, planning documents, and user manuals. However, the LOC-metrics is not effective in dealing with non-code software deliverables.

TABLE 9.17   SEI CMM Software Quality Targets for Each Level
(Expressed in defects per function point)

SEI CMM levels	Defect potentials	Removal efficiency	Delivered defects
SEI CMM 1	5.00	85%	0.75
SEI CMM 2	4.00	90%	0.40
SEI CMM 3	3.00	95%	0.15
SEI CMM 4	2.00	97%	0.06
SEI CMM 5	1.00	99%	0.01

The combination of function point metrics coupled with direct measurement of defect-removal efficiency levels is making software quality results tangibly demonstrable. Now that software quality can be measured directly and predicted accurately, significant improvements are starting to occur.

Sizing Test Cases

The effort, costs, and schedule time devoted to testing software can, in some cases, exceed the effort, costs, and time devoted to coding the software. This situation means that test case sizing and testing estimation are critical features of software cost-estimating tools.

Fortunately, the function point metric has made a useful contribution to the ability to predict test case volumes. Recall the fundamental structure of function points:

- Inputs
- Outputs
- Logical files
- Inquiries
- Interfaces

These factors are the very aspects of software that need to be tested and, hence, the function point metric is actually one of the best tools ever developed for predicting test case volumes, because derivation from function points is an excellent way of dealing with a problem that was previously quite difficult.

An emerging and very important topic in the context of test estimating is that of predicting the number of bugs or errors in test cases themselves. As many commercial software vendors have come to realize, the error density of software test cases may actually exceed the error density of the software being tested. As previously noted, the defect volume in test libraries approximates 2.0 defects per function point. This means that there may be more defects in test cases than in the code being tested!

Because function points can be derived during both the requirements and early design stages, this approach offers a method of predicting test case numbers fairly early. The method is still somewhat experimental, but the approach is leading to interesting results and its usage is expanding.

Table 9.18 shows preliminary data for 18 kinds of testing on the number of test cases that have been noted among SPR's clients, using test cases per function point as the normalizing metric.

TABLE 9.18   Range of Test Cases per Function Point for 18 Forms of Software-Testing Projects in the United States

Testing stage	Minimum	Average	Maximum
Clean-room testing	0.60	1.00	3.00
Regression testing	0.40	0.60	1.30
Unit testing	0.20	0.45	1.20
New function testing	0.25	0.40	0.90
Integration testing	0.20	0.40	0.75
Subroutine testing	0.20	0.30	0.40
Independent testing	0.00	0.30	0.55
System testing	0.15	0.25	0.60
Viral testing	0.00	0.20	0.40
Performance testing	0.00	0.20	0.40
Acceptance testing	0.00	0.20	0.60
Lab testing	0.00	0.20	0.50
Field (beta) testing	0.00	0.20	1.00
Usability testing	0.00	0.20	0.40
Platform testing	0.00	0.15	0.30
Stress testing	0.00	0.15	0.30
Security testing	0.00	0.15	0.35
Special date testing	0.00	0.15	0.30
Total	2.00	5.50	13.25

This table has a high margin of error, but as with any other set of preliminary data points, it is better to publish the results in the hope of future refinements and corrections than to wait until the data is truly complete.

It should be noted that no project in our knowledge base has utilized all 18 forms of testing concurrently. The maximum number of test stages that the author has observed has been 16.

Much more common is a series of about half a dozen discrete forms of testing, which would include the following:

- Subroutine testing
- Unit testing
- New function testing
- Regression testing
- System testing
- Acceptance or field testing

Another way of looking at test case sizing is in terms of the patterns of testing by industry, rather than simply examining all 18 kinds of testing (see Table 9.19).

As can be seen, the numbers of test cases produced will vary widely, but quite a bit of this variance can be reduced by utilizing the typical patterns found in the class and type of software application.

TABLE 9.19   Number of Test Cases Created per Function Point

	Systems software	MIS software	Military software	Commercial software
Unit testing	0.30	0.20	0.50	0.30
New function testing	0.35	0.25	0.35	0.25
Regression testing	0.30	0.10	0.30	0.35
Integration testing	0.45	0.25	0.75	0.35
System testing	0.40	0.20	0.55	0.40
Total test cases	1.80	1.00	2.45	1.65

To a very significant degree, modern software cost-estimating tools operate as pattern-matching engines. Once the nature, scope, class, and type parameters are known to the software cost-estimating tool, it can begin to extract and utilize similar projects from its built-in knowledge base or from the portfolio of projects stored by users.

Of course, there is always a finite probability that any given project will deviate from the normal patterns of its class and type. This is why software cost-estimating tools allow users to override many predictions and make adjustments to the estimating assumptions.

Although functional metrics are not perfect, the advent of function points has expanded the number of software artifacts that can be sized, and has greatly simplified the tasks of sizing multiple deliverables.

The Event Horizon for Sizing Software Artifacts

We are now approaching the event horizon for software sizing technology. Beyond this horizon are a number of software artifacts where sizing is outside the scope of current software estimation capabilities.

Sizing Database Volumes

The technology for sizing database volumes is far less sophisticated than the technology for sizing other artifacts, such as documents, source code, test cases, and defects. The reason for this is because there are no current metrics for enumerating either the size of a database or for normalizing the number of errors that a database may contain.

Sizing Multimedia Artifacts

Modern software packages distributed and executed via CD-ROM are no longer severely limited by storage constraints and storage costs. As a result, software packages are no longer restricted to static displays of graphics and to the use of alphanumeric information for tutorial information.

These very modern multimedia artifacts are currently the edge of the event horizon for software cost-estimating tools. Recall that before accurate cost-estimating algorithms can be developed, it is necessary to have a solid body of empirical data available from accurate project measurements.

Since many of the advanced multimedia applications are being produced by the entertainment segment of the software industry, such as game vendors, these companies have seldom commissioned any kind of measurement or benchmarking studies. Therefore, there is an acute shortage of empirical data available on the effort associated with the creation of multimedia applications.

Some of these exotic technologies will move into business software. The business software community does tend to commission benchmarking and measurement studies, so in the future enough empirical data may become available to create estimating algorithms for software projects that feature multimedia, animation, music and voice soundtracks, and three-dimensional graphics.

It is entirely possible to build business software applications with features that were quite impossible ten years ago, including but not limited to the following:

- Audio soundtracks with instruction by human voices
- Music soundtracks
- Full animation for dynamic processes
- Three-dimensional graphics
- Photographs or video clips
- Neural-net engines that change the software's behavior

As this edition is being written, these multimedia artifacts are outside the scope of current software cost-estimating tools and are also outside the scope of software-measurement technology.

There are a few other topics that are also outside the event horizon for commercial estimating tools, but are probably known by those with a need for this kind of information. Many military, defense, and intelligence software packages utilize very sophisticated protective methods, such as encryption and multiple redundancy of key components.

Some of these critical applications may even execute from read-only memory (ROM) in order to minimize the risks of viral intrusion, so the software may have to be burned into special secure ROM devices. For obvious reasons of security, these methods are not widely discussed, and the specific approaches utilized are not covered by normal commercial software estimating tools and methods.

Suffice it to say that software applications with significant national security implications will include activities and forms of representation that are beyond the event horizon of standard estimating methods, and this is by reason of deliberate policy.

What Is Known as a Result of Sizing Software Projects

Because the main work of software estimating requires some kind of size information in order to proceed; sizing is a very important preliminary stage of constructing software cost estimates.

When using an automated estimating tool, users supply quite a bit of data by means of checklists or multiple-choice questions that enable the estimating tools to produce size predictions and later to produce full estimates.

Assuming that a user is working with one of the many commercial estimating tools, the list in Table 9.20 shows the kinds of information that are normally used to prime the estimating engine and allow the estimating tool to perform sizing and estimating tasks.

Note that much of the information is optional or the estimating tools include default values, which the users can either accept or override by substituting their own values.

TABLE 9.20   Project Information Normally Provided by Users

Project name	Optional
Project manager's name	Optional
Project estimator's name	Optional
Standard industry classification	Optional
Project start date	Optional; default is "today"
Desired delivery date	Optional
Salary levels	Optional or default value
Burden rates	Optional or default value
Burdened salary	Optional or default value
Inflation rate	Optional or default value
Special costs	Optional
Project goals	Optional or default value
Project nature	Required or default value
Project scope	Required or default value
Project class	Required or default value
Project type	Required or default value
Programming languages	Optional or default value
Complexity of problem	Optional or default value
Complexity of source code	Optional or default value
Complexity of data elements	Optional or default value

If the estimating tool includes sizing logic, it can produce project size estimates that the users can either accept or adjust as appropriate. However, in order to generate an accurate cost estimate, the commercial software estimating tools utilize the kinds of size information shown in Table 9.21, regardless of whether the information is generated by the tool itself, is supplied by the user, or both in some cases (the tool predicts a suggested value and the user may adjust or replace the value if desired).

Software projects have many different kinds of deliverable artifacts besides the code itself, and accurate software cost estimates must include these non-code deliverables in order to ensure that the estimate is complete and useful.

Similar kinds of information are required for estimating other types of projects besides software projects. For example, if you were working with an architect on designing and building a custom home, you would have to provide the architect with some basic information on

TABLE 9.21   Predicted Size Information or User-Supplied Size Information

Size in function points/feature points (initial value)	Approximated or supplied by user
Algorithms	Approximated or supplied by user
Inputs	Approximated or supplied by user
Outputs	Approximated or supplied by user
Inquiries	Approximated or supplied by user
Logical files	Approximated or supplied by user
Interfaces	Approximated or supplied by user
Rate of function point creep	Predicted—adjusted by user
Size in function points/feature points (final value)	Predicted—adjusted by user
Size in physical lines of source code	Predicted—adjusted by user
Size in logical source code statements	Predicted—adjusted by user
Size in terms of input/output screens	Predicted—adjusted by user
Size in terms of database volumes	Predicted—adjusted by user
Number of probable defects or bugs	Predicted—adjusted by user
Number of probable test cases	Predicted—adjusted by user
Size of volume of use cases	Predicted -- adjusted by user
Size of initial requirements	Predicted—adjusted by user
Rate of requirements creep	Predicted—adjusted by user
Size of final requirements	Predicted—adjusted by user
Size of external specifications	Predicted—adjusted by user
Size of internal specifications	Predicted—adjusted by user
Size of planning documents	Predicted—adjusted by user
Size of quality control documents	Predicted—adjusted by user
Size of user manuals	Predicted—adjusted by user
Size of training and tutorial information	Predicted—adjusted by user
Size of translations into other languages	Predicted—adjusted by user

how many square feet you wanted the house to be. A luxury house with 6000 square feet of living space and a three-car garage will obviously be more expensive to construct than a starter home with 1500 square feet and a one-car carport.

Strengths and Weaknesses of Software Size Metrics

Unfortunately, the current conflict between rival metrics enthusiasts is slowing down progress in software sizing and estimating technology. In fact, the conflicts are so sharp that it often escapes notice that none of the currently available metrics can measure every important aspect of software.

- The LOC-metrics have major problems for dealing with non-coding activities and for comparisons between unlike programming languages. Also, for certain languages, such as Visual Basic and its competitors, coding is only one way of developing applications. The LOC-metric has no relevance for software constructed using button control and pull-down menus.

- The function point metrics in all varieties have problems with counting precision for any specific variant, and even larger problems with converting data between variants. There are also severe problems across all function point variants for very small projects where certain constants in the counting rules tend to artificially inflate the results below about 15 function points.

- The object-oriented (OO) metrics are totally devoid of relevance for non-OO projects, and do not seem to deal with OO quality or defect rates. The OO metrics are also lacking the ability to predict the non-code aspects of software development. There are no known conversion rules between the OO metrics and the other size metrics.

- The more obscure size metrics, such as the Halstead software-science metrics, are yet additional variants. The original studies for software science appear to have methodological flaws, and the volume of published data for software-science metrics is only marginally greater than zero.

- In addition to basic size metrics, there are also metrics that are used for size adjustments, such as complexity. Of the 24 known forms of complexity that influence software projects, only two (cyclomatic and essential complexity) have significant literature. Unfortunately, many of the more critical complexity metrics have no literature in a software context, although psychologists and linguists deal with them.

- There are also attempts to use "natural" metrics, such as number of pages of specifications or number of staff hours. Here, too, there are problems with accuracy and with data conversion from these metrics to any other known metric.

- There are no known metrics of any form that can deal with the topic of the size of databases, nor with the important topic of data quality. Fundamental metrics research is needed in the database arena.

- The explosive growth of web-based applications brings up another metrics gap: the ability to measure web content in terms of size, cost, and quality.

- The literature on metrics conversion between the competing function point methods, the competing LOC methods, and the other methods (object-oriented metrics, software-science metrics, etc.) is only marginally better than a null set.

The following would be advantageous to the software industry overall:

- A complete analysis of the strengths and weaknesses of all current metrics

- A concerted effort to develop industrial-strength function metrics that can support all software activities

- Development of a standard activity table for the major software activities, so that such terms as *requirements* or *design* have the same general meaning and include the same task sets

- The elimination of the scores of minor function point variants with few users and little published data or, at the very least, publication of conversion rules between minor variants and major function point forms

- A consistent set of source code counting rules that could be applied to all programming languages, including visual languages

- Development of a *data point* metric derived from the structure of function point metrics, but aimed at quantifying the sizes of databases, repositories, data warehouses, and flat files

- Development of metrics for dealing with the size and quality of web content in the forms of images, sounds, animation, links, etc.

If multiple and conflicting metrics continue to be used, then metrics-conversion tools should be added to the software management toolkit to facilitate international comparisons when the data originates using multiple metrics.

The eventual goal of metrics research would be to facilitate the sizing and estimating of complex hybrid systems where software, microcode, hardware, data, and service components all contribute to the final constructed artifact.

What would probably be of immediate use to the software industry would be to publish formal rules for conversion logic between the major competing metrics. Even better would be automated metrics conversion tools that could handle a broad range of current metrics problems, such as the following:

- Rules for size conversion between IFPUG Versions 3.4 and 4.1 counting methods

- Rules for size conversion between IFPUG, COSMIC, NESMA, and Mark II counting methods

- Rules for size conversion between source code and function point metrics

- Rules for code size conversion between SPR and SEI code counting methods

- Rules for size conversion between object-oriented metrics and any other metric

- Rules for size conversion between two unlike programming languages

As an experiment, the author has constructed a prototype metric conversion tool that can handle some of these conversion problems, such as conversion between the SPR logical statement counts and the SEI physical line counts for selected programming languages.

While the prototype demonstrates that automatic conversion is feasible, the total number of variations in the industry is so large that a full-scale metric-conversion tool that can handle all common variants would be a major application in its own right. For such a tool to stay current, it would be necessary to keep it updated on an almost monthly basis, as new languages and new metrics appear.

Summary and Conclusions

Software sizing is a critical but difficult part of software cost estimating. The invention of function point metrics has simplified the sizing of non-code artifacts, such as specifications and user documents, but sizing is still a complicated and tricky undertaking.

While function points in general have simplified and improved software sizing, the unexpected fragmentation of function point metrics into more than 38 variants has added an unnecessary amount of confusion to the task of sizing, without contributing much in terms of technical precision.

The most accurate and best method for software sizing is to keep very good historical data of the sizes of software project deliverables. This way it will be possible to use the known sizes of artifacts from completed projects as a jumping-off place for predicting the sizes of similar artifacts for projects being estimated.

References

Abran, A., and P. N. Robillard: "Function Point Analysis: An Empirical Study of Its Measurement Processes," *IEEE Transactions on Software Engineering*, **22**(12):895–909 (1996).

Abrieu, Fernando Brito e: "An email information on MOOD," *Metrics News*, Otto-von-Guericke-Univeersitaat, Magdeburg, **7**(2):11 (1997).

Albrecht, A. J.: "Measuring Application Development Productivity," *Proceedings of the Joint IBM/SHARE/GUIDE Application Development Symposium*, October 1979, reprinted in *Programming Productivity—Issues for the Eighties* by Capers Jones, IEEE Computer Society Press, New York, 1981.

Artow, J. and I Neustadt: UML and the Unified Process, Addison-Wesley, Boston, Mass., 2000.

———: *AD/M Productivity Measurement and Estimate Validation*, IBM Corporation, Purchase, N.Y., 1984.

Boehm, Barry: *Software Engineering Economics*, Prentice-Hall, Englewood Cliffs, N.J., 1981.

Booch, Grady, Ivar Jacobsen, and James Rumbaugh: *The Unified Modeling Language User Guide, Second Edition*, Addison-Wesley, Boston, Mass., 2005.

Bogan, Christopher E., and Michael J. English: *Benchmarking for Best Practices*, McGraw-Hill, New York, 1994.

Brown, Norm (ed.): *The Program Manager's Guide to Software Acquisition Best Practices*, Version 1.0, U.S. Department of Defense, Washington, D.C., 1995.

Chidamber, S. R., D. P. Darcy, and C. F. Kemerer: "Managerial Use of Object Oriented Software Metrics," Working Paper no. 750, Joseph M. Katz Graduate School of Business, University of Pittsburgh, Pittsburgh, Pa., November 1996.

———, and C. F. Kemerer: "A Metrics Suite for Object Oriented Design," *IEEE Transactions on Software Engineering*, **20**:476–493 (1994).

Cockburn, Alistair: *Agile Software Development*, Addison-Wesley, Boston, Mass., 2001.

Cohn, Mike: *Agile Estimating and Planning*, Prentice-Hall PTR, Englewood Cliffs, N.J., 2005.

———: *User Stories Applied: For Agile Software Development*, Addison-Wesley, Boston, Mass., 2004.

DeMarco, Tom: *Controlling Software Projects*, Yourdon Press, New York, 1982.

———: *Why Does Software Cost So Much?*, Dorset House, New York, 1995.

Department of the Air Force: *Guidelines for Successful Acquisition and Management of Software Intensive Systems*, vols. 1 and 2, Software Technology Support Center, Hill Air Force Base, Utah, 1994.

Dreger, Brian: *Function Point Analysis*, Prentice-Hall, Englewood Cliffs, N.J., 1989.

Fenton, Norman, and Shari Lawrence Pfleeger: *Software Metrics—A Rigorous and Practical Approach, Second Edition*, IEEE Press, Los Alamitos, Calif., 1997.

Fetchke, Thomas, Alain Abran, Tho-Hau Nguyen: *Mapping the OO-Jacobsen Approach into Function Point Analysis*, University du Quebec a Montreal, Software Engineering Management Research Laboratory, 1997.

Fuqua, Andrew M.: *Using Function Points in XP—Considerations*, Springer Berlin/ Heidelberg, 2003.

Galea, R. B.: *The Boeing Company: 3D Function Point Extensions*, V2.0, Release 1.0, Boeing Information Support Services, Seattle, Wash., June 1995.

Gamma, Erich, Richard Helm, Ralph Johnson, and John Vlissides: *Design Patterns: Elements of Reusable Object Oriented Design*, Addison-Wesley, Boston Mass., 1995.

Garmus, David, and David Herron: *Measuring the Software Process: A Practical Guide to Functional Measurement*, Prentice-Hall, Englewood Cliffs, N.J., 1995.

Grady, Robert B.: *Practical Software Metrics for Project Management and Process Improvement*, Prentice-Hall, Englewood Cliffs, N.J., 1992.

————, and Deborah L. Caswell: *Software Metrics: Establishing a Company-Wide Program*, Prentice-Hall, Englewood Cliffs, N.J., 1987.

Halstead, Maurice H.: *Elements of Software Science*, Elsevier North Holland, NY, 1977.

Howard, Alan (ed.): *Software Metrics and Project Management Tools*, Applied Computer Research (ACR), Phoenix, Ariz., 1997.

IFPUG Counting Practices Manual, Release 3, International Function Point Users Group, Westerville, Ohio, April 1990.

————, Release 4, International Function Point Users Group, Westerville, Ohio, April 1995.

International Organization for Standards, ISO 9000 / ISO 14000 (http://www.iso.org/iso/en/iso9000-14000/index.html).

Jones, Capers: *SPQR/20 Users Guide*, Software Productivity Research, Cambridge, Mass., 1986.

————: *Critical Problems in Software Measurement*, Information Systems Management Group, 1993a.

————: *Software Productivity and Quality Today—The Worldwide Perspective*, Information Systems Management Group, 1993b.

————: *Assessment and Control of Software Risks*, Prentice-Hall, Englewood Cliffs, N.J., 1994.

————: *New Directions in Software Management*, Information Systems Management Group,

————: *Patterns of Software System Failure and Success*, International Thomson Computer Press, Boston, 1995.

————: *Applied Software Measurement, Second Edition*, McGraw-Hill, New York, 1996a.

————: *Table of Programming Languages and Levels* (8 Versions from 1985 through July 1996), Software Productivity Research, Burlington, Mass., 1996b.

————: *The Economics of Object-Oriented Software*, Software Productivity Research, Burlington, Mass., April 1997a.

————: *Software Quality—Analysis and Guidelines for Success*, International Thomson Computer Press, Boston, 1997b.

————: *The Year 2000 Software Problem—Quantifying the Costs and Assessing the Consequences*, Addison-Wesley, Reading, Mass., 1998.

Kan, Stephen H.: , Addison-Wesley Longman, Boston, Mass., 2003.

Kemerer, C. F.: "Reliability of Function Point Measurement—A Field Experiment," *Communications of the ACM*, **36:**85–97 (1993).

Love, Tom: *Object Lessons*, SIGS Books, New York, 1993.

McCabe, Thomas J.; A Complexity Measure; IEEE Transactions on Software Engineering; Vol. SE-2, No. 4; 1976; pg. 308-318.

McConnell, Steve: *Software Estimating: Demystifying the Black Art*, Microsoft Press, Redmond, WA; 2006.

Marciniak, John J. (ed.): *Encyclopedia of Software Engineering*, vols. 1 and 2, John Wiley & Sons, New York, 1994.

McCabe, Thomas J.: "A Complexity Measure," *IEEE Transactions on Software Engineering*, (December 1976) pp. 308–320.

Muller, Monika, and Alain Abram (eds.): *Metrics in Software Evolution*, R. Oldenbourg Vertag GmbH, Munich, 1995.

Oman, Paul, and Shari Lawrence Pfleeger (eds.): *Applying Software Metrics*, IEEE Press, Los Alamitos, Calif., 1996.

Pressman, Roger: *Software Engineering – A Practitioner's Approach, Sixth Edition*, McGraw-Hill, New York, 2005.

Putnam, Lawrence H.: *Measures for Excellence—Reliable Software on Time, Within Budget,* Yourdon Press/Prentice-Hall, Englewood Cliffs, N.J., 1992.

———, and Ware Myers: *Industrial Strength Software—Effective Management Using Measurement,* IEEE Press, Los Alamitos, Calif., 1997.

Rethinking the Software Process, CD-ROM, Miller Freeman, Lawrence, Kans., 1996. (This CD-ROM is a book collection jointly produced by the book publisher, Prentice-Hall, and the journal publisher, Miller Freeman. It contains the full text and illustrations of five Prentice-Hall books: *Assessment and Control of Software Risks* by Capers Jones; *Controlling Software Projects* by Tom DeMarco; *Function Point Analysis* by Brian Dreger; *Measures for Excellence* by Larry Putnam and Ware Myers; and *Object-Oriented Software Metrics* by Mark Lorenz and Jeff Kidd.)

Shavisprasad Koirala: "How to Prepare Quotations Using Use Case Points" (http://www.codeproject.com/gen/design//usecasepoints.asp).

Shepperd, M.: "A Critique of Cyclomatic Complexity as a Software Metric," *Software Engineering Journal,* **3**:30–36 (1988).

St-Pierre, Denis, Marcela Maya, Alain Abran, and Jean-Marc Desharnais: *Full Function Points: Function Point Extensions for Real-Time Software, Concepts and Definitions,* TR 1997-03, University of Quebec, Software Engineering Laboratory in Applied Metrics (SELAM), March 1997.

Stukes, Sherry, Jason Deshoretz, Henry Apgar, and Ilona Macias: *Air Force Cost Analysis Agency Software Estimating Model Analysis—Final Report,* TR-9545/008-2, Contract F04701-95-D-0003, Task 008, Management Consulting & Research, Inc., Thousand Oaks, Calif., September 1996.

Symons, Charles R.: *Software Sizing and Estimating—Mk II FPA (Function Point Analysis),* John Wiley & Sons, Chichester, U.K., 1991.

———: "ISMI—International Software Metrics Initiative—Project Proposal" (private communication), June 15, 1997.

———: "Software Sizing and Estimating: Can Function Point Methods Meet Industry Needs?" (unpublished draft submitted to the IEEE for possible publication), Guild of Independent Function Point Analysts, London, U.K., August 1997.

Whitmire, S. A.: "3-D Function Points: Scientific and Real-Time Extensions to Function Points," *Proceedings of the 1992 Pacific Northwest Software Quality Conference,* June 1, 1992.

Zuse, Dr. Horst; *Software Complexity: Measures and Methods*; Walter de Gruyter, Berlin, 1990.

4

Cost-Estimating Adjustment Factors

Software cost estimating is a complex activity with a host of interlocking factors and hundreds of adjustment rules to evaluate. In general, commercial software cost-estimation tools assume that a project is average in every major factor unless the users state otherwise. This means that users need deal only with topics where they know their project will be much better or much worse than normal.

However, there are some adjustments that are so important that industry averages should not be used and, indeed, may even be hazardous. Some of these critical factors where local information should be used in place of industry averages include the following:

- *Compensation levels for project personnel*
- *Burden or overhead rates to be applied to the projects*
- *Work patterns in terms of paid and unpaid overtime*
- *Specific methodologies to be used*
- *Specific tools to be used*
- *Specific programming languages to be used*
- *The specific kinds of reviews and inspections to be used*
- *The specific kinds of testing to be used*

The normal method of operation of dealing with programming adjustments is to present the users of estimating tools with the current default values, which they can either accept or modify as the situation warrants.

Compensation and Work-Pattern Adjustments

Estimating software development projects and the related topic of estimating software maintenance and enhancement projects are the real heart of commercial software estimating tools. Hundreds of factors can influence the outcomes of software projects for better or for worse. Modern software estimating tools are designed to deal with three classes of adjustment factors:

- Average situations where tools or methods have no significant impact
- Situations where the project is much better than average in key areas
- Situations where the project is much worse than average in key areas

The factors that influence the outcomes of software projects number in the hundreds, but for convenience in evaluating them they can be placed into seven main topical areas:

- Attributes of the project itself (novelty, complexity, and size)
- Personnel and management experience levels (similar projects, tools, and languages)
- Methodology and development processes utilized (Agile, waterfall, OO, etc.)
- Tools utilized (management, development, quality, maintenance, etc.)
- Geographic separation of team members for multisite projects
- Programming languages utilized
- Reusable materials available

The default value for most software cost-estimating tools is to assume that the project is average for all topics, unless the user states otherwise. But accurate estimation depends upon more than default values and average assumptions. Users of software cost-estimation tools must deal truthfully with situations where the project is worse than normal, and should also identify situations where the project may be better than average.

Manual and Automated Methods of Adjustment

One of the advantages of using computers and commercial software estimating tools is that really accurate estimation for software projects is very complicated and involves hundreds of rules. Commercial software estimation tools can handle many factors and adjustments quickly, and can also deal with the more granular activity-based and task-based cost estimates much more conveniently than would be possible using manual approaches.

However, even with automated software cost-estimating tools, managerial experience and judgment are helpful, as is input by the technical staff members who must actually do the work in real life.

Software cost estimates are important business tools, but important business decisions depend upon human judgment. It is interesting to examine a detailed work-breakdown structure of software estimating itself and evaluate whether automated or manual methods are most appropriate for each step (see Table 10.1).

As can easily be seen, for all of the steps that depend primarily on calculations and rule-based decisions, the automated approach is preferred. However, for the steps where judgment and business knowledge come into play, the human mind is preferred.

In addition, there are many activities where an automated cost-estimating tool can provide a default or starting value, but manual adjustments and overrides to match specific situations may be desirable.

For example, determining whether to build a software application or buy a commercial package remains a human choice. Also, while automated estimating tools may have adjustments for staff experience levels and expertise, human performance varies so widely that it is useful to allow project managers to override default assumptions and substitute their own values for teams of exceptional capabilities.

In addition, the amount of overtime applied to a software project can only be approximated by software cost-estimating tools. The work ethics of the team and the amount of schedule pressure applied by clients or executives remain factors that must be interpreted by human minds.

TABLE 10.1   A 35-Step Breakdown for Constructing Software Cost Estimates

Step	Definition	Method preferred for maximum accuracy
Step 1	Understanding software requirements	Manual
Step 2	Evaluating creeping user requirements	Automated
Step 3	Exploring similar historical projects	Automated/manual
Step 4	Sizing software deliverables	Automated/manual
Step 5	Preliminary estimates and rules of thumb	Automated/manual
Step 6	Make or buy decisions based on estimate	Manual
Step 7	Identifying activities to be performed	Automated/manual
Step 8	Estimating the impact of reusable materials	Automated
Step 9	Estimating software defect potentials	Automated
Step 10	Estimating software defect removal efficiency	Automated
Step 11	Estimating staffing needs based on project size	Automated/manual
Step 12	Staffing adjustments based on schedule pressure	Automated
Step 13	Staffing adjustments based on specialists	Automated
Step 14	Staffing adjustments based on team experience	Automated/manual
Step 15	Estimating software effort (hours/days/months)	Automated
Step 16	Effort adjustments based on unpaid overtime	Automated
Step 17	Effort adjustments based on class and type	Automated
Step 18	Effort adjustments based on team capability	Automated/manual
Step 19	Effort adjustments based on process	Automated
Step 20	Effort adjustments based on tools	Automated
Step 21	Effort adjustment based on languages	Automated
Step 22	Estimating software schedules	Automated
Step 23	Schedule adjustments based on scope creep	Automated/manual
Step 24	Schedule adjustments based on overtime	Automated/manual
Step 25	Schedule adjustments based on critical paths	Automated
Step 26	Applying basic salary cost structures	Automated
Step 27	Cost adjustments based on unpaid overtime	Automated
Step 28	Cost adjustments based on paid overtime	Automated
Step 29	Cost adjustments based on compensation levels	Automated
Step 30	Cost adjustment based on burden rate levels	Automated
Step 31	Cost adjustments based on inflation rates	Automated
Step 32	Cost adjustments based on special factors	Automated
Step 33	Estimating post-release maintenance	Automated
Step 34	Estimating post-release enhancements	Automated
Step 35	Validating software cost estimates	Automated/manual

It is interesting to focus on the activities where human judgment is often used to override the default values provided by software estimating tools (see Table 10.2).

As can be seen, almost a third of the activities associated with software cost estimating benefit from the experience and judgment of human participants in the estimating process. Only for activities that are purely rule-based or mechanical, such as applying inflation rates, performing

TABLE 10.2   Software Estimating Activities Depending upon Human Judgment

Step	Definition	Method preferred for maximum accuracy
Step 1	Understanding software requirements	Manual
Step 3	Exploring similar historical projects	Automated/manual
Step 4	Sizing software deliverables	Automated/manual
Step 5	Preliminary estimates and rules of thumb	Automated/manual
Step 6	Make or buy decisions based on estimate	Manual
Step 7	Identifying activities to be performed	Automated/manual
Step 14	Staffing adjustments based on team experience	Automated/manual
Step 18	Effort adjustments based on team capability	Automated/manual
Step 23	Schedule adjustments based on scope creep	Automated/manual
Step 24	Schedule adjustments based on overtime	Automated/manual
Step 35	Validating software cost estimates	Automated/manual

currency conversions, or dealing with critical path analysis, can software estimating tools work in a wholly automated fashion.

Software cost estimates must also deal with a number of specific technologies that are known to affect the projects where these technologies come into play. A few examples of the technical factors that can affect the outcome of software projects both in real life and in the context of cost estimates are shown in Table 10.3.

With commercial software estimating tools, the normal mode for dealing with specific technologies is that of either constructing or acquiring

TABLE 10.3   Special Factors and Adjustments for Software Cost Estimation

Agile development methods
Application generators
CASE and I-CASE tools
Client/Server project estimation
Component-based software development
Deferral or deletion of planned project functions
Distributed international development
Department of Defense standards
Eurocurrency support
ERP deployment
Extreme programming (XP)
Frame-based development
Hybrid hardware/firmware/software projects
Hypertext links in text files
Information-engineering (IE) project estimation
International projects and translation expenses
Interactive tutorials on CD-ROM or DVD
ISO 9000–9004 standards
Music or special soundtracks
Pattern-based design methods
Processes or methodologies utilized

TABLE 10.3   Special Factors and Adjustments for Software Cost Estimation
(Continued)

Prototyping before main project commences
Object-oriented (OO) analysis and design methods
Object-oriented (OO) programming languages
Object-oriented (OO) metrics
Migration to multiple platforms
Multiplatform projects
Multicompany projects
Multimedia software project estimation
Rapid application development (RAD) projects
Reusable design
Reusable source code
Reusable test cases
Reusable user information
Scrum meetings
SEI CMM or CMMI level of the development organization
Training and tutorial material
Use cases for requirements
Videotape tutorials
World Wide Web applets

a *template* or *pattern* that includes the activities and default values associated with the technology in question.

A software cost-estimating template for a technology is a kind of special estimating *object* that includes the set of development activities associated with the technology and default or starting values for assignment scopes, production rates, and other key factors.

Some of the standard software estimating templates available with commercial software estimating tools include but are not limited to those shown in Table 10.4.

TABLE 10.4   Software Estimating Templates for Specific Methods and Processes

Agile development
Clean-room development
Client/server development
ERP deployment
Eurocurrency updates
Extreme programming (XP)
Information engineering (IE)
Object-oriented (OO) development
Rapid Application Development (RAD)

SEI CMM level 1
SEI CMM level 2
SEI CMM level 3
SEI CMM level 4
SEI CMM level 5

In addition to commercial estimating templates created by estimating-tool vendors, a number of commercial software estimating tools include a template construction utility that allows users to create custom templates for technologies that are used locally.

Exclusions from Normal Software Cost Estimates

It is also significant that even with very powerful automated software cost-estimating tools, there are a number of cost topics that are usually excluded from general-purpose software cost estimates because they either occur infrequently or vary so widely that no overall rules have been developed for predicting their outcomes (see Table 10.5).

Although these activities are outside the scope of normal software cost estimates, some of the expenses can be very significant. Indeed, the costs

TABLE 10.5   Normal Exclusions from Software Cost Estimates

Advertising costs for commercial software
Assessments of projects during development
Benchmark studies of projects during development
Bonuses or awards to key employees
External management consultants
Legal expenses for trademark searches
Legal expenses for patent filings
Legal expenses for copyright filings
Legal expenses for any litigation affecting the project
Nationalization or translating material into other languages
Off-site rents for JAD or Scrum meetings
Moving and living expenses for new hires
Postmortem analyses of projects after completion
Signing bonuses for new hires
Stock or equity awarded to employees
Training costs for learning new methods or languages
Travel expenses for meetings and conferences
Transfer costs for moving projects from site to site

Personnel hiring expenses and agency fees
Capital equipment such as new computers
Software licenses and maintenance fees for tools
Marketing and advertising fees
Work performed by clients or customers
Focus group expenses
Customer survey expenses
Customer association funding
Online forum costs

of travel for projects involving multiple locations can actually achieve third place out of the top six major software cost elements:

- Defect-removal costs
- Paperwork costs
- Travel and meeting costs
- Coding costs
- Project management costs
- Change-control costs

A number of software cost-estimating tools allow these special costs to be added to the overall project by providing empty "cost buckets" that can be filled with whatever special costs are known to be included for the project but are outside the scope of the normal estimate.

Some of these cost buckets are even identified and set up for various kinds of costs that often occur, but that are too variable and irregular for rule-based estimation. Some examples of these prepared cost buckets include the following:

- Hiring expenses for the project
- Legal expenses for the project
- Travel expenses for the project
- Nationalization expenses for the project
- Assessment expenses for the project
- Management consulting fees for the project

Without multiplying examples, it can be seen that software cost estimating requires dealing with a very large number of factors. One of the advantages of automated cost estimating as opposed to manual cost estimating is that the obscure and infrequent factors are not likely to be forgotten or left out by accident.

Setting Up the Initial Conditions for a Cost Estimate

Once a user has turned on a cost-estimating tool and entered administrative information such as the name of the project, the next step is to establish the initial conditions for the project being estimated.

Although commercial estimating tools vary in how they deal with the initial conditions, many of them operate in a similar manner. By means of pull-down menus, buttons, or explicit statements, users need to narrow down the universe of all possible projects to the specific kind of project for which the estimate is to be made. The estimating tools narrow their focus with such basic kinds of topics as the following:

- Is the project a military project or a civilian project?
- Is the project for internal use or for delivery to external customers?
- Is the project a new project or an enhancement project?
- Is the project a small program or a large system?
- Is the project embedded software, an information system, or something else?
- Will the project use Agile methods, OO methods, waterfall methods, or something else?
- Will the staff receive payment for overtime work or not?
- Will the project involve work in more than one city or country?
- Are subcontracts or multiple companies involved in the project?
- Are there schedule or cost limits for completing this project?
- Should the estimate be set at project, phase, activity, or task level?

These are the kinds of factors with such an obvious impact on the outcome of the project that it is apparent why the information is needed. To ease the work of users, however, some commercial estimating tools have default or assumed settings so that the only information that users have to supply is regarding things that are different from the default values.

For example, the estimating tools that the author's company builds includes the following set of assumptions as the initial default values, although every factor in the list can be changed by users if needed:

Project nature	New project
Project scope	Standalone program
Project class	Internal software
Project type	Information system
Staff availability	100%
Staff compensation	$5000 per month
Burden rate	50%
Burdened compensation	$7500
Overtime premium	50%
Annual inflation rate	5%
Exempt personnel (no overtime pay)	100%
Nonexempt personnel (overtime pay)	0%
Overtime premium	100%
Hiring costs	0
Moving and living costs	0
Development locations	1

Maintenance locations	1
Work days per week	5.00
Work hours per day	8.00
Effective hours per day	6.00
Unpaid overtime hours per day	1.00
Holidays per year	10.00
Vacation days per year	15.00
Sick days per year	3.00
Education/training days per year	10.00
Meetings/travel days per year	5.00
Work days per calendar year	218

The purpose of providing default values is to simplify estimating mechanics by having at least reasonable information available for topics that not every project manager will know or have immediate access to.

Although these are reasonable default values for software projects produced in the United States, they are by no means absolute values that can safely be applied to projects in every country. Even in the United States, the ranges of possible values are extremely broad and users will need to replace such default assumptions with their own organization's real values.

There are several major problems in the cost domain that have existed for more than 50 years, but which escaped notice so long as software used inaccurate metrics like lines of code that tended to mask a host of other important problems. These same problems occur for other industries besides software, incidentally. They tend to be more troublesome for software than for most other industries because software is so labor-intensive.

The topic of software costs has a very large range of variability within any given country, and an even larger range for international software studies. There are seven interconnected sets of cost factors that need to be evaluated to determine software costs, and every one is an independent variable, as shown in Table 10.6.

A fundamental problem with software cost measures is the fact that salaries and compensation vary widely from job to job, worker to worker, company to company, region to region, industry to industry, and country to country.

TABLE 10.6   Compensation Variations That Impact Software Cost Estimates

1. Variations due to industry compensation averages
2. Variations due to sizes of companies
3. Variations due to geographic regions or locations
4. Variations due to merit appraisals or longevity
5. Variations due to burden rate or overhead differences
6. Variations due to work patterns and unpaid overtime
7. Variations due to bonuses or special one-time payments

For example, among SPR's clients in the United States the basic salary for software project managers ranges from a low of about $55,000 per year to a high of more than $120,000 per year. When international clients are included, the range for the same position runs from less than $15,000 per year to more than $130,000 a year.

For example, large urban areas, such as the San Francisco Bay Area or the urban areas in New York and New Jersey, have much higher pay scales than do more rural areas or smaller communities in other locations, such as Arkansas, Nebraska, or West Virginia.

Also, some industries, such as banking and financial services and telecommunications manufacturing, tend to have compensation levels that are far above U.S. averages, while other industries, such as government service and education, tend to have compensation levels that are significantly lower than U.S. averages.

The huge variances in basic compensation mean that it is unsafe and inaccurate to use "U.S. averages" for cost comparisons of software. In fact, although "average cost per function point" is the single question that is most often posed to software cost-estimating companies, that specific factor is one of the most volatile and unreliable of all metrics.

At the very least, cost comparisons should be within the context of the same or related industries, and comparisons should be made against organizations that are of similar size and are located in similar geographic areas.

Other software-related positions besides project management have similar ranges, and there are now more than 75 software-related occupations in the United States. This means that in order to do software cost studies it is necessary to deal with major differences in costs based on industry, on company size, on geographic location, on the kinds of specialists that are present on any given project, and on years of tenure or merit appraisal results.

Even if only basic compensation is considered, it can easily be seen that software projects developed by large companies in such large cities as New York, Chicago, and San Jose will have higher cost structures than the same applications developed by small companies in smaller cities.

One of the more complex issues of software cost estimating is dealing with all of the elements that actually go into the cost structures of modern corporations and their payment and benefit plans.

Variations in Burden Rates or Overhead Costs

An even more significant problem associated with software cost studies is the lack of generally accepted accounting practices for determining the burden rate or overhead costs that are added to basic salaries to create a metric called the *fully burdened salary rate*, which corporations use for determining business topics such as the charge-out rates for cost centers. The fully burdened rate is also used for other business purposes, such as contracts, outsourcing agreements, and return on investment (ROI) calculations.

The components of the burden rate are highly variable from company to company. Some of the costs included in burden rates can be social security contributions, unemployment benefit contributions, various kinds of taxes, rent for office space, utilities, security, postage, depreciation, portions of mortgage payments on buildings, various fringe benefits (medical plans, dental plans, disability, moving and living, vacations, etc.), and sometimes the costs of indirect staff (human resources, purchasing, mail room, etc.).

As this edition is being written, one of the major gaps in the software literature, and for that matter in accounting literature as well, is the almost total lack of international comparisons of the typical burden rate methodologies used in various countries. So far as can be determined, there are no published studies that explore burden rate differences between countries, such as the United States, Canada, India, the European Union countries, Japan, China, and so forth.

Among SPR's clients, the range of burden rates runs from a low of perhaps 15 percent of basic salary levels to a high of approximately 300 percent. In terms of dollars, that range means that the fully burdened charge rate for the position of senior systems programmer in the United States can run from a low of about $15,000 per year to a high of $350,000 per year.

Unfortunately, the software literature is almost silent on the topic of burden or overhead rates. Indeed, many articles on software costs not only fail to detail the factors included in burden rates, but often fail to even state whether the burden rate itself was used in deriving the costs that the articles discuss.

Of all of the cost-estimating adjustment factors, there is the greatest scarcity of industry average data for burden rates. This is because many companies regard the structure of their burden or overhead rates as being proprietary information.

Table 10.7 illustrates some of the typical components of software burden rates, and also shows how these components might vary between a large corporation with a massive infrastructure and a small startup corporation that has very few overhead cost elements.

When the combined ranges of basic salaries and burden rates are applied to software projects in the United States, they yield almost a 6 to 1 variance in personnel costs for projects where the actual number of work months or work hours are identical.

When the salary and burden rate ranges are applied to international projects, they yield about a 15 to 1 variance between such countries

TABLE 10.7   Generic Components of Typical Burden or Overhead Costs in Large and
Small Companies

Component	Large company		Small company	
	Cost	Percentage	Cost	Percentage
Average Annual Salary	$50,000	100.0	$50,000	100
Personnel burden				
Payroll taxes	5,000	10	$5,000	10
Bonus	5,000	10	0	0
Benefits	5,000	10	2,500	5
Profit sharing	5,000	10	0	0
Subtotal	$20,000	40	$7,500	15
Office burden				
Office rent	$10,000	20	$5,000	10
Property taxes	2,500	5	1,000	2
Office supplies	2,000	4	1,000	2
Janitorial service	1,000	2	1,000	2
Utilities	1,000	2	1,000	2
Subtotal	$16,500	33	$9,000	18
Corporate burden				
Information systems	$5,000	10	0	0
Finance	5,000	10	0	0
Human resources	4,000	8	0	0
Legal	3,000	6	0	0
Subtotal	$17,000	34	0	0
Total burden	$53,500	107	$16,500	33
Salary+burden	$103,500	207	$66,500	133
Monthly rate	8,625		5,542	

as India, China, or the Ukraine at the low end of the spectrum and
Germany or Switzerland or Japan at the high end of the spectrum.

Hold in mind that this 15 to 1 range of cost variance is for projects
where the actual number of hours worked is identical. When productivity differences are considered, too, there can be more than a 100 to 1
variance between the most productive projects in companies with the
lowest salaries and burden rates and the least productive projects in
companies with the highest salaries and burden rates.

On the whole, throughout the world, large corporations in major metropolitan areas have higher compensation and burden rates than smaller
corporations in rural areas. Consider a plain ordinary management information system of 1000 function points written in COBOL. It might cost
$1500 per function point for a major corporation to build this application
in New York or San Francisco, but only $600 per function point for a small
company to build it in St. Petersburg, Florida or Lincoln, Nebraska, with
exactly the same number of people and exactly the same number of work

hours for the project. The large metropolitan version will be built by personnel whose salaries are 10 to 15 percent higher than the rural version, while the overhead factors of rent, taxes, utilities, and other components may be 100 percent greater in the large metropolitan areas.

Variations in Work Habits and Unpaid Overtime

From an estimating viewpoint, one of the most troublesome aspects of software cost estimating is predicting the work patterns of the development team. Software development and maintenance are very labor intensive. So long as software is built using human effort as the primary tool, all of the factors associated with work patterns and overtime will continue to be significant.

Assume that a typical month contains four work weeks, each comprised of five 8-hour working days. The combination of 4 weeks × 5 days × 8 hours = 160 available hours in a typical month. However, at least in the United States, the *effective* number of hours worked each month is often less than 160, due to such factors as coffee breaks, meetings, slack time between assignments, interruptions, and the like. (The *effective* hours are sometimes termed *ideal* hours with some of the Agile methods.)

Thus, in situations where there is no intense schedule pressure, the effective number of work hours per month may only amount to about 80 percent of the available hours, or about 128 hours per calendar month.

On the other hand, software projects are often under intense schedule pressures and overtime is quite common. The majority of professional U.S. software personnel are termed *exempt*, which means that they do not receive overtime pay for work in the evening or on weekends. Indeed, many software cost-tracking systems do not even record overtime hours.

Thus, for situations where schedule pressures are intense, not only might the software team work the available 160 hours per month, but they might also work late in the evenings and on weekends, too. Thus, on crunch projects the work might amount to 110 percent of the available hours, or about 176 hours per month.

Table 10.8 compares two versions of the same project, which can be assumed to be a 1000–function point information systems application written in COBOL.

The first version, shown in the left column, is a *normal* version, where only about 80 percent of the available hours each month are worked. The second version, shown in the right column, is the same project in *crunch mode*, where the work hours total 110 percent, with all of the extra hours being in the form of unpaid overtime by the software team.

Since exempt software personnel are normally paid on a monthly basis rather than an hourly basis, the differences in apparent results

TABLE 10.8   Differences Between Normal and Intense Work Patterns

| | Work habits | | | |
Activity	Project 1, normal	Project 2, intense	Difference	Percentage
Size, FP	1,000	1,000	0	0.00
Size, LOC	100,000	100,000	0	0.00
LOC per FP	100	100	0	0.00
A scope, FP	200	200	0	0.00
Nominal P rate, FP	10	10	0	0.00
Availability	80.00%	110.00%	30.00%	37.50
Hours per month	128.00	176.00	48.00	37.50
Salary per month	$5,000.00	$5,000.00	$0.00	0.00
Staff	5.00	5.00	0.00	0.00
Effort months	125.00	90.91	−34.09	−27.27
Schedule months	31.25	16.53	−14.72	−47.11
Cost	$625,000	$454,545	−$170,455	−27.27
Cost per FP	$625.00	$454.55	−$170.45	−27.27
Work hours per FP	16.00	16.00	0.00	0.00
Virtual P rate, FP	8.00	11.00	3.00	37.50
Cost per LOC	$6.25	$4.55	−$1.70	−27.27
LOC per month	800	1100	300	37.50

between normal and intense work patterns are both significant and tricky when performing software cost analysis.

As can be seen from Table 10.8, applying intense work pressure to a software project in the form of unpaid overtime can produce significant and visible reductions in software costs and software schedules. (However, there may also be invisible and harmful results in terms of staff fatigue and burnout.)

Table 10.8 introduces five terms that are significant in software measurement and also cost estimating, but which need to be defined.

The first term is *assignment scope* (A scope), which is the quantity of function points normally assigned to one staff member. The assignment scope varies from activity to activity, but in general is approximately one staff member for every 150 function points for new development projects. During maintenance, one staff member is needed for about every 750 function points of deployed software. Both variables can vary significantly.

The second term is *production rate* (P rate), which is the monthly rate in function points at which the work will be performed. Here, too, there are major variations based on the expertise of the staff members, and the reusable materials and overtime applied to the project. (Other metrics are also used for production rates, such as lines of code for programmers, pages for technical writers, or bugs fixed per month for maintenance specialists.) The *production rate* is somewhat equivalent to the term *velocity* as used by some of the Agile methods.

The third term is *nominal production rate*, which is the rate of monthly progress measured in function points without any unpaid overtime being applied.

The fourth term is *virtual production rate*, which is the apparent rate of monthly productivity in function points that will result when unpaid overtime is applied to the project or activity.

The fifth term is *work hours per function point*, which simply accumulates the total number of work hours expended and divides that amount by the function point total of the application. In the more sophisticated corporate measurement programs, normal paid hours, unpaid overtime hours, and paid overtime hours would be recorded separately. Incidentally, similar metrics could be calculated such as work hours per use case point, work hours per object point, work hours per story point, and so forth.

Because software technical staff members are usually paid monthly but work hourly, the most visible impact of unpaid overtime is to decouple productivity measured in work hours per function point from productivity measured in function points per staff month. This is a complicated topic, and an illustration can clarify what happens.

Assume that a small 60–function point project would normally require two calendar months, or 320 work hours, to complete. Now assume that the programmer assigned works double shifts and finishes the project in one calendar month, although 320 work hours are still needed.

If the project had been a normal one stretched over two months, the productivity rate would have been 30 function points per staff month and 5.33 work hours per function point.

By applying unpaid overtime to the project and finishing in one month instead of two, the virtual productivity rate appears to be 60 function points per staff month, but the actual number of hours required remains 5.33 work hours per function points—only a large portion of these work hours are in the form of unpaid overtime, and hence, have no effect on the costs of the project. The unpaid overtime hours tend to elevate productivity rates when measured at monthly intervals.

Variations in work patterns are extremely significant variations when dealing with international software projects. There are major national differences in terms of work hours per week, quantities of unpaid overtime, numbers of annual holidays, and annual vacation periods.

In fact, it is very dangerous to perform international studies without taking this phenomenon into account. Variations in work practices are a major differentiating factor for international software productivity and schedule results.

Table 10.9 makes a number of simplifying assumptions and does not deal with the specifics of sick time, lunch and coffee breaks, meetings, courses, and non-work activities that might occur during business hours. The table is derived from basic assumptions about national holidays and

TABLE 10.9   Approximate Number of Work Hours per Year in Ten Countries

Country	Work days per year	Work hours per day	Overtime per day	Work hours per year	Percentage of U.S. results
Japan	260	9.00	2.5	2990	139
China	260	9.00	1.5	2730	127
India	245	8.50	2	2573	120
Italy	230	9.00	1	2300	107
United States	239	8.00	1	2151	100
Brazil	234	8.00	1	2106	98
United Kingdom	232	8.00	1	2088	97
France	230	8.00	1	2070	96
Germany	228	8.00	0	1824	85
Russia	230	7.50	0	1725	80
Average	238.8	8.30	1.1	2245	104

average annual vacation times. It also ignores telecommuting, home offices, flex time, and a number of other factors that are important for detailed analyses.

Since there are significant local and industry differences within every country, the data in Table 10.9 should be used as just a starting point for more detailed exploration and analysis.

This table has a very large margin of error, because within any given country there are significant variances in work habits and compensation by industry, by geographic region, and by size of the organization.

Software is currently among the most labor-intensive commodities on the global market. Therefore, work practices and work effort applied to software exerts a major influence on productivity and schedule results. In every country, the top software personnel tend to work rather long hours, so Table 10.10 can only be used for very rough comparisons.

The differences in national work patterns compounded with differences in burdened cost structures can lead to very significant international differences in software costs and schedules for the same size and kind of application.

Table 10.10 illustrates how wide the global cost variances can actually be. This table examines the cost ranges of building exactly the same 1000–function point software project in ten countries throughout the world.

Table 10.10 artificially holds the effort constant at 20 work hours per function point, and then applies typical local compensation levels and burden rates for the ten countries illustrated.

Although there are very large ranges within each country, it can be seen that there also are very large national differences, as well. Expressed in terms of cost per function point, the observed range for exactly the same size and kind of software projects around the world spans amounts that run from less than $350 per function point on the low end to more than $1500 per function point on the high end.

Table 10.10   International Cost Comparison for 1000 Function Points

Country	Work hours per FP	Effort in work hours	Cost per work hour	Project cost	Cost per FP	Percent of U.S.
Germany	20	20000	$68.75	$1,375,000	$1,375.00	125%
France	20	20000	$59.50	$1,190,000	$1,190.00	108%
United States	20	20000	$55.00	$1,100,000	$1,100.00	100%
United Kingdom	20	20000	$52.25	$1,045,000	$1,045.00	95%
Brazil	20	20000	$48.50	$970,000	$970.00	88%
Italy	20	20000	$44.75	$895,000	$895.00	81%
Japan	20	20000	$43.50	$870,000	$870.00	79%
Russia	20	20000	$32.75	$655,000	$655.00	60%
India	20	20000	$22.20	$444,000	$444.00	40%
China	20	20000	$17.50	$350,000	$350.00	32%
AVERAGE	20	20000	68.75	$889,400	$889.40	81%

Although it is easily possible to calculate the arithmetic mean, harmonic mean, median, and mode of software costs, any such cost value would be dangerous to use for estimating purposes when the ranges are so broad.

This is why the author has always been reluctant to publish general software cost data, and instead uses costs only in the context of country, industry, regional, and project norms. In fact, cost data varies so much that work hours or person months are much more stable for software productivity studies.

Obviously, for international comparisons the daily fluctuations in currency exchange rates and the longer fluctuations in national rates of inflation also need to be considered.

In fact, one interesting phenomenon has only recently been noticed. Countries that are successful in attracting large outsource contracts such as India and China tend to have inflation rates that are higher than the countries issuing the outsource contracts such as the United States. The implications are that within perhaps ten years, the current cost savings from international outsourcing will diminish due to the fact that successful outsource countries have high inflation rates that will drive up their costs. This phenomenon has already occurred in the countries that were low-cost providers 25 years ago such as Japan and Taiwan. Today their costs are so high that they are no longer the preferred locations for labor-intensive outsourcing such as software.

When clients ask for data on average cost per function point so that they can use this data for estimating purposes, the only safe answer is that costs vary so much due to compensation and burden rate differences that it is better to base the comparison on the client's own industry and geographic locale. General industry cost data is much too variable for casual comparisons at national levels.

On the whole, a great deal more work is needed on software adjustment factors in terms of showing their impacts in both positive and negative directions. The current literature sometimes exaggerates the impact of positive factors, and is extremely limited in empirical findings on negative factors that can degrade productivity and stretch out schedules.

References

Barrow, Dean, Susan Nilson, and Dawn Timberlake: *Software Estimation Technology Report*, Air Force Software Technology Support Center, Hill Air Force Base, Utah, 1993.

Boehm, Barry: *Software Engineering Economics*, Prentice-Hall, Englewood Cliffs, N.J., 1981.

DeMarco, Tom: *Controlling Software Projects*, Yourdon Press, New York, 1982.

————: *Why Does Software Cost So Much?*, Dorset House, New York, 1995.

Harmon, Paul, and David King: *Expert Systems*, John Wiley & Sons, New York, 1985.

Humphrey, Watts S.: *Managing the Software Process*, Addison-Wesley/Longman, Reading, Mass., 1989.

————: *A Discipline of Software Engineering*, Addison-Wesley, Reading, Mass., 1995.

Jones, Capers: *Critical Problems in Software Measurement*, Information Systems Management Group, 1993a.

————: *Software Productivity and Quality Today—The Worldwide Perspective*, Information Systems Management Group, 1993b.

————: *Assessment and Control of Software Risks*, Prentice-Hall, Englewood Cliffs, N.J., 1994.

————: *New Directions in Software Management*, Information Systems Management Group,.

————: *Patterns of Software System Failure and Success*, International Thomson Computer Press, Boston, 1995.

————: *Applied Software Measurement, Second Edition*, McGraw-Hill, New York, 1996.

————: *The Economics of Object-Oriented Software*, Software Productivity Research, Burlington, Mass., April 1997a.

————: *Software Quality—Analysis and Guidelines for Success*, International Thomson Computer Press, Boston, 1997b.

————: *The Year 2000 Software Problem—Quantifying the Costs and Assessing the Consequences*, Addison-Wesley, Reading, Mass., 1998.

Love, Tom: *Object Lessons*, SIGS Books, New York, 1993.

Putnam, Lawrence H.: *Measures for Excellence—Reliable Software on Time, Within Budget*, Yourdon Press/Prentice-Hall, Englewood Cliffs, N.J., 1992.

————, and Ware Myers: *Industrial Strength Software—Effective Management Using Measurement*, IEEE Press, Los Alamitos, Calif., 1997.

Rethinking the Software Process, CD-ROM, Miller Freeman, Lawrence, Kans., 1996. (This CD-ROM is a book collection jointly produced by the book publisher, Prentice-Hall, and the journal publisher, Miller Freeman. It contains the full text and illustrations of five Prentice-Hall books: *Assessment and Control of Software Risks* by Capers Jones; *Controlling Software Projects* by Tom DeMarco; *Function Point Analysis* by Brian Dreger; *Measures for Excellence* by Larry Putnam and Ware Myers; and *Object-Oriented Software Metrics* by Mark Lorenz and Jeff Kidd.)

Robbins, Brian, and Howard Rubin: *The Year 2000 Planning Guide*, Rubin Systems, Pound Ridge, N.Y., 1997.

Roetzheim, William H., and Reyna A. Beasley: *Best Practices in Software Cost and Schedule Estimation*, Prentice-Hall PTR, Upper Saddle River, N.J., 1998.

Rubin, Howard: *Worldwide Software Benchmark Report for 1997*, Rubin Systems, Pound Ridge, N.Y., 1997.

————: *Study of the Global Software Shortage*, Rubin Systems, Pound Ridge, N.Y., 1998. (Study produced for the ITAA.)

Symons, Charles R.: *Software Sizing and Estimating—Mk II FPA (Function Point Analysis)*, John Wiley & Sons, Chichester, U.K., 1991.

Activity Pattern Adjustment Factors

It is obvious that serious studies of software processes and practices need data that gets down to the levels of activities and tasks. Data measured only to the project level is inadequate for any kind of in-depth economic analysis, and is worthless for process improvement analysis. This is also true for phase-level measurements based on rudimentary phase structures, such as requirements, design, coding, integration, and testing. However, as of 2007 , there are no standard definitions for the sets of activities that should be included in activity-based software measurement studies.

It is very interesting to realize that much of the observed difference in productivity rates among various industries and kinds of software is due to the fact that not all software is built using the same sets of activities. For example, it takes much more work to build U.S. military software than any other kind of software in the world. This is because Department of Defense standards mandate activities, such as *independent verification and validation*, that civilian software projects almost never use.

Further, the intensive oversight requirements in military contracts cause various specifications and control documents on military software projects to be two to three times larger than equivalent documents on civilian projects. Among SPR's military clients, the effort associated with producing paper documents on software projects often exceeds 50 percent of the entire work of the project. In some military software projects, as many as 400 English words are written for every line of Ada code produced!

Some software methodologies include more than 50 activities and tasks, and there are countless variations when local customizations of methodologies are considered. For example, all of these methodologies have specialized activity sets associated with them: Agile development, extreme programming (XP), information engineering (IE), Rapid Application Development (RAD), object-oriented (OO) analysis and design, and the European Merise and SPICE methodologies. And both the traditional waterfall and more recent spiral and iterative models have activity patterns that are partly unique and partly generic.

There are also specialized activities outside the scope of normal project development work that need to be considered. For example, some of the specialized activities are those associated with formal design and code inspections, ISO 9000–9004 certification, SEI assessments and the capability maturity model (CMM), capturing *cost of quality* information, total quality management (TQM), Six-Sigma, and business process reengineering (BPR) studies.

Twenty Five Common Activities for Software Projects

SPR has analyzed many software development methodologies from around the world, and has constructed a generic checklist of 25 activities that occur with high frequency. This list of activities is used for our baseline and benchmark cost collections, for schedule measurement, and as the basis for exploring the effectiveness of various kinds of tools and practices.

One of the interesting by-products of exploring software projects down to the level of activities is the set of *patterns* that are often associated with various sizes and kinds of software projects.

To illustrate some of the variations at the activity level, Table 11.1 gives examples of activity pattern differences noted during SPR assessment and baseline studies for various classes of software, based on the checklist of 25 activities that SPR utilizes for data collection. These same patterns are discussed in previous sections, but they remain key differentiating factors that explain much of the cost variances among different software classes.

Estimates for large software projects need to include many more activities than just coding or programming. Table 11.1 shows typical activity patterns for six different kinds of projects: web-based applications, management information systems (MIS), outsourced software, commercial software, systems software, and military software projects.

In the context of Table 11.1, "web" projects are applications designed to support corporate web sites. The letters "MIS" stand for management information systems. "Outsource" software is similar to MIS, but performed by an outside contractor. "Systems" software controls physical devices such as computers or telecommunication systems. Military software

TABLE 11.1   Patterns of Software Development Activities for Six Types of Application (Data indicates the percentage of work effort by activity)

Activities performed	Web	MIS	Outsource	Commer.	System	Military
01 Requirements	5.00%	7.50%	9.00%	4.00%	4.00%	7.00%
02 Prototyping	10.00%	2.00%	2.50%	1.00%	2.00%	2.00%
03 Architecture		0.50%	1.00%	2.00%	1.50%	1.00%
04 Project plans		1.00%	1.50%	1.00%	2.00%	1.00%
05 Initial design		8.00%	7.00%	6.00%	7.00%	6.00%
06 Detail design		7.00%	8.00%	5.00%	6.00%	7.00%
07 Design reviews			0.50%	1.50%	2.50%	1.00%
08 Coding	30.00%	20.00%	16.00%	23.00%	20.00%	16.00%
09 Reuse acquisition	5.00%		2.00%	2.00%	2.00%	2.00%
10 Package purchase		1.00%	1.00%		1.00%	1.00%
11 Code inspections				1.50%	1.50%	1.00%
12 Independent verification and validation						1.00%
13 Configuration mgt.		3.00%	3.00%	1.00%	1.00%	1.50%
14 Formal integration		2.00%	2.00%	1.50%	2.00%	1.50%
15 User documentation	10.00%	7.00%	9.00%	12.00%	10.00%	10.00%
16 Unit testing	30.00%	4.00%	3.50%	2.50%	5.00%	3.00%
17 Function testing		6.00%	5.00%	6.00%	5.00%	5.00%
18 Integration testing		5.00%	5.00%	4.00%	5.00%	5.00%
19 System testing		7.00%	5.00%	7.00%	5.00%	6.00%
20 Field testing				6.00%	1.50%	3.00%
21 Acceptance testing		5.00%	3.00%		1.00%	3.00%
22 Independent testing						1.00%
23 Quality assurance			1.00%	2.00%	2.00%	1.00%
24 Installation/training		2.00%	3.00%		1.00%	1.00%
25 Project management	10.00%	12.00%	12.00%	11.00%	12.00%	13.00%
Total	100.00%	100.00%	100.00%	100.00%	100.00%	100.00%
Activities	7	16	20	21	22	25

constitutes all projects that are constrained to follow various military standards. Commercial software refers to ordinary packaged software such as word processors, spreadsheets, and the like.

Table 11.1 is merely illustrative, and the actual numbers of activities performed and the percentages of effort for each activity can vary. For estimating actual projects, the estimating tool would present the most likely set of activities to be performed. Then the project manager or estimating specialist would adjust the set of activities to match the reality of the project. Some estimating tools allow users to add additional activities that are not part of the default set.

It is also interesting to look at the activities that are performed for some of the newer development methods such as Agile and extreme programming and contrast them to the traditional waterfall model. The list of activities is not a perfect match to the Agile and XP approaches, but if a few of the names are changed, such as using "Scrum" in place of "reviews," the list is close enough to show the differences in numbers of activities and percentages of total effort. Table 11.2 illustrates five of the newer methods plus the waterfall method.

Note that over and above the average values shown, there can be significant variations. For example, small client/server projects may only perform 8 of the 16 activities listed under the MIS domain, which simultaneously explains why client/server productivity can be high and client/server quality can be low.

From activity-based analysis such as this, it becomes easy to understand a number of otherwise ambiguous topics. For example, it can easily be seen why U.S. military software projects are more expensive than any other kind of software. For a project of any given size, military standards trigger the performance of more activities and tasks than any other software methodology or process of development.

It can also be seen why the quality levels of client/server projects often tend to be embarrassingly bad, and why client/server maintenance costs are alarmingly high. The processes used to build client/server applications are among the skimpiest and least rigorous of any kind of software yet analyzed.

It can also be seen why the Agile and extreme programming methods are quicker than some of the older approaches: they eliminate much of the paperwork associated with the older methods.

Some questions frequently asked of software cost-estimating experts are "What percentage of effort goes to testing?" and "What percentage of effort goes to programming?" Unfortunately, these questions are dangerous ones either to ask or to answer.

There are no fixed percentages for any known activity that can safely be used for estimating software projects of all sizes and kinds. It is much better to consider the percentages associated with specific activities, and to do so in the context of a specific type of application and a specific size range.

When variations in costs and variations in activity patterns are melded together, the overall results are very broad indeed. Table 11.3 illustrates the burdened and unburdened costs per function point for the same six industries and methods shown in Tables 11.1 and 11.2.

Table 11.3 illustrates average U.S. data and the ranges would be even broader if global data were used.

Table 11.3 is somewhat misleading because it uses simple arithmetic averages, rather than weighted averages. However, it is only included

TABLE 11.2   Patterns of Software Development Activities Associated with Six Methods (Percentage of staff months by activity)

Activities performed	Agile	Extreme	Iterative	Spiral	OO	Waterfall
01 Requirements			10.00%	4.00%	6.00%	7.00%
02 Prototyping	15.00%	20.00%	3.00%	5.00%	5.00%	2.00%
03 Architecture			1.00%	2.00%	3.00%	1.00%
04 Project plans			1.00%	1.00%	1.00%	1.00%
05 Initial design			5.00%	5.00%	8.00%	6.00%
06 Detail design			7.00%	5.00%	6.00%	8.00%
07 Reviews or Scrum	5.00%	10.00%	5.00%	1.50%	3.00%	3.00%
08 Coding	35.00%	40.00%	16.00%	22.00%	15.00%	15.00%
09 Reuse acquisition	10.00%	5.00%	2.00%	2.00%	5.00%	2.00%
10 Package purchase			1.00%			1.00%
11 Code inspections				1.50%		1.00%
12 Independent verification and validation				1.0%		
13 Configuration mgt.			3.00%	1.00%	2.00%	1.50%
14 Formal integration			2.00%	1.50%	2.00%	1.50%
15 User documentation	10.00%	10.00%	10.00%	10.00%	10.00%	10.00%
16 Unit testing	25.00%	15.00%	5.00%	2.50%	5.00%	3.00%
17 Function testing			5.00%	6.00%	5.00%	5.00%
18 Integration testing			5.00%	4.00%	5.00%	5.00%
19 System testing			5.00%	7.00%	5.00%	6.00%
20 Field testing				5.00%		3.00%
21 Acceptance testing			3.00%		1.00%	3.00%
22 Independent testing						1.00%
23 Quality assurance			1.00%	2.00%	2.00%	1.00%
24 Installation/ training				1.00%	1.00%	1.00%
25 Project management			10.00%	10.00%	10.00%	12.00%
Total	100.00%	100.00%	100.00%	100.00%	100.00%	100.00%
Activities	6	6	20	20	20	24

TABLE 11.3   U.S. Cost per Function Point in 2007 With and Without Burden Rates

	Web	MIS	Outsource	Commercial	Systems	Military	Average
Compensation	$6,000	$4,750	$4,500	$5,000	$5,250	$4,500	$5,000
Burdened cost	$9,600	$7,600	$13,500	$8,000	$8,400	$14,625	$10,288
Unburdened, $/FP	$145	$1,053	$890	$1,281	$1,733	$2,601	$1,284
Burdened, $/FP	$232	$1,684	$2,671	$2,049	$2,773	$8,453	$2,977

to illustrate the basic fact that variations in compensation levels by industry, and variations in burden rates or overhead structures, can exert a significant impact. Indeed, the impact is so significant that it is quite unsafe and hazardous to use *average cost per function point* for any business purpose unless the average in question is taken from information that meets the following restrictions:

- Similar companies
- Similar geographic region
- Similar staffing patterns
- Similar work habits
- Similar burden rate structures

Cost data is far too variable for more global averages to be valid for specific projects or estimating purposes.

Table 11.3 originally appeared in the companion book *Applied Software Measurement*, (McGraw-Hill publisher, 1996) and is repeated with the same message: Software costs are highly variable and unstable. Variations are so large from region to region, industry to industry, and company to company that only local cost data should be used for estimating purposes.

Of course, Table 11.3 does not show the full range of costs for software, since there are also major variations by size of the application, as well as variations due to the industry, the geographic region, the company size, and the variations in occupations utilized on the projects in question.

Software costs have a very wide range of possible results, although the reasons for the variations are at last starting to be well understood. For every item in Table 11.2, the range in the United States can run from less than 50 percent of the nominal average value to more than 150 percent of the nominal average value.

To illustrate the approximate amount of effort and costs for specific activities, Table 11.4 shows the approximate average amount of work hours per function point for each of the 25 activities in the standard SPR chart of accounts for software projects.

The information shown in Table 11.4 illustrates one basic form of activity-based software costing. It is not a substitute for one of the commercial software cost-estimating tools that support activity-based costs in a much more sophisticated way, such as allowing each activity to have its own unique cost structure and to vary the nominal hours expended based on experience, methods, tools, and so forth.

Note that only large military projects will use all of the 25 activities shown in Table 11.4. Indeed, small civilian client/server projects

TABLE 11.4   Example of Activity-Based Costs for Software Development

Average monthly salary	$5000
Burden rate	50%
Fully burdened monthly rate	$7500
Work hours per calendar month	132

Activities	Staff assignment scope, FP	Monthly production rate, FP	Work hours per FP	Salary cost per FP	Burdened cost per FP
01 Requirements	333	175	0.75	$28.57	$42.86
02 Prototyping	500	150	0.88	$33.33	$50.00
03 Architecture	1000	300	0.44	$16.67	$25.00
04 Project plans	1000	500	0.26	$10.00	$15.00
05 Initial design	250	175	0.75	$28.57	$42.86
06 Detail design	250	150	0.88	$33.33	$50.00
07 Design reviews	200	225	0.59	$22.22	$33.33
08 Coding	175	50	2.64	$100.00	$150.00
09 Reuse acquisition	500	600	0.22	$8.33	$12.50
10 Package purchase	2000	400	0.33	$12.50	$18.75
11 Code inspections	150	150	0.88	$33.33	$50.00
12 Independent verification and validation	500	125	1.06	$40.00	$60.00
13 Configuration management	1000	1750	0.08	$2.86	$4.29
14 Integration	1000	250	0.53	$20.00	$30.00
15 User documentation	1000	70	1.89	$71.43	$107.14
16 Unit testing	200	150	0.88	$33.33	$50.00
17 Function testing	200	150	0.88	$33.33	$50.00
18 Integration testing	250	175	0.75	$28.57	$42.86
19 System testing	250	200	0.66	$25.00	$37.50
20 Field (beta) testing	1000	250	0.53	$20.00	$30.00
21 Acceptance testing	1000	350	0.38	$14.29	$21.43
22 Independent testing	750	200	0.66	$25.00	$37.50
23 Quality assurance	1000	150	0.88	$33.33	$50.00
24 Installation and training	2000	350	0.38	$14.29	$21.43
25 Project management	1000	100	1.32	$50.00	$75.00
Cumulative results	130.18	6.77	19.49	$738.29	$1107.44

or World Wide Web applets may utilize only a few of the 25 activities, which simultaneously explains their high productivity levels but often questionable quality levels.

Here, too, these default values are a good starting point, but the range around every value is at least 2 to 1 and not every activity will be used on every project. Software cost estimating is a very complex task, and involves thousands of rules and hundreds of adjustments if it is to be done with high precision.

Once activity-based costing is started, it can be extended to include many other activities in a similar fashion. For example, the set of activities shown here is common for waterfall development projects.

If you are concerned with maintenance of aging legacy applications, with porting software from one platform to another, or with bringing out a new release of a commercial software package, then you will need to deal with other activities outside of those shown in the tables.

There are also specific activity patterns associated with Agile development, extreme programming (XP), object-oriented (OO) development, information engineering (IE), RAD, and a host of methodologies and software processes. The fundamental concept of activity-based costing can still be used, even though the activities and their patterns may vary.

The literature on adjustments to match specific activity patterns is very poorly covered in a software cost-estimation context. Indeed, many books on software cost estimation do not even deal with activity-based costs but stop at the level of complete projects or rudimentary phase structures.

The worst result of this lack of empirical data on activity-based costs is the false belief that a small set of ratios and percentages can be used as estimating rules of thumb for any class, size, and type of software project. This is roughly the equivalent of assuming that any U.S. citizen could fit into a size 40-regular suit of clothes with a 34-inch waist. Both in software estimation and in buying clothes, it is important to have the results custom-fitted to match the reality of the client.

References

Ambler, S.: *Process Patterns—Building Large-Scale Systems Using Object Technology*, Cambridge University Press, SIGS Books, 1998.

Artow, J. and I. Neustadt: *UML and the Unified Process*, Addison-Wesley, Boston, Mass., 2000.

Beck, K.: *Extreme Programming Explained: Embrace Change*, Addison-Wesley, Boston, Mass., 1999.

Boehm, Barry: *Software Engineering Economics*, Prentice-Hall, Englewood Cliffs, N.J., 1981.

———: "A Spiral Model of Software Development and Enhancement," Proceedings of the Int. Workshop on Software Process and Software Environments, ACM Software Engineering Notes, Aug. 1986, pp. 22-42.

Bogan, Christopher E., and Michael J. English: *Benchmarking for Best Practices*, McGraw-Hill, New York, 1994.

Booch, Grady: *Object Solutions: Managing the Object-Oriented Project*, Addison-Wesley, Reading, Mass., 1995.

Brown, Norm (ed.): *The Program Manager's Guide to Software Acquisition Best Practices*, Version 1.0, U.S. Department of Defense, Washington, D.C., July 1995.

Cockburn, Alistair: *Agile Software Development*, Addison-Wesley, Boston, Mass., 2001.

Cohen, D., M. Lindvall, and P. Costa: "An Introduction to Agile Methods," Advances in Computers, Elsevier Science, New York, 2004, pp.1–66.

Cohn, Mike: *Agile Estimating and Planning*, Prentice-Hall PTR, Englewood Cliffs, N.J., 2005.

DeMarco, Tom: *Controlling Software Projects*, Yourdon Press, New York, 1982.

Department of the Air Force: *Guidelines for Successful Acquisition and Management of Software Intensive Systems*, vols. 1 and 2, Software Technology Support Center, Hill Air Force Base, Utah, 1994.

Highsmith, Jim: *Agile Software Development Ecosystems*, Addison-Wesley, Boston, Mass., 2002.

Jones, Capers: *Critical Problems in Software Measurement*, Information Systems Management Group, 1993a.

———: *Software Productivity and Quality Today—The Worldwide Perspective*, Information Systems Management Group, 1993b.

———: *Assessment and Control of Software Risks*, Prentice-Hall, Englewood Cliffs, N.J., 1994.

· ———: *New Directions in Software Management*, Information Systems Management Group,

———: *Patterns of Software System Failure and Success*, International Thomson Computer Press, Boston, Mass.,1995.

———: *Applied Software Measurement, Second Edition*, McGraw-Hill, New York, 1996.

———: *The Economics of Object-Oriented Software*, Software Productivity Research, Burlington, Mass., April 1997a.

———: *Software Quality—Analysis and Guidelines for Success*, International Thomson Computer Press, Boston, Mass., 1997b.

———: *Software Assessments, Benchmarks, and Best Practices*, Addison-Wesley Longman, Boston, Mass., 2000.

Larman, Craig and Victor Basili: "Iterative and Incremental Development—A Brief History," IEEE Computer Society, June 2003, pp 47-55.

Love, Tom: *Object Lessons*, SIGS Books, New York, 1993.

McConnell: *Software Estimating: Demystifying the Black Art*, Microsoft Press, 2006

Pressman, Roger: *Software Engineering—A Practitioner's Approach, Sixth Edition*, McGraw-Hill, N.Y., 2005.

Putnam, Lawrence H.: *Measures for Excellence—Reliable Software on Time, Within Budget*, Yourdon Press/Prentice-Hall, Englewood Cliffs, N.J., 1992.

———, and Ware Myers: *Industrial Strength Software—Effective Management Using Measurement*, IEEE Press, Los Alamitos, Calif., 1997.

Roetzheim, William H., and Reyna A. Beasley: *Best Practices in Software Cost and Schedule Estimation*, Prentice-Hall PTR, Upper Saddle River, N.J., 1998.

Rubin, Howard: *Worldwide Software Benchmark Report for 1997*, Rubin Systems, Pound Ridge, N.Y., 1997.

———: *Study of the Global Software Shortage*, Rubin Systems, Pound Ridge, N.Y., 1998. (Study produced for the ITAA.)

Symons, Charles R.: *Software Sizing and Estimating—Mk II FPA (Function Point Analysis)*, John Wiley & Sons, Chichester, U.K., 1991.

Software Technology
Adjustment Factors

Once we have completed the administrative, sizing, and chart of accounts selection aspects of our estimate, we are ready to deal with one of the most important of all estimating tasks, which is that of dealing with software technology adjustment factors.

Here the commercial estimating tools really come into their own, because knowledge of how any particular tool, method, programming language, or skill set can affect the outcome of a software project is obviously a job for a rule-based expert system, where the rules themselves are derived from empirical data taken from hundreds, or even thousands, of software projects.

Estimating tool vendors also need active consulting and research groups in order to stay current with rapid changes in the technologies themselves. For example, in the past ten years Agile development, extreme programming, and web applications have all become prominent technologies.

The methodology for dealing with adjustment factors varies widely from tool to tool. Since most commercial estimating-tool vendors regard their knowledge of adjustment factors as being a proprietary trade secret, this discussion will of necessity deal with the ways of adjustment in general rather than with the specific adjustments of individual tools, which are often closely guarded trade secrets.

Software estimating-tool vendors are usually for-profit corporations rather than nonprofit corporations. Although it would be very beneficial if the knowledge of adjustment factors were in the public domain, the value of this kind of information is so high that it is unlikely that the details of more than a few adjustment factors will be made publicly available.

Not only do the software estimating-tool companies derive revenues from their proprietary knowledge bases, but so do some other kinds of information service providers. Companies such as Gartner Group and Forester Research also sell proprietary data for many millions of dollars in annual revenues.

Adjustment Factors and Macro-Estimation Tools

In the commercial software-estimating domain, the way macro-estimation tools and micro-estimation tools deal with adjustments is rather different. The macro-estimation tools typically accumulate information from various kinds of adjustments, such as skill levels, tools, and methods, and create a single value that is used as a multiplier over the entire project.

For example, if an average team using average tools and methods has a monthly productivity rate of 10 function points or 1000 lines of code, then a superstar team equipped with state-of-the-art tools and methods might experience a doubled productivity rate of 20 function points per staff month or 2000 lines of code per month.

Conversely, a novice team equipped with marginally adequate tools and methods might experience a monthly productivity rate of only 5 function points or 500 lines of code.

In this situation, team abilities and methodological sophistication can be converted into productivity multipliers, each of which span a range of 2 to 1. Inside a typical commercial software cost-estimating tool itself may be found a table of values similar to the following.

Although these nine combinations are not taken from any specific estimating tool, they show how various combinations of factors might be converted into productivity adjustments by means of a table-lookup function.

Example of Macro-Estimating Adjustment Assumptions

Factor combinations	Multiplier
Superior team with superior tools	2.00
Superior team with average tools	1.75
Average team with superior tools	1.50
Superior team with marginal tools	1.25
Average team with average tools	**1.00**
Average team with marginal tools	0.90
Novice team with superior tools	0.75
Novice team with average tools	0.65
Novice team with marginal tools	0.50

As can be seen, the nine permutations of these two factors yield an average central value, and then there are four adjustments on either side of the average value for dealing with situations that are either better or worse than average. This illustration of how adjustments might be made is only an example and is not intended to provide actual estimating adjustment weights or multipliers, although in fact these combinations are not unreasonable in their range of impact.

Micro-estimation tools also deal with adjustment factors, but typically apply each factor independently rather than developing an aggregated adjustment that covers multiple factors concurrently.

Example of Micro-Estimating Adjustment Assumptions

Evaluation	Team capability multiplier	Tool capability multiplier
Excellent	1.50	1.20
Good	1.25	1.10
Average	**1.00**	**1.00**
Below average	0.75	0.90
Poor	0.50	0.80

This micro-estimating method of applying each factor individually allows specific factors to be included or excluded as the situation warrants. This is a useful feature, because software productivity is a complex phenomenon with at least 100 known factors at play that can influence the outcomes of software projects.

Further, applying each factor individually opens up the range of possible outcomes. For example, it is now possible to consider what happens when an excellent team has poor tools, or what happens when a poor team is given excellent tools.

For example, assuming that an average team with average tools has a productivity rate of 10 function points per staff month, any of the following combinations can be explored:

Excellent team	10*1.5 = 15 function points per staff month
Excellent tools	15*1.2 = 18 function points per staff month
Excellent team	10*1.5 = 15 function points per staff month
Poor tools	15*0.8 = 12 function points per staff month
Poor team	10*0.5 = 5 function points per staff month
Excellent tools	5*1.2 = 6 function points per staff month
Poor team	10*0.5 = 5 function points per staff month
Poor tools	5*0.8 = 4 function points per staff month

This methodology of applying each factor in sequence can be continued indefinitely. But note that if a factor is average it is assumed to have a multiplying effect of 1 so that only factors where the project is better or worse than normal need to be dealt with.

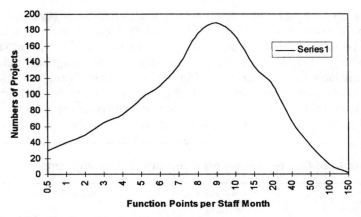

Figure 12.1   Distribution of productivity rates of 1500 software projects.

The Software Productivity Research (SPR) knowledge base of roughly 12,500 software projects spans a range that runs from a low of 0.13 function points per staff month to a high of about 140 function points per staff month. Figure 12.1 shows the approximate distribution of 1500 software development projects from the SPR knowledge base.

As can be seen from Figure 12.1, the range of software productivity results is very broad. This brings up a key question: What causes productivity to be significantly better or worse than average results?

Some of the factors that influence software productivity results are outside the control of the software project team. Although these factors are important, there is little ability to change them. For example:

- Large systems of more than 10,000 function points in size have lower productivity rates than small projects of less than 100 function points in size.

- Military software projects that follow the older Department of Defense (D0D) standards, such as DoD 2167, have lower productivity than similar civilian projects because of the huge volume of required paperwork.

There is little value in discussing factors that are outside the control of the software development team. What this section is concerned with are the factors over which there is a measure of control, such as the choice of tools, programming languages, and development processes.

Before discussing the positive and negative factors, it may be of interest to show a relatively typical average project, such as a COBOL application of 1000 function points in size, in order to give a context of why changes can occur in both positive and negative directions (see Table 12.1).

TABLE 12.1 Example of an Average COBOL Application of 1000 Function Points

Assumptions	
Application class	Information system
Programming language(s)	COBOL
Size in function points	1,000
Source lines per function point	100
Size in source code statements	100,000
Average monthly salary	$5,000
Burden rate percent	50%
Fully burdened compensation	$7,500
Nominal work hours per month	160
Effective work hours per month	128

Activity	Assignment scope	Production rate	Hours per FP	Staff	Effort months	Schedule months	Burdened cost	Cost per FP	Cost per LOC	Percent of total
Requirements	333	95.00	1.35	3.00	10.53	3.51	$78,947	$78.95	$0.79	8.42
Prototyping	500	60.00	2.13	2.00	1.67	0.83	12,500	12.50	0.13	1.33
Design	250	75.00	1.71	4.00	13.33	3.33	100,000	100.00	1.00	10.66
Design inspections	200	150.00	0.85	5.00	6.67	1.33	50,000	50.00	0.50	5.33
Coding	200	25.00	5.12	5.00	40.00	8.00	300,000	300.00	3.00	31.99
Code inspections	165	150.00	0.85	6.06	6.67	1.10	50,000	50.00	0.50	5.33
Change control	1000	175.00	0.73	1.00	5.71	5.71	42,857	42.86	0.43	4.57
Testing	200	60.00	2.13	5.00	16.67	3.33	125,000	125.00	1.25	13.33
User documents	1000	140.00	0.91	1.00	7.14	7.14	53,571	53.57	0.54	5.71
Project management	1500	60.00	2.13	0.67	16.67	25.00	125,000	125.00	1.25	13.33
Net result	199	8.00	17.93	5.02	125.05	24.93	$937,876	$937.88	$9.38	100.00

Because Table 12.1 is being used for illustrative purposes, it simplifies a number of topics and uses rounded data in order to arrive at a net productivity result of exactly 8 function points per staff month, which is a very representative average value for COBOL applications on mainframe computers.

Table 12.1 also uses an even value of 100 COBOL statements per function point even though the real-life results for COBOL applications average about 107 statements per function point. This approach serves to make the "Cost per FP" and "Cost per LOC" columns more comprehensible by having the two values differ by 100 to 1.

The main point to be gained from examining the table is that for typical software projects coding may be the largest single activity, but it constitutes only a relatively small percentage of total effort and expense. This means that the productivity improvement or degradation can affect some activities more than others, or may affect only one activity.

A strong lesson from the table is that productivity estimates or measurements that center on coding and do not include paper-based software work, such as specifications and user documents, are not complete enough for serious business purposes, such as contracts and budgets.

Of course, some of the modern Agile approaches are based on the hypothesis that a lot of software paperwork in the form of written requirements and detailed design specifications are not of great value and indeed slow down progress towards the end result of having operational software.

Factors That Influence Software Development Productivity

We turn now to the factors that can exert either a positive or negative influence on software development projects.

Table 12.2 shows a number of factors that can exert a positive impact on software productivity and raise results higher than average values.

The three most influential factors for elevating software productivity are the use of *high-quality reusable materials* and the *experience levels of both the managers and the technical staff*, respectively, in building similar kinds of applications.

Let us now consider some of the factors that can reduce or degrade software productivity and cause it to lag average values (see Table 12.3).

What is most interesting about Table 12.3 is that the same factor, *software reuse*, that can exert the largest positive impact on improving software productivity can also exert the largest negative impact on reducing productivity. How is it possible for software reuse to exert such a large influence in both directions?

The critical difference between the positive and negative influences of software reuse can be expressed in one word: *quality*. The positive

TABLE 12.2 Impact of Key Adjustment Factors on Development Productivity
(Sorted in order of maximum positive impact)

New development factors	Plus range, %
Reuse of high-quality deliverables	350
High management experience	65
High staff or team experience	55
Clear and understandable requirements	40
Effective methods or process	35
Effective management tools	30
Effective technical tools	27
High-level programming languages	24
Effective defect prevention	19
Specialist occupations for key skills	18
Effective client participation	18
Formal cost, quality, and schedule estimates	17
Unpaid overtime	15
Use of formal design and code inspections	15
Good office ergonomics	15
Quality measurement	14
Low project complexity	13
Quick computer response time	12
Moderate schedule pressure	11
Productivity measurements	10
Low or controlled requirements creep	9
Annual training of 10 days in new methods	8
No geographic separation of team	8
High team morale	7
Effective team organization	5
Total	840

value of software reuse occurs when the reusable artifacts approach or achieve zero-defect levels.

The negative value of software reuse, on the other hand, will occur if the reusable materials are filled with errors or bugs. Imagine the result of reusing a software module in 50 applications only to discover that it contains a number of high-severity errors that trigger massive recalls of every application!

Note that software reuse encompasses much more than just source code. An effective corporate reuse program will include at least the following five reusable artifacts:

- Reusable requirements
- Reusable designs
- Reusable source code
- Reusable test materials
- Reusable user documentation

TABLE 12.3   Impact of Key Adjustment Factors on Development Productivity
(Sorted in order of maximum negative impact)

New development factors	Minus range, %
Reuse of poor-quality deliverables	−300
Management inexperience	−90
Staff or team inexperience	−87
High or uncontrolled requirements creep	−77
Inadequate technical tools	−75
No use of design and code inspections	−48
Inadequate management tools	−45
Ineffective methods or process	−41
Ineffective defect prevention	−40
High project complexity	−35
Excessive schedule pressure	−30
Slow computer response time	−30
Crowded office space	−27
Low-level programming languages	−25
Geographic separation of team	−24
Inaccurate cost and schedule estimates	−22
Generalist occupations for key skills	−15
Ineffective client participation	−13
No annual training in new methods	−12
No quality measurements	−10
Cumbersome organization	−8
No productivity measurements	−7
Poor team morale	−6
No unpaid overtime	0
Total	−1067

In order to gain the optimum positive value from software reuse, each major software deliverable should include at least 75 percent reused material, which is certified and approaches zero-defect levels.

Another interesting aspect of Table 12.3 is that the negative cumulative results are much larger than those of Table 12.2, which shows positive results. Essentially, this means that it is far easier to make mistakes and degrade productivity than it is to get things right and improve productivity.

In general, there is often a lack of symmetry between the positive influences and the negative influences. For example, a good development process will exert a moderate positive influence on software productivity, but a really bad development process can exert a very severe negative impact on productivity.

When considering the fundamental goals of new approaches such as Agile development, the object-oriented (OO) approach, spiral development, extreme programming (XP), and others, keep in mind that they are all trying to minimize the number of harmful factors and increase the number of beneficial factors that occur with software projects.

Factors That Influence Software Maintenance Productivity

The word *maintenance* is highly ambiguous in the software domain. The common meaning for the term *maintenance* includes both repair of defects and making enhancements in response to new requirements. Sometimes the term *maintenance* also includes customer support. Although this general definition of maintenance is not perfect, it will serve to show the positive and negative factors that influence the modification of existing software applications.

Table 12.4 illustrates a number of factors that have been found to exert a positive impact on the work of updating aging applications.

TABLE 12.4   Impact of Key Adjustment Factors on Maintenance Productivity
(Sorted in order of maximum positive impact)

Maintenance factors	Plus range, %
Maintenance specialists	35
High staff or team experience	34
Table-driven variables and data	33
Low complexity of base code	32
Static analysis search engines	30
Code restructuring tools	29
Reengineering tools	27
High-level programming languages	25
Reverse-engineering tools	23
Complexity-analysis tools	20
Defect-tracking tools	20
Multitier defect response teams	20
Automated change-control tools	18
Unpaid overtime	18
Quality measurements	16
Formal base code inspections	15
Regression-test libraries	15
Excellent response time	12
Annual training of 10 days	12
High management experience	12
HELP desk automation	12
No error-prone modules	10
Online defect reporting	10
Maintenance productivity measurements	8
Excellent ease of use	7
User satisfaction measurements	5
High team morale	5
Total	503

Because software reuse is not a factor in either repairing defects or adding features to existing applications, the overall positive impacts in the maintenance domain are not as strong as those for new development projects.

The top three factors that exert a positive influence are those associated with the use of *full-time maintenance specialists*, with having extensive *experience in the application* being updated, and with the use of *tables for holding variables and constants* rather than embedding them in the source code itself.

Let us now consider some of the factors that exert a negative impact on the work of updating or modifying existing software applications (see Table 12.5). Note that the top-ranked factor that reduces maintenance productivity, the presence of *error-prone modules*, is very asymmetrical.

The top-ranked factor that degrades maintenance productivity is the presence of *error-prone modules* in the applications being updated.

TABLE 12.5   Impact of Key Adjustment Factors on Productivity
(Sorted in order of maximum negative impact)

Maintenance factors	Minus range, %
Error-prone modules	−50
Embedded variables and data	−45
Staff or team inexperience	−40
High complexity of base code	−30
No static analysis search engines	−28
Manual change-control methods	−27
Low-level programming languages	−25
No defect-tracking tools	−24
Single tier defect response teams	−22
Poor ease of use	−18
No quality measurements	−18
No maintenance specialists	−18
Poor response time	−16
Management inexperience	−15
No base code inspections	−15
No regression-test libraries	−15
No HELP desk automation	−15
No online defect reporting	−12
No annual training	−10
No code restructuring tools	−10
No reengineering tools	−10
No reverse-engineering tools	−10
No complexity-analysis tools	−10
No productivity measurements	−7
Poor team morale	−6
No user satisfaction measurements	−4
No unpaid overtime	0
Total	−500

Indeed, as a class, error-prone modules are the most expensive artifacts in the software world and can cost as much as five times more than high-quality modules.

Error-prone modules were discovered in the 1960s when IBM began a methodical study of the factors that influence software maintenance. It was discovered that errors or bugs in IBM software products, such as the Information Management System (IMS) database and the Multiple Virtual Storage (MVS) operating system tended to clump in a very small number of modules that were extremely buggy indeed.

In the case of MVS, about 38 percent of customer-reported errors were found in only 4 percent of the modules. In the case of IMS, an even more extreme skew was noted. There were 300 zero-defect modules out of a total of 425, and 57 percent of all customer-reported errors were found in only 31 modules, which coincidentally were in one department under one manager.

Although IBM first discovered the existence of error-prone modules, they are remarkably common and have been found by dozens of companies and government agencies, too. Wherever they are found, they are expensive and troublesome.

Fortunately, error-prone modules are a completely curable problem, and the usage of formal design and code inspections has the effect of completely immunizing software projects against these troublesome entities.

However, some error-prone modules are so poorly designed and implemented that they require surgical removal of the original module followed by complete redevelopment of at least one new module to replace it.

Patterns of Positive and Negative Factors

The author and his colleagues at Software Productivity Research (SPR) collect quantitative and qualitative data on about 50 to 70 software projects every month. Other companies such as the Davids Consulting Group, Quantitative Software Management, Galorath, and many others also gather historical data in order to understand the factors that influence software projects. Software projects and software organizations tend to follow relatively normal bell-shaped curves. There are comparatively few projects and companies that are good in almost every aspect of software, and also few that are really bad in almost every aspect of software.

The most common pattern that SPR encounters is that of projects and companies where the technical work of building software in terms of design and coding are reasonably good, but project management factors and quality control factors are fairly weak. This combination of factors is a reasonable characterization of the information systems domain, which numerically is the most common form of software development.

A variant of information systems projects, those produced by out-source contractors, have a somewhat better chance of having good project management methods than do the other forms of information systems development. However, not all outsource projects use good project management tools and methods, either.

For a variety of reasons, the systems software domain has a greater likelihood of having fairly good quality control as well as fairly good development skills. Here, too, project management is often the weak link. Quality control is better in the systems software domain because the hardware devices that the software controls (switching systems, computers, aircraft, etc.) need stringent quality control in order to operate.

The military software domain, like the systems software domain, is often characterized by rather good development methods and fairly good quality control methods, but marginal or deficient project management methods.

The large commercial software vendors tend to have better than average software development methods and much better than average maintenance methods. Here, too, quality control and project management are the weaknesses noted most often in assessment and benchmarking studies.

Among the organizations whose productivity rates are in the top 10 percent of SPR's client's results, there is a very strong tendency for most of the following factors to be better than average:

- Project management tools and methods are excellent.

- Quality control tools and methods are excellent.

- Maintenance tools and methods are excellent.

- Development tools and methods are excellent.

- Team experience is excellent.

- Client cooperation with team is excellent.

Conversely, among the clients who bring up the rear in terms of productivity, there is a strong tendency for this pattern to be noted:

- Project management tools and methods are poor.

- Quality control tools and methods are poor.

- Maintenance tools and methods are poor.

- Development tools and methods are adequate.

- Team experience is low or marginal.

- Client cooperation with team is poor.

On the whole, those in the software technical community of analysts and programmers seem to be better trained and equipped for their jobs than do those in the software project management community.

Most of the adjustment factors are treated as independent variables, and their impact is then calculated and used to adjust the overall productivity multiplier. Essentially, the macro-estimating tools start with a null productivity multiplier of 1.00 and then apply the results of various plus or minus adjustment factors to reach a final productivity multiplier, which can range from a low or minimum value of about 0.1 to a high or maximum value of perhaps 10.

However, since any real-life set of adjustments will include both positive and negative changes, the most common range of adjustments is much narrower and usually runs from about 0.75 to 1.25 for most projects.

For example, using the familiar five stages of the Software Engineering Institute (SEI) capability maturity model, a macro-estimating tool might yield overall productivity adjustments for each level that resemble the following.

Macro-Estimating Productivity Adjustments for the Five Levels of the SEI CMM

SEI CMM Level	Multiplier	Nominal Rate, FP per Month
SEI CMM level 1	1.00	5.00
SEI CMM level 2	1.10	5.50
SEI CMM level 3	1.25	6.25
SEI CMM level 4	1.50	7.50
SEI CMM level 5	2.00	10.00

In real life, some activities can improve much further than others. Indeed, some activities can even regress or get worse while others improve significantly. To deal with this phenomenon, it is necessary to move to the way adjustment factors are handled by the micro-estimating tools.

Adjustment Factors and Micro-Estimating Tools

The activity-based micro-estimating tools deal with adjustments at a more granular level than do the macro-estimating tools. For the micro-estimating tools, each activity is adjusted separately, although there are some factors that tend to affect every activity, such as *team experience*.

The micro-estimating adjustment factors can have an impact on any combination of these four dimensions of a software project:

- The *assignment scope*, or the amount of work that is normally assigned to one person

- The *production rate*, or amount of work that one person can perform in a standard time period such as an hour, a day, a week, a month, or a year

- The *defect potential*, or probable number of errors or bugs that might be created

- The *defect-removal efficiency*, or probable number of errors or bugs that will be detected and removed prior to external deployment of the software package

The micro-estimating tools usually have many more adjustment factors than the macro-estimating tools. Sometimes more than 100 factors can be adjusted.

It would obviously be inconvenient to adjust 100 factors every time an estimate is made, so the normal mode of operation for micro-estimating tools is to provide a nominal or default value for every factor. That way, only factors that are significantly better or worse than average need to be entered: Sometimes, fewer than 10 out of 100 may require adjustment above or below nominal values.

It is also possible for users to establish custom templates with adjustments preset to match local conditions. For example, a telecommunications company with a stable personnel group that has been building switching software for a number of years might preset the factor for *application experience* to *all experts*. This way the number of adjustments that have to be made to estimate a specific project is reduced. Sometimes 50 percent or more of the variable adjustments might be preset to match local conditions, which greatly speeds up the amount of setup work needed to complete an estimate.

The estimating tools designed by the author use a five-point scale for adjustment factors, with the following meaning for each point of the five-point scale:

1 = Much better than average	(Excellent)
2 = Better than average	(Very good)
3 = Average or nominal value	(Average)
4 = Worse than average	(Marginal)
5 = Much worse than average	(Poor)

(The five-point scale is not the only kind used for adjustments. Some estimating tools use binary adjustment factors, such as yes or no answers to adjustment questions; some estimating tools use a three-point scale; and a very few use a seven-point scale.)

However, the five-point adjustment scale on the author's estimating tools do allow two-decimal-place precision to fine-tune the responses. Thus responses of 3.25 or 3.75 are perfectly acceptable inputs, and allow fine adjustments between integer scores. To illustrate how the author's estimating tools capture adjustment data, following are sample adjustment factors that deal with various aspects of management, staff, and client experience levels.

Examples of the Software Productivity Research Method for Capturing Adjustment Data

PROJECT MANAGEMENT EXPERIENCE   _____

1 Experts (implemented many priority projects).
2 Extensive experience (implemented some projects).
3 Average experience (implemented some priority projects).
4 Limited experience (previous project management experience).
5 Novice experience (has never managed a project).

DEVELOPMENT PERSONNEL APPLICATION
EXPERIENCE   _____

1 All are experts in the type of program being developed.
2 Majority are experts, but some are new hires or novices.
3 Even mixture of experts, new hires, and novices.
4 Majority are new hires or novices, with few experts.
5 All personnel are new to this kind of program.

DEVELOPMENT PERSONNEL TOOL AND METHOD
EXPERIENCE   _____

1 All are experts in the tools and methods for the project.
2 Majority are experts in the tools and methods.
3 Even mixture of experts, new hires, and novices.
4 Majority are new hires or novices in tools and methods.
5 All personnel are new to the tools and methods.

DEVELOPMENT PERSONNEL ANALYSIS AND DESIGN
EXPERIENCE   _____

1 All are experts in analysis and design methods.
2 Majority are experts in analysis and design methods.
3 Even mixture of experts, new hires, and novices.
4 Majority are new hires or novices in analysis and design.
5 All personnel are inexperienced in analysis and design.

DEVELOPMENT PERSONNEL PROGRAMMING LANGUAGE
EXPERIENCE   _____

1 All are experts in the languages used for the project.
2 Majority are experts in the hardware used for the project.
3 Even mixture of experts, new hires, and novices.
4 Majority are new hires or novices in the languages.
5 All personnel are new to the languages used.

DEVELOPMENT PERSONNEL HARDWARE EXPERIENCE _____

1 All are experts in the hardware used for the project.
2 Majority are experts in the hardware used for the project.
3 Even mixture of experts, new hires, and novices.
4 Majority are new hires or novices in the hardware.
5 All personnel are new to the hardware for the project.

PRETEST DEFECT-REMOVAL EXPERIENCE _____

1 All personnel are experienced in reviews/inspections.
2 Most personnel are experienced in reviews/inspections.
3 Even mixture of experienced and inexperienced personnel.
4 Most personnel are inexperienced in reviews/inspections.
5 All personnel are inexperienced in reviews/inspections.

TESTING DEFECT-REMOVAL EXPERIENCE _____

1 All personnel are experienced in software test methods.
2 Most personnel are experienced in software test methods.
3 Even mixture of experienced and inexperienced personnel.
4 Most personnel are inexperienced in test methods.
5 All personnel are inexperienced in software test methods.

USER PERSONNEL EXPERIENCE WITH SOFTWARE PROJECTS _____

1 User experience with software is not a key factor.
2 All or a majority of users have software experience.
3 Even mixture of experts and inexperienced users.
4 Majority of users have no prior software experience.
5 All personnel have no prior software experience.

USER PERSONNEL EXPERIENCE WITH APPLICATION TYPE _____

1 User expertise is not a major factor for the project.
2 All or a strong majority of users are experts.
3 Even mixture of experts, new hires, and novices.
4 Majority are new hires and novices, with few experts.
5 All personnel are new to this kind of program.

MAINTENANCE PERSONNEL STAFFING _____

1 All are full-time professional maintenance personnel.
2 Majority are full-time professional maintenance personnel.
3 Some are full-time professional maintenance personnel.
4 Most maintenance is done by development personnel.
5 All maintenance is done by development personnel.

MAINTENANCE PERSONNEL EXPERIENCE   _____

1 All are experts in system being maintained.
2 Majority are experts, but some are new hires or novices.
3 Even mixture of experts, new hires, and novices.
4 Majority are new hires, with few experts.
5 All maintenance personnel are new to the system.

MAINTENANCE PERSONNEL EDUCATION   _____

1 Maintenance training is not required for the project.
2 Adequate training in projects and tools is available.
3 Some training is available in projects and tools.
4 Some training in projects to be maintained is available.
5 Little or no training in projects or tools is available.

As can be seen, these questions use a scoring pattern resembling the Richter scale for earthquakes. Low numbers are the safe direction, while larger numbers represent the dangerous or hazardous direction. In all of these questions, the approximate average value is set at 3.00. Lower scores of 1.00 through 2.50 indicate better than average performance, while scores of 3.50 through 5.00 represent worse than average performance.

However, if the project hovers around average or 3.00 for most responses, the user of an estimating tool does not have to take any overt action because average values are the default, or nominal, assumption.

As with the macro-estimating adjustments, the direction of the adjustment can be either positive or negative. However, the micro-estimating adjustment factors do not provide universal adjustments but are used to adjust specific activities, such as requirements, specifications, coding, unit testing, or user documentation.

The range of impact of each adjustment factor varies, and indeed the impacts are often regarded as proprietary trade secrets. However, most factors will have a small adjustment of about 5 percent, while only a few factors can exert a really major impact and can top a range of plus or minus 10 to 15 percent from the midpoint or nominal default value.

A typical pattern of adjustments might span a range of plus or minus 10 percent, as shown in Table 12.6. Assume that the range in the table is associated with the following question about software development process rigor:

SYSTEM DEVELOPMENT PROCESS   _____

1 Automated and effective system development process
2 Automated but cumbersome system development process
3 Manual and effective system development process
4 Manual and cumbersome system development process
5 Informal development: no formal system development process

Assuming that these five questions reflect the topic, then the range of impact of how the questions are answered might exert the range of productivity adjustments shown in Table 12.6.

Obviously, there will be interpolation for scores with decimal values, such as 2.35 or 4.50, but these are exactly the kinds of calculations at which automated estimating tools excel.

Incidentally, the micro-estimating adjustment factors are applied independently and, hence, have a cumulative impact. For example, if every one of the experience adjustment factors is in the good to excellent range, then the cumulative impact of all of these factors can generate results that are more than 60 percent better than average values, and more than 120 percent better than marginal to poor adjustment values.

Of course, a random combination of good and bad factors can achieve an effective adjustment that is close to zero in its impact. However, random factors seldom occur in real-life software projects.

Software projects usually follow typical patterns where many adjustments are either average, better than average, or worse than average depending upon the company, its culture, and the importance of software to corporate operations.

Let us examine some typical micro-estimating adjustments and also nominal or default values for a sample of ten common software development activities that occur on many different classes, types, and sizes of software applications.

- Requirements
- Prototyping
- Specifications and design
- Design inspections
- Coding
- Code inspections
- Change management
- Testing

TABLE 12.6   Typical Ranges of Software Adjustment Factors

Score	Definition	Productivity impact, %
1	Excellent	+10
2	Good	+5
3	Average	0
4	Below average	−5
5	Poor	−10

- User documentation

- Project management

These ten activities occur with high enough frequency that almost every commercial estimating tool can deal with them. Certainly, all of the micro-estimating tools can deal with them.

It should be noted that there are no constant or fixed ratios for the expense patterns of these ten activities. Indeed, if there were constant ratios, then there would be no need for software cost-estimating tools, and there would be no software cost-estimating industry. Each of these ten can range from less than 10 percent of development expenses to more than 50 percent, depending upon the nature, scope, class, and type of the software application in question.

For example, the generic topic of *testing* actually encompasses no less than 18 discrete kinds of software testing. The observed range of costs for the testing of software applications runs from a low of about 5 percent for small personal applications to more than 70 percent for large and complex systems with stringent safety or reliability requirements.

It is obvious that there are huge ranges for every activity, and this is why adjustments are necessary. However, these ten are also major components of software development schedules and expenses, although there are certainly other important activities besides these ten, such as quality assurance, integration, independent verification and validation, and many others.

Before considering the details of how each of these activities might be estimated, let us consider what a complete estimate might look like with all ten activities displayed simultaneously. Table 12.7 illustrates a systems software project of 1500 function points constructed in the C programming language.

Table 12.7 differs from Table 12.1, which uses the same format. Table 12.7 assumes a systems software project in C rather than an MIS project in COBOL, and the size is 1500 function points rather than 1000 function points. More significant, Table 12.7 assumes a different company and, hence, uses a burden rate of 100 percent rather than 50 percent.

The columns in Table 12.7 reflect a number of basic kinds of information that the family of automated cost-estimating tools can usually provide.

Column 1, "Activity," is self-explanatory and simply lists the activities included in the software estimate. It should be noted that the activities in Table 12.7 represent a standard "waterfall" project. For Agile development, XP, and some of the other new approaches, the sets of activities would differ. For example, "Scrum meetings" might be an activity.

TABLE 12.7   Examples of Estimating Values for 10 Software Activities

Assumptions	
Application class	Systems software
Programming language(s)	C
Size in function points	1,500
Source lines per function point	125
Size in source code statements	187,500
Average monthly salary	$5,000
Burden rate percent	100%
Fully burdened compensation	$10,000
Work hours per month	160
Effective work hours per month	128

Activity	Assignment scope	Production rate	Hours per FP	Staff	Effort months	Schedule months	Burdened cost	Cost per FP	Cost per LOC	Percent of total
Requirements	500	75.00	1.71	3.00	20.00	6.67	$200,000	$133.33	$1.07	9.16
Prototyping	750	50.00	2.56	2.00	3.00	1.50	30,000	20.00	0.16	1.37
Design	300	60.00	2.13	5.00	25.00	5.00	250,000	166.67	1.33	11.45
Design inspections	250	150.00	0.85	6.00	10.00	1.67	100,000	66.67	0.53	4.58
Coding	250	25.00	5.12	6.00	60.00	10.00	600,000	400.00	3.20	27.48
Code inspections	200	100.00	1.28	7.50	15.00	2.00	150,000	100.00	0.80	6.87
Change control	1500	150.00	0.85	1.00	10.00	10.00	100,000	66.67	0.53	4.58
Testing	200	50.00	2.56	7.50	30.00	4.00	300,000	200.00	1.60	13.74
User documents	750	125.00	1.02	2.00	12.00	6.00	120,000	80.00	0.64	5.50
Project management	1500	45.00	2.84	1.00	33.33	33.33	333,333	222.22	1.78	15.27
Net result	245	6.87	20.94	6.13	218.33	35.65	2,183,333	1,455.56	11.64	100.00

Column 2, "Assignment scope," is the amount of work normally assigned to one technical staff member. Although the table expresses the assignment scope in terms of function point metrics, assignments in real life are often given in terms of natural metrics, such as pages of specifications, screens, volumes of source code, number of customers supported, and a host of other possibilities. For example, assignment scopes can be expressed in terms of object points, use case points, COSMIC function points, or any of a variety of metrics.

Column 3, "Production rate," is the amount of work that a staff member can be expected to complete in a standard time period. In this table the standard time period is the *month*, which the table itself defines as consisting of 128 hours of effective work time, once coffee breaks, meetings, and other non-work tasks have been backed out. Here, too, it is possible to substitute natural metrics for function points, such as pages of specifications, screens, source code, and the like.

Column 4, "Hours per FP," provides the same information as column 3, but expresses the results in a different mathematical form. Rather than expressing the results in terms of *function points per staff month*, column 4 uses the reciprocal value of *work hours per function point* derived by dividing the number of effective work hours per month by the nominal rate. That is, a productivity rate of 100 function points and a rate of 128 work hours per month yields the result of 1.28 work hours per function point.

Column 5, "Staff," is a predicted value of the number of full-time personnel required for the project. Since some staff members will work only part-time, this information is normally expressed using decimal values. For example, one person working half-time would be expressed as a staffing level of 0.5.

Column 6, "Effort months," is also a predicted value, and shows the amount of effort for each activity. Although effort in the table is expressed in months, it could also have been expressed in terms of any other work period: hours, days, weeks, months, or years.

Column 7, "Schedule months," is also a predicted value, and shows the schedule in terms of calendar months. Since activities overlap and never really follow a "waterfall" model, the actual schedule for software projects is always shorter than the sum of the activity schedules. For example, if requirements takes two months and design takes four months, the arithmetic sum of these two activities would be six months. However, design usually starts when requirements are about 50 percent complete, so the effective schedule would be five months rather than six, because design overlaps requirements by 50 percent, meaning that half of the requirements are still unfinished at the time design commences.

Column 8, "Burdened cost," shows the cost for the activity, which is calculated by multiplying the "Effort" column by the burdened compensation rate. If there were more space on the page, it might also be possible to show the costs without burden rates.

Column 9, "Cost per FP," shows the normalized data of cost per function point. Since this is a 1500–function point example, the costs of each activity are simply divided by 1500.

Column 10, "Cost per LOC," shows the normalized data of cost per line of code. Since this project is written in the C programming language and requires 187,500 source code statements, each data item in column 7 is divided by 187,500. This column will obviously vary widely from language to language. If the application had been written in Smalltalk rather than in C, then the amount of source code might have only been around 30,000 source code statements. If it had been written in assembly language, the volume of source code might have been 320,000 source code statements. This is one of the reasons why function points are preferred for normalizing data across different languages.

Column 11, "Percent of total," shows the percentage of the total effort devoted to each activity. Readers should be cautioned that percentages are not a safe method for estimating software effort or costs. Because of wide ranges and fluctuations in many factors, percentages vary far too widely to be used for software cost estimating. For example, the percentage of testing for this project is only 13.74 percent of the total effort. This is due to the use of formal design and code inspections. If inspections were absent, then testing could easily absorb 35 percent to more than 50 percent of the total effort.

Table 12.7 reveals quite a few interesting facts at the same time, and is a useful example of the kinds of outputs available from commercial software cost-estimating tools. One of the advantages of using estimating tools is that they can produce all kinds of useful information very easily. For example, commercial software estimating tools can easily show cost per function point, cost per line of code, and percentage of costs simultaneously. Some can also show data expressed in terms of use case points, object points, story points, COSMIC function points, or other newer metrics.

Because Table 12.7 illustrates micro-estimation where each activity is subject to multiple adjustment factors, it is interesting to consider some of the factors that affect each row of the estimate, as follows:

- Requirements adjustment factors
  1. Overall size of the project
  2. Experience of the clients in working with software teams
  3. Experience of the clients in the knowledge that is to be automated

4. Experience of the development team with similar applications
5. Availability of commercial software that satisfies some requirements
6. Rate of creeping requirements after requirements phase
7. Use of prototyping
8. Use of joint application design (JAD)
9. Use of Quality Function Deployment (QFD)
10. Use of Agile, XP, or object-oriented methods

- Prototyping adjustment factors
  1. Experience of the prototype developers
  2. Experience of the clients
  3. Percentage of total features included in prototype
  4. Programming languages utilized for the prototype
  5. Reusable materials utilized within the prototype
  6. Time allowed to construct the prototype, i.e. time boxes or sprints

- Design adjustment factors
  1. Experience of the development team
  2. Geographic separation of the team
  3. Reusable materials utilized for the design
  4. Use of formal or informal design methodologies
  5. Use or failure to use design-automation tools
  6. Use or failure to use design inspections

- Design inspections
  1. Size of specifications
  2. Schedule pressure applied by management or clients
  3. Geographic dispersal of the design team
  4. Percentage of specifications to be inspected, up to 100 percent
  5. Experience of the development team in inspections
  6. Design representation methods utilized
  7. Use or failure to use automated inspection tools

- Coding
  1. Experience of the development team with similar applications
  2. Schedule pressure applied to developers by management or clients

    3. Programming languages utilized

    4. Experience of the team with the programming languages

    5. Use of pair programming or individual programming

    6. Programming environment and automated tools available

    7. Volume of reusable source code utilized

    8. Programming office space and ergonomics

- Code inspections

    1. Experience of the development team

    2. Schedule pressure applied to developers by management or client

    3. Programming languages utilized

    4. Percentage of code inspected, up to 100 percent

    5. Structure and complexity of the code being inspected

    6. Use or failure to use code inspection automation

- Change control

    1. Use of Agile or waterfall methods

    2. Presence or absence of a change-control board

    3. Rate of requirements creep during development

    4. Rate of design changes during development

    5. Rate of coding development

    6. Use or failure to use change-control automation

    7. Continuous or discrete build strategy

    8. Geographic dispersal of the development groups

- Testing

    1. Experience of the test personnel

    2. Number and kind of test stages utilized

    3. Number and severity levels of defects found during testing

    4. Rate at which discovered defects are repaired

    5. Schedule pressure applied by managers or clients

    6. Number of existing regression tests

    7. Structure and complexity of the code being tested

    8. Use or failure to use test-automation tools

    9. Use or failure to use test-coverage analysis

    10. Use of failure to use defect tracking

- User documentation

  1. Experience of the technical writers
  2. Communication between technical writers and developers
  3. Schedule pressure applied by managers or clients
  4. Nature of documentation to be produced (tutorial, reference, etc.)
  5. Mixture of text and graphics utilized
  6. Use or failure to use document-automation tools
  7. Volume of reusable document items available

- Project management

  1. Experience of the project managers
  2. Presence or absence of historical data from similar projects
  3. Schedule and other pressures applied by higher management or clients
  4. Use or failure to use software cost-estimating tools
  5. Use of failure to use software project-planning tools

As can easily be seen, each software development activity is sensitive to a large number of adjustment factors. Further, there are complex interactions among the activities themselves. For example, source code that is well structured and has few defects is easier and quicker to inspect and to test than source code that is poorly structured and buggy.

Table 12.8 shows a general ranking of eight key adjustment factors in terms of their overall impacts. As might be expected using just common sense, small projects with capable teams and excellent tools will be much more productive than large systems with marginal teams and questionable tools.

Because activity-based costing is the heart of modern software cost estimation, let us now explore a selection of key activities in depth to discover the nature of the problems that cost-estimation tool vendors are attempting to solve.

TABLE 12.8   General Ranking of Key Adjustment Factors

1. Size of project
2. Team experience
3. Reusable material
4. Schedule pressure
5. Creeping changes
6. Methodologies
7. Tools
8. Ergonomics

The most effective mode of software cost estimation is to estimate each activity individually, and then consolidate the overall estimate from the partial estimates of discrete activities.

This method ensures that no important activities will be accidentally omitted. Further, estimating each activity individually minimizes the chances that estimating errors will flow from activity to activity. In other words, estimating errors may occur, but they will tend to be localized to specific activities.

Table 12.9 illustrates some typical assignment scopes and production rates for 25 standard activities that are often found in new development projects that utilize the "waterfall" approach.

This same approach can also be used for Agile development, object-oriented development, web site development, and other new approaches. Table 12.10 illustrates the same kinds of information for a sample of new activities.

TABLE 12.9: Example of Activity-Based Cost Chart of Accounts
(Assumes new waterfall development projects)

Assumptions	
Work hours per month	132
Unpaid overtime per month	0
Average monthly salary	$5,000
Burden rate	100%
Burdened monthly rate	$10,000
Burdened daily rate	$500
Burdened hourly rate	$76

Activities	Staff FP. assignment	Monthly FP production	Work hours per FP	Burdened cost per FP	Staffing per 1000 FP
01 Requirements	250.00	175.00	0.75	$57.14	4.00
02 Prototyping	350.00	150.00	0.88	$66.67	2.86
03 Architecture	2000.00	300.00	0.44	$33.33	0.50
04 Project plans	1000.00	500.00	0.26	$20.00	1.00
05 Initial design	250.00	175.00	0.75	$57.14	4.00
06 Detail design	250.00	150.00	0.88	$66.67	4.00
07 Design reviews	200.00	225.00	0.59	$44.44	5.00
08 Coding	150.00	50.00	2.64	$200.00	6.67
09 Reuse acquisition	250.00	600.00	0.22	$16.67	4.00
10 Package purchase	5000.00	400.00	0.33	$25.00	0.20
11 Code inspections	150.00	150.00	0.88	$66.67	6.67
12 Independent verification & validation.	2000.00	125.00	1.06	$80.00	0.50
13 Configuration management	1000.00	1750.00	0.08	$5.71	1.00

TABLE 12.9: Example of Activity-Based Cost Chart of Accounts *(Continued)*
(Assumes new waterfall development projects)

Activities	Staff FP. assignment	Monthly FP production	Work hours per FP	Burdened cost per FP	Staffing per 1000 FP
14 Integration	2000.00	250.00	0.53	$40.00	0.50
15 User documentation	750.00	70.00	1.89	$142.86	1.33
16 Unit testing	150.00	150.00	0.88	$66.67	6.67
17 Function testing	350.00	150.00	0.88	$66.67	2.86
18 Integration testing	700.00	175.00	0.75	$57.14	1.43
19 System testing	2500.00	200.00	0.66	$50.00	0.40
20 Field (beta) testing	1500.00	225.00	0.59	$44.44	0.67
21 Acceptance testing	750.00	350.00	0.38	$28.57	1.33
22 Independent testing	2500.00	200.00	0.66	$50.00	0.40
23 Quality assurance	2000.00	150.00	0.88	$66.67	0.50
24 Installation/ training	5000.00	350.00	0.38	$28.57	0.20
25 Project management	750.00	100.00	1.32	$100.00	1.33
Cumulative results	203.39	6.75	19.55	$1,481.03	4.92

TABLE 12.10: Example of Activity-Based Data
(Assumes Agile or object-oriented development)

Assumptions	
Work hours per month	132
Unpaid overtime per month	0
Average monthly salary	$5,000
Burden rate	100%
Burdened monthly rate	$10,000
Burdened hourly rate	$76

Activities	Staff FP assignment	Monthly FP production	Work hours per FP	Burdened cost per FP	Staffing per 1,000 FP
01 User stories	300	200	0.66	$50.00	3.33
02 UML design	250	150	0.88	$66.67	4.00
03 Use case design	350	225	0.59	$44.44	2.86
04 Class library design	500	175	0.75	$57.14	2.00
05 Web page design	400	250	0.53	$40.00	2.50
06 Scrum sessions	350	500	0.26	$20.00	2.86
07 Pair programming	100	50	2.64	$200.00	10.00

Table 12.10 illustrates that the key values of "assignment scopes" and "production rates" can be applied to essentially any software development activity. The logic is equally valid with Agile development, XP, OO development, spiral development, or anything else. Of course, the activities themselves will vary, but for any known activity there will still be typical assignment scopes and production rates. Once the logic of assignment scopes and production rates is grasped, the software estimating can be modified to match any form of development from the classic waterfall approach to full pattern-based development with almost 100 percent reusable materials.

The "assignment scope" is the amount of work normally assigned to a single individual. It is expressed in terms of function points in Table 12.10, but it could just as easily be expressed in terms of use cases, object points, lines of code, story points, or any other metric.

The "production rate" is the average amount of work normally completed in a standard time period. In Table 12.10 the standard times periods are work months and work hours. But the time period can also be weeks, years, or even minutes.

The use of assignment scope and production rate logic is the key to unified estimates for all activities. The only additional criteria is that each activity must be expressed in the same unit of measure. This is why function point metrics have become so valuable for software estimating tools. They can be applied to all known activities without exception.

References

Ambler, S.: *Process Patterns—Building Large-Scale Systems Using Object Technology,* Cambridge University Press, New York, SIGS Books, 1998.

Artow, J. and I. Neustadt: *UML and the Unified Process,* Addison-Wesley, Boston, Mass., 2000.

Beck, K: *Extreme Programming Explained: Embrace Change,* Addison-Wesley, Boston, Mass., 1999.

Boehm, Barry: *Software Engineering Economics,* Prentice-Hall, Englewood Cliffs, N.J., 1981.

————: "A Spiral Model of Software Development and Enhancement," Proceedings of the Int. Workshop on Software Process and Software Environments, ACM Software Engineering Notes, Aug. 1986, pp. 22–42.

Booch, Grady: *Object Solutions: Managing the Object-Oriented Project,* Addison-Wesley, Reading, Mass., 1995.

————, Ivar Jacobsen, and James Rumbaugh: *The Unified Modeling Language User Guide, Second Edition,* Addison-Wesley, Boston, Mass., 2005.

Brown, Norm (ed.): *The Program Manager's Guide to Software Acquisition Best Practices,* Version 1.0, U.S. Department of Defense, Washington, D.C., July 1995.

Chidamber, S.R. and C.F. Kemerer: "A Metrics Suite for Object-Oriented Design," IEEE Trans. On Software Engineering, Vol. SE20, No. 6, June 1994, pp. 476–493.

Cockburn, Alistair: *Agile Software Development,* Addison-Wesley, Boston, Mass., 2001.

Cohen, D., M. Lindvall, and P. Costa: "An Introduction to Agile Methods, Advances in Computers, Elsevier Science, New York, 2004, pp. 1–66.

Cohn, Mike: *User Stories Applied: For Agile Software Development,* Addison-Wesley, Boston, Mass., 2004.

————: *Agile Estimating and Planning*, Prentice-Hall PTR, Englewood Cliffs, N.J., 2005.
Curtis, Bill, William E. Hefley, and Sally Miller: *People Capability Maturity Model*, Software Engineering Institute, Carnegie Mellon University, Pittsburgh, Pa., 1995.
DeMarco, Tom: *Controlling Software Projects*, Yourdon Press, New York, 1982.
————: *Why Does Software Cost So Much?*, Dorset House, New York, 1995.
————, and Tim Lister: *Peopleware*, Dorset House Press, New York, 1987.
Fuqua, Andrew M.: *Using Function Points in XP—Considerations*, Springer Berlin/Heidelberg, 2003.
Gamma, Erich, Richard Helm, Ralph Johnson, and John Vlissides: *Design Patterns: Elements of Reusable Object Oriented Design*, Addison-Wesley, Boston Mass., 1995.
Garmus, David and David Herron: *Function Point Analysis*, Addison-Wesley Longman, Boston, Mass., 2001.
————: *Measuring the Software Process: A Practical Guide to Functional Measurement*, Prentice-Hall, Englewood Cliffs, N.J., 1995.
Highsmith, Jim: Agile Software Development Ecosystems, Addison-Wesley, Boston, Mass., 2002.
Humphrey, Watts S.: *Managing the Software Process*, Addison-Wesley/Longman, Reading, Mass., 1989.
International Function Point Users Group (IFPUG) (http://www.IFPUG.org).
Jeffries, R. et al: *Extreme Programming Installed*, Addison-Wesley, Boston, Mass., 2001.
Jones, Capers: *SPQR/20 Users Guide*, Software Productivity Research, Cambridge, Mass., 1986.
————: *Critical Problems in Software Measurement*, Information Systems Management Group, Carlsbad, CA 1993a.
————: *New Directions in Software Management*, Information Systems Management Group, Carlsbad, CA 1993b.
————: *Assessment and Control of Software Risks*, Prentice-Hall, Englewood Cliffs, N.J., 1994.
————: *Patterns of Software System Failure and Success*, International Thomson Computer Press, Boston, Mass.,1995.
————: *Applied Software Measurement*, 2d ed., McGraw-Hill, New York, 1996a.
————: *Table of Programming Languages and Levels* (8 Versions from 1985 through July 1996), Software Productivity Research, Burlington, Mass., 1996b.
————: *The Economics of Object-Oriented Software*, Software Productivity Research, Burlington, Mass., April 1997a.
————: *Software Quality—Analysis and Guidelines for Success*, International Thomson Computer Press, Boston, Mass.,1997b.
————: "Sizing Up Software," *Scientific American*, New York, December 1998, Vol. 279, No. 6; pp 104–109.
————: *Software Assessments, Benchmarks, and Best Practices*, Addison-Wesley Longman, Boston, Mass., 2000.
Keys, Jessica: *Software Engineering Productivity Handbook*, McGraw-Hill, New York, 1993.
Koirala, Shavisprasad: "How to Prepare Quotations Using Use Case Points" (http://www.codeproject.com/gen/design//usecasepoints.asp).
Larman, Craig and Victor Basili: "Iterative and Incremental Development—A Brief History," IEEE Computer Society, June 2003, pp 47–55.
Love, Tom: *Object Lessons*, SIGS Books, New York, 1993.
Marciniak, John J. (ed.): *Encyclopedia of Software Engineering*, vols. 1 and 2, John Wiley & Sons, New York, 1994.
McConnell, Steve: *Software Estimating: Demystifying the Black Art*, Microsoft Press, Redmond, WA, 2006.
Paulk Mark, et al.: *The Capability Maturity Model: Guidelines for Improving the Software Process*, Addison-Wesley, Reading, Mass., 1995.
Pressman, Roger: *Software Engineering—A Practitioner's Approach, Sixth Edition*, McGraw-Hill, New York, 2005.
Putnam, Lawrence H.: *Measures for Excellence—Reliable Software on Time, Within Budget*, Yourdon Press/Prentice-Hall, Englewood Cliffs, N.J., 1992.

————, and Ware Myers: *Industrial Strength Software—Effective Management Using Measurement,* IEEE Press, Los Alamitos, Calif., 1997.

Rethinking the Software Process, CD-ROM, Miller Freeman, Lawrence, Kans., 1996. (This CD-ROM is a book collection jointly produced by the book publisher, Prentice-Hall, and the journal publisher, Miller Freeman. It contains the full text and illustrations of five Prentice-Hall books: *Assessment and Control of Software Risks* by Capers Jones; *Controlling Software Projects* by Tom DeMarco; *Function Point Analysis* by Brian Dreger; *Measures for Excellence* by Larry Putnam and Ware Myers; and *Object-Oriented Software Metrics* by Mark Lorenz and Jeff Kidd.)

Roetzheim, William H., and Reyna A. Beasley: Best Practices in Software Cost and Schedule Estimation, Prentice-Hall PTR, Upper Saddle River, N.J., 1998.

Rubin, Howard: *Software Benchmark Studies For* 1997, Howard Rubin Associates, Pound Ridge, N.Y., 1997.

Stapleton, J.: *DSDM—Dynamic System Development in Practice,* Addison-Wesley, Boston, Mass., 1997.

Stukes, Sherry, Jason Deshoretz, Henry Apgar, and Ilona Macias: *Air Force Cost Analysis Agency Software Estimating Model Analysis—Final Report,* TR-9545/008-2, Contract F04701-95-D-0003, Task 008, Management Consulting & Research, Inc., Thousand Oaks, Calif., September 1996.

Symons, Charles R.: *Software Sizing and Estimating—Mk II FPA (Function Point Analysis),* John Wiley & Sons, Chichester, U.K., 1991.

Yourdon, Ed: Death March—The Complete Software Developer's Guide to Surviving "Mission Impossible" Projects, Prentice-Hall PTR, Upper Saddle River, N.J., 1997.

5

Activity-Based Software Cost Estimating

Software cost estimating at the activity level, or micro-estimating, is far more accurate than macro-estimating, but is also more difficult. The advantages of activity-based estimation are twofold: (1) key activities will not be accidentally left out, and (2) estimating errors, if they occur, tend to stay local within a specific activity rather than affecting the entire suite of activities.

This section explores the software cost-estimating implications of ten key software development activities:

- *Requirements*
- *Prototyping*
- *Design and specifications*
- *Design inspections*
- *Coding*
- *Code inspections*
- *Change management and configuration control*
- *Testing*
- *User documentation and project documentation*
- *Project management*

These ten activities comprise a minimum set for activity-based software cost estimating, although not every one of these activities occurs on every project. Also, most of these ten activities occur with very high frequency and, hence, can be encountered on many large software development projects.

However, the maximum set of activities for very large systems is more than 25 activities, which can be decomposed into many hundreds of sub-activities and tasks. Discussing the implications of estimating 25 or more software activities would require a book more than twice as large as the current volume.

13

Estimating Software Requirements

Software requirements are the starting point for every new project, and are a key contributor to enhancement projects, as well. Software requirements are also very ambiguous, often filled with bad assumptions and severe errors, and are unusually difficult to pin down in a clear and comprehensive way.

From a software cost-estimating standpoint, the most tricky part of estimating requirements is the fact that requirements are usually unstable and grow steadily during the software development cycle in the coding and even the testing phases.

The observed rate at which requirements change after their initial definition runs between 1 percent and more than 3 percent per month during the subsequent analysis, design, and coding phases. The U.S. average circa 2007 is for an average growth rate of new requirements of about 2 percent per calendar month. This is based on a standard waterfall model of development. With some of the Agile approaches that start coding as soon as a minimal set of requirements are understood, the average rate of growth is about 12 percent per calendar month.

Equally as troublesome, software requirements are the source of about 20 percent of all software bugs or defects, and are the source of more than 30 percent of really severe and difficult defects. (For example, the year-2000 software problem originated as a requirement. Believe it or not, military software projects and many civilian projects were required to use only two digits for dates, even though many programmers knew that two-digit date fields would eventually cause trouble.)

Because software projects depend heavily upon the accuracy and completeness of software requirements, it is urgent that requirements be done well. Both software sizing and software cost estimates are derived from the requirements themselves, so the precision with which requirements are defined affects the accuracy of the software size and cost estimates. Unfortunately, the available technologies for gathering and analyzing software requirements are troublesome and incomplete, although some progress is underway.

Although many books on requirements contain thoughtful analyses of requirements methods and offer interesting suggestions for improving software requirements gathering and analysis, they tend to omit two key topics:

- Quantification of requirements sizes, schedules, effort, and costs
- Quantification of requirements errors and defect-removal efficiency

From a software cost-estimating viewpoint, the nominal or default values for producing software requirements specifications are shown in Table 13.1.

If you were to utilize these nominal default values for a case study software project of 1500 function points, the results would approximate the following, assuming systems software as the class of the application.

For a 1500–function point systems software project, the nominal or average requirements would be about 375 pages in size and would be

TABLE 13.1   Nominal Default Values for Requirements Estimates

Activity sequence	Initial activity of software projects
Performed by	Client representatives and development representatives
Predecessor activities	None
Overlap	None
Concurrent activities	Prototyping
Successor activities	Analysis, specification, and design
Initial requirements size	0.25 U.S. text pages per function point
Requirements size in story points	0.50 U.S. text pages per story point
Requirements size in use cases	35 use cases per function point
Size in use case points	0.20 U.S. text pages per use case point
Graphics volumes	0.01 illustrations per function point
Reuse	10% from prior or similar projects
Assignment scope	500 function points per technical staff member
Production rate	175 function points per staff month
Production rate	0.75 work hours per function point
Schedule months	Function points raised to the 0.15 power
Rate of creep or change	2.0% per month (12% for Agile projects)
Defect potential	1.0 requirements defects per function point
Defect removal	75% via requirements inspections
Delivered defects	0.25 requirements defects per function point
High-severity defects	30% of delivered requirements defects
Bad fix probability	10% of requirements fixes may yield new errors

produced by a team of three technical personnel (working with about the same number of client personnel). The effort would amount to about nine staff months. The schedule would be about three calendar months.

If you were doing requirements with use cases, the application would require about 43 use cases, or roughly 35 function points per use case.

If you were doing requirements with user stories, the application would require about 3000 story points. Each user story is perhaps five story points in size so there would be about 600 stories. That is roughly equivalent to about 2.5 function points per user story.

If you were doing the same application using Agile methods, the written requirements would only be about half the size of the example. Further, the application would probably be subdivided into perhaps five separate iterations or sprints, each of which would total to about 300 function points in size.

More ominously, there would be about 1500 potential defects in the requirements themselves. About 30 percent of the requirements errors or bugs would be very serious, which would amount to about 450 high-severity requirements errors—more than any other source of serious error.

Since many companies are careless about attempting to remove errors or defects in software requirements, defect-removal efficiency levels against requirements are lower than for other sources of error and average only about 75 percent.

A nominal defect-removal efficiency of only 75 percent means that when the project is deployed there will still be about 375 requirements defects and about 112 high-severity defects still latent. Indeed, latent requirements defects comprise the most troublesome form of after-deployment defects in software systems, because they are highly resistant to defect-removal methods.

Among the more sophisticated software companies the significance of requirements and requirements errors is recognized. Several defect-prevention technologies that are deployed fairly widely are available:

- Joint application design (JAD) for gathering user requirements

- Quality Function Deployment (QFD) for focusing on quality issues

- Prototyping of key application features

- Extreme programming for writing test cases for each requirement

Formal requirements inspections are useful and can top 75 percent defect-removal efficiency, but this powerful method is seldom deployed because too many companies have adopted the false concept that *quality* means *conformance to requirements*. The problem with this concept is that it ignores the volume and severity levels of errors in requirements themselves and, hence, leads to downstream problems with incorrect and ambiguous requirements.

The growth in unplanned creeping requirements would amount to about 20 percent during the analysis, design, and coding stages, which is equivalent to a monthly change rate of about 2 percent. The growth in unplanned new requirements affects the size of the requirements themselves, affects the size of the internal and external specifications, and also increases the source code size and ups the number of test cases that must be constructed. Also, the unplanned new requirements will have at least as many defects as the original requirements, and probably more.

For Agile projects, the initial requirements will be only about 300 function points when coding begins. Since the final application is a nominal 1500 function points in size, it can be seen that the growth rate for the Agile approach is much larger than for the waterfall approach.

Although the default or nominal values for requirements estimates provide a useful starting place, the range of variance around each of the default values can be more than 3 to 1. The adjustment factors account for much of the variance, but other factors, such as whether the requirements are being created for a military or a civilian project, also exert an impact.

Military software projects usually have much larger and more formal requirements than similar civilian projects of the same size, and also require much more extensive work in order to define the requirements than is normal for civilian projects.

In real-life situations, the effort for requirements definition fluctuates more than almost any other software activity, and can range from close to zero effort for small personal applications to more than 3.0 work hours per function point for large military software systems.

Table 13.2 illustrates some of the ranges in requirements productivity rates associated with various sizes and kinds of software projects.

In addition to the initial default assumptions, software requirements also have a number of attributes associated with them that should be recorded, including but not limited to the following.

TABLE 13.2   Ranges in Requirements Productivity Rates by Class of Software

Software class	Requirements productivity, FP/staff month	Requirements productivity, hours/FP
End user	1000	0.128
Web applications	500	0.256
Commercial	200	0.640
Small MIS	175	0.750
Large MIS	75	1.710
Outsource	90	1.422
Embedded	80	1.600
Systems	75	1.710
Military	35	3.657

Performed by   Clients, marketing staff, sales staff, engineering staff, systems analysts, programmers, quality-assurance staff, and software project managers are the normal participants in requirements, although not every category will be present on every project. It is useful to record who provided the basic set of application requirements. For Agile projects the client will be an actual part of the team. For large commercial software projects such as Microsoft Office, some clients may be interviewed or participate in focus groups. But when the number of potential clients tops 10,000,000 which is the case for many commercial applications, most of the requirements come in from marketing groups and competitive analysis rather than from the clients themselves.

Formal methodologies   Numerous requirements methods exist, including those of information engineering (IE), Rapid Application Development (RAD), object-oriented (OO) design and the unified modeling language (UML), use cases, Quality Function Deployment (QFD), joint application design (JAD), finite-state machines, and state transition diagrams. For the newer Agile methods there are also user stories. Since these methods affect both the error density and the productivity of requirements, it is useful to record which method or combination of methods will be utilized.

Requirements tools   Software requirements automation is only just becoming a major product arena, and a host of new tools, such as Rational's Requisite, are beginning to speed up the effort of requirements management. However, the next generation of requirements tools should include additional features, such as automatic derivation of function points, use case points, object points, story points, and linkages to software sizing, cost estimating, and project management tools, which are often lacking. Indeed, some tools, such as the Bachman Analyst Workbench and the Texas Instruments Information Engineering Facility (IEF), do provide automatic derivation of function point metrics from requirements. Pattern matching, or selecting requirements from libraries of historical requirements, is also an emerging but not yet developed technology.

Defect prevention   The most effective defect-prevention method for requirements defects is the construction of a working prototype. Disposable prototypes are much more effective than evolutionary prototypes. (Disposable prototypes typically contain about 10 percent of the functionality of the final product.) Time box prototypes and the methods of JAD and QFD are also effective in preventing requirements defects. If any of these are used, the fact should be recorded. The extreme programming method of developing a test case for each requirement serves as both a defect prevention method and a defect removal method.

Defect removal   Requirements defects are highly resistant to removal (consider the year-2000 problem). However, formal requirements inspections have been successfully utilized and deserve more widespread usage. After requirements are complete, downstream activities, such as design inspections, code inspections, and testing, are not very effective in removing requirements defects. Indeed, once major defects (such as the year-2000 problem) are embedded in requirements, they tend be immune to most standard forms of defect removal and are especially resistant to being found via testing. The extreme programming approach of writing a test case for each requirement seems to be fairly effective.

Requirements defects   Software requirements errors comprise about 20 percent of the total errors found in software applications, but comprise more than 30 percent of the intractable, difficult errors.

The current U.S. averages for software defect origins, expressed in terms of defects per function point, are shown in Table 13.3.

Software requirements are the third highest source of all defects, but the second highest source of major defects that are likely to cause serious trouble after the application is deployed. It should not be forgotten that the year-2000 problem originated as an explicit and deliberate requirement rather than as an accidental coding error. Although the Y2K problem is now behind us, it remains a good example of what happens when a bad requirement gets into software.

Some examples of the kinds of errors that can be found in software requirements include but are not limited to the following:

- **Errors of Omission**   The most common problem with requirements is that they are incomplete for any application larger than trivial. Given the number of permutations of features possible with large software projects, it is very likely that incompleteness will always occur, because a complete requirements specification might approach infinite size.

TABLE 13.3   Requirements Defects and Other Categories

Defect origins	Total defects per FP	High-severity defects per FP
Requirements	1.00	0.30
Design	1.25	0.50
Code	1.75	0.25
Documentation	0.60	0.10
Bad fixes	0.40	0.15
Total	5.00	1.30

- **Errors of Ambiguity** Because requirements specifications are usually expressed using natural languages, such as English, Japanese, German, or Spanish, they are subject to all of the sources of ambiguity and misunderstanding of any other text document. For example, such phrases as "high-speed transaction processing" or "very high reliability" will be understood differently by almost everyone who reads them.

- **Errors of Commission** It is very common for software requirements to insist that the application do something that may be incorrect or hazardous. The famous year-2000 problem originated as a specific requirement to "economize storage by recording year dates using only the last two digits."

- **Conflicting Requirements** Some software requirements for applications where several or many users are contributing their specific needs may end up with conflicts. For example, the requirements for a state motor vehicle registration system contained conflicting requirements in two sections: (1) proof of insurance had to be input before a registration could be issued, and (2) a registration had to be issued before a proof of insurance certificate could be granted. These two requirements were in direct conflict, and yet both were actually implemented!

The most important aspect of requirements errors is that if they escape detection, it is very difficult to find them downstream via testing. Usually, if an incorrect requirement eludes removal, subsequent testing will confirm the error rather than find it. For example, once the Y2K requirement to use two-digit date formats was accepted, then no test cases were ever created that could find this problem until just before the century ended. When the problem was finally realized, an entirely new suite of test cases was built specifically in response to this classic requirements problem.

Creeping requirements The rate of *creeping requirements*, or changes after the initial set of requirements are defined, is a major software problem. The U.S. average is about 2 percent per month during the design and coding phases. The maximum amount of creep has sometimes topped 150 percent, so this is a major consideration. Prototyping plus such methods as JAD can reduce this rate down to a small fraction, such as 0.5 percent per month.

For Agile projects, the rate of change is about 12 percent per calendar month. This is because the Agile method does not seek to gather 100 percent of the requirements before starting development. Instead, the most obvious initial requirements are analyzed and then coded into a working model. After usage, the next wave of requirements are created and then coded. The approach typically results in a series of increments, each of which contains between 10 percent and 20 percent of the ultimate set of requirements.

The fundamental root cause of changing requirements is that software applications are expanding the horizon of the ways companies operate. In a sense, the creation of software requirements is reminiscent of hiking in a fog that is gradually lifting. At first only the immediate surroundings within a few feet of the path are visible, but as the fog lifts more and more of the terrain can be seen.

Reuse of software requirements In theory, software requirements should be one of the key artifacts of a formal software reuse program. Indeed, because so many software applications are so similar, the level of requirements reuse should top 75 percent for many software applications, although the actual volume of reuse hovers around only 10 percent or so.

Unfortunately, the technologies of requirements gathering, using primarily natural-language text and documents with random formats, makes effective reuse of software requirements rather difficult. As a result, the requirements for far too many applications are treated as being unique when in fact they may be only minor variations of existing software applications. One of the most important software technologies of the next 20 years would be to improve the methodology of software requirements so that reusability becomes a standard attribute. Use cases and the UML are steps on the path to reusable requirements. The eventual goal is to capture requirements "patterns" in such a fashion that widespread reuse becomes feasible.

Function Points and Software Requirements

The function point metric has proven to be a useful tool for gathering requirements, and also for exploring the impact and costs of creeping requirements. Recall that the function point metric is a synthetic metric derived from the following five external attributes of software systems:

- Inputs
- Outputs
- Inquiries
- Logical files
- Interfaces

The normal reason that requirements grow or creep is that one or more of the five attributes also associated with function points grows. The single most common growth factor is the need for additional outputs, but any of the five function point elements can and do expand as software projects proceed through development.

In the context of exploring creeping requirements, the initial use of function point metrics is simply to size the application at the point where the requirements are first considered to be firm. At the end of the development cycle, the final function point total for the application will also be counted.

For example, suppose the initial function point count is for a project of 100 function points, and at delivery the count has grown to 125. This provides a direct measurement of the volume of creep in the requirements.

From analysis of the evolution of requirements during the development cycle of software applications, it is possible to show the approximate rates of monthly change. The changes in Table 13.4 are shown from the point at which the requirements are initially defined through the design and development phases of the software projects.

Table 13.4 is derived from the use of function point metrics, and the data is based on differences in function point totals between: (1) the initial estimated function point total at the completion of software requirements, and (2) the final measured function point total at the deployment of the software to customers.

If the first quantification of function points at requirements definition is 1000 function points and the final delivered number of function points is 1120, that represents a 12 percent net growth in creeping requirements. If the time span from completing the requirements through the design and code phases is a 12-month period, then it can be seen that the rate of growth in creeping requirements averages 1 percent per month.

In Table 13.4 the changes are expressed as a percentage change to the function point total of the original requirements specification. Note that there is a high margin of error, but even so it is useful to be able to measure the rate of change at all. With Agile projects, which start only with the most immediate of requirements, the rate of growth is about 12 percent per month.

TABLE 13.4   Monthly Growth Rate of Software Creeping Requirements

Software type	Monthly rate of requirements change, %
Contract or outsource software	1.0
Information systems software	1.5
Systems software	2.0
Military software	2.0
Commercial software	3.5
Web-based software	12.0

It is interesting that although the rate of change for contract software is actually less than for many other kinds of applications, the changes are much more likely to lead to disputes or litigation. The data in these tables is taken from the author's book, *Patterns of Software Systems Failure and Success* (International Thomson Computer Press, Boston, MA publisher, 1996).

Since the requirements for more than 90 percent of all software projects change during development, creeping user requirements is numerically the most common problem of the software industry, which should not be a surprise to anyone.

A number of technologies have been developed that can either reduce the rate at which requirements change or, at least, make the changes less disruptive. Space does not permit a full discussion of each, but following are the technologies with positive value in terms of easing the stress of creeping user requirements.

Joint Application Design (JAD)

Joint application design (JAD) is a method for developing software requirements under which user representatives and development representatives work together with a facilitator to produce a joint requirements specification that both sides agree to.

The JAD approach originated in Canada in the 1970s and has now become very common for information systems development. Books, training, and consulting groups that offer JAD facilitation are also very common.

Compared to the older style of adversarial requirements development, JAD can reduce creeping requirements by almost half. The JAD approach is an excellent choice for large software contracts that are intended to automate information systems.

In order to work well, JAD sessions require active participation by client representatives, as well as by the development organization. This means that JAD technology may not be appropriate for some kinds of projects. For example, for projects such as Microsoft's Windows Vista, where there are many millions of users, it is not possible to have a small subset of users act for the entire universe.

The JAD method works best for custom software, where there is a finite number of clients and the software is being built to satisfy their explicit requirements. It does not work well for software with hundreds or thousands of users, each of whom may have slightly different needs.

Agile Development

Because of the well-known failures of software projects, many researchers have been seeking alternative approaches. The genesis of the set of "agile" methods can be traced to the publication of the "agile manifesto" in 2001. This manifesto recommended collaborative development, meeting evolving requirements with working versions, and growing the final application organically from a number of iterations.

The essence of agile development is that requirements for software projects will always be fluid and changing. Rather than attempting to document every known requirement prior to starting development, under the Agile methods small teams of developers build working versions of key features in very short intervals called "time boxes" or "increments." In order to do this, there must be daily contact with the application's customer and with each other. Under the Agile methods, requirements growth is viewed as a natural organic phenomenon.

Prototypes

Since many changes don't start to occur until clients or users begin to see the screens and outputs of the application, it is obvious that building early prototypes can move some of these changes to the front of the development cycle instead of leaving them at the end.

Prototypes are often effective in reducing creeping requirements, and they can be combined with other approaches, such as JAD. Prototypes by themselves can reduce creeping requirements by somewhere between 10 and about 25 percent.

There are three common forms of software prototypes:

- Disposable prototypes
- Evolutionary prototypes
- Time box prototypes

Of these three, the disposable and time box methods have the most favorable results. The problem with evolutionary prototypes that grow to become full projects is that during the prototyping stage, too many short cuts and too much carelessness is usually present. This means that evolutionary prototypes seldom grow to become stable, well-structured applications that are easy to maintain.

Use Cases

The technique termed *use cases* originated as a method for dealing with the requirements of object-oriented applications, but has subsequently expanded and is moving toward becoming a formal approach for dealing with software requirements.

The use case technique deals with the patterns of usage that typical clients are likely to have and, hence, concentrates on clusters of related requirements for specific usage sequences. The advantage of the use case approach is that it keeps the requirements process at a practical level and minimizes the tendency to add "blue sky" features that are not likely to have many users.

Change-Control Boards

Change-control boards are not exactly a technology, but rather a group of managers, client representatives, and technical personnel who meet and decide which changes should be accepted or rejected.

Change-control boards are often encountered in the military software systems domain, although they are not common for information systems. Such boards are most often encountered for large systems in excess of 10,000 function points in size.

In general, change-control boards occur within large organizations and are utilized primarily for major systems. These boards are seldom encountered within small companies and are almost never utilized for small projects.

Change-control boards are at least twice as common among military software procedures as they are among civilian software producers. Within the civilian domain, change-control boards are more common for systems, commercial, and outsourced software projects than they are for internal management information systems.

The members of a change-control board usually represent multiple stakeholders and include client representatives, project representatives, and sometimes quality-assurance representatives. For hybrid projects that include hardware, microcode, and software components, the change-control board for software is linked to similar change-control boards for the hardware portions.

The change-control board concept has been very successful whenever it has been deployed, and tends to have long-range value across multiple releases of evolving systems. Change-control boards are now a standard best practice for the construction of large and complex applications, such as telephone switching systems, operating systems, defense systems, and the like.

Quality Function Deployment (QFD)

The technique called *Quality Function Deployment* (QFD) originated in Japan as a technique for exploring the quality needs of engineered products, and then moved to software. QFD is now expanding globally, and many of SPR's high-technology clients who build hybrid products, such as switching systems and embedded software, have found QFD to be a valuable method for exploring and controlling software quality issues during requirements.

Procedurally, QFD operates in a fashion similar to JAD in that user representatives and design team representatives work together with a facilitator in focused group meetings. However, the QFD sessions center on the quality needs of the application rather than on general requirements.

The QFD method has developed some special graphical design methods for linking quality criteria to product requirements. One of these methods shows product feature sets linked to quality criteria. Visually, this method resembles the peaked roof of a house, so QFD drawings are sometimes termed *the house of quality*.

Sliding Cost per Function Point Scales

For software development contracts, perhaps the most effective way of dealing with changing user requirements is to include a sliding scale of costs in the contract itself. For example, suppose a hypothetical contract is based on an initial agreement of $500 per function point to develop an application of 1000 function points in size, so that the total value of the agreement is $500,000.

The contract might contain the following kind of escalating cost scale for new requirements added downstream:

Initial 1000 function points	$500 per function point
Features added more than 3 months	$600 per function point after contract signing
Features added more than 6 months	$700 per function point after contract signing
Features added more than 9 months	$900 per function point after contract signing
Features added more than 12 months	$1200 per function point after contract signing
Features deleted or delayed at user request	$150 per function point

Similar clauses can be utilized with maintenance and enhancement outsource agreements, on an annual or specific basis, such as the following:

Normal maintenance and defect repairs	$125 per function point per year
Mainframe to client/server conversion	$200 per function point per system
Special date search and repair	$65 per function point per system

(Note that the actual cost per function point for software produced in the United States runs from a low of less than $100 per function point for small end-user projects to a high of more than $5000 per function point for large military software projects. The data shown here is for illustrative purposes, and should not actually be used in contracts as it stands.)

The advantage of the use of function point metrics for development and maintenance contracts is that they are determined from the user requirements and cannot be unilaterally added by the contractor.

One of the many problems with the older lines-of-code (LOC) metrics is that there is no objective way of determining the minimum volume of code needed to implement any given feature. This means that contracts based on cost per LOC could expand without any effective way for the client to determine whether the expansions were technically necessary.

Function points, on the other hand, cannot be unilaterally determined by the vendor and must be derived from explicit user requirements. Also, function points can easily be understood by clients while the LOC-metrics is difficult to understand in terms of why so much code is needed for any given contract.

Gathering and understanding software requirements has been a weak link in the software development process since the industry began more than 50 years ago, and shows signs of staying troublesome for the foreseeable future. The basic problems with software requirements are the following:

- The clients who provide requirements vary widely in their understanding of fundamental business processes and the rules for the activities needing automation.

- The clients who provide requirements vary widely in their ability to explain the requirement clearly, even if they understand the requirements.

- Requirements-gathering methodologies and requirements-representation methods are not as well formed or sophisticated as software design approaches. For many projects, requirements are casually collected and expressed primarily in natural-language text documents. Such requirements are highly ambiguous, contain many severe errors, and tend to creep at alarming rates.

- Because clients are seldom software professionals, they may lack understanding of key topics such as development schedules and quality control, and, hence, may make impossible or even dangerous demands.

- For some applications, such as Microsofts operating systems and office suites, the total number of users can top 10,000,000. With so many users doing so many different things, the actual set of requirements can approach infinity. Even if the requirements are finite, there are so many thousands of them that full documentation is not feasible.

The topic of errors in requirements is often ignored under the common software aphorism that *quality* means *conformance to requirements*. In fact, requirements errors are plentiful and often are very severe.

It should never be forgotten that the very serious year-2000 problem originated as an explicit requirement. This is why all test libraries and test cases throughout the world failed to identify this problem for 25 years.

Only in about 1995 did the software world wake up to the fact that the end of the century would lead to catastrophic failure of software applications if calendar-year dates were recorded in two-digit format (i.e., 97 for the year 1997).

Conformance to the requirement that calendar years be recorded in two-digit rather than four-digit form became one of the most expensive single problems in human history. This should be a lesson to us to examine requirements very carefully in terms of possible errors and long-range consequences.

The ability to measure the rate at which requirements creep is due to the advent of the function point metric. At the end of the requirements phase the function point total of the application can be quantified with high precision. Then, each change in requirements is evaluated in terms of how the function point total will be adjusted in response. When the application is delivered to users the final total is enumerated, and the difference between the initial and final totals is then noted.

Primary Topics for Software Requirements

By fortunate coincidence, the structure of the function point metric and the related feature point metric are a good match to the fundamental issues that should be included in software requirements. In chronological order, these seven fundamental topics should be explored as part of the requirements process:

- The *outputs* that should be produced by the application
- The *inputs* that will enter the software application
- The *logical files* that must be maintained by the application
- The *entities, actors, and relationships* that will be in the logical files of the application
- The *inquiry types* that can be made to the application
- The *interfaces* between the application and other systems
- Key *algorithms* that must be present in the application

Five of these seven topics are the basic elements of the International Function Point Users Group (IFPUG) function point metric. In the fourth topic, *entities* and *relationships* are part of the British Mark II function point metric; *actors* are part of use case and object points. The seventh topic, *algorithms*, is a standard factor of the feature point metric, which adds a count of algorithms to the five basic function point elements used by IFPUG.

The similarity between the topics that need to be examined when gathering requirements and those used by the functional metrics makes the derivation of function point totals during requirements a straight-forward task.

Indeed, several companies, such as Bachman and Texas Instruments, produced automated requirements tools that can also calculate function point totals directly from the requirements themselves.

There is such a strong synergy between requirements and function point analysis that it would be possible to construct a combined require-ments-analysis tool with full function point sizing support as a natural adjunct, although the current generation of automated requirements tools is not quite at that point.

Secondary Topics for Software Requirements

In addition to the 7 fundamental requirements topics, there are also 12 other ancillary topics that should be resolved during the requirements-gathering phase:

- The *size* of the application in function points, use case points, object points, and source code
- The *schedule* of the application from requirements to delivery
- The *cost* of the application by activity and also in terms of cost per function point
- The *quality levels* in terms of defects, reliability, and ease of use cri-teria
- The *hardware platform(s)* on which the application will operate
- The *software platform(s)*, such as operating systems and databases
- The *security criteria* for the application and its companion databases
- The *performance criteria*, if any, for the application
- The *training requirements* or form of tutorial materials that may be needed
- The *installation requirements* for putting the application onto the host platforms
- The *reuse criteria* for the application in terms of both reused materials going into the application and also whether features of the application may be aimed at subsequent reuse by downstream applications
- The *use cases* or major tasks users that are expected to be able to perform via the application

These 12 supplemental topics are not the only items that can be included in requirements, but none of these 12 should be omitted by accident since they can all have a significant effect on software projects.

Positive and Negative Requirements Adjustment Factors

For estimating software requirements, schedules, effort, costs, and quality, both positive and negative factors must be considered.

Positive Requirements Factors

The positive factors that can benefit software requirements production by perhaps 10 percent for assignment scopes, production rates, and defect potentials include the following:

- High client experience levels
- High staff experience levels
- Joint application design (JAD)
- Prototyping
- Quality Function Deployment (QFD)
- Use cases
- Requirements inspections
- Reusable requirements (patterns or frameworks)
- Requirements derived from similar projects
- Requirements derived from competitive projects
- Effective requirements representation methods

Negative Requirements Factors

The negative factors that can slow down or degrade the software requirements production by perhaps 5 percent, or that can raise defect potentials, include the following:

- Inexperienced clients
- Inexperienced development team
- Novel applications with many new features
- Requirements creep of more than 3 percent per month (except for Agile projects)

- Ineffective or casual requirements-gathering process
- Failure to prototype any part of the application
- Failure to review or inspect the requirements
- No reusable requirements

The way the author's estimating tools collect data about requirements approaches can be illustrated by the following sample questions using SPR's standard five-point weighting scale. These questions are not the only ones that affect software requirements, of course.

DEVELOPMENT PERSONNEL APPLICATION EXPERIENCE _____

1 All are experts in the type of program being developed.
2 Majority are experts, but some are new hires or novices.
3 Even mixture of experts, new hires, and novices.
4 Majority are new hires or novices, with few experts.
5 All personnel are new to this kind of program.

DEVELOPMENT PERSONNEL REQUIREMENTS EXPERIENCE _____

1 All are experts (have successfully gathered requirements from many projects).
2 Majority are experts but some are new hires or novices.
3 Even mixture of experts, new hires, and novices.
4 Majority are new hires or novices, with few experts.
5 All personnel are inexperienced in requirements analysis.

REQUIREMENTS ANALYSIS PROCESS _____

1 Formal methods are used rigorously, such as JAD, QFD, Warnier-Orr, and the like.
2 Formal methods are used in a semi-rigorous manner.
3 Formal methods are mixed with informal methods.
4 Requirements methods are primarily informal and unstructured.
5 Requirements methods are informal and unstructured.

REQUIREMENTS PROTOTYPING PROCESS _____

1 Application is too small to need prototyping or prototyping is not necessary.
2 Formal prototyping of key features, algorithms, and interfaces.
3 Informal prototyping of selected features, algorithms, and interfaces.
4 Partial prototyping of a few features or algorithms.
5 No prototyping at all for this project.

REQUIREMENTS INSPECTION EXPERIENCE _____

1 All personnel are experienced in requirements reviews/inspections.
2 Most personnel are experienced in requirements reviews/inspections.
3 Even mixture of experienced and inexperienced personnel.
4 Most personnel are inexperienced in requirements reviews/inspections.
5 All personnel are inexperienced in requirements reviews/inspections.

USER PERSONNEL EXPERIENCE WITH SOFTWARE PROJECTS _____

1 User experience with software is not a key factor.
2 All or a majority of users have software experience.
3 Even mixture of experts and inexperienced users.
4 Majority of users have no prior software experience.
5 All personnel have no prior software experience.

USER PERSONNEL EXPERIENCE WITH APPLICATION TYPE _____

1 User expertise is not a major factor for the project.
2 All or a strong majority of users are experts.
3 Even mixture of experts, new hires, and novices.
4 Majority are new hires and novices, with few experts.
5 All personnel are new to this kind of program.

USER INVOLVEMENT DURING REQUIREMENTS _____

1 User involvement is not a major factor for this project.
2 Users are heavily involved during requirements.
3 Users are somewhat involved during requirements.
4 Users are seldom involved during requirements.
5 Users are not involved during requirements.

As can be seen, projects whose responses to these questions are in the range of 1.00 through 2.00 are much more likely to succeed than similar projects where the responses are in the upper range of 4.00 and 5.00.

Software requirements are a pivotal topic for software projects. If requirements are done well, the rest of the project has a good chance of being done well. If requirements are poorly formed, incomplete, or highly unstable, then it will be very difficult to have a successful project no matter what kinds of tools and methods or processes are utilized later on.

There are a number of interesting differences in how requirements are gathered and analyzed based on industry differences, and also on differences in the type of software being produced.

Requirements and End-User Software

There is very little to say about requirements when the application is being developed for the personal use of the developer.

Except for a few notes on possible alternatives, the requirements for end-user software exist primarily in the mind of the developer. This is not to say that the user can't change his or her mind during development. However, changes in end-user requirements usually have no serious implications.

Requirements and Agile Applications

One of the interesting attributes of the Agile approach is that a customer or client becomes an integral part of the development team. This means that issues relating to requirements can be discussed face to face and resolved in a very short time. The limits of this method are for applications that might have hundreds or thousands of users, each of whom may be doing something different. The Agile approach works best for applications with only a few kinds of users, all of whom use the software in a similar fashion.

Requirements and Management Information Systems (MIS) Projects

MIS projects usually derive software requirements directly from users or the users' authorized representatives.

For MIS projects the most effective methods for gathering requirements include JAD, prototypes, and requirements reviews. The combination of JAD sessions plus prototyping can reduce the rate of creeping requirements from 2 percent per month down to perhaps 0.5 percent per month.

The older method of gathering MIS requirements consisted of drafting a basic set of requirements more or less unilaterally by the client organization, and then presenting them to the software development organization. This method leads to a high rate of requirements creep, and also to adversarial feelings between the clients and the developers.

The requirements approach with the RAD methodology leads to a form of evolutionary prototyping without much in the way of written requirements. While the RAD approach is acceptable for small or simple applications, the results are not usually satisfactory for large applications above 1000 function points, nor for critical applications with stringent security, safety, performance, or reliability criteria.

MIS requirements can begin by exploring either the functions that the software is intended to perform or the data that is intended to be utilized. On the whole, beginning the requirements by exploring data and defining the outputs appears to give the best results.

Several well-known requirements approaches are in this general domain, including the Warnier-Orr method, the Jackson method, and several varieties of the information engineering method. Some of the OO requirements approaches meet the general criteria, although as usual with OO methods there are also unique attributes due to the OO class and method concepts.

Even if user requirements can be satisfied by a package, it is still important to gather, evaluate, and review them in a careful manner. This means that even when commercial software is planned, such as SAP R/3, Oracle, IBM, or Computer Associates products, it is still desirable to match package capabilities against fundamental needs and requirements.

Requirements and Outsourced Projects

Outsourced projects in the MIS domain are similar in style and content to normal MIS projects with two important exceptions:

- Outsource vendors often apply a cost per function point rate to the initial requirements in order to give the clients a good idea of the costs of the project. Some modern outsource contracts also include a sliding cost scale, so that the costs of implementing creeping requirements will be higher than the costs of the initial set of requirements.

- Outsource vendors that serve many clients within the same industry often have substantial volumes of reusable materials and even entire packages available that might be utilized with minor or major customization. For certain industries, such as banking, insurance, telecommunications, and health care, almost every company uses software with the same generic feature sets, so reusable requirements are possible.

Requirements and Systems Software

In the author's books the phrase *systems software* is defined as software that controls a physical device, such as a computer, switching system, fuel injection system, or aircraft controls.

Because of the close and intricate relationship between the hardware and software, many requirements changes in the systems software domain are due to changes in the associated hardware. This close linkage between hardware and software requirements is one of the reasons why QFD technology has been effective in the systems software domain.

Requirements gathering in the systems software domain seldom comes directly from the users themselves. Instead the software requirements usually come in from hardware engineers and/or the marketing organization that is in direct contact with the users, although for custom software applications users may be direct participants in requirements sessions.

Requirements, and also specification methods, in the system software domain are closely linked to hardware requirements, and the approaches for the software and hardware domains overlap. Special representation methods, such as Petri nets or state-transition diagrams, are sometimes used in the context of systems software requirements, and even hardware representation methods, such as the Verilog design language, may be applied to software requirements.

Because quality is a key criterion for systems software, approaches that can deal with quality issues during the requirements phase are common practices for systems software.

Traditional quality-assurance methods for systems software include formal inspections, full configuration control, and sometimes JAD that may include both hardware and software requirements.

An interesting new approach called *Quality Function Deployment* (QFD) is starting to move rapidly through the systems software domain. The QFD approach is similar to JAD in structure, although the primary emphasis of the QFD approach is on the quality and reliability of the application.

The usual starting point for the analysis of systems software requirements is determining the functions and features that are needed by the system.

Requirements and Commercial Software

Gathering requirements for commercial software has some unique aspects that are not found with the requirements for the other kinds of software projects.

For some kinds of commercial software products there may be hundreds, thousands, or even millions of possible users. There may also be many competitors whose software has features that might also have to be imitated.

These two factors imply that commercial software requirements seldom come directly from one or two actual clients. Instead, commercial software requirements may arrive from any or all of the following channels:

- From the minds of creative development personnel who envision new products or useful new features
- From customer surveys aimed at eliciting customer needs and requests for new features
- From marketing and sales personnel, based on their perceptions of what users have requested
- From sophisticated customer support personnel who recognize needed improvements due to incoming customer complaints
- From user associations, focus groups, and online product forums on services such as CompuServe or the World Wide Web, where inputs from thousands of customers may be received
- From focus groups—selected sets of customers who volunteer to meet with design representatives and discuss the features that they like or dislike about possible new products
- From analyzing the feature sets of competitive packages and imitating the more useful competitive features

Because the seven channels are more or less independent, the requirements for commercial software packages tend to be highly volatile. For example, if a competitor comes out with a striking new feature, a vendor may well have to implement a similar feature even if a product release is rather far along.

Requirements and Military Software Projects

Military software requirements are usually the most precise and exacting of any class of software. This phenomenon is due to the long-standing military requirement of *traceability*, or the need to identify exactly which requirement triggered the presence of any downstream design feature or source code module.

The military form of requirements tends toward large, even cumbersome, requirements specifications that are about three times larger than civilian norms. Although these military requirements documents are large and sometimes ambiguous, the specificity and completeness of military software requirements makes it easier to derive function point totals than for any other kind of software application.

On the whole, military software requirements have somewhat more positive attributes than negative for major systems that affect national defense or weapons. For smaller and less serious projects, the military requirements methods are something of an overkill.

Requirements and Web-Based Applications

Modern web-based applications are dynamic and rapidly evolving. Web applications may feature animation, sound, graphics, links to other web sites, music, online questionnaires, and a host of topics that are far from traditional. Because of the visual impact of web sites and the high degree of interaction with possibly millions of people, the most effective method for gathering web requirements is to construct working prototypes. A secondary method for gathering requirements is to copy the features of the more interesting web sites that already exist. Some aspects of web requirements do need to be expressed in more conventional terms, such as security criteria or failure recovery modes.

Evaluating Combinations of Requirements Factors

The author and his colleagues at Software Productivity Research are often asked to deal with combinations of factors at the same time. SPR has developed a useful method of showing how a number of separate topics interact.

SPR's method is to show the 16 permutations that result from changing four different factors. This method is not perfect and makes some simplifying assumptions, but it is useful to show the ranges of possible outcomes.

Table 13.5 shows the 16 permutations that result from four key factors that affect software requirements:

- The use of or failure to use prototypes
- The use of or failure to use joint application design (JAD)
- The use of or failure to use formal requirements inspections
- The presence or absence of experienced staff familiar with the application type

In this table we assume fairly complex applications of at least 1000 function points or 125,000 C statements in size. For smaller projects, requirements defects and rates of change would be less, of course. For really large systems in excess of 10,000 function points or 1,125,000 C statements, requirements errors would be larger and removal efficiency would be lower.

TABLE 13.5   Sixteen Permutations of Software Requirements Technologies
(Data expressed in defects per function point; best-case options appear in boldface type)

	Defect potential per FP	Defect-removal efficiency, %	Residual defects per FP	Rate of creep, % monthly
No prototypes No use of JAD No inspections Inexperienced staff	2.00	60	0.80	4.0
No prototypes No use of JAD No inspections **Experienced staff**	2.00	65	0.70	3.5
Prototypes used No use of JAD No inspections Inexperienced staff	1.50	70	0.45	1.5
No prototypes No use of JAD **Inspections used** Inexperienced staff	2.00	80	0.40	3.0
No prototypes **JAD used** No inspections Inexperienced staff	1.50	75	0.38	1.0
Prototypes used No use of JAD No inspections **Experienced staff**	1.50	77	0.35	0.9
No prototypes No use of JAD **Inspections used** **Experienced staff**	2.00	84	0.32	1.0
No prototypes **JAD used** No inspections **Experienced staff**	1.50	80	0.30	0.9
Prototypes used **JAD used** No inspections **Inexperienced staff**	1.00	77	0.23	0.6
Prototypes used No use of JAD **Inspections used** Inexperienced staff	1.50	86	0.21	0.6
No prototypes **JAD used** **Inspections used** Inexperienced staff	1.50	86	0.21	0.5

TABLE 13.5   Sixteen Permutations of Software Requirements Technologies
(Continued)
(Data expressed in defects per function point; best-case options appear in boldface type)

	Defect potential per FP	Defect-removal efficiency, %	Residual defects per FP	Rate of creep, % monthly
No prototypes **JAD used** **Inspections used** **Experienced staff**	1.35	88	0.16	0.5
Prototypes used **JAD used** No inspections **Experienced staff**	1.00	87	0.13	0.3
Prototypes used No use of JAD **Inspections used** **Experienced staff**	1.50	94	0.09	0.3
Prototypes used **JAD used** **Inspections used** Inexperienced staff	1.00	94	0.06	0.2
Prototypes used **JAD used** **Inspections used** **Experienced staff**	0.70	97	0.02	0.1

The table shows polar extreme conditions; that is, each factor is illustrated in binary form and can switch between best-case and worst-case extremes.

Note that the function point (FP) values used in the table assume the IFPUG Version 4.1 counting rules.

As can be inferred from the 16 permutations, software requirements outcomes cover a very broad range of possibilities. The combination of effective requirements-gathering technologies coupled with effective defect-removal technologies and a capable team lead to a very different outcome from casual requirements methods utilized by inexperienced staff.

The best-in-class technologies for dealing with requirements are highly proactive, and include the following components:

- Formal requirements gathering, such as JAD for large systems above 10,000 function points

- Use of Agile methods for applications below 1000 function points

- Augmentation of written requirements with prototypes

- Use of requirements-automation tools

- Attention to requirements quality control using such methods as Quality Function Deployment (QFD) and requirements inspections.

- Use of function point metrics or equivalent based on requirements to determine overall application size, schedules, and costs

- Use of requirements change-control approaches, such as change-control boards, change-control tools, and the use of a sliding *cost per function point* scale

- Use of *reusable requirements* from similar or competitive projects

If the initial requirements for a software project are done well, the project has a fair chance to succeed regardless of size. If the requirements are done poorly and are filled with errors and uncontrolled changes, the project has a distressingly large chance of being canceled or running out of control.

References

Ambler, S.: *Process Patterns—Building Large-Scale Systems Using Object Technology*, Cambridge University Press, SIGS Books, 1998.

Artow, J. and I. Neustadt: *UML and the Unified Process*, Addison-Wesley, Boston, Mass., 2000.

Beck, K.: *Extreme Programming Explained: Embrace Change*, Addison-Wesley, Boston, Mass., 1999.

Boehm, Barry: "A Spiral Model of Software Development and Enhancement," Proceedings of the Int. Workshop on Software Process and Software Environments, ACM Software Engineering Notes, Aug. 1986, pp. 22–42.

Booch, Grady: *Object Solutions: Managing the Object-Oriented Project*, Addison-Wesley, Reading, Mass., 1995.

———, Ivar Jacobsen, and James Rumbaugh: *The Unified Modeling Language User Guide, Second Edition,* Addison-Wesley, Boston, Mass., 2005.

Cockburn, Alistair: *Agile Software Development*, Addison-Wesley, Boston, Mass., 2001.

Cohen, D., M. Lindvall, and P. Costa: "An Introduction to Agile Methods," *Advances in Computers*, Elsevier Science, New York, 2004, pp. 1–66.

Cohen, Lou: *Quality Function Deployment: How to Make QFD Work for You*, Prentice-Hall PTR, Englewood Cliffs, NJ, 1995 Mass.

Cohn, Mike: *User Stories Applied: For Agile Software Development*, Addison-Wesley, Boston, Mass., 2004.

Davis, Alan M.: *Software Requirements—Objects, Functions, and States, Second Edition*, Prentice-Hall, Englewood Cliffs, N.J., 1993.

Fuqua, Andrew M.: *Using Function Points in XP—Considerations*, Springer Berlin/ Heidelberg, 2003.

Gause, Donald C., and Gerald M. Weinberg: *Exploring Requirements—Quality Before Design*, Dorset House Press, New York, 1989.

Jeffries, R. et al.: *Extreme Programming Installed*, Addison-Wesley, Boston, Mass., 2001.

Jones, Capers: *Assessment and Control of Software Risks*, Prentice-Hall, Englewood Cliffs, N.J., 1994.

———: *Patterns of Software Systems Failure and Success*, International Thomson Computer Press, Boston, Mass., 1995.

———: *Software Quality—Analysis and Guidelines for Success*, International Thomson Computer Press, Boston, Mass., 1997.

————: *Applied Software Measurement*, McGraw-Hill, New York, 1996.

————: "Sizing Up Software," Scientific American, New York, December 1998, Vol. 279, No. 6, pp 104–109.

————: *Software Assessments, Benchmarks, and Best Practices*, Addison-Wesley Longman, Boston, Mass., 2000.

————: *Conflict and Litigation Between Software Clients and Developers*, Software Productivity Research, Burlington, Mass., 2003.

Larman, Craig and Victor Basili: "Iterative and Incremental Development—A Brief History,; IEEE Computer Society, June 2003, pp 47-55.

Love, Tom: *Object Lessons*, SIGS Books, New York, 1993.

Orr, Ken: *Structured Requirements Definition*, Ken Orr & Associates, Topeka, Kans., 1981.

Pressman, Roger: *Software Engineering—A Practitioner's Approach, Sixth Edition*, McGraw-Hill, New York, 2005.

Quality Function Deployment (http://en.wikipedia.org/wiki/Quality_function_deployment).

Robertson S. and J. Robertson: *Requirements-Led Project Management*, Addison-Wesley, Boston, Mass., 2005.

Thayer, Richard H., and Merlin Dorfman: *Software Requirements Engineering, Second Edition*, IEEE Computer Society Press, Los Alamitos, Calif., 1997.

Estimating Software Prototypes

Prototyping and requirements gathering are often parallel activities. In some situations such as the Agile development methods, the prototypes may even substitute for other forms of requirements gathering, although this is not often a safe practice.

Among SPR's clients, prototyping is a very common practice. For projects between about 100 and 5000 function points in size, about 80 percent of them have had some form of prototype development prior to full development. Of the prototypes, about 65 percent were disposable, 10 percent were time box, and 25 percent were evolutionary in nature.

To have an optimal effect, prototypes should serve as a method for augmenting written requirements and written specifications, not for replacing them. When prototypes are used in place of written specifications, the results are more often hazardous rather than beneficial. The reason for the hazard is because the prototype is not a sufficient source of information to enable formal design and code inspections, effective test case construction, or later downstream maintenance.

High-speed prototypes can be useful adjuncts to both joint application design (JAD) sessions and Quality Function Deployment (QFD) sessions, but prototypes are not a complete substitute for written requirements because prototypes have no long-range archival value. Also, for military and defense projects, prototypes have no traceability, so they do not support the military requirement of a backwards linkage between application features and specific requirements.

Prototypes are an interesting technology because they are most successful for midsized projects in the 500– to 2500–function point size range. For very small projects of less than 100 function points, they are usually not needed. For very large systems in excess of 10,000 function points, they may not be effective.

Prototypes are seldom used below a size of about 100 function points, although a few screens or user sequences might be constructed. This is because the entire application will be developed so quickly that a prototype is superfluous.

Above 10,000 function points, prototypes are used but may be large projects in their own right. For example, prototyping 10 percent of a 10,000–function point application would yield a project of 1000 function points, which is an application of substantial size in its own right and might take a year to complete. (A size of 10,000 function points is roughly equivalent to 1,250,000 C statements. A size of 1000 function points is roughly equivalent to 125,000 C statements.)

In every engineering field a *prototype* is an early or partial version of a complex artifact assembled to test out design principles and, sometimes, operational characteristics. The same concept is true for software projects. A software prototype is an early and partial replica of a software application constructed to test out design principles and operational characteristics.

Prototyping is usually carried out with fairly high-level languages of level 5 or higher because lower-level programming languages are too cumbersome for high-speed prototypes. (The level of a language refers to the number of source code statements required to encode 1 function point. Level 1 starts with basic assembly language where about 320 statements are needed for each function point. As language levels go up, fewer statements are needed, so that for level-10 languages only 32 statements are needed for each function point.)

Table 14.1 illustrates the ranges of possibilities for creating a prototype of 100 function points in size using language levels that range from 1 through 20. To simplify the situation, the coding rate is held constant at a fairly representative rate of 1600 lines of code per month for all 20 examples. The size of the prototype is also held constant at 100 function points. However, the volume of source code varies significantly, as does apparent productivity when considering the effort required or productivity rates expressed in terms of *function points per person month* (FP/PM).

Some examples of languages with levels lower than 5 include Assembly language in all forms, C, COBOL, and Fortran.

Some examples of mid-range languages with levels between 5 and 10 include C++, Lisp, Forth, Java, Simula, and Quick Basic.

Some examples of high-level languages with levels higher than 10 include APL, Visual Basic, Objective-C, and Smalltalk.

As can be seen, the volume of source code needed to implement a constant size of 100 function points declines as the level of the language rises. This, in turn, translates into less effort to produce the prototype and, hence, leads to higher productivity rates when the results are expressed in terms of function points per person month. In general, the

TABLE 14.1 Relationship Between Function Point and Lines-of-Code Productivity Rates for Software Prototypes by Language Level

Language level	Size, FP	Size, LOC	Monthly coding rate, LOC/PM	Effort to code prototype, months	Function point productivity, FP/PM
1	100	32,000	1,600	20.00	5
2	100	16,000	1,600	10.00	10
3	100	10,667	1,600	6.67	15
4	100	8,000	1,600	5.00	20
5	100	6,400	1,600	4.00	25
6	100	5,333	1,600	3.33	30
7	100	4,571	1,600	2.86	35
8	100	4,000	1,600	2.50	40
9	100	3,556	1,600	2.22	45
10	100	3,200	1,600	2.00	50
11	100	2,909	1,600	1.82	55
12	100	2,667	1,600	1.67	60
13	100	2,462	1,600	1.54	65
14	100	2,286	1,600	1.43	70
15	100	2,133	1,600	1.33	75
16	100	2,000	1,600	1.25	80
17	100	1,882	1,600	1.18	85
18	100	1,778	1,600	1.11	90
19	100	1,684	1,600	1.05	95
20	100	1,600	1,600	1.00	100

economics of prototyping favors using languages of level 5 and higher regardless of the language used to create the actual application.

Incidentally, the ease of constructing prototypes is greatly facilitated when reusable artifacts are also available. Thus, prototyping derived from patterns, frameworks, class libraries, and the like can have even higher productivity rates than prototypes based on "pure coding" approaches.

Languages often used for prototyping include Visual Basic, Realizer, Eiffel, Smalltalk, Java, and a host of other languages whose nominal levels range between 5 and 20. In general, low-level languages, such as assembly, C, Fortran, and COBOL, are not used very often for prototyping purposes because these languages are bulky in terms of code volumes and hence low in productivity for quick and dirty work, such as prototyping.

The phrase *software prototyping* actually encompasses a number of discrete forms of prototype, including but not limited to the following:

- Disposable prototypes
- Time box prototypes
- Evolutionary prototypes

Let us consider the pros and cons of these three forms of software project prototyping from the standpoint of how to estimate not only the prototypes themselves, but also their impact on downstream development.

Disposable Prototypes

As the name implies, disposable prototypes are created to demonstrate aspects of a software project, and when they have served that purpose they are no longer needed, so they are discarded.

Many of SPR's client companies do not limit the development of prototypes to the requirements phase of software development. If at any point in the development cycle an algorithm is difficult or there is some question as to how a screen element should appear, they continue to build disposable prototypes as the need arises.

Disposable prototypes are usually done rapidly, without formal specifications or much in the way of up-front planning. High-speed prototyping using such tools as Visual Basic and Realizer, or even special prototyping tools, such as the Bricklin Demo tool, is rather common.

The observed effects of disposable prototyping are a reduction in requirements defects and a very significant reduction in the rate of creeping requirements. Requirements creep for prototyped projects is usually well below the 1 to 2 percent per month range noted for conventional requirements gathering. Indeed, prototypes often reduce downstream requirements creep during design and coding to less than 0.5 percent per month.

Interestingly, disposable prototypes also yield a reduction in design defects and coding defects, although they yield no discernible impact on the user documentation or bad fix defect categories. Prototypes also seem to have little or no impact on bad test case defects or data errors, either.

Disposable prototypes interact in a synergistic fashion with two other requirements approaches: JAD and QFD. Indeed, disposable prototypes are often produced in real time during JAD or QFD sessions.

Disposable prototypes are usually only partial replicas of the software applications themselves, and usually contain only 10 to 25 percent of the features of the final product. Their main purpose is to test out interfaces, usability, and perhaps try out key algorithms or complex processing sequences.

Time box Prototypes

So far as can be determined, the concept of time box prototypes originated circa 1986 at Du Pont. A specific time period, such as one month or six weeks, is dedicated to developing a prototype of the final project, in order to demonstrate that it is feasible and implementable. The time box concept was adopted by several of the Agile methods and also by extreme programming (XP).

Compared to disposable prototypes, which are often discrete and not unified, time box prototypes are often partial replicas of full applications and are intended to show how the features and functions interact.

If the average size of disposable prototypes totals 10 to 15 percent of the eventual features, the average size of time box prototypes is about 15 to 25 percent of the eventual features.

Because the time box period may be less than a month and is almost never more than three months, it is obvious that time box prototypes are most effective for projects that range from about 500 function points up to a maximum of about 5000 function points, with an optimal node point of about 1000 function points.

For really large systems that top 10,000 function points, the time box would have to stretch out to more than 12 months to prototype 10 percent of the system, and the prototype would be 1000 function points in size, which is a significant application itself.

Time box prototyping works best for new kinds of applications where the development team needs to practice in order to be sure that it can build the final product. While time box prototypes are often constructed using such languages as Visual Basic, Realizer, or Objective C, they are sometimes built using conventional procedural languages, such as C.

The observed effects of time box prototypes are twofold: (1) many requirements defects are prevented, and (2) the rate of requirements creep is significantly reduced and is often less than 0.5 percent per month after the prototype is finished.

Although harder to validate, time box prototypes also seem to benefit design and coding defects slightly, although perhaps not as much as a staggered set of disposable prototypes.

Time box prototypes are usually too extensive to be part of JAD or QFD sessions. Often the time box method serves as a replacement for JAD, although QFD can still be included for high-technology projects.

The time box concept sometimes overlaps the hazardous *evolutionary prototype* form if the time box prototype is used as the actual base for growing a final product. This situation is dangerous for a number of reasons, as will be explained in the section on evolutionary prototypes.

A time box prototype is usually a disposable prototype constructed during a specific time interval inserted into the overall project schedule. Typical time box intervals might be one week for prototypes of less than 10 function points in size, one month for prototypes of less than 50 function points in size, or three months for prototypes of really massive systems where the prototype itself tops 100 function points.

Evolutionary Prototypes

As their name implies, evolutionary prototypes are intended to grow into finished products. Often the evolutionary prototypes are used as parts of various methodologies, such as some of the Agile methods, spiral development, XP, iterative development, and RAD. There are some decided hazards associated with the approach that need to be dealt with very carefully.

By definition, *prototypes* are built without formal specifications or much in the way of quality control, such as design or code inspections. This carelessness means that the structure of the application may be far from optimal, the comment density may be below safe levels, and the number of latent defects in the application may be significant.

The exceptions to this rule are evolutionary prototypes built under the protocols of XP. With the XP approach, test cases are built before the actual prototype code is written and hence are immediately available. Since the XP method is used primarily for applications smaller than 1000 function points (roughly 125,000 C statements) there is no solid information on how this method might scale up to really large applications.

For really large systems in the 10,000–function point range and higher, attempting to grow a prototype into a final product is a very dangerous practice. Indeed, for contracted software, such systems show up in court often enough that evolutionary prototyping can be considered professional malpractice on larger applications in the 10,000–function point range (which is equivalent to about 1,250,000 C statements.)

The evolutionary prototype method leaves a lot of important issues more or less unresolved until late in the coding and testing phases. This means that testing itself is severely handicapped by the lack of any kind of formal specification document for the basis of constructing test cases.

Indeed, unless the development personnel are also the test personnel, it is difficult to do any serious testing at all, because the details of the evolutionary prototypes are not stable and may not even have been worked out at the normal time when test-case construction should be ramping up during the design and coding phases.

Also, the evolutionary prototype method usually does not have any finished materials that are capable of going through formal design and code inspections. This explains why inspections are seldom used in conjunction with evolutionary prototypes.

Obviously, users and developers have whatever levels of prototypes are available at the moment, but a casual examination of a prototype is far less efficient in finding errors than are formal design and code inspections.

The hazards of the evolutionary prototyping approach for software applications larger than roughly 1000 function points are the following:

- Design rigor is often absent.

- Design inspections are seldom utilized.

- Written specifications are missing or perfunctory.
- Coding structure may be questionable.
- Code inspections are seldom utilized.
- Both cyclomatic and essential complexity levels may be high.
- Comments in code may be sparse.
- Test plan development is difficult and uncertain.
- Test cases may have major gaps in coverage.
- Quality and reliability levels are usually below average.
- Maintenance costs are usually well above average.
- Follow-on releases are expensive and troublesome.
- Customer support is difficult.
- User satisfaction levels are often below average.
- Litigation probability is alarmingly high.

These problems occur most severely at the larger end of the size spectrum. It is not fair to be totally dismissive of the evolutionary prototyping approach because it has been used more or less successfully on hundreds of applications by SPR's clients who use the Agile and XP methods for smaller applications.

However, the literature on evolutionary prototyping has manifested a common software flaw. There has been a tendency to assume that because the evolutionary prototype method works well on smaller applications of less than 1000 function points, it can be scaled up for larger applications of more than 10,000 function points. This is a dangerous fallacy, although it is a common failing in the software engineering literature.

Also, the evolutionary prototype method would be very dangerous to use for software that affects the operation of complex physical devices. This means that extreme caution is indicated when attempting evolutionary prototypes for weapons systems, aircraft flight control applications, medical instrument systems, or any other kind of application where failure can mean death, injury, or the probability of a major disaster.

Against the background of average results for MIS projects using disposable prototypes, evolutionary prototypes are a decided step backward in terms of quality results. Using COBOL information systems as an example, evolutionary prototypes tend to yield defect potentials about 15 percent higher than projects using JAD, while defect-removal efficiency levels are about 15 percent lower than average and may drop below 80 percent. This is a hazardous combination of results.

With evolutionary prototypes, the short-term advantages derived from working out the requirements early are quickly offset by sloppy design and poor coding structure, which elevates overall defect volumes and degrades defect-removal efficiency levels.

An evolutionary prototype is an attempt to build a full product by constructing a series of successively more complete partial versions, each of which includes features that are operational and usable by the intended clients.

The first stage of a series of evolutionary prototypes might include perhaps 25 percent of the features of the final product, and successive prototypes would then be constructed at the 50-, 75-, and 100-percent levels.

Default Values for Estimating Disposable Prototypes

The default values and initial assumptions shown here are for the *disposable prototype* form, which implies that the prototype is intended to clarify key algorithms or interfaces and, once it has served its purpose, will be replaced by a more rigorous version developed using normal quality controls.

Software estimating tools can also deal with the more complex forms of prototyping associated with time box prototypes, disposable prototypes, and the form of prototyping associated with XP, which is another variant on the evolutionary prototyping form. The initial assumptions for creating disposable prototypes are shown in Table 14.2.

TABLE 14.2   Nominal Default Values for Disposable Prototypes

Activity sequence	Initial or second activity of software projects
Performed by	Development software engineers; client representatives
Predecessor activities	Early requirements or none
Overlap	50% with normal requirements
Concurrent activities	Requirements
Successor activities	Analysis, specification, and design
Initial prototype size	25 function points or 10% of final application size
Initial prototype size	750 source code statements
Reuse	35% from prior or similar projects
Assignment scope	500 function points or actual prototype
Production rate	75 function points per staff month
Production rate	1.76 work hours per function point
Production rate	2500 LOC per staff month (level-5 languages)
Language level	Level 5 or higher
Schedule months	Function points raised to the 0.1 power
Rate of creep or change	5% per month
Defect potential	1.5 defects per function point
Defect removal	90%
Delivered defects	0.15 defects per function point
High-severity defects	15% of delivered requirements defects
Bad fix probability	10% of prototype fixes may yield new errors

Prototyping is a highly variable activity, and in particular, the size range of software prototypes can vary by more than 50 to 1. The smallest prototypes observed are only a fraction of a function point and may be only 10 to 20 source code statements in size. These prototypes are typically created for proving key algorithms.

The largest prototypes, on the other hand, can almost be applications in their own right and can exceed 500 function points or 15,000 source code statements in size.

To illustrate the range of variability of prototypes, Table 14.3 illustrates three typical forms of prototyping: (1) disposable, (2) time box, and (3) evolutionary.

Assume that the total size of the project for which the prototypes are being constructed will be 1000 function points. The prototypes are constructed using Visual Basic, which is one of the more common programming languages for prototyping.

TABLE 14.3 Three Forms of Prototypes
(Size expressed in both function points and source code statements)

Assumptions			
Programming language	Visual Basic		
Project size in function points	1,000		
Lines of code per function point	30		
Source code size	30,000		
Work hours per staff month	132		
Burdened salary rate	$10,000		

Factor	Disposable prototype	Time box prototype	Evolutionary prototype
Prototype percent	10.00%	15.00%	100.00%
Prototype FP	100	150	1000
Source code size	3000	4500	30000
Assignment, LOC	3000	2250	10000
Production, LOC	2500	2500	2000
Assignment, FP	150	112.5	500
Production, FP	125	125	100
Staff	1.00	2.00	3.00
Effort months	1.20	1.80	15.00
Schedule months	1.20	0.90	5.00
Cost	$12,000.00	$18,000.00	$150,000.00
Cost per FP	$120.00	$120.00	$150.00
Cost per LOC	$4.00	$4.00	$5.00
Defect potential per KLOC	50	50	75
Defect potential per FP	1.5	1.5	2.25
Defects	150	225	2250
Removal efficiency	90.00%	92.00%	93.00%
Delivered defects	15	18	158
per FP	0.15	0.12	0.16
per KLOC	5.00	4.00	5.25

One of the reasons why evolutionary prototypes are often hazardous is because prototypes of any kind are often built with casual development processes and no particular rigor during testing. Usually, no formal inspections or other quality-control approaches will be used, so the removal of prototype errors will depend primarily on desk checking and unit testing by the developers themselves.

For disposable and time box prototypes, the value of the prototypes for revealing possible requirements and design problems outweighs the number of errors or defects in the prototypes themselves.

But if the prototype is aimed at actually being grown into the final, finished product, the casual development approaches and lack of rigorous quality-control methods become a cause for concern.

As can be seen, the outcomes of software prototypes vary significantly based on which specific kind of prototype is being constructed.

Positive and Negative Factors That Influence Software Prototypes

The major positive adjustment factors for prototyping include the following:

- The prototyping language itself, if it is a high-level language
- Experience in the programming language used to construct the prototype
- Experience in the application or problem domain being prototyped
- Available reusable materials from similar projects or commercial sources
- Construction of test cases prior to the prototype, as with XP

Some of the negative adjustment factors for prototyping include the following:

- Clients who are unsure of what features they want in the prototype
- Inadequate development tools
- The prototyping language itself, if it is a low-level language
- Inadequate computer power or response time
- Inexperience of various kinds
- No reusable artifacts available
- Lack of formal testing and thorough test cases

To illustrate some of the adjustment factors that affect prototyping, consider the impact of the following topics.

DEVELOPMENT PERSONNEL APPLICATION EXPERIENCE _____

1 All are experts in the type of program being developed.
2 Majority are experts, but some are new hires or novices.
3 Even mixture of experts, new hires, and novices.
4 Majority are new hires or novices, with few experts.
5 All personnel are new to this kind of program.

DEVELOPMENT PERSONNEL TOOL AND METHOD EXPERIENCE _____

1 All are experts in the tools and methods for the project.
2 Majority are experts in the tools and methods.
3 Even mixture of experts, new hires, and novices.
4 Majority are new hires or novices in tools and methods.
5 All personnel are new to the tools and methods.

DEVELOPMENT PERSONNEL PROGRAMMING LANGUAGE EXPERIENCE _____

1 All are experts in the languages used for the project.
2 Majority are experts in the languages used for the project.
3 Even mixture of experts, new hires, and novices.
4 Majority are new hires or novices in the languages.
5 All personnel are new to the languages used.

DEVELOPMENT PERSONNEL HARDWARE EXPERIENCE _____

1 All are experts in the hardware used for the project.
2 Majority are experts in the hardware used for the project.
3 Even mixture of experts, new hires, and novices.
4 Majority are new hires or novices in the hardware.
5 All personnel are new to the hardware for the project.

USER PERSONNEL EXPERIENCE WITH APPLICATION TYPE _____

1 User expertise is not a major factor for the project.
2 All or a strong majority of users are experts.
3 Even mixture of experts, new hires, and novices.
4 Majority are new hires and novices, with few experts.
5 All personnel are new to this kind of program.

USER INVOLVEMENT DURING REQUIREMENTS   _____

1 User involvement is not a major factor for this project.
2 Users are heavily involved during requirements.
3 Users are somewhat involved during requirements.
4 Users are seldom involved during requirements.
5 Users are not involved during requirements.

PROGRAM DEBUGGING TOOLS   _____

1 Full screen editor and automated testing tool are used.
2 Full screen editor, traces, and cross-references are used.
3 Full screen editor traces, but little else, is used.
4 Full screen editor, but no trace or other flow aids, is used.
5 Line editor with little or no trace and flow aids is used.

DEVELOPMENT PLATFORM NOVELTY   _____

1 All hardware is familiar and well understood by staff.
2 Most hardware is familiar and well understood by staff.
3 Mixture of familiar and new or unfamiliar hardware.
4 Most hardware is new or unfamiliar to staff.
5 Hardware is new or experimental or unfamiliar.

DEVELOPMENT HARDWARE STABILITY   _____

1 Stable, single-vendor hardware with high compatibility is used.
2 Single-vendor hardware with moderate compatibility is used.
3 Mixed-vendor hardware with high mutual compatibility is used.
4 Mixed-vendor hardware with moderate compatibility is used.
5 Unstable, changing, or incompatible development hardware is used.

RESPONSE TIME OF DEVELOPMENT ENVIRONMENT   _____

1 Response time is not a factor for this project.
2 Subsecond response time is the norm.
3 One- to five-second response time is the norm.
4 Five- to ten-second response time is the norm.
5 More than 10-second response time is the norm.

DEVELOPMENT COMPUTING SUPPORT   _____

1 Computer support is ample, reliable, and effective.
2 Computer support is adequate, reliable, and effective.
3 Computer support is usually adequate and effective.
4 Computer support is sometimes inadequate or ineffective.
5 Computer support is seriously deficient for the project.

WORKSTATION ENVIRONMENT _____

1 Individual workstations networked with LAN and mainframe are used.
2 Individual workstations on LAN are used.
3 Individual workstations for all staff members are used.
4 Shared workstations (two employees per workstation) are used.
5 Batch development/more than two employees per workstation.

Here, too, a pattern of responses that are in the range of 1 or 2 indicates above-average performance levels, while a pattern of responses that sags into the 4 and 5 range indicates below-average responses.

Prototypes are useful adjuncts to design and are very useful in working out usability and human interface problems. However, great care must be exercised if a prototype is intended to be turned into a finished application.

References

Ambler, S.: *Process Patterns—Building Large-Scale Systems Using Object Technology*, Cambridge University Press, New York SIGS Books, 1998.

Artow, J. and I. Neustadt: *UML and the Unified Process*, Addison-Wesley, Boston, Mass., 2000.

Beck, K.:; *Extreme Programming Explained: Embrace Change*, Addison-Wesley, Boston, Mass., 1999.

Boar, Bernard: *Application Prototyping*, John Wiley & Sons, New York, 1984.

Boehm, Barry: "A Spiral Model of Software Development and Enhancement," Proceedings of the Int. Workshop on Software Process and Software Environments, ACM Software Engineering Notes, Aug. 1986, pp. 22–42.

Booch, Grady: *Object Solutions: Managing the Object-Oriented Project*, Addison-Wesley, Reading, Mass., 1995.

———, Ivar Jacobsen, and James Rumbaugh: *The Unified Modeling Language User Guide, Second Edition*, Addison-Wesley, Boston, Mass., 2005.

Cockburn, Alistair: *Agile Software Development*, Addison-Wesley, Boston, Mass., 2001.

Cohen, D., M. Lindvall, and P. Costa: "An Introduction to Agile Methods," *Advances in Computers*, Elsevier Science, New York, 2004, pp. 1–66.

Highsmith, Jim: *Agile Software Development Ecosystems*, Addison-Wesley, Boston, Mass., 2002.

Isensee, Scott, and Jim R. Rudd: *The Art of Rapid Prototyping*, International Thomson Computer Press, Boston, Mass., 1997.

Jeffries, R. et al.: *Extreme Programming Installed*, Addison-Wesley, Boston, Mass., 2001.

Jones, Capers: Applied Software Measurement, McGraw-Hill, New York, 1996.

———: *Software Quality—Analysis and Guidelines for Success*, International Thomson Computer Press, Boston, Mass., 1997.

———: "Sizing Up Software," *Scientific American*, New York, December 1998, Vol. 279, No. 6, pp 104–109.

———: *Software Assessments, Benchmarks, and Best Practices*, Addison-Wesley Longman, Boston, Mass., 2000.

Larman, Craig and Victor Basili: "Iterative and Incremental Development—A Brief History," IEEE Computer Society, June 2003, pp 47–55.

Love, Tom: *Object Lessons*, SIGS Books, New York, 1993.

Pressman, Roger: *Software Engineering—A Practitioner's Approach, Sixth Edition*, McGraw-Hill, New York, 2005.

Rapid Application Development (http://en.wikipedia.org/wiki/Rapid_application_ development).

Reilly, John P.: *Rapid Prototyping*, International Thomson Computer Press, Boston, Mass., 1997.

Robertson S., and J. Robertson: *Requirements-Led Project Management*, Addison-Wesley Boston, Mass., 2005.

Estimating Software Specifications and Design

Software specifications and design are a technical response to the user requirements, and serve to describe the way the user requirements will be handled in an automated fashion by the software application that is being constructed.

The term *specifications and design* covers a very broad range of actual forms of design, including but not limited to the following:

- Rough preliminary specifications
- Detailed final specifications
- External specifications of the features visible and usable by clients
- Internal specifications of the control flow and structure of the application
- Data specifications of the information created, used, or modified by the application
- Performance specifications of the desired response times and throughput
- Security specifications of the various protections against hacking and unlawful use

Also, prior to the commencement of design itself, there may be a moderate to lengthy period of systems analysis, which is sometimes subsumed under the design phase, too.

Estimating software design and specification activities is complicated by the fact that there are a host of formal and semi-formal methodologies, each of which will produce a somewhat different volume of design materials and also will trigger somewhat different work patterns.

The list in Table 15.1 of 43 different forms of specification representation methods illustrates some of the diversity of the software design situation.

TABLE 15.1 Forty-Three Common Software Design Methods

1. Conventional flowcharts
2. Natural language text
3. Control-flow diagrams
4. Data-structure diagrams
5. Gane & Sarson data-flow diagrams
6. DeMarco bubble diagrams
7. DeMarco structured English
8. Entity-relationship diagrams (generic)
9. Chen entity-relationship diagrams
10. Action diagrams
11. Structured analysis and design technique (SADT)
12. James Martin entity-relationship diagrams
13. James Martin information engineering (IE) diagrams
14. Texas Instruments information engineering (IE) diagrams
15. Nassi-Shneiderman diagrams
16. Chapin chart diagrams
17. Decision tables
18. Jackson design diagrams
19. Hierarchy plus input, output, and process (HIPO) diagrams
20. Yourdon-Constantine structured design diagrams
21. Yourdon object-oriented diagrams
22. Shlaer-Mellor object-oriented analysis diagrams
23. Booch object-oriented diagrams
24. Rumbaugh object-oriented diagrams
25. Jacobsen object-oriented diagrams
26. Universal modeling language (UML) diagrams in 13 forms
27. Use cases
28. User stories
29. Petri nets
30. Leighton diagrams
31. State-transition diagrams
32. Warnier-Orr diagrams
33. Structured analysis and design technique (SADT) diagrams
34. Merise diagrams
35. Three-dimensional control structure diagrams
36. Animated (dynamic) flow diagrams
37. Quality # (QFD) house of quality diagrams
38. Root-cause analysis fishbone diagrams
39. Text-based specifications using structured English
40. Formal mathematical notation-based specifications
41. Pseudocode design
42. Z
43. Pattern-based reusable designs.

This list of 43 methods of dealing with software specifications and design is not a complete list of all possible methods, which might well exceed 100 alternatives in all. It merely reflects the fact that the phrase *software design* can mean a very wide range of topics, and the huge number of possibilities represents a challenge to software cost-estimating vendors.

The literature on software design methods is quite extensive and totals more than 250 books. However, the great bulk of the software design literature concentrates on how-to-do-it treatments of specific design representation methods. Books that deal with the interaction of software design issues with software cost estimating are far more limited. Also limited are books that attempt to relate various software design approaches to the development of function point analysis.

The usual estimating response to the very large number of software design and specification approaches is to utilize templates for the more common design methods. However, templates are not a perfect solution for several reasons:

- A significant number of software projects use multiple or hybrid design methods rather than one "pure" design method. For many projects, designers may start using one of the object-oriented design methods, such as the universal modeling language (UML), but find that it has such a steep learning curve that they augment it with something else, such as the Yourdon structured design approach.

- A significant number of software projects utilize private or custom specification methods for which no published general data is available. Although templates are possible for private design methods, they must be constructed by users of estimating tools rather than by vendors, who may not even be aware of their existence.

However, clients of software cost-estimating tool vendors can construct software cost-estimating templates no matter what combinations of specification methods they use. But if an enterprise uses its own proprietary or highly modified design approach, then commercial templates from software cost-estimating tool vendors will obviously not be available.

As an example of a proprietary custom design method, the ITT corporation used the structured analysis and design technique (SADT), both in its pure form and in the form of a customized ITT variation created and used for switching software projects.

As an example of multiple design methods, it is very common to see a mixture of flowcharts, one or more of the object-oriented specification methods, use cases, and some kind of entity-relationship charts all in the specifications for a single project.

The nominal or default values for software specifications and design are not the same for every class and type of software project. The major variants are those of: (1) civilian versus military software projects, (2) systems software versus information systems projects, and (3) new applications versus enhancements to existing software.

The default values shown in Table 15.2 are for civilian systems software projects. Two design methods are shown: 1) conventional structured design methods, such as those first defined by the late Wayne Stevens, and 2) the unified modeling language (UML). Conventional structured design methods and the UML are the most widely deployed design methods for systems software, and have default values in many commercial software cost-estimating tools.

For military projects, the size of the full specifications would be two to three times larger than for civilian projects. If the older DoD 2167 standard is followed, then the designs are about three times larger than civilian norms. If the newer DoD 498 standard is followed, the design is roughly twice as large as civilian norms.

Using the default values for a systems software project of 1500 function points, the size of the design specifications would amount to perhaps 750 pages. The design team would consist of about six people, and

TABLE 15.2   Nominal Default Values for Systems Software Specifications and Design

Activity sequence	Third with prototypes; second without prototypes
Performed by	Systems analysts; development staff; architects
Predecessor activities	Requirements and prototypes
Overlap	75% with requirements and with prototypes
Concurrent activities	Reverse engineering for enhancement projects
Successor activities	Coding
Initial size	0.50 pages per function point
Initial size (UML)	0.50 pages per function point
Graphics	0.25 illustrations per function point
Reuse	35% from prior or similar projects
Assignment scope	250 function points
Production rate	125 function points per staff month
Production rate	1.06 work hours per function point
Schedule months	Function points raised to the 0.25 power
Rate of creep or change	2% per month for 6 months; then 1% per month
Defect potential	1.25 defects per function point
Defect potential (UML)	0.25 defects per function point
Defect removal	90%
Delivered defects	0.125 defects per function point
Delivered defects (UML)	0.025
High-severity defects	15% of delivered defects
Bad fix probability	5% of design fixes may yield new errors

the effort would amount to about 30 staff months. The schedule for the design would amount to roughly five calendar months.

Alarmingly, the design will contain about 1875 bugs or defects, and around 5 percent of these, or 94 of them, will be high-severity bugs that can have very serious consequences if they are not removed.

Assuming a 90 percent defect-removal efficiency, the number of residual design errors at the time of deployment will be about 190, and perhaps 10 of them will be quite serious. Design defects are often pervasive and require extensive changes, unlike coding defects, which are typically localized and concise.

Table 15.3 illustrates some of the nominal or default estimating variations associated with a number of widely utilized software design methodologies. Table 15.3 is merely a rough approximation of samples of various design methodologies. Actual cost estimates would require further adjustment based on such factors as the experience of the design team, the use or absence of design automation, and the rate at which requirements change during the design phase. Table 15.3 is in alphabetical order by the name of the design method.

As can easily be seen, estimating software specifications and design requires knowledge of the specific kinds of design methods that are going to be utilized.

TABLE 15.3   Estimating Assumptions for Software Design Methods

Design method	Size, pages per FP	Graphics content, %	Defect potential per FP	Defect-removal efficiency, %	Residual defects deployed
Structured design	1.25	30.00	1.20	85.00	0.18
Booch	1.50	50.00	1.35	80.00	0.27
Constantine	1.20	45.00	1.25	87.00	0.16
DoD 2167	2.75	25.00	1.10	90.00	0.11
Gane and Sarson	1.20	45.00	1.25	80.00	0.25
HIPO	1.15	60.00	1.30	75.00	0.33
Information engineering	1.25	45.00	1.15	85.00	0.17
Merise	1.50	40.00	1.15	85.00	0.17
RAD	0.35	60.00	1.75	70.00	0.53
Agile	0.25	65.00	1.30	70.00	0.39
Extreme (XP)	0.25	65.00	1.20	85.00	0.18
Rumbaugh	1.50	50.00	1.35	80.00	0.27
SADT	1.25	50.00	1.10	90.00	0.11
Shlaer-Mellor	1.50	50.00	1.35	80.00	0.27
UML	2.00	50.00	1.15	80.00	0.23
Warnier-Orr	1.20	60.00	1.00	90.00	0.10
Yourdon	1.20	35.00	1.25	87.00	0.16
Average	1.25	48.53	1.25	82.29	0.23

Positive Design Adjustment Factors

Software projects have been designed and developed continuously for more than 50 years. This means that quite a few applications circa 2007 are actually third- or fourth-generation applications whose "grandparents," so to speak, were originally conceived for such computers as the IBM 650 or IBM 1401, more than 35 years ago.

As a result, comparatively few applications are truly new in the sense that they represent novel uses of computers that have never been seen before. Because so many new applications are basically replacements of prior applications, the topic of reusable design material is now quite common. Among SPR's clients in 2007, more than two-thirds of the software design projects consisted of either:

- Designing modern replacements for aging legacy software
- Designing new features and enhancements to existing applications
- Designing customized features for such packages as ERP or databases

Unfortunately, the original specifications are seldom useful as they stand, but the existence of the aging software itself provides at least a starting point. Also, the usage of such tools as reverse engineering and reengineering tools also facilitates capturing some of the original design assumptions, which may not even exist in paper form any more.

The general impact of reusable material from previous projects is to streamline and truncate the analytical portion of the design process, and also to reduce the overall bulk of written specifications that need to be created. Table 15.4 shows a rough approximation of software design from 1960 forward at ten-year intervals for a hypothetical 1000–function point billing application.

By the time an enterprise is on its fifth or sixth generation of billing software, the accumulated knowledge of what needs to be done is quite extensive, and this tends to shrink the size of the paper specifications.

TABLE 15.4   Evolution of Software Design Reuse at Ten-Year Intervals

Year	Application generation	Size, FP	Size of new design, pages	Percent of reusable materials
1960	First	1000	600	0
1970	Second	1000	600	10
1980	Third	1000	500	25
1990	Fourth	1000	350	60
2000	Fifth	1000	300	65
2010	Sixth	1000	250	75

Staff and client experience with similar applications is a major benefit for software design work, and can have an impact of 15 percent or more.

Software design methodologies also have an impact, although this impact can swing between positive and negative directions.

For information systems, design methods that deal with data flow, such as the Warnier-Orr and Jackson design methods, have a positive impact, as do several of the variants of IE.

For systems, embedded, and real-time software, design methods that deal with control flow and state changes, such as finite-state design the UML and Petri nets, have a beneficial impact.

As this book is being written, design patterns and frameworks are beginning to achieve publicity in the software press, while the topic of component-based development is now a standard topic. After many years of false starts, it appears that software reuse is finally beginning to move from a research topic to a day-to-day development approach.

Negative Design Adjustment Factors

For large systems, one of the major negative factors is the failure to utilize formal design methods. Surprisingly, exactly which formal design method is comparatively unimportant, but a total lack of rigor exerts a significant downward trend in design completion coupled with an upward trend in serious design defects.

Perhaps the most significant factor of all is failure to utilize formal design inspections, or at least some form of design review. Design defects are both plentiful and serious, and are highly resistant to later discovery via testing.

Other negative influences on the software design process include the following:

- Using natural language as the primary medium of expressing design

- Using graphical design approaches without automated tools

- Failure to place specifications under formal configuration control

- Failure to utilize formal design inspections

- Substituting prototypes for specifications

- The very steep learning curve for OO design methods such as the UML

As a prime example, consider the implications of the year-2000 problem. Once this problem moved from requirements (where it originated) into design, it was no longer possible to find it via testing because test cases are derived from both requirements and design specifications. Hence, major errors in the design such as the classic Y2K issue were *tested into* a project rather than being *tested out*.

Some of the factors that influence software specifications and design, either for good or for ill, include the following:

PROJECT ORGANIZATION STRUCTURE _____

1 Individual project.
2 Small team project (less than four staff members).
3 Conventional departments, with hierarchical organization.
4 Conventional departments, with matrix organization.
5 Ambiguous or uncertain organization.

DEVELOPMENT PERSONNEL APPLICATION EXPERIENCE _____

1 All are experts in the type of program being developed.
2 Majority are experts, but some are new hires or novices.
3 Even mixture of experts, new hires, and novices.
4 Majority are new hires or novices, with few experts.
5 All personnel are new to this kind of program.

DEVELOPMENT PERSONNEL ANALYSIS AND DESIGN EXPERIENCE _____

1 All are experts in analysis and design methods.
2 Majority are experts in analysis and design methods.
3 Even mixture of experts, new hires, and novices.
4 Majority are new hires or novices in analysis and design.
5 All personnel are inexperienced in analysis and design.

DEVELOPMENT PERSONNEL HARDWARE EXPERIENCE _____

1 All are experts in the hardware used for the project.
2 Majority are experts in the hardware used for the project.
3 Even mixture of experts, new hires, and novices.
4 Majority are new hires or novices in the hardware.
5 All personnel are new to the hardware for the project.

DESIGN REVIEW DEFECT-REMOVAL EXPERIENCE _____

1 All personnel are experienced in reviews/inspections.
2 Most personnel are experienced in reviews/inspections.
3 Even mixture of experienced and inexperienced personnel.
4 Most personnel are inexperienced in reviews/inspections.
5 All personnel are inexperienced in reviews/inspections.

USER PERSONNEL EXPERIENCE WITH APPLICATION TYPE _____

1 User expertise is not a major factor for the project.
2 All or a strong majority of users are experts.
3 Even mixture of experts, new hires, and novices.
4 Majority are new hires and novices, with few experts.
5 All personnel are new to this kind of program.

USER INVOLVEMENT DURING DESIGN REVIEWS _____

1 User involvement is not a major factor for the project.
2 Users are heavily involved during design reviews.
3 Users are somewhat involved during design reviews.
4 Users are seldom involved during design reviews.
5 Users are not involved during design reviews.

DESIGN AUTOMATION ENVIRONMENT _____

1 Design-to-code automation with reusable code library is applied.
2 Formal design methods and automated text/graphics support are applied.
3 Semiformal design with some text/graphics support is applied.
4 Semiformal design with text automation only is applied.
5 Informal design with no automation is applied.

TOOL INTEGRATION _____

1 Integration across all phases of life cycle is achieved.
2 Integration across multiple phases is achieved.
3 Integration between phases is achieved.
4 Integration within a phase is achieved.
5 No integration is achieved.

PROJECT DOCUMENTATION LIBRARY _____

1 Full project library with automated support is used.
2 Partial project library with automated support is used.
3 Minimal automated library for documentation is used.
4 Manual documentation control is used.
5 No formal library control for documentation is used.

DEVELOPMENT PLATFORM NOVELTY _____

1 All hardware is familiar and well understood by staff.
2 Most hardware is familiar and well understood by staff.
3 Mixture of familiar and new or unfamiliar hardware.
4 Most hardware is new or unfamiliar to staff.
5 Hardware is new or experimental or unfamiliar.

DEVELOPMENT HARDWARE STABILITY _____

1 Stable, single-vendor hardware with high compatibility is used.
2 Single-vendor hardware with moderate compatibility is used.
3 Mixed-vendor hardware with high mutual compatibility is used.
4 Mixed-vendor hardware with moderate compatibility is used.
5 Unstable, changing, or incompatible development hardware is used.

WORKSTATION ENVIRONMENT _____

1 Individual workstations networked with LAN and mainframe are used.
2 Individual workstations on LAN are used.
3 Individual workstations for all staff members are used.
4 Shared workstations (two employees per workstation) are used.
5 Shared workstations (more than two employees per workstation).

Here, too, projects with a majority of answers in the 1.0 to 2.5 range will end up with significantly better results than projects with a majority of answers in the 3.5 to 5.0 range.

Software specifications and design are critical aspects of software development projects, and, hence, critical to software cost-estimation methods, too. However, the variations and ranges associated with software specifications and design make this a particularly difficult estimating domain.

Also, the fact that neither the size nor the effort associated with most forms of specification and design can be measured using the traditional lines-of-code-metrics has led to a shortage of solid empirical data. Only studies using natural metrics (such as pages of text) or function point metrics have been published.

References

Ambler, S.: *Process Patterns—Building Large-Scale Systems Using Object Technology*, Cambridge University Press, New York, NY, SIGS Books, 1998.

Artow, J., and I. Neustadt: *UML and the Unified Process*, Addison-Wesley, Boston, Mass., 2000.

Beck, K.: *Extreme Programming Explained: Embrace Change*, Addison-Wesley, Boston, Mass., 1999.

Boehm, Barry: *Software Engineering Economics*, Prentice-Hall, Englewood Cliffs, N.J., 1981.

———: "A Spiral Model of Software Development and Enhancement," Proceedings of the Int. Workshop on Software Process and Software Environments, ACM Software Engineering Notes, Aug. 1986, pp. 22–42.

Booch, Grady: *Object Solutions: Managing the Object-Oriented Project*, Addison-Wesley, Reading, Mass., 1995.

———, Ivar Jacobsen, and James Rumbaugh: *The Unified Modeling Language User Guide, Second Edition*, Addison-Wesley, Boston, Mass 2005.

Cockburn, Alistair: *Agile Software Development*, Addison-Wesley, Boston, Mass., 2001.

Cohen, D., M. Lindvall, and P. Costa: "An Introduction to Agile Methods," *Advances in Computers*, Elsevier Science, New York, 2004, pp.1–66.

Cohn, Mike: *User Stories Applied: For Agile Software Development*, Addison-Wesley, Boston, Mass., 2004.

DeMarco, Tom: *Controlling Software Projects*, Yourdon Press, New York, 1982.

Dreger, Brian: *Function Point Analysis*, Prentice-Hall, Englewood Cliffs, N.J., 1989.

Enterprise Resource Planning (http://en.wikipedia.org/wiki/Enterprise_resource_planning).

Feature Driven Development (http://en.wikipedia.org/wiki/Feature_Driven_Development).

Gamma, Erich, Richard Helm, Ralph Johnson, and John Vlissides: *Design Patterns: Elements of Reusable Object Oriented Design*, Addison-Wesley, Boston Mass., 1995.

Garmus, David and David Herron: *Measuring the Software Process: A Practical Guide to Functional Measurement*, Prentice-Hall, Englewood Cliffs, N.J., 1995.

————: *Function Point Analysis*, Addison-Wesley Longman, Boston, Mass., 2001.

Jeffries, R. et al.: *Extreme Programming Installed*, Addison-Wesley, Boston, Mass., 2001.

Jones, Capers: *Assessment and Control of Software Risks*, Prentice-Hall, Englewood Cliffs, N.J., 1994.

————: *Patterns of Software System Failure and Success*, International Thomson Computer Press, Boston, Mass., 1995.

————: *Applied Software Measurement, Second Edition*, McGraw-Hill, New York, 1996.

————: *Software Quality—Analysis and Guidelines for Success*, International Thompson Computer Press, Boston, Mass., 1997.

————: "Sizing Up Software," *Scientific American*, New York, December 1998, Vol. 279, No. 6, pp 104-109.

————: *Software Assessments, Benchmarks, and Best Practices*, Addison-Wesley Longman, Boston, Mass., 2000.

Larman, Craig, and Victor Basili: "Iterative and Incremental Development—A Brief History," IEEE Computer Society, June 2003, pp 47-55.

Love, Tom: *Object Lessons*, SIGS Books, New York, 1993.

Pressman, Roger: *Software Engineering—A Practitioner's Approach, Sixth Edition*, McGraw-Hill, New York, 2005.

Putnam, Lawrence H.: *Measures for Excellence—Reliable Software on Time, Within Budget*, Yourdon Press/Prentice-Hall, Englewood Cliffs, N.J., 1992.

————, and Ware Myers: *Industrial Strength Software—Effective Management Using Measurement*, IEEE Computer Society Press, Washington, D.C., 1997.

Rapid Application Development (http://en.wikipedia.org/wiki/Rapid_application_development).

Rubin, Howard: *Software Benchmark Studies for 1997*, Howard Rubin Associates, Pound Ridge, N.Y., 1997.

Stapleton, J.: *DSDM—Dynamic System Development in Practice*, Addison-Wesley, Boston, Mass., 1997.

Stevens, Wayne: *Using Structured Design*, John Wiley & Sons, Chichester, U.K., 1981.

Symons, Charles R.: *Software Sizing and Estimating—Mk II FPA (Function Point Analysis)*, John Wiley & Sons, Chichester, U.K., 1991.

Chapter

16

Estimating Design Inspections

The defect-removal method of formal inspections was developed at IBM Kingston in the 1970s by Michael Fagan and his colleagues. The inspection process has more than 35 years of continuous data available and has proven to be one of the most effective and efficient defect-removal operations ever developed. As a general rule, formal inspections are about twice as effective in finding bugs as any known form of testing. Most forms of testing are less than 30 percent efficient in finding bugs, but formal inspections on average are more than 60 percent efficient and sometimes top 95 percent. As an additional benefit, inspections also raise testing efficiency levels and they serve as surprisingly effective defect prevention methods.

The phrase *defect-removal efficiency* refers to the percentage of latent errors actually detected. For example, if a formal inspection is 60 percent efficient, that implies that it found six out of ten errors that were actually present. Obviously, it is necessary to measure defects over a lengthy period to calibrate defect-removal efficiency rates.

Inspection Literature

There is an extensive literature on both design and code inspections, but much of the literature is devoted to how-to-do-it books, such as the excellent Handbook of Walkthroughs, Inspections, and Technical Reviews by Gerald Weinberg and Daniel Friedman (Dorset House, 1990) and the more recent treatment by Tom Gilb and D. Graham in *Software Inspections* (Addison-Wesley, 1993), although this book does deal with the defect-removal results of formal inspections.

There are few books that attempt to quantify the economics of inspections, such as Robert Dunn and Richard Ullman's *Quality Assurance for Computer Software* (McGraw-Hill, 1982) and the author's own more recent *Patterns of Software Systems Failure and Success* (International

Thomson Computer Press, 1995) and *Software Quality—Analysis and Guidelines for Success* (International Thomson Computer Press, 1997). Also, Larry Putnam has discussed inspections in an estimating context in *Industrial Software* (IEEE Computer Society Press, 1997), and Howard Rubin usually includes interesting data on inspections in his annual benchmark handbooks (Howard Rubin Associates, 1997).

Inspections continue to attract interest and research. One interesting recent book is *Peer Reviews in Software* by Karl Wiegers (Addison-Wesley, 2002). Another useful book is *High-Quality, Low-Cost Software Inspections* by Ron Radice (Paradoxican Publishing, 2002). Ron was a colleague of Michael Fagan at IBM Kingston when the first design and code inspections were being tried out. Thus, Ron has been an active participant in formal inspections for almost 35 years.

An even newer book that discusses not only inspections per se, but also their economic value and the measurement approaches for collecting inspection data is Stephen Kan's *Metrics and Models in Software Quality Engineering* (Addison-Wesley, 2003). This is the second edition of Kan's popular book.

Roger Pressman's book *Software Engineering—A Practitioner's Approach* (McGraw-Hill, 2005) also discusses various forms of defect removal. The sixth edition of this book includes new chapters on Agile development, extreme programming, and several other of the newer methods. It provides an excellent context for the role of quality in all of the major development approaches.

It should be noted that design inspections work perfectly well on every known kind of design and specification document. Formal inspections are a good fit for text-based specifications, for the unified modeling language (UML), Nassi-Shneiderman charts, user stories, and every other form of written specification.

Not every software cost-estimating tool can deal with the impact of inspections, although inspections have been included in some cost-estimating tools since SPQR/20 in 1985.

The initials SPQR stand for "software productivity, quality, and reliability" and "20" is the number of estimating parameters that can be adjusted with the model.

Because quality plays such a major role in software schedules and costs, and because formal inspections are a leading quality method, modern software cost-estimating tools deal explicitly with inspections and can predict the following data points:

- The number of defects in the application
- The defect-removal efficiency of formal inspections
- The bad-fix injection of defect repairs, which leads to new errors
- The number of latent defects still present at delivery of the software

- The severity levels of latent defects
- The post-release discovery rate of defects by users of the software
- The post-release maintenance costs to repair latent defects

In real life as well as with estimating tools, the presence of formal inspections makes the outcome of a project much easier to predict.

Inspection Process

The term *inspection* refers to a formal procedure in which a trained group of practitioners examine a software artifact, such as a specification, page by page in a planned fashion. Each inspection session is limited to a two-hour duration, and no more than two such sessions can be held in any business day. Prior to the inspection, each participant will have received the material to be inspected no less than a week prior to the start of the first inspection process.

It should be noted that informal reviews of another person's work, which often occurs with the pair-programming concept, is not the same as a formal inspection. Informal reviews are useful, of course, but their measured level of defect-removal efficiency is usually less than 50 percent. Incidentally, the defect efficiency of programmers in finding errors in their own work is only about 30 percent. Most testing steps are also only about 30 percent efficient. Formal inspections have the highest average defect-removal efficiency levels of any form of defect removal yet studied.

The participants in the inspection process normally include the following set, although there is some flexibility and doubling up, such as having one person perform two roles:

- The *producer* of the material being inspected
- A *moderator*, charged with keeping the inspection on track
- A *recorder*, charged with keeping track of problems identified
- A *reader*, charged with paraphrasing each section
- One or more *reviewers*, charged with performing the inspection
- One or more *observers*, normally novices there to learn how inspections operate

In really large organizations that use inspections, such as IBM or AT&T, there are other specialized personnel associated with the inspection process, too:

- A *coordinator*, charged with scheduling inspections and reserving rooms
- One or more *trainers*, charged with instructing novices in the inspection protocols

The minimum number of participants needed to actually perform a formal inspection is three: the producer, the moderator, and the recorder. In this minimum complement, the moderator and recorder are, of course, also serving as reviewers.

For an average inspection held within a major corporation on specifications associated with large systems, the normal complement is five personnel: the producer, the moderator, the recorder, and two reviewers.

The maximum number of participants in formal inspections is limited to no more than eight. This is a practical limitation caused by the fact that large meetings tend to be discursive and inefficient, coupled with the fact that rooms big enough to hold more than eight people are not readily available in many corporations.

The most difficult role to fill when performing inspections is that of the moderator, because the moderator must deal with rather delicate human relationship issues. It is sometimes stressful to have other individuals performing a close scrutiny of one's work, and from time to time producers challenge the validity of whether or not a particular finding is really an error or defect or not. The moderator has to keep such disagreements from growing into full-scale disputes.

The reviewers also must be selected carefully, since they have to understand the work being inspected. For large projects, the reviewers are normally selected from the project team for the practical reason that other team members have the best prospect of being able to contribute meaningful observations.

From an estimating standpoint, there is a substantial body of empirical data available on both inspection effort and inspection effectiveness. However, in spite of the available data, inspections are somewhat tricky and complex to estimate. The reason for the difficulty is because inspections are intermittent activities that occur in a series of discrete two-hour packets that may occur at almost random intervals due to the need to juggle the schedules of the participants. The nominal default values for design inspections are the parameters shown in Table 16.1.

Estimating inspections often use natural metrics, such as pages. Typical rules of thumb using pages of specifications might be the following:

Preparation	10 to 15 pages per hour
Inspection sessions	5 to 10 pages per hour
Preparation	5 to 10 use cases per hour
Inspection session	3 to 10 use cases per hour

Since the purpose of design inspections is finding and fixing errors, the number and severity level of design problems exert a major influence on the timing and costs of the inspection process.

TABLE 16.1   Nominal Default Values for Design Inspections

Activity sequence	Fourth
Performed by	Developers; quality assurance; testing staff; observers
Predecessor activities	Requirements, prototypes, design, and specification
Overlap	75% with specification and design
Concurrent activities	Both design and code
Successor activities	Coding
Initial size	1.50 pages per function point
Graphics	0.25 illustrations per function point
Reuse	15% from prior or similar projects
Assignment scope	200 function points
Assignment scope	300 specification pages
Production rate	225 function points per staff month
Production rate	0.59 work hours per function point
Production rate	15 pages inspected per 2-hour session
Schedule months	2-hour packets with no more than 2 per day
Rate of creep or change	None
Defect potential	1.25 design defects per function point
Defect removal	65% average removal efficiency (peak is 95%)
Delivered defects	Design defects −65% = 0.44 defects per function point
High-severity defects	10% of delivered defects
Bad fix probability	3% of design inspection fixes may yield new errors

On average, software designs and specifications contain about 1.25 errors or defects per function point, which for a project of 1000 function points can amount to about 1250 design bugs. Of these, about 15 percent, or almost 200, will be serious.

Design inspections average about 65 percent defect-removal efficiency overall, but against serious design defects the efficiency of formal design inspections tops 95 percent. Therefore, after a series of formal design inspections on this 1000–function point example, only about ten serious design issues may remain under best-case conditions.

By contrast, most forms of testing are less than 30 percent efficient in finding bugs, and are even less efficient in finding design defects. If design errors stay in the design, there is a strong chance that testing will not find them at all, because test cases are constructed using the design specifications as the basis. The efficiency of testing in finding design errors is less than 10 percent, which is a very low value indeed.

(Recall that for many years no test cases were constructed that could find the two-digit year-2000 problem, because the two-digit form of date representation originated as a requirement and then passed into design, so testing had a 0 percent efficiency against this problem.)

Inspections are fairly expensive and time-consuming activities. Having from three to six participants moving through a specification at a rate of less than 10 pages per hour amounts to only about 1.25 pages per staff hour. If the specification being reviewed is large, say 500 pages, then the total costs can amount to 400 staff hours.

Value of Inspections

Surprisingly, formal inspections have proven both to benefit overall project costs and to shorten project schedules. Indeed, the inventor of the inspection process, Michael Fagan, received an IBM outstanding contribution award for determining that inspections shorten schedules as well as improve quality when applied to major systems software projects.

Assume you have a software project of 1000 function points in size and that the specifications are 500 pages in size. Now assume that preparation and inspection of these specifications requires 500 staff hours, but finds 250 defects, of which 50 are serious. The testing for this project will probably take about 500 staff hours, too.

Now assume that the same 1000–function point project is developed without using design inspections. The 250 design defects—including the 50 serious defects—are not discovered before development, and they find their way into the code. Under this second scenario, when testing occurs it will probably take 2000 staff hours, because serious design flaws are difficult to eliminate during the testing stage.

Thus, the 500 staff hours invested in formal design inspections trigger a savings of 1500 staff hours during testing, and shorten the overall project schedule for delivery. These claims are solidly based on empirical observations.

There is a simple experiment that anyone can perform to validate the schedule and cost assumptions associated with formal design and code inspections:

1. Record the effort, schedule, costs, and number of bug reports for a trial application, such as a 100–function point enhancement that uses both inspections and testing.

2. Record the effort, schedule, costs, and number of bug reports for a similar trial application that does not use inspections, but uses only testing.

Although results will vary, the inspection trials will usually end up with about 15 percent shorter schedules, 20 percent less effort, and perhaps 200 percent more bugs eliminated prior to release of the application. The front end of the inspection trials will take longer and cost more, but when testing begins it won't even be a contest: The inspected portions will usually exit testing in between one-third and one-fourth of the elapsed time, and with less than one-third of the effort devoted to bug repairs, as the uninspected portions.

Although formal design and code inspections originated more than 35 years ago, they still are the top-ranked methodologies in terms of defect-removal efficiency. Further, inspections have a synergistic relationship with other forms of defect removal, such as testing, and also are quite successful as defect-prevention methods.

Recent work on software inspections by Tom Gilb, Ron Radice, Karl Wiegers, and other colleagues continues to support the early finding that the human mind remains the tool of choice for finding and eliminating complex problems that originate in requirements, design, and other non-code deliverables. Indeed, for finding the deeper problems in source code, formal code inspections still outrank testing in defect-removal efficiency.

The most effective usage of formal inspections among SPR's clients occurs among large corporations that produce systems software, such as computer manufacturers, telecommunication system manufacturers, aerospace equipment manufacturers, and the like. These companies have learned that if software is going to control complex physical devices it has to have state-of-the-art quality levels, and only inspections can achieve the necessary quality.

Formal inspections have not yet played a major role in the Agile methodologies. Extreme programming is interested in quality and is good in testing, but has not adopted formal inspections. The daily Scrum sessions that identify and discuss problems are useful, but they are not as efficient as formal inspections.

A combination of formal inspections, formal testing by test specialists, and a formal (and active) quality-assurance group are the methods that are most often associated with projects achieving a cumulative defect-removal efficiency higher than 99 percent.

Formal inspections are manual activities in which three to eight colleagues go over design specifications page by page, using a formal protocol. In order to term this activity an *inspection*, certain criteria must be met, including but not limited to the following:

- There must be adequate preparation time before each session.
- Effort expended during preparation and during the inspections is recorded.
- Records must be kept of the defects discovered.
- Defect data should not be used for appraisals or punitive purposes.

The original concept of inspections was based on actual meetings with live participants. The advent of effective online communications and tools for supporting remote inspections, now means that inspections can be performed electronically, which saves on travel costs for teams that are geographically dispersed.

Any software deliverable can be subject to a formal inspection, and the following deliverables have now developed enough empirical data to indicate that the inspection process is generally beneficial:

- Architecture inspections
- Requirements inspections
- Design inspections
- Database design inspections
- Quality Function Deployment (QFD) diagrams
- Code inspections
- Test plan inspections
- Test case inspections
- User documentation inspections
- Web page inspections

For every software artifact where formal inspections are used, they range from just under 60 percent to more than 90 percent in defect-removal efficiency and have an average efficiency level of roughly 65 percent. Overall, this is the best defect-removal efficiency level of any known form of error elimination.

Further, thanks to the flexibility of the human mind and its ability to handle inductive logic as well as deductive logic, inspections are also the most versatile form of defect removal and can be applied to essentially any software artifact. Indeed, inspections have even been applied recursively to themselves, in order to fine-tune the inspection process and eliminate bottlenecks and obstacles.

It is sometimes asked why everyone doesn't use inspections if they are so good. The answer to this question reveals a basic weakness of the software industry. Inspections have been in the public domain for more than 35 years. Therefore, except for a few training companies, no company tries to *sell* inspections, while there are many vendors selling testing tools. If you want to use inspections, you have to seek them out and adopt them.

Most software development organizations don't actually do research or collect data on effective tools and technologies. They make their technology decisions, to a large degree, by listening to tool and methodology vendors and adopting those represented by the most persuasive sales personnel. Since there is comparatively little money to be made in selling inspections, sales personnel tend to concentrate on things like testing tools, where the commissions are greater.

It is even easier if the sales personnel make the tool or method sound like a "silver bullet" that will give miraculous results immediately upon deployment with little or no training, preparation, or additional effort. Since inspections are not sold by tool vendors and do require training and effort, they are not a glamorous technology. Hence, many software organizations don't even know about inspections and have no idea of their versatility and effectiveness.

The companies that are most likely to use inspections are those that for historical or business reasons have some kind of research capability that looks for *best practices* and tries to adopt them.

It is a telling point that all of the top-gun quality software houses, and even industries, in the United States tend to utilize pretest inspections. For example, formal inspections are very common among computer manufacturers, telecommunication systems manufacturers, aerospace equipment manufacturers, defense systems manufacturers, medical instrument manufacturers, and systems software and operating systems developers. All of these need high-quality software to market their main products, and inspections top the list of effective defect-removal methods.

One of the most effective ways of illustrating the effectiveness of formal inspections is to produce graphs that connect the points where software defects are *discovered* with the points in software development where the defects *originate*.

Whenever there is an acute angle in the line connecting a defect's discovery and origin points, there is a serious problem with software quality control, because the gap between making an error and finding it can amount to many months.

The goal of defect removal is to have the angle connecting defect origins and discoveries approach 90 degrees. Although a 90-degree angle is unlikely, formal inspections can at least bring the angle up from perhaps 30 degrees to more than 60 degrees (see Figures 16.1 and 16.2).

As can easily be seen in Figure 16.1, software projects that do not utilize formal inspections enter a *zone of chaos* during the test cycle. This is because deep problems with requirements and specifications suddenly emerge that require extensive and expensive repair and rework.

Note in Figure 16.2 how the lines connecting the discovery points of defects with their origins have obtuse angles. Even more important, note how defects that originate within a phase tend to be eliminated during that phase, and do not pass on to downstream activities.

Normal Defect Origin/Discovery Gaps

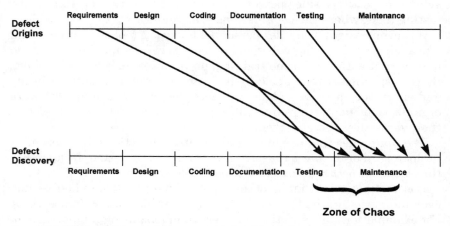

Figure 16.1   Defect origins and discovery points without usage of formal inspections.

One of the greatest contributions of formal inspections is that they tend to find errors closer to their original source than testing. Further, inspections also find errors that testing cannot easily discover, such as requirements defects. Overall, inspections have a solid record of success.

Defect Origins/Discovery With Inspections

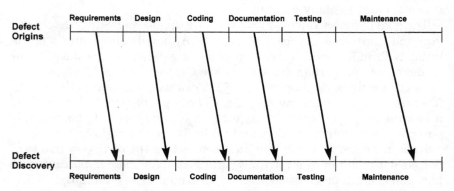

Figure 16.2   Defect origins and discovery points with usage of formal inspections.

Some of the adjustment factors for dealing with software design inspections include the following set:

PROJECT GOALS _____

1 Find the standard estimate of schedule, staff, and quality.
2 Find the shortest development schedule with extra staff.
3 Find the lowest effort with reduced staff.
4 Find the highest quality with normal staff.
5 Find the highest quality with shortest schedule.
6 Find the highest quality with least effort.

PROBLEM COMPLEXITY _____

1 Simple algorithms and simple calculations.
2 Majority are simple algorithms and calculations.
3 Algorithms and calculations are of average complexity.
4 Some difficult or complex calculations.
5 Many difficult and complex calculations.

DATA COMPLEXITY _____

1 Simple data, few variables, and little complexity.
2 Several data elements, but simple data relationships.
3 Multiple files, switches, and data interactions.
4 Complex data elements and complex data interactions.
5 Very complex data elements and data interactions.

DEVELOPMENT PERSONNEL APPLICATION
EXPERIENCE _____

1 All are experts in the type of program being developed.
2 Majority are experts, but some are new hires or novices.
3 Even mixture of experts, new hires, and novices.
4 Majority are new hires or novices, with few experts.
5 All personnel are new to this kind of program.

DEVELOPMENT PERSONNEL ANALYSIS AND DESIGN
EXPERIENCE _____

1 All are experts in analysis and design methods.
2 Majority are experts in analysis and design methods.
3 Even mixture of experts, new hires, and novices.
4 Majority are new hires or novices in analysis and design.
5 All personnel are inexperienced in analysis and design.

PRETEST DEFECT-REMOVAL EXPERIENCE   _____

1 All personnel are experienced in reviews/inspections.
2 Most personnel are experienced in reviews/inspections.
3 Even mixture of experienced and inexperienced personnel.
4 Most personnel are inexperienced in reviews/inspections.
5 All personnel are inexperienced in reviews/inspections.

USER PERSONNEL EXPERIENCE WITH SOFTWARE
PROJECTS   _____

1 User experience with software is not a key factor.
2 All or a majority of users have software experience.
3 Even mixture of experts and inexperienced users.
4 Majority of users have no prior software experience.
5 All personnel have no prior software experience.

USER PERSONNEL EXPERIENCE WITH APPLICATION
TYPE   _____

1 User expertise is not a major factor for the project.
2 All or a strong majority of users are experts.
3 Even mixture of experts, new hires, and novices.
4 Majority are new hires and novices, with few experts.
5 All personnel are new to this kind of program.

USER INVOLVEMENT DURING REQUIREMENTS   _____

1 User involvement is not a major factor for this project.
2 Users are heavily involved during requirements.
3 Users are somewhat involved during requirements.
4 Users are seldom involved during requirements.
5 Users are not involved during requirements.

USER INVOLVEMENT DURING DESIGN REVIEWS   _____

1 User involvement is not a major factor for the project.
2 Users are heavily involved during design reviews.
3 Users are somewhat involved during design reviews.
4 Users are seldom involved during design reviews.
5 Users are not involved during design reviews.

Both in real life and in software cost estimating, the combination of having quality as a key project goal, keeping complexity low, and having experienced users and experienced team members pays off in lower costs, quicker schedules, and higher quality than result through the opposite situations.

Formal design and code inspections are fairly major discriminators between best-in-class organizations and the rest of the software industry. The really good groups tend to use inspections because nothing else can find so many bugs or errors, nor find so many deep and subtle problems, as the human mind.

References

Dunn, Robert, and Richard Ullman: *Quality Assurance for Computer Software*, McGraw-Hill, New York, 1982.

Fagan, M. E.: "Design and Code Inspections to Reduce Errors in Program Development," *IBM Systems Journal*, 12(3):219–248 (1976).

Friedman, Daniel P., and Gerald M. Weinberg: *Handbook of Walkthroughs, Inspections, and Technical Reviews*, Dorset House Press, New York, 1990.

Gilb, Tom, and D. Graham: *Software Inspections*, Addison-Wesley, Reading, Mass., 1993.

Jones, Capers: *Assessment and Control of Software Risks*, Prentice-Hall, Englewood Cliffs, N.J., 1994.

———: *Patterns of Software System Failure and Success*, International Thomson Computer Press, Boston, Mass., 1995.

———: *Software Quality—Analysis and Guidelines for Success*, International Thomson Computer Press, Boston, Mass., 1997.

———: *Software Assessments, Benchmarks, and Best Practices*, Addison-Wesley Longman, Boston, Mass., 2000.

———: *Conflict and Litigation Between Software Clients and Developers*, Software Productivity Research, Burlington, Mass., 2003.

Kan, Stephen H.: *Metrics and Models in Software Quality Engineering, Second Edition*, Addison-Wesley Longman, Boston, Mass., 2003.

Larman, Craig, and Victor Basili: "Iterative and Incremental Development—A Brief History," IEEE Computer Society, June 2003, pp. 47–55.

Mills, H., M. Dyer, and R. Linger: "Cleanroom Software Engineering," *IEEE Software*, 4, 5 (Sept. 1987), pp. 19–25.

Pressman, Roger: *Software Engineering—A Practitioner's Approach, Sixth Edition*, McGraw-Hill, New York, 2005.

Putnam, Lawrence H.: *Measures for Excellence—Reliable Software on Time, Within Budget*, Yourdon Press/Prentice-Hall, Englewood Cliffs, N.J., 1992.

———, and Ware Myers: *Industrial Strength Software—Effective Management Using Measurement*, IEEE Computer Society Press, Washington, D.C., 1997.

Quality Function Deployment (http://en.wikipedia.org/wiki/Quality_function_deployment).

Radice, Ronald A.: *High-Quality Low-Cost Software Inspections*, Paradoxican Publishing, Andover, Mass., 2002.

Rubin, Howard: Software Benchmark Studies for 1997, Howard Rubin Associates, Pound Ridge, N.Y., 1997.

Weinberg, Dr. Gerald and Friedman, Daniel; Handbook of Walkthroughs, Inspections, and Technical Reviews; Dorset House, New York, NY, 1990.

Wiegers, Karl E.: *Peer Reviews in Software—A Practical Guide*, Addison-Wesley, Boston, Mass., 2002.

Estimating Programming
or Coding

Programming or coding presents an interesting challenge to software cost estimators. As this edition is being written in 2007, the total number of known programming languages and dialects in the software industry exceeds 600. There are probably another 100 or so proprietary languages created for use in specific companies but unknown outside of them.

These languages range in power from very low-level assembly languages to very high level languages such as APL and Smalltalk. There are also "quasi-languages" that allow certain kinds of programming to be performed via things like buttons and pull-down menus. Visual Basic is an example of such a hybrid language that mixes up conventional code statements with a variety of shortcuts using menus and buttons rather than coded statements.

For more than half of the 600 known programming languages, there are no published rules for counting lines of code in the form of logical statements. While physical lines can be counted for any language, the actual work of programming is more closely related to logical statements than it is to physical lines.

Adding to the plethora of languages, many large software applications are written in more than one language. For example, the combination of COBOL and SQL is very common. Many newer applications use a combination of Java and HTML. The author has noted some applications that contain as many as 12 different programming languages at the same time.

In addition, there may be reused or inherited code that can be extracted from copy books, class libraries, or even purchases in the form of "software-integrated circuits" from commercial vendors.

From this short summary of issues, it is easy to see that accurate estimation of programming is more challenging than might be thought. A very typical situation that faces cost estimators almost every day is trying to size a large application that is to be written in several programming languages and will also include an unknown volume of reused code. It is not impossible to estimate or measure the volume of code in such a situation, but it is not a trivial or easy task.

All of these variations in programming languages explain why function point metrics were developed. In order to study the economics of software engineering, there was a need for a stable metric that would stay constant no matter how many different programming languages were being used in a specific application.

For small to medium software projects, estimating the coding effort is the oldest and most important single aspect of cost estimation. Surprisingly for such a critical activity, there is a shortage of solid empirical data on this key task.

There is no shortage of information about the specifics of various programming languages. Most common languages have at least two books in print that discuss syntax and programming styles. Some popular languages, such as Visual Basic, Java, Smalltalk, C, and COBOL, have more than 25 books in print. The total number of books in print that deal with programming in various languages tops 2000 titles, and several new books appear every month.

What is more surprising than the large number of books is the fact that brand-new programming languages continue to appear at frequent intervals. The author and his colleagues at Software Productivity Research monitor the appearance of new programming languages so they can be added to SPR's master list of programming languages. At least one new programming language, or a new dialect, has appeared every month for the past 20 years, and some months more than one new language shows up.

The frequent appearance of new programming languages presents a continuous challenge to the developers of software estimating tools, because when a new language first appears there is usually no available data on the use of the language, so evaluating its impact in an estimating context is quite difficult.

Even though there are hundreds of programming languages, millions of programmers, and millions of software applications, only a few controlled studies have been performed. Also, many of the benchmarking comparisons do not reach the level of specific activities, such as coding, but include the whole universe of software activities, such as requirements, design, coding, testing, and so forth.

When controlled studies of programming are performed, they usually reveal that programmers can code at more or less the same rates in almost every language they are familiar with, but they vary widely in individual capabilities. However, most controlled studies are based on small and simple examples that can be completed in a matter of hours at most.

There are annual contests of programming speed where various contestants utilize different languages to code the same trial application. These contests are interesting, but the trial examples are not necessarily representative of how a language will perform in real-life situations.

In real-life situations where programmers are working on very large applications that may have creeping requirements, and where they need to interact with many other programmers who are all working on the same system, production rates are much lower than for small projects or projects where one person can handle the entire programming assignment.

The nominal default values for estimating coding or programming include those shown in Table 17.1.

Although the set of default values given in Table 17.1 are useful, the range of programming performance is very wide and can range to more than 100 percent greater, or more than 75 percent worse, than the starting default values. Note that Table 17.1 is based on the assumption of individual programmers. If you are using one of the Agile approaches that features pair-programming, or assigning two programmers to the

TABLE 17.1 Nominal Default Values for Programming or Coding

Activity sequence	Fifth
Performed by	Development staff
Predecessor activities	Prototypes, design, and specification
Overlap	75% with design and specification
Concurrent activities	Design and unit testing
Successor activities	Function testing; integration testing
Reuse	15% from prior or similar projects
Assignment scope	175 function points
Assignment scope	17,500 logical source code statements
Production rate	25 function points per staff month
Production rate	5.28 work hours per function point
Production rate	2,500 source code statements per month
Production rate	20 source code statements per work hour
Schedule months	Application code size divided by production rate
Rate of creep or change	Identical to requirements (about 2% per month)
Defect potential	1.75 coding defects per function point
Defect potential	17.5 coding bugs per KLOC
Defect removal	90% average removal efficiency
Delivered defects	0.175 coding defects per function point
Delivered defects	0.175 defects per KLOC
High severity defects	15% of delivered defects
Bad fix probability	7% of coding defect fixes may yield new errors

same code segments, Table 17.1 would need adjustment. The assignment scope would be only 50 percent of the value shown in the table. Production rate would be roughly the same.

From the author's analysis and benchmarks at the level of specific activities, the major factors that influence coding rates are the 12 listed in Table 17.2, in descending order of overall significance.

Adding to the difficulty of estimating programming performance, the ranking of factors that influence programming in a positive or beneficial direction is not exactly the same as the ranking of factors that influence programming in a negative or harmful direction.

Tables 17.3 and 17.4 illustrate the ranges of *maximum* impact in both positive and negative directions. The first ranking is sorted in descending order of the factors that can influence programming productivity in a positive direction, with the availability of reusable code now moving above team experience in terms of maximum positive value. (In Dr. Barry Boehm's previous study of influential factors, reported in his 1981 book *Software Engineering Economics*, team experience was the dominant factor. However, software reuse was not a well-known technology in 1981.)

By contrast, Table 17.4 gives the same factors, but ranks them in terms of the maximum negative impacts that can degrade software productivity, with bugs and errors topping the list, followed fairly closely by the impact of creeping user requirements.

In any real-life software project, the positive and negative factors will be present simultaneously, and because the overall impact in both positive and negative directions is roughly equivalent, the net result often approximates average values for programming productivity.

However, for projects where either positive factors or negative factors are dominant, the net results can be either much better than average values or much worse than average values, depending upon which sets of factors predominate.

TABLE 17.2   Twelve Factors That Influence Programming Productivity

1. The availability of reusable code
2. The experience of the programming team
3. The number of bugs or errors introduced
4. The amount of unpaid overtime applied
5. The rate at which requirements change or creep during coding
6. The structure or complexity of the application
7. The number of unplanned workday interruptions
8. The size of the application
9. The size and noise level of the programming office space
10. The features of the programming languages used
11. The power of the programming tools available
12. Schedule pressure applied to the team

TABLE 17.3 **Maximum Positive Impacts of 12 Programming Factors**
(Ranked in terms of maximum positive impact)

Factor	Maximum negative impact, %	Maximum positive impact, %
Reusable code	–50	300
Team experience	–115	150
Bugs or errors	–175	100
Unpaid overtime	–30	75
Requirements creep	–125	50
Unplanned interruptions	–100	40
Code complexity	–65	35
Size of the application	–50	35
Programming office space	–55	25
Programming tools	–40	30
Programming languages	–30	25
Schedule pressure	–50	20
Total	–885	885

The fact that both positive and negative factors may be present in unequal amounts explains why it is necessary to be totally honest when using software cost-estimating tools. If you are not truthful and indicate to the estimating tool that your team is more experienced or better equipped than they really are, then the estimating tool will generate a much better than average cost estimate but your team may not be better than average in real life.

It is obvious that to achieve really good programming results, enterprises should strive to maximize the positive influential factors and minimize the negative influential factors.

TABLE 17.4   **Maximum Negative Impacts of 12 Programming Factors**
(Ranked in terms of maximum negative impact)

Factor	Maximum negative impact, %	Maximum positive impact, %
Bugs or errors	–175	100
Requirements creep	–125	50
Team experience	–115	150
Unplanned interruptions	–100	40
Code complexity	–65	35
Programming office space	–55	25
Reusable code	–50	300
Size of the application	–50	35
Schedule pressure	–50	20
Programming tools	–40	30
Unpaid overtime	–30	75
Programming language(s)	–30	25
Total	–885	885

As might be expected, experienced programmers can outperform novices by several hundred percent. However, even very experienced programmers have to deal with changing requirements, schedule pressures, and the fact that bugs or errors are very easy to make but often are hard to eliminate.

Table 17.5 summarizes an overall picture of the coding activity from 1 source code statement through major systems of 100 million source code statements in order to illustrate some of the trends associated with increasing application sizes.

Recall that the term *assignment scope* (A scope) refers to the amount of work assigned to one person.

The term *production rate* (P rate) refers to the amount of work that one person can do in a standard time period, such as a work month.

Below about 15,000 source code statements, the entire programming task is usually assigned to one person (unless your project uses the pair-programming concept). The table assumes that the programmer will work full-time, but below about 1000 source code statements programmers often work part-time on any single project, because they are dividing their time among several small projects.

Above 15,000 source code statements, the coding activity usually involves multiple programmers, although SPR's data contains examples of projects of up to 75,000 source code statements carried out by only one programmer. When multiple programmers are involved, problems begin to occur with the interfaces between the work of separate programmers.

For the larger application sizes in excess of 100,000 source code statements, a number of factors tend to come into play simultaneously. First, because these large systems are often complicated and involve fairly large teams, defect rates begin to escalate (as do creeping requirements).

When defect rates go up, the amount of time that programmers spend debugging must also increase, which, in turn, means that coding productivity must decline as more and more time goes to finding and fixing

TABLE 17.5   General Programming Productivity and Defect Rates
(Size data expressed in logical source code statements)

Size, LOC	A scope, LOC	P rate, LOC	Staff	Effort months	Schedule months	Coding defects	Defect removal	Delivered defects
1	1	2,500	1	0.0004	0.0004	0	99	0
10	10	2,500	1	0.0040	0.0040	0	99	0
100	100	2,500	1	0.0400	0.0400	1	99	0
1,000	1,000	2,250	1	0.4444	0.4444	10	98	0
10,000	10,000	2,000	1	5.0000	5.0000	125	96	5
100,000	20,000	1,750	5	57.1429	11.4286	1,500	95	75
1,000,000	25,000	1,500	40	666.6667	16.6667	17,500	94	1,050
10,000,000	30,000	1,200	333	8,333.3333	25.0000	200,000	92	16,000
100,000,000	35,000	1,000	2,857	100,000.0000	35.0000	2,500,000	90	250,000

bugs and, in particular, to interface problems. Not only do defect levels rise, but it becomes harder to remove defects, so removal efficiency suffers. Also, programmers must devote a higher percentage of their time to meetings with other programmers and to making revisions in response to changing requirements.

Because of client and executive demands for fairly short coding schedules, organizations tend to raise the numbers of programmers assigned to a project, which, in turn, increases the complexity and defect levels associated with interfaces.

However, for really large systems above 1 million source code statements, a new problem exists: Keeping the programming assignment scope low (<15,000 source code statements) is not usually possible because literally thousands of programmers would be needed on the application. Therefore, at the high end of the size spectrum, the programming assignment scopes begin to stretch out because of the fact that most organizations do not employ enough programmers to have any other choice!

Even if the enterprise had unlimited resources and could assign 10,000 programmers to a large system, that would not necessarily lead to satisfactory results. Such large teams would probably have to devote half of the workday to meetings and communication, and perhaps another quarter to finding and fixing bugs or dealing with changing requirements.

As can be seen, the needs of really large systems tend to be conflicting, and it is hard to reach an optimal point. Wealthy corporations, such as Microsoft, can approach optimization because of their ability to attract and keep only top-gun programming personnel. This allows Microsoft to have very large assignment scopes (sometimes in excess of 50,000 source code statements) and, hence, keep team sizes within reasonable bounds. However, for applications the size of Windows XP(in the range of 12 million source code statements) even Microsoft has trouble with schedules and with quality levels.

Coding is the only software development activity for which the older lines-of-code metrics can be used without undue error and distortion. Table 17.5 uses *logical source code statements* as the basis of the productivity data. Logical statements correlate more closely to the work of programming than do physical lines. Also, logical statements are more stable than the use of *physical lines of code* because of the distressing tendency of physical code counts to include blank lines, comments, and dead code.

The same information can also be expressed in terms of function points, with the caveat that each language will have a more or less unique ratio of source code statements to function points. For example, COBOL averages about 106.7 logical source code statements per function point, using the procedure and data divisions as the base. Table 17.6 shows the same information, only using function points.

TABLE 17.6   General Programming Productivity and Defect Rates
(Size data expressed in function points for COBOL applications)

Size, FP	A scope, FP	P rate, FP	Staff	Effort months	Schedule months	Coding defects	Defect removal, %	Delivered defects
0.01	0.01	23.36	1	0.0004	0.0004	0	99	0
0.09	0.09	23.36	1	0.0040	0.0040	0	99	0
0.93	0.93	23.36	1	0.0400	0.0400	0	99	0
9.35	9.35	21.03	1	0.4444	0.4444	0	98	0
93.46	93.46	18.69	1	5.0000	5.0000	1	96	0
934.58	186.92	16.36	5	57.1429	11.4286	14	95	1
9,345.79	233.64	14.02	40	666.6667	16.6667	164	94	10
93,457.94	280.37	11.21	333	8,333.3333	25.0000	1,869	92	150
934,579.44	327.10	9.35	2,857	100,000.0000	35.0000	23,364	90	2,336

Although the first three columns are different when using function points, the remaining columns of Tables 17.5 and 17.6 are identical. This should not be unexpected. For example, the costs and effort of building a home will be the same whether the area is measured in square feet or square meters. Changing the metric between square feet and square meters does not change the actual cost of construction in the slightest.

Let us consider the implications of the 12 factors on estimating the work of coding individually, and then in groups or patterns that occur frequently.

The Impact of Reusability on Programming

Informal and personal reuse of source code have been part of the programming occupation since it began. In recent years, the topic of reusability has been elevated to a formal discipline. Reusability is one of the central themes of object-oriented development (OO). Some enterprises have established internal libraries of reusable source code. In addition, there is a growing business of marketing reusable code for some programming languages, with Visual Basic, Java, and various object-oriented languages, such as Smalltalk and Objective-C, leading the set of languages where reusable routines can be acquired from commercial vendors.

The most recent trend in software reuse is to acquire reusable assets for applications written in Java from the Internet and the World Wide Web. Table 17.7 illustrates both *private* and *commercial* reuse for a sampling of common programming languages.

The column labeled "Private Reuse" refers to several different forms of software reuse, including personal reuse by individual programmers and shared reuse within the same company, where no fees or charges are levied.

TABLE 17.7   Software Reuse by Language
(Percentage)

Language	Private reuse	Commercial reuse	Total reuse
Visual Basic	30.00	50.00	80.00
Java	40.00	30.00	70.00
Objective-C	25.00	30.00	55.00
Smalltalk	30.00	25.00	55.00
Eiffel	25.00	25.00	50.00
Forte	25.00	25.00	50.00
Ada 83	20.00	25.00	45.00
Ada 95	20.00	25.00	45.00
ABAP/4	20.00	25.00	45.00
C++	30.00	15.00	45.00
Macro assembly	20.00	20.00	40.00
COBOL	30.00	10.00	40.00
FORTRAN	15.00	20.00	35.00
C	20.00	10.00	30.00
Quick Basic	15.00	15.00	30.00
Pascal	20.00	5.00	25.00
RPG	20.00	5.00	25.00
SQL	20.00	1.00	21.00
CMS2	15.00	5.00	20.00
Jovial	15.00	5.00	20.00
Algol	15.00	5.00	20.00
Modula II	15.00	1.00	16.00
Basic assembly	5.00	10.00	15.00
PL/I	10.00	5.00	15.00
CHILL	12.50	0.10	12.60
CORAL	12.50	0.10	12.60
Average	20.56	16.01	36.56

The column labeled "Commercial Reuse" also refers to several different forms of software reuse, including purchasing reusable materials from commercial vendors or downloading them from the World Wide Web in the form of shareware or freeware.

Note that the column labeled "Total Reuse" indicates the *maximum* amount of an application that could be constructed from reusable materials. This does not imply averages or indicate day-to-day reuse in ordinary applications.

Furthermore, in order for code reuse to be beneficial, the reused code needs to be certified as being approximately zero-defect level. It is hazardous in the extreme to attempt to reuse uncertified material, which may contain serious bugs or even viruses. Either of these situations would damage the application and degrade productivity to unacceptable levels.

The availability of high-quality reusable code modules is now the major positive factor that can influence software coding productivity, ranking even above team experience. However, attempts to reuse code that is buggy and filled with errors can exert a significant impact that degrades or reduces productivity. Reuse is only effective for high-quality deliverables, and is hazardous and uneconomical in the presence of excessive defect levels.

The Impact of Experience on Programming

The word *experience* is multifaceted and can apply to several dimensions. The best results occur when the programmers are experienced in the following topics:

- The application type
- The programming language
- The programming tools or environment

Programmers who, for example, are working on a familiar kind of application in a language they know well are very likely to make few mistakes, and are also likely to have reusable materials available.

Conversely, programmers working on novel kinds of applications, using a programming language with which they have limited experience, and using new tools tend to make quite a few mistakes, which will degrade their overall performance.

The Impact of Bugs or Errors on Programming

Computer programming is an exacting discipline that is much more difficult than writing text. To make an analogy with text, the only form of writing that needs as much precision as computer programming is the writing of medical prescriptions by a physician. In both computer programming and prescriptions, errors involving only a single word can, at least potentially, be fatal.

If it were not for the enormous numbers of bugs or errors that might occur, writing a computer program would be a much easier occupation and productivity levels would be at least twice as high as they actually are.

Designers of programming languages have not always been successful in developing language syntax and notations that can minimize the natural human tendency to make errors. In general, languages with regular syntax, minimal use of complex symbols, and built-in features for dealing with memory utilization have lower levels of bugs than do more arcane languages. Also, the built-in debugging facilities of the compilers, interpreters, and supporting environments can also affect the bug totals.

Table 17.8 illustrates the ranges of coding bugs typically encountered in a sample of programming languages, using both *defects per 1000 lines of code* (KLOC) and *defects per function point* (FP) as the metrics.

Individual programmers' knowledge of the language, experience, schedule pressures, and other factors can cause variations of more than 3 to 1 for each language shown.

The high bug levels for some of the languages, such as C and assembly language, explains why programmers may spend more time and effort on debugging than on actually coding. Bug removal is a major component of software costs, and the bugs that are not removed are a major component of downstream maintenance costs after the release of the software to clients and users.

Overall, the effort and costs required to remove bugs constitute the major cost driver of the programming occupation. There can be no serious or significant productivity gains for software projects without reducing

TABLE 17.8   Programming Bug Patterns by Language
(Coding and syntax bugs only)

Language	Bugs or errors per KLOC	Bugs or errors per FP
Ada 95	9.00	0.50
Ada 83	9.50	0.67
Eiffel	10.00	0.21
Forte	10.00	0.18
Visual Basic	10.50	0.21
Objective C	11.00	0.19
Smalltalk	11.00	0.14
Modula II	12.00	0.84
Java	12.50	0.50
ABAP/4	13.00	0.21
Pascal	13.00	1.18
SQL	13.50	0.18
COBOL	14.00	1.50
RPG	14.50	0.54
CMS2	15.00	1.58
Jovial	15.00	1.59
C++	15.50	0.82
FORTRAN	16.00	1.68
Algol	16.00	1.71
PL/I	16.00	1.30
Quick Basic	17.00	1.11
CHILL	17.50	1.87
CORAL	19.50	2.09
C	20.00	2.50
Macro assembly	23.50	5.01
Basic assembly	29.00	9.28
Average	14.57	1.40

the numbers of bugs that must be removed or maximizing the speed with which bugs are removed.

One of the major economic advantages of software reusability is prefaced on the assumption that reusable code approaches the level of zero defects. If indeed a reusable module is at a zero-defect level, then it's affect on productivity would be about 500 percent. It takes about four times as long to debug 1000 lines of source code as it does to actually write the code. Therefore, if you substitute a zero-defect code segment of 1000 source code statements, you have eliminated both the coding and the debugging.

The Impact of Unpaid Overtime on Programming

The software occupation is very labor intensive and, hence, is extraordinarily sensitive to work habits and the use or absence of overtime, and particularly of unpaid overtime. In the United States, the great majority of software technical workers, including programmers of various kinds, are termed *exempt*, which means they are classed as salaried employees who are legally exempt from receiving paid overtime if they work late or on weekends. The opposite term is *nonexempt*, used by the Bureau of Labor Statistics to classify hourly employees who must receive overtime pay for all work over and above their normal shifts.

Long hours with massive doses of unpaid overtime is more or less a normal cultural phenomenon in the software industry. If you drive by major software companies, such as Microsoft, at night or on weekends you will find most of the lights on, many cars in the parking lot, and more or less continuous activity every day of the week.

The impact of unpaid overtime is important and adds quite a bit of complexity to the tasks of estimation and software measurement. The main impact of unpaid overtime is that it decouples the *cost* of coding from the *effort* devoted to coding.

Table 17.9 presents two different scenarios, with one scenario showing programming effort using only 80 percent of the available monthly work hours, while the other scenario assumes unpaid overtime, and, hence, utilizes 110 percent of the nominally available monthly work hours.

As can be seen, although the actual work hours are the same in both columns, the costs for the application and the apparent productivity expressed in monthly form clearly favors the *intense* column with unpaid overtime.

In the Project 1 column, the "leisurely" rate of 128 hours per month times 50 calendar months totals 6400 work hours.

For the Project 2 column, the intense rate of 176 hours per month times 36.36 calendar months also totals 6400 work hours.

TABLE 17.9   Effects of Unpaid Overtime on Software Costs and Schedules

| Activity | Work habits | | Difference | Percentage |
	Project 1, normal	Project 2, intense		
Size, FP	1,000	1,000	0	0.00
Size, LOC	100,000	100,000	0	0.00
LOC per FP	100	100	0	0.00
Reuse, %	0.00	0.00	0	0.00
A scope, FP	250	250	0	0.00
Nominal P rate, FP	25	25	0	0.00
Availability, %	80.00	110.00	30.00	37.50
Hours per month	128.00	176.00	48.00	37.50
Salary per month	$5,000.00	$5,000.00	$0.00	0.00
Programming staff	4.00	4.00	0.00	0.00
Effort months	50.00	36.36	−13.64	−27.27
Schedule months	15.63	8.26	−7.36	−47.11
Cost	$250,000	$181,818	−$68,182	−27.27
Cost per FP	$250.00	$181.82	−$68.18	−27.27
Work hours per FP	6.40	6.40	0.00	0.00
Virtual P rate, FP	20.00	27.50	7.50	37.50
Cost per LOC	$2.50	$1.82	−$0.68	−27.27
LOC per month	2000	2750	750	37.50

There is no difference in the absolute number of work hours needed between the two versions, but there is a very significant difference in the costs and schedules, because much of the work consists of unpaid overtime in the *intense* example.

Because programmers, for the most part, are treated as salaried professionals who are paid on a monthly rather than an hourly basis, the impact of unpaid overtime creates a major split between productivity measured using *hours of effort* and productivity measured using *costs*.

Unpaid overtime also introduces anomalies in apparent monthly productivity, because projects will require fewer months if unpaid overtime is significant. For example, assume that a 50–function point, 5000–code statement programming project requires 320 hours of programming time. Assuming standard eight-hour workdays, the project would normally require two calendar months. Assuming two calendar months, the productivity for this project would be 25 function points per month, or 2500 lines of code per month. Expressed in hourly form, the project would proceed at a rate of 6.4 work hours per function point or 15.6 LOC per work hour. Assuming that the programmer is paid $5000 per month, the total cost amounts to $10,000. Hence, the project has a cost of $200 per function point or $0.50 per line of code.

Now assume that the programmer who does the project works Saturdays and Sundays plus evening overtime, and finishes the project in one calendar month even though it still requires 320 hours of programming.

Under this alternate scenario with 50 percent unpaid overtime, the apparent monthly productivity has doubled to 5000 lines of code or 50 function points per month. However, because the project still takes 320 hours, the actual effort is still 6.4 work hours per function point and 15.6 LOC per work hour.

The cost structure has changed dramatically: Now the project only costs $5000 because the overtime is not paid for, so the apparent cost of the project has dropped to $100 per function point and only $0.25 per LOC.

As can be seen, the presence of massive quantities of unpaid overtime exerts a very tricky impact on productivity studies and also needs to be carefully included in software cost-estimating assumptions. Most software cost-estimating tools provide default values for paid and unpaid overtime assumptions, and also allow users both to override these defaults and to specify such factors as overtime premium payments if they exist.

The Impact of Creeping Requirements on Programming

One of the chronic problems of the software industry is the fact that programming requirements are seldom stable, and change during the development cycle. Indeed, the monthly rate of change after the requirements are first identified runs from 1 percent to more than 3 percent per month during the subsequent design and coding stages. The U.S. average is about 2 percent per calendar month.

Note that with the Agile methods the rate of change is about 12 percent per calendar month. This is because the Agile methods have a user or client as part of the team. The Agile approach starts coding when the most immediate and obvious requirements are defined. In the Agile view, requirements growth is a natural and organic phenomenon.

The major impact of creeping requirements on the task of programming is that making late additions to software tends to exert negative impacts in terms of the following:

- Damaging the control-flow structure of the application
- Raising the cyclomatic and essential complexity of the applications
- Raising the number of coding defects
- Reducing the defect-removal efficiency
- Damaging long-range maintenance

The overall impact of creeping requirements has both a near-term and a long-term effect. In the near term, it makes it difficult to predict when the project will be done, and in the long term creeping requirements tend to degrade quality and elevate maintenance costs.

Incidentally, the rate at which requirements creep can be measured directly by calculating the function point total of the application at the end of requirements, and then keeping track of the change in function point volumes for every new feature that the clients demand. This use of function points is now showing up in outsourcing contracts, where costs are expressed in terms of cost per function point.

In contracts, there is often a sliding scale so that the original set of function points might be constructed for a fixed cost, such as $500 per function point. But new requirements added later would have elevated costs, such as $750 per function point for requirements added more than six months later.

The Impact of Code Structure and Complexity on Programming

It has been known for more than 40 years that the structure of a software application exerts a major impact on every important software result, including the following:

- Defect levels
- Defect-removal efficiency
- Productivity
- Schedules
- Maintenance
- Reliability

In spite of the fact that well-structured applications are beneficial and poorly structured applications are harmful, structural deficiencies are endemic in the software world. An exact statistical distribution of structural problems has not been published, but among SPR's clients complex structures with hazardous control-flow patterns occur in more than 50 percent of larger applications of 10,000 source code statements and above.

The reasons for this unfortunate situation can be traced to several interrelated factors:

- Excessive schedule pressure
- Misguided attempts to improve execution speed

- Misguided attempts to conserve space
- Misguided attempts by programmers to do clever things
- Lack of training in structured programming

Software code complexity can be measured directly using a number of commercial or even shareware and freeware tools. The two most common metrics for source code structure are *cyclomatic complexity* and *essential complexity*. Both measure the numbers of branches and the control flow through source code.

In general, programming productivity declines as complexity goes up. Since cyclomatic and essential complexity are measured in integer values, optimum programming productivity tends to occur when cyclomatic and essential complexity levels are close to 1, and in any case stay below 10, at the module level.

Conversely, high levels of cyclomatic and essential complexity, with values greater than 20, are often associated with excessive defect rates and reduced productivity.

There are some anomalies with this general rule, however. Sometimes applications with high levels of cyclomatic and essential complexity have higher productivity rates than similar applications with low complexity levels. When this situation occurs, it is usually because the low-complexity application has been assigned to novices, while the high-complexity application has been assigned to top-gun experts with a great deal of experience in similar applications.

The Impact of Unplanned Interruptions on Programming

Computer programming is a very labor-intensive occupation; hence, it is best to allow programming personnel to work with few interruptions, and especially with very few unplanned interruptions.

One of the most frequent and damaging forms of interruption occurs in situations where programmers are performing both development and maintenance tasks at the same time. Often maintenance is driven by the unexpected discovery and reporting of bugs, and sometimes the bugs are very severe and need immediate repairs.

In this kind of situation, development work must be suspended while the programmer attempts to repair the bugs. Since development work is often under schedule pressure, the programmers are anxious to get back to it and may be careless when fixing bugs, hence raising the possibility of a *bad fix*, or a new bug resulting from attempts to fix a prior bug.

Obviously, it is very difficult to estimate development for a programming team that is time-slicing between maintenance and development work, where the maintenance portion is subject to random unplanned bug reports.

(It is interesting that neither the Agile methods nor XP have yet addressed the issue of handling development and maintenance at the same time with the same team. Most of the Agile and XP projects to date have been pure development, rather than enhancements of legacy applications that may be receiving daily bug reports from users.)

The mutual interference of development programming and maintenance programming is significant enough that most top software companies divide the tasks in two and establish full-time maintenance departments. By separating maintenance from development, the performance of both sides will improve, and estimating is a great deal easier.

Also see the section on the impact of office space on programming, because having programmers share offices can lead to very disruptive unplanned interruptions.

The Impact of Application Size on Programming

The amount of code that is normally assigned to one programmer is called the *assignment scope*. Typical ranges of programming assignments on large projects run from about 10,000 statements up to about 50,000 statements.

The determining factors for programming assignment scopes include the skill levels of the programmers and the schedule pressure for completing the project. In theory it would be possible to assign one programmer the coding of a 100,000 statement application, but it might take more than three calendar years to complete the code.

It would be more common to divide the 100,000 statement application up among four or five programmers in order to reduce the elapsed time. For example, four programmers might complete the project in less than 15 calendar months, while five programmers could finish up in perhaps 12 calendar months.

However, as the number of programmers increases the number of interfaces between their components or modules also increases.

Complex interfaces mean more bugs and more time spent on meetings and communication in order to deal with the transfer of information across the interfaces. These interfaces are notoriously troublesome, so defect levels will also increase, and, hence, productivity and quality will decline.

Some of the Agile approaches make use of the pair-programming concept, or assigning two programmers to the same modules or programs. This method offers some advantages in terms of defect prevention and defect removal. Having each member of the team review the other's work leads to quicker and more thorough debugging. Since finding and fixing bugs usually takes about four times as much effort as actually writing the code, the pair concept can be justified economically if it reduces defect levels and speeds up defect removal. Preliminary evidence indicates that both factors do occur.

However, to work successfully the pair-programming concept requires that both members of the pair be compatible and more or less at the same skill level. It sometimes happens that a new or novice programmer is assigned to work with an expert in order to pick up skills in a hurry. That can be successful.

But what would not be successful would be to pair a competent programmer with one of marginal competence.

The Impact of Office Space and Ergonomics on Programming

One very significant factor that has a surprisingly strong influence on programming productivity is that of the size, noise level, and ergonomic layout of the programmers' office space. This topic is often ignored and is underreported in the software literature, although there are a few truly excellent studies on programming office environments.

In the mid-1970s when software was becoming a major industry, the IBM corporation built a number of new programming laboratories. One of these labs, the Santa Teresa lab located in the foothills of the coast range in San Jose, California, was intended to be an IBM showpiece for software excellence. This was a major software location, which was originally planned for about 2000 software professionals.

The architect selected to design this lab was Dr. Gerald McCue, the Dean of Architecture at Harvard University. Dr. McCue and the IBM team working with him interviewed several hundred software developers about what they regarded as an optimal office arrangement, and then the Santa Teresa programming laboratory was constructed in response to their expressed requirements.

The IBM Santa Teresa programming laboratory won a number of architectural awards and featured many interesting innovations, such as using the excess heat from the computer rooms for heating the office space. However, the most notable feature of the Santa Teresa programming laboratory was the fact that every programmer was able to have a full private office that was 10 feet by 10 feet in size, or 100 square feet overall.

The rationale for giving all programmers private offices is based on the typical work patterns of the programming occupation. For at least 75 percent of a typical business day, programmers need to concentrate on programming; hence, interruptions and noise should be minimized or eliminated.

The other 25 percent of the day, programmers need to communicate and coordinate with their peers if they are working on sizable projects that have other programmers involved. In order to deal with this situation, the Santa Teresa office complex featured small conference rooms for every department, and a scattering of larger conference rooms as well.

The overall impact of the Santa Teresa office complex was surprisingly positive. The same IBM programmers who had been working in shared cubicles at the adjacent San Jose and Palo Alto programming centers achieved productivity gains of about 11 percent after the first year of occupancy of Santa Teresa. This was not a case of a *Hawthorn complex*, or measurements themselves artificially introducing higher productivity rates. The IBM productivity measurement system had been in existence for some years, and was the same at Santa Teresa as everywhere else.

Another surprising effect of the Santa Teresa office complex was on morale. The annual opinion surveys carried out throughout IBM noted that the morale levels at the Santa Teresa office complex were the highest of any of IBM's 26 programming centers.

A more recent study of the impact of office environments on software productivity was published by Tom DeMarco and Tim Lister in their well-known book *Peopleware* (Dorset House, 1987). Their study consisted of programming war games, in which more than 300 programmers took part. The programmers each wrote the same trial application in their own offices, using their own computers and tools, and using any programming language they preferred.

After the data was collected, it was discovered that the size and the noise level of the programmer's office space actually seemed to have a stronger influence than almost any other variable, including the programming language used.

The programmers in the high quartile had more than 80 square feet of noise-free private office space, while those in the low quartile had less than about 44 square feet of rather noisy office space, such as open offices or cubicles with two to three programmers in the same space.

However, programmers' office space is not universally a factor in every country. For example, the impact of crowded office space is quite significant in the United States and Europe, but appears not to be a factor in Japan, where office space is quite expensive.

In recent years some of the Agile methods and XP have emphasized development by small teams that are co-located and work together cooperatively. Often these teams are set up with adjacent work stations or shared offices. This arrangement does optimize the communication aspects of team members. But over and above communication, there are times when programming requires intense concentration with no interruptions. This is called "ideal time" in some of the Agile jargon.

In the author's opinion, based on observations of various kinds of office arrangements, the most effective arrangement for team programming consists of individual offices for each team member, but all offices are next to a dedicated meeting area that can hold the entire team. In other words, if you have a team of six programmers you would need six adjacent private offices plus a small conference room that is in close proximity. When the programmers want to work privately they use their offices. When the team needs to meet, it uses the meeting room.

The Impact of Tools on Programming

Thirty years ago, when the author was a practicing programmer using assembly language, the only kinds of programming tools that were readily available were the assemblers themselves. Today, as this book is being written, programming tools are extremely sophisticated and growing more sophisticated each day. A full suite of programming support tools circa 2007 supports most of the software life cycle, and includes the following features:

- Assemblers
- Compilers
- Interpreters
- Software design tools
- Interface design tools
- Database design tools
- Reusability-support tools
- Reverse-engineering tools
- Reengineering tools
- Code restructuring tools
- Change management tools
- Code editors
- Static analysis tools
- Standards-checking tools
- Complexity-analysis tools
- Bounds checkers
- Execution simulation tools
- Record/playback tools

- Debugging tools
- Defect-tracking tools
- Inspection-support tools
- Testing-support tools
- Groupware/communication support tools
- Viral protection tools

While specific tool vendors vary widely in features, costs, and usefulness, the overall impact of programming-support tools is positive. Compared to programming in the 1970s, the sets of programming-support tools circa 2007 can greatly facilitate such key activities as design, debugging, and enabling software reuse.

The Impact of Programming Languages on Programming

It is something of a mystery to understand why the programming industry has managed to create more than 600 different programming languages and dialects of programming languages, but there are more than 600 languages in the master table of programming languages SPR uses with its commercial software cost-estimating tools. (See the companion book *Applied Software Measurement* for the full list , or refer to SPR's Web site for the master list: http://www.spr.com.)

Choosing a programming language is more of an art than a science, and many languages' supporters almost resemble members of a cult. However, when considering the various kinds of software that are programmed, certain patterns of language use emerge. Some of the languages noted include the following:

- ABAP/4
- Ada
- Algol
- APL
- C
- C++
- CHILL
- CMS2
- COBOL
- CORAL
- Eiffel

- Forte
- Forth
- FORTRAN
- HTML
- Java
- Jovial
- Macro assembly
- Magic
- Modula II
- Mumps
- Pascal
- Netron CAP
- Objective-C
- PL/I
- RPG
- QBE
- RPG
- Smalltalk
- SQL
- Visual Basic

This list could be, and indeed has been, extended to include over 600 programming languages and dialects. (See the Software Productivity Research overall list of levels and languages for the full 2007 table of languages.) It is an unanswered question of the software engineering world as to whether or not all of these languages and dialects have any real value. Of course, the same question could be posed about natural languages such as English, French, German, Swahili, Japanese, etc. In both situations it is a fact of life that hundreds of languages exist.

To show the effects of various programming languages, Tables 17.10 and 17.11 show the same application developed in ten different programming languages. The application in the example is a private branch exchange (PBX) switching system. Actually, data from a number of PBX switches was collected, and then modified slightly to convert all of the sizes into exactly 1500 function points. Note the very large range of source code among the ten languages for exactly the same set of features.

The next topic of interest is the amount of effort required to develop the ten examples of the project. Table 17.11 gives the effort for the six

TABLE 17.10 Function Point and Source Code Sizes for Ten Versions of the Same Project
(A PBX Switching System of 1500 Function Points in Size)

Language	Size in FP	Lang. level	LOC per FP	Size in LOC
Assembly	1500	1	250	375,000
C	1500	3	127	190,500
CHILL	1500	3	105	157,500
PASCAL	1500	4	91	136,500
PL/I	1500	4	80	120,000
Ada83	1500	5	71	106,500
C++	1500	6	55	82,500
Ada95	1500	7	49	73,500
Objective-C	1500	11	29	43,500
Smalltalk	1500	15	21	31,500
Average	1500	6	88	131,700

major activities and the overall quantity of effort expressed in terms of "staff months." Note that the term "staff month" is defined as a typical working month of about 22 business days, and includes the assumption that project work occurs roughly six hours per day, or 132 work hours per month. The data normalization feature of the CHECKPOINT tool was used to make these assumptions constant, even though the actual data was collected from a number of companies in different countries, where the actual number of work hours per staff month varied.

None of the projects were exactly 1500 function point in size, and the original sizes ranges from about 1300 to 1750 function points in size. Here too, the data normalization feature was used to make all ten versions identical in factors that would conceal the underlying similarities of the examples.

TABLE 17.11 Staff Months of Effort for Ten Versions of the Same Software Project
(A PBX Switching System of 1500 Function Points in Size)

Language	Req. (months)	Design (months)	Code (months)	Test (months)	Doc. (months)	Mgt. (months)	TOTAL (months)
Assembly	13.64	60.00	300.00	277.78	40.54	89.95	781.91
C	13.64	60.00	152.40	141.11	40.54	53.00	460.69
CHILL	13.64	60.00	116.67	116.67	40.54	45.18	392.69
PASCAL	13.64	60.00	101.11	101.11	40.54	41.13	357.53
PL/I	13.64	60.00	88.89	88.89	40.54	37.95	329.91
Ada 83	13.64	60.00	76.07	78.89	40.54	34.99	304.13
C++	13.64	68.18	66.00	71.74	40.54	33.81	293.91
Ada 95	13.64	68.18	52.50	63.91	40.54	31.04	269.81
Objective-C	13.64	68.18	31.07	37.83	40.54	24.86	216.12
Smalltalk	13.64	68.18	22.50	27.39	40.54	22.39	194.64
Average	13.64	63.27	100.72	100.53	40.54	41.43	360.13

It can readily be seen that the overall costs associated with coding and testing are much less significant for object-oriented languages than for procedural languages. However, the effort associated with initial requirements, design, and user documentation are comparatively inelastic and do not fluctuate in direct proportion to the volume of code required.

Tables 17.10 and 17.11 illustrated some of the challenges associated with sizing and cost estimating when different programming languages are part of the picture.

Table 17.12 shows productivity rates for all ten versions using both function points and lines-of-code metrics. Note the paradox that measurements based on lines of code penalize high-level and object-oriented programming languages.

As can easily be seen, the LOC data does not match the assumptions of standard economics, and indeed moves in the opposite direction from real economic productivity. It has been known for many hundreds of years that when manufacturing costs have a high proportion of fixed costs and there is a reduction in the number of units produced, the cost per unit will go up.

The same logic is true for software. When a "line of code" is defined as the unit of production, and there is a migration from low-level procedural languages to object-oriented languages, the number of units that must be constructed declines. The costs of paper documents such as requirements and user manuals do not decline, and tend to act like fixed costs. This inevitably leads to an increase in the "cost per LOC" for object-oriented projects, and a reduction in "LOC per staff month" when the paper-related activities are included in the measurements.

On the other hand, the function point metric is a synthetic metric totally divorced from the amount of code needed by the application.

TABLE 17.12   Productivity Rates for ten Versions of the Same Software Project
(A PBX switching system of 1500 Function Points in Size)

Language	Effort (months)	FP per staff month	Work hrs. per FP	LOC per staff month	LOC per staff hour
Assembly	781.91	1.92	68.81	480	3.38
C	460.69	3.26	40.54	414	3.13
CHILL	392.69	3.82	34.56	401	3.04
PASCAL	357.53	4.20	31.46	382	2.89
PL/I	329.91	4.55	29.03	364	2.76
Ada 83	304.13	4.93	26.76	350	2.65
C++	293.91	5.10	25.86	281	2.13
Ada 95	269.81	5.56	23.74	272	2.06
Objective-C	216.12	6.94	19.02	201	1.52
Smalltalk	194.64	7.71	17.13	162	1.23
Average	360.13	4.17	31.69	366	2.77

Therefore function point metrics can be used for economic studies involving multiple programming languages and object-oriented programming languages without bias or distorted results. The function point metric can also be applied to non-coding activities such as requirements, design, user documentation, integration, testing, and even project management.

The Impact of Schedule Pressure on Programming

The most common problem in the software industry for large systems is that of intense but artificial schedule pressure applied to the programmers by their managers, by senior executives in their companies, or by their clients.

Unfortunately, intense schedule pressure leads to carelessness, which in turn drives up the chances of making errors and introducing bugs. The overall impact of intense schedule pressure is not what is desired, but instead tends to lengthen schedules because the software does not work well enough to be released.

Look carefully at the assignment scopes and production rates shown in the tables in this chapter. If you know the size of a software application, and set schedules that are much shorter than those shown in the tables, you will have a very small chance of achieving the schedules and a very large chance of running late and over budget, because the schedule pressure you apply will cause haste and carelessness and will drive up the bug or error probability to dangerous levels.

References

Ambler, S.: *Process Patterns—Building Large-Scale Systems Using Object Technology*, Cambridge University Press, New York, NY, SIGS Books, 1998.

Artow, J., and I. Neustadt: *UML and the Unified Process*, Addison-Wesley, Boston, Mass., 2000.

Beck, K.: *Extreme Programming Explained: Embrace Change*, Addison-Wesley, Boston, Mass., 1999.

Boehm, Barry, Dr.: *Software Engineering Economics*, Prentice-Hall, Englewood Cliffs, N.J., 1981.

Booch, Grady: *Object Solutions: Managing the Object-Oriented Project*, Addison-Wesley, Reading, Mass., 1995.

———, Ivar Jacobsen, and James Rumbaugh: *The Unified Modeling Language User Guide, Second Edition*, Addison-Wesley, Boston, Mass., 2005.

Cockburn, Alistair: *Agile Software Development*, Addison-Wesley, Boston, Mass.; 2001.

Cohen, D., M. Lindvall, and P. Costa: "An Introduction to Agile Methods," *Advances in Computers*, Elsevier Science, New York, 2004, pp. 1–66.

Cohen, Lou: *Quality Function Deployment: How to Make QFD Work for You*, Addison-Wesley, Boston, Mass.

Cohn, Mike: *Agile Estimating and Planning*, Prentice-Hall PTR, Englewood Cliffs, N.J., 2005.

DeMarco, Tom: *Controlling Software Projects*, Yourdon Press, New York, 1982.

————, and Timothy Lister: *Peopleware*, Dorset House Press, New York, 1987.

Fuqua, Andrew M.: *Using Function Points in XP—Considerations*, Springer Berlin/ Heidelberg, 2003.

Garmus, David, and David Herron: *Measuring the Software Process: A Practical Guide to Functional Measurement*, Prentice-Hall, Englewood Cliffs, N.J., 1995.

————: *Function Point Analysis*, Addison-Wesley Longman, Boston, Mass., 2001.

Humphrey, Watts: *Managing the Software Process*, Addison-Wesley, Reading, Mass., 1989.

————: *Personal Software Process*, Addison-Wesley/Longman, Reading, Mass., 1997

Jeffries, R. et al.: *Extreme Programming Installed*, Addison-Wesley, Boston, 2001.

Jones, Capers: *Programming Productivity*, McGraw-Hill, New York, 1986.

————: *Assessment and Control of Software Risks*, Prentice-Hall, Englewood Cliffs, N.J., 1994.

————: *Patterns of Software System Failure and Success*, International Thomson Computer Press, Boston, Mass., 1995.

————: *Applied Software Measurement, Second Edition*, McGraw-Hill, New York, 1996a.

————: *Table of Programming Languages and Levels* (8 Versions from 1985 through July 1996), Software Productivity Research, Burlington, Mass., 1996b.

————: "Sizing Up Software," *Scientific American*, New York, December 1998, Vol. 279, No. 6, pp 104–109.

————: *Software Assessments, Benchmarks, and Best Practices*, Addison-Wesley Longman, Boston, Mass., 2000.

————: *Conflict and Litigation Between Software Clients and Developers*, Software Productivity Research, Burlington, Mass., 2003.

Kan, Stephen H.: *Metrics and Models in Software Quality Engineering, Second Edition*, Addison-Wesley Longman, Boston, Mass., 2003.

Larman, Craig, and Victor Basili: "Iterative and Incremental Development—A Brief History," *IEEE Computer Society*, June 2003, pp 47–55.

Love, Tom: *Object Lessons*, SIGS Books, New York, 1993.

McConnell, Steve: *Software Estimating: Demystifying the Black Art*, Microsoft Press, Redmond, WA, 2006.

McCue, Gerald: "The IBM Santa Teresa Laboratory—Architectural Design for Program Development," *IBM Systems Journal*, 17(1):4–25 (1978). Reprinted in *Programming Productivity—Issues for the Eighties, Second Edition*, by Capers Jones, IEEE Computer Society Press, Los Alamitos, Calif., year???.

Pressman, Roger: *Software Engineering—A Practitioner's Approach, Sixth Edition*, McGraw-Hill, New York, 2005.

Putnam, Lawrence H.: *Measures for Excellence—Reliable Software on Time, Within Budget*, Yourdon Press/Prentice-Hall, Englewood Cliffs, N.J., 1992.

————, and Ware Myers: *Industrial Strength Software—Effective Management Using Measurement*, IEEE Computer Society Press, Washington D.C., 1997.

Roetzheim, William H., and Reyna A. Beasley: *Best Practices in Software Cost and Schedule Estimation*, Prentice-Hall PTR, Upper Saddle River, N.J., 1998.

Rubin, Howard: *Software Benchmark Studies for 1997* Howard Rubin Associates, Pound Ridge, N.Y., 1997.

Software Productivity Research LLC: "Table of Programming Languages and Levels," 2007 (http://www.spr.com).

Symons, Charles R., *Software Sizing and Estimating—Mk II FPA (Function Point Analysis)*, John Wiley & Sons, Chichester, U.K., 1991.

Yourdon, Ed: *Death March—The Complete Software Developer's Guide to Surviving Mission Impossible Projects*, Prentice-Hall PTR, Upper Saddle River, N.J., 1997.

18

Estimating Code Inspections

The topic of formal code inspections has a continuous stream of empirical data that runs back to the early 1970s. Formal code inspections were originally developed at the IBM Kingston programming laboratory by Michael Fagan and his colleagues, and have since spread throughout the programming world.

(It is interesting that Michael Fagan, the inventor of inspections, received an IBM outstanding contribution award for the discovery that design and code inspections benefit software quality, schedules, and costs simultaneously.)

Code Inspection Literature

Other researchers, such as Tom Gilb, Dr. Gerald Weinberg, and the author of this book, have followed the use of inspections in recent years, and the method is still the top-ranked method for achieving high levels of overall defect-removal efficiency.

Even in 2007 inspections continue to attract interest and research. One interesting new book is *Peer Reviews in Software* by Karl Wiegers (Addison-Wesley, 2002). Another interesting and useful book is *High-Quality Low-Cost Software Inspections* by Ron Radice (Paradoxican Publisher, 2002). Ron was a colleague of Michael Fagan at IBM Kingston when the first design and code inspections were being tried out. Thus, Ron has been an active participant in formal inspections for almost 35 years.

An even newer book that discusses not only inspections per se, but also their economic value and the measurement approaches for collecting inspection data is Stephen Kan's *Metrics and Models in Software Quality Engineering* (Addison-Wesley, 2003). This is the second edition of Kan's popular book.

Roger Pressman's book *Software Engineering—A Practitioner's Approach* (McGraw-Hill, 2005) also discusses various forms of defect removal. The sixth edition of this book includes new chapters on Agile development, extreme programming, and several other of the newer methods. It provides an excellent context for the role of quality in all of the major development approaches.

It should be noted that code inspections work perfectly well on every known programming language. They have been successfully utilized on APL, assembly language, Basic, C, C++, HTML, Java, Smalltalk, and essentially all known languages. Inspections can be a bit tricky on languages where "programming" can be performed via buttons or pull-down menus such as those used in Visual Basic.

Effectiveness of Code Inspections

Formal code inspections are about twice as efficient as any known form of testing in finding deep and obscure programming bugs, and are the only known method to top 85 percent in defect-removal efficiency.

However, formal code inspections are fairly expensive and time-consuming, so they are most widely utilized on software projects where operational reliability and safety are mandatory, such as the following:

- Mainframe operating systems
- Telephone switching systems
- Aircraft flight control software
- Medical instrument software
- Weapons systems software

It is an interesting observation, with solid empirical data to back it up, that large and complex systems (>1000 function points or >100,000 source code statements) that utilize formal code inspections will achieve shorter schedules and lower development and maintenance costs than similar software projects that use only testing for defect removal. Indeed, the use of formal inspections has represented a *best practice* for complex systems software for more than 35 years.

The reason for this phenomenon is based on the fact that for complex software applications the schedule, effort, and costs devoted to finding and fixing bugs take longer and are more expensive than any other known cost factors. In fact, the cost of finding coding errors is about four times greater than the cost of writing the code. Without inspections, the testing cycle for a large system is often a nightmare of numerous bug reports, hasty patches, retests, slipping schedules, and lots of overtime.

Formal inspections eliminate so many troublesome errors early that when testing does occur, very few defects are encountered; hence, testing costs and schedules are only a fraction of those experienced when testing is the first and only form of defect removal. When considering the total cost of ownership of a major software application, the return on investment (ROI) from formal inspections can top $15 for every $1 spent, which ranks as one of the top ROIs of any software technology.

Formal code inspections overlap several similar approaches, and except among specialists the terms *inspection, structured walkthrough,* and *code review* are often used almost interchangeably. Following are the major differences among these variations.

Formal code inspections are characterized by the following attributes:

- Training is given to novices before they participate in their first inspection.

- The inspection team is comprised of a moderator, a recorder, one or more inspectors, and the person whose work product is being inspected.

- Schedule and timing protocols are carefully adhered to for preparation time, the inspection sessions themselves, and follow-up activities.

- Accurate data is kept on the number of defects found, hours of effort devoted to preparation, and the size of the work product inspected.

- Standard metrics are calculated from the data collected during inspections, such as defect-removal efficiency, work hours per function point, work hours per KLOC, and work hours per defect.

The less formal methods of structured walkthroughs and code reviews differ from the formal code inspection method in the following key attributes:

- Training is seldom provided for novices before they participate.

- The usage of a moderator and recorder seldom occurs.

- Little or no data is recorded on defect rates, hours expended, costs, or other quantifiable aspects of the review or walkthrough.

As a result, it is actually harder to estimate the less formal methods, such as code walkthroughs, than it is to estimate formal code inspections. The reason is that formal code inspections generate accurate quantitative data as a standard output, while the less formal methods usually have very little data available on either defects, removal efficiency, schedules, effort, or costs.

However, there is just enough data to indicate that the less formal methods are not as efficient and effective as formal code inspections, although they are still better than many forms of testing.

Formal code inspections will average about 65 percent in defect-removal efficiency, and the best results can top 85 percent.

Less formal structured walkthroughs average about 45 percent in defect-removal efficiency, and the best results can top about 70 percent.

For peer reviews in small applications using the Agile "pair-programming" concept, the reviews of one colleague on the code of the second colleague will average about 50 percent efficient. The best results can top about 75 percent, assuming a very experienced and capable programmer.

In general, the Agile methods and XP have not adopted formal inspections. This is due to the fact that inspections are somewhat time-consuming and perhaps not fully necessary for the kinds of smaller applications that are typically being developed under the Agile and XP methods.

However, since most forms of testing are less than 30 percent efficient in finding bugs, it can be seen that either formal code inspections or informal code walkthroughs can add value to defect-removal operations.

Another common variant on the inspection method is that of doing partial inspections on less than 100 percent of the code in an application. This variant makes estimating tricky, because there is no fixed ratio of code that will be inspected. Some of the variants that the author's clients have utilized include the following:

- Inspecting only the code that deals with the most complex and difficult algorithms (usually less than 10 percent of the total volume of code)

- Inspecting only modules that are suspected of being error prone due to the volumes of incoming defect reports (usually less than 5 percent of the total volume of code)

- Using time box inspections (such as setting aside a fixed period such as one month), and doing as much as possible during the assigned time box (often less than 50 percent of the total volume of code)

However, for really important applications that will affect human life or safety (i.e., medical instrument software, weapons systems, nuclear control systems, aircraft flight control, etc.), anything less than 100 percent inspection of the entire application is hazardous and should be avoided.

Another aspect of inspections that makes estimation tricky is the fact that the inspection sessions are intermittent activities that must be slotted into other kinds of work. Using the formal protocols of the inspection process, inspection sessions are limited to a maximum of two hours each, and no more than two such sessions can be held in any given business day.

These protocols mean that for large systems, the inspection sessions can be strung out for several months. Further, because other kinds of work must be done and travel might occur, and because re-inspections may be needed, the actual schedules for the inspection sessions are unpredictable using simple algorithms and rules of thumb.

Using a sophisticated scheduling tool, such as Microsoft Project, Timeline, Artemis, and the like, what usually occurs is that inspections are slotted into other activities over a several-month period. A common practice is to run inspections in the morning, and leave the afternoons for other kinds of work.

However, one of the other kinds of work is preparing for the next inspection. Although preparation goes faster than the inspection sessions themselves, the preparation for the next code inspection session can easily amount to one hour per inspector prior to each planned inspection session.

Although the programmer whose work is being inspected may not have as much preparation work as the inspectors, after the inspection he or she may have to fix quite a few defects that the inspection churns up.

Yet another aspect of inspections that adds complexity to the estimation task is the fact that with more and more experience, the participants in formal code inspection benefit in two distinct ways:

- Programmers who participate in inspections have reduced bug counts in their own work.

- The inspectors and participants become significantly more efficient in preparation time and also in the time needed for the inspection sessions.

Table 18.1 illustrates these simultaneous improvements for a scenario that assumes that six different software projects will be inspected over time by more or less the same set of programmers. As can be seen, by the time the sixth project is reached, the team is quite a bit better than when it started with its first inspection.

As can be observed, inspections are beneficial in terms of both their defect-prevention aspects and their defect-removal aspects. Indeed, one

TABLE 18.1   Improvement in Code Inspection Performance with Practice
(Time in hours)

Number of projects	Size, in LOC	Defects found	Prep time	Session time	Repair time	Total time
1	1000	20	10.0	12.0	60.0	82.0
2	1000	17	9.0	10.0	55.0	74.0
3	1000	15	7.0	8.0	50.0	65.0
4	1000	12	5.0	7.0	40.0	52.0
5	1000	10	4.0	5.0	30.0	39.0
6	1000	7	3.0	3.0	20.0	26.0
Average	1000	14	6.3	7.5	42.5	56.3

of the most significant benefits of formal design and code inspections is that they raise the defect-removal efficiency of testing.

Some of the major problems of achieving high-efficiency testing are that the specifications are often incomplete, the code often does not match the specifications, and the poor and convoluted structure of the code makes testing of every path difficult. Formal design and code inspections will minimize these problems by providing test personnel with more complete and accurate specifications and by eliminating many of the problem areas of the code itself.

Considerations for Estimating Code Inspections

A simple rule of thumb is that every hour spent on formal code inspections will probably save close to three hours in subsequent testing and downstream defect-removal operations.

Estimating both design and code inspections can be tricky, because both forms of inspection have wide ranges of possible variance, such as the following:

- Preparation time is highly variable.
- The number of participants in any session can range from three to eight.
- Personal factors (flu, vacations, etc.) can cancel or delay inspections.
- Inspections are intermittent events limited to two-hour sessions.
- Inspections have to be slotted into other kinds of work activities.

The nominal default values for code inspections are shown in Table 18.2, although these values should be replaced by local data as quickly as possible. Indeed, inspections lend themselves to template construction because local conditions can vary so widely.

Although design and code inspections are time-consuming and admittedly expensive, they will speed up test cycles to such a degree that follow-on test stages such as new-function test, regression test, system test, stress test, and customer acceptance test will often be reduced in time and cost by more than 50 percent. Thus, when estimating the costs and schedule impacts of formal inspections, don't forget that testing costs and test schedules will be significantly lower.

When inspections become a normal part of software development processes in large corporations, there may be several, or even dozens, of inspections going on concurrently on any given business day. For some large systems, there may even be dozens of inspections for different components of the same system taking place simultaneously.

TABLE 18.2   Nominal Default Values for Code Inspections

Activity sequence	Sixth
Activity performed by	Development personnel; quality assurance; testers
Predecessor activities	Coding
Overlap	50% with coding
Concurrent activities	Both coding and unit testing
Successor activities	Unit testing, regression testing, and function testing
Initial size	2 function points per inspection session
Initial size	250 code statements per inspection session
Assignment scope	2 function points per team member per session
Assignment scope	250 source code statements per team member per session
Production rate	2 function points per hour (0.5 per team member)
Production rate	250 source statements per hour (50 per team member)
Schedule months	2-hour packets, with no more than 2 per day
Rate of creep or change	1%
Defect potential	1.5 code defects present per function point
Defect potential	15 code defects present per 1000 source code statements
Defect removal	65% average removal efficiency
Delivered defects	Code defects –65% or roughly 0.5 per function point
High-severity defects	12% of delivered defects
Bad fix probability	5% of code inspection fixes may yield new errors

This phenomenon raises some practical issues that need to be dealt with:

- Possible conflicts in scheduling inspection conference rooms.
- Possible conflicts in scheduling inspection participants.

Often, large companies that use inspections have an inspection coordinator, who may be part of the quality-assurance organization. The inspection coordinator handles the conference room arrangements and also the scheduling of participants. For scheduling individual participants, some kind of calendar management tool is usually used.

Although the inspection process originated as a group activity in which all members of the inspection team met face to face, software networking technologies are now powerful enough that some inspections are being handled remotely. There is even commercial software available that allows every participant to interact, to chat with the others, and to mark up the listings and associated documentation.

These online inspections are still evolving, but the preliminary data indicates that they are slightly more efficient than face-to-face inspections. Obviously, with online inspections there is no travel to remote buildings, and another less obvious advantage also tends to occur.

In face-to-face inspection sessions, sometimes as much as 15 to 20 minutes out of each two-hour session may be diverted into such unrelated topics as sports, the weather, politics, or whatever. With online inspections idle chat tends to be abbreviated, and, hence, the work at hand goes quicker. The usual result is that the inspection sessions themselves are shorter, and the online variants seldom run much more than 60 minutes, as opposed to the two-hour slots assigned to face-to-face inspections.

Alternatively, the production rates for the online inspection sessions are often faster and some can top 400 source code statements per hour—and with experienced personnel who make few defects to slow down progress, inspections have been clocked at more than 750 source code statements per hour.

Given the power and effectiveness of formal inspections, it is initially surprising that they are not universally adopted and used on every critical software project. The reason why formal inspections are noted only among best-in-class organizations is that the average and lagging organizations simply do not know what works and what doesn't.

In other words, both the project managers and the programming personnel in lagging companies that lack formal measurements of quality, formal process improvement programs, and the other attributes of successful software production do not know enough about the effectiveness of inspections to see how large an ROI they offer.

Consider the fact that lagging and average companies collect no historical data of their own and seldom review the data collected by other companies. As a result, lagging and average enterprises are not in a position to make rational choices about effective software technologies. Instead, they usually follow whatever current cult is in vogue, whether or not the results are beneficial. They also fall prey to pitches of various tool and methodology vendors, with or without any substantial evidence that what is being sold will be effective.

Leading companies, on the other hand, do measure such factors as defect-removal efficiency, schedules, costs, and other critical factors. Leading companies also tend to be more familiar with the external data and the software engineering literature. Therefore, leading enterprises are aware that design and code inspections have a major place in software engineering because they benefit quality, schedules, and costs simultaneously.

Another surprising reason why inspections are not more widely used is the fact that the method is in the public domain, so none of the testing-tool companies can generate any significant revenues from the inspection technology. Thus, the testing-tool companies tend to ignore inspections as though they did not even exist, although if the testing companies really understood software quality they would include inspection support as part of their offerings.

Judging from visits to at least a dozen public and private conferences by testing-tool and quality-assurance companies, inspections are sometimes discussed by speakers but almost never show up in vendor's showcases or at quality tool fairs. This is unfortunate, because inspections are a powerful adjunct to testing and, indeed, can raise the defect-removal efficiency level of downstream testing by perhaps 15 percent as compared to the results from similar projects that do only testing. Not only will testing defect removal go up, but testing costs and schedules will go down once formal inspections are deployed.

From a software-estimating standpoint, the usage of formal inspections needs to be included in the estimate, of course. Even more significant, the usage of formal design and code inspections will have a significant impact on downstream activities that also need to be included in the estimate. For example, the usage of formal inspections will probably have the following downstream effects:

- At least 65 percent of latent errors will be eliminated via inspections, so testing will be quicker and cheaper. The timeline for completing testing will be about 50 percent shorter than for similar projects that do not use inspections.

- The inspections will clean up the specifications and, hence, will allow better test cases to be constructed, so the defect-removal efficiency levels of testing will be about 12 to 15 percent higher than for similar projects that do not use inspections.

- The combined defect-removal efficiency levels of the inspections coupled with better testing will reduce maintenance costs by more than 50 percent compared to similar projects that don't use inspections.

- Projects that use formal inspections will usually score higher on customer-satisfaction surveys.

There are some psychological barriers to introducing formal inspections for the first time. Most programmers are somewhat afraid of inspections because they imply a detailed scrutiny of their code and an evaluation of their programming styles.

One effective way to introduce inspections is to start them as a controlled experiment. Management will ask that formal inspections be used for a six-week period. At the end of that period, the programming team will decide whether to continue with inspections, or revert back to previous methods of testing and perhaps informal reviews.

When this approach is used and inspections are evaluated on their own merits, rather than being perceived as something forced by management, the teams will vote to continue with inspections about 75 percent of the time.

References

Dunn, Robert, and Richard Ullman: *Quality Assurance for Computer Software*, McGraw-Hill, New York, 1982.

Fagan, M.E.: "Design and Code Inspections to Reduce Errors in Program Development," *IBM Systems Journal*, **12**(3):219–248 (1976).

Friedman, Daniel P., and Gerald M. Weinberg: *Handbook of Walkthroughs, Inspections, and Technical Reviews*, Dorset House Press, New York, 1990.

Gilb, Tom, and D. Graham: *Software Inspections*, Addison-Wesley, Reading, Mass., 1993.

Jones, Capers: *Assessment and Control of Software Risks*, Prentice-Hall, Englewood Cliffs, N.J., 1994.

———: *Patterns of Software System Failure and Success*, International Thomson Computer Press, Boston, Mass., 1995.

———: *Software Quality—Analysis and Guidelines for Success*, International Thomson Computer Press, Boston, Mass., 1997.

———: *Software Assessments, Benchmarks, and Best Practices*, Addison-Wesley Longman, Boston, Mass., 2000.

———: *Conflict and Litigation Between Software Clients and Developers*, Software Productivity Research, Burlington, Mass., 2003.

Kan, Stephen H.: *Metrics and Models in Software Quality Engineering, Second Edition*, Addison-Wesley Longman, Boston, Mass., 2003.

Larman, Craig, and Victor Basili: "Iterative and Incremental Development—A Brief History," *IEEE Computer Society*, June 2003, pp 47–55.

Mills, H., M. Dyer, and R. Linger: "Cleanroom Software Engineering," *IEEE Software*, 4, 5 (Sept. 1987), pp. 19–25.

Pressman, Roger: *Software Engineering—A Practitioner's Approach, Sixth Edition*; McGraw-Hill, New York, 2005.

Putnam, Lawrence H.: *Measures for Excellence—Reliable Software on Time, Within Budget*, Yourdon Press/Prentice-Hall, Englewood Cliffs, N.J., 1992.

———, and Ware Myers: *Industrial Strength Software—Effective Management Using Measurement*, IEEE Computer Society Press, Washington D.C., 1997.

Quality Function Deployment (http://en.wikipedia.org/wiki/Quality_function_deployment).

Radice, Ronald A.: *High-Quality Low-Cost Software Inspections*, Paradoxican Publishing, Andover, Mass., 2002.

Rubin, Howard: *Software Benchmark Studies for 1997*, Howard Rubin Associates, Pound Ridge, N.Y., 1997.

Wiegers, Karl E.: *Peer Reviews in Software—A Practical Guide*, Addison-Wesley, Boston, Mass., 2002.

Estimating Software Configuration Control and Change Management

Software projects change as rapidly as any product ever conceived by the human mind. Therefore, one of the major challenges of the software industry has been to manage change as efficiently as possible.

Estimating the work of change management is also important, not only because change management itself can be expensive, but because the rate of change of various software deliverables is a major factor in the accuracy of overall software cost and schedule estimation. Table 19.1 shows historical data on the monthly rates of change for requirements and the cumulative totals of change for six kinds of software projects:

As can be seen from Table 19.1, an average of almost one-third of the final features that are in software applications when they are delivered to clients were not defined in the initial set of requirements.

Every software project changes during development. But the rates of change vary widely from project to project, as do the set of artifacts that are created for the project. In general, estimating change management requires separate estimates for the following variable items:

- The set of artifacts (requirements, specifications, code, documents, tests, bugs, etc.)
- The rates of change of each artifact
- The way proposed changes are evaluated and accepted or rejected
- The presence or absence of a formal change-control board
- The way changes to various artifacts are stored and recorded
- The presence or absence of configuration audits

TABLE 19.1   Monthly Rate of Changing Requirements for Six Application Types
(From end of requirements to start of coding phases)

	Web	MIS	Outsource	Commercial	System	Military	Average
Monthly Rate	4.00%	2.50%	1.50%	3.50%	2.00%	2.00%	2.58%
Months	6.00	12.00	14.00	10.00	18.00	24.00	14.00
TOTAL	24.00%	30.00%	21.00%	35.00%	36.00%	48.00%	32.33%

- The tools available for building and controlling versions of the application
- The frequency with which new versions are built

Estimating change management is also a fairly difficult task, because of several unique characteristics of this activity:

- Not every software project uses formal change management methods.
- Agile projects often use informal change-control methods.
- Not every software project has a change-control board.
- For projects that have change-control boards, their sizes and memberships vary.
- For projects that have change-control boards, their meetings are intermittent.
- Not every project uses configuration-control automation.
- The automated configuration-control tools vary widely in capabilities.

For example, military projects of almost any size usually include formal change management approaches because they are required by various military standards such as DoD 2167A and DoD 973. Military configuration management starts early, during the requirements phase. Once started, change control is continuous and includes intermittent audits of configuration status.

Civilian projects are less likely to utilize formal change management unless the corporation is certified using the ISO 9000–9004 standards or is climbing the SEI capability maturity model above level 2, where change management becomes a standard activity. Civilian configuration control typically starts later than military configuration control, and may support fewer artifacts. Indeed, some civilian projects use only rudimentary configuration control for the source code, and no formal methods at all for specifications, user documents, or other artifacts.

Civilian projects using the new Agile methods have very dynamic changing requirements. Because a client is part of the development team and requirements are worked out on the fly, the monthly rates of change for Agile projects is about 12 percent. Usually, the set of initial requirements for Agile projects define only between 15 and 30 percent of the final features that eventually are included. The other features are defined during subsequent iterations or sprints.

However, civilian systems and embedded software typically uses more thorough configuration control than does information systems software, and often follows formal change management standards, such as IEEE Standard 1042-1987 on software configuration management.

Thus, estimating the nature of change management activity requires a knowledge of the nature of the enterprise, the nature of the project, the size of the application in question, and the forms of change management methods to be utilized.

The Literature on Change Management

There is fairly extensive literature on software change management in both its civilian and military forms. For example, Tim Mikkelsen and Suzanne Pherigo of Hewlett-Packard have published an interesting primer entitled *Practical Software Configuration Management* (Prentice-Hall, 1997). There are also a number of older books on software configuration control, such as H. R. Berlack's *Software Configuration Management* (John Wiley & Sons, 1992).

In addition to standalone books on software configuration control, the topic is also covered in chapters on general software engineering and management principles in such books as Fred Brooks's classic *The Mythical Man-Month* (Addison-Wesley, 1974) and Roger Pressman's *Software Engineering—A Practitioner's Approach* (McGraw-Hill, 2005). Note that Roger Pressman's book has gone through six editions, and each edition adds new material. The latest edition has new data on change management for Agile projects.

The nominal default values for estimating the activity of software change management or configuration control are shown in Table 19.2.

Once change management and configuration control begin for an application, some aspects of change management are daily events, such as updating records in response to repaired bugs.

Other aspects of change management are intermittent. For example, the change management board may meet at weekly, biweekly, or monthly intervals. The duration of each meeting can run from less than one hour to more than one day.

From time to time on large systems, there may be a configuration audit. Such audits are required for military software and are formal milestones. For civilian projects, configuration audits are not as common and are not as formal when they occur. Variable factors, such as the presence or absence of configuration audits, make estimating change control rather tricky.

TABLE 19.2   Nominal Default Values for Change Management and Configuration Control

Activity sequence	Seventh
Activity performed by	Change-control specialists; developers; auditors; clients
Predecessor activities	Requirements, design, coding, and inspections
Overlap	25% with design; then continuous
Concurrent activities	Multiple: design, coding, testing, and documentation
Successor activities	Release of the project to clients
Assignment scope	1000 function points per change team member
Production rate	1500 function points per staff month
Schedule months	Continuous once begun through release
Rate of creep or change	Varies with artifact: overall about 2% per month
Defect potential	0.2 defects per function point due to change errors
Defect removal	75% average removal efficiency
Delivered defects	0.2 defects −75% or roughly 0.05 per function point
High-severity defects	10% of delivered defects due to change
Bad fix probability	3% of change-control modifications may yield new errors

In general, large systems of more than 5000 function points in size will utilize very formal change management methods; will have change-control boards; and will have an extensive suite of change management tools that can handle changes to requirements, specifications, code, defects, user documents, and other artifacts.

Software projects between 1000 and 5000 function points may utilize formal change management methods, but often deploy only subsets of the methods used on larger systems. Among SPR's clients, a significant portion use change management automation only for source code, and handle changes to requirements and specifications in a manual fashion. For projects toward the low end of this spectrum, change-control boards are rare rather than the norm.

At the low end, for small projects of only a few hundred function points or less, formal change control tends to concentrate on source code and is handled by the developers themselves. Formal change-control boards essentially never are used, unless the project is an enhancement to a much larger system.

For very small projects of less than 100 function points with a one-person development team, change control is never formal. Unless change management features are part of the development tool suite, there is seldom any automation utilized.

The overall challenge of software change management was poorly met for many years. The primary change management tools for source code were standalone file-based version control systems that supported code only.

Change management for text specification and planning documents, cost estimates, test libraries, graphics and illustrations, and the inventories of bugs reported against software projects were all performed using only rudimentary standalone tools that often did not communicate or coordinate across domains. Indeed, some projects utilized only source code change-control tools, and handled changes of all other artifacts in an informal, manual fashion.

In recent years, since about 1990, it has been recognized that source code is not the only deliverable that changes. In fact, for many projects source code is not even the major item that changes. For large software projects, there are many more words created than source code and the words change more rapidly! There are also large volumes of bug reports, which need constant surveillance and monitoring during software development and maintenance.

Therefore, modern change management tools, or *configuration-control* tools as they are commonly called, must be capable of dealing with every kind of software deliverable and artifact, as follows:

- Changing requirements
- Changing project plans
- Changing project cost estimates
- Changing contracts
- Changing design
- Changing source code
- Changing user documents
- Changing illustrations and graphics
- Changing test materials
- Changing volumes of bug reports

Ideally, the change management tools can use hypertext capabilities to handle cross-references between deliverables so that when something changes, the corresponding places in related material can be highlighted or even modified semi-automatically.

Measuring Software Change

Another recent development in the software world is the newfound ability to understand the economics of changes. For many years, software costs were normalized using *lines of code* (LOC) as the primary metric. This metric was useless for dealing with the costs of producing text materials, graphics, test cases and all other non-code software artifacts. Therefore, both the development and the modification costs of non-code material were essentially invisible to the software world.

The function point metric can be applied to plans, estimates, specifications, test materials, source code, and all software deliverables. The function point metric has helped enormously in understanding the costs and economic consequences of changes to every software artifact.

Other new metrics such as use case points, story points, object points, or COSMIC function points can also be used to measure rates of requirements change.

In order to discuss the rate at which software deliverables change, it is necessary to know at least approximately how big they are under normal conditions. The function point metric has given the software industry a useful way of normalizing various deliverable items, so that volumes of materials can be discussed using a stable size dimension.

The function point metric is also beginning to be used to assign fairly accurate cost and value amounts to changes. Outsource vendors, for example, are beginning to include *cost per function point* on sliding scales in contracts, so that new features added late in development have higher charges than function points derived during the actual requirements phase.

Table 19.3 shows the nominal sizes and rates of monthly change associated with a generic average systems software project of 1000 function points in size. This project can be assumed to use the C programming language.

If the project shown in Table 19.3 were an object-oriented project designed with the unified modeling language (UML) and use cases, the volumes of requirements and design would be roughly the same as the volumes indicated.

The typical calendar time for developing a systems software application of 1000 function points would be about 18 months from the start of requirements to the initial delivery to the first customer.

The overall effort to produce this project would total about 200 person months. The productivity rate can be seen to be five function points ˙

TABLE 19.3   Average Deliverable Sizes and Rates of Change for a 1000–Function Point System Software Application Using a Waterfall Method

Deliverable	Size per FP	Basic size	Monthly change rate, %
Requirements	0.3 pages	300 pages	2
Plans/estimates	0.2 pages	200 pages	10
External design	0.5 pages	500 pages	5
Logical design	0.7 pages	700 pages	4
Source code	125.0 LOC	125,000 LOC	7
Test cases	5.0 test cases	5,000 cases	10
User manuals	0.4 pages	400 pages	5
Defects (bug reports)	5.0 bugs	5,000 reports	15

per month. Assuming an average burdened salary rate of $8000 per month, the total cost would be $16 million and the cost per function point would be $1600.

Because the Agile methods reduce the volume of requirements and design paperwork, it is interesting to show what the same project might look like using the Agile approach. Table 19.4 illustrates typical document volumes and rates of change in an Agile context.

With Agile methods the formal documentation at the start of a project, such as requirements and specifications, are reduced in volume. This reduction in paperwork requires that one or more clients become an actual part of the development team. Since client participation is not usually included in waterfall cost estimates, but is included in Agile cost estimates, there will be at least one more staff member for Agile projects than for waterfall projects. The reduction in paperwork volumes usually raises overall productivity by about 30 percent.

Because such non-code materials as text and graphics actually comprise the bulk of software deliverables, it is of interest to include some information on the approximate volumes of these two items.

Table 19.5 shows the approximate volumes of the major paper deliverables associated with software that uses the waterfall approach. There are, of course, many more ephemeral documents produced, such as letters, memos, presentations, progress reports, and the like. (A total of more than 50 kinds of paper document can be produced for large software projects.) However, these ephemeral documents may not come under configuration control, while the basic specifications, contracts, plans, estimates, and user documents often do.

Because the volume of source code in this example is 125,000 logical statements, it can be seen that more than 184 words are created for every source code statement. (Had this been a military project, the total would have been more than 400 English words per source code statement.)

TABLE 19.4   Average Deliverable Sizes and Rates of Change for a 1000–Function Point System Software Application Using Agile Methods

Deliverable	Size per FP	Basic size	Monthly change rate, %
Requirements	0.1 pages	100 pages	12
Plans/estimates	0.1 pages	100 pages	10
External design	0.2 pages	200 pages	10
Logical design	0.1 pages	100 pages	10
Source code	125.0 LOC	125,000 LOC	15
Test cases	5.0 test cases	5,000 cases	10
User manuals	0.4 pages	400 pages	5
Defects (bug reports)	5.0 bugs	5,000 reports	15

TABLE 19.5   Volume of Text and Words Produced for a Generic 1000–Function Point System Software Project

Deliverable	Basic size, pages	English words	English words per FP
Requirements	300	120,000	120
Plans/estimates	100	40,000	40
External design	500	200,000	200
Internal design	700	245,000	245
User manuals	400	160,000	160
Bug reports	5000	1,350,000	1350
Total	7000	2,115,000	2115

Of course, if this were an Agile project, the volume of paperwork would be less than 50 percent of the volume shown in Table 19.5. The only paper documents that would be the same size in both the waterfall and Agile methods of development would be the user manuals and the bug reports. All of the front-end requirements and specification volumes would be reduced.

Both the large volume of information associated with bug reports and the significance of this topic imply a need for very strong defect-tracking capabilities in configuration-control tool suites.

Graphics and illustrations vary widely and are more difficult to quantify. Even so, the volume of graphical material in support of software is too large to ignore and is becoming larger very rapidly as better graphics production tools become widespread. Table 19.6 shows the approximate volumes of graphical materials that might be produced for this sample waterfall application.

Even as this is being written, graphics and illustrations tend to remain somewhat troublesome for configuration-control purposes. In the future, when dynamic or animated models and simulations become common for software, and when multimedia approaches are used for software representation, change control will become both more difficult and more important.

TABLE 19.6   Volume of Graphic Illustrations Produced for a Generic 1000–Function Point System Software Project

Deliverable	Basic size, pages	Graphics	Graphics per FP
Requirements	300	100	0.10
Plans/estimates	100	50	0.05
External design	500	50	0.05
Logical design	700	200	0.50
User manuals	600	300	0.30
Total	2200	700	1.00

If the project illustrated in Table 19.6 were an object-oriented project that used the UML, the volume of graphics would be about 25 percent larger for the requirements and design documents. Plans and user manuals would not change.

Changes in User Requirements

Requirements changes, or creeping requirements, are the most important topic for change management, because they cause updates of all downstream deliverables. Requirements changes become progressively more troublesome after the nominal completion of the requirements phase, as discussed earlier in this book.

The exception to the rule that requirements changes become progressively more troublesome are projects that use the Agile methodology. These projects start coding when only basic and obvious requirements are understood, and the remainder of the requirements grow organically. This method requires that a client be an actual part of the development team, and that each increment or sprint be used in order to plan the next wave of change.

Of course for projects where the number of users is large, say more than 1,000,000 people, the Agile methods are not applicable. Neither are they applicable for projects that might be developed under a fixed-cost contract.

During the subsequent design phase, the average rate of requirements change may exceed 3 percent per month for many software projects (and 12 percent for Agile projects). This burst of rapid requirements changes may last as long as a year for large systems, but would occur only for about three months on this sample project. The burst of new requirements slows down to about 1 percent per month during coding, and eventually stops by the time testing commences. (Requirements changes don't really stop, of course, but the requirements tend to get pushed downstream into follow-on releases.)

For systems software, such as this example, and for commercial software, changes may be due to market needs or competitive products. The average rate is about 2 percent per month from the end of initial requirements until start of testing. But if a competitor suddenly announces a new product, monthly change rates can top 15 percent!

For internal software, requirements changes are driven by user needs and average about 1 percent per month from the start of design until well into coding. For military software, the average is about 2 percent per month.

Military software requirements call for very strict *requirements traceability*. This means that all downstream deliverables need to identify which requirements they include to a very granular level. This implies, ideally, that software requirements would be the base for hypertext linkages to other downstream software artifacts.

Software outsourcers and contractors can now derive the function point totals of software during the requirements phase, and this is leading to a newfound ability to quantify the subsequent downstream costs of changing requirements.

Because the *cost per function point* is now being used to price software features, tools such as Function Point Workbench, which can assign function point totals to various features of an application, are starting to become important business tools. Currently, these are standalone tools, but it is obvious that direct linkages will be needed so that changes in requirements or design can automatically trigger new size and cost estimates.

For example, assume that this project is performed as a contract development effort rather than as an internal project. The contract might include phrasing or concepts similar to the following:

- Development costs for requirements derived during months 1 to 3 or the requirements phase of the project = $1500 per function point.
- Development costs for new requirements added during months 4 to 6 = $1750 per function point.
- Costs for requirements deleted during months 4 to 6 = $150 per function point.
- Development costs for new requirements added during months 6 to 12 = $2250 per function point.
- Costs for requirements deleted during months 6 to 12 = $500 per function point.
- Development costs for new requirements added during months 12 to 18 = $5000 per function point.
- Costs for requirements deleted during months 12 to 18 = $1000 per function point.

The usage of cost per function point as a contractual metric means that clients, accountants, project managers, contract officers, attorneys, and others now have a much better understanding of software economics than was possible during the primitive lines-of-code era. It is also significant that the Internal Revenue Service is now exploring cost per function point as a way of determining the taxable value of software.

Changes in Specifications and Design

Since the design and specifications for a software project are in response to fundamental user requirements, most of the design changes after the initial creation of the design can be attributed to changes in the user requirements.

However, a significant number of design modifications are due to suggested improvements by the development team members themselves, or to factors that only come to light during the detailed design phase. For example, if a software application has very stringent performance targets it may be necessary to revise the design in order to squeeze extra speed out of the system.

A study performed by the author on IBM systems software noted that the design and development team introduced a number of changes for what appeared to be insufficient justification. Some changes were made because of personal preferences by the design personnel, or for somewhat nebulous reasons, such as "Someone might need this feature and it was easy to put it in."

On the whole, large systems benefit from the costs of having a formal change-control board with representatives from the client community, the development community, the quality-assurance community, and the testing community.

A multi-skilled change-control board with a broad outlook can save time and money by eliminating unnecessary changes and ensuring that when changes do occur, all affected organizations are brought up to speed.

It should be noted that there are more than 40 different kinds of design methodology in the software engineering world. Obviously, the volumes and costs of producing design documents will vary from method to method. UML and use cases are not increasing in usage. As it happens, their volume is roughly commensurate with some of the older design approaches such as standard structured design.

Changes Due to Bugs or Defect Reports

Software development and maintenance are intellectually difficult tasks during which a large number of bugs or defects will be created (and hopefully found and eliminated). Defect removal is the most expensive cost component of software, and the volume of information associated with software defects or bugs is the largest of any software artifact.

Because there are so many bugs in software, so much information about bugs, and the costs of bug removal is such a major component of overall software costs, it is mandatory that configuration-control tools have powerful defect tracking and reporting capabilities.

Bugs are not just found in source code, of course. Table 19.7 shows approximate U.S. national averages for software defects and the percentages of defects removed prior to the initial deployment.

A simple rule of thumb can lead to useful approximations of software defects or bugs. Take the size of the application in function points and raise the size to the 1.25 power. That will yield a rough approximation of the total number of bugs that may be faced during development.

TABLE 19.7 U.S. Averages for Software Defects and Defect-Removal Efficiency
(Data expressed in defects per function point)

Defect origins	Defect potentials	Removal efficiency, %	Delivered defects
Requirements	1.00	77	0.23
Design	1.25	85	0.19
Coding	1.75	95	0.09
Documentation	0.60	80	0.12
Bad fixes	0.40	70	0.12
Total	5.00	85	0.75

For enhancement projects, the size is that of the enhancement rather than the base size of the application.

This approximation method for defects works for waterfall projects, Agile projects, object-oriented projects, web projects and most other kinds of software projects.

There are three interesting exceptions, however. Projects that are at level 3 or higher on the capability maturity model (CMM) should use a power of 1.15 rather than 1.25. Projects developed in organizations that utilize six-sigma for software should use a power of 1.2 rather than 1.25. Projects that utilize QFD should use a power of 1.12 rather than 1.25. These three methods have proven to be fairly effective in preventing defects from occurring.

Assuming that the hypothetical project discussed here is an average project, there would be about 1000 errors found in requirements, 1250 in design, 1750 in the source code, and 600 in the user manuals. Another 400 bugs would be secondary errors or bad fixes introduced when a bug repair itself contains a new error. A total of about 5000 bugs would have to be found and eliminated in this average project.

Because of the costs and importance of quality control, it can be seen that defect tracking is a vital component of software change management. Defect tracking spans the entire life cycle of a software project. Defect tracking starts during requirements and proceeds all the way through the development cycle and out into the maintenance cycle for as long as the product is used—20 years or more in some cases.

Summary and Conclusions

Change management is one of the most important aspects of successful software development. Recognition of this fact is leading to an interesting new sub-industry of companies that build integrated change management tools that can handle far more than just source code revisions.

Part of the impetus for the development of this sub-industry is the impact of function point metrics, which allow quantifying the costs of change with a precision that was impossible for many years.

Costs of changes are now beginning to appear in development and maintenance contracts for software, and this, in turn, is leading to a new business understanding of the economics of changing software.

There is still a long way to go before software changes are fully explored and understood, but the rate of progress is now very rapid and even accelerating.

References

Ambler, S.: *Process Patterns—Building Large-Scale Systems Using Object Technology*, Cambridge University Press, New York, SIGS Books, 1998.

Arthur, Jay: *Software Evolution*, John Wiley & Sons, New York, 1988.

Artow, J., and I. Neustadt: *UML and the Unified Process*, Addison-Wesley, Boston, Mass., 2000.

Beck, K.: *Extreme Programming Explained: Embrace Change*, Addison-Wesley, Boston, Mass., 1999.

Berlack, H.R.: *Software Configuration Management*, John Wiley & Sons, New York, 1992.

———: "Configuration Management," in, *Encyclopedia of Software Engineering*, John Marciniak, (ed.), vol. 1, John Wiley & Sons, New York, 1994, pp. 180–206.

Boehm, Barry: "A Spiral Model of Software Development and Enhancement," Proceedings of the Int. Workshop on Software Process and Software Environments, ACM Software Engineering Notes, Aug. 1986, pp. 22–42.

Booch, Grady: *Object Solutions: Managing the Object-Oriented Project*, Addison-Wesley, Reading, Mass., 1995.

———, Ivar Jacobsen, and James Rumbaugh: *The Unified Modeling Language User Guide, Second Edition*, Addison-Wesley, Boston, Mass., 2005.

Brooks, Fred: *The Mythical Man-Month, Second Edition*, Addison-Wesley, Reading, Mass., 1995.

"Capability Maturity Model Integration," Version 1.1, Software Engineering Institute, Carnegie-Mellon Univ., Pittsburgh, PA, March 2003, (http://www.sei.cmu.edu/cmmi/).

Cockburn, Alistair: *Agile Software Development*, Addison-Wesley, Boston, Mass., 2001.

Cohen, D., M. Lindvall, and P. Costa: "An Introduction to Agile Methods," *Advances in Computers*, Elsevier Science, New York, 2004, pp. 1–66.

Cohen, Lou: *Quality Function Deployment: How to Make QFD Work for You*, Prentice-Hall PTR, 1995.

Cohn, Mike: *User Stories Applied: For Agile Software Development*, Addison-Wesley, Boston, Mass., 2004.

———: *Agile Estimating and Planning*, Prentice-Hall PTR, Englewood Cliffs, N.J., 2005.

Gack, Gary: "Applying Six-Sigma to Software Implementation Projects," (http://software.isixsigma.com/library/content/c040915b.asp).

Gamma, Erich, Richard Helm, Ralph Johnson, and John Vlissides: *Design Patterns: Elements of Reusable Object Oriented Design*, Addison-Wesley, Boston Mass., 1995.

Garmus, David, and David Herron, David: *Measuring the Software Process: A Practical Guide to Functional Measurement*, Prentice-Hall, Englewood Cliffs, N.J., 1995.

———: *Function Point Analysis*, Addison-Wesley Longman, Boston, Mass., 2001.

Hallowell, David L.: "Six-Sigma Software Metrics, Part 1" (http://software.isixsigma.com/library/content/03910a.asp).

Highsmith, Jim: *Agile Software Development Ecosystems*, Addison-Wesley, Boston, Mass., 2002.

Humphrey, Watts: *Managing the Software Process*, Addison-Wesley, Reading, Mass., 1989.

———: *TSP—Leading a Development Team*, Addison-Wesley, Boston, Mass., 2006.

IEEE Standard 828-1990: Software Configuration Management, IEEE Standards Department, Piscataway, N.J., 1990.

Mikkelsen, Tim, and Suzanne Pherigo: *Practical Software Configuration Management*, Prentice-Hall PTR, Upper Saddle River, N.J., 1997.

MIL STD 973: Configuration Management, Department of Defense, Naval Publications Center, Philadelphia, Pa., 1992.

MIL STD 2167A: Defense System Software Development and Data Item Descriptions, Department of Defense, Naval Publications Center, Philadelphia, Pa., 1988.

Jones, Capers: *Assessment and Control of Software Risks*, Prentice-Hall, Englewood Cliffs, N.J., 1994.

———: *Patterns of Software System Failure and Success*, International Thomson Computer Press, Boston, Mass., 1995.

———: *Applied Software Measurement*, McGraw-Hill, New York, 1996.

———: *Software Quality—Analysis and Guidelines for Success*, International Thomson Computer Press, Boston, 1997.

———: "Sizing Up Software," *Scientific American*, New York, December 1998, Vol. 279, No. 6, pp 104–109.

———: *Software Assessments, Benchmarks, and Best Practices*, Addison-Wesley Longman, Boston, Mass., 2000.

———: *Conflict and Litigation Between Software Clients and Developers*, Software Productivity Research, Burlington, Mass., 2003.

Kan, Stephen H.: *Metrics and Models in Software Quality Engineering, Second Edition*, Addison-Wesley Longman, Boston, Mass., 2003.

Koirala, Shavisprasad: *"How to Prepare Quotation Using Use Case Points,"* (http://www.codeproject.com/gen/design//usecasepoints.asp).

Larman, Craig, and Victor Basili: "Iterative and Incremental Development—A Brief History," *IEEE Computer Society*, June 2003, pp 47–55.

Love, Tom, *Object Lessons*, SIGS Books, New York, 1993.

McConnell, Steve: *Software Estimating: Demystifying the Black Art*, Microsoft Press, Redmond, WA, 2006.

Mikkelsen, Tim and Pherigo, Suzzanne; *Practical Software Configuration Management: The Latenight Developer's Handbook*; Prentice-Hall PTR, Englewood Cliffs, NJ; 1997.

Mills, H., M. Dyer, and R. Linger: "Cleanroom Software Engineering," *IEEE Software*, 4, 5 (Sept. 1987), pp. 19–25.

Pressman, Roger: *Software Engineering—A Practitioner's Approach, Sixth Edition*, McGraw-Hill, New York, 2005.

Putnam, Lawrence H.: *Measures for Excellence—Reliable Software on Time, Within Budget*, Yourdon Press/Prentice-Hall, Englewood Cliffs, N.J., 1992.

———, and Ware Myers: *Industrial Strength Software—Effective Management Using Measurement*, IEEE Computer Society Press, Washington D.C., 1997.

Quality Function Deployment (http://en.wikipedia.org/wiki/Quality_function_deployment).

Rapid Application Development (http://en.wikipedia.org/wiki/Rapid_application_development).

Stapleton, J.: *DSDM—Dynamic System Development in Practice*, Addison-Wesley, Boston, Mass., 1997.

20

Estimating Software Testing

From an estimating standpoint, estimating testing effort, testing schedules, and testing costs are rather complex topics because of the many different forms of testing that might be performed, and the fact that the numbers of discrete test stages for applications can run from a single perfunctory form of testing up to a high of about 18 formal test operations.

Test estimation is also complicated by the fact that the defects that are actually present when testing begins can vary widely. For example, projects that use formal design and code inspections enter testing with about 80 percent fewer defects than projects that do not use inspections.

The best way to start a discussion of software test estimating is to show the approximate volumes of defects in various kinds of software applications. Then it is useful to show the typical patterns of software defect removal and testing activities that are likely to occur. Table 20.1 shows defects from all major sources, while Table 20.2 illustrates typical patterns of defect removal and testing.

The typical sequence is to estimate defect volumes for a project, and then to estimate the series of reviews, inspections, and tests that the project utilizes. The defect-removal efficiency of each step will also be estimated. The effort and costs for preparation, execution, and defect repairs associated with each removal activity will also be estimated.

Table 20.1 illustrates the overall distribution of software errors among the six project types. In Table 20.1 bugs or defects are shown from five sources: requirements errors, design errors, coding errors, user documentation errors, and "bad fixes." A "bad fix" is a secondary defect accidentally injected in a bug repair. In other words, a bad fix is a failed attempt to repair a prior bug that accidentally contains a new bug. On average about 7 percent of defect repairs will themselves accidentally inject a new defect, although the range is from less than 1 percent to more than 20 percent bad-fix injections.

TABLE 20.1   **Average Defect Potentials for Six Application Types**
(Data expressed in terms of "defects per function point")

Source	Web	MIS	Outsource	Commercial	System	Military	Average
Requirements	1.00	1.00	1.10	1.25	1.30	1.70	1.23
Design	1.00	1.25	1.20	1.30	1.50	1.75	1.33
Code	1.25	1.75	1.70	1.75	1.80	1.75	1.67
Documents	0.30	0.60	0.50	0.70	0.70	1.20	0.67
Bad fix	0.45	0.40	0.30	0.50	0.70	0.60	0.49
TOTAL	4.00	5.00	4.80	5.50	6.00	7.00	5.38

(The data in Table 20.1, and in the other tables in this chapter, are based on a total of about 12,000 software projects examined by the author and his colleagues circa 1984–2007. Additional information on the sources of data can be found in other publications by the author and by Stephen H. Kan, as listed in the References section at the end of this chapter.)

Table 20.1 presents approximate average values, but the range for each defect category is more than 2 to 1. For example, software projects developed by companies who are at level 5 on the capability maturity model (CMM) might have less than half of the potential defects shown in Table 20.1. Similarly, companies with several years of experience with the "six-sigma" quality approach will also have lower defect potentials than those shown in Table 20.1. Several commercial estimating tools make adjustments for such factors.

A key factor for accurate estimation involves the removal of defects via reviews, inspections, and testing. The measurement of defect removal is actually fairly straightforward, and many companies now do this. The U.S. average is about 85 percent, but leading companies can average more than 95 percent removal efficiency levels.

Measuring defect-removal efficiency levels is actually one of the easiest forms of measurement. For example, suppose a programmer finds 90 bugs or defects during the unit test of a small program. Then the program is turned over to its client, who finds an additional 10 bugs in the first three months of use. Calculating defect-removal efficiency only requires adding the number of bugs found during a particular test step to the bugs found afterwards, and deriving the percentage. Thus, in this simple example the 90 bugs found during unit test and the 10 bugs found afterwards total to 100 defects. As can be seen, the removal efficiency of this unit test was 90 percent.

In real life the calculations are not quite so simple, because a percentage of the bug repairs will accidentally inject new bugs back into the software. (The U.S. average for such "bad fixes" is about 7 percent.) Even so, measuring defect-removal efficiency is fairly straightforward. Measuring defect-removal efficiency does not even require knowledge of lines of code, function points, object points, or other metrics. It is one of the simplest and yet most revealing of all forms of software measurement.

It is much easier to estimate software projects that use sophisticated quality control and have high levels of defect removal in the 95 percent range. This is because there usually are no disasters occurring late in development when unexpected defects are discovered. Thus projects performed by companies at the higher CMM levels or by companies with extensive six-sigma experience for software often have much greater precision than average.

Table 20.2 illustrates the variations in typical defect prevention and defect-removal methods among the six kinds of projects shown in Table 20.1. Of course, many variations in these patterns can occur. Therefore, it is important to adjust the set of activities, and their efficiency levels, to match the realities of the projects being estimated. However, since defect removal in total has been the most expensive cost element of large software applications for more than 50 years, it is not possible to achieve accurate estimates without being very thorough in estimating defect-removal patterns.

(The cumulative efficiency values in Table 20.2 are calculated as follows. If the starting number of defects is 100, and there are two consecutive test stages that each remove 50 percent of the defects present, then the first test will remove 50 defects and the second test will remove 25 defects. The cumulative efficiency of both tests is 75 percent, because 75 out of a possible 100 defects were eliminated.)

Readers who are not experienced quality-assurance or test personnel may be surprised by the low average levels of defect-removal efficiency shown in Table 20.2. However, the data is derived from empirical studies of reviews, inspections, and tests taken from many large corporations. It is an unfortunate fact of life that most forms of testing are less than 50 percent efficient in finding bugs or defects and many are less than 30 percent efficient. Formal design and code inspections have the highest measured removal efficiencies of any known form of defect elimination and are usually at least twice as efficient as any standard test stage such as new function testing or regression testing.

The comparatively low average values for defect-removal efficiency levels explains why leading companies typically deploy several kinds of inspections before testing begins, and up to 10 discrete testing steps. For really critical applications such as military weapons systems there may be as many as six inspection stages and a dozen discrete testing stages utilized.

Table 20.2 oversimplifies the situation, since defect-removal activities have varying efficiencies for requirements, design, code, documentation, and bad-fix defect categories. Also, bad fixes during testing will be injected back into the set of undetected defects.

TABLE 20.2   Patterns of Defect Prevention and Removal Activities

Prevention activities	Web	MIS	Outsource	Commercial	System	Military
Prototypes	20.00%	20.00%	20.00%	20.00%	20.00%	20.00%
Clean rooms					20.00%	20.00%
JAD sessions		30.00%	30.00%			
QFD sessions					25.00%	
Subtotal	20.00%	44.00%	44.00%	20.00%	52.00%	36.00%
Pretest Removal						
Desk checking	15.00%	15.00%	15.00%	15.00%	15.00%	15.00%
Requirements review			30.00%	25.00%	20.00%	20.00%
Design review			40.00%	45.00%	45.00%	30.00%
Document review				20.00%	20.00%	20.00%
Code inspections				50.00%	60.00%	40.00%
Independent verification and validation						20.00%
Correctness proofs						10.00%
Usability labs				25.00%		
Subtotal	15.00%	15.00%	64.30%	89.48%	88.03%	83.55%
Testing Activities						
Unit test	30.00%	25.00%	25.00%	25.00%	25.00%	25.00%
New function test		30.00%	30.00%	30.00%	30.00%	30.00%
Regression test			20.00%	20.00%	20.00%	20.00%
Integration test		30.00%	30.00%	30.00%	30.00%	30.00%
Performance test				15.00%	15.00%	20.00%
System test		35.00%	35.00%	35.00%	40.00%	35.00%
Independent test						15.00%
Field test				50.00%	35.00%	30.00%
Acceptance test			25.00%		25.00%	30.00%
Subtotal	30.00%	76.11%	80.89%	91.88%	92.69%	93.63%
Overall Efficiency	52.40%	88.63%	96.18%	99.32%	99.58%	99.33%
Number of Activities	3	7	11	14	16	18

The low efficiency of most forms of defect removal explains why a lengthy series of defect removal activities is needed. This in turn explains why estimating defect removal is critical for overall accuracy of software cost estimation for large systems. Below 1000 function points, the series of defect removal operations may be as few as three. Above 10,000 function points the series may include more than 15 kinds of review, inspection, and test activity.

Table 20.3 provides some nominal default values for estimating testing activities, although these defaults need to be adjusted and applied to each specific form of testing, as will be discussed later in this chapter.

TABLE 20.3 Nominal Default Values for Testing

Activity sequence	Eighth
Activity performed by	Developers; test specialists; quality assurance; clients
Predecessor activities	Coding and code inspections
Overlap	25% with coding
Concurrent activities	Coding, quality assurance, change control, and documentation
Successor activities	Release of the project to clients
Assignment scope	500 function points per test specialist
Production rate	250 function points per staff month
Schedule months	Varies with number of defects found and test stage
Rate of creep or change	5% per month
Defect potential	0.3 defects per function point in test cases themselves
Defect removal	75% average removal efficiency against defective test cases
Defect removal	30% average against defects in code itself
Delivered defects	0.3 defects −75% or roughly 0.1 per function point
High-severity defects	5% of test-case defects
Bad-fix probability	5% of test-case changes may yield new errors

It is obvious from Table 20.3 that testing can vary significantly in who performs it, and even more significantly in the number of kinds of tests that are likely to be performed. Let us consider the implications of these test estimating complexities.

The exact definition of what *testing* means is quite ambiguous. In this book and the author's previous books on software quality and software measurement the basic definition of testing is:

> The dynamic execution of software and the comparison of the results of that execution against a set of known, predetermined criteria. Determining the validity of a specific application output in response to a specific application input is termed a *test case*.

Under this definition of testing, static defect-removal methods, such as formal design and code inspections, are not viewed as *testing*. However, under a broader definition of *defect removal*, both inspections and testing would be considered as complementary activities. Formal inspections actually have higher levels of defect-removal efficiency than almost any form of testing.

It may also be significant to define what *software* means in a testing context. The term *software* can mean any of the following:

- An individual instruction (about .001 function points)

- A small subroutine of perhaps 10 instructions in length (about .01 function points)

- A module of perhaps 100 instructions in length (about 1 function point)

- A complete program of perhaps 1000 instructions in length (10 function points)

- A component of a system of perhaps 10,000 instructions in length (100 function points)

- An entire software system of perhaps 100,000 instructions

- A mega-system of perhaps 1 to more than 10 million instructions in length

Any one of these software groupings can be tested, and often tested many times, in the course of software development activities.

Also significant in a testing context is the term *execution*. As used here, the term *execution* means running the software on a computer with or without any form of instrumentation or test-control software being present.

The phrase *predetermined criteria* means that what the software is supposed to do is known prior to its execution, so that what the software actually does can be compared against the anticipated results to judge whether or not the software is behaving correctly.

The term *test case* means recording a known set of conditions so that the response of the application to a specific input combination is evaluated to determine that the outputs are valid and fall within predetermined, acceptable ranges.

There are dozens of possible forms of testing, but they can be aggregated into three forms of testing that can be defined as the following broad categories:

- General testing of applications for validity of outputs in response to inputs

- Specialized testing for specific kinds of problems, such as performance or capacity

- Testing that involves the users or clients themselves to evaluate ease of use

The general forms of testing are concerned with almost any kind of software and seek to eliminate common kinds of bugs, such as branching errors, looping errors, incorrect outputs, and the like.

The specialized forms of testing are more narrow in focus and seek specific kinds of errors, such as problems that only occur under full load, or problems that might slow down performance.

The forms of testing involving users are aimed primarily at usability problems and at ensuring that all requirements have, in fact, been implemented.

Not every form of testing is used on every software project, and some forms of testing are used on only 1 project out of every 25 or so.

TABLE 20.4 **Distribution of Testing Methods for Large Software Projects**

Testing stage	Projects utilizing test stage, %
General testing	
Subroutine testing	100
Unit testing	99
System testing of full application	95
New function testing	90
Regression testing	70
Integration testing	50
Specialized testing	
Viral protection testing	45
Stress or capacity testing	35
Performance testing	30
Security testing	15
Platform testing	5
Supply chain testing	5
Independent testing	3
User testing	
Customer-acceptance testing	35
Field (beta) testing	30
Usability testing	20
Lab testing	1
Clean-room statistical testing	1

The distribution in Table 20.4 shows the frequency with which various test forms have been noted among SPR's clients for projects of 500 function points or larger.

It is interesting to note that the only form of testing that is truly universal is testing of individual subroutines. Unit testing of entire modules is almost universal, although a few projects have not utilized this method (such as those using the clean-room method). Testing of the entire application upon completion is also very common, although here, too, not every project has done so.

For the other and more specialized forms of testing, such as performance testing or security testing, only a minority of projects among SPR's clients perform such testing. Sometimes the specialized forms of testing are not needed, but sometimes they are needed and are skipped over due to schedule pressure or poor decision making by project managers.

General Forms of Software Testing

The general forms of software testing occur for almost every kind of software: systems software, commercial software, military software, information systems, or anything else.

While the general forms of software testing are common and well understood, not all companies use the same vocabulary to describe them.

The following brief definitions explain the general meanings of the general forms of testing discussed here.

Subroutine Testing   This is the lowest-level form of testing noted among SPR's clients. Recall that a *subroutine* is a small collection of code that may constitute less than ten statements, or perhaps one-tenth of a function point.

Subroutine testing is performed almost spontaneously by developers, and is very informal. Essentially, this form of testing consists of executing a just-completed subroutine to see if it compiles properly and performs as expected. Subroutine testing is a key line of defense against errors in algorithms in spite of its being informal and underreported in the testing literature.

Subroutine testing is too informal to be included in test plans and because it is done by developers themselves, there is usually no data kept on either effort or efficiency in terms of numbers of bugs found. However, since subroutine testing is done immediately after the code is written, it is a key first-line defense against coding defects.

Unit Testing   This is the lowest-level form of testing normally discussed in the testing literature. Unit testing is the execution of a complete module or small program that will normally range from perhaps 100 to 1000 source code statements, or roughly from 1 to 10 function points.

Although unit testing may often be performed informally, it is also the stage at which actual test planning and deliberate test-case construction begins. Unit testing is usually performed by the programmers who write the module and, hence, seldom includes data on defect levels or removal efficiency. (Note that for testing under clean-room concepts, unit testing is *not* performed by the developers, so data on defect removal may be recorded in this situation.)

One of the interesting attributes of XP is that unit tests are written before the code itself. The hypothesis is that starting with test cases focuses the mind of the programmers on various kinds of error conditions, and leads to few defects. Although the evidence is incomplete, the concept of starting with test cases does seem to provide value in terms of reduced defects and higher levels of defect-removal efficiency.

Even in the normal situation of unit testing being performed by developers, enough companies have used volunteers who record the defects found during unit testing to have at least an idea of how efficient this form of testing is. Unit testing is also often plagued by bad test cases, which themselves contain errors. Unit testing is the lowest-level form of testing provided for by software estimating tools.

New Function Testing   This is often teamed with regression testing, and both forms are commonly found when existing applications are being updated or modified. As the name implies, new function testing is aimed at validating new features that are being added to a software package.

For entirely new projects, as opposed to enhancements, this form of testing is also known as *component testing* because it tests the combined work of multiple programmers whose programs in aggregate may comprise a component of a larger system.

This form of testing would roughly be tests against perhaps half a dozen or more use cases, or perhaps five user stories. In other words, while new function testing is not aimed at a full system, it does aim at testing common usage patterns.

New function testing is often performed by testing specialists because it covers the work of a number of programmers. For example, typical size ranges of major new functions added to existing software packages can exceed 10,000 source code statements, 100 function points, or five detailed use cases.

New function testing is normally supported by formal test plans and planned test cases, and is performed on software that is under full configuration control. Also, defect reporting for new function testing is both common and reasonably accurate.

New function testing is a key line of defense against errors in inter-module interfaces and the movement of data from place to place through an application. New function testing is also intended to verify that the new or added features work correctly.

Regression Testing   This is the opposite of new function testing. The word *regression* means to slip back, and in the context of testing regression means accidentally damaging an existing feature as an unintended by-product of adding a new feature. Regression testing also checks to ensure that prior known bugs have not inadvertently stayed in the software after they should have been removed.

After a few years of software evolution, regression testing becomes one of the most extensive forms of testing because the library of available test cases from prior releases tends to grow continuously. Also, regression testing involves the entire base code of the application, which for major systems can exceed 10 million lines of code or 100,000 function points.

Regression testing can be performed by developers, professional test personnel, or software quality-assurance personnel. Regardless of who performs regression testing, the application is usually under full configuration control.

Regression test libraries, though often extensive, are sometimes troublesome and have both redundant test cases and test cases that themselves contain errors.

Regression testing is a key line of defense as systems evolve and age. It should be noted that the average growth rate of new features in software after the initial release is about 7 percent per calendar year. Each new feature or change includes a small chance of damaging some existing feature. Therefore, regression testing is a very common and important test activity.

Integration Testing   As the name implies, this is testing on a number of modules or programs that have come together to comprise an integrated software package. Since integration testing may cover the work of dozens, or even hundreds, of programmers, it also deals with rather large numbers of test cases.

Integration testing often occurs in waves as new builds of an evolving application are created. Microsoft, for example, performs daily integration of developing software projects and, hence, also performs daily integration testing. Other companies may have longer intervals between builds, such as weekly or even monthly builds.

Applications undergoing integration testing are usually under formal configuration control. Integration testing normally makes use of formal test plans, formal test scripts, planned suites of test cases, and formal defect-reporting procedures. Integration testing can be performed by developers themselves, by professional test personnel, or by software quality-assurance personnel, but professional test or Quality assurance (QA) personnel are usually more efficient and effective than developers.

System Testing of Full Application   This is usually the last form of internal testing before customers get involved with field testing (beta testing). For large systems, a formal system test can take many months and can involve large teams of test personnel. Also, the entire set of development programmers may be needed in order to fix bugs that are found during this critical test stage.

System testing demands formal configuration control and also deserves formal defect-tracking support. System testing can be performed by developers, professional test personnel, or quality-assurance personnel.

For software that controls physical devices (such as telephone switching systems) the phrase *system test* may include concurrent testing of hardware components. In this case, other engineering and quality-assurance specialists may also be involved, such as electrical or aeronautical engineers dealing with the hardware. Microcode may also be part of system testing. For complex hybrid products, system testing is a key event.

System testing may sometimes overlap a specialized form of testing termed *lab testing*, where special laboratories are used to house complex new hardware and software products that will be tested by prospective clients under controlled conditions.

Specialized Forms of Software Testing

These specialized forms of software testing occur with less frequency than the general forms. The specialized forms of testing are most common for systems software, military software, commercial software, contract software, and software with unusually tight criteria for things like high performance or ease of use.

Stress or Capacity Testing   This is a specialized form of testing aimed at judging the ability of an application to function when nearing the boundaries of its capabilities in terms of the volume of information used. For example, capacity testing of the word processor used to create this book (Microsoft Word for Windows Version 7) might entail tests against individual large documents of perhaps 300 to 600 pages to judge the upper limits that can be handled before MS Word becomes cumbersome or storage is exceeded.

It might also entail dealing with even larger documents, say 2000 pages, segmented into master documents and various sections. For a database application, capacity testing might entail loading the database with 10,000; 100,000; or 1 million records to judge how it operates when fully populated with information.

Capacity testing is often performed by testing specialists rather than developers primarily because ordinary developers may not know how to perform this kind of testing. Capacity testing may either be a separate test stage, or be performed as a subset of integration or system testing. Usually, it cannot be performed earlier, since the full application is necessary.

Performance Testing   This is a specialized form of testing aimed at judging whether or not an application can meet the performance goals set for it. For many applications performance is only a minor issue, but for some kinds of applications it is critical. For example, weapons systems, aircraft flight control systems, fuel injection systems, access methods, and telephone switching systems must meet stringent performance goals or the devices the software is controlling may not work.

Performance testing is also important for information systems that need to process large volumes of information rapidly, such as credit card authorizations, airline reservations, and bank ATM transactions.

Performance testing is often performed by professional testers and sometimes is supported by performance or tuning specialists. Some aspects of performance testing can be done at the unit-test level, but the bulk of performance testing is associated with integration and system testing because interfaces within the full product affect performance.

Note that in addition to performance testing, software systems with high performance needs that run on mainframe computers are often *instrumented* by using either hardware or software performance monitoring equipment. Some of these performance monitors can analyze the source code and find areas that may slow down processing, which can then be streamlined or modified.

However, some forms of software with real-time, high-speed requirements are not suitable for performance-monitoring equipment. For example, the onboard flight control software package of a cruise missile has high performance requirements but needs to achieve those requirements prior to deployment.

Viral Spyware Protection Testing   This is rapidly moving from a specialized form of testing to a general one, although it still has been noted on less than half of SPR's client's projects. The introduction of software viruses or spyware by malicious hackers has been a very interesting sociological phenomena in the software world. Viruses number in the thousands, and more are being created daily. Spyware also numbers in the thousands.

Virus and spyware protection has now become a growing sub-industry of the software domain. Virus testing is a white-box form of testing. Although commercial virus protection software can be run by anybody, major commercial developers of software also use special proprietary tools to ensure that master copies of software packages do not contain viruses.

Security Testing   This is most common and most sophisticated for military software, followed by software that deals with very confidential information, such as bank records, medical records, tax records, and the like.

The organizations most likely to utilize security testing include the military services, the National Security Agency (NSA), the Central Intelligence Agency (CIA), the Federal Bureau of Investigation (FBI), and other organizations that utilize computers and software for highly sensitive purposes.

Security testing is usually performed by highly trained specialists. Indeed, some military projects use *penetration teams* that attempt to break the security of applications by various covert means, including but not limited to hacking, theft, bribery, and even picking locks or breaking into buildings.

It has been noted that one of the easiest ways to break into secure systems involves finding disgruntled employees, so security testing may have psychological and sociological manifestations.

Platform Testing   This is a specialized form of testing found among companies whose software operates on different hardware platforms under different operating systems. Many commercial software vendors market the same applications for Windows XP, the Macintosh, UNIX, LINUX, and sometimes for other platforms as well.

While the features and functions of the application may be identical on every platform, the mechanics of getting the software to work on various platforms requires separate versions and separate test stages for each platform. Platform testing is usually a white-box form of testing.

Another aspect of platform testing is ensuring that the software package correctly interfaces with any other software packages that might be related to it. For example, when testing software cost-estimating tools, this stage of testing would verify that data can be passed both ways between the estimating tool and various project management tools. For example, suppose cost-estimating tools, such as CHECKPOINT or KnowledgePlan, are intended to share data with Microsoft Project under Windows XP. This is the stage where the interfaces between the two would be verified.

Platform testing is also termed *compatibility testing* by some companies. Regardless of the nomenclature used, the essential purpose remains the same: to ensure that software that operates on multiple hardware platforms, under multiple operating systems, and interfaces with multiple tools can handle all varieties of interconnection.

Independent Testing   This is very common for military software, because it was required by Department of Defense standards. It can also be done for commercial software, and indeed there are several commercial testing companies that do testing on a fee basis. However, independent testing is very rare for management information systems, civilian systems software projects, and outsourced or contracted software. Independent testing, as the name implies, is performed by a separate company or at least a separate organization from the one that built the application. Both white-box and black-box forms of independent testing are noted.

A special form of independent testing may occur from time to time as part of litigation when a client charges that a contractor did not achieve acceptable levels of quality. The plaintiff, defendant, or both may commission a third party to test the software.

Another form of independent testing is found among some commercial software vendors who market software developed by subcontractors or other commercial vendors. The primary marketing company usually tests the subcontracted software to ensure that it meets the company's quality criteria.

Forms of Testing Involving Users or Clients

For many software projects, the clients or users are active participants at various stages along the way, including but not limited to requirements gathering, prototyping, inspections, and several forms of testing. The testing stages where users participate are generally the following.

Usability Testing   This is a specialized form of testing sometimes performed in usability laboratories. Usability testing involves actual clients who utilize the software under controlled and sometimes instrumented conditions so that their actions can be observed. Usability testing is common for commercial software produced by large companies, such as IBM and Microsoft. Usability testing can occur with any kind of software, however. Usability testing usually occurs at about the same time as system testing. Sometimes usability testing and beta testing are concurrent, but it is more common for usability testing to precede beta testing.

Field (Beta) Testing   This is a common testing technique for commercial software. *Beta* is the second letter in the Greek alphabet. Its use in testing stems from a testing sequence used by hardware engineers that included alpha, beta, and gamma testing. For software, alpha testing more or less dropped out of the lexicon circa 1980, and gamma testing was almost never part of the software test cycle. Thus, beta is the only one left for software, and is used to mean an external test involving customers.

Microsoft has become famous by conducting the most massive external beta tests in software history, with more than 10,000 customers participating. High-volume beta testing with thousands of customers is very efficient in terms of defect-removal efficiency levels and can exceed 85 percent removal efficiency if there are more than 1000 beta-test participants. However, if beta-test participation comprises less than a dozen clients, removal efficiency is usually around 35 to 50 percent.

Beta testing usually occurs after system testing, although some companies start external beta tests before system testing is finished (to the dismay of their customers). External beta testing and internal usability testing may occur concurrently. However, beta testing may involve special agreements with clients to avoid the risk of lawsuits should the software manifest serious problems.

Lab Testing This is a special form of testing found primarily with hybrid products that consist of complex physical devices that are controlled by software, such as telephone switching systems, weapons systems, and medical instruments. It is obvious that conventional field testing or beta testing of something like a PBX switch, a cruise missile, or a CAT scanner is infeasible due to the need for possible structural modifications to buildings, special electrical wiring, and heating and cooling requirements, to say nothing of zoning permits and authorization by various boards and controlling bodies.

Therefore, the companies that build such devices often have laboratories where clients can test out both the hardware and the software prior to having the equipment installed on their own premises.

Customer-Acceptance Testing This is commonly found for contract software and often is found for management information systems, software, and military software. The only form of software where acceptance testing is rare or does not occur is high-volume commercial shrink-wrapped software. Even here, some vendors and retail stores provide a money-back guarantee, which permits a form of acceptance testing. How the customers go about acceptance testing varies considerably. Customer-acceptance testing is not usually part of software cost estimates, since the work is not done by the software vendors but rather by the clients. However, the time in the schedule is still shown, and the effort for fixing client-reported bugs is shown.

Clean-Room Statistical Testing This is found only in the context of clean-room development methods. The clean-room approach is unusual in that the developers do not perform unit testing, and the test cases themselves are based on statistical assertions of usage patterns. Clean-room testing is inextricably joined with formal specification methods and proofs of correctness. Clean-room testing is always performed by testing specialists or quality-assurance personnel rather than the developers themselves, because under the clean-room concept developers do no testing.

Number of Testing Stages

Looking at the data from another vantage point, if each specific kind of testing is deemed a *testing stage*, it is interesting to see how many discrete testing stages occur for software projects (see Table 20.5). The overall range of testing stages among SPR's clients and their software projects runs from a low of 1 to a high of 16 out of the total number of 18 testing stages discussed here.

TABLE 20.5   Approximate Distribution of Testing Stages for U.S. Software Projects

Number of testing stages	Projects utilizing test stages, %
1	2
2	8
3	12
4	14
5	16
6	18
7	5
8	5
9	7
10	5
11	3
12	1
13	1
14	1
15	1
16	1
17	0
18	0
Total	100

As can be seen from the distribution of results, the majority of software projects in the United States (70 percent) use six or fewer discrete testing stages, and the most common pattern of testing observed includes the following:

- Subroutine testing
- Unit testing
- New function testing
- Regression testing
- Integration testing
- System testing

These six forms of testing are very common on applications of 1000 function points or larger. These six also happen to be generalized forms of testing that deal with broad categories of errors and issues.

Below 1000 function points, and especially below 100 function points, sometimes only three testing stages are found, assuming the project in question is new and not an enhancement:

- Subroutine testing
- Unit testing
- New function testing

The other forms of testing that are less common are more specialized, such as performance testing or capacity testing, and deal with a narrow band of problems that not every application is concerned with.

Testing Pattern Variations by Industry and Type of Software

There are, of course, very significant variations between industries and between various kinds of software in terms of typical testing patterns utilized, as follows.

End-User Software   This is the sparsest in terms of testing, and the usual pattern includes only two test stages: subroutine testing and unit testing. Of course, end-user software is almost always less than 100 function points in size.

Web Software   These new kinds of applications are beginning to develop some new and specialized kinds of testing. With web sites that link to many other sites, or that use animation and sound, it is obvious that these features need to be tested to work correctly. Also, web applications that are intended to accept customer orders or payments need special security testing and also various kinds of encryption. Usually, five to ten kinds of testing will occur for large web sites. Small personal web sites will probably use two to five kinds of testing. Some of the kinds of testing include subroutine testing, unit testing, new function testing, regression testing, user interface testing, hyperlink testing, performance testing, and security testing.

Management Information Systems (MIS)   MIS software projects use from three up to perhaps eight forms of testing. A typical MIS testing-stage pattern would include subroutine testing, unit testing, new function testing, regression testing, system testing, and user-acceptance testing. MIS testing is usually performed by the developers themselves, so that testing by professional test personnel or by quality-assurance personnel is a rarity in this domain.

Outsource Software   Vendors doing information systems are similar to their clients in terms of testing patterns. MIS outsource vendors use typical MIS patterns; systems software vendors use typical systems software patterns; and military outsource vendors use typical military test patterns. This means that the overall range of outsource testing can run from as few as 3 kinds of testing up to a high of 16 kinds of testing. Usually, the outsource vendors utilize at least one more stage of testing than their clients.

Commercial Software   Commercial software developed by major vendors, such as Microsoft, IBM, and Computer Associates, will typically use a 12-stage testing series: (1) subroutine testing, (2) unit testing, (3) new function testing, (4) regression testing, (5) performance testing, (6) stress testing, (7) integration testing, (8) usability testing, (9) platform testing, (10) system testing, (11) viral testing, and (12) field testing, which is often called *external* or *beta testing*.

However, small software vendors who develop small applications of less than 1000 function points may only use six testing stages: (1) subroutine testing, (2) unit testing, (3) new function testing, (4) regression testing, (5) system testing, and (6) beta testing.

Major software vendors, such as Microsoft and IBM, utilize large departments of professional testers who take over after unit testing and perform the major testing work at the higher levels, such as integration testing, system testing, and such specialized testing as performance testing or stress testing.

Systems Software   This is often extensively tested and may use as many as 14 different testing stages. A typical testing pattern for a software system in the 10,000–function point range would include subroutine testing, unit testing, new function testing, regression testing, performance testing, stress/capacity testing, integration testing, usability testing, system testing, viral testing, security testing, special date tests such as daylight savings, and lab testing and/or field testing, which is often called *external* or *beta testing*.

The larger systems software companies such as AT&T, Siemens-Nixdorf, IBM, and the like, typically utilize professional testing personnel after unit testing. Also, the systems software domain typically has the largest and best-equipped software quality-assurance groups and the only quality-assurance research labs.

Some of the large systems software organizations may have three different kinds of quality-related laboratories:

- Quality research labs
- Usability labs
- Hardware and software product testing labs

Indeed, the larger systems software groups are among the few kinds of organizations that actually perform research on software quality, in the classical definition of *research* as formal experiments using trial and error methods to develop improved tools and practices.

Military Software   This uses the most extensive suite of test stages, and large weapons or logistics systems may include 16 discrete testing stages: (1) subroutine testing; (2) unit testing; (3) new function testing; (4) regression testing; (5) performance testing; (6) stress testing; (7) integration testing; (8) independent testing; (9) usability testing; (10) lab testing; (11) system testing; (12) viral testing; (13) security testing; (14) special date testing; (15) field testing, which is often called *external* or *beta testing*; and (16) *customer-acceptance testing.*

Only military projects routinely utilize *independent testing*, or testing by a separate company external to the developing or contracting organization. Military projects often utilize the services of professional testing personnel and also quality-assurance personnel.

However, there are several companies that perform independent testing for commercial software organizations. Often, smaller software companies that lack full in-house testing capabilities will utilize such external testing organizations.

Testing Pattern Variations by Size of Application

Another interesting way of looking at the distribution of testing stages is to look at the ranges and numbers of test stages associated with the various sizes of software applications, as shown in Table 20.6.

As can be seen, the larger applications tend to utilize a much more extensive set of testing stages than do the smaller applications, which is not unexpected.

It is interesting to consolidate testing variations by industry and testing variations by size of application. The following table shows the typical number of test stages observed for six size plateaus and six software classes (see Table 20.7).

There are wide variations in testing patterns, so this table has a significant margin of error. However, the data is interesting and explains why the commercial, systems, and military software domains often have higher reliability levels than others.

TABLE 20.6 Ranges of Test Stages Associated with the Size of Software Applications

Application size, FP	Number of test stages performed		
	Minimum	Average	Maximum
1	0	3	4
10	1	4	5
100	2	5	8
1,000	3	9	11
10,000	4	10	13
100,000	6	12	16

TABLE 20.7   Average Number of Tests Observed by Application Size and Class of Software
(Application size in function points)

Class of software	1	10	100	1,000	10,000	100,000	Average
End-user	1	2	2				1.67
MIS	2	3	4	6	7	8	5.00
Web	2	3	4	7	8	10	5.67
Outsource	2	3	5	7	8	9	5.67
Commercial	3	4	6	9	11	12	7.50
Systems	3	4	7	11	12	14	8.50
Military	4	5	8	11	13	16	9.50
Average	2.43	3.43	5.14	8.50	9.80	11.5	6.22

This table also illustrates that there is no single pattern of testing that is universally appropriate for all sizes of software and all classes of software. The optimal pattern of defect-removal and testing stages must be matched to the nature of the application.

Testing Stages Noted in Lawsuits Alleging Poor Quality

It is an interesting observation that for outsourced, military, and systems software that ends up in court for litigation involving assertions of unacceptable or inadequate quality, the number of testing stages is much smaller, while formal design and code inspections are not utilized at all.

Table 20.8 shows the typical patterns of defect-removal activities for software projects larger than 1000 function points in size where the developing organization was sued by the client for producing software of inadequate quality.

TABLE 20.8   Defect Removal and Testing Stages Noted During Litigation for Poor Quality

Stages	Reliable software	Software in litigation
Formal design inspections	Used	Not used
Formal code inspections	Used	Not used
Subroutine testing	Used	Used
Unit testing	Used	Used
New function testing	Used	Rushed or omitted
Regression testing	Used	Rushed or omitted
Integration testing	Used	Used
System testing	Used	Rushed or omitted
Performance testing	Used	Rushed or omitted
Capacity testing	Used	Rushed or omitted

The table simply compares the pattern of defect-removal operations observed for reliable software packages with high quality levels to the pattern noted during lawsuits where poor quality and low reliability were at issue. The phrase *rushed or omitted* indicates that the vendor departed from best standard practices by eliminating a stage of defect removal or by rushing it in order to meet an arbitrary finish date or commitment to the client.

It is interesting that during the depositions and testimony of litigation, the vendor often countercharges that the shortcuts were made at the direct request of the client. Sometimes the vendor asserts that the client ordered the shortcuts even in the face of warnings that the results might be hazardous.

As can be seen, software developed under contractual obligations is at some peril if quality control and testing approaches are not carefully performed.

Using Function Points to Estimate Test-Case Volumes

IFPUG function points and related metrics such as COSMIC function points, object points, and use case points are starting to provide some preliminary but interesting insights into test-case volumes. This is not unexpected, because the fundamental parameters of both function points and feature points all represent topics that need test coverage, as follows:

- Inputs
- Outputs
- Inquires
- Logical files
- Interfaces
- Algorithms (feature points only)

Since function points can be derived during the requirements and early design stages, this approach offers a method of predicting test-case numbers fairly early. The method is still somewhat experimental, but the approach is leading to interesting results and its usage is expanding. Currently, IFPUG function points have the largest numbers of examples for estimating test cases.

Table 20.9 shows preliminary data on the number of test cases that have been noted among SPR's clients, using *test cases per function point* as the normalizing metric. This table has a high margin of error, but as with any other set of preliminary data points, it is better to publish the

TABLE 20.9   Ranges of Test Cases per IFPUG Function Point (Version 4.1)

Testing stage	Minimum	Average	Maximum
Clean-room testing	0.60	1.00	3.00
Regression testing	0.40	0.60	1.30
Unit testing	0.20	0.45	1.20
Web testing	0.20	0.40	1.20
New function testing	0.25	0.40	0.90
Integration testing	0.20	0.40	0.75
Subroutine testing	0.20	0.30	0.40
Independent testing	0.00	0.30	0.55
System testing	0.15	0.25	0.60
Viral testing	0.00	0.20	0.40
Performance testing	0.00	0.20	0.40
Acceptance testing	0.00	0.20	0.60
Lab testing	0.00	0.20	0.50
Field (beta) testing	0.00	0.20	1.00
Usability testing	0.00	0.20	0.40
Platform testing	0.00	0.15	0.30
Stress testing	0.00	0.15	0.30
Security testing	0.00	0.15	0.35
Total	2.00	5.55	13.75

results in the hope of future refinements and corrections than to wait until the data is truly complete.

The usage of function point metrics also provides some rough rules of thumb for predicting the overall volumes of test cases that are likely to be created for software projects.

- Raising the function point total of the application to the 1.15 power will give an approximation of the minimum number of test cases.

- Raising the function point total to the 1.2 power gives an approximation of the average number of test cases.

- Raising the function point total to the 1.3 power gives an approximation of the maximum number of test cases.

These rules of thumb are based on observations of software projects whose sizes range between about 100 and 10,000 function points. Rules of thumb are not accurate enough for serious business purposes, such as contracts, but are useful in providing estimating sanity checks. See the section on "Function Point Sizing Rules of Thumb" in Chapter 6 for additional rules of thumb involving these versatile metrics.

Because of combinatorial complexity, it is usually impossible to write and run enough test cases to fully exercise a software project larger than about 100 function points in size. The number of permutations of inputs, outputs, and control-flow paths quickly becomes astronomical.

For really large systems that approach 100,000 function points in size, the total number of test cases needed to fully test every condition can be regarded, for practical purposes, as infinite. Also, the amount of computing time needed to run such a test suite would also be an infinite number, or at least a number so large that there are not enough computers in any single company to approach the capacity needed.

Therefore, the volumes of test cases shown here are based on empirical observations and the numbers assume standard reduction techniques, such as testing boundary conditions rather than all intermediate values and compressing related topics into equivalency classes.

Using Function Points to Estimate the Numbers of Test Personnel

One of the newest but most interesting uses of function point metrics in a testing context is for predicting the probable number of test personnel that might be needed for each test stage, and then for the overall product.

Table 20.10 has a high margin of error, but the potential value of using function points for test-staffing prediction is high enough to make publication of preliminary data useful.

This table is a bit misleading. While the average test stage might have a ratio of about 1300 function points for every tester, the range is very broad.

TABLE 20.10   Ranges in Number of Function Points per Software Tester

Testing stage	Minimum	Average	Maximum
Subroutine testing	0.1	1.0	3.0
Unit testing	1.0	3.0	12.0
New function testing	100.0	350.0	1500.0
Clean-room testing	100.0	350.0	1000.0
Performance testing	150.0	400.0	1000.0
Web testing	150.0	450.0	1750.0
Integration testing	150.0	700.0	2500.0
Acceptance testing	250.0	750.0	1500.0
Regression testing	500.0	1500.0	7500.0
Platform testing	350.0	1500.0	5000.0
Security testing	200.0	1500.0	3500.0
Field (beta) testing	250.0	1500.0	5000.0
Usability testing	150.0	2000.0	4500.0
Lab testing	750.0	2500.0	4000.0
Viral testing	250.0	2500.0	5000.0
System testing	750.0	2500.0	5000.0
Independent testing	500.0	2500.0	8500.0
Capacity testing	400.0	3000.0	7500.0
Average	277.8	1339.1	3598.0

Also, the table does not show the ratio of testers to software for testing performed in parallel.

For example, if a common four-stage combination of test stages where professional testers or quality-assurance personnel handle the testing is done in parallel rather than sequentially, the ratio for the entire combination is in the range of one testing staff member for about every 250 function points for the following test stages:

- New function testing
- Regression testing
- Integration testing
- System testing

For some of the test stages, such as subroutine testing and unit testing, the normal practice is for the testing to be performed by developers. In this case, the data simply indicates the *average* sizes of subroutines and standalone programs.

Testing and Defect-Removal Efficiency Levels

Most forms of testing, such as unit testing by individual programmers, are less than 30 percent efficient in finding bugs. That is, less than one bug out of three will be detected during the test period. Sometimes a whole string of test steps (unit testing, function testing, integration testing, and system testing) will find less than 50 percent of the bugs in a software product. By itself, testing alone has never been sufficient to ensure really high quality levels.

Consider also the major categories of defects that affect software:

- Errors of omission
- Errors of commission
- Errors of clarity or ambiguity
- Errors of speed
- Errors of capacity

Table 20.11 shows the approximate defect-removal efficiency level of the common forms of testing against these five error categories (with a very large margin of error).

This data is derived in part from measurements by the author's clients, and in part from discussion with software testing and quality-assurance personnel in a number of companies. The data is based on anecdotes rather than real statistical results because none of the author's clients

TABLE 20.11   Average Defect-Removal Efficiency Levels of Software Test Stages Against Five Defect Types
(Percentage of defects removed)

Testing stage	Omission	Commission	Clarity	Speed	Capacity	Average
Web testing	40	40	60	50	40	46
Beta testing	40	40	35	40	35	38
Lab testing	25	35	30	50	50	38
System testing	20	30	30	50	50	36
Clean-room testing	35	40	35	25	40	35
Usability testing	55	50	60	10	0	35
Acceptance testing	30	35	35	35	30	33
Independent testing	20	30	30	35	40	31
Stress testing	0	40	0	25	80	29
New function testing	30	30	30	20	20	26
Integration testing	20	35	20	25	25	25
Unit testing	10	60	10	20	20	24
Platform testing	20	70	0	30	0	24
Regression testing	10	45	20	20	20	23
Performance testing	0	10	0	75	30	23
Subroutine testing	10	50	0	20	15	19
Virus testing	0	80	0	0	0	16
Security testing	50	30	0	0	0	16
Average	23	42	22	31	28	29

actually record this kind of information. However, the overall picture the data gives of testing is interesting and clarifies testing's main strengths and weaknesses.

This table is ranked in descending order of overall efficiency against all forms of defects and, hence, is slightly misleading. Some of the specialized forms of testing, such as stress and performance testing or viral protection testing, are highly efficient but against only one narrow class of problem.

The most obvious conclusion from this table is that testing is much more effective in finding errors of *commission*, or things that are done wrong, than it is in finding errors of *omission*, or things that are left out by accident.

Note that there are wide ranges of observed defect-removal efficiency over and above the approximate averages shown here. Any given form of testing can achieve defect-removal efficiency levels that are perhaps 15 percent higher than these averages, or about 10 percent lower. However, no known form of testing has yet exceeded 90 percent in defect-removal efficiency, so a series of inspections plus a multistage series of tests is needed to achieve really high levels of defect-removal efficiency, such as 99.9999 percent.

Although testing is often the only form of defect removal utilized for software, the performance of testing is greatly enhanced by the use of formal design and code inspections, both of which tend to elevate testing efficiency levels in addition to finding defects themselves.

Using Function Points to Estimate Testing Effort and Costs

Another use of the function point metric in a testing context is to estimate and later measure testing effort and costs. A full and formal evaluation of testing requires analysis of three discrete activities:

- Test preparation
- Test execution
- Defect repair

Test preparation involves creating test cases, validating them, and putting them into a test library.

Test execution involves running the test cases against the software and recording the results. Note that testing is an iterative process, and the same test cases can be run several times if needed, or even more.

Defect repair concerns fixing any bugs that are found via testing, validating the fix, and then rerunning the test cases that found the bugs to ensure that the bugs have been repaired and that no bad fixes have inadvertently been introduced.

With a total of 18 different kinds of testing to consider, the actual prediction of testing effort is too complex for simplistic rules of thumb. Several commercial estimating tools, such as CHECKPOINT, COCOMO II, KnowledgePlan, PRICE-S, SEER, and SLIM, can predict testing costs for each test stage and then aggregate overall testing effort and expenses for any kind or size of software project. These same tools and others within this class can also predict testing defect-removal efficiency levels.

There are too many variables involved for a static representation in a published table or graph to be really accurate. Therefore, for the purposes of this book, a major simplifying assumption will be used. The assumption is that the proportion of total software effort devoted to testing correlates exactly with the number of test stages that are utilized. This assumption has a few exceptions, but seems to work well enough to have practical value.

The percentages shown in Table 20.12 for testing are based on the total development budget for the software project in question.

The same table also shows the approximate defect-removal efficiency correlated with number of test stages for coding defects. Here, too, as the number of test stages grows larger, defect-removal efficiency

TABLE 20.12   Number of Testing Stages, Testing Effort, and Defect-Removal
Efficiency

Number of testing stages	Effort devoted to testing, %	Cumulative defect-removal efficiency, %
1	10	50
2	15	60
3	20	70
4	25	75
5	30	80
6*	33*	85*
7	36	87
8	39	90
9	42	92
10	45	94
11	48	96
12	52	98
13	55	99
14	58	99.9
15	61	99.99
16	64	99.999
17	67	99.9999
18	70	99.99999

*Six test stages, 33 costs, and 85 percent removal efficiency are approximate U.S. averages for software projects = >1000 function points in size.

levels increase. The essential message is that if you want to approach zero-defect levels, be prepared to perform quite a few testing stages.

This simplified approach is not accurate enough for serious project planning or for contracts, but it shows overall trends well enough to make the economic picture understandable.

This table also explains why large systems have higher testing costs than small applications, and why systems and military software have higher testing costs than information systems: More testing stages are utilized.

Note, however, that the table does not show the whole picture (which is why commercial estimating tools are recommended). For example, if formal pre-test design and code inspections are also utilized, they alone can approach 80 percent in defect-removal efficiency and also raise the efficiency of testing.

Thus, projects that utilize formal inspections plus testing can top 99 percent in cumulative defect-removal efficiency with fewer stages than shown here, since this table illustrates only testing. See Chapters 16 and 18 for additional information.

There is no shortage of historical data that indicates that formal inspections continue to be one of the most powerful software defect-removal operations since the software industry began.

Testing by Developers or by Professional Test Personnel

One of the major questions concerning software testing is who should do it. The possible answers to this question include:

- The developers themselves
- Professional test personnel
- Professional quality-assurance personnel
- Some combination of the three

Note that several forms of testing, such as external beta testing and customer-acceptance testing, are performed by clients themselves or by consultants that the clients hire to do the work.

There is no definitive answer to this question, but some empirical observations may be helpful.

- The defect-removal efficiency of almost all forms of testing is higher when performed by test personnel or by quality-assurance personnel rather than by the developers themselves. The only exceptions are subroutine and unit tests.
- For usability problems, testing by clients themselves outranks all other forms of testing.
- The defect-removal efficiency of specialized kinds of testing, such as special date testing or viral protection testing, is highest when performed by professional test personnel rather than by the developers themselves.

Table 20.13 shows the author's observations of who typically performs various test stages from among SPR's client organizations. Note that since SPR's clients include quite a few systems software, military software, and commercial software vendors, there probably is a bias in the data. The systems, commercial, and military software domains are much more likely to utilize the services of professional testing and quality-assurance (QA) personnel than are the MIS and outsource domains.

The table is sorted in descending order of the development column. Note that this order illustrates that the early testing is most often performed by development personnel, but the later stages of testing are most often performed by testing or quality-assurance specialists.

As can be seen from this table, among SPR's clients testing by developers and testing by professional test personnel are equal in frequency, followed by testing involving software quality-assurance personnel, and, finally, testing by customers or their designated testers.

TABLE 20.13   Observations on Performance of Test Stages by Occupation Group
(Percentage of testing performed)

Testing stage	Developers	Testers	QA personnel	Clients
Subroutine testing	100	0	0	0
Unit testing	90	10	0	0
New function testing	50	30	20	0
Integration testing	50	30	20	0
Viral testing	50	30	20	0
System testing	40	40	20	0
Regression testing	30	50	20	0
Performance testing	30	60	10	0
Platform testing	30	50	20	0
Stress testing	30	50	20	0
Security testing	30	40	30	0
Web testing	20	50	30	0
Usability testing	10	10	30	50
Acceptance testing	0	0	0	100
Lab testing	0	0	0	100
Field (beta) testing	0	0	0	100
Clean-room testing	0	50	40	10
Independent testing	0	60	40	0
Average	31	31	18	20

Testing by development personnel is much more common for the smaller forms of testing, such as subroutine and unit testing. Testing by development personnel is also more common for the Agile development methods and for XP. For the larger forms (i.e., system testing) and for the specialized forms (i.e., performance testing, stress testing, etc.), testing by professional test personnel or by quality-assurance personnel become more common.

Testing should be part of a synergistic and integrated suite of defect-prevention and defect-removal operations that may include prototyping, quality-assurance reviews, pretest inspections, formal test planning, multistage testing, and measurement of defect levels and severities.

For those who have no empirical data on quality, the low average defect-removal efficiency levels of most forms of testing will be something of a surprise. However, it is because each testing step is less than 100 percent efficient that multiple test stages are necessary in the first place.

Testing is an important technology for software. For many years, progress in testing primarily occurred within the laboratories of major corporations who built systems software. However, in recent years a new sub-industry of commercial testing tool and testing-support companies has appeared. This new sub-industry is gradually improving software test capabilities as the commercial vendors of testing tools and methodologies compete within a fast-growing market for test-support products and services.

Test Case Coverage

One of the reasons that test stages only average about 30 percent in defect-removal efficiency is because testing does not actually cover all of the code in large applications. It is theoretically possible to test every instruction in a software application for applications up to about 1000 logical statements in size. Above that size, testing coverage declines sharply.

Table 20.14 shows the approximate relationships between volumes of source code, numbers of test cases, and test coverage or the percentage of code actually tested when running the test case suite.

What happens, of course, is that as applications get larger in size the number of paths through the code grows geometrically. It is not economically feasible to write enough test cases to cover all of the paths and every individual instruction in really large software applications.

Also, other factors tend to drive up the numbers of test cases too. Software that is high in cyclomatic and essential complexity will need more test cases for a given number of source code statements than would the same volume of code with lower complexity scores.

There is no simple method for predicting number of test cases, number of test runs, and number of bugs that will be detected and need repairs. The rules for predicting these variables are numerous and complex, and this is why automated estimating tools usually outperform individual project managers and quality-assurance personnel.

The Factors That Affect Testing Performance

The key factors that affect testing from the point of view of estimating test schedules, costs, and efficiency levels include the following:

- The number of bugs or defects in the application being testing
- The number of test stages selected for the application

TABLE 20.14   Application Size, Test Cases, and Test Coverage
(Size expressed in logical source code statements)

Source code statements	Test cases	Test coverage
1	1	100.00%
10	2	100.00%
100	5	95.00%
1,000	15	75.00%
10,000	250	50.00%
100,000	4,000	35.00%
1,000,000	50,000	25.00%
10,000,000	350,000	15.00%

- The structure of the application, measured with cyclomatic and essential complexity
- The test-tool suite available to the testing personnel
- The training and experience of the testing personnel
- Whether or not precursor code inspections were utilized
- The amount of time allotted to testing in project schedules
- The number of defects found during each test stage
- The method used to route defects to the appropriate repair team
- Interruptions that might occur during testing or defect repairs

Unfortunately, these ten factors tend to be independent variables and each of them can vary significantly. It is interesting to bracket the possible outcomes by means of *best-case, expected-case,* and *worst-case* scenarios for a generic application of 1000 function points or 100,000 procedural source code statements.

The *best-case* scenario would comprise a combination of experienced test personnel with very sophisticated test tools performing a sequence of at least eight test stages on software that is well structured and low in defects.

The forms of testing used in the best-case scenario would include (at a minimum) subroutine testing, unit testing, new function testing, regression testing, integration testing, system testing, performance testing, and external testing. Note that with the best-case scenario, there is a high probability that formal inspections would also have been utilized.

The *expected-case* scenario would include moderately experienced personnel using a few test tools, such as record/playback tools and test execution monitors, performing half a dozen test stages on fairly well structured code that contains a moderate quantity of defects. The forms of testing used would include subroutine testing, unit testing, new function testing, regression testing, system testing, and external testing.

The *worst-case* scenario would consist of inexperienced test personnel with few test tools, attempting to test a very buggy, poorly structured application under tremendous schedule pressure.

However, under the worst-case scenario it is likely that only five kinds of testing might be performed: subroutine testing, unit testing, new function testing, system testing, and external testing.

References

Beizer, Boris: *Software Testing Techniques*, Van Nostrand Reinhold, New York, 1988.
Black, Rex: *Managing the Testing Process, Second Edition*, Wiley,Indianapolis, Indiana, 2002.
———: *Black Box Testing*, IEEE Computer Society Press, Los Alamitos, Calif., 1995.

Boehm, Barry: *Software Engineering Economics*, Prentice-Hall, Englewood Cliffs, N.J., 1981.

Brown, Norm (ed.): *The Program Manager's Guide to Software Acquisition Best Practices*, Version 1.0, U.S. Department of Defense, Washington, D.C., July 1995.

DeMarco, Tom: *Controlling Software Projects*, Yourdon Press, New York, 1982.

Department of the Air Force: *Guidelines for Successful Acquisition and Management of Software Intensive Systems*, vols. 1 and 2, Software Technology Support Center, Hill Air Force Base, Utah, 1994.

Dreger, Brian: *Function Point Analysis*, Prentice-Hall, Englewood Cliffs, N.J., 1989.

Dustin, Elfriede, Jeff Rashka, and John Paul: *Automated Software Testing: Introduction, Management, and Performance*, Addison-Wesley, Boston, Mass., 1999.

Grady, Robert B.: *Practical Software Metrics for Project Management and Process Improvement*, Prentice-Hall, Englewood Cliffs, N.J., 1992.

———, and Deborah L. Caswell: *Software Metrics: Establishing a Company-Wide Program*, Prentice-Hall, Englewood Cliffs, N.J., 1987.

Howard, Alan (ed.): *Software Testing Tools*, Applied Computer Research (ACR), Phoenix, Ariz., 1997.

Hutchinson, Marnie L.: *Software Testing Methods and Metrics*, McGraw-Hill, New York, 1997.

———: *Software Testing Fundamentals*, Wiley, 2003.

Jones, Capers: *New Directions in Software Management*, Information Systems Management Group, Carlsbad, California 1993.

———: *Assessment and Control of Software Risks*, Prentice-Hall, Englewood Cliffs, N.J., 1994.

———: *Patterns of Software System Failure and Success*, International Thomson Computer Press, Boston, Mass., 1995.

———: *Applied Software Measurement, Second Edition*, McGraw-Hill, New York, 1996a.

———: *Table of Programming Languages and Levels* (8 Versions from 1985 through July 1996), Software Productivity Research, Burlington, Mass., 1996.

———: *The Economics of Object-Oriented Software*, Software Productivity Research, Burlington, Mass., April 1997a.

———: *Software Quality—Analysis and Guidelines for Success*, International Thomson Computer Press, Boston, Mass., 1997b.

———: *The Year 2000 Software Problem—Quantifying the Costs and Assessing the Consequences*, Addison-Wesley, Reading, Mass., 1998.

———: *Software Assessments, Benchmarks, and Best Practices*, Addison-Wesley Longman, Boston, Mass., 2000.

———: *Conflict and Litigation Between Software Clients and Developers*, Software Productivity Research, Burlington, Mass., 2003.

Kan, Stephen H.: *Metrics and Models in Software Quality Engineering, Second Edition*, Addison-Wesley Longman, Boston, Mass., 2003.

Kaner, C., J. Faulk, and H. Q. Nguyen: *Testing Computer Software*, International Thomson Computer Press, Boston, Mass., 1997.

Kaner, Cem, James Bach, and Bret Pettichord: *Lessons Learned in Software Testing*, Wiley, Indianapolis, Indiana, 2001.

Linegaard, G.: *Usability Testing and System Evaluation*, International Thomson Computer Press, Boston, Mass., 1997.

Love, Tom: *Object Lessons*, SIGS Books, New York, 1993.

Marciniak, John J. (ed.): *Encyclopedia of Software Engineering*, vols. 1 and 2, John Wiley & Sons, New York, 1994.

McCabe, Thomas J.: "A Complexity Measure," *IEEE Transactions on Software Engineering*, December 1976, pp. 308–320.

Mills, H., M. Dyer, and R. Linger: "Cleanroom Software Engineering," *IEEE Software*, 4, 5 (Sept. 1987), pp. 19–25.

Mosley, Daniel J.: *The Handbook of MIS Application Software Testing*, Yourdon Press/Prentice-Hall, Englewood Cliffs, N.J., 1993.

Perry, William: *Effective Methods for Software Testing*, IEEE Computer Society Press, Los Alamitos, Calif., 1995.

Pressman, Roger: *Software Engineering—A Practitioner's Approach, Sixth Edition*, McGraw-Hill, New York, 2005.

Putnam, Lawrence H.: *Measures for Excellence—Reliable Software on Time, Within Budget*, Yourdon Press/Prentice-Hall, Englewood Cliffs, N.J., 1992.

———, and Ware Myers: *Industrial Strength Software—Effective Management Using Measurement*, IEEE Press, Los Alamitos, Calif., 1997.

Rethinking the Software Process, CD-ROM, Miller Freeman, Lawrence, Kans., 1996. (This CD-ROM is a book collection jointly produced by the book publisher, Prentice-Hall, and the journal publisher, Miller Freeman. It contains the full text and illustrations of five Prentice-Hall books: *Assessment and Control of Software Risks* by Capers Jones; *Controlling Software Projects* by Tom DeMarco; *Function Point Analysis* by Brian Dreger; *Measures for Excellence* by Larry Putnam and Ware Myers; and *Object-Oriented Software Metrics* by Mark Lorenz and Jeff Kidd.)

Symons, Charles R.: *Software Sizing and Estimating—Mk II FPA (Function Point Analysis)*, John Wiley & Sons, Chichester, U.K., 1991.

Whittaker, James: *How to Break Software: A Practical Guide to Testing*, Addison-Wesley, Boston, Mass., 2002.

21

Estimating User and Project Documentation

Every manager and cost-estimating specialist who deals with large applications needs to understand that a typical software system produces more than a hundred English words for every line of source code. The costs and schedules for creating these words are greater than the cost of actually writing the source code.

The software industry has developed three characteristics that are visibly distinct from almost every other industry:

- Software is the most labor-intensive of any U.S. industry in terms of the amount of human effort required to create a product.

- Software, being abstract, has become a document-intensive industry and tends to create a larger volume of text and graphics-based documents than almost any other industry.

- Learning to use software applications often requires more training and more tutorial information than any other consumer product.

The second and third of these attributes explain a significant proportion of the first attribute. Software is labor-intensive not only because of the source code itself, but because of the enormous number of paper documents that are created to define and explain the source code.

As discussed several times elsewhere in this book, the five major cost drivers for software projects in rank order of total effort are the following:

1. Finding and fixing bugs

2. Producing paper documents (requirements, specifications, plans, etc.)

3. Meetings and communications

4. Coding

5. Project management

The new Agile methods have correctly identified paperwork as a major cost and schedule issue. The Agile methods also assert, with somewhat less justification, that paperwork may lack relevance in actually understanding user requirements. The sequence of cost drivers with Agile projects is

1. Finding and fixing bugs

2. Meetings and communications

3. Coding

4. Producing paper documents (bug reports, user manuals)

5. Project management

Although the Agile methods have had some successes, there are issues. The problems with the Agile approach of replacing paper specifications with face-to-face client meetings are these: For projects with thousands of different users, the method is not suitable, for projects such as military projects that require traceability between requirements and coded features, the method is not suitable, and for long-range topics such as maintenance, the lack of documentation may prove to be troublesome.

Over the past ten years the unified modeling language (UML) and use cases have increased in popularity and usage. While UML and use cases add to the precision of software specifications, they are if anything slightly larger than older forms of specifications using other techniques such as HIPO diagrams and structured English.

The object-oriented (OO) community has emphasized reusability as a key virtue. For source code with class libraries and OO programming languages, those claims are justified. However, the OO community has not yet made much progress with reusing various kinds of documentation.

Several new mandates have affected the volume and costs of the documents that support software projects. Any software project that must either adhere to ISO 9000–9004 quality standards or Department of Defense standards, or support the Sarbanes-Oxley reporting requirements will produce enormous volumes of compliance reports. These are "unfunded mandates" whose costs are passed on to the software developers. Needless to say, the Agile approaches are not going to be suitable for projects with mandated documentation sets.

Indeed, software paperwork is so cumbersome that for some kinds of software, such as large military applications, the sequence of cost drivers

1 and 2 are reversed, and *paperwork* is the topmost cost element. Some of SPR's military clients have produced as many as 400 English words for every Ada source code statement. The cost of these words is more than twice that of the code itself.

Curiously, although the production of paper documents is one of the most expensive and time-consuming activities in the history of software, the literature on this topic is almost nonexistent. The most probable reason why such a major topic has little or no quantification is due to the historical use of lines-of-code (LOC) metrics. This unfortunate metric cannot be used for estimating or measuring paper documents, hence, to most software engineering authors, paperwork has been essentially invisible.

Indeed, the primary books that discuss estimation and measurement of software documentation are those written by function point users, such as Charles Symons's *Software Sizing and Estimating* (John Wiley & Sons, 1991), the author's own *Applied Software Measurement* (McGraw-Hill, 1996), and the IFPUG collection of essays entitled *IT Measurement* (Addison-Wesley, 2002).

There is, of course, an extensive how-to-do-it literature that covers scores of individual documents, including requirements, various forms of specifications, planning documents, user manuals, and a number of others. However, the books that discuss specific kinds of documents are often silent on document costs, schedules, staffing, and even on such basic factors as the size of the documents correlated with the size of the software projects themselves.

Estimating Tools and Software Documentation

From an estimating standpoint, only a handful of commercial software estimating tools include predictive capabilities for software paper documents. Some of the estimating tools that can estimate paper documents include SPQR/20 (1985), CHECKPOINT (1989), and KnowledgePlan (1997). It is no coincidence that the designer of these tools (the author) was formerly the manager of a software documentation department within IBM.

Other estimating tools, such as COCOMO, COCOMO II, SLIM, and the like, have also added support for estimating some forms of software documentation, such as specification sets, but may not support user manuals, training materials, or some forms of planning documents.

In general, software document production is under-reported in the software literature and under-supported in both project management and estimating tools. Even configuration-control tools do not always support the major documents and often concentrate on source code rather than on specifications and user documents.

The nominal default values for estimating software documentation are shown in Table 21.1, although there are very large ranges for every factor.

Software documentation has never lent itself to being estimated or measured using lines-of-code-metrics but does have a number of traditional rules of thumb based on text pages or on ratios to other activities. For example, as long ago as 1965 the IBM corporation used rules of thumb for estimating software user manuals that included the following:

- The effort for user manuals comprises about 10 percent of coding effort for assembly language applications.

- One technical writer can support the work of ten programmers, if they are coding in low-level languages such as assembly language.

- Technical writers can produce final text at an average rate of one page per working day.

The problem with rules of thumb based on ratios of programming effort is that with 600 or so programming languages in existence, the rules are too erratic to be useful. It is hardly a good estimating practice to assume that if one technical writer can support the work of ten programmers using assembly language, then this ratio would also apply to

TABLE 21.1   Nominal Default Values for Documentation Estimates

Activity sequence	Ninth
Performed by	Technical writers, developers, clients
Predecessor activities	Design, coding, and partial testing
Overlap	50% with coding
Concurrent activities	Coding and testing
Successor activities	System testing, beta, or field testing
Initial requirements size	0.50 U.S. text pages per function point
Detailed specification size	3.0 U.S. text pages per function point
All document types in total	17.0 U.S. text pages per function point
Graphics volumes	0.02 illustrations per function point
Reuse	15% from prior or similar projects
Assignment scope	1500 function points per technical staff member
Production rate	125 function points per staff month
Production rate	1.06 work hours per function point
Schedule months	Function points raised to the 0.15 power
Rate of creep or change	2.0% per month
Defect potential	0.6 documentation defects per function point
Defect removal	75% via editing and document inspections
Delivered defects	0.15 document defects per function point
High-severity defects	10% of delivered document defects
Bad fix probability	5% of document fixes may yield new errors

Visual Basic, C++, Java, Smalltalk, or any of the more powerful modern programming languages.

However, in modern software cost-estimating tools, documentation estimates based on function point metrics are now the norm, although some estimating tools support the older methods as well.

Software documentation is rapidly being transformed under the impact of modern graphics-production tools, the World Wide Web, and the more or less unlimited storage capacity of CD-ROM and equivalent optical devices.

Quantifying the Number and Sizes of Software Document Types

Documentation for software during the 1970s and 1980s was primarily textual, with only such rudimentary graphics as flowcharts and simple structure diagrams. Today, circa 2007, much of the software documentation is available online, is highly graphical and perhaps even animated, and the sizes of normal text-based user manuals are smaller today than 10 years ago.

Before continuing with a discussion of estimating documentation costs, it is appropriate to illustrate the many kinds of documents associated with software products, to make clear why software paperwork in all its manifestations is a key software cost element.

Table 21.2 illustrates typical sizes for nine general kinds of documents associated with software projects: (1) planning documents, (2) financial documents, (3) project-control documents, (4) technical documents, (5) legal documents, (6) marketing documents, (7) user documents, (8) support documents, and (9) quality-control documents.

The table also shows the ranges for management information system (MIS) software, systems software, military projects software, and commercial software packages. Both the numbers of documents produced and their average sizes vary significantly by class of application, and also by size of application.

With an average of 69 kinds of documents produced for large software applications, it should come as no surprise to see why the sum of all documents under the heading of *paperwork* is the most expensive software cost element for military software projects and the second most expensive software cost element for civilian software projects.

However, because document sizes and costs cannot be easily measured using the lines-of-code-metrics, the cost implications of software paperwork remained invisible until the advent of function point metrics, which suddenly revealed that paperwork costs are far larger than coding costs for major software systems. Some of the other new metrics, such as COSMIC function points, use case points, object points, etc., can also be used to measure documentation volumes.

TABLE 21.2   Universe of Software Project Document Types
(Size in pages per function point)

Document type	MIS	Systems	Military	Commercial	Average
Planning documents					
Marketing plans				0.020	0.020
Project staffing plans	0.010	0.010	0.010	0.010	0.010
Building and integration plans	0.012	0.020	0.030	0.020	0.021
Distribution and support plans				0.017	0.017
Documentation plans		0.020	0.020	0.020	0.020
Design review plans		0.010	0.010	0.010	0.010
Code inspection plans		0.015	0.015	0.015	0.015
Unit test plans		0.010	0.015	0.010	0.012
Function test plans	0.010	0.012	0.015	0.010	0.012
Regression test plans		0.010	0.010	0.010	0.010
Integration test plans		0.010	0.015	0.012	0.012
Performance test plans		0.012	0.017	0.012	0.014
Component test plans		0.010	0.015	0.010	0.012
System test plans	0.010	0.012	0.020	0.012	0.014
Independent test plans			0.020		0.020
Field (beta) test plans		0.010	0.010	0.012	0.011
Lab test plans		0.010	0.150		0.080
Usability test plans		0.010	0.200	0.012	0.074
Maintenance and support plans	0.010	0.012	0.250	0.020	0.073
Nationalization plans				0.010	0.010
Special date containment plans	0.020	0.025	0.030	0.015	0.023
Subtotal	0.072	0.218	0.852	0.257	0.350
Financial documents					
Market forecasts				0.010	0.010
Cost estimates	0.010	0.015	0.020	0.010	0.014
Department budgets	0.001	0.001	0.001	0.001	0.001
Capital expenditure requests	0.001	0.001	0.001	0.001	0.001
Travel authorization requests	0.001	0.001	0.002	0.001	0.001
Maintenance cost estimates	0.010	0.020	0.025	0.015	0.018
Special date repair cost estimates	0.010	0.015	0.015	0.010	0.013
Subtotal	0.033	0.053	0.064	0.048	0.050
Control documents					
Budget variance reports	0.010	0.010	0.010	0.010	0.010
Computer utilization reports	0.015	0.020	0.020		0.018
Milestone tracking reports	0.010	0.010	0.015	0.015	0.013
Design inspection reports	0.010	0.025	0.030	0.015	0.020
Code inspection reports	0.010	0.015	0.017	0.010	0.013
Quality-assurance status reports	0.010	0.020	0.025	0.015	0.018
Control documents					
Test status reports	0.020	0.035	0.045	0.035	0.034
Build status reports	0.010	0.025	0.030	0.030	0.024
Phase review reports		0.010	0.030		0.020

TABLE 21.2   Universe of Software Project Document Types *(Continued)*
(Size in pages per function point)

Document type	MIS	Systems	Military	Commercial	Average
Independent verification and validation reports			0.025		0.025
Audit reports	0.010	0.010	0.020		0.013
Project postmortem reports		0.015	0.017		0.016
Special date status reports	0.025	0.045	0.050	0.025	0.036
Subtotal	0.130	0.240	0.334	0.155	0.215
Technical documents					
Requirements specifications	0.150	0.450	0.800	0.200	0.400
Initial functional specifications	0.250	0.550	0.700	0.250	0.438
Final functional specifications	0.600	1.200	2.000	0.550	1.088
Logic specifications	0.500	1.150	1.600	0.600	0.963
System structure specifications	0.100	0.400	0.800	0.100	0.350
Database specifications	0.375	0.250	0.900	0.150	0.419
Data dictionaries	0.030	0.020	0.030	0.020	0.025
Design change requests	0.250	0.400	0.700	0.300	0.413
Configuration-control status	0.010	0.025	0.030	0.030	0.024
Invention/patent disclosures		0.010		0.010	0.010
Subtotal	2.265	4.455	7.560	2.210	4.123
Legal documents					
Trademark search reports				0.010	0.010
Patent applications		0.001	0.001	0.001	0.001
Copyright registrations		0.001	0.001	0.001	0.001
Outsource contracts	0.500	0.500		0.500	0.500
Package acquisition contracts	0.015	0.015	0.100	0.015	0.036
Custom software contracts	0.020	0.020	0.030	0.020	0.023
Employment agreements	0.001	0.001	0.001	0.001	0.001
Non-competition agreements	0.001	0.001	0.001	0.001	0.001
Sarbanes-Oxley compliance disclosures	0.010	0.010	0.010	0.010	0.010
Litigation materials	4.000	4.000	4.000	4.000	4.000
Subtotal	4.547	4.549	4.144	4.559	4.450
Marketing Documentation					
Marketing brochures				0.001	0.001
World Wide Web materials				0.010	0.010
Advertisements				0.001	0.001
Television ad copy				0.001	0.001
Marketing Documentation					
Sales manual updates		0.001		0.001	0.001
Customer satisfaction surveys	0.010	0.010		0.010	0.010
Competitive analysis reports		0.003	0.004	0.002	0.003
Subtotal	0.010	0.014	0.004	0.026	0.014
User documentation					
Quick-start users guide				0.010	
Full users guides	0.200	0.400	0.800	0.300	0.425
Feature users guides	0.100	0.200	0.500	0.300	0.275

TABLE 21.2 Universe of Software Project Document Types *(Continued)*
(Size in pages per function point)

Document type	MIS	Systems	Military	Commercial	Average
HELP text	0.010	0.100	0.150	0.200	0.115
README files				0.010	0.010
Training course materials	0.100	0.150	0.400	0.150	0.200
Instructors guides	0.010	0.050	0.060	0.040	0.040
Reference manuals	0.600	1.000	1.700	0.700	1.000
Glossaries		0.200	0.350	0.150	0.233
CD-ROM information				1.000	1.000
Subtotal	1.020	2.100	3.960	2.860	2.485
Support documentation					
Operators guides	0.100	0.150	0.220		0.157
Programmers guides	0.100	0.200	0.300	0.250	0.213
Systems programmers guides		0.250	0.650	0.330	0.410
Maintenance guides	0.250	0.350	0.600	0.250	0.363
Message and code guides		0.150	0.150		0.150
Subtotal	0.450	1.100	1.920	0.830	1.075
Quality-control documentation					
Design inspection defect reports	0.500	0.750	0.900	0.650	0.700
Code inspection defect reports	0.300	1.200	1.000	0.800	0.825
Test defect reports	1.650	1.500	1.650	1.500	1.575
Customer defect reports	0.500	0.400	0.500	1.900	0.825
Usability survey reports		0.020		0.150	0.085
Subtotal	2.950	3.870	4.050	5.000	3.968
Total pages per function point	11.477	16.599	22.888	15.945	16.727
Document types produced	52	74	71	79	69

Software document estimation is normally carried out in the following sequence:

1. Determine the specific set of documents to be produced for the application.

2. Determine the size of each document to be produced.

3. Determine the effort to create each basic document.

4. Determine the rate at which each document may change due to new requirements.

5. Determine the defect potential of each document.

6. Determine the additional effort to accommodate changing requirements.

7. Determine the additional effort to repair documentation defects.

8. Determine the mechanical costs of document production and distribution.

In many cases, documentation can be even more extensive than what is shown here, because for international commercial software, many of the technical, user, and marketing document types may be produced in multiple natural languages, so documents may concurrently exist in any or all of the following languages:

- English
- Japanese
- Korean
- Chinese
- German
- French
- Italian
- Spanish
- Portuguese
- Dutch
- Norwegian
- Swedish
- Finnish
- Polish
- Russian

Obviously, when estimating overall documentation costs it is necessary to include the costs of nationalization, or translation into various national languages. For example, many Canadian software projects are required to produce key documents in both French and English, even for internal use.

Software Documentation Tools on Lagging and Leading Projects

When estimating software documentation costs and schedules, automation applied to the production of documents has an impact. Table 21.3 shows some of the differences in documentation automation noted in lagging, average, and leading organizations.

TABLE 21.3   Numbers and Size Ranges of Software Documentation Tools
(Size data expressed in terms of function point metrics)

Documentation support	Lagging	Average	Leading
Word processing	3,000	3,000	3,000
Web publishing		3,000	3,000
Desktop publishing	2,500	2,500	2,500
Graphics support	500	500	2,500
Multimedia support		750	2,000
Grammar checking			500
Dictionary/thesaurus	500	500	500
Hypertext support		250	500
Scanning			300
Spell checking	200	200	200
Function point subtotal	6,700	10,700	15,000
Number of tools	5	8	10

Almost all software projects require documentation, but very few are documented extremely well. The set of documentation tools is undergoing profound transformation as online publishing and the World Wide Web begins to supplant conventional paper documents.

Note that some of these tools included here are also used for requirements, specifications, plans, and other documents throughout the software development cycle. For example, almost every knowledge worker today makes use of "word processing" tools, so these tools are not restricted only to the software documentation domain.

As online publishing grows, this category is interesting in that the "average" and "leading" categories are fairly close together in terms of document tool usage. However, the laggards are still quite far behind in terms of both numbers of tools and overall capacities deployed.

As web publishing and DVD drives become more common, it is likely that conventional paper documents will gradually be supplanted by online documents. The advent of the "paperless office" has been predicted for years but stumbled due to the high costs of storage.

Now that optical storage is exploding in capacities and declining in costs, optical online storage is now substantially cheaper than paper storage, so the balance is beginning to shift towards online documentation and the associated tool suites.

In the documentation domain the variance between the leaders and the laggards is 2 to 1 in the number of tools deployed, and also just over 2 to 1 in the volumes of tools deployed. The differences in the documentation category are interesting, but not so wide as the differentials for project management and quality assurance tools.

References

Ambler, S.: *Process Patterns—Building Large-Scale Systems Using Object Technology*, Cambridge University Press, New York, NY, SIGS Books, 1998.

Artow, J., and I. Neustadt: *UML and the Unified Process*, Addison-Wesley, Boston, Mass., 2000.

Beck, K.: *Extreme Programming Explained: Embrace Change*, Addison-Wesley, Boston, Mass., 1999.

Boehm, Barry: "A Spiral Model of Software Development and Enhancement," Proceedings of the Int. Workshop on Software Process and Software Environments, ACM Software Engineering Notes, Aug. 1986, pp. 22–42.

Booch, Grady: *Object Solutions: Managing the Object-Oriented Project*, Addison-Wesley, Reading, Mass., 1995.

————, Ivar Jacobsen, and James Rumbaugh: *The Unified Modeling Language User Guide, Second Edition*, Addison-Wesley, Boston, Mass., 2005.

Cockburn, Alistair: *Agile Software Development*, Addison-Wesley, Boston, Mass., 2001.

Cohen, D., M. Lindvall, and P. Costa: "An Introduction to Agile Methods," *Advances in Computers*, Elsevier Science, New York, 2004, pp. 1–66.

Cohen, Lou: *Quality Function Deployment: How to Make QFD Work for You*, Prentice-Hall, Englewood Cliffs, NJ; 1995.

Cohn, Mike: *User Stories Applied: For Agile Software Development*, Addison-Wesley, Boston, Mass., 2004.

————: *Agile Estimating and Planning*, Prentice-Hall PTR, Englewood Cliffs, N.J., 2005.

Gamma, Erich, Richard Helm, Ralph Johnson, and John Vlissides: *Design Patterns: Elements of Reusable Object Oriented Design*, Addison-Wesley, Boston Mass., 1995.

Garmus, David, and David Herron: *Measuring the Software Process: A Practical Guide to Functional Measurement*, Prentice-Hall, Englewood Cliffs, N.J., 1995.

————: *Function Point Analysis*, Addison-Wesley Longman, Boston, Mass., 2001.

IFPUG: IT Measurement, Addison-Wesley, Boston, Mass., 2002.

International Organization for Standards: ISO 9000 / ISO 14000 (http://www.iso.org/iso/en/iso9000-14000/index.html).

Jeffries, R. et al.: *Extreme Programming Installed*, Addison-Wesley, Boston. Mass., 2001.

Jones, Capers: *Patterns of Software System Failure and Success*, International Thomson Computer Press, Boston, 1995.

————: *Applied Software Measurement, Second Edition*, McGraw-Hill, New York, 1996.

————: *Software Quality—Analysis and Guidelines for Success*, International Thomson Computer Press, Boston, Mass., 1997.

————: "Sizing Up Software," *Scientific American*, New York, December 1998, Vol. 279, No. 6, pp 104–109.

————: *Software Assessments, Benchmarks, and Best Practices*, Addison-Wesley Longman, Boston, Mass., 2000.

Kan, Stephen H.: *Metrics and Models in Software Quality Engineering, Second Edition*, Addison-Wesley Longman, Boston, Mass., 2003.

Larman, Craig, and Victor Basili: "Iterative and Incremental Development—A Brief History," *IEEE Computer Society*, June 2003, pp 47–55.

Love, Tom, *Object Lessons*, SIGS Books, New York, 1993.

McConnell, Steve: *Software Estimating: Demystifying the Black Art*, Microsoft Press, Redmond, WA, 2006.

Mikkelsen, Tim, and Suzanne Pherigo: *Practical Software Configuration Management*, Prentice-Hall PTR, Upper Saddle River, N.J., 1997.

MIL STD 2167A: Defense System Software Development and Data Item Descriptions, Department of Defense, Naval Publications Center, Philadelphia, Pa., 1988.

Pressman, Roger: *Software Engineering—A Practitioner's Approach, Sixth Edition*, McGraw-Hill, New York, 2005.

Putnam, Lawrence H.: *Measures for Excellence—Reliable Software on Time, Within Budget*, Yourdon Press/Prentice-Hall, Englewood Cliffs, N.J., 1992.

————, and Ware Myers: *Industrial Strength Software—Effective Management Using Measurement*, IEEE Computer Society Press, Washington D.C., 1997.

Quality Function Deployment (http://en.wikipedia.org/wiki/Quality_function_ deployment).

Rapid Application Development (http://en.wikipedia.org/wiki/Rapid_application_ development).

Robertson S. and Robertson J.: *Requirements-Led Project Management*, Addison-Wesley Boston, Mass., 2005, ISBN 0-321-18062-3.

Rubin, Howard: *Software Benchmark Studies for* 1997, Howard Rubin Associates, Pound Ridge, N.Y., 1997.

Symons, Charles R.: *Software Sizing and Estimating—Mk II FPA (Function Point Analysis)*, John Wiley & Sons, Chichester, U.K., 1991.

Estimating Software Project Management

In round numbers, the project management function will contribute between 10 and 20 percent to the cost of software projects. Project managers also exert a strong influence on schedules, quality, and team morale. For large software projects, failures and disasters are more closely correlated to poor project management than to poor technical work. In fact, poor project management can cause poor technical work by skimping on inspections and quality control activities and by creating excessively optimistic cost and schedule estimates.

Estimating the work of software project managers is surprisingly complicated, and is supported by very little in the way of solid empirical data. In fact, even the roles and responsibilities of project managers can vary from company to company, and from project to project within the same company.

The literature on software project management is extensive, but slanted heavily toward how-to-do-it books. Books that contain quantitative data on the costs of project management or even on such rudimentary topics as the ranges on software project spans of control are quite rare.

Some of the books that do deal with software project management include Fred Brooks's *Mythical Man-Month* (Addison-Wesley, 1974), Barry Boehm's *Software Engineering Economics* (Prentice-Hall, 1981), and several of the author's own books, such as *New Directions in Software Management* (Information Systems Management Group, 1993) and *Patterns of Software Systems Failure and Success* (International Thomson Computer Press, 1995). Lois Zells comes at software project management from the viewpoint of the tools utilized in *Managing Software Projects* (QED Information Sciences, 1990).

Although not a book about estimating management, Watts Humphrey's book *Managing Technical People* (Addison-Wesley, 1997) provides valuable insights. The cognitive psychologist Dr. Bill Curtis succeeded Watts as head of the SEI's assessment research group, and has also contributed to the management literature in the form of the SEI's people capability model.

Some more recent books include Donald Reifer's *Software Management, Sixth Edition* (IEEE Press, 2002) and the sections from Roger Pressman's *Software Engineering—A Practitioner's Approach, Sixth Edition* (McGraw-Hill, 2005) that discuss planning, estimating, and measurement.

The Project Management Institute (PMI) has dozens of relevant titles dealing with multiple issues. PMI is the largest non-profit association in the project management world. Membership in PMI opens up many programs and additional sources of information for project managers.

The nominal default values for software project management are easy to state (see Table 22.1), but these values are not very useful because the range of project management functions is extremely broad. Also, the span of control or number of staff reporting to a project manager can range from a low of 1 to a high of more than 30 technical staff members.

The activity of software project management has not traditionally been estimated or measured using lines-of-code-metrics. Project management cannot be directly measured using function points either, but it is possible to reconstruct both function point and LOC values.

Suppose for example a 1500–function point (roughly equivalent to a size of 150,000 C statements) project has a team of eight programmers and one manager. In this example the assignment scope for the programmers will be 188 function points or 18,750 source code statements. That is the

TABLE 22.1   Nominal Project Management Default Estimating Values

Activity sequence	Continuous: Initial and final activity of software projects
Performed by	Project managers, supervisors, or client representatives
Predecessor activities	None
Overlap	100% with requirements
Concurrent activities	All other development activities
Successor activities	Maintenance
Assignment scope	1500 function points per manager
Span of control	8 employees per manager
Production rate	100 function points per staff month
Production rate	1.32 work hours per function point
Schedule months	Concurrent with overall project schedule
Defect potential	1.0 management defects per function point
Defect removal	75% via various kinds of inspections
Delivered defects	0.25 management defects per function point
High-severity defects	30% of delivered management defects
Bad-fix probability	10% of management fixes may yield new errors

average amount assigned to each team member. Since there is only one manager, the assignment scope for him or her will be 1500 function points or 150,00 source code statements. This is not to say that the manager actually develops any code (although some do). It is merely a mathematical expression for the quantity of technical material that one manager might be able to handle.

The standard way of dealing with project management, which is used for many kinds of projects and not just software, centers around the *span-of-control* concept.

The management span of control refers to the number of technical employees who report to a specific project manager. The concept has been studied and explored for various industries for more than a century. The nominal average for the number of employees reporting to a manager in the United States is about eight employees per manager.

However, for software projects among SPR's clients, the observed ratios of employees to managers has run from 1 to 1 to as high as 30 to 1.

Software project managers have personnel responsibilities as well as project management responsibilities. Most project managers are also responsible for appraisals and personnel counseling, for hiring, and for other aspects of human resource management, such as approving education and training requests.

In addition, software project managers have departmental roles for budgets, arranging for office space, approving travel requisitions, ordering supplies, and so forth. The generic rules of thumb for software project managers among SPR's clients resemble the following:

- One project manager for every eight technical staff members
- One full-time project manager for every 1500 function points
- One project manager for roughly every 150,000 source code statements
- Project management starts before requirements and runs after the project ends
- Project management work = 35 percent of available management time
- Personnel work = 30 percent of available management time
- Meetings with other managers or clients = 22 percent of available management time
- Departmental work = 8 percent of available management time
- Miscellaneous work = 5 percent of available management time

To understand why these nominal default values fluctuate very widely, it is necessary to understand the real-life situations that often affect the work of software project managers. The main variable factors that can influence software project managers' jobs, and hence also influence cost estimates, include the following:

- The roles assigned to (or assumed by) the project manager for activities such as sizing, cost estimating, quality estimating, departmental budgeting, personnel hiring and appraisals, space allocation, milestone tracking, cost tracking, quality tracking, measurement, and the like.

- Whether the project manager is a *pure* manager, or also contributes to the project in a technical way. For example, some software project managers may also serve as *chief programmers* and, hence, perform technical work as well as managerial work.

- The nature of the project, and whether it is a *pure* software project or a hybrid project that also involves engineered components, manufactured components, microcode, or some other kinds of work besides software development.

- External pressures applied to the project, and hence to the project manager, from clients or senior management, in terms of schedule pressure, cost-containment pressure, or some other forms of pressure that occur less often, such as the need to achieve very high performance levels.

- The suite of project management tools available and utilized by the project manager, including cost-estimating tools, project-scheduling tools, methodology management tools or process management tools, quality-estimation tools, tracking tools, and the like.

- The number of other managers involved on the project simultaneously, and whether large projects are organized in a hierarchical or matrix fashion. Surprisingly, software productivity for entire projects tends to correlate very strongly, and inversely, with the number of managers engaged. Large software projects with many managers have a very strong probability of running late, exceeding budgets, being canceled, or even all three at once.

- Time-splitting among multiple projects, which can occur when a project manager is simultaneously responsible for several small projects, rather than one discrete project or one component of a really large system.

- The span of control, or the number of technical workers assigned to any given manager.

- The number of different kinds of software occupations among the workers assigned to a given manager.

- The presence or absence of a *project office* for larger projects, and the division of work between individual project managers and the project office.

- The experience level of the project manager in terms of having managed projects similar to the current project.

- The set of quality-control activities that the project manager establishes for the project.

Let us consider the implications of all of these project management factors in turn.

The Roles of Software Project Management

The responsibilities and roles of a software project manager can be divided into three distinct components:

- The role of personnel management
- The role of departmental management
- The role of specific project management

Personnel management may not always be delegated to a project manager under the matrix method of organization, although it is a normal responsibility under the hierarchical method of organization. When present, the personnel role includes, but is not limited to the following:

- Interviewing candidates
- Creating job offers and benefits packages, within human resources guidelines
- Performing personnel appraisals
- Approving training or education requests
- Issuing awards, if indicated
- Disciplinary matters, if needed
- Terminations and layoffs, if necessary
- Participation in various human resources programs
- Receiving guidance based on morale surveys

The personnel aspects of the project manager's job are important, and personnel-related issues can often occupy 25 to 40 percent of a manager's daily time. In some situations, such as when there are "open door" issues or some kind of serious morale problems present, personnel-related work can top 60 percent of a manager's daily time.

From an estimating point of view, not all of the manager's personnel activities are related to a specific project. Therefore, it is important to know whether the manager's personnel work is to be charged to a specific project, or is general in nature and should be classed as overhead work.

The departmental management role includes, but is not limited to the following:

- Participating in annual or semiannual budget creation exercises
- Dealing with facilities management on space and office issues
- Approving travel plans
- Requesting or approving requisitions for computers and equipment
- Participating in special studies, such as SEI or SPR assessments, ISO audits, or business process reengineering (BPR) reviews

In larger corporations, the creation of annual departmental budgets is often one of the most expensive "products" that the company builds. Every project manager can devote from two weeks to more than a month each year to budget preparation, budget review meetings, and budget revision work.

The budgeting process is usually a departmental exercise, hence, the work may affect many different software projects, although for very large software systems an entire budget may be devoted to only a single project. However, it is more common for a typical department of eight technical staff members and a manager to have dozens of projects in the course of a single calendar year, and some projects that surface toward the end of the year may not even be visible at the time the annual budgets are first being planned.

Because project managers are often department managers too, the overhead work of managing a department can amount to about 1 month out of 12, or perhaps 8 percent of a project manager's annual effort. Here, too, the departmental work can be much larger, but is seldom smaller.

The project management role, which is the primary focus of this chapter, generally includes 12 key activities that are specifically associated with the project management function:

- Coordinating with clients on the project
- Coordinating with higher management on project resources and status
- Coordinating with other managers on large projects
- Technology and tool selection for the project
- Sizing, or predicting the volumes of deliverables to be created
- Cost estimating, or predicting the probable total expenses for the project
- Schedule estimating, or predicting the nominal end date for the project

- Quality estimating, or predicting the probable numbers of bugs or defects
- Milestone estimating, or predicting the dates of key events
- Tracking, or monitoring progress against key milestones
- Progress reporting, or creating monthly (or weekly) status reports
- Measurement, or collecting and normalizing data about the project

It is the set of key activities associated with actually estimating, planning, and tracking projects that is the heart of the project manager's role. These are the activities that can spell success for projects when they are done well, or failure for projects if they are done poorly or contain significant errors.

Estimating, tracking, and reporting are interleaved activities that can occur almost continuously during the development cycles of software projects. The work of these key tasks will vary significantly based on whether manual methods or automated methods are utilized. If manual methods are used, estimating and planning can absorb about 35 percent of a project manager's time on major projects. If automated estimating and planning tools are used, estimating and planning can drop well below 10 percent.

Project Managers Who Are Also Technical Contributors

Because one of the most common origins for software project managers is a promotion from programmer to project manager, it is not surprising that many project managers also perform technical work, too. In fact, it is extremely common in the software industry for project managers to continue to serve as chief programmers on the projects that they manage.

Obviously, for estimating the work of project managers, it is necessary to separate the managerial tasks from the technical tasks. When project managers are also technical contributors, the task of estimating both the managerial component and the technical component becomes complex.

Many managers who wear two hats and also do technical work tend to have very intense work ethics and put in a lot of overtime. Usually, technical work dominates and absorbs about 60 percent of the manager's time, while the usual managerial work absorbs about 40 percent. However, we're dealing with work weeks that often include 20 hours or more of unpaid overtime.

The reason that software project managers often do technical work is because many of them were promoted into management from programming or software engineering work. There is a school of thought that asserts that the personality attributes of good programmers are so different from the personality attributes of good managers that a career progression from software engineer to software manager may not be effective. Although there may be some truth to this hypothesis, there is no other source of software management that has been proven to be more effective than the available pool of programming talent.

Project Management for Hybrid Projects Involving Hardware and Software

Many complex systems include hardware, software, and microcode at the same time. When hybrid projects are being developed, the project management tasks for estimating, schedule planning, and other activities grow more complicated and more time-consuming. Obviously, the final estimate and plan for hybrid projects must integrate the software and hardware components.

Also, from the point of view of cost tracking and cost management, it is more complicated to keep track of software costs versus hardware costs when both are going on simultaneously.

The distribution of management time between hardware and software components of hybrid systems is seldom a 50/50 split. Obviously, the proportions will vary with the magnitude of software work versus the magnitude of engineering work. However, there are also variations with a sociological origin. For example, if the project manager has an electrical or mechanical engineering background, then less time might be spent on software than if the project manager has a computer science or software engineering background.

However, because software is usually the component that has the greatest chance of running late and exceeding budgets, project managers from all backgrounds will need to concentrate their energies on the software component if problems begin to accumulate.

Project Management and External Schedule Pressures

One of the more difficult aspects of being a project manager is that of being subject to external pressures from both clients and senior executives. The most common pressure applied to project managers is that of schedule pressure, but other topics may also be under external pressures, such as costs or (less frequently) quality.

The best defense for dealing with external pressure is accurate historical data derived from similar projects. For example, suppose you are a project manager responsible for a project of 1000 function points or

100,000 source code statements. You have a team of five, and a planned 18-month development schedule based on team capabilities. It would not be surprising for either the clients or senior management (or both) to try to force the project schedule to be cut back to 12 months.

If you have no empirical data from similar projects, it is hard to defend your plans against this kind of external pressure. But if you know that based on a sample of 50 similar projects, 0 percent have been completed in 12 months, 50 percent have been completed in 18 months, 40 percent have run longer than 18 months, and 10 percent have been completed in 15 to 18 months, then you have a solid basis for defending your plan, and it is not likely to be overturned in an arbitrary manner.

The primary value of mounting a rational defense against irrational schedule pressure from outside is because project managers who succumb to these external pressures often see their projects fail or suffer severe cost and schedule overruns. Unfortunately, if the project manager has no empirical data from similar projects, and is not using any of the automated estimating tools with a built-in knowledge base, then succumbing to external schedule pressures is hard to avoid.

Many major software disasters occur because clients or executives with little or no knowledge about the realities of software estimating and software schedules force impossible delivery dates on helpless project managers, whose own knowledge of estimating and scheduling is not sufficient or not credible enough to keep the project on a realistic schedule.

Project Management Tools

The phrase *project management* has been artificially narrowed by vendors so that many people think the phrase describes only a limited set of tools that can produce Gantt charts and PERT diagrams, perform critical path analysis, and handle the mechanics of scheduling and cost accumulation.

However, there are a number of specialized software project management tools that are aimed specifically at software projects and can augment the somewhat limited software abilities of the traditional project management tools, such as Microsoft Project, Timeline, Primavera, Artemis, and the like. (The traditional project management tools have no built-in software knowledge base and cannot deal with many important software topics, such as sizing, creeping requirements, and quality estimating.)

Among the specialized tools aimed specifically at software project managers can be found specialized software cost-estimating tools and specialized methodology or process management tools. There are also automated "project offices" for capturing progress and historical data.

Table 22.2 discusses some of the differences in project management tools noted in lagging, average, and leading organizations. Both counts

TABLE 22.2   Numbers and Size Ranges of Project Management Tools
(Size data expressed in terms of function point metrics)

Project management	Lagging	Average	Leading
Project planning	1,000	1,250	3,000
Project cost estimating			3,000
Statistical analysis			3,000
Methodology management		750	3,000
Project office analysis			3,000
Quality estimation			2,000
Assessment support		500	2,000
Project measurement			1,750
Portfolio analysis			1,500
Risk analysis			1,500
Resource tracking	300	750	1,500
Value analysis		350	1,250
Cost variance reporting		500	1,000
Personnel support	500	500	750
Milestone tracking		250	750
Budget support		250	750
Function point analysis		250	750
Backfiring: LOC to FP			750
Function point subtotal	1,800	5,350	31,250
Number of tools	3	10	18

of numbers of tools and also the usage of the features of those tools is illustrated.

The counts of the numbers of tools is simply based on assessment and benchmark results and our interviews with project personnel. Although projects vary, of course, deriving the counts of tools is reasonably easy to perform.

The sizes of the tools expressed in function points are more difficult to arrive at, and have a larger margin of error. For some kinds of tools such as cost-estimating tools actual sizes are known in both function point and lines-of-code form because the author's company builds such tools.

For many tools, however, the size data is only approximate and is derived either from "backfiring," which is conversion from lines of code to function points, or from analogy with tools of known sizes. The size ranges for tools in this report are interesting, but not particularly accurate. The purpose of including the function point size data is to examine the utilization of tool features in lagging and leading projects.

In general, the lagging projects depend to a surprising degree on manual methods and have rather sparse tool usage in every category except software engineering, where there are comparatively small differences between the laggards and the leaders.

The differences in project management tool usage is both significant and striking. The lagging projects typically utilize only three general kinds of project management tools, while the leading projects utilize 18. Indeed, the project management tool family is one of the key differentiating factors between lagging and leading projects.

In general, the managers on the lagging projects typically use manual methods for estimating project outcomes and measuring progress, although quite a few may use schedule planning tools such as Microsoft Project. However, project managers on lagging projects tend to be less experienced in the use of planning tools and to utilize fewer of the available features.

The sparseness of project management tools does much to explain why so many lagging software projects tend to run late, to exceed their budgets, or to behave in more or less unpredictable fashions.

By contrast, the very significant use of project management tools on the leading projects results in one overwhelming advantage: "No surprises." The number of on-time projects in the leading set is far greater than in the lagging set, and all measurement attributes (quality, schedules, productivity, etc.) are also significantly better.

Differences in the software project management domain are among the most striking in terms of the huge differential of tool usage between the laggards and leaders. Variances in the number of tools deployed is about 6 to 1 between the leaders and the laggards, while variances in the tool capacities expressed in function points has a ratio of almost 17 to 1 between the leaders and the laggards. These differences are far greater than almost any other category of tool.

Since this book is about software cost estimating rather than overall project management, it is appropriate to discuss the pros and cons of automated software cost-estimating tools. Among the most important advantages is that these tools contain extensive built-in knowledge bases derived from hundreds or thousands of software projects, and can handle such specialized topics as predicting the number of bugs or defects, estimating the rate of creeping user requirements, or automatically changing the estimate in response to different technologies, such as making an adjustment if the programming language switches from C to C++. These specialized software cost-estimating tools can interface with traditional project management tools, and together the results can be very useful. Another advantage is that the accuracy of software cost-estimating tools is often better than manual estimates by project managers. Indeed, from time to time the accuracy of cost-estimating tools has been shown to be higher than the historical data used to calibrate the tool! (Sometimes the historical data had gaps such as production of user manuals and the work of software quality assurance (SQA) specialists. These activities were present in the automated cost estimates. When the reasons why the cost estimates showed higher costs than historical data, it was discovered that the historical data was incomplete.)

The "cons" of acquiring and using commercial software cost-estimating tools are threefold:

- The learning curve to use the tools effectively is not trivial.
- The tools need to be calibrated to local conditions.
- Some of the better cost-estimating tools are fairly expensive.

The best-in-class software organizations have a suite of very powerful and effective project management tools, of which traditional project management or scheduling tools are only one component. Cost-estimating and tracking tools are also major components of the project management suites.

Overall, successful projects have more than an order of magnitude more project management tools available than do the set of failing projects. In fact, the two most significant differences between failing projects and successful ones are the suites of available tools for project management and for quality control. In both project management and quality-control tools, the leaders outrank the laggards by about an order of magnitude in terms of tool deployment.

(Interestingly, the suites of software development tools do not show any major differences between successful, average, and failing projects. All three tend to use between 30,000 and 50,000 function points of software design and development tools.)

The use of function point metrics for evaluating tool suites is one of the newer uses of function point metrics, but one that is already producing very interesting results.

Note that the tools shown here are those directly associated with software project management roles. In addition to these tools, project managers may have another 10,000 function points of human-resource tools and about 5000 function points of departmental tools for such things as budgets, capital expenditures, travel cost reporting, and the like.

Project Management on Large Systems with Many Managers

Really large systems in the 100,000–function point range may have more than 500 technical staff members and 50 or more project managers. These large systems are very difficult to manage, and a considerable amount of project management effort is devoted to meetings and coordination with other managers.

Indeed, assuming that the system is large enough to have ten project managers engaged, about 30 percent of monthly project management time will be spent in meetings with other managers. These coordination meetings can absorb even more than 38 percent of managerial effort, because these large systems usually have multiple layers of management so that the planning meetings may involve first-line managers to whom the technical staff reports, second-line managers to whom the first-line managers report, and perhaps even third-line and fourth-line managers on really large systems. (Above the third line, management titles usually change to something like *director* or *vice president*.)

It is an interesting phenomenon that software productivity, like any other human activity, declines as the number of workers simultaneously engaged grows larger. However, for software projects the rate at which software productivity declines is directly proportional to the number of managers that are concurrently engaged in the overall system.

This phenomenon explains some otherwise curious results, such as the fact that software projects organized in a *matrix* fashion often have lower productivity than the same size project organized in a *hierarchical* fashion. The matrix style of organization deploys more managers for any given project size than does the hierarchical style, and that alone may be sufficient to explain the reduced productivity levels.

In the matrix organization, the set of project management roles may not include personnel functions. Often, under a matrix organization there are permanent department or *career managers* to whom employees report for appraisal and salary review purposes, and project managers to whom the employees report temporarily for the duration of the project.

The matrix organization more or less resembles a *task force* in the military sense. Under the task force concept military units are aggregated together for a specific mission, and then return to their usual locations when the mission is over. For example, during World War II ships from the American Fifth Fleet and the Seventh Fleet were combined for several months for a specific campaign, and then reverted to their normal commands afterwards.

Under the matrix organization personnel from a number of departments are aggregated together for a specific project, and when the project is over they return to their normal organizations for reassignment.

Under the matrix organization, as previously noted, technical employees usually report simultaneously to two managers:

- Their departmental managers, for personnel and salary matters
- The project manager, for technical matters

Under a hierarchical organization, on the other hand, the personnel on larger projects are organized in a pyramidal fashion like a traditional military organization, with the overall project director at the top and all subordinate units reporting upward in a standard chain of command.

For example, suppose you are concerned with a software project that is 10,000 function points or 1 million lines of code in size. If this project is organized in a hierarchical fashion, there might be 50 programmers and 6 project managers involved.

If it is organized in a matrix fashion, there might still be 50 programmers, but now the management complement is up to 10. There is a good chance that the productivity of the matrix version might be about 10 to 15 percent below the productivity of the hierarchical version.

Part of the reduction can be attributed to the four additional managers, but another portion of the reduction is because matrix management tends to add a certain level of confusion to projects which is absent in the hierarchical fashion.

Not all matrix projects fail or even are below the hierarchical style in net results, because many other factors are at play. However, from considering the results of 100 matrix projects and comparing them to 100 hierarchical projects, the matrix projects often lag the hierarchical ones.

Time-Splitting, or Managing Several Projects Simultaneously

In addition to having multiple managers on large systems, it is also common to have multiple small projects assigned to a given project manager. The reason for this is because department sizes are often constant within a company and average about eight employees per manager, but project sizes can range from a low of less than 1 function point to more than 100,000 function points.

Suppose your company has a traditional department structure with one manager for every eight technical staff members. Now suppose your company is interested in building two small projects that are each 800 function points in size and will require about four programmers.

Since department sizes are more or less fixed but project sizes are not, it would be typical to see both of these projects assigned to the same department and, hence, both have the same project manager.

This is merely a simple example. Suppose your company wants to do eight simultaneous projects, each of which is 200 function points in size. Under this second scenario, the same project manager would be responsible for all eight projects concurrently.

Although small projects do not require as much technical effort as large systems, there is a certain amount of irreducible overhead associated with projects in many companies. For example, each project may need its own cost estimate, its own monthly report, its own status meetings, and the like.

This means that project managers supporting multiple projects concurrently will have a much different time distribution than project managers supporting only one project. More time must be devoted to administrative matters and, sometimes, to additional meetings with clients.

This means that time devoted to personnel matters may be reduced, or managerial overtime may go up. In any case, estimating project management time when the manager is supporting multiple, independent projects is a tricky situation.

In companies that do not separate new development work from maintenance work, it is very common for a department that is doing development work in the form of an enhancement to an existing application to also be responsible for bug repairs on prior releases.

Because each incoming bug can be viewed as a kind of microproject, it is very common to have both technical personnel and project managers dealing with new development and maintenance simultaneously. This situation makes project cost estimating very complex, because the maintenance work interferes with the development work, and, hence, development will become erratic and hard to predict.

The Span of Control, or Number of Staff Members per Manager

If every manager had the same number of technical employees reporting in, then estimating project management work would be a great deal easier than it is. The span of control, or number of technical workers reporting to a manager, averages about eight employees, but the range runs from a low of 1 to a high of about 30.

The span-of-control concept originated more than 100 years ago in some of the pioneering work on army units after the close of the U.S. Civil War. The original purpose was to discover how fast troop units of various sizes could move from one place to another. It was quickly discovered that small units of less than 20 (squads, platoons) could get started and cover ground more quickly than larger units, such as companies, regiments, and brigades.

This research was soon applied to business situations, and led to the development of the span-of-control concept. For many kinds of office work, including software, the average value is roughly eight employees per manager.

Although a ratio of eight employees per manager is widely accepted, it may not be optimal for software projects. There is a great deal of debate in the Agile and XP domains about small teams of three to five being able to outperform normal departments of eight to ten. However, the literature on small teams tends to overlook the fact that the software projects that the small teams are concerned with are often much smaller than the projects assigned to larger groups. In other words, the apparent benefits of small teams may be at least partly due to the volume of work, rather than to the team size itself.

The author's own research has centered on really large systems in the 10,000– to 100,000–function point size range being constructed in large corporations, such as IBM, AT&T, Microsoft, and ITT. In the larger size ranges, what appears to be the optimal team size is a ratio of about a dozen technical workers reporting to a single project manager.

Although managers often state that large teams are hard to manage and keep track of, a careful analysis of how managers spend their time indicates that managers often spend more time with other managers than with their own employees.

The reason that larger teams appear to be more effective than smaller teams is not very flattering to software managers: Larger teams mean that less-capable managers can be removed from management and return to technical work, where their skills may be better utilized. Hence, larger teams give companies the ability to be more selective in choosing their managers, while also giving their managers better tools and support.

Larger teams and fewer managers also means less time spent in meetings with other managers, and less difficulty coordinating complex projects.

Other advantages of larger teams are that the amount of work that can be assigned to a given team goes up, and every student of management knows that cross-department coordination is much more difficult than coordination within a department. A department or team of a dozen technical workers and a manager can be assigned projects as large as 3000 function points or more than 300,000 source code statements. Conversely, a smaller team of five programmers and a manager can usually only handle about 1000 function points or 100,000 source code statements.

Managing Multiple Occupation Groups

As the software industry grows and expands, it is following the path of other industries and is developing a considerable number of specialists. One of the challenges of modern software project management is to select the optimum set of specialists for any given project. Another challenge is to develop organization structures that can place specialists so that their many diverse talents can best be utilized.

In 1995 AT&T commissioned SPR to perform a research study on the numbers and kinds of specialists utilized in large corporations and government groups. Some of the participants in this study included AT&T itself, IBM, Texas Instruments, and the U.S. Air Force. More recently several other organizations such as NASA, several Naval groups, and about a dozen large civilian companies were visited.

Table 22.3 shows the overall occupation group percentages noted among SPR's clients in the original and more recent studies.

Although there is some ambiguity in the available data, the presence of specialist occupation groups appears to be beneficial for software development and maintenance work.

The corporations that use specialists for key activities, such as testing and maintenance, usually outperform similar organizations that use generalists by 15 to 20 percent in terms of both quality and productivity levels.

The presence or absence of specialists is severely skewed based upon the overall size of the total software population in the company or enterprise. Small companies with less than about 100 total software personnel usually make use of generalists who perform development programming, maintenance programming, testing, quality duties, and sometimes even technical writing. Except for technical writing, generalists also predominate in the Agile and XP programming domains. There are some specialists such as "scrummasters" in the Agile world, however. The object-oriented (OO) domain, on the other hand, does utilize specialists in about the same numbers as older development methods.

TABLE 22.3   Overall Distribution of Software Occupations in Large Corporations

Occupation groups	Percent
Maintenance programming	20.0
Development programming	18.0
Project managers	11.5
Testing specialists	10.5
Systems analysts	9.0
Supply chain specialists	6.0
Technical writing specialists	4.0
Administration specialists	3.5
Quality-assurance specialists	3.0
Customer-support specialists	2.5
Database administration specialists	2.0
Cost-estimating specialists	1.5
Measurement specialists	1.5
Network specialists	1.5
Configuration-control specialists	1.0
Function point and measurement specialists	1.0
Web master specialists	1.0
Systems-support specialists	1.0
Process improvement specialists	1.0
Architecture specialists	0.5
Total	100.0

TABLE 22.4   **Number of Specialist Occupations and Total Software Employment**

Total software population	Number of specialist occupations
10	2
100	4
1,000	15
10,000	75

As the overall software population grows larger, more and more kinds of specialist occupations are noted, as in Table 22.4.

Although other factors may be involved, the use of specialists rather than generalists is strongly indicated as a possible explanation for an otherwise curious phenomenon. When software productivity rates are normalized based on the size of the software populations, the very large corporations with more than 10,000 software employees (i.e., Andersen, AT&T, EDS, IBM, Microsoft, etc.) have higher productivity rates than midsize organizations with 100 to 1000 total software personnel.

Very small corporations with fewer than 100 total software personnel have the highest productivity rates and don't use specialists very much at all. However, small companies only build small applications where generalists and specialists are roughly equivalent in performance.

Within midsized corporations, some rather large software applications in excess of 10,000 function points may be attempted. If the development personnel are generalists and are attempting every aspect of large systems construction (i.e., design, coding, quality control, testing, etc.), these various roles tend to be conflicting and slow down progress.

In particular, if the same people are simultaneously attempting to do new development and maintenance of earlier versions, the maintenance work will interfere with development work and make both activities inefficient and hard to estimate.

The Presence or Absence of Project Offices for Large Systems

Large software applications in the 100,000–function point size class (equivalent to roughly 10 million source code statements) are often supported by a specialized group of planning, estimating, and tracking specialists organized into what has come to be known as a *project office.*

Software projects in the 100,000–function point class may have 500 or more technical personnel and 50 to 70 managers deployed, so obviously there is a need for some kind of a central coordinating unit for such mammoth undertakings.

The size of the project office itself for a huge application in the 100,000–function point domain is likely to be about ten personnel, including the project office manager.

For very large projects that have a project office, a number of the tasks that might normally be assigned to the project managers themselves are instead performed by the specialists in the project office: Sizing, function point analysis, cost estimating, measurement, and so forth are often delegated to the project office.

The project managers' work is made easier by the presence of project offices, but they still have considerable responsibilities for coordinating their own teams, tracking progress against milestones, and reporting on any *red flag* items, which are serious technical or logistical problems that might affect the project's outcome.

In recent years tools that automate some of the project office functions have begun to be commercially available. Preliminary data indicates that these tools are fairly effective when used on large projects within large companies.

Experience Levels of Software Project Managers

Experience is a factor in every human activity, and software is no exception. Novice project managers are seldom entrusted with major projects, for very good reasons. The work of software project management is eased considerably with experience on similar projects—especially on similar projects with a successful outcome, rather than similar projects that were failures or disasters.

A fairly sensitive issue needs to be discussed. The overall population of the software world seems to have a shortage of qualified project management candidates. In large companies, that means that at least some of the project managers will not be very good.

Studies of the exit interview of software engineers who were leaving large companies to take new jobs revealed two disturbing findings:

- The best technical workers with the highest appraisal scores leave in the greatest numbers.

- The most common reason for leaving was stated to be "bad project management."

The implication is that bad project managers cannot attract and keep good technical workers. Therefore, bad project managers present a serious problem to large companies. So long as there are fewer qualified candidates for project management than there are job openings, the only short-term solution is to raise the span of control in order to weed out ineffective project managers. If you raise the span of control from eight employees per manager to ten employees per manager, then the weakest 20 percent of project managers can be reassigned.

Quality-Control Methods Selected by Project Managers

Although quality control is listed last in this discussion of project management roles, it is actually one of the most important factors of all. As discussed several times already, a ranked listing of the five major cost drivers for software projects has *finding and fixing* bugs as the most expensive single activity:

1. Finding and fixing bugs
2. Producing paper documents
3. Meetings and communication
4. Coding
5. Project management

In general, projects that run out of control and are terminated or end up in court usually have skimped on quality control, with the result that the projects could not be successfully delivered or deployed.

Consider the well-known disaster associated with the luggage-handling system at the Denver airport, which delayed the opening of the airport for approximately one year at a cost of roughly $1 million per day.

The two chief problems leading to this disaster were:

- Bad project management methods
- Inadequate quality-control methods

It is quite unfortunate that the impact of inadequate quality control is very deceptive and does not manifest itself until so late in the project that it is difficult to recover from the problem.

Usually, projects that are skimping on software quality methods, such as failing to use pretest design and code inspections, formal test methods, and the like, appear to be ahead of schedule and below cost estimates during the requirements, analysis, design, and even coding phases of development.

It is not until testing begins that the magnitude of the disaster starts to be realized. Then, when testing starts, it is painfully revealed that all of the quality shortcuts made earlier have produced an application that does not work and possibly cannot be made to work without major revisions and repairs.

All of the apparent early schedule and cost savings disappear in a huge frenzy of round-the-clock overtime as developers and managers frantically try to fix enough bugs so that the project stabilizes and can, perhaps, be released.

Project Managers and Metrics

Every project manager should understand the pros and cons of various metrics. Every project manager should understand what U.S. and industry averages are when expressed in terms of common metrics such as function points, use case points, object points, COSMIC function points, and the like. Every project manager should understand quality metrics such as defect-removal efficiency levels. It would also be helpful for every project manager to understand the basics of the six-sigma approach and of QFD.

However, actually counting function points or determining the sizes of applications with lines of code or use case points requires expertise that goes beyond normal management skills. In fact, actually counting function points accurately is a task that should only be done by certified counting specialists.

Managers need to understand how metrics work and what the data means, but it is not a project management job to count function points, lines of code, use case points, or other metrics. The counting tasks are better done by staff members and certified specialists.

Summary of Project Management Findings

The project management position is one of the most critical jobs in the software world. Good management correlates very strongly with successful projects. Bad management correlates strongly with failing projects. Good managers are good with people, understand estimating, are good planners, and recognize the value of excellent quality control and accurate measurements. Good managers also use a variety of automated tools to simplify their jobs.

Bad managers are often bad with people. They are marginal with estimating and planning, and they seldom understand the importance of quality control. Bad managers tend to fear measurements rather than embrace them, because accurate measurements are going to reveal their deficiencies. Bad managers also tend to use "seat of the pants" methods rather than automated methods for critical tasks such as schedule planning and cost estimating.

The worst aspect of bad managers is that they tend to drive away the strongest technical workers and the best software engineers. Good technical workers do not have to put up with bad managers because they can easily change jobs.

References

Boehm, Barry: *Software Engineering Economics*, Prentice-Hall, Englewood Cliffs, N.J., 1981.

Booch, Grady: *Object Solutions: Managing the Object-Oriented Project*, Addison-Wesley, Reading, Mass, 1995.

Brennan, E.M.: *Software Project Management—A Practitioner's Approach*, McGraw-Hill, New York, 1995.

Brooks, Fred: *The Mythical Man Month, Revised Edition*, Addison-Wesley, Reading, Mass., 1995.

Brown, Norm (ed.): *The Program Manager's Guide to Software Acquisition Best Practices*, Version 1.0, U.S. Department of Defense, Washington, D.C., July 1995.

Hughes, Bob, and Mike Cottrell: *Software Project Management, Third Edition*, McGraw-Hill, New York, 2002.

Cohn, Mike: *Agile Estimating and Planning*, Prentice-Hall PTR, Englewood Cliffs, N.J., 2005.

Curtis, Bill, William E. Hefley, and Sally Miller: *People Capability Maturity Model*, Software Engineering Institute, Carnegie Mellon University, Pittsburgh, Pa., 1995.

DeMarco, Tom, and Tom Lister: *Peopleware—Productive Projects and Teams, Second Edition*, Dorset House, New York, 1998.

Gack, Gary: "Applying Six-Sigma to Software Implementation Projects," (http://software .isixsigma.com/library/content/c040915b.asp).

Garmus, David, and David Herron, David: *Measuring the Software Process: A Practical Guide to Functional Measurement*, Prentice-Hall, Englewood Cliffs, N.J., 1995.

————: *Function Point Analysis*, Addison-Wesley Longman, Boston, Mass., 2001.

Hallowell, David L.: "Six Sigma Software Metrics, Part 1.," (http://software.isixsigma .com/library/content/03910a.asp).

Humphrey, Watts: *Managing the Software Process*, Addison-Wesley, Reading, Mass, 1989.

————: *Managing Technical People*, Addison-Wesley/Longman, Reading, Mass., 1997.

————: *TSP—Leading a Development Team*, Addison-Wesley, Boston, Mass, 2006.

International Organization for Standards: ISO 9000 / ISO 14000, (http://www.iso.org/iso/ en/iso9000-14000/index.html).

Jones, Capers: *New Directions in Software Management*, Information Systems Management Group, 1993.

————: *Assessment and Control of Software Risks*, Prentice-Hall, Englewood Cliffs, N.J., 1994.

————: *Applied Software Measurement, Second Edition*, McGraw-Hill, New York, 1996.

————: *Patterns of Software System Failure and Success*, International Thomson Computer Press, Boston, Mass., 1995.

————: "Sizing Up Software," *Scientific American*, New York, December 1998, Vol. 279, No. 6, pp 104–109.

————: *Software Assessments, Benchmarks, and Best Practices*, Addison-Wesley, Boston, Mass., 2000.

————: *Conflict and Litigation Between Software Clients and Developers*, Software Productivity Research, Burlington, Mass., 2003.

Kan, Stephen H.: *Metrics and Models in Software Quality Engineering, Second Edition*, Addison-Wesley Longman, Boston, Mass., 2003.

Kemerer, Chris F.: *Software Project Management Readings and Cases*, McGraw-Hill, New York, 1997.

Koirala, Shivprasad: "How to Prepare Quotations Using Use Case Points," (http://www .codeproject.com/gen/design//usecasepoints.asp).

McConnell, Stevel: *Software Estimating: Demystifying the Black Art*, Microsoft Press, Redmond, Washington, 2006.

Pressman, Roger: *Software Engineering—A Practitioner's Approach, Sixth Edition*, McGraw-Hill, New York, 2005.

Project Management Institute (PMI) (http://www.pmi.org).

Putnam, Lawrence H., and Ware Myers: *Industrial Strength Software—Effective Management Using Measurement*, IEEE Computer Society Press, Washington, D.C., 1997.

Quality Function Deployment (http://en.wikipedia.org/wiki/Quality_function_ deployment).

Rapid Application Development (http://en.wikipedia.org/wiki/Rapid_application_development).

Reifer, Don; Software Management; IEEE Press, Washington DC, 1997.

Rubin, Howard: *Software Benchmark Studies for* 1997, Howard Rubin Associates, Pound Ridge, New York, 1997.

Stapleton, J.: *DSDM—Dynamic System Development in Practice*, Addison-Wesley, Boston, Mass., 1997.

Stellman, Andrew, and Jennifer Green: *Applied Software Project Management*, O'Reilly Books, Cambridge, Mass., 2005.

Stephens M., and D. Rosenberg: *Extreme Programming Refactored: The Case Against XP*, APress L.P., Berkeley, Calif., 2003.Thayer, Richard H. (ed.): *Software Engineering and Project Management*, IEEE Press, Los Alamitos, Calif., 1988.

Umbaugh, Robert E. (ed.): *Handbook of IS Management, Fourth Edition*, Auerbach Publications, Boston, Mass., 1995.

Zells, Lois: *Managing Software Projects*, QED Information Sciences, Wellesley, Mass., 1990.

Zvegintzov, Nicholas: *Software Management Technology Reference Guide*, Dorset House Press, New York, 1994.

6

Maintenance and Enhancement Cost Estimating

Estimating software maintenance and estimating software enhancements are technically quite different, but these two post-release activities are often treated as though they were one and the same. Maintenance and enhancement are alike in that both deal with modifications to existing software. Maintenance and enhancement are different in the sources of funds and the rigor of the development methods.

For a variety of reasons, software maintenance and enhancement estimates are far more complex than estimates of new projects. One reason for this complexity is the fact that the phrase maintenance and enhancement can actually encompass at least 23 discrete activities, each of which has unique attributes in terms of costs, staffing, schedules, and influential factors.

Maintenance and Enhancement Estimating

In today's world more than 50 percent of the global software population is engaged in modifying existing applications rather than writing new applications. This implies that maintenance and enhancement estimating is actually the most critical aspect of software cost estimating.

Surprisingly, for such an important topic as maintenance, less than half of the current software cost-estimating tools have special *maintenance* and *enhancement* estimating modes. The reason for this lack will be discussed later in this chapter, but the essence of the situation is that maintenance and enhancement estimation is much more difficult than estimating brand-new software projects.

In this book the word *maintenance* is defined as repairing defects in software applications in order to correct errors. The word *enhancement* is defined as adding new features to software applications. These new features either meet new user requirements, or are caused by new government rules and mandates such as changes in tax laws.

Some additional terms also require discussion. Several books on maintenance and/or enhancement use the word "evolution" as a definition for what happens to software after it is first deployed. This term is used because it implies continuous change over time. However, since software systems are subject to the law of entropy, many of them decay over time instead of changing for the better. Unfortunately, aging software applications resemble aging humans in some respects. Both gain weight with advancing age, and both become increasingly subject to illness and other signs of age.

In fact, one of the supplemental terms for modifying aging software captures the essence of the situation: "geriatric care." The phrase *"geriatric care"* implies attempting to alleviate the chronic conditions of aging software.

Another new term became popular in the literature associated with extreme programming (XP) and some of the other Agile approaches: *"refactoring."* The term derives from mathematics, and its meaning in a software context is to improve the structure and readability of code without changing or damaging its operations or the features that users care about.

The phrase *"total cost of ownership"* is also an important topic in a maintenance context. The total cost of ownership includes development or acquisition costs, defect repairs, enhancements, customer support, and computing and platform expenses over the entire life of a software application from the first day of initial planning until the application is finally retired from use.

Although software enhancements and software maintenance in the sense of defect repairs are usually funded in different ways and have quite different sets of activity patterns associated with them, many companies lump these disparate software activities together for budgeting and cost estimates. The author does not recommend this practice, but it is very common.

Consider some of the basic differences between enhancements, or adding new features to applications, and maintenance, or defect repairs, as shown in Table 23.1.

Development estimating is a difficult problem, but estimating maintenance and enhancements is even more complex because of the very tricky relationship between the base application that is being modified and the changes being made to accommodate new features or repair defects.

Indeed, maintenance and enhancement estimating is so complex that a number of first-generation estimating tools could not deal with the intricacies and were limited to new project estimates. However, the newer generation of software estimating tools, such as COCOMO II, SLIM, PRICE-S, and KnowledgePlan, can handle many forms of modification to existing applications as standard features.

TABLE 23.1   Key Differences Between Maintenance and Enhancements

Activity	Enhancements (new features)	Maintenance (defect repairs)
Funding source	Clients	Absorbed
Requirements	Formal	None
Specifications	Formal	None
Inspections	Formal	None
User documentation	Formal	None
New function testing	Formal	None
Regression testing	Formal	Minimal

The literature on maintenance estimating is very sparse compared to development estimating. Indeed, any kind of literature on software maintenance is sparse compared to the equivalent literature on software development. Books on software development outnumber books on maintenance by more than 100 to 1, based on the catalogs of such software book publishers as Addison-Wesley, McGraw-Hill, Prentice-Hall, Dorset House, John Wiley & Sons, and the like.

A small number of pioneering software engineers recognized that maintenance would eventually become the dominant work of the software community because applications are being created much faster than they are being withdrawn. Girish Parikh and Nicholas Zvegintzov are perhaps the best known of the early maintenance pioneers who started their research in the 1970s and 1980s.

There are now a number of books on maintenance itself, but the literature on maintenance cost estimating is still fairly sparse. Some books with valuable insights into maintenance topics include the *Handbook of Software Maintenanc* (John Wiley & Sons, 1986), *Software Evolution—The Software Maintenance Challenge* (John Wiley & Sons, 1988), *Practical Software Maintenance* (IEEE Computer Press, 1997), *Software Maintenance: The Problem and its Solutions* (Prentice-Hall, 1983), *Managing Systems in Transition* (International Thomson Computer Press, 1996), and *Software Maintenance* (International Thomson Computer Press, 1997). A book on object-oriented maintenance is *Object-Oriented Software: Design and Maintenance* by Luiz Fernando and Miriam Capretz (Word Scientific Publishing, 1996).

There are also a number of books on maintenance in more specialized forms, such as reengineering, and on available tools, such as the annual catalogs published by ACR and the discussion by the maintenance pioneer Nicholas Zvegintzov. There are also specialized books in the area of Agile and XP and object-oriented programming.

One of the newer books on software maintenance is *Software Maintenance—Concepts and Practice* by Penny Grubb and Armstrong A. Takang (World Scientific Publishing, 2003).

Many of the author's other books deal with issues that are troublesome during maintenance, such as bad-fix injection and the low status of maintenance personnel. See also the author's books *Software Quality—Analysis and Guidelines for Success* (International Thomson Computer Press, 1997), *Patterns of Software Systems Failure and Success* (International Thomson Computer Press, 1995), *Applied Software Measurement* (McGraw-Hill 1996), *Assessment and Control of Software Risks* (Prentice-Hall, 1994), and *Software Assessments, Benchmarks, and Best Practices* (Addison-Wesley, 2000).

In terms of maintenance estimation, some of the standard volumes discuss this topic, such as *Software Engineering Economics*

(Prentice-Hall,1981) and *Industrial Strength Software* (Prentice-Hall, 1997). The well-known software researcher Dr. Howard Rubin also publishes useful information on software maintenance topics, often in the context of his large-scale annual reports. The British software metrics researcher Charles Symons also discusses maintenance estimation using Mark II function points.

Because the general topic of maintenance is so complicated and includes so many different kinds of work, some companies merely lump all forms of maintenance together and use gross metrics, such as the overall percentage of annual software budgets devoted to all forms of maintenance summed together.

This method is crude, but can convey useful information. Organizations that are proactive in using geriatric tools and services can spend less than 30 percent of their annual software budgets on various forms of maintenance, while organizations that have not used any of the geriatric tools and services can top 60 percent of their annual budgets on various forms of maintenance.

A new and expanding trend since the first edition of this book has been using outsource vendors for software maintenance in the sense of defect repairs, customer support, and some small enhancements. Because maintenance tends to interfere with development work, it is more cost-effective to have full-time maintenance specialists than it is to assign maintenance tasks to developers. Maintenance outsourcing one of the areas where the performance of the outsource vendors is usually good enough to provide significant economic justification for the outsource contract.

This section deals with 23 topics that are often coupled together under the generic term *maintenance* in day-to-day discussions, but which are actually quite different in many important respects (see Table 23.2).

Some of the 23 forms of updates such as warranty repairs and retirement of applications have legal and business aspects over and above the technical work involving software and, hence, are not completely encompassed by any commercial software-estimating tool or methodology.

The fact that there are 23 separate kinds of work subsumed under the general term "maintenance" explains why maintenance cost estimates are more complicated than development cost estimates. Later in this chapter we will consider the differences among these disparate maintenance tasks.

When applications are first put into production and begin to be used by customers, they still have hundreds of latent defects. Therefore, a significant amount of maintenance will be required to repair these defects. Also, once applications are put into production they continue to grow and add new features at a rate of about 7 percent per calendar year. Therefore, another significant amount of work will be required to add

TABLE 23.2   Major Kinds of Work Performed Under the Generic Term *Maintenance*

1. Major enhancements (new features of >20 function points)
2. Minor enhancements (new features of <5 function points)
3. Maintenance (repairing defects for good will)
4. Warranty repairs (repairing defects under formal contract)
5. Customer support (responding to client phone calls or problem reports)
6. Error-prone module removal (eliminating very troublesome code segments)
7. Mandatory changes (required or statutory changes)
8. Complexity analysis (quantifying control flow using complexity metrics)
9. Code restructuring (reducing cyclomatic and essential complexity)
10. Optimization (increasing performance or throughput)
11. Migration (moving software from one platform to another)
12. Conversion (Changing the interface or file structure)
13. Reverse engineering (extracting latent design information from code)
14. Reengineering (transforming legacy applications to client/server form)
15. Dead code removal (removing segments no longer utilized)
16. Dormant application elimination (archiving unused software)
17. Nationalization (modifying software for international use)
18. Mass updates such as date changes (date format expansion or masking)
19. Mass updates such as Eurocurrency conversion (adding the new unified currency to financial applications)
20. Retirement (withdrawing an application from active service)
21. Field service (sending maintenance members to client locations)
22. Refactoring software to improve its readability and understanding
23. Installing new releases from software vendors

these enhancements. The life expectancy of software applications vary, but for those in the 10,000–function point size range they typically are utilized for more than ten calendar years. It usually happens that by about the fifth calendar year the sum of the costs of defect repairs and enhancements becomes greater than the costs of initial development.

When an application is nominally retired or withdrawn from service there may be a legal obligation to continue to support users who do not wish to stop using the software package. Several lawsuits have been filed by clients who felt that a vendor's retirement of a software package violated warranty or service agreements. Hence, there may be a need for special kinds of service and support for individual clients even after a package has been withdrawn from general use.

Although the 23 maintenance topics cited in this section are different in many respects, they all have one common feature that makes a group discussion possible: They all involve modifying an existing application rather than starting from scratch with a new application.

The 23 forms of modifying existing applications have different reasons for being carried out, and it often happens that several of them take place concurrently. For example, enhancements and defect repairs are very common in the same release of an evolving application.

There are also common sequences or patterns to these modification activities. For example, reverse engineering often precedes reengineering and the two occur together so often as to almost comprise a linked set.

Nominal Default Values for Maintenance and Enhancement Activities

The nominal default values for estimating these 23 kinds of maintenance are shown in Table 23.3 However, each of the 23 has a very wide range of variability and reacts to a number of different technical factors, and also to the experience levels of the maintenance personnel.

Let us consider some generic default estimating values for these various maintenance tasks using three common metrics: *assignment scopes* (A scopes), *production rates* (P rates) in terms of *function points* (FP) *per staff month* and the similar but reciprocal metric, *work hours per function point*. We will also include *lines of code* (LOC) *per staff month* with the caveat that the results are merely based on an expansion of

TABLE 23.3   Default Values for Maintenance Assignment Scopes and Production Rates

Activities	A scopes, FP	P rates, FP per month	P rates, work hours per FP	P rates, LOC per staff month
Installing new releases	7,500	3500	0.03	350,000
Customer support	5,000	3,000	0.04	300,000
Code restructuring	5,000	1,000	0.13	100,000
Complexity analysis	5,000	500	0.26	50,000
Reverse engineering	2,500	125	1.06	12,500
Retirement	5,000	100	1.32	10,000
Field service	10,000	100	1.32	10,000
Dead code removal	750	35	3.77	3,500
Enhancements (minor)	75	25	5.28	2,500
Reengineering	500	25	5.28	2,500
Maintenance (defect repairs)	750	25	5.28	2,500
Refactoring	750	25	5.28	2,500
Warranty repairs	750	20	6.60	2,000
Migration to new platform	300	18	7.33	1,800
Enhancements (major)	125	15	8.80	1,500
Nationalization	250	15	8.80	1,500
Conversion to new interface	300	15	8.80	1,500
Mandatory changes	750	15	8.80	1,500
Performance optimization	750	15	8.80	1,500
Mass updates: date repairs	2,000	15	8.80	1,500
Mass updates:	1,500	15	8.80	1,500
Error-prone module removal	300	12	11.00	1,200

100 statements per function point, which is only a generic value and should not be used for serious estimating purposes.

Each of these forms of modification or support activity have wide variations, but these nominal default values at least show the ranges of possible outcomes for all of the major activities associated with support of existing applications.

None of these values are sufficiently rigorous by themselves for formal cost estimates, but are sufficient to illustrate some of the typical trends in various kinds of maintenance work. Obviously, adjustments for team experience, complexity of the application, programming languages, and many other local factors are needed as well.

To illustrate the ranges of possibilities, consider the permutations of four different variables, with 16 combinations in all.

Table 23.4 shows some of the factors and ranges that are associated with assignment scopes, or the amount of software that one programmer can keep running in the course of a typical year.

In Table 23.4 the term "experienced staff" means that the maintenance team has worked on the applications being modified for at least six months and is quite familiar with the available tools and methods.

TABLE 23.4   Variations in Maintenance Assignment Scopes Based on Four
Key Factors
(Data expressed in terms of function points per maintenance team member)

	Worst case	Average case	Best case
Inexperienced staff Poor structure Low-level language No maintenance tools	100	200	350
Inexperienced staff Poor structure **High-level language** No maintenance tools	150	300	500
Inexperienced staff Poor structure Low-level language **Full maintenance tools**	225	400	600
Inexperienced staff **Good structure** Low-level language No maintenance tools	300	500	750
Experienced staff Poor structure Low-level language No maintenance tools	350	575	900
Inexperienced staff **Good structure**	450	650	1,100

TABLE 23.4   **Variations in Maintenance Assignment Scopes Based on Four Key Factors** *(Continued)*
(Data expressed in terms of function points per maintenance team member)

	Worst case	Average case	Best case
High-level language No maintenance tools Inexperienced staff **Good structure**	575	800	1,400
Low-level language **Full maintenance tools** **Experienced staff** **Good structure**	700	1,100	1,600
Low-level language No maintenance tools Inexperienced staff Poor structure	900	1,400	2,100
High-level language **Full maintenance tools** **Experienced staff** Poor structure	1,050	1,700	2,400
Low-level language **Full maintenance tools** **Experienced staff** Poor structure	1,150	1,850	2,800
High-level language No maintenance tools **Experienced staff** **Good structure**	1,600	2,100	3,200
High-level language No maintenance tool Inexperienced staff **Good structure**	1,800	2,400	3,750
High-level language **Full maintenance tools** **Experienced staff** Poor structure	2,100	2,800	4,500
High-level language **Full maintenance tools** **Experienced staff** **Good structure**	2,300	3,000	5,000
Low-level language **Full maintenance tools** **Experienced staff** **Good structure**	2,600	3,500	5,500
High-level language **Full maintenance tools** **Average**	1,022	1,455	2,278

The term "good structure" means that the application adheres to the basic tenets of structured programming, has clear and adequate comments, and has cyclomatic complexity levels that are below a value of 10.

The term "full maintenance tools" implies the availability of most of these common forms of maintenance tools: 1) defect tracking and routing tools; 2) change-control tools; 3) complexity analysis tools; 4) code restructuring tools; 5) reverse engineering tools; 6) reengineering tools; 7) maintenance "workbench" tools; 8) test coverage tools; and 9) static analysis tools.

The term "high-level language" implies a fairly modern programming language that requires less than 50 statements to encode one function point. Examples of such languages include most object-oriented languages such as Smalltalk, Java, and Objective-C.

By contrast "low-level languages" implies language requiring more than 100 statements to encode one function point. Obviously, assembly language would be in this class since it usually takes more than 200 to 300 assembly statements per function point. Other languages that top 100 statements per function point include many mainstream languages such as C, Fortran, and COBOL.

In between the high-level and low-level ranges are a variety of mid-level languages that require roughly 70 statements per function point, such as Ada 95, PL/I, and Pascal.

The variations in maintenance assignment scopes are significant in understanding why so many people are currently engaged in maintenance of aging legacy applications. If a company owns a portfolio of 100,000 function points maintained by generalists, many more people will be required than if maintenance specialists are used. If the portfolio consists of poorly structured code written in low-level languages, then the assignment scope might be less than 500 function points or a staff of 200 maintenance personnel.

If the company has used complexity analysis tools, code restructuring tools, and has a staff of highly trained maintenance specialists, then the maintenance assignment scope might top 3000 function points. This implies that only 33 maintenance experts are needed, as opposed to 200 generalists. Table 23.4 illustrates how maintenance assignment scopes vary in response to four different factors, when each factor switches from "worst case" to "best case." Table 23.4 assumes Version 4.1 of the International Function Point Users Group (IFPUG) counting practices manual.

None of the values in Table 23.4 are sufficiently rigorous by themselves for formal cost estimates, but are sufficient to illustrate some of the typical trends in various kinds of maintenance work. Obviously, adjustments for team experience, complexity of the application, programming languages, and many other local factors are needed as well.

However, the table does illustrate the inner workings of automated software estimating tools when they deal with maintenance estimates. The impact of various factors is analyzed and then aggregated together to calculate maintenance expenses.

Metrics and Measurement Problems with Small Maintenance Projects

There are several difficulties in exploring software maintenance costs with accuracy. One of these difficulties is the fact that maintenance tasks are often assigned to development personnel who interleave both development and maintenance as the need arises. This practice makes it difficult to distinguish maintenance costs from development costs because the programmers are often rather careless in recording how time is spent.

Another very significant problem is the fact that a great deal of software maintenance consists of making very small changes to software applications. Quite a few bug repairs may involve fixing only a single line of code. Adding minor new features such as perhaps a new line-item on a screen may require less than 50 source code statements.

These small changes are below the effective lower limit for counting function point metrics. The function point metric includes weighting factors for complexity, and even if the complexity adjustments are set to the lowest possible point on the scale, it is still difficult to count function points below a level of perhaps 15 function points.

Quite a few maintenance tasks involve changes that are either a fraction of a function point, or may at most be less than 10 function points or about 1000 COBOL source code statements. Although normal counting of function points is not feasible for small updates, it is possible to use the "backfiring" method or converting counts of logical source code statements into equivalent function points. For example, suppose an update requires adding 100 COBOL statements to an existing application. Since it usually takes about 105 COBOL statements in the procedure and data divisions to encode 1 function point, it can be stated that this small maintenance project is "about 1 function point in size."

If the project takes one work day consisting of six hours, then at least the results can be expressed using common metrics. In this case, the results would be roughly "6 staff hours per function point." If the reciprocal metric "function points per staff month" is used, and there are 20 working days in the month, then the results would be "20 function points per staff month."

Another area of measurement difficulty is that of refactoring applications. Refactoring is common with XP. Since refactoring does not add any features to the software, but only improves its readability, refactoring does not add any function points to the application. In order to measure productivity with function points, the size of the code segment being refactored would be the basis of the measurement. For example, if a programmer refactors 10 function points or 1000 source code statements in five working days of 6 hours each or 30 hours in all, the productivity rate could be expressed either as 33 lines of code per hour, or 3 work hours per function point.

Another measurement problem involves the installation of new releases from software vendors, or the installation of patches and bug repairs. Since most vendors do not release information on either the size of the entire application or the size of a new release or the size of a bug repair, there is no really good way of expressing the effort and costs in normalized forms. In fact, source code counts are not provided by vendors either.

Best and Worst Practices in Software Maintenance

Because maintenance of aging legacy software is very labor-intensive it is quite important to explore the best and most cost-effective methods available for dealing with the millions of applications that currently exist. The sets of best and worst practices are not symmetrical. For example, the practice that has the most positive impact on maintenance productivity is the use of trained maintenance experts. However, the factor that has the greatest negative impact is the presence of "error-prone modules" in the application that is being maintained.

Table 23.5 illustrates a number of factors that have been found to exert a beneficial positive impact on the work of updating aging applications and shows the percentage of improvement compared to average results.

At the top of the list of maintenance "best practices" is the utilization of full-time, trained maintenance specialists rather than turning over maintenance tasks to untrained generalists such as development programmers. The positive impact from utilizing maintenance specialists is one of the reasons why maintenance outsourcing has been growing so rapidly. The maintenance productivity rates of some of the better maintenance outsource companies are roughly twice that of their clients prior to the completion of the outsource agreement. Thus, even if the outsource vendor costs are somewhat higher, there can still be useful economic gains.

Let us now consider some of the factors that exert a negative impact on the work of updating or modifying existing software applications. Note that the top-ranked factor that reduces maintenance productivity, the presence of error-prone modules, is very asymmetrical. The absence of error-prone modules does not speed up maintenance work, but their presence definitely slows down maintenance work.

TABLE 23.5   Impact of Key Adjustment Factors on Maintenance
(Sorted in order of maximum positive impact)

Maintenance factors	Plus range
Maintenance specialists	35%
High staff experience	34%
Table-driven variables and data	33%
Low complexity of base code	32%
Special search engines	30%
Restructuring tools/refactoring	29%
Reengineering tools	27%
High level programming languages	25%
Reverse engineering tools	23%
Complexity analysis tools	20%
Defect tracking tools	20%
"Mass update" specialists	20%
Automated change control tools	18%
Unpaid overtime	18%
Quality measurements	16%
Formal base code inspections	15%
Regression test libraries	15%
Excellent response time	12%
Annual training of > 10 days	12%
High management experience	12%
Help desk automation	12%
No error prone modules	10%
Online defect reporting	10%
Productivity measurements	8%
Excellent ease of use	7%
User satisfaction measurements	5%
High team morale	5%
Sum	503%

Error-prone modules were discovered by IBM in the 1960s when IBM's quality measurements began to track errors or bugs down to the levels of specific modules. For example, it was discovered that IBM's IMS database product contained 425 modules, but more than 300 of these were zero-defect modules that never received any bug reports. About 60 percent of all reported errors were found in only 31 modules, and these were very buggy indeed.

When this form of analysis was applied to other products and used by other companies, it was found to be a very common phenomenon. In general, more than 80 percent of the bugs in software applications are found in less than 20 percent of the modules. Once these modules are identified, then they can be inspected, analyzed, and restructured to reduce their error content down to safe levels.

Table 23.6 summarizes the major factors that degrade software maintenance performance. Not only are error-prone modules troublesome,

TABLE 23.6   Impact of Key Adjustment Factors on Maintenance
(Sorted in order of maximum negative impact)

Maintenance factors	Minus range
Error-prone modules	−50%
Embedded variables and data	−45%
Staff inexperience	−40%
High complexity of base code	−30%
No special search engines	−28%
Manual change control methods	−27%
Low-level programming languages	−25%
No defect-tracking tools	−24%
No "mass update" specialists	−22%
Poor ease of use	−18%
No quality measurements	−18%
No maintenance specialists	−18%
Poor response time	−16%
Management inexperience	−15%
No base code inspections	−15%
No regression test libraries	−15%
No Help desk automation	−15%
No online defect reporting	−12%
No annual training	−10%
No restructuring or refactoring	−10%
No reengineering tools	−10%
No reverse engineering tools	−10%
No complexity analysis tools	−10%
No productivity measurements	−7%
Poor team morale	−6%
No user satisfaction measurements	−4%
No unpaid overtime	0%
Sum	−500%

but many other factors can degrade performance too. For example, very complex "spaghetti code" is quite difficult to maintain safely. It is also troublesome to have maintenance tasks assigned to generalists rather than to trained maintenance specialists.

A very common situation that often degrades performance is lack of suitable maintenance tools, such as defect-tracking software, change management software, test library software, complexity analyzers, and so forth. In general it is very easy to botch up maintenance and make it such a labor-intensive activity that few resources are left over for development work. At the end of the 20th century the simultaneous arrival of the year 2000 and Euro problems basically saturated the available maintenance teams, and also drew developers into the work of making mass updates. Similar problems in the future will also be troublesome.

Given the enormous amount of effort that is now being applied to software maintenance, and that will be applied in the future, it is obvious that every corporation should attempt to adopt maintenance "best practices" and avoid maintenance "worst practices" as rapidly as possible.

Software Entropy and Total Cost of Ownership

The word "*entropy*" means the tendency of systems to destabilize and become more chaotic over time. Entropy is a term from physics and is not a software-related word. However, entropy is true of all complex systems, including software applications. All known compound objects decay and become more complex with the passage of time unless effort is exerted to keep them repaired and updated. Software is no exception. The accumulation of small updates over time tends to gradually degrade the initial structure of applications and makes changes grow more difficult over time.

For software applications entropy has long been a fact of life. If applications are developed with marginal initial quality control, they will probably be poorly structured and contain error-prone modules. This means that every year, the accumulation of defect repairs and maintenance updates will degrade the original structure and make each change slightly more difficult. Over time, the application will destabilize and "bad fixes" will increase in number and severity. Unless the application is restructured or fully refurbished, eventually it will become so complex that maintenance can only be performed by a few experts who are more or less locked into the application.

By contrast, leading applications that are well structured initially can delay the onset of entropy. Indeed, well-structured applications can achieve declining maintenance costs over time. This is because updates do not degrade the original structure, as happens in the case of "spaghetti bowl" applications where the structure is almost unintelligible when maintenance begins.

The total cost of ownership of a software application is the sum of four major expense elements: 1) the initial cost of building an application; 2) the cost of enhancing the application with new features over its lifetime; 3) the cost of repairing defects and bugs over the application's lifetime; and 4) the cost of customer support for fielding and responding to queries and customer-reported defects.

Table 23.7 illustrates the total cost of ownership of three similar software applications under three alternate scenarios. Assume the applications are nominally 1000 function points in size. (To simplify the table, only a five-year ownership period is illustrated.)

The "lagging" scenario in the left column of Table 23.7 assumes inadequate quality control, poor code structure, up to a dozen severe error-prone modules, and significant "bad-fix" injection rates of around

TABLE 23.7   Five-Year Cost of Software Application Ownership
(Costs are in dollars per function point)

	Lagging projects	Average projects	Leading projects
DEVELOPMENT	$1,200.00	$1,000.00	$800.00
Year 1	$192.00	$150.00	$120.00
Year 2	$204.00	$160.00	$112.00
Year 3	$216.00	$170.00	$104.00
Year 4	$240.00	$180.00	$96.00
Year 5	$264.00	$200.00	$80.00
MAINTENANCE	$1,116.00	$860.00	$512.00
TOTAL COST	$2,316.00	$1,860.00	$1,312.00
Difference	$456.00	$0.00	-$548.00

20 percent. Under the lagging scenario maintenance costs will become more expensive every year due to entropy and the fact that the application never stabilizes.

The "average" scenario assumes marginal quality control, reasonable initial code structure, one or two error-prone modules, and an average bad-fix injection rate of around 7 percent. Here too, entropy will occur. But the rate at which the application's structure degrades is fairly slow. Thus, maintenance costs increase over a five-year period, but not at a very significant annual rate.

The "leading" scenario assumes excellent quality control, very good code structure at the initial release, zero error-prone modules, and a very low bad-fix injection rate of 1 percent or less. Under the leading scenario, maintenance costs can actually decline over the five-year ownership period. Incidentally, such well-structured applications of this type are most likely to be found for systems software and defense applications produced by companies at or higher than the level 3 on the Software Engineering Institute (SEI) capability maturity model (CMM) scale.

Under the lagging scenario, the five-year maintenance costs for the application (which include defect repairs, support, and enhancements) are almost equal to the original development costs. Indeed, the economic value of lagging applications is questionable after about three to five years. The degradation of initial structure and the increasing difficulty of making updates without "bad fixes" tends toward negative returns on investment (ROI) within a few years.

For applications in COBOL there are code restructuring tools and maintenance workbenches available that can extend the useful economic lives of aging legacy applications. But for many languages such as assembly language, Algol, Bliss, CHILL, CORAL, and PL/I, there are few maintenance tools and no commercial restructuring tools. Thus for poorly structured applications in many languages, the ROI may be marginal or negative within less than a ten-year period. Of course, if the applications are vital or mission critical (such as air traffic control or the IRS income tax applications), there may be no choice but to keep the applications operational regardless of cost or difficulty.

Under the average scenario, the five-year maintenance costs for the application are below the original development costs. Most average applications have a mildly positive ROI for up to ten years after initial deployment.

Under the leading scenario with well-structured initial applications, the five-year maintenance costs are only about 63 percent of the original development costs. Yet the same volume of enhancements is assumed in all three cases. For leading applications, the ROI can stay positive for 10 to 20 years after initial deployment. This is due to the low entropy and the reduced bad-fix injection rate of the leading scenario. In other words, if you build applications properly at the start, you can get many years of useful service. If you build them poorly at the start, you can expect high initial maintenance costs that will grow higher as time passes. You can also expect a rapid decline in ROI.

The same kinds of phenomena can be observed outside of software. If you buy an automobile that has a high frequency of repair as shown in *Consumer Reports* and you skimp on lubrication and routine maintenance, you will fairly soon face some major repair problems—usually well before 50,000 miles.

By contrast, if you buy an automobile with a low frequency of repair as shown in *Consumer Reports* and you are scrupulous in maintenance, you should be able to drive the car more than 100,000 miles without major repair problems.

Let us consider the nature of some of these 23 kinds of modifications to existing software.

Installing New Releases and Patches from Software Vendors

Every large organization uses software applications acquired from vendors. Examples of these include enterprise resource planning (ERP) packages, operating systems, human resource systems, payroll and accounting systems, spreadsheets, word processors, and dozens of others.

However, most software vendors do not provide information on the size of their applications in terms of lines of code, function points, use case points, or any other metric. Customers have costs associated with all vendor packages. Obviously, they pay for the package either once or through monthly lease arrangements. Customers also pay for maintenance agreements, which imply periodic updates in the form of new releases and bug repairs or patches.

In the absence of size information, about the only metrics and measurements that can be taken are the financial costs of the software itself, and the effort and costs required to install new releases or bug repairs when the vendors make them available.

Some of these installations have major costs and effort associated with them. For example, a new release of a mainframe operating system or a major ERP package can take more than a calendar month and more than ten staff months for installation, tuning, and regression testing to ensure that all applications still work correctly. IBM once did a survey of major customers and found that deploying a new release of the MVS operating system typically cost more than $500,000 per customer. Due to the effort and costs, customers did not want more than one major release per year.

ERP packages are even more costly. In fact, keeping ERP packages up to date with defect repairs, minor changes, and new releases can occupy a full-time team of up to ten people.

When viewed from a distance, sometimes as much as 25 percent of the annual maintenance costs of large companies are devoted to keeping vendor software running smoothly. Not only do new releases have to be installed and tested, but there are usually latent defects in vendor software that have to be reported. If the defects are high-severity, the customers may have to assign their own personnel to the repairs rather than waiting for the vendor.

If the client has permission to modify the code in the vendor package, then there will be significant expenses devoted to creating enhancements. These enhancements can be estimated with commercial estimating tools, although there may be gaps in the data for topics such as the size of the base application being updated.

Unfortunately, as of 2007 some of the costs of keeping vendor packages running are outside the scope of most commercial software cost-estimating tools. There are not very many informal algorithms available either. Without knowing the size of the vendor application packages, there is no easy way to estimate what it will cost to install new versions, perform regression testing, and make the transition of applications from the old release of the software to the new release.

Major Enhancements

Major enhancements are concerned with adding or changing features in existing software in response to explicit user requests. Because the new features meet new user requirements, the funding for enhancements is usually derived from user organizations, or at any rate there will be new charges for the augmented version.

An exception to the rule that major enhancements originate with users involves changes in government rules and regulations. For example, a major change in tax law can cause major changes to financial applications. The cost of these unfunded mandates must be absorbed by the application owners.

There is no fixed size for differentiating *major* and *minor* enhancements. The author suggests that the term *minor enhancement* be restricted to application updates that can be done in a calendar week or less, which would imply a size of no more than about 5 function points or 500 source code statements. This size is sufficient for adding a new report or a new screen element.

For the term *major enhancement*, a size of 20 function points or larger (roughly 2000 source code statements) approximates the amount of code that can be added to an application in a month. At this size and larger significant updates, such as those dealing with changes in tax law or adding a new feature to a system, are often found.

Major enhancements to very large systems, such as IBM's MVS operating system or Microsoft Windows XP, can top 1000 function points or 100,000 source code statements. Of course, both of these large systems are now in the vicinity of 100,000 function points or 10 million source code statements.

Between updates that are definitely minor and those that are definitely major is an ambiguous zone that can be defined either way based on specific circumstances.

(The annual rate of enhancements to existing applications averages a net increase in the function point totals of the applications of about 7 percent per year, although there are, of course, wide variations.)

Major enhancements are usually formal in terms of development methods and use the same kinds of rigor as new projects—that is, formal specifications, design reviews, test plans, quality-assurance involvement, technical writers, formal cost estimates, milestone tracking, and so forth.

From an estimating standpoint, the main difference between estimating a new project and estimating a major enhancement is the fact that the current version of the application needs to be included in the estimate. Some activities, such as gathering requirements, are aimed primarily at the new features to be added. But for many key software activities, such as design, coding, integration, and testing, both the new features and the existing application must be dealt with as a linked system.

Minor Enhancements

Minor enhancements are those that add some small improvement from the user's point of view, such as improving an interface or adding a new report. Most minor enhancements among the author's clients are usually less than 5 function points in size, or less than about 500 source code statements.

Minor enhancements are difficult to estimate and measure using function point metrics, because they are below the size range of about 50 function points where function point accuracy starts to decay due to the lower limits of the weighting factors. However, the use of *backfiring*, or creating function points from source code statements, can work down to even a fraction of a function point.

Minor enhancements are often small enough that they are not explicitly budgeted or charged back to users, which makes accumulating empirical data difficult. Indeed, some very minor enhancements can be accomplished in less than a day, have no formal specifications, cost estimates, budgets, or even any written record that the enhancement occurred at all!

The development methodologies for minor enhancements are seldom rigorous. Minor enhancements may lack formal specifications, may not have written test plans, and may not even utilize formal inspections or reviews by quality-assurance personnel.

The combination of informal practices and the difficulty of calibrating function point metrics for very small projects makes estimating minor enhancements a troublesome zone. Indeed, this is one of the rare domains where manual estimates by experienced project managers can exceed automated estimates in terms of accuracy.

It is an interesting phenomenon that the productivity rates for minor enhancements are often lower than for major enhancements. The reason for this unexpected situation is one of the complicating factors associated with enhancement estimating: the impact of the base application.

Let us assume that you are planning to add 5 function points or 500 source code statements to an existing application of 10,000 function points or 1,000,000 source code statements in size. At this low end, it is obvious that the requirements for the new feature are likely to be easy to understand and the design and coding tasks will probably be fairly simple, too.

What is troublesome for small enhancements, and degrades productivity substantially, is the fact that the connection between the new feature and the existing application may be complicated and require small but significant modifications to a number of attachment points within the parent application.

These multiple attachment points, in turn, require extensive recompilation of the entire application and, of course, very extensive regression testing to ensure that the changes have not degraded or shut down existing capabilities.

Compared to a small stand-alone application of the same size (5 function points or 500 source code statements), the basic tasks of gathering requirements and coding the main features are roughly equivalent in effort and costs. However, the work of testing the application will probably cost at least five times more for the enhancement than for the standalone application. Indeed, for changes to large and poorly structured applications, sometimes the testing costs can be 100 times more expensive for enhancements than for an equivalent amount of new development work.

The complex interactions between the enhancement itself and the size, structure, and state of decay of the parent application are factors that make enhancement estimating very tricky. Adding to the complexity of enhancement estimation are the usual problems of dealing with large software projects. There will probably be latent bugs or defects that will arise unexpectedly, and the specifications for the existing application may be out of date.

Also, as the years go by, the accumulated changes begin to degrade the structure of the original application and make adding any new feature progressively more troublesome as time goes by. For example, adding a 5–function point addition to a poorly structured 15-year-old system can be twice as costly as making the same update to a well-structured 1-year-old system.

Maintenance (Defect Repairs)

One of the reasons why the author makes a sharp distinction between maintenance in the sense of defect repairs and enhancements in the sense of adding new features is due to a court order associated with an antitrust suit involving IBM. The judge ordered IBM to provide "maintenance information" to a direct competitor, but did not define what the word *maintenance* meant in the context of the order. As a result, IBM's attorneys suggested that the primary definition of the word *maintenance* was that of defect repair, and that the term *enhancement* should be used for adding new features.

Maintenance, or normal defect repairs, is aimed at keeping software in operational condition after a crash or bug report. The costs for maintenance are usually absorbed by the software group that built the application, or covered under an explicit warranty agreement.

Software defect repairs are endemic because U.S. averages for defect-removal efficiency prior to release of software are only about 85 percent. For the first year or two after the release of a software package, repairing defects reported by users is a significant expense for both internal and commercial software packages. There are also "bad fixes" or new defects injected as an accidental by-product of fixing previous defects. The bad-fix injection rate averages about 7 percent, but can top 20 percent for poorly structured and complex software systems.

Maintenance in the sense of defect repairs is seldom measured using normal function point calculations, because the majority of maintenance defects are less than 25 source code statements in size, or perhaps one-quarter of a function point. There are no counting rules for fractional function points, so the only way of enumerating the function point totals of small updates is by means of *backfiring*, or direct conversion from source code statements.

The most common way of estimating and measuring the productivity of maintenance in the sense of defect repairs is to evaluate the number of defect repairs made per month. U.S. norms are about eight to ten bug or defect repairs per month. Of course, in some months fewer than eight bugs will be reported, so this metric is not very reliable.

There is also a substantial range in terms of monthly defect repair rates. Some maintenance organizations staffed by experienced maintenance personnel and fully supported by change-control tools, defect-tracking tools, and the like can achieve average rates of 16 to 20 bugs repaired per month.

On the other hand, novice maintenance personnel or those who are splitting their time between defect repairs and new development tasks can drop below six bugs repaired per month.

The *cost per defect* metric is also used for maintenance repairs, and here, too, there are severe problems with accuracy of the results. The main problem lies in situations where maintenance personnel are charging time to a project's maintenance budget but no defects have been reported.

In practice, the cost per defect metric tends to be cheaper for applications that are very buggy than for applications that are approaching zero-defect status. For example, one month there may be no defects reported, but the project has a maintenance programmer standing by whose time is being charged to the project's maintenance budget.

The overall financial impact of cost per defect is to penalize high-quality applications and make low-quality applications look better than they really are.

Estimating maintenance in the sense of defect repairs is a rather tricky problem. Usually, maintenance estimates are broken down into discrete categories based on the severity level of the reported defects, as shown in Table 23.8, using the four-point severity scale developed by the IBM corporation in the 1960s.

For high-severity defects in the Severity 1 category, maintenance is often performed on an emergency basis. Indeed, some maintenance personnel have beepers and home computers and are often roused in the middle of the night when Severity 1 bugs are reported. Once such a bug is reported, it is not uncommon for the repair activity to proceed around the clock until the problem is fixed or, at least, a temporary work-around is developed.

TABLE 23.8   Nominal Response Time or Turnaround for Defect Repairs by
Severity Level

Severity level	Meaning	Turnaround time from report to initial repair	Percent reported
Severity 1	Application does not run	24 hours	1
Severity 2	Major function disabled	48 hours	12
Severity 3	Minor function disabled	30 days	52
Severity 4	Cosmetic error	120 days	35

Defect repair estimating has some other complicating factors besides severity levels that must be considered: abeyant defects, invalid defects, bad fix injection, and duplicate defects all add to the complexity of software maintenance estimation.

Incidentally, there are some *maintenance factories* used by outsource vendors that are extremely efficient and highly productive. Some of these are staffed on a 24-hour basis and use very capable staff members and full suites of complexity analyzers and maintenance-support tools.

When estimating the performance of specialized groups such as this, it is obvious that *industry norms* should not be used, because a normal maintenance group works only part time, may also be assigned to development work, and seldom has a full maintenance tool suite available.

The difference between a fully equipped group of maintenance specialists and normal casual maintenance can be several hundred percent in productivity, and more than 50 percent in quality and bad-fix injection levels.

Some of the factors that affect maintenance estimates include the following.

Abeyant Defects   For about 10 percent of incoming defect reports by clients, the software maintenance team cannot make the same problem occur. In other words, the client's version of the software may be dead on the floor, but the same version operating under similar or identical conditions at the maintenance repair center works just fine.

These troublesome bugs or defects are usually based on some unique combination of events, or on a specific combination of applications being run simultaneously on the client's system. Obviously, if the maintenance team can't make a bug occur, they will have trouble fixing it. These troublesome defects were termed *abeyant* by IBM when they were first noted there in the 1960s.

The costs for finding and repairing abeyant defects may be as much as an order of magnitude more expensive than normal defects of any given severity level, and the time required may also be stretched out significantly. Sometimes it is necessary to send field service personnel to the client's location and find out what the problem is on the client's own system. At the very least, quite a bit of additional diagnostic work will be needed.

Invalid Defects For about 15 percent of incoming defect reports by clients, the error is not actually caused by the software application against which it has been reported. Sometimes the client simply makes a mistake, sometimes the error is really a hardware problem, and sometimes the error is caused by some other software application and misdiagnosed.

Whatever the reason for the invalid defect reports, they still must be dealt with by the maintenance group and the client must be given a prompt and courteous reply. For commercial software packages with hundreds or thousands of users, at least 15 percent of the time spent by customer-support personnel and 10 percent of the time spent by maintenance programmers is wrapped up with invalid defect reports.

The reason that so much energy is devoted to invalid defect reports is that until substantial diagnostic work is performed, it may not be immediately obvious that the defect report is invalid. Unless the problem is completely obvious or has occurred before, both customer-support personnel and maintenance programmers can spend quite a bit of time processing invalid defect reports before they are discovered to be errors in something other than the application against which they were initially reported.

Bad-Fix Injection Any time a software defect is repaired, there is a finite probability that the repair itself may contain a new defect. The general term for these derivative errors or bugs is *bad fix*, and they are surprisingly common. The observed range of bad fix injection runs from less than 1 percent of repaired defects to more than 20 percent. The approximate U.S. average, based on long-range data from such major software corporations as IBM, is that about 7 percent of all defect repairs may trigger a new defect.

The factors that affect the probability of bad fixes being injected into software applications include the structure of the application, the experience of the development team, and the schedule pressure under which the repairs are being made. Other factors include the use or lack of use of repair inspections and the thoroughness with which the application is tested.

Bad fixes are very likely to occur when poorly structured legacy applications are being fixed under severe schedule pressure by developers who are inexperienced with the application. Bad fixes are less likely to occur when the application is well structured, and when the repairs are made carefully without undue haste. However, bad fixes are endemic within the software industry and have been a chronic problem for more than 50 years at relatively constant rates.

From an estimating standpoint, bad fixes need to be included because the secondary bad-fix defects are at least as expensive as the primary defects, and the practical impact of bad fixes is to add roughly an unplanned 10 percent or so to both testing and maintenance costs.

Incidentally, both the year-2000 repair work and the Eurocurrency updates had bad fix rates in the 5 to 10 percent range. When companies assign two separate change teams to make both modifications on identical schedules, expect the overall bad-fix injection rate to approach or exceed 15 percent.

Duplicate Defects   For any software package with multiple users, it is very likely that more than one user will find and report the same problem. A few years ago an article appeared in several newspapers about a bug in the install procedure of the WordPerfect word-processing application. This bug was found and reported by more than 10,000 clients on the same day, which temporarily saturated the telephone lines leading into the WordPerfect maintenance facilities.

From an estimating standpoint, duplicate defect reports only need to be fixed once, of course. However, a substantial amount of customer-support time is devoted to dealing with these duplicates. For companies like Computer Associates, IBM, or Microsoft, about 10 percent of customer-support time will go to dealing with multiple complaints about the same defect. In fact, it is duplicate defect reports that cause most of the delays and hold time when trying to contact the customer-support groups of commercial software vendors.

Error-Prone Modules   The distribution of errors through the modules of large systems is usually not random. Errors or bugs tend to concentrate in a small number of places. An empirical rule of thumb based on observations from more than 100 large systems is that 5 percent of the modules will accumulate more than 50 percent of all customer-reported defects. Error-prone modules are often high in complexity and poor in structure. The bad-fix injection rate when attempting to update error-prone modules averages more than 20 percent, and in a few cases tops 50 percent. Error-prone modules are the most expensive single kind of problem in the history of software. Error-prone modules can be detected by analysis of incoming defect reports, if your tracking system is sophisticated enough to show defects against specific modules. If not, your maintenance programmers will probably know which modules are error prone. Formal inspections of legacy software will also diagnose error-prone modules. The only true cure for error-prone modules is surgical removal followed by redevelopment. This is an expensive operation, but it will pay for itself in less than 18 months.

Warranty Repairs

Warranty repairs are technically similar to normal maintenance defect repairs, but differ in a business or legal sense due to the fact that clients who report the defects are covered by an explicit warranty. For business and tax reasons, it may be desirable to record warranty repairs as a separate category. Warranty repairs are primarily of concern to software vendors and to clients with maintenance contracts.

Repairs made under warranty are often assigned severity codes, with values ranging from 1 (total failure of the application) to 4 or 5 (minor cosmetic errors). Software vendors repair high-severity defects much more rapidly than low-severity defects. Usually, repairs on Severity 1 or catastrophic defects are made in less than 24 hours, while repairs for low-severity defects may not occur until the next planned release of the software package.

Commercial software vendors usually have separate groups responsible for defect repairs, rather than turning over this work to the development teams. If the same team handles both new features and defect repairs, it is difficult to keep accurate records of work and very difficult to estimate new development, because maintenance tends to occur at random intervals and intrude on the work of new development.

On the whole, software warranties have been sparse since the software industry began. It would be beneficial to both clients and the software industry if more robust warranties were provided with commercial software, and also were included as part of custom development contracts.

Customer Support

Customer support refers to the personnel and activities in direct contact with users of software applications. Much of the work of customer support is interrupt-driven and is initiated by the customers themselves when they have problems or need to have questions answered.

For commercial software the bulk of customer-support work is driven by telephone contacts, although faxes, e-mail, and such online information services such as CompuServe, America Online, and similar utilities have many forums sponsored by software and computing companies.

For in-house customer support within specific companies, the work can also include face-to-face meetings between clients and customer-support personnel.

Customer-support estimates are based in part on the anticipated number of bugs in applications, but a more significant estimating variable is the number of users or clients. As a rough rule of thumb, assuming phone contact as the primary channel, one customer support specialist can handle the monthly calls from roughly 150 clients, assuming software of average quality with no major Severity-1 defects at the time of release.

For e-mail and electronic contacts with clients the ratios are much larger, and one customer support person can sometimes handle queries from as many as 1000 clients or users. An added benefit of the online customer support forums is that other customers may step in with suggestions or helpful advice. For example, Microsoft monitors the responses of clients on its forums and will sometimes invite customers who provide useful insights to speak at Microsoft conferences or events.

For in-house customer support with some face-to-face meetings, the typical ratio would be one customer support person for about every 75 to 100 users of a software application.

A variety of tools and automation are available for customer-support use. Contact-logging software and defect-tracking software are two common examples. The customer-support function is a key activity in the commercial software world, and provides very useful information not only for quality-control purposes, but also surprisingly helpful suggestions about desirable new features and functions.

The role of customer support is one of interfacing between the clients and the defect-repair teams. The customer-support personnel usually do not fix the problems themselves. For new problems, the customer-support role is to record the symptoms and route the problem to the correct repair group.

However, the same problems tend to occur over and over. Therefore, after a problem has been fixed, customer-support personnel are often able to guide clients through work-arounds or temporary repairs.

Customer-support groups can also gather very useful information about customer usage patterns and requests for new or missing features. Customer-support organizations should be viewed as an integral part of the software domain, and their advice and counsel should be included in the planning for new releases and even for new products.

In recent years many companies have been outsourcing customer support to countries with lower labor costs than the United States, such as India. The number of clients that can be handled is roughly equivalent to U.S. averages for these international outsource agreements.

One technical problem with customer support that needs improvement is dealing with defect reports from people who are hearing impaired or completely deaf. There is a need for better TTY support and also expanded use of automatic voice translation software so that answers to questions can be displayed on the client's screen.

Economics of Error-Prone Modules

Although most companies don't know this, almost 50 percent of their maintenance budgets goes to repairing less than 5 percent of the code in their aging legacy applications. That is because many large software applications have small segments or modules with enormous numbers of latent bugs. The annual maintenance costs of error-prone modules can top $1000 per function point, which is basically what it cost to develop the module in the first place. Maintenance of error-prone modules is in fact the most expensive activity in all of software. And with error-prone modules, these costs occur every year that the modules exist!

The surgical removal of an error-prone module and its replacement with a new and better module is expensive. It can cost about $1500 per function point to excise an error-prone module and redevelop it. But if you are spending $1000 per function point every year, the ROI for replacement will be positive in 18 months or less.

Error-prone module removal projects have been part of the systems software domain for more than 40 years. Research at IBM in the 1960s discovered that software bugs in large systems are seldom randomly distributed. Instead, they tend to clump in a small number of very buggy portions, termed *error-prone modules*.

As an example, in the 1970s IBM's large database product, the Information Management System (IMS), contained 425 modules. About 300 of these modules never received a customer-reported bug. But 31 modules out of 425 received more than 2000 customer bug reports each year in all, or roughly 60 percent of the total bug reports against the entire product.

Some error-prone modules are on record that have received as many as 5 bugs or defects per function point (or 50 bugs per KLOC) per year after release to customers. Error-prone modules may never stabilize because the bad-fix injection rate can approach 100 percent, which means that each attempt to repair a bug may introduce a new bug.

Other companies besides IBM soon performed similar research, and it was discovered that error-prone modules were very common among large systems and applications above about 5000 function points or 500,000 source code statements in size. Error-prone modules are so common and so expensive to maintain that every sophisticated software organization should eliminate them completely.

Error-prone modules are the most expensive artifacts in the software domain, and their cumulative costs can be higher than those of normal modules by almost 500 percent. The reason is that the costs of defect repairs exceed the original development costs in less than a year, and continue to grow indefinitely until the error-prone module is totally eliminated.

Extensive research has been performed as to why these modules exist in the first place, and the four most common reasons are

- Excessive schedule pressure
- Poorly trained programmers who lack knowledge of structured techniques

- Failure to utilize code inspections
- Failure to track defects well enough to realize that error prone modules were present

Of these four, the use of code inspections can essentially immunize against error-prone modules, and this explains in part why formal inspections are used by all best-in-class organizations, which also have zero error-prone modules in their production software.

Any organization that builds large software projects in excess of 1000 function points or 100,000 source code statements should do periodic surveys of the error-prone module status of all deployed software applications. Error-prone modules are a fully treatable and controllable problem, so only companies that are careless in quality control have them today.

There is insufficient data to judge the frequency of error-prone modules in Agile projects or those using XP. However, the average size of Agile and XP projects circa 2007 is below the size where error-prone modules have been troublesome. Error-prone modules tend to occur with high frequency for applications larger than 5000 function points or 500,000 source code statements. Most Agile and XP projects to date have been below 2000 function points or 200,000 source code statements in size.

Incidentally, since the bad-fix injection rate of repairs to error-prone modules approaches 50 percent, they should definitely be removed prior to commencing major enhancements.

Mandatory Changes

Mandatory changes are modifications to software made in response to changes in law or policy. For example, a change in tax rates or a change in health-care benefits will require modifications to many software packages. The source of funds for mandatory changes is ambiguous and can vary from case to case.

The most notable recent example of a mandatory change was conversion work for the unified European currency, or *euro*, that ran from 1999 through 2002. Many applications in Western Europe and some in the U.S. were updated to accommodate the euro. A more recent change will be the software updates necessary to accommodate the lengthened period of daylight savings time that will occur starting in 2007. Although the total duration of daylight savings time is changing only by a few weeks, thousands of software applications will require updates. Unfortunately many smaller devices where date routines are embedded in microcode cannot actually be updated, and will require complete replacement.

It is a source of dispute between companies and government agencies that government regulations can require extensive and expensive updates to software, without providing any funding or financial relief.

Making matters worse, governments may demand that the changes be made on impossibly short deadlines. Indeed, some mandatory changes are even retroactive!

Mandatory changes are one of the more troubling forms of software maintenance because the costs are often high, the schedule pressure is intense, and there may be severe penalties for noncompliance. For example, non-compliance with the Sarbanes-Oxley financial reporting requirements can actually lead to criminal charges.

Historically, the unwise decision of the European community to attempt to roll out a common European currency in January 1999 without realizing that year-2000 repairs would be peaking at the same time was one of the worst combinations of mandatory changes in software history, or indeed in human history.

Complexity Analysis

Complexity analysis is not usually an independent project with its own budget. Usually, complexity analysis is a preliminary stage prior to some other form of maintenance work, such as the following:

- Code restructuring
- Error-prone module removal
- Mandatory updates for new government regulations
- Major enhancements
- Migration to another platform
- Conversion to another language

Complexity analysis cannot easily be done using manual methods. (However, refactoring has been observed to reduce complexity in a number of examples.) A variety of commercial complexity-analysis tools, some smaller shareware tools, and even a few freeware tools are available that can examine source code in a number of languages, graph control flow, and calculate one or more quantitative indicators of complexity levels, such as cyclomatic complexity or essential complexity.

Unfortunately, of the 24 kinds of complexity known to affect software projects, only cyclomatic and essential complexity have fully automated tools available. As a result, many of the other kinds of complexity that can impact software projects (combinatorial complexity, computational complexity, fan complexity, topologic complexity, syntactic complexity, semantic complexity, etc.) are seldom used for software projects, and almost never are used for source code complexity analysis.

It would be highly valuable to apply some of the semantic complexity models to software requirements and specifications, such as using the

FOG index to calculate the reading difficulty of the text documents. Unfortunately, none of the major complexity vendors have yet started to deal with complexity of the non-code portions of software applications.

The phrase *cyclomatic complexity* is derived from graph theory. The concept is basically a measure of the control flow and branching structure of software applications. Cyclomatic complexity is derived from a flowchart or graph of the application's control flow, using the formula edges – nodes + 2. An application which has no branches at all but consists entirely of one straight-through coding sequence has a cyclomatic complexity of 1. In this simple case, *start* and *end* are the two nodes. The control flow is a straight line or *edge* connecting the two nodes.

Applying the formula of edges – nodes + 2 yields the following sequence. There is 1 edge or line and – nodes, so the first part of the formula subtracts the – nodes from the single line, yielding a value of – 1. The second part of the formula adds a constant of + 2, and the final result is a cyclomatic complexity of 1.

Essential complexity uses similar logic, but involves more complex analysis to eliminate duplication of the same patterns in the graph.

In practice, software applications that are low in cyclomatic and essential complexity (with values <5) are easier to maintain than applications that are high in cyclomatic and essential complexity (say, values >20). The correlation between complexity and maintenance difficulty is not perfect, but it is fairly strong.

On the whole, the impact of software complexity is not well covered in the software literature. Indeed, only cyclomatic and essential complexity have any significant citations in a software context, and the pioneering report by Tom McCabe is one of the few examples of actual research into software complexity issues.

Code Restructuring and Refactoring

Code restructuring projects are very common for COBOL, because a number of excellent commercial restructuring tools entered the market many years ago. The pioneering restructuring tools entered the market circa 1985, and include Recoder, Structured Retrofit, and Superstructure. Code restructuring tools are also available for C, FORTRAN, and PL/I, but the market for these tools is clearly aimed at COBOL because that language is dominant for business applications.

Code restructuring is usually done by an automated tool, and has the effect of lowering both cyclomatic and essential complexity levels. This, in turn, eases maintenance. The restructuring tools also create fresh flowcharts and maintenance documentation. The tools may also allow changes to names and modernization in other fashions. Usually, restructuring is benign in that it does not degrade performance or introduce errors. However, some restructured applications do contain about 10 percent more code than they did previously.

Although the method of operation of code restructuring tools varies from vendor to vendor, a common pattern is that these tools first evaluate the cyclomatic and essential complexity of the applications and produce a structure chart of the current situation. Then, using graph theory, the tools simplify the structure chart and eliminate harmful branching patterns. The actual source code is then taken apart and the application is reconstructed using the simplified graph as the basis.

Code restructuring is most commonly used for aging legacy software that has some long-range strategic value and can't be replaced for several more years. Code restructuring is also showing up as a precursor to making large enhancements, because it is faster and easier to find things in well-structured software than in highly complex software.

Refactoring is also a form of code restructuring. The concept of refactoring became popular with XP and some of the Agile methods. The purpose of refactoring is primarily to improve the logic and clarity of the code itself, not to add features or fix bugs. Refactoring occurs after functional updates are made to the code.

Since refactoring is performed by the original programmers who developed the code, productivity rates are fairly high—in the range of 25 function points of 2500 source code statements per staff month, or higher.

However, the technology exists to do refactoring in an automated manner at rates of perhaps 2500 source code statements per second. Why manual refactoring is preferred instead of automated refactoring is perhaps a sociological issue more than a technical issue. Although automated restructuring tools are more common for aging legacy languages such as COBOL and assembly than they are for more recent languages such as Smalltalk and Java. However, the underlying technology of automated restructuring can be applied to any programming language.

In theory and sometimes in practice refactoring will reduce both the cyclomatic and essential complexity of code segments. Here too, automation is available to handle the same kinds of complexity improvements.

Restructuring of software applications involves reducing the complexity of the control flow, as commonly measured using cyclomatic or essential complexity metrics. For common languages, such as COBOL and C, automated restructuring tools are available that can reduce complexity with little or no human involvement.

However, there are more than 600 programming languages in use, and automated restructuring tools are available only for about a dozen of these languages. For languages where restructuring automation is not available, such as mumps or CHILL, the work effort is so enormous that manual restructuring is seldom attempted.

Performance Optimization

Optimization projects are normally performed for applications and systems with very high transaction rates, such as credit card processing or real-time applications.

Optimization is concerned with minimizing delays in transactions by looking for approaches that slow things down. Sometimes for really old legacy software, optimization can include obvious steps, such as switching from tape files to disks. However, optimization is also concerned with control flow, loops, calls, caching, and everything else known to affect the speed with which applications perform.

It is interesting that optimization is such a rare commodity that large companies employ performance specialists to do the work. There are also commercial performance-monitoring tools in both hardware and software variants that are used to monitor execution speeds and help identify sections that may need tuning for performance purposes.

There are a number of vendors who build special performance-monitoring tools and software packages, usually aimed at high-transaction mainframe applications. Examples of applications where performance is critical include credit card processing, gasoline pump credit wand processing, and, of course, software that controls automatic teller machines.

Migration Across Platforms

Migration projects are those associated with moving an application from one platform to another. Historical examples of migration include porting an application from DOS to Windows, from UNIX to Windows, from Windows to a Macintosh, or from Windows to Linux.

Migration projects can be made for a variety of reasons, such as user requests, a desire to open up new markets, or to preserve important applications that were written for processors or operating systems now being withdrawn from service.

Funding for migration projects varies from case to case, although a majority of migration projects for internal software are paid for by the user group. For commercial software, migration is usually performed in order to expand markets or reach new ones.

Migration can be either very easy or very difficult depending upon the status of the original software. If the software is written in languages such as COBOL, with extensive tools available for renovation, and if the specifications have been kept up, migration can proceed at rates in excess of 50 function points per staff month.

If the software is written in obscure languages, and if the specifications are missing or obsolete, migration might proceed at a rate of less than 5 function points per staff month—if, indeed, it can be successfully completed at all.

Migration often requires changing hardware platforms, changing operating systems, and changing programming languages all at the same time. Automation to accomplish all three of these changes is not widely available, and may reduce performance if it can be done at all. What is available are tools that can extract latent design information from source code. For example, it is possible to extract and print latent design information from assembly language applications as a precursor to migrating them to some newer or more widely used language such as COBOL or Java.

Conversion to New Architectures

Conversion projects are those that change the interface and file structure of applications, such as switching from flat files to relational databases, or switching from a monolithic mainframe application to a client/server application.

Because conversion projects often add features or facilities that benefit users, the users are often motivated to fund these projects.

Conversion projects are often much more troublesome than anticipated because maintenance practices have historically been lax and unprofessional. For many aging legacy applications that are targets for conversion, the specifications are out of date or missing; the original designers have retired or changed jobs; and in some cases, even the source code is missing or is no longer compilable.

Conversion projects can be done using manual methods, or be supported by reverse-engineering and reengineering tools. Also, before the conversion gets under way, the application may be given a thorough complexity analysis and possibly be restructured using a commercial code restructuring tool. All of these situations can be estimated, but add complexity to the estimation process.

Reverse Engineering

Reverse-engineering projects are usually concerned with aging legacy applications where the original specifications are missing or incomplete, but where the application has strategic value and cannot be simply replaced. By means of reverse-engineering tools, some of the missing design information can be extracted from the source code itself. Reverse engineering is usually a prelude to reengineering, and may often be performed in conjunction with complexity analysis, code restructuring, or both.

The need for reverse engineering is because the specifications for many aging software applications no longer exist or are in such bad shape that the essential design information is no longer up to date or complete. Reverse engineering via automated tools is the most common approach.

Reverse engineering is normally a precursor stage for applications that are slated to be reengineered, or converted into modern client/server forms.

Note that another form of reverse engineering is sometimes used: Some companies reverse-engineer competitive software packages in an attempt to extract possible trade secrets or proprietary algorithms. This form of reverse engineering is very likely to end up in court, and a number of lawsuits for theft of intellectual property have occurred in recent years in which reverse engineering of trade-secret material was one of the claims by the plaintiff.

Reengineering

Reengineering projects are most often concerned with migrating aging legacy software into a more modern client/server form with a graphical user interface (GUI). These projects are highly variable, based upon the programming languages and platforms involved. Straightforward reengineering involving COBOL applications can be done in a highly automated fashion, which can reduce human programming effort by 70 percent or more compared to manual conversions. It is also possible to reengineer applications written in assembly language and develop replacements in more modern languages.

Funding for reengineering projects varies, but often comes from the user or client budget as a (hopefully) cheaper alternative to building an entirely new application.

Dead Code Removal

Dead code removal projects are fairly uncommon, but started to occur in the context of year-2000 and Euro updates and repairs. It usually happens that when programmers make repairs to software, they do not physically remove the old code but merely change the structure so that the old code can no longer be reached and, hence, is never executed. The rationale for this is that the new modifications may not work, so it is safer to leave the old code untouched in case the new changes fail or have to be backed out.

Over time, as many changes are made to aging legacy applications, the volume of dead code can approximate 30 percent in some cases. It is not difficult to identify dead code, because many commercial complexity-analysis tools that trace application control flows produce maps that highlight dead code segments.

Until recently, the only major harm from dead code was that it made maintenance by novice programmers more difficult because they would not immediately be aware of which code was dead and which was still active.

However, in the former year-2000 context dead code turned out to be an expensive problem. The billing algorithms for many year-2000 service companies were based on counts of total physical lines of code in the application. If an application of 10,000 physical lines contains 3000 lines of dead code, then the year-2000 repair vendor charged at a rate of between $1 and $2 per line for the dead code as well as for the active portion of the application. Thus, the cost implications of dead code can grow to a substantial amount of money.

Although the Y2K problem and the Euro are history, similar issues will occur in the future. In a few years it may be necessary to add a digit to telephone numbers because of the explosive increase in cell phones. Some kind of national registration system may change the structure of social security numbers. In the year 2038 the Unix calendar will reset. In other words, future "mass update" software problems may make dead code an economic liability.

Dormant Application Removal

Dormant application removal projects were also a by-product of the year-2000 problem. A large-scale study of eight IBM data centers found that almost 50 percent of the software applications in the portfolio had not been run for several years, and probably would never be run again. Some of these were systems developed for previous hardware, or prior versions of applications that had undergone major revisions. Some were also packages that were no longer utilized.

Before the year-2000 problem there was no overwhelming reason to remove these dormant applications. But since year-2000 repairs cost between $1 and $2 per physical line of code when contractors were used, it was obvious that dormant applications needed to be removed from the suite of active software packages before making expensive updates. Since similar problems will occur in the future, companies should at least identify and catalog dormant applications.

Nationalization

The term *nationalization* concerns the need to translate screens, text, and sometimes comments and programming information into other natural languages so software projects can be successfully marketed abroad. English is the most widely used language in the software world, but many commercial software products also have versions available in French, Italian, Japanese, Korean, Portuguese, Russian, Spanish, or many other languages for countries where a significant number of possible clients may not be able to use technical English.

When nationalization occurs, it is a significant expense element. The overall costs of translating materials into other languages runs from 5 percent of original development to more than 25 percent, based on the availability of translation tools and bilingual personnel for the target languages.

Nationalization is tricky for estimation purposes because the levels of nationalization can run from surface changes of key user manuals and Help screens through full-bore renovation of the entire application, possibly including comments if the application is likely to be transferred to an off-shore outsource company.

Mass Update Projects

Starting with the famous Y2K problem and continuing with the Euro conversion, a new kind of maintenance activity became both common and expensive. This new form of maintenance can be termed "mass updates." The meaning of the phrase "mass update" is that simultaneous changes may be needed to every legacy application in a portfolio. In fact, some mass update changes may affect the majority of legacy software applications in an entire country or even the entire world.

Some future mass update projects will occur on specific dates but others are not yet predictable. Two of the mass updates that are predictable deal with Unix and Microsoft date formats.

On January 18th of the year 2038, yet another date problem will occur when the UNIX operating system and the C programming language internal date representations expire. UNIX stores dates in terms of the number of seconds accrued after January 1, 1970 using a four-byte storage area.

Using normal 32-bit storage, this method works until UNIX time reaches 2,147,483,647 accumulated seconds, when a roll-over occurs. Thus, the UNIX clock will roll over on January 19, 2038 at 3:14:07, at which point it will seem to be 1970 again, or at least the number of seconds from January 1, 1970 will seem to be 0.

Some applications may then revert to January 1, 1970 as the current date, but some may revert to a date of December 13, 1901 based on implementation logic.

Here too, the root cause of the problem is conservation of storage by using only four digits. Using six digits instead of four would have extended the useful UNIX and C date life for many thousands of year, but the use of four digits will cause another mass migration of dates in less than 40 years.

The C runtime library has a time function that reports time as a 31-bit signed integer. Jan Huffman of Software Productivity Research (SPR) has suggested creating a new data type that would be an unsigned integer, and hence allow the 32nd bit to be used for dates. This would provide an additional 68 years before roll-over occurs.

If the UNIX problem follows the same pattern as the year-2000 problem, it will not be covered in the press until about 2033 and major repairs won't begin until 2036, when it is almost too late to get the affected applications updated before the roll-over occurs.

Because software from Microsoft is used in more computers than all other vendors combined, how Microsoft handles dates is a very serious issue. Based on Microsoft's congressional testimony in 1996 and the former Microsoft year-2000 web site, information on all Microsoft products is available for review and analysis. Readers can start at the basic Microsoft web site and branch to relevant sections: http://www.Microsoft.com is the basic URL to get started.

There are a number of Microsoft date expirations that users should know about. For example, the very popular Excel 95 spreadsheet package handles dates only up to 2019 using two-digit dates, or up to 2078 using four-digit dates. The Microsoft Project planning tool can handle dates only up to 2049. The Microsoft Access database product will stop at 1999 using two-digit date formats, but goes all the way to 9999 using four-digit dates.

According to Microsoft's congressional testimony, these rather close-in dates are going to be stretched out in future versions with the year 9999 being the stated end point for many new Microsoft product releases.

Some unpredictable future mass update problems will occur if it is necessary to add a digit to U.S. telephone numbers, or to change the structure or add a digit to social security numbers.

Other unpredictable mass update problems include changes in tax laws, health care benefits, retirement ages, and scores of other items that are determined by Congress or by regulatory agencies. Indeed, a fairly significant mass update project is occurring as this book is being written—the expansion of the duration of daylight savings time in the United States.

Mass updates are tricky from an estimating standpoint because what top management needs to know is not what it will cost to update one specific application, but what it might cost to update more than 1000 applications in current portfolios.

Retirement or Withdrawal of Applications

Software retirement is also a special case, and involves withdrawing a software package from active service. For commercial software, many users are reluctant to give up applications or move to newer versions, so it may be necessary to provide continued support for packages long past the nominal end of their useful lives. Failure to provide such support has sometimes led to litigation if the software in question was covered by warranty or maintenance agreement.

Estimating software retirement is not a standard feature of software cost-estimating tools. In fact, the costs of retirement are so variable that they can range from 0 to more than $1,000,000 based on contractual obligations and the kind of good will that vendors wish to provide to key clients. Sometimes to encourage retirement of obsolete software vendors provide deep discounts on new versions. When retirement costs do occur, they are part of the total cost of ownership of an application.

Field Service

Field service at customer locations is a special form of support offered primarily to major customers of large mainframe applications. As the name implies, field-service personnel visit the customer location (or may even be assigned there full time) and carry out defect repairs, update installations, and other tasks at the customer location.

In the 1970s and 1980s, field service was a common aspect of mainframe software, and sometimes the costs were bundled in with the lease of the application itself. Since the 1990s, field service has become rare for a number of reasons. One obvious reason is that there is a shortage of software personnel and costs are rising, so software and computer companies are trying to minimize or eliminate field-service expenses. If software maintenance is outsourced to an offshore vendor, then on-site field service in the United States becomes logistically difficult. Also, the availability of the Internet, e-mail, and other direct computer-to-computer linkages means that remote maintenance is now technically possible.

Field service is still available, and some personal computer manufacturers offer on-site service. (Indeed, the computer used to write the first edition of this book had its hard drive replaced under a field-service contract.)

Combinations and Concurrent Maintenance Operations

Although 23 discrete forms of maintenance have been discussed separately, it is very common for a number of them to take place simultaneously. This adds complexity to maintenance estimating. For example, some of the common mixtures of maintenance work can include any or all of the following sets:

Set 1: Normal maintenance operations
1. Maintenance (defect repairs)
2. Enhancement (major or minor)
3. Installation of software updates from vendors

Set 2: Restructuring preceding a major enhancement
1. Complexity analysis
2. Restructuring or refactoring
3. Enhancement (major)

Set 3: Restructuring for quality improvement
1. Complexity analysis
2. Restructuring or refactoring
3. Error-prone module removal
4. Maintenance (defect repairs)
5. Enhancement (major)

Set 4: Mass update conversion work
1. Complexity analysis
2. Reengineering
3. Restructuring or refactoring
4. Initial updates
5. Reoptimization to restore lost performance
6. Secondary bad-fix repairs

This same practice of concurrent maintenance and enhancement also raises the complexity of estimation, since the two separate forms of modification tend to interfere with each other, and it adds complexity to change management, configuration control, and other administrative tasks. Sometimes development programmers working on an enhancement and maintenance programmers working on defect repairs may try and change the same code at the same time, with problems occurring. Obviously, cooperation, coordination, and a controlled source code library are needed to prevent simultaneous changes from interfering with each other.

Essentially any combination of the 23 separate maintenance activities can occur at the same time for the same software application.

Maintenance estimation when combinations of different kinds of maintenance are occurring is far more difficult and complex than estimating any of the individual forms. For example, in controlled experiments involving the same application before and after complexity analysis and code restructuring, the effort of making the same update was 40 percent lower for the team working on the well-structured, low-complexity version than for the team working on the poorly structured, high-complexity version.

Estimating tools vary widely in the approaches they utilize for dealing with hybrid forms of maintenance, such as adding new features at the same time that bug repairs are taking place. To illustrate some of the implications, consider the following five types of maintenance in ascending order of complexity.

Type 1 Maintenance: Additions Without Internal Modification

The first type of maintenance is that of adding new features to an application, without the new features causing any extensive internal changes to the original source code. This form of addition is uncommon and requires that the original application be designed and developed with expansion in mind. An example of this kind of addition might be adding a dictionary module to a word-processing component.

The productivity rates of Type 1 updates are roughly equivalent to new stand-alone development, with the exception that testing of both the old and new versions is somewhat more extensive. Typical productivity rates are in the 5 to 15 function points per staff month range. Assignment scopes are usually 1000 function points or higher.

Type 2 Maintenance: Additions with Internal Modifications to the Base Application

With Type 2 updates, it is necessary to make internal changes to the original application in order to attach the additional features. Type 2 updates are possible only for applications that were originally designed in a very modular, well-structured manner.

With Type 2 updates, all of the interfaces are concise and are located in one area of the original application. The productivity rate for adding the new features is close to that of new development work, but when the modifications to the existing application are included there is some minor reduction due primarily to the need for extensive regression testing to ensure that no accidental damages have occurred. Productivity rates run from about 3 to just over 10 function points per staff month. Assignment scopes are in the range of 750 function points.

Type 3 Maintenance: New Feature Replaces an Existing Feature

With Type 3 updates, the new feature being added to the software replaces a current feature that is actually being eliminated. This kind of update may occur with software that handles tax calculation or withholding rates, when there is a change in tax law.

Type 3 modifications are sometimes a source of concern. The reason for the problem is the very common habit by programmers of *not* removing the original code when a new feature is added. The reason for this practice is that until the new feature is fully installed and tested, there is a chance that it might not work and, indeed, may have to be backed out. Therefore, it is simple prudence to leave the prior work alone, in case it has to be used again.

This habit of making updates without removing the former code or modules results in a phenomenon called *dead code*, which was discussed earlier in this chapter. Dead code consists of source code resident in an application that can no longer be executed, and which probably cannot even be reached via branching or normal operation of the software package.

Because updates for software can occur over many years, dead code can accumulate in substantial volumes—for some applications, as much as 30 percent of the actual volume of source code is dead and is no longer part of the working application.

Normally, dead code causes a reduction in maintenance productivity when new maintenance personnel take over, because they have to learn to avoid it. For some outsource agreements, the dead code is often quite troublesome for two reasons:

- The vendor may charge $1 to $2 per line of code for the dead code.

- Accidentally searching the dead code slows down repairs to active code.

Both situations are so troublesome that many companies go through a dead code removal stage before starting maintenance outsource work. Productivity rates for Type 3 updates run from 2 to about 8 function points per staff month. Assignment scopes are around 500 function points or less.

Type 4 Maintenance: New Features
Accompanied by Scatter Updates

Because well-structured code is something of a rarity in the software world and is found in less than 30 percent of SPR's clients' legacy applications, the most common situation for making updates to software is the Type 4 category, or *scatter updates*.

With Type 4 modifications, several new features are being added at the same time. For poorly structured code, the interfaces between the new features and the existing application are not neat or tidy, but instead require extensive changes scattered in almost random patterns throughout the entire base application.

Type 4 modifications are very common and very troublesome. Productivity is much lower than normal development, and the incidence of bad fixes, or new bugs introduced as a by-product of the updates, can approach unity; that is, a new bug may be added for every change.

Productivity rates for Type 4 updates range between 1 and 5 function points per staff month. Maintenance assignment scopes are in the 300– to 500–function point range.

Type 5 Maintenance: Scatter Updates, Deletions, and Conflicting Repairs

When we arrive at Type 5 updates, we encounter the classic form of maintenance of poorly structured, aging legacy applications. Here all of the bad problems are occurring at the same time, and in addition, a special kind of problem can occur. When updates are occurring at the same time by different programmers, some of their changes may be in conflict and interfere with each other!

Type 5 updates have a number of both chronic and acute problems associated with them. Obviously, productivity is very low because the original code is quite difficult to work with. Also obviously, bad fix injection rates are very high, which is to say that new bugs will be accidentally introduced with almost every change.

In addition, Type 5 projects are very hard to put under proper configuration control, which means that several programmers may be updating the same modules of the existing application without being aware of each other's work. Only when testing begins will it be noted that some of the changes have interfered with each other, so rework is common and expensive in Type 5 situations.

The problems of Type 4 and Type 5 updates can be alleviated by a number of commercial software tools that provide geriatric services to aging legacy applications:

- Complexity-analysis tools
- Code restructuring tools
- Configuration-control tools
- Defect-tracking tools
- Reverse-engineering tools
- Reengineering tools
- Maintenance workbenches

Not every tool will work for every application or every programming language. Obviously, for common languages, such as COBOL, FORTRAN, and C, there is a large number of tools available. For more uncommon languages, such as CHILL, CORAL, Forth, or mumps, the number of geriatric tools is rather limited.

Productivity for Type 5 updates ranges from about 0.5 to perhaps 3 function points per staff month. Maintenance assignment scopes are below 300 function points.

In conclusion, estimating the various forms of maintenance and enhancement work is among the most difficult problems facing software cost-estimating tool developers. It is perhaps appropriate to close the discussion of maintenance estimating by paraphrasing the observation of the eighteenth-century wit, Samuel Johnson, upon seeing a dog that had been trained to walk on its hind legs: "It is not done well, but it is surprising that it can be done at all."

The literature on software maintenance is slowly expanding and rapidly improving. Maintenance tools are also improving. In addition, maintenance outsource contracts are becoming one of the most popular and also most successful forms of outsource agreement. Maintenance work is most efficient when performed by trained specialists supported by a suite of maintenance tools. This is what the larger outsource vendors can supply. Maintenance work is least efficient when done by developers who must divide their time between defect repairs and adding new features. In the current era, the importance of maintenance finally began to achieve mainstream status.

References

Arnold, Robert S.: *Software Reengineering*, IEEE Computer Society Press, Los Alamitos, Calif., 1993.

Arthur, Lowell Jay: *Software Evolution—The Software Maintenance Challenge*, John Wiley & Sons, New York, 1988.

Boehm, Barry: *Software Engineering Economics*, Prentice-Hall, Englewood Cliffs, N.J., 1981.

Brown, Norm (ed.): *The Program Manager's Guide to Software Acquisition Best Practices*, Version 1.0, U.S. Department of Defense, Washington, D.C., July 1995.

Capretz, Luis Fernandez, and Miriam Capretz: *Object-Oriented Software: Design and Maintenance*, World Scientific Pub. Co, Hackensack, NJ., 1996.

Demeyer, Serge et al.: *Object-Oriented Reengineering Patterns*, World Scientific Pub. Co, Hackensack NJ., 2002.

Department of the Air Force: *Guidelines for Successful Acquisition and Management of Software Intensive Systems*, vols. 1 and 2, Software Technology Support Center, Hill Air Force Base, Utah, 1994.

Fowler, Martin et al.: *Refactoring: Improving the Design of Existing Code*, Addison-Wesley, Boston, Mass., 2003.

Gallagher, R. S.: *Effective Customer Support*, International Thomson Computer Press, Boston, Mass., 1997.

Grady, Robert B.: *Practical Software Metrics for Project Management and Process Improvement*, Prentice-Hall, Englewood Cliffs, N.J., 1992.

———, and Deborah L. Caswell: *Software Metrics: Establishing a Company-Wide Program*, Prentice-Hall, Englewood Cliffs, N.J., 1987.

Grubb, Penny, and Armstrong Takang: *Software Maintenance: Concepts and Practice*, World Scientific Pub. Co,Hackensack, NJ 2003.

Howard, Alan (ed.): *Software Maintenance Tools*, Applied Computer Research (ACR), Phoenix, Ariz., 1997.

Jones, Capers: *Critical Problems in Software Measurement*, Information Systems Management Group, Carlsbad, Califorina, 1993a.

———: *New Directions in Software Management*, Information Systems Management Group, Carlsbad California, 1993b.

———: *Software Productivity and Quality Today—The Worldwide Perspective*, Information Systems Management Group, Carlsbad, California, 1993c.

———: *Assessment and Control of Software Risks*, Prentice-Hall, Englewood Cliffs, N.J., 1994.

———: *Patterns of Software System Failure and Success*, International Thomson Computer Press, Boston, Mass., 1995.

———: *Applied Software Measurement, Second Edition*, McGraw-Hill, New York, 1996.

———: *Software Quality—Analysis and Guidelines for Success*, International Thomson Computer Press, Boston, Mass., 1997.

———: *The Year 2000 Software Problem—Quantifying the Costs and Assessing the Consequences*, Addison-Wesley, Reading, Mass., 1998.

———: *Software Assessments, Benchmarks, and Best Practices*, Addison-Wesley, Boston, Mass., 2000.

Kan, Stephen H.: *Metrics and Models in Software Quality Engineering, Second Edition*, Addison-Wesley, Boston, Mass., 2003.

Kerievsky, Joshua: *Refactoring to Patterns*, Addison-Wesley, Boston, Mass., 2004.

Lehman, Meir M., and L.A. Belady: *Program Evolution: Process of Software Change*, Academic Press, Burlington, Mass.,1985.

Marciniak, John J. (ed.): *Encyclopedia of Software Engineering*, vols. 1 and 2, John Wiley & Sons, New York, 1994.

McCabe, Thomas J.: "A Complexity Measure," *IEEE Transactions on Software Engineering*, 308–320 (December 1976).

Mertes, Karen R.: *Calibration of the CHECKPOINT Model to the Space and Missile Systems Center (SMC) Software Database (SWDB)*, Thesis AFIT/GCA/LAS/96S-11, Air Force Institute of Technology (AFIT), Wright-Patterson AFB, Ohio, September 1996.

Muller, Monika, and Alain Abram (eds.): *Metrics in Software Evolution*, R. Oldenbourg Vertag GmbH, Munich, 1995.

Parikh, Girish: *Handbook of Software Maintenance*, John Wiley & Sons, New York, 1986.

Pigoski, Thomas M.: *Practical Software Maintenance—Best Practices for Managing Your Software Investment*, IEEE Computer Society Press, Los Alamitos, Calif., 1997.

Polo, Macario et al.: *Advances in Software Maintenance, Management, Technologies, and Solutions*, World Scientific Pub. Co., Hackensack, NJ, 1996.

Putnam, Lawrence H.: *Measures for Excellence—Reliable Software on Time, Within Budget*, Yourdon Press/Prentice-Hall, Englewood Cliffs, N.J., 1992.

———, and Ware Myers: *Industrial Strength Software—Effective Management Using Measurement*, IEEE Press, Los Alamitos, Calif., 1997.

Rethinking the Software Process, CD-ROM, Miller Freeman, Lawrence, Kans., 1996. (This CD-ROM is a book collection jointly produced by the book publisher, Prentice-Hall, and the journal publisher, Miller Freeman. It contains the full text and illustrations of five Prentice-Hall books: *Assessment and Control of Software Risks* by Capers Jones; *Controlling Software Projects* by Tom DeMarco; *Function Point Analysis* by Brian Dreger; *Measures for Excellence* by Larry Putnam and Ware Myers; and *Object-Oriented Software Metrics* by Mark Lorenz and Jeff Kidd.)

Rada, Roy: *Reengineering Software: How to Reuse Programming to Build New State of the Art Software, Second Edition*, Fitzroy Dearborn Publishers, 1999.

Rubin, Howard: *Software Benchmark Studies for 1997*, Howard Rubin Associates, Pound Ridge, N.Y., 1997.

Seacord, Robert C. et al.: *Modernizing Legacy Systems*, Addison-Wesley, Boston, Mass., 2003.

Sharon, David: *Managing Systems in Transition—A Pragmatic View of Reengineering Methods*, International Thomson Computer Press, Boston, Mass., 1996.

Shepperd, M.: "A Critique of Cyclomatic Complexity as a Software Metric," *Software Engineering Journal*, **3:**30–36 (1988).

Stukes, Sherry, Jason Deshoretz, Henry Apgar, and Ilona Macias: *Air Force Cost Analysis Agency Software Estimating Model Analysis*, TR-9545/008-2, Contract F04701-95-D-0003, Task 008, Management Consulting & Research, Inc., Thousand Oaks, Calif., September 1996.

Symons, Charles R.: *Software Sizing and Estimating—Mk II FPA (Function Point Analysis)*, John Wiley & Sons, Chichester, U.K., 1991.

Takang, Armstrong, and Penny Grubh: *Software Maintenance Concepts and Practice*, International Thomson Computer Press, Boston, Mass., 1997.

Yang, Hongji, and Ward, Martin: *Successful Evolution of Software Systems*, Artech House, Norwood, Mass., 2003.

Yang, Hongji (ed.): *Software Evolution with UML and XML*, Idea Group Publishing, Hershey, Pennsylvannia, 2005.

Zvegintzov, Nicholas: *Software Management Technology Reference Guide*, Dorset House Press, New York, 1994.

Software Cost-Estimating Research Issues

In spite of the progress in software development methods and software cost-estimation tools, accurate estimation remains a difficult task circa 2007. Some of the difficulty is due to the intrinsic ambiguity and complexity of large software applications. But some of the difficulty associated with accurate estimation is self-inflicted and due to lack of research into key problem areas. This chapter discusses ten estimating problem areas that are in need of additional study and research:

1. Metrics conversion

2. Automatic sizing from user requirements

3. Activity-based costs for Agile projects, object-oriented projects, and web projects

4. Complexity analysis of software applications

5. Value analysis and estimation

6. Risk analysis and estimation

7. Including specialists in software cost estimates

8. Reuse analysis and software cost estimates

9. Process improvement estimation

10. Methodology analysis and software cost estimating

These ten problem areas are all important for achieving both a better understanding of software cost estimating and a better understanding of the most effective methods of developing complex software applications.

Metrics Conversion

In gathering the information for this second edition, no fewer than 38 separate metrics for measuring software size were noted. The author believes that, for unknown reasons, the software industry has created more kinds of sizing metrics than any other engineering field in human history. Not only does the software industry utilize an excessive number of sizing metrics, but there are very few rules or algorithms for converting size between one metric and another.

This issue is not a new one. As far back as the 1970s ambiguity began to occur with productivity measurements and cost estimates due to the large differences in software size when applications were measured with either *physical lines of code* or with *logical statements*. Based on the programming language used, there can be as much as a 500 percent difference in apparent size between these two metrics.

For some languages there are more logical statements than physical lines. This is true for COBOL with case statements. For other languages there are more physical lines than logical statements. This is true for Quick Basic, which allows logical statements to be concatenated. For yet other languages (such as Visual Basic) it is even possible to create code without any lines of code at all, due to using buttons and pull-down menus. There is also the issue of reusable code that is copied into an application or is available from class libraries.

Analysis of published data in software journals by the author found that about one-third of technical articles used physical lines, one-third used logical statements, and one-third did not state which method was used. There are very few studies or rules for converting size between physical lines and logical statements for any of the 600 or so programming languages that have been developed. There are also very few studies on the volumes of reused code in completed applications.

Suppose you had published data from an Objective-C program that indicated it was 10,000 physical lines in size. You also had published data from a C++ program of 10,000 logical statements in size. You had published data from a third program in C that stated it was 10,000 lines of code in size, but did not say whether logical or physical lines were used. Are these three programs the same size? Is one of them bigger than the others? If so, which one is largest and which is smallest? There is no effective answer to this question as of 2007.

More recently, no fewer than 15 forms of functional metrics have been developed and have started to be used for estimation and measurement purposes. Some of these in alphabetical order include

- 3D function points
- COSMIC function points

- Engineering function points
- Feature points
- IFPUG function points
- Mark II function points
- NESMA function points
- Object points
- Story points
- Unadjusted function points
- Use case points
- Web object points

There are almost no published rules for converting size between any of these function point variants. If one application is measured with COSMIC function points and is 1000 function points in size, another is measured with IFPUG function points and is also 1000 function points in size, and a third is measured with NESMA function points and is also 1000 function points in size, are these three the same size or not? As of 2007 there is no effective answer to this basic question.

For maintenance of legacy applications where code exists but there are often no current specifications, the most common technique for sizing is "backfiring." The term *backfiring* means calculating size in function points by mathematical conversion from logical source code statements.

There are several sets of published rules for converting size between source code size and function points via backfiring, but the rules are inconsistent from study to study. Conversion between logical source code statements and IFPUG function points is the most widely cited, and there are rules for about 600 programming languages. However, there are very few conversion rules between physical lines of code and any of the function point counting methods.

Backfiring has not been particularly accurate. One reason is that aging legacy applications often have significant quantities of "dead" code that is no longer operational but is still present. An application's cyclomatic and essential complexity levels are known to affect backfire ratios.

Several kinds of tools such as automated complexity analyzers and static analysis tools could be modified to produce backfire function point counts whenever they are run on a legacy application. This would improve the accuracy of backfire ratios and ensure greater consistency of backfire data. For one thing, these tools could quantify the volume of dead code and exclude it from the backfire calculations.

Given the popularity and widespread use of the backfiring method, it is surprising that none of the international metrics organizations such as IFPUG or COSMIC have formed backfiring committees to standardize this approach.

The large number of inconsistent metrics used for expressing software size is a barrier to effective cost estimating. The problem with all of these metrics is that they damage the validity of historical data, and make constructing benchmarks extremely difficult. If all of these metrics are included in software cost-estimating tools, it would be hard to keep the tools current because all of the various metrics change counting rules at random intervals.

The author believes that it is the responsibility of metric developers to produce conversion rules between any new metric and all of the older metrics that have been in existence for some time. Since IFPUG function points are the oldest form of functional metric, the developers of the newer variants should be the ones to produce the conversion rules.

The industry would benefit from the publication of a general table of conversion rules that included differences between physical lines and logical statements for all programming languages, as well as conversion ratios among the various functional metrics now in use. While some preliminary conversion rules appeared earlier in Chapter 9, their margin of error is rather high. Additional research into metrics conversion is needed.

Automatic Sizing from User Requirements

As of 2007 the work of ascertaining the size of a new software application during the requirements gathering and analysis phase depends upon five different sizing methods:

- Mathematical projections from the taxonomy of the application
- Analogy with existing applications of the same kind
- Having a certified function point consultant manually count function points from the requirements documents
- Having developers count story points, use case points, object points, web object points, or one of the other new metrics
- Guesswork or some kind of Monte Carlo approach

The second method, analogy with historical projects, needs additional research. Currently, looking for similar applications to use as patterns for sizing or for feature analysis is pretty much a manual operation. In-house data may have one or two legacy examples, but if there were data available on an industry basis then there might be dozens of prior examples.

Unfortunately, industry data is only available from a few consulting companies. A lot of the data is somewhat ambiguous due to the metrics issues discussed in the previous section.

As this second edition is being prepared for 2007, a new consortium of companies, including the Software Engineering Institute (SEI), Software Productivity Research (SPR), and the David's Consulting Group, is beginning work on establishing an industry benchmark data base. This could lead to much more sophisticated pattern matching in the future. However, the work is only just getting started as this edition is being prepared.

If each software application is defined using an exact taxonomy, and if these taxonomies and other historical data are placed in a large database of software histories, then it should be possible to search for analogous projects in a fully automated way. Since almost all new applications are similar to older applications, the combination of pattern matching and a large multicompany repository of historical projects should allow as many as 50 previous projects to be considered. These would provide useful information not only on size, but also on schedules, costs, quality and other estimating topics of interest.

Function point counting, as well as counting story points, use case points, object points, etc., are primarily manual operations by trained personnel or by certified experts. Manual counting is fairly accurate when performed by certified personnel, but it is painfully slow. Typically manual counting of function point metrics proceeds at rates of between 500 and 1500 function points per day. That may sound like a lot, but for an application of 10,000 function points or larger, the costs quickly mount up. In fact just counting the function points in a large application can have costs in excess of $100,000.

It is technically possible to derive function points (and other metrics too) automatically from requirements expressed in structured English, HIPO diagrams, use cases, Class responsibility collaboration (CRC), or in the unified modeling language (UML). Over the past ten years, several experimental tools have been built to automate function point counting. However, these tools were built to operate with some specific design tools such as the Bachman Analyst. When the companies did not continue to market the design tools, the function point counting features were not ported to other platforms. There would be a fairly large untapped market in the future automating the sizing of applications by derivation from requirements and specifications.

The different topics that combine together to form the basis of the size of a software application include the following elements:

- The *outputs* that should be produced by the application
- The *inputs* that will enter the software application

- The *logical files* that must be maintained by the application
- The *entities, actors, classes, and relationships* of the application
- The *inquiry types* that can be made to the application
- The *interfaces* between the application and other systems
- The *algorithms* that will be in the application
- The *use cases* or major tasks users can perform
- The *hardware platforms* on which the application operates
- The *software platforms* on which the application operates
- The *reused material* going into application
- The *national languages* the application must support

The similarity between the topics that need to be examined when gathering requirements and those used by the functional metrics makes the derivation of function point totals during requirements a fairly straightforward task.

There is such a strong synergy between requirements and function point analysis that it would be possible to construct a combined requirements-analysis tool with full function point sizing support as a natural adjunct. However, the current generation of automated requirements tools is not quite at that point. Additional research is needed.

Activity-Based Costs for Agile, Object-Oriented, and Web Projects

The waterfall development method has more than 50 years of accumulated history and several thousand measured projects. Although some of the data is ambiguous and inaccurate, at least there is a lot of it. For waterfall projects enough data has been accumulated and analyzed for estimating tools to predict with reasonable accuracy dozens of specific activities. Earlier in this book costs and effort tables were shown for 25 of these activities.

The Agile, web, and object-oriented approaches have developed interesting and unique patterns of development activities that are not found in standard waterfall projects. These include activities such as scrum sessions, development sprints, refactoring, object-oriented analysis, object-oriented design, use case development and many others.

As of 2007 there is a shortage of solid empirical data on the effort, schedules, costs, and quality of many of these newer activities. Because of the newness of some of these approaches, there is a significant shortage of long-range studies that include maintenance and enhancement information.

In order to really evaluate the effectiveness of a specific approach, a minimum of about 50 projects should use the method and report application sizes, schedules, costs, productivity, quality, and other quantified results. Table 24.1 shows some of the methods and approaches where there is a shortage of enough historical data to evaluate the effectiveness of the techniques.

This is not to say that there is no information at all about these approaches. However, for many of them there is either insufficient information for statistical analysis, or the available data is expressed in more than one metric so analysis is difficult.

TABLE 24.1   Methods Lacking Historical Data

 1. Actor-based development
 2. Assembly, disassembly, reassembly (ADR)
 3. Capability maturity model integration (CMMI)
 4. Clean-room development
 5. CRC diagrams
 6. Crystal development approach
 7. Data flow diagrams
 8. Data structured system design (DSSD)
 9. Dynamic system development method (DSDM)
10. Entity-relationship diagrams
11. Extreme programming (XP)
12. Feature-driven development (FDD)
13. Finite state diagrams
14. Incremental development
15. ISO 9000–9004 standards
16. Jackson diagrams
17. Object-oriented development (OO)
18. Open-source components
19. Pattern-based development
20. Petri nets
21. Quality Function Deployment (QFD)
22. Rapid Application Development (RAD)
23. Rational development method
24. Scrum
25. Six-sigma for software
26. Spiral development
27. State transition diagrams
28. Team Structured Process (TSP)
29. Total Quality Management (TQM)
30. Tropos software development method
31. Unified modeling language (UML)
32. Use cases
33. User stories
34. Vienna development method (VDM)
35. Zermelo-Frankel Z Notation

For example, there are hundreds of object-oriented (OO) projects with some kind of historical data available. But some of these OO projects were measured with physical lines of code, some with logical statements, some with IFPUG function points, some with object points, some with use case points, some with web object points, and some with Mark II function points. Statistical analysis of projects that were measured with incompatible metrics is not effective.

Estimating accuracy depends upon reliable historical data. And that historical data should either be measured with the same kind of metrics, or at least with metrics where there are known conversion rules among all of the metrics in the sample. Thus, the lack of conversion rules, discussed earlier in the chapter, is delaying the full understanding of many interesting software technologies.

Complexity Analysis of Software Applications

There is a substantial body of data that indicates that complex software will cost more, have more defects, and be more difficult to update safely than simple software. However, complexity itself is either a subjective opinion, or derived from measuring the cyclomatic and essential complexity of source code or the Halstead complexity level.

Whether the complexity of the code is necessary or simply due to poor judgment by the developers is an unanswered question. From the fact that there is a significant market for tools that can restructure software code, and that manual "refactoring" of code is quite common, it appears that much of the complexity is accidental rather than necessary.

Several of the function point metrics have complexity adjustment factors. However, these adjustments are essentially subjective. Surprisingly, none of the function point complexity adjustments make use of cyclomatic and essential complexity or Halstead complexity.

As discussed earlier in this book, the general scientific literature cites some 24 forms of complexity. Most of these would seem to have an impact on software projects, but only two of them, cyclomatic and essential complexity, have any solid empirical data associated with them. The Halstead complexity metric has very little data associated with it.

There is a need for additional research on the other forms of complexity and how they affect the outcomes of software projects and also how they affect function point metrics. Some of the other forms of complexity that need additional research include fan complexity, flow complexity, and Halstead complexity. There is also a need to examine the complexity of the many text documents associated with software projects such as requirements and specifications. For example, it is suspected that requirements with a high FOG index are more error prone and difficult to develop than requirements with a low FOG index.

There is also a need for research into some topics of sociological complexity. There are assertions among the Agile development enthusiasts that small teams are the best solution for software development. This is an interesting but unproven hypothesis. There is a need for additional research on a variety of software organization structures including hierarchical, matrix, small teams, large teams, and virtual teams.

There is one other aspect of complexity that has a direct bearing on automated software cost-estimating tools and also on benchmarks. As of 2007 the software industry uses some 600 different programming languages and creates about 120 different kinds of software applications, each of which can contain about 23 different features. The software industry employs 90 kinds of specialists, creates 53 kinds of paper documents, uses 43 different design methods, and measures with 38 different size metrics. Software applications are built utilizing 26 different development methods that include at least 35 different activities. About 25 international standards affect software projects. Software projects face 30 different kinds of risk factors. The software industry must also deal with 24 kinds of complexity, perform 23 different kinds of maintenance activities, and may perform 18 different kinds of testing. The combinatorial complexity of these topics is enormous. There is no way for either project managers or estimating tool developers to include all of these factors at the same time. It is obvious from the plethora of choices and alternatives in the software industry that we are groping for better ways of doing things, but have not yet found optimal approaches.

Value Analysis of Software Applications

The opposite side of cost estimating is value estimating. Cost-estimating tools and manual methods can predict with fair accuracy how much a software application will cost to build and maintain, but what will be the value of the application once it is deployed? Will the application have a positive return on investment (ROI)? Will there be other kinds of value than financial value such as improvements in customer satisfaction or employee morale?

Financial value can be calculated using net present value, accounting rates of return, or internal rates of return. In fact, several commercial software cost-estimating tools include value-analysis features that can predict financial value. There are also earned-value calculations. But the non-financial value of software applications is a very difficult issue to deal with.

It would be useful to consider performing research on and developing a "value point" metric that could be used to handle both the financial and non-financial kinds of value that software applications provide.

Currently, almost the only kinds of "value" considered for software applications are either cost reductions or revenue increases. While these are no doubt important topics, there are a host of other aspects of value that also need to be examined and measured—customer satisfaction, employee morale, national security, safety, and many other topics. A hypothetical *value point metric* might include the following factors:

- Financial value
  1. Cost reduction
  2. Revenue increases
- Business value
  1. Market share increases
  2. Schedule improvement
  3. Quality and reliability improvement
  4. Competitive advantages
  5. Risk reduction
  6. Hardware synergy (software that leads to hardware sales)
  7. Software synergy (software that leads to other software sales)
  8. Consulting synergy (software that leads to consulting sales)
- Intangible value
  1. Corporate prestige
  2. Improvement in client operations
  3. Morale improvement of employees
  4. Attrition reduction of employees
  5. Health or safety improvement
  6. Corporate security improvement
  7. National security improvement
  8. Government mandates

The way such a value point metric might work is as follows. For the two forms of financial value, cost reduction and revenue increases, a fixed amount such as $1000 might be assigned to each value point.

For the other forms of value, various weights would be assigned. For example if an application is going to increase the market share of a company, each new customer might be equivalent to one value point. If the application is going to improve the work performance of its users, a value point might be assigned for each 1 percent gain by each user.

The eventual usage of value points would be to aid in the determination of whether a software application should be built or not. For example, a corporation might set a goal that each application had to return 10 value points for each function point in the application itself. Thus, an application of 2500 function points would need to achieve a target of 25,000 value points in order to get funded.

Some of these value points would be derived from cost reductions and revenue increases, but other value points might derive from enhancing corporate prestige or improving customer operational effectiveness.

The main purpose of a hypothetical value point metric would be to provide some kind of tangible weight to all aspects of value and not just those that are purely based on dollars. While value based on cost reduction and revenue increases are no doubt important, they are not a complete justification for software that deals with issues such as medical diagnostic studies, national security, policy analysis, or government mandates.

As an example, both the Democratic and Republican political parties have fairly sophisticated software that analyzes voting patterns and sorts registered voters by address, party, zip code, and the like. These applications are about 3000 function points in size. They are not easily justified based on financial ROI. The justification of these applications is to improve the election chances of the candidates from each party. Such applications might assign one value point to each voter. Value could then be calculated, approximately, by the number of voters added to the total for various candidates.

As another example, the Veterans Administration has a large application in excess of 15,000 function points in size for keeping track of the medical histories of millions of veterans. This is an effective application that performs a vital task. However, it would be hard to justify this application using only financial value. The real value is in the way it speeds up making information available to physicians and thereby benefits the health care of the veterans who are being treated. With value points, each veteran's record could be assigned a value point, while each 1 percent improvement in the speed of accessing the information by each physician could also be assigned a value point. Under such an approach, this 15,000 function point application probably would have in excess of 5,000,000 value points and hence clearly be considered a vital application.

Risk Analysis and Software Cost Estimates

It is a known fact that many large software applications are cancelled without completion due to excessive delays or poor quality. It is also a known fact that about half of the large software applications that are completed will be late by as much as a year, and overrun their budgets by as much as 100 percent. These two phenomena appear to be an indictment of software cost estimates as being fundamentally flawed. However, in many cases accurate estimates were arbitrarily rejected by clients and senior managers, who substituted their own cost and schedule targets based on business needs rather than on team capabilities.

What is not so widely known is that delays and cancellations for large software projects are usually caused by the same five factors:

- Excessive defect levels in key deliverables
- Inadequate defect removal activities
- Excessive changes in requirements late in development
- Inadequate change-control procedures
- Rejection of accurate estimates and replacement by arbitrary schedule and cost targets

Since the problems that cause delays and cancellations are known, it would be prudent to include a formal risk analysis and risk abatement stage for every software development project larger than 1000 function points or 100,000 source code statements in size.

Such a risk analysis would include the known problem areas for large software applications. These include problems associated with project management, problems associated with defects, and problems associated with changing requirements:

- Project management risks
  1. Cost estimates optimistic by > 10 percent
  2. Quality estimates optimistic by > 25 percent
  3. Milestones missed by > 1 week
  4. Failure to track progress daily
  5. Failure to report problems to higher management
  6. Failure to revise estimates to match new requirements
- Requirements change risks
  1. New requirements growth > 2 percent per calendar month
  2. No cost or schedule adjustments for new requirements
  3. No quality estimates for new requirements
  4. No inspections or reviews of new requirements
  5. Ineffective change-control methods
- Quality control risks
  1. Errors in requirements > 1 defect per function point
  2. Errors in design > 1 defect per function point
  3. Errors in new code > 1.5 defect per function point

4. Errors in reused code > 0.5 defects per function point

5. Error-prone modules present in code

6. Errors in user documents > 0.5 per function point

7. Errors caused by bad fixes > 5 percent

8. No usage of pre-test inspections

9. Inadequate test planning

10. Insufficient test cases for changing requirements

11. Defect-removal efficiency < 95 percent

The set of problems in this list has been noted in more than 90 percent of the software applications that ended up in litigation for breach of contract where the author worked as an expert witness. In-house project failures do not end up in court for breach of contract, but these problems have been found in very close to 100 percent of the large failing projects studied by the author.

Additional research is needed on various forms of risk. Also, there is a need for including a standard risk taxonomy in the estimates of all large software projects.

Including Specialists in Software Cost Estimates

Empirical studies have indicated that for a number of software tasks and activities, specialists outperform generalists in significant ways. Some of the occupations where trained or certified specialists have been shown to be beneficial include in alphabetic order:

- Configuration control
- Cost estimating
- Customer support
- Database administration
- Function point counting
- Maintenance
- Technical writing
- Testing

That brings up the point that the presence or absence of specialists is a factor that should be included both in historical benchmarks and also in cost estimates.

A large software development laboratory has a surprisingly diverse set of personnel employed. In a study the author and his colleagues carried out involving large organizations such as the Air Force, IBM, and Texas Instruments, no fewer than 90 kinds of specialists were noted in the entire study. However, no single company employed more than 50 of these.

One of the major topics in the domain of specialization is how many specialists of various kinds are needed to support the overall work of the software community? This is a topic that needs additional research. The ratios shown in Table 24.2 are not known to be optimal, but reflect the numbers of specialists observed during the study for a number of common specialties. For some kinds of specialization there are not yet any normative ratios available. Not all of the specialists shown here occur within the same company or even the same industry, it should be noted. They are ranked in Table 24.2 in descending order.

It was noted during the study that only a few kinds of software specialization have formal training and certification available. For example, project managers and function point counters can both be certified.

In other technical disciplines such as medicine, law, and engineering there are certification boards for many kinds of specialists. The software industry needs to perform additional studies on the kinds of specialists needed. There is also a need for improved training and certification in almost all software specialties.

TABLE 24.2   Approximate Ratios of Specialists to General Software Populations

Specialist occupations	Specialists		Generalists	Generalist %
Maintenance and enhancement specialists	1	to	4	25.0%
Testing specialists	1	to	8	12.5%
Technical writing specialists	1	to	15	6.6%
Quality assurance specialists	1	to	25	4.0%
Database administration specialists	1	to	25	4.0%
Configuration control specialists	1	to	30	3.3%
Systems software support specialists	1	to	30	3.3%
Function point counting specialists	1	to	50	2.0%
Integration specialists	1	to	50	2.0%
Measurement specialists	1	to	50	2.0%
Network specialists	1	to	50	2.0%
Performance specialists	1	to	75	1.3%
Architecture specialists	1	to	75	1.3%
Cost-estimating specialists	1	to	100	1.0%
Reusability specialists	1	to	100	1.0%
Package acquisition specialists	1	to	150	0.6%
Process improvement specialists	1	to	200	0.5%
Education and training specialists	1	to	250	0.4%
Standards specialists	1	to	300	0.3%

The performance difference between specialists and generalists is sometimes surprisingly large. In the case of function point counting, for example, certified specialists have been tested and came within 3 percent of providing the same count for the test examples. Counts by uncertified function point counters varied by more than 30 percent for the same examples.

Another aspect of the issue is that specialists and generalists may have different levels of compensation. If so, then these levels of compensation need to be included in the cost estimate.

More research is indicated on the performance levels of specialists versus generalists for many software activities.

Reuse Analysis and Software Cost Estimates

There is an interesting and simple exercise that makes it easy to see why software is expensive. Simply consider what these three activities have in common?

- Building a 12-meter yacht to compete in the America's Cup race
- Building a successful Formula 1 racing car
- Building a new software order-entry system

What the three have in common is that they can all cost more than $10,000,000 for the same reason. Each of these products is designed and constructed manually as a custom product by skilled and highly paid craftsmen.

These three have something more subtle in common too: not one of the three is likely to stay competitive for more than a few years. Another similarity is that all three are difficult and costly to modify or update once they are built.

It is obvious that none of the three activities will ever drop down significantly in cost just because the craftsmen use better tools or have more efficient processes and methods.

If any of these three expensive activities are to become really efficient and cost effective, it will be because of a fundamental principle of manufacturing economics: the substitution of standard reusable parts in place of custom development.

There are at least 12 different software artifacts that lend themselves to reusability. Unfortunately, much of the literature on software reuse has concentrated only on reusing source code, with a few sparse and intermittent articles devoted to other topics such as reusable design. Some very important aspects of reuse, such as testing materials, have almost no citations in the current literature.

From analyzing the cost breakdown of manual production of these 12 artifacts on software projects, it is possible to create a preliminary analysis of the ROI of reusing these 12 artifacts, with an admittedly large margin of error.

Table 24.3 lists the 12 artifacts that are potentially reusable for software projects, and the approximate reuse value of each, in terms of dollars returned for each dollar invested. The value approximation is based on reuse of each artifact in up to 24 software projects over a four-year period.

As an example of how reuse value is calculated for a specific project, consider the following hypothetical model. Assume a financial software project of 1000 function points (equal to roughly 100,000 COBOL statements) is being constructed with no reuse at all for a net cost of $1000 per function point or $1,000,000 in total. Then consider three different plateaus of reusability: 25 percent, 50 percent, and 75 percent reuse of key artifacts such as design and source code. Table 24.4 shows the cost breakdown for this project.

It is important to note that there is not a one-to-one linear relationship between the volume of reused material and costs. For example, reusing 50 percent of the source code in an application does not translate into an exact 50 percent savings in coding costs. There may be internal charges for acquiring the reusable materials. Even if the reusable component is acquired for free, there is still work involved in linking the reused material to the custom developed material, testing the link, and ensuring that the combination works properly.

There may be subtle impacts on other activities as well. Not all of the impacts are necessarily positive. It may sometimes cost more than

TABLE 24.3   Value of Software Reusability Over a Four-Year Period

Reusable artifact	Return on each $1.00 invested after four years and 24 uses
Reusable source code	$8.00
Reusable designs	$7.00
Reusable requirements	$6.00
Reusable test cases	$5.00
Reusable data	$4.00
Reusable project plans	$3.00
Reusable test plans	$3.00
Reusable cost estimates	$3.00
Reusable screens	$2.50
Reusable user documents	$2.50
Reusable architecture	$1.50
Reusable human interfaces	$1.50
Overall value of all reuse	*$47.00*

TABLE 24.4   Cost per Function Point with 0%, 25%, 50%, and 75% Reusability

	0% Reuse	25% Reuse	50% Reuse	75% Reuse
Development				
Requirements	$75.00	$67.50	$52.50	$37.50
Planning & estimating	$25.00	$20.00	$17.50	$12.50
Design	$150.00	$127.50	$97.50	$67.50
Coding	$225.00	$191.25	$168.75	$112.50
Integration	$75.00	$67.50	$60.00	$52.50
Testing	$275.00	$233.75	$192.50	$96.25
User documents	$75.00	$60.00	$52.50	$45.00
Project management	$100.00	$80.00	$65.00	$55.00
Subtotal	$1,000.00	$847.50	$706.25	$478.75
Maintenance				
Year 1	$250.00	$200.00	$150.00	$75.00
Year 2	$265.00	$215.00	$155.00	$75.00
Year 3	$280.00	$225.00	$165.00	$75.00
Year 4	$300.00	$240.00	$175.00	$70.00
Year 5	$325.00	$260.00	$185.00	$65.00
Subtotal	$1,420.00	$1,140.00	$830.00	$360.00
TOTAL	$2,420.00	$1,987.50	$1,536.25	$838.75
SAVINGS	$0.00	$432.50	$883.75	$1,581.25

normal to handle the requirements, design, configuration control, testing, and user documentation in a way that reflects a high volume of code reuse. Doing reuse analysis well actually requires a much more extensive activity-based reuse model that can deal with all 12 artifacts and their mutual interactions, handle customization of reused materials, deal with acquisition or creation of reused materials, and can amortize the savings or costs across multiple projects and time periods.

Successful entry to software reuse is not inexpensive and cannot happen overnight. From analysis of the steps utilized by the most successful reuse programs, the following five step sequence is recommended:

1. Identification of reusable artifacts

2. Acquisition of reusable artifacts

3. Validation of reusable artifacts

4. Cataloging of reusable artifacts

5. Deployment of reusable artifacts

The first step toward reuse is identification of the major artifacts that will be needed. Normally, a reusability committee or task force is convened that analyzes existing applications and selects functions that have significant reuse potential. This activity will typically run for a period of roughly three calendar months and can involve from three to more than a dozen software personnel depending upon the size and geographic distribution of the software organization.

Reusable materials can either be constructed or acquired from commercial vendors. Construction is preferred for reusable materials that are highly proprietary or will have significant competitive value. Construction may also be preferred due to quality control. Commercial acquisition of reusable materials is normally for standard functions.

The object-oriented (OO) paradigm supports the concept of source code reusability by means of class libraries, inheritance, polymorphism, and several other constructs as well. However, the OO paradigm is still not totally comprehensive in its approach to software reuse. For example, reuse of design elements is still somewhat difficult under any of the standard OO design approaches. There are no current OO methods for dealing with reuse of user manual materials at all. Reuse of test cases is also still in evolution under the OO paradigm.

The construction of reusable material such as source code is normally up to twice as expensive and takes up to 50 percent longer in calendar time than single-use development. This is because of two main factors: (1) reusable materials are normally built by the most experienced and capable (and therefore expensive) software engineers; and (2) artifacts constructed for reusable purposes need very high quality levels and therefore require full 100 percent inspections and extensive testing and validation.

Because successful reuse demands very high quality, all reusable artifacts need to be certified to approximate zero-defect levels. It is uneconomical and indeed highly dangerous to attempt large-scale reuse of unvalidated material. A single "recall" of a defective component that has been used in multiple applications can damage the economic return of software reuse.

There are some fairly serious barriers that must be overcome before software reuse can even approach its economic potential. Here is a short summary of the major obstacles:

- First, you cannot safely reuse garbage. Successful reuse demands that the reusable materials be certified to levels of quality that approach or achieve zero defects. To be blunt, some companies are not good enough today to build anything that is worth reusing. Therefore, the primary barrier to reuse is poor quality control and careless practices that are common today.

- Second, when you set out to reuse something you have to construct that artifact with reuse in mind. It is usually not possible to casually extract reusable artifacts from ordinary software projects for high-volume corporate reuse (although individual programmers do so all the time). The second barrier is finding the time and funds to construct reusable materials initially, given the intense schedule and cost pressure most software projects are under. Software life cycles, estimating tools, planning tools, company standards, and design methods need to include specific capabilities for dealing with reusable materials. As the situation now stands, most software management tools and practices have no provision for reuse.

- Third, once you accumulate a useful library of reusable artifacts you need to offer some incentives to project managers and technical personnel to make use of the materials. This is not as easy as it sounds, and requires both cultural and financial changes to current practices. For example, your current measurement system may not give credit for reuse. There may also be staff resistance to making use of someone else's work. In general, a successful reuse program must deal with social issues as well as technical issues.

There are many other important factors associated with reuse besides the ones discussed here, but the basic points are clear enough. Reuse has the best potential for improving financial software costs and schedules of any known technology, but there are serious barriers that must be eliminated before reuse can take its place as a major software technology.

Successful reuse requires careful validation, and many existing applications are of such marginal quality that reuse would be uneconomical and even dangerous. The fundamental point of this analysis is that a reusability program has substantial start-up costs that must be funded.

Incidentally, reusability requires that two kinds of productivity measurements be used: *development productivity* and *delivery productivity*. Suppose that you are building an application of 1000 function points in size. Now suppose that you are able to supply half of the desired features by means of reused materials.

With 50 percent reuse, that means that you will actually be developing only 500 function points. If your *development productivity* is 10 function points per staff month, then the project will take 50 staff months of effort for the 500 function points you must develop.

However, what you deliver to the customer will be a final application that contains 1000 function points. If you measure your *delivery productivity* you have supplied the customer with 1000 function points of useful features and used only 50 staff months of effort. Therefore, your *delivery productivity* rate is 20 function points per staff month, or twice the rate of your *development productivity*.

While both metrics are important and should be measured, the metric that is most important from an economic standpoint is your *delivery productivity*. At some point in the future it might be possible to develop the same application with 90 percent reused material or 900 function points out of 1000. In that case, your *development productivity* might still be only 10 function points per staff month and the project will require 10 staff months of effort. But with 90 percent reuse, your *delivery productivity* will have climbed to 100 function points per staff month.

Suppose it were possible to provide the same application with 100 percent reusable material. In this case, the *development productivity* would be zero because nothing actually got developed! But the *delivery productivity* would be at least 1000 function points per staff month.

As can easily be seen from these examples, it is important to distinguish between the *development* and the *delivery* of software applications.

Process Improvement Estimation

The standard form of software cost estimating is aimed at a specific project. Standard cost estimates will show the costs, schedules, and resources from the beginning of requirements of the project until deployment, and sometimes for maintenance as well.

However, many companies are anxious to improve their software development and maintenance practices. This indicates a growing need for a new kind of estimating tool that will predict the costs and schedules of moving through the stages of a software process improvement cycle.

Often such a cycle is built around the patterns of the capability maturity model (CMM) developed by the SEI. However, there is a need to estimate the costs, schedules, and value of improving software practices, whether the specific method used is the CMM, six-sigma, or something else.

It is technically possible to produce an estimating tool that can deal with process improvements. However, while there are prototypes and in-house tools circa 2007, there are no major commercial tools that deal with the economics of software process improvements.

Significant software process improvements do not occur in random patterns. When you generalize the patterns used by companies that have gone the farthest and are the best overall, you can see that the initial activity is an assessment and a baseline, followed by a six-stage improvement program:

Stage 0:   Software Process Assessment, Baseline, and Benchmark
Stage 1:   Focus on Management Technologies
Stage 2:   Focus on Software Processes and Methodologies
Stage 3:   Focus on New Tools and Approaches
Stage 4:   Focus on Infrastructure and Specialization
Stage 5:   Focus on Reusability
Stage 6:   Focus on Industry Leadership

The first place to start for a process improvement program is management. The reason for this is because managers need to produce the ROI and cost data to fund the rest of the improvement program.

Following is some general information based on the overall size of companies in terms of software personnel. The cost data in Table 24.5 is expressed in terms of "cost per capita," or the approximate costs for each employee. The cost elements include training, consulting fees, capital equipment, software licenses, and improvements in office conditions.

The sizes in Table 24.5 refer to the software populations, and divide organizations into four rough size domains: less than 100 software personnel, less than 1000, less than 10,000, and more than 10,000, which implies giant software organizations such as IBM, Microsoft, and EDS, all of which have more than 25,000 software personnel corporate wide.

Table 24.5 is not a substitute for an actual estimating tool aimed at process improvement and tailored for a specific company. It simply provides generic data and approximate values. The information should not be used for serious business purposes.

As can be seen from Table 24.5, a formal process improvement program is not inexpensive. Therefore, part of the estimate must be to show the value of such a significant pattern of expenses. However, there is other data needed first.

The next topic shown in Table 24.6 is how long it will take to move through each of the stages of the process improvement sequence.

A process improvement program is of necessity a multiyear endeavor. As can be seen, smaller companies can move much more rapidly than large corporations and government agencies.

Large corporations and government agencies cannot move quickly even if everyone is moving in the same direction. When there is polarization of opinion or political opposition within the organization, progress can be very slow or nonexistent.

The next topic is what kind of value or return on investment will occur from software process improvements?

Table 24.7 shows only the approximate improvements for productivity, costs, and quality (here defined as reductions in software

TABLE 24.5   Process Improvement Expenses Per Capita

Stage	Meaning	Small < 100 staff	Medium < 1000 staff	Large < 10,000 staff	Giant > 10,000 staff	Average
0	Assessment	$100	$125	$150	$250	$156
1	Management	$1,500	$2,500	$3,500	$5,000	$3,125
2	Process	$1,500	$2,500	$3,000	$4,500	$2,875
3	Tools	$3,000	$6,000	$5,000	$10,000	$6,000
4	Infrastructure	$1,000	$1,500	$3,000	$6,500	$3,000
5	Reuse	$500	$2,500	$4,500	$6,000	$3,375
6	Industry Leadership	$1,500	$2,000	$3,000	$4,500	$2,750
	Total Expenses	$9,100	$17,125	$22,150	$36,750	$21,281

TABLE 24.6   Process Improvement Stages in Calendar Months

Stage	Meaning	Small < 100 staff	Medium < 1000 staff	Large < 10,000 staff	Giant > 10,000 staff	Average
0	Assessment	2.00	2.00	3.00	4.00	2.75
1	Management	3.00	6.00	9.00	12.00	7.50
2	Process	4.00	6.00	9.00	15.00	8.50
3	Tools	4.00	6.00	9.00	12.00	7.75
4	Infrastructure	3.00	4.00	9.00	12.00	7.00
5	Reuse	4.00	6.00	12.00	16.00	9.50
6	Industry Leadership	6.00	8.00	9.00	12.00	8.75
	Sum (Worst Case)	26.00	38.00	60.00	83.00	51.75
	Overlap (Best Case)	16.90	26.60	43.20	61.42	33.64

defect levels). The results are expressed as percentage improvements compared to the initial baseline at the start of the improvement process.

As can be seen from this rough analysis, the maximum benefits do not occur until stage 5, when full software reusability programs are implemented. Since reusability has the best return and greatest results, it is frequently asked why it is not the first stage.

The reason that software reuse is offset to stage 5 is that a successful reusability program depends upon mastery of software quality and a host of precursor software technologies such as formal inspections and formal development processes. Unless software quality is at state of the art levels, any attempt to reuse materials will result in longer schedules and higher costs than you have right now!

When a multiyear software process improvement is in about its third year, the following kinds of results should be achievable:

- Set aside 12 days a year for training in software management topics
- Set aside 10 days a year for training in software engineering topics
- Establish a software "center for excellence" to pursue continuous improvements

TABLE 24.7   Improvements in Software Defect Levels, Productivity, and Schedules

Stage	Meaning	Delivered defects	Development production	Development schedule
0	Assessment	0.00%	0.00%	0.00%
1	Management	−10.00%	10.00%	−12.00%
2	Process	−50.00%	30.00%	−17.00%
3	Tools	−10.00%	25.00%	−12.00%
4	Infrastructure	−5.00%	10.00%	−5.00%
5	Reuse	−85.00%	70.00%	−50.00%
6	Industry Leadership	−5.00%	50.00%	−5.00%
	Total	−95.00%	365.00%	−75.00%

- Budget $1500 per capita per year for improved tools and training
- Achieve Level 3 status on the SEI CMM or CMMI maturity scale
- No more than 5 percent difference between estimated schedules and real delivery dates
- No more than 5 percent difference between estimated costs and actual costs
- Defect-removal efficiency averages above 97 percent as the corporate average
- Defect potentials average below 3.0 per function point as the corporate average
- Development schedules reduced by 50 percent from requirements until delivery
- Development productivity rates increased by more than 50 percent
- Development costs reduced by more than 40 percent
- Maintenance costs reduced by 50 percent for all maintenance work
- More than 50 percent reusability by volume for design, code, and test artifacts
- Establish an in-house measurement department
- Monthly reports on software quality and defect removal produced
- Annual "state of the art" report produced to show accomplishments

Not every software process improvement program is a success. In fact, the rate of change is proportional to the level of management and technical sophistication at the beginning of the improvement campaign. If an organization is really lagging the state of the art, the costs and schedules to achieve tangible improvements may be so high that perhaps switching over to an outsource model would provide a better return on investment.

Methodology Analysis and Software Cost Estimating

Suppose you are a project manager who is going to be responsible for the software development effort connected with a PBX switching system. You know from previous PBX applications constructed by your company that the size of the application will be about 1500 function points or roughly 187,500 statements in the C programming language.

You also know, because of the nature of the application, that high levels of reliability are mandatory. This implies that quality control must be at state-of-the-art levels.

The vice president in charge of both the hardware and software sides of the product has a joint meeting with you and the hardware engineering manager. One of the questions that the vice president asks is this: "What software methodology are you planning to use on this project?"

Table 24.8 lists a sample of some of the possible answers to this basic question.

TABLE 24.8　Software Development Methods

1. Action diagrams
2. Actor-based development
3. Adaptive system development
4. Assembly, disassembly, reassembly (ADR)
5. Agile development
6. Capability maturity model (CMM)
7. Capability maturity model integration (CMMI)
8. Clean-room development
9. Code inspections
10. Commercial off-the-shelf software (COTS)
11. Component-based development (CBD)
12. CRC diagrams
13. Crystal development approach
14. Data flow diagrams
15. Data structured system design (DSSD)
16. Decision tables
17. Decision trees
18. Design inspections
19. Dynamic system development method (DSDM)
20. Enterprise Resource Planning (ERP)
21. Entity-relationship diagrams
22. Extreme programming (XP)
23. Feature-driven development (FDD)
24. Finite state diagrams
25. Flowcharts
26. HIPO diagrams
27. Incremental development
28. Information Engineering (IE)
29. ISO 9000–9004 standards
30. Iterative development
31. Jackson diagrams
32. Nassi-Shneiderman charts
33. Object-oriented development (OO)
34. Open-source components
35. Outsourcing – Domestic
36. Outsourcing – International
37. Pattern-based development
38. Petri nets
39. Pseudocode
40. Quality Function Deployment (QFD)
41. Rapid Application Development (RAD)

TABLE 24.8 Software Development Methods *(Continued)*

42.	Rational development method
43.	Scrum
44.	Six-sigma for software
45.	Spiral development
46.	State transition diagrams
47.	Structured development
48.	Structured English
49.	Team Structured Process (TSP)
50.	Total Quality Management (TQM)
51.	Tropos software development method
52.	Unified modeling language (UML)
53.	Use cases
54.	User stories
55.	Vienna development method (VDM)
56.	Warnier-Orr diagrams
57.	Waterfall development
58.	Zermelo-Frankel Z Notation

Not all of these methods are relevant to the project in question. Recall that this is a joint hardware/software project. Also recall the need for high reliability and excellent quality control. With these two constraints, the most likely subset of these 58 possible approaches might be the following:

1. Capability maturity model integration (CMMI)
2. Code inspections
3. Design inspections
4. Object-oriented development (OO)
5. Quality Function Deployment (QFD)
6. Six-sigma for software
7. Unified modeling language (UML)
8. Use cases

If these eight approaches are utilized, then the development productivity of the PBX software would probably be about 10 function points per staff month. The schedule would probably be about 18 calendar months. The defect potential would be around 4.0 defects per function point, and the defect removal efficiency would probably be about 98 percent. The number of latent defects at delivery would be about 120, of which perhaps 10 would be of high severity levels.

Once deployed, the maintenance and customer support costs would be about $150 per function point per year. Therefore, the maintenance and support costs for the first two years of deployment would be about $225,000 per year, or $450,000 in all.

This kind of situation is a daily occurrence for software cost estimation. In order to deal with such situations, estimating tool vendors need to be cognizant of essentially all of the common software design and development methods in use.

Since the nature, scope, and class of a software application is a preliminary input to many software cost-estimation tools, such basic information can allow the tool to select the most appropriate sets of development approaches from the full repertory that might be available. The tool's choices will be displayed to the person doing the estimate, and the choices can either be accepted or replaced by some other choice.

There is no guarantee that a particular project will use the most probable set of development approaches. For the same PBX project, suppose the project manager selected a completely different set:

1. Agile development
2. User stories

Under this alternate scenario the development productivity would be about 15 function points per staff month. The development schedule would be about 14 calendar months. However, the defect potential for this method of development would be about five defects per function point. The defect-removal efficiency would be about 90 percent. The number of defects at delivery would be about 750, of which perhaps 75 would be of high severity levels.

Under this alternate scenario, the annual maintenance costs would be about $300 per function point per year for the first two years. Therefore, the annual maintenance costs would be about $450,000 per year or $900,000 in all.

Here too we have a fairly typical situation for commercial software cost-estimating tools: predicting the outcome of two very different ways of designing and building the same application.

Note that the two examples discussed in this chapter are hypothetical, and merely illustrate the fact that there are many different ways of designing and building software applications. Each of these many ways will have a characteristic productivity, schedule, and quality pattern associated with it.

What makes this a complex and challenging task for the software estimating vendors is the fact that for about 35 of the 58 possibilities shown in Table 24.8, there is little or no empirical data available from historical projects. Adding to the problems of calibrating all of the various development approaches that might be used, some of the historical data will have been measured with lines-of-code-metrics, some with function point metrics, and some with newer metrics such as object points or use case points. For these disparate measurement methods, there is no easy way of analyzing the results to find out which was the most effective approach.

There is a need for much more research on various alternative methods for building software applications in order know the actual results that have been achieved. For each approach there is a need to evaluate costs, schedules, staffing, productivity, and quality results. There is also a need to know how the method works on applications that range from less than 100 function points in size to more than 100,000 function points in size. And there is a need to know how the method works on many different kinds of software including but not limited to web-based applications, information systems, embedded software, military software, systems software, and perhaps even game and entertainment software.

Summary and Conclusions About Software Cost-Estimating Research

Software cost estimating is a fairly sophisticated technology circa 2007 but it is far from perfect. Like any other technology, there are boundaries that have not yet been crossed. The ten issues discussed in this chapter illustrate some of the problems that need to have additional research and development in order to improve software cost-estimating technologies in the future. These are not the only topics that need additional exploration. The software cost-estimating world needs to evolve and improve over time like any other successful technology.

Index